MODERN FRANCE

*PROBLEMS OF THE THIRD
AND FOURTH REPUBLICS*

CONTRIBUTORS

WARREN C. BAUM

JOHN BOWDITCH

ROBERT F. BYRNES

RICHARD D. CHALLENER

JOHN B. CHRISTOPHER

KENNETH DOUGLAS

EDWARD MEAD EARLE

HENRY W. EHRMANN

EDWARD WHITING FOX

HENRY E. GUERLAC

FRED LATIMER HADSEL

ELLEN HAMMER

DONALD J. HARVEY

HENRY BERTRAM HILL

H. STUART HUGHES

EDWARD L. KATZENBACH, JR.

DUDLEY KIRK

DAVID S. LANDES

VAL R. LORWIN

SCOTT H. LYTLE

CHARLES A. MICAUD

L. ARTHUR MINNICH, JR.

DAVID H. PINKNEY

RICHARD RUGGLES

JOHN E. SAWYER

ANDRÉ SIEGFRIED

VERNON VAN DYKE

JOHN B. WOLF

GORDON WRIGHT

MODERN FRANCE

Problems of the Third and Fourth Republics

EDITED BY

EDWARD MEAD EARLE

PRINCETON

PRINCETON UNIVERSITY PRESS

1951

Printed in the United States of America by
Vail-Ballou Press, Inc., Binghamton, N.Y.

INTRODUCTION

EDWARD MEAD EARLE

IT WAS being said in Europe in 1949 that in England the situation was rapidly deteriorating in perfect order, whereas in France recovery was proceeding steadily midst complete chaos. This was another way of stating an old paradox—that the basic situation of the French nation is sound, however unstable its parliamentary institutions and however mercurial its political behavior. The authors of this book are impressed by the extent and speed of French recovery and, with some reservations, they are optimistic concerning the future. They take a less hopeful view of French politics and French political institutions; they are gravely concerned that France may not be sufficiently unified and sufficiently determined to do, and to do before it is too late, the things which must be done if France is to survive and to play her indispensable role in Europe. If France can consolidate and extend her economic gains of the past five years; if she can achieve a larger measure of political stability; if she can bring into being a military force which, along with the forces of the other Atlantic powers, can effectively deter or resist aggression—if she can do these things, and do them in time—there is reason to believe that the security of Western Europe will have been won. If, on the other hand, France should fail in any essential respect, it is difficult to see how the other European members of the Atlantic bloc can long survive as altogether free and independent.

For three centuries and more the French nation has enjoyed high estate in the European community, a fact which even the defeat of 1940 should not be permitted to obscure. The French people are vital, tough, devoted to their independence and freedom; therefore their future should not be too heavily discounted. But even the most ardent Francophile would hardly contend that the France of 1950 faces Europe and the world with the same confidence, the same esprit or élan, as the France of 1914. How has this condition of affairs come to pass? And what are the prospects for the Fourth French Republic?

These are the principal questions which this book asks and attempts to answer.

For thirty years or more France has been living in a state of chronic crisis. In its most acute phases the crisis dates from the February Days of 1934. But in a larger sense it goes back to 1919 or 1899, to 1870 or 1848, to 1793 or 1789, according to the depth and spectrum of one's historical perspective. The prevailing political instability, like the military defeat of 1940, has its roots deep in the past and cannot be quite understood without regard to the traditional forces which operate in French society. But the crisis cannot be understood solely, or indeed principally, in terms of history, legends, and *mystique*. France does not live of or to herself; she is part of Europe and the world and, above all, she is part of present-day Europe and the present-day world. Some of the factors which must be considered in studying modern France are peculiarly or predominantly French; others are European—to cite a single instance, France might be a different France if her neighbor Germany had been a different sort of neighbor.

This volume is analytical rather than historical, but it does not slight the historical factor which operates so powerfully in France. What is the nature of the thirty years' crisis in France? What are its origins? What have been and what are its consequences to France and to Europe? What are the reasonable hopes that the crisis may be resolved? The several chapters of the book are concerned with these issues, among others. The authors are critical, as an affectionate friend would be critical; they are not carping. They are sympathetic, since they are Americans who care enough about France to devote the major part of their professional activities to French studies. They are objective, as a physician would be objective, not merely for the sake of objectivity but for the larger purpose as well of understanding the situation and seeking its improvement. One will gather from these pages a somewhat discouraging picture of the number and the complexity of the critical situations which confront the Fourth Republic, but one will not find dark pessimism or hopelessness—quite the contrary. What one will encounter is an informed, an honest, and a sympathetic grappling with the problems of modern France and an eager, tough-minded determination to reach solutions for them. Taken as a whole, too, these essays are impressive evidence of the competence, the maturity, and the vitality of the younger American scholars who are concerning themselves with French affairs.

The several chapters of this book, with some subsequent amendment, were read as papers at a Conference on Modern France held in Princeton, February 1–3, 1950. The Conference was organized, sponsored, and partially financed by the Committee on International and Regional Studies, Harvard University; the Institute of International Studies, Yale University; the School of International Affairs, Columbia University; the Woodrow Wilson School of Public and International Affairs, Princeton University; the School of Historical Studies, the Institute for Advanced Study at Princeton. The Carnegie Corporation of New York generously assisted in financing the conference and hence deserves a large share of credit for the present volume. The Government of the French Republic provided the services, and defrayed the expenses, of Professor Siegfried, who at considerable personal inconvenience made a hurried visit to the United States for the purpose of participating in the conference. By arrangement with the Yale Institute of International Studies, Chapter 25 appeared (in a slightly different form) in *World Politics* for July 1950; otherwise material in the book has not been published heretofore. Chapter 18 was not read at the conference but was specially prepared for inclusion with the other papers, in view of the significance which the problem of population holds for modern France. Miss Jean MacLachlan, research assistant at the Institute for Advanced Study, has prepared the manuscript for the printer and seen the volume through the press. Mr. Joseph Kraft, of the Institute for Advanced Study, has read the proofs and prepared the index. M. Claude Cellier has been most helpful in editing portions of the text.

EDWARD MEAD EARLE

Princeton, New Jersey
15 August 1950

CONTENTS

I

1

++

APPROACHES TO

AN UNDERSTANDING OF MODERN FRANCE

ANDRÉ SIEGFRIED

++

THE relative importance of France in Europe has greatly increased in the years following World War II. With the countries of Eastern Europe looking in a new direction, with a defeated Germany no longer in a dominant position economically or politically, France has of necessity become the center of the entire Continental system. This situation readily justifies the study of modern France as being critical to Western Europe and the Atlantic community. What can a Frenchman like myself contribute to a sympathetic American understanding of my native country?

France is always difficult to understand—more so, perhaps, than any other nation. It is not that France is particularly hard to know: the French people speak freely of themselves and of their national problems. Yet it is a perplexing country to judge and to interpret, notably because of its peculiar psychology, which is the result of its geographical and cultural position among the diverse civilizations of Europe, Asia, Africa and America. This difficulty of interpretation has been augmented by the recent upheavals of two world wars, the German occupation, the overthrow of the Third Republic, and the weight of Communist ideology. Nor must it be forgotten that the Industrial Revolution has shaken traditional concepts of production that were more deeply rooted in France than in any other European state.

The aim of this chapter is not to deal with the problem of modern France as a whole, but to introduce it and, I hope, to throw some light upon it. As one who has followed French politics for half a century, I offer from my experience some impressions and suggestions which may provide a key to the French psychology.

I

First of all, it is important to locate France geographically. France has a threefold character: she is an Atlantic, occidental country; she is Continental and European; she is Mediterranean. On her Atlantic front, France looks west, beyond her own frontiers, onto the immensity of the ocean. Historically she has thus been exposed to extra-Continental attractions, endowed with an expansionist spirit, tempted by far-off adventures. This maritime, colonial, expansionist France belongs to the liberal family of the Anglo-American civilizations, and from this point of view she is authentically occidental.

On the other hand, as a Continental unity, France is joined to Europe by her own flesh and blood, in a manner impossible for insular England. Her eastern territory belongs to Central Europe, by virtue of its climate and its way of life. From this point of view she is no longer an Atlantic country, but a society rooted in the European soil and, in that respect, more typically European than any other Continental nation. Without France, there is no Europe; without Europe, there would be no France.

However—and this is perhaps the most interesting point of all—on her Mediterranean front France maintains direct contact with Africa and Asia—even, to some extent, with the Far East. She is thereby in touch not only with an important group of extra-European countries, but with the entire illustrious tradition of ancient times. The Mediterranean culture is extraordinarily homogeneous, and by her relation to it France possesses a true sense of the Indo-European civilization which the West has largely lost. To a certain degree, the gardener of the French Riviera may be said to be a cousin of the small farmer of the Orient.

The unique character of the French is probably due to these complex anomalies. At one and the same time their nation looks West and East, toward the future and back to the past, toward progress and back to tradition. Whatever may be the angle of vision, there is always something to admire about France, but there is also always something to criticize.

It is no more simple to locate France ethnically. There is no such thing as a French race—the very expression should be avoided. In the north and east are the Germanic peoples; in the west and the central plateau are found the Celts; in the south, the Mediterraneans, the Latins. "We are a race of half-breeds," the great historian Seignobos said, but he added, "Mongrels are often more intelligent than pure-bred dogs." To the Latins the French owe their gift for expression and their intellectual lucidity; to the Celts their artistic nature as well as their individual anarchism; to the Germans what they possess of seriousness and constructive capabilities. These diverse qualities have fused into a strong national unity, but not a unity based on race, for no one element has been allowed to dominate the rest as is the case in England. All Frenchmen consider themselves wholly French, no matter what their racial origin may be. They are, indeed, the least race-minded of any nation in Europe. Their unity has been effected, instead, by a perfect adaptation to the soil, by a long tradition which has produced a special way of life, and, above all, by a common culture. The strength of the French nation (and its weakness as well) lies not in the state, but in the individual or the family group.

In contrast to many other nations, France is a country with a long history and deeply rooted traditions. Germany, in its modern form, dates only from 1870; the United States is largely a creation of the twentieth century; Russia has been regenerated, for better or for worse, by the Bolshevik Revolution of 1917. France, however, was a finished product by the end of the eighteenth century. Hers is an adult civilization, and as such it is less adaptable to the dynamic forces of the present-day world. For this reason, the twentieth century has been for France a century of crisis.

Since the completion of the French national individuality, two events of tremendous consequence have taken place: the Industrial Revolution has transformed all methods of production and indeed every aspect of material life; and, secondly, the center of gravity of the world has shifted away from Europe, altering all our traditional measures of greatness. As a result, France is doubly disoriented: mass production conflicts with her traditional individualism, and her weight among the nations of the world has been diminished. A certain loss of confidence in her national destiny has been inevitable.

Conceived and constructed for another age, France must adapt herself to the new situation, but the best qualities of her people are not readily available for mass production and the formulation of world policy, while their defects become only too apparent. What really is at stake is the French personality and the unique character of a civilization: herein lies the true French crisis.

II

An understanding of the French psychology is essential to any study of France. While this observation may be true of any country, it is particularly so of France, for her political life can be explained only from that point of view—to a degree that is rarely recognized or comprehended by foreigners.

The French mind reveals two contradictory propensities. On the one hand, it is extremely practical and matter of fact—a tendency derived, I believe, from our peasant background ("peasant" being used, of course, in the French sense, which is not pejorative). This element in our national character is a Celtic heritage, and distinguishes the French from the Anglo-Saxons or, generally speaking, the Nordic peoples; a similar trait may be found in northern Spain and the west of the British Isles where Celtic blood prevails. It should be noted carefully that this characteristic pertains to the individual, not the citizen, for French behavior is entirely different in private and in political life.

As an individual or as the head of a family, the Frenchman's sense of his material interests is keenly developed. He believes deeply in private ownership, in the sense derived from Roman law. In the management of his affairs, he reveals an abounding good sense and a remarkable gift for measure: his house is well kept, his wife's linen, although mended, is in perfect order; he has contrived to balance his private budget—even though the state finances show a deficit. In short, he is a realist, not to be taken in with fine words; his feet are firmly on the ground. So strong is his sense of thrift that at times it is almost sordid, but—whatever may be the case, and contrary to repute—he is, in the organization of his private life, at his most orderly and most serious.

On the other hand, because of the second dominant trait in his character, this same Frenchman will manifest a greater idealism and universalism in his thought than any other human being. Once reassured about his private interests (and he does not make excessive demands), he releases his mind, as though he were throwing out a clutch, and his thought evolves independently, in perfect freedom, without initiating any action. In this fashion he achieves a high measure of intellectual disinterestedness, a maturity of mind shared only by the Chinese and, perhaps, the Spaniards—also the products of an ancient civilization.

By this process of thought, the Frenchman oversteps the narrow limits of racial or nationalistic prejudices, and attains effortlessly a humanist, international, conception of man. He possesses a certain intellectual radiance, a Latin gift distinguishing him from the Anglo-Saxon, who is practical, mystical, and racist, all at one and the same time. In contrast, the French are intellectual realists, with a skepticism which unfits them for action, but they are more widely humane than those nations which have retained their racial prejudices. This sense of humanity, enabling them to say sincerely, *"Nihil humani a me alienum puto,"* I find to be the finest quality of the French character.

It is when we consider the Frenchman as an individual that we have come to the heart of the problem. In France, nearly everything that is good, as well as nearly everything that is bad, derives from one's conception of the individual. That conception may be splendid . . . but it is also pathological. It has as its foundation a claim for intellectual independence. The Frenchman demands the right to think and judge for himself, as an independent being. His is a critical mind, nonconformist and antitotalitarian. He will not willingly bow before any sort of mandarinate—whether it be that of a priest, a professor, or an "expert." But, at the same time, he reveres a principle to such an extent that he occasionally becomes its slave, attaining in the name of that principle and its logic such fanaticism that he loses his judgment and his critical sense. Such worship of principle can act as a dangerous ferment, contradicting the wisdom that lies behind *"Quieta non movere. . . ."*

In addition to his demand for intellectual independence, the Frenchman desires independence in his private life. He hates to be a debtor, to be dependent on others or on one person in particular. It is this that lies at the very heart of his democratic convictions, in which jealousy and a sense of equality take precedence over any notion of liberty. His desire for economic security has the same basis; it is fundamentally a desire to be economically self-sufficient. In the France of yesterday, security could be achieved by thrift, and the typical Frenchman devoted his life to acquiring a little property, a little house, a little business, a little income from investments, for his old age. Today inflation and the depreciation of the franc have made such modest objectives difficult to attain, and the average citizen has to rely on social security, although a collective form of insurance is less in keeping with his native genius.

We have said that there is something sordid about the astonishing instinct for saving that lies deep in the character of every Frenchman. He knows that money, since it is difficult to earn, is meant to be kept —I speak of his *own* money, of course: state money can be lavishly dispensed. Such is the peasant tradition, skeptical of the future, distrustful of life, of society, of one's fellow creatures, lacking any civic-mindedness. On the other hand, there is a favorable side to this element of the French character. The Frenchman is essentially an adult. He looks life straight in the face, with no trace of hypocrisy or childishness and with no illusions. He is a wise man, who accepts things as they are. In this philosophical attitude toward life lies, to my mind, the true charm of the French. And it is found at its best less among the upper and middle classes than among the man of the people—the "common man"—who is the most interesting Frenchman of them all.

The Frenchman, then, is primarily humane, a civilized man, with a sense of measure which is repelled by anything chaotic or too big. He is moderate; he does not aim too high. "The biggest in the world" is not his slogan; he prefers the phrase *"rien de trop,"* the proverb, *"Mon verre est petit, mais je bois dans mon verre."* Instinctively, he relies on reason: the Englishman will admonish his child, "Be a good boy"; *"Sois raisonnable,"* say the French. Their rather skeptical, somewhat cynical philosophy is perfectly expressed in the fables of La Fontaine, which every Frenchman learns at school and which later exactly correspond to his experience of life. Here is the treasure house of wisdom of the French tradition.

III

The psychological tendencies which we have tried to analyze are essential factors in the behavior of the French people, not only in their private life, but in public and political affairs. Let us consider this behavior in relation to production, to religion, to politics, and to intellectual activity. This will, I believe, provide the best introduction to an understanding of modern France.

There is a traditional conception of work, of production, which is peculiarly French, rooted in the very soil. It involves the honor of work well done; it requires an intelligent collaboration of the mind with the hand and the tool. An affirmation of the personality of the Frenchman is found in his work. Many a craftsman insists on inscribing his signature in some way or other on what he has produced; others, when they have completed their work, fall back in the manner of the artist to contemplate it. Péguy writes in illustration: "We have known that devotion carried out, maintained, to its most extreme limits and demands. Throughout my youth, I saw chairs recaned in exactly the same spirit, with the same heart and the same hands, as those of that same people when they were building their cathedrals. These workers were not serving, they were working. Their honor was absolute, as it is the character of honor to be absolute. A chair rung had to be well done—that was admitted as a paramount principle. If it had to be well done, it was not for the employer, it was not for the experts, neither was it for the customers of the employer. It had to be well done as such in the very conception of the chair itself."

Such a conception, while essentially *artisanale,* is also that of the artist—the two words are the same. The French love creation above everything, but they have no comparable interest in further application; they sow, while others reap. They are the creators of the prototype—the automobile, for instance, the airplane, the submarine—but when the profits are shared and dispensed, they are conspicuous by their absence. In the words of Cocteau in *Le Coq et l'arlequin:* "France, unconcerned, had her pockets full of seeds and let them fall carelessly behind her. Others came and picked them up and carried them away to their own countries, to plant them in a chemically fertilized soil, where they bore huge and scentless flowers."

This conception of work cannot fail to produce a crisis in the age of the machine. It should be noted that the French appreciate standardization; they are, after all, the inventors of the metric system, and the author of *Discours de la méthode* was certainly the ancestor of Taylor, the apostle of scientific management. There is a strongly constructive character to French thought; the French language seems especially contrived for clarity and order of expression. It is not that the French are incapable of understanding mass production; they simply fail in its large-scale application. It is not enough to conceive: plans must be carried out, and modern production entails cooperative assembly-line techniques, an enormous amount of mechanical equipment, and the resources of a big national market. Obviously, France is not well endowed in these respects. The Frenchman, as we have said, does things from a sense of honor, or because he is keenly interested, or proud of creating something fine or unique. In the modern factory, on the other hand, where work is essentially collective, he will not be asked to do his job better than his fellow workers, but to adapt his own activity to the corporate enterprise. The qualities required of him will be endurance, conscientiousness, a capacity for resistance to the boredom of the assembly line, and above all team spirit.

France, rightly or wrongly, has been loath to see the machine threaten craftsmanship or the individual craftsman. If she has been slower than other countries to accept mechanical progress, it was because machinery displaces her precious artisan tradition. If she responds at all to the demands of the age of mass production, it is from necessity, and not with the alacrity and ease manifested by Germany and America. Devoted to what they call *production de qualité,* French industrialists continue to hope that they will be able to mechanize production as far as necessary and yet maintain the old artistic and individualistic tradition of the land.

IV

In considering the French conception of religion, the fundamental factor to take into account is that France is essentially a Roman Catholic country. Faithful to the Church or not (and faith is widespread), the Frenchman is indelibly marked by Catholicism. Herein lies the main contrast between France and the Protestant nations; in fact, I would go so far as to suggest that any lack of comprehension, any sense of mistrust, that exists between France and the Anglo-

Saxon countries can be attributed very largely to this single fact. English-speaking Protestants have equal difficulty in understanding and in placing confidence in France, whether they regard her as a Catholic country or as a country which has broken away from her religious ties. In the first case they dislike her as non-Protestant; in the second, as a nation of non-believers.

French Catholicism—like all Catholicism—is a religion of authority, encasing France in an armor of ecclesiastical discipline. The Church has given the French neither a tradition of individual moral responsibility nor an education in political liberty. As a result, the nation is divided among those who accept religious discipline and respect it; those who defend themselves by a skeptical adaptation to the external ritual of the Church without sacrificing their critical liberty; and those who, in violent reaction, have left the Church entirely. (Theirs is more than a silent indifference; the separation is openly admitted and even asserted. France is a country where the absence of faith is in itself a faith.)

The consequences of this Catholic influence in France are considerable. There are proportionally very few Protestants (hardly more than 800,000), with the result that practically every Frenchman bears the stamp of Catholicism—believers and non-believers alike, as we have said. It is this mark and the countermark borne by the avowed enemies of the Church that characterize the French mind. Voltaire provides a typical example of the reverse side of the coin: only a Catholic country could have produced him. In effect, France has attained a degree of critical liberty of mind which Protestant countries, liberated from Rome but never completely emancipated from some sort of moral prejudice, generally fail to achieve. She stands in subtle comparison here with Spain, also a Catholic country, in that she has never wholly accepted the domination of the Church.

The influence of Catholicism has had decisive political consequences as well. The ancien régime was founded on the double absolutism of King and Church, and modern France (the France since 1789) is the product of a double revolt. Our democracy is thus based on a twofold negation that has profoundly perverted the idea of authority, which we are apt to consider as absolutist and tyrannical, and of liberty, which in France is not a constructive conception. The nation still suffers from these basic misunderstandings.

V

The varied ethnical origins of the French are reflected in their political behavior, and it must be admitted that, politically speaking, the combination of Latin, Celtic, and Germanic traits is not an entirely happy one. In the sphere of politics, some of the defects of the French character are aggravated, while admirable qualities in turn become defects, through either excess of zeal or unwise utilization. Thus, although it has escaped the pathological régimes that have befallen some erratic Latin countries, France has never succeeded in achieving a really stable political structure. She has tried Bonapartism, royalty both absolute and liberal, and four republics—but nothing has ever been completely satisfactory.

To its Latin origin, France owes primarily its solid familial structure, founded on a deep and sincere devotion to domestic ties—comparable, perhaps, to the clan, the clientele, in the Roman meaning of the word. In France the family is stronger than the state; it provides a social foundation of extraordinary stability.

Also from the Latins comes the French concept of the law and a great respect for the legal document, for what is written and solemnly confirmed, ritually, as it were. French law is statute law, a written law, born of Rome. Its lines are rigid. It is based on realism, on a mistrust of man, convinced of man's original sin and of the need to take every precaution against him. Such a premise is in sharp contrast with the British legal code, which does not place this emphasis on the letter of the law and adheres to equity rather than to a rigid interpretation of the statute. The French believe in the sanctity of the written contract and of private property, again as expressed and embodied in Roman law. Waldeck-Rousseau, one of the greatest statesmen of the Third Republic, defined the position clearly: "We are an old nation. We have a long history. We cling to the past by the deepest roots, and the very roots which one might expect to be withered still retain a sensitiveness which the least wound revives and which spreads to the entire organism. We are a country of legality, we are Latins, we belong to that race which considered the written law to be more necessary, which not only sees in it an abstract synthesis, but the measure and the safeguard of its rights."

It is again from the Latins that the French have inherited their conception of the state, and in a more general way of political authority. The power of the state is conceived as separate from and exterior to the individual, possibly even dangerous to him, a power considered as the ancient races considered God. One can lay hold of the state in order to acquire domination, the *imperium* of the Romans, but at the same time it may be prudent to shield oneself against it, since the state, in the hands of one's antagonists, is apt to abuse its power. There is a striking difference here from the Anglo-American idea of the state as a protective, community delegation of powers. The latter conception is in line with the Protestant tradition, while the French point of view bears a relation to the Roman Catholic concept of authority: the hierarchy of the Church stands outside and above the individual.

Above all, the French owe to their Latin heritage their special type of culture, their particular way of thought and their notable gift for expression. They have at their disposal, all of them, an extraordinary capacity for analysis, the power to perceive at once the principle implicated in a problem. They can grasp the nicest distinctions, foresee the remotest consequences, penetrate a question to its core. Indeed, the facility with which the French can pose a problem is intrinsically dangerous, because nothing is ever left unsaid—even that which should be unsaid. In countries which are politically self-disciplined, parties can tacitly agree to reserve certain awkward questions: such restraint has always been impossible in France. A gift for lucid analysis is not necessarily a political asset.

The Celtic heritage has also made itself felt in French political behavior, and I would not say that its influence has been good. From the Celts, as has been suggested, the French derive a strong sense of their private interests, an anxiety to retain the money they have earned, a remarkable capacity for thrift. While this tendency contributes to the probity of their private life, politically it makes for instability, urging them alternately to withhold and to extort from the government everything they can. They are only too well aware of how to keep what they have earned, how to defend themselves against the rapacity of the state: they do not like to pay taxes. This individual anarchism in the Celtic blood brought the Gauls to ruin and defeat as early as the time of Caesar. In the provinces today, the same persistent hostility prevails against collective interference with the private citizen. When the typical Frenchman enters into an association, he always thinks he brings more to it than he will receive.

Lastly, from the northern and eastern parts of France, from the Germanic peoples, comes the seriousness, the solidity and strength of the French character. One finds here, as much as anywhere else in Central Europe, a constructive spirit and a sense of order, not only in private but in public life. The French Republic was the creation of the serious elements of the East; Jules Ferry, Jules Méline, Raymond Poincaré, were men typical of the region. Unfortunately, the people of that portion of France are as a rule more attracted by business than by the forum, and—the contrary being the case in the south—Latin ebullience is more in evidence in French politics than Germanic poise.

The consequences of this combination of elements in the French political character are numerous, and occasionally they are dangerous to the state. In his political behavior the Frenchman is prone to excess in one of two directions: in his devotion to principles, and in his individual or familial egoism. Both tendencies, though apparently contradictory, may even be found in the same man.

It is impossible to exaggerate the decisive role of principles in French politics. Principles and ideals are its heart and soul, but their eventual application often seems a matter of indifference. A subtle commentator, Robert de Jouvenel, observed in *La République des camarades:* "Our legislators are far less interested in the contents of the bills before them than in the resolution closing the debate." In French elections, the voters base their choice on principle more often than on interest. I do not know whether or not the famous phrase, *"Périssent les colonies plutôt qu'un principe,"* was ever actually uttered, but it expresses to a nicety the French point of view.

Such devotion to principle may lead to a fanaticism more absolute than any other, and herein lies the explanation as to why French politics are so often both unrealistic and passionately ideological. The recent nationalizations, for example, were not effected to achieve greater efficiency of service through state control, but on the principle that private enterprise should be eliminated. The choice between Right and Left is made on the same basis: the French vote on various conceptions of life, and ideological distinctions between political parties assume profound and even decisive importance in the conduct of their politics.

However, this concern for principle does not, as I have indicated, prevent the existence of vested interests or of their occasional defense on a sordid basis. You may not be able to win an election in France on a slogan of interest, but other means are found by the French to safeguard that which they want to safeguard. At bottom they place little reliance on collective solutions of their difficulties, considering it more prudent by far to look after one's own affairs— the state cannot be trusted for that. According to the Chinese, it is right and proper to steal from the state to support an aged parent; at heart the French share this opinion. Of course, the Frenchman does have recourse to the state, especially now that inflation has undermined the efficacy of private thrift. But the state is viewed as something of a prey which must be overcome by threat, by patronage, by privilege. The role of the deputy is significant in this respect: his mandate to the Chamber is less that of a lawmaker than an agent-ambassador, who must always be within reach of the electors, to right the wrongs inflicted by an arbitrary administration—unless he is, on the contrary, asking arbitrary favors. Americans, who make similar use of their Congressmen, will understand this point of view.

Moreover, strongly as a Frenchman may assert a principle, he remains unconvinced that the consequences of that principle should apply to him. He wears his heart on the Left and his pocket on the Right—and in practice every Frenchman has a pocket. His innate love of order—his own interests, to put it more crudely—counteracts the extreme political ideas which delight him. As Jouvenel wrote: "France is a happy country where the soil is fertile, where the craftsman is ingenious, where wealth is evenly distributed. Politics is the hobby of men: it is not the condition of their lives." One is reminded of President Taft's observation about some of his political friends: "They pray one way and vote the other." Many a Communist in France is a small proprietor who is politically attracted to the Left, but who has not the slightest desire to be deprived of his private property: he votes Communist, but he prays bourgeois. This political dichotomy explains why foreigners treat the French as dangerous revolutionaries when we talk, and as slow bourgeois of the old type when we do not come to the point.

With fine gifts and a wealth of talent at its disposal, the French political system yet remains inefficient, very largely through misuse of what should be its assets. Some observers say it is impossible to understand French politics; despairingly, they quote Shakespeare's "It is a tale told by an idiot, full of sound and fury, signifying nothing." Of course, they are utterly wrong. Nothing is more logical, nothing is based more firmly on intelligence than French politics: perhaps it is too intelligent—for intelligence, as we have seen, does not ensure success. The doctrinaire prefers theory to application; devotion to principle goes so far as to endanger interest; the individualist fails to identify himself with the community. There is unfortunately a sound basis for the clever commentary on French idiosyncrasies: "One Frenchman: an intelligent man. Two Frenchmen: conversation. Three Frenchmen: an awful mess." (This is in contrast to "One Englishman: a good fellow. Two Englishmen: sport. Three Englishmen: the British Empire.")

So far no satisfactory solution of the nation's political problems has appeared. When France asserted the principle of authority, she ended not with a Washington, but with a Bonaparte. When she instituted a republican régime, authority was seriously vitiated. Her nationalization program, instead of being a step in the direction of administrative progress, was essentially a negation of the principle of free enterprise. Her small landowners, jealous of their progressive

political convictions, vote so far to the Left that they support the abolition of private property. This record is not inexcusable from the point
of view of principle, but the practical result is shocking, and only the
great essential strength of France prevents political chaos.

VI

We now come to a wider aspect of the problem—the French conception of the intellect and their way of making use of it. No analysis
of the country would be complete which does not take this into consideration. When intelligence is at stake, France adopts a special attitude—one, indeed, that is unique. She brings to bear something
which she alone can contribute to the world; herein lies the source
of her international intellectual influence.

France has a magnificent confidence in human intelligence, that
is to say, in humanity itself. She believes that there is a human verity,
belonging to all men, and that this underlying truth is such that the
intelligence can understand it and the word express it. For the Frenchman—and this is of basic significance—thought has no validity unless it is expressed; form is an essential condition of its true existence.
The French language, famous for its clarity, is a precision instrument,
and an authentic national heritage. Any thought whatsoever, filtered
through the French spirit, thereby receives clarity and order. Even
more, it acquires universality; it becomes transmissible, like a medium
of exchange acceptable everywhere and usable by everyone.

In this universality we find that sense of order which French politics may lack but which the French mind possesses. France knows
how to pose a problem, how to analyze a question. Having laid bare
the various elements involved, her intelligence can go to work con-
structively, placing each factor in its proper relationship, transforming the chaos of nature into the cosmos of the spirit, tracing openings
in the virgin forests of the mind. The basis of such a conception of
the intelligence is a sincere respect for human values, a religion of
the spirit in the cultural sense of the word. This is the lesson France
can teach the world—a lesson not to be learned from any other
country.

VII

Any study of France can profit from the use of these keys to French
character and behavior. They are equally applicable to the problem
of production and industry, of relations between social classes, of
divisions between parties, of the establishment of a foreign and colo-

nial policy. But the question arises: to what extent do they remain valid in the aftermath of two world wars?

Many factors have appeared during the last two generations which might tend to transform the French psychology. There is the remorseless development of mechanized production: France nowadays has more industrial workingmen than peasants. There is the inflationary trend of economic life: can the native thrift survive? There is the demoralization which is a natural concomitant of war, especially when war means invasion, as it does for France, rather than a sort of colonial expedition. As a result of war and invasion, problems have arisen in France that sometimes seem too big to be dealt with or even measured intellectually, undermining the national confidence of men who have hitherto relied on reason. Last but not least, there is the shifting of the center of gravity of the world, with the loss for Europe of her place at the heart of world events. Taking all these grave circumstances into account, we can only ask ourselves: will they prove stronger than the French tradition of twenty centuries? *Je me pose la question.*

II

THE DECLINE OF THE FRENCH
ÉLAN VITAL

2

++

THE ÉLAN VITAL OF FRANCE:

A PROBLEM IN HISTORICAL PERSPECTIVE

JOHN B. WOLF

++

IT WOULD be easy for a discussion of the *élan vital* * of France to degenerate into relatively meaningless and insignificant generalizations unless some criteria for analysis can be established. The usual meaning of the term is constrained by context, so that it is not very useful in a discussion dealing with an organic unit like a nation. Bergsonian philosophers, the revolutionary labor leaders, and the "Young Turks" in the French army personalized the conception and thereby narrowed it so that it hardly applies to a whole people. If, therefore, we are to arrive at any significant conclusions about the effectiveness and survival value of the French nation, we must associate the idea *élan vital* with the total psychological-biological process of its historical development in modern times. Only after we have applied the conception to the totality of French life can we profitably turn our attention to the more intimate problem of the *élan vital* of individuals or groups within the society.†

When we focus our attention on the historical process, we must also avoid postulating a mysterious force, a spring of vital energy or drive, that somehow molds the evolution of a people. Such an assumption may be useful to patriotic orators on festive occasions, but even Rousseau never went so far in elaborating his General Will, and the sober-minded historian will be chary of such postulates. On the other hand, it seems reasonable to assume that the *élan vital* of a people can be

* This term is difficult to translate or define, although its meaning is reasonably clear. See discussion of *élan vital* in Chapter 3, especially p. 33.

† Throughout the book authors' footnotes are in Arabic numerals, editor's are indicated by asterisks, daggers, or similar devices.

judged by their ability to adjust their national life to the larger historical processes of the development of Western Europe. This assumption postulates a community, perhaps in the sense that Rousseau described it; it assumes that the community as a political-biological fact
does develop in the same environment with other similar communities; and lastly it presupposes that there is a characteristic form of
development in the larger community that can be used as a measur-
ing stick. Since these are the hypotheses that every historian must
assume if he is to discuss the rise of modern Europe, they are not un-
reasonable and they may be useful in our discussion.

There are several levels of achievement that we must consider.
The most obvious is purely materialistic: does the community provide for the economic well-being of its people on a standard comparable with that maintained by other communities? The second is political: is the community sufficiently in agreement on the popular
mythology and the fundamental aims of the group to assure homogeneity? In other words, is there a general will that can be implemented
politically? A third level is psychological: do the people have confidence in their future and their destiny—a confidence strong enough
to encourage them to maintain and increase their numbers, to induce
them to take social and economic risks, and to impel them to defend
their lands whatever the personal sacrifice? Lastly, does the vigor of
the community lead to creative social and intellectual development?
Obviously the answers to these questions must be relative to the larger
processes in the European community if they are to measure the *élan
vital* as we have described it.

Let us recognize at the outset that these criteria are loaded against
the French. They ask no questions about spiritual well-being, about
refinements in manners and morals, about *civilisation* as the French
often use the term. Nor do they take into consideration the inner
psychological fact that a man's success or failure, his happiness or
misery, in the last analysis, depends upon his individual values and
may well be quite independent of the destiny of the nation. However, by defining the community as the unit that we are to consider,
we automatically reject the atomistic conception of society, and assume that all values ultimately stem from the organic development
of the group. Without economic, political, and military stability, no
society has long maintained either high standards of civilization or a
creative social life.

Our criteria, even without further discussion, will warn anyone
familiar with French history that there has been a serious decline in
the *élan vital* of France. This discovery is not very startling; publicists and philosophers have been expressing it for half a century.

But if we are to understand the forces underlying our problem, we must try to discover when this decline began so that we can assess the problem at hand. Many writers have assumed that the watershed is to be found somewhere in the first decade of the twentieth century; the fact that the Third Republic survived in spite of the hostility of its opponents is thus confused with underlying forces in the historical process. A better point of departure, if one is not too deeply committed to the *mystique* of 1789, is the era of the Revolution and the Empire. With the exception of a few years under the government of Louis Napoleon, the entire period since Waterloo has seen the progressive failure of the French to adjust their development to the process in the other advanced countries of Europe. In the period before the Revolution, France was a leader, perhaps *the* leader, in Europe; her curve of development set the standard for Western society. A cursory glance at the history of France in the last three centuries will give us the evidence we need.

The modern French state, as contrasted with the Medieval and Renaissance kingdom of France, is the creation of the seventeenth century. Henry IV, Richelieu, and Louis XIV were agents of the forces that gave characteristic form to the centralized, bureaucratic, military police state. The forms that came into being in the latter seventeenth century continued to assert themselves, to extend themselves, and to facilitate further development in the characteristic pattern even though the constitutional provisions of the country might indicate Monarchy, Empire, or Republic. Historical processes have a way of asserting their power to survive revolution and violence, and to control the development of characteristic form.

In the century and a half before the Revolution the *élan vital* of France was maintained at a very high level. That was an era in which the French—despite the social strains which precipitated the Revolution—were essentially in agreement about their social and political myths, and in which the economic structure of the Western world gave France relative advantages that maintained the standards of living and the economic vigor of the people. In this period the people were able to accept a common ideal: One God, One Law, One King over a society organized in social hierarchies that assured to each the privileges of his class and the economic status appropriate to the station in life to which God had called him. It is true that the *politique* of the society, to borrow Péguy's term, did not always correspond to this *mystique*. Vauban's famous report at the opening of the eighteenth century, for example, lifts the curtain to show dissatisfaction, distress, and misery. Nevertheless, in the same decade that Vauban wrote the *Dîme royale* (1707) the French people responded to

Louis XIV's cry, "The Kingdom is in danger," and supplied Villars
with the men, money, and material necessary to beat off a coalition of
all Europe led by two of the foremost captains of modern times. The
myths of a society often fit the facts but poorly; they do, however,
establish the goals, and it is the essential unity of the aspirations and
aims of a people that make them a people, not the events of a year
or a decade.

From the moment that Henry IV claimed the throne to the fatal
day on which Louis XVI lost it, Bourbon France suffered chronic
financial malaise. The organization of the monarchy was such that it
was almost impossible for the king to tap the wealth of the kingdom
for the use of government. When one thinks of the burden of taxation
of the old régime, this statement seems paradoxical; it is nonetheless
true. Even a Sully or a Colbert was unable to reorganize the fiscal
structure of the kingdom to correspond to the realities of economic
life. The financial instability of the Bourbon kings, however, must
not be regarded as evidence that France under the Old Régime was a
poor country, economically behind her neighbors. Quite the contrary
was true. France showed striking economic vitality throughout the
seventeenth and eighteenth centuries. The sensational recoveries
that followed both the disaster of the forty years of civil and religious
warfare in the later sixteenth century and the depression resulting
from the wars and the drought years in the last two and a half decades
of Louis XIV's reign provide ample evidence of the essential sound-
ness of French economy. Even the bad government of Louis XV could
not check this growth or impair the confidence of the nation in its
future. The *cahiers* that the deputies brought to Versailles in 1789
testify eloquently to the faith of the people; they recognized abuses
and problems, but they were not beaten down by economic distress.

Nor was this fundamentally sound picture of the *élan vital* of the
nation confined to economics and politics. Throughout most of the
seventeenth and eighteenth centuries the French were the intellectual
leaders of Europe. For only a few years at the opening of the eighteenth
century the intellectual hegemony temporarily passed to the England
of Newton, Locke, and the Augustine writers; by the mid-eighteenth
century French astronomers, chemists, mathematicians, naturalists,
and philosophers had regained the brilliant position that their forefathers had held under the *Roi Soleil*. French artists and architects
took the place of the Italians in the last quarter of the seventeenth
century as the leaders of Europe and maintained their position for two
hundred years.

Obviously there were gross injustices in the society of the old régime, but this is not the place to pass judgment upon them. There

were gross inequities, from the viewpoint of the twentieth century, in every society in Europe, and it would be difficult to prove that France under the Bourbons was strikingly worse than her neighbors. Indeed a strong argument might be made to show exactly the contrary. The France that so successfully stood off all Europe for twenty-five years after 1789 obviously was not a nation beaten to the ground by internal distress.

When we shift our attention to the France of the nineteenth century, the first thing that attracts our notice is the fragmentation that appears in the national will. The old myth, One God, One King, One Law, no longer compels loyalty; in its place we find slogans that proclaim programs: "Liberty, Equality, Fraternity"; "Equality, Order, Obedience"; "Social Justice"; "Property is theft"; "Workers of the world unite." The Revolution of 1789 shifted the axis of political life from the organic conception of the state to an atomistic one, and at the same time expanded the number of political wills to include all members of society. This sharp break with traditions opened wide the possibility of divergent political and social mythology, and granted to every group, indeed to every individual, the right to proclaim a program and to elevate it to the status of a political absolute.

The differences that appear in the course of the nineteenth century are fundamental; they imply a wide diversity of social and political goals and, indeed, mutually exclusive conceptions of God. Furthermore, the process of fragmentation was progressive; by the end of the century there were three major mythologies clamoring vehemently for supremacy, and within each of the major divisions cults were beginning to appear further to atomize the national will. The crisis did not reach proportions implying the nonexistence of a General Will until the 1930's, but even by 1900 the seeds of the disaster were well sprouted. Unless the process is checked the General Will of the nation will be destroyed, leaving only particular wills and anarchy or tyranny as the ultimate result.

At the end of the seventeenth century Bishop Bossuet explained in his *Variations of the Protestant Churches* that the process of religious fragmentation must lead to indifference to God and anarchy in society. The Bishop's predictions were partially wrong, because he did not understand that the state could take the role that religion had traditionally played as the custodian of the beliefs and practices of the community. Were he to see the France of the early twentieth century with its variations in political cults, he would be sure that the Reformation was finally producing its fruit. The same process that had broken the Christian community of Europe in his day seemed to be at work to destroy the political community of France.

The dissociation on the political level was undoubtedly symptomatic of deeper forces at work in the society. This same nineteenth century saw French economy fall behind the developments in the other advanced nations of Europe. It saw the intellectual hegemony of the Continent pass to England and Germany. French artists cultivated flowers from their environment, a few distinguished individuals made great contributions to the science that the Western world was developing, but the creative political and economic forces that had made France paramount in the seventeenth and eighteenth centuries seem either to have lost dynamic power or to have been dissipated in fruitless controversy.

It is unnecessary to pile up evidence of the tragic failure of France to adjust herself to the emerging industrial-scientific society of the twentieth century, but it should be profitable to inquire into the underlying forces that were at work in the society. Perhaps we will be on firmer ground if we follow Goethe's admonition, *"Am Anfang war die Tat,"* and regard brute fact before we attempt to probe political or psychological processes.

France seems to have had little difficulty in adjusting herself to the historical processes of the seventeenth and eighteenth centuries. That was an era in which agriculture, commerce, and handicraft production dominated economic life. The masses made their living from the soil in villages that were relatively self-sufficient; manufacturing was largely confined to small enterprises employing few men; the commercial and financial entrepreneur was the representative of the capitalism of the period. It was a society that depended upon wind, water, and the backs of men and animals for power, and relied upon wood for its principal material. France was eminently fitted to function efficiently in such a civilization. Her soil was fertile, her climate mild, her agriculture as advanced as any in Europe, and her peasants were industrious. The French craftsmen were skillful, and French merchants aggressive. Located so that her harbors faced both the Levant and the Atlantic, France enjoyed a favored position to compete for the commerce of the world.

Furthermore, the form of seventeenth and eighteenth century commerce was favorable to France. The market was weighted to cater to the needs of the wealthy in society, and therefore the items of the luxury trade loomed relatively large in the total commerce. From the sixteenth century onward French manufacturing tended to emphasize the luxury trade; actually, even in the preceding two centuries this tendency was already in evidence. Fine wines, expensive textiles, jewelry, glassware, mirrors, and other articles *de luxe* were the products of France. Even at this early date there was a significant difference in the economies of France and England; the latter emphasized the workaday world—hardware, cheaper textiles, and other articles with relatively wide mass appeal—while the "finer things of life" came from France. The French reputation for quality was so great that certain English manufacturers shipped their products to France for reexport to England so that the goods could be marked "Made in France." Seventeenth- and eighteenth-century France thus was admirably suited to function efficiently in Europe. The economy of the kingdom was well within the norm of European development; even the regulations that Bourbon kings placed upon commerce and manufacturing in their effort to use economic life as a state-building process was characteristic of the whole European picture.

In the nineteenth century, however, France progressively lost the favorable position that she had enjoyed earlier. This was an age of coal and iron and science, and the center of gravity of the market shifted from luxury items to capital goods and commodities for mass consumption. By the opening of the twentieth century the great industrial machine, using enormous quantities of power and substituting the laboratory for the skill of the craftsman, became the characteristic form for European economy.

France was ill-equipped to adjust herself to this new economic process. Her beautiful countryside was lacking in the one essential commodity: coal. At no time after 1815 did the domestic production of coal satisfy the total demand. This fact meant that she was in no position to exploit her great deposits of ferrous metals, since these minerals normally move to coal for efficient production. France did develop heavy industry; she did build factories and foundries comparable to those of her neighbors, but she was unable to do so on the same scale as Britain and Germany. The handicap in fuel made her competitive position hazardous and prevented her from achieving the productive capacity of her neighbors. This fact brought another problem in its train: French industry was not equipped to make full use of the science that was transforming the face of the economy of Europe. Only large enterprises could afford to maintain the expensive laboratories that were developing new processes and new commodities. This in turn affected the educational system, for without the market for engineers and scientists, the French technical schools fell behind those of Germany, England, and the United States. In the eighteenth century French technical education was second to none; in the nineteenth and twentieth centuries it lagged behind. Thus lack of coal and comparative inability to utilize scientific information left France in a disadvantageous position in the economic society of the West.

While she fell behind in the race for heavy industry, her position in the luxury trades seemed secure. The tendency in human behavior to extend a mode of action is nowhere better illustrated than in the emphases on luxury production in France. French workers had an advantage in this traffic, and this in turn strengthened their ability to extend their markets. It was a traffic that eminently fitted the skill and the temperament of the French artisan class, and this facilitated the further development of the industry. In the nineteenth century when machine-made and shoddy were almost synonymous, the luxury industry could easily support the handworker and even assure him an advantageous position in the market, but in the twentieth century when the gap between machine- and hand-quality narrowed, the French artisan as well as his employer faced a crisis, a relative decline in the value of their products. Furthermore, the emphasis on luxury goods worked another disadvantage upon the nation. In the twentieth century the ability to produce steel and sulphuric acid counted more in a contest of military and political power than the ability to produce a subtle perfume or a lady's hat. The world that was making bigger and better guns, bigger and better atom bombs, even bigger and better hogs and cows, had small favor for a society that emphasized uniqueness, artistry, and personal skill. These are values that pay dividends in personal satisfaction, but they count little in the play of power in the modern world.*

Agricultural progress in the nineteenth century was not much more encouraging. French farmers resisted change during the whole period. In spite of the freedom granted by the Revolutionary legislation, the change from old to new methods of agriculture was painfully slow, and by the time that methods grounded in the Middle Ages were largely eradicated, startling new developments in agriculture elsewhere again left the French peasants far behind. In the last quarter of the century rural France received a terrible blow. New methods of transportation brought the cheaply produced foodstuffs of the Americas to Europe on a heretofore inconceivable scale, at the very time when pests and disease blighted French fields. Land values that had reached a peak under Napoleon III were cut in half, and large tracts of French agricultural land became submarginal. The readjustments were painful and slow. Whole districts lost heavily in population; others were forced to find new uses for the land. Unfortunately the structure of French landholdings and the traditional contracts between tenants and landlords were badly adapted to the new conditions, so tradition added its weight to the problems of change.

* Concerning the role of the luxury trades in the present-day French economy see below Chapter 22, especially p. 383.

An ungracious Nature that failed to endow the land with coal cannot be held solely responsible for the failure of the nation to adjust itself to the economic civilization of the nineteenth and twentieth centuries. The traditional ideals of the French must bear their share of blame. Somehow the French bourgeoisie accepted the feudal code that branded trade and manufacturing as ignoble. One does not find this stated overtly, but the very fact that so many of the French entrepreneurs seem to have looked upon their business efforts as a means for providing the wealth necessary for retirement is indicative of a moral value. Sons of retired men did not regard the creation of great economic institutions as a suitable goal for their efforts; they became officials in the government, entered the professions, or joined the country gentry. Again, these values probably provide personal satisfactions, but they do not build industrial concentrations on the modern scale.* On a lower level of aspiration, as André Siegfried has pointed out, the French penchant for the "little"—a little business, a little farm, even a little graft—has further limited the economic vision; France is a nation of small enterprises and, paradoxically, the *Petit Parisien* became its largest newspaper.

In another age these values would have created no serious difficulty, but in the century 1850–1950 they were out of line with the dominant trend in the world, and thereby had within them the seeds of disaster. The French themselves became acutely aware of the gap that was appearing between their economy and that of their more advanced neighbors when the World Fair at the opening of the twentieth century dramatically called attention to the technological and industrial developments elsewhere. Coming as it did after twenty-odd years of economic stagnation, this fair at Paris aroused considerable self-criticism. The nation became painfully aware of its declining birth rate, the flight from the land, and the relative backwardness of its industries. Clearly the same France that functioned so well in an age of wood, wind, and water was falling behind in an age of steam and iron. A glance at the files of any of the more thoughtful French periodicals in the first years of the twentieth century will reveal that this problem, even as much as the more inflammable Dreyfus Case, engaged the attention of thoughtful Frenchmen. It was at this very time that the term *élan vital* came into currency; perhaps the French themselves understood the danger that was threatening the vital springs of the nation.

It is probably an unwarranted assumption that either economic institutions or economic values can fully explain the course of human

* For further discussion of this point see below Chapter 19, dealing with French business and the French businessman.

behavior. It would be attractively simple to show that lack of coal and a limited aspiration are at the roots of the disorder in French society, but such an explanation would have to meet the objection that other societies in Europe where coal is also scarce and men's economic aspirations also limited have not followed the French pattern. Thus to escape the pitfalls of economic determinism we must look to other aspects of French life that also worked to the detriment of the *élan vital* of the nation.

The most important of these, I believe, is to be found in an understanding of the basic postulates of French society. As limiting to man as his economic environment are his postulates about the world. The things that men believe are the true limits of their vision, and these limits, in turn, circumscribe their development.

Bourbon France rested firmly upon a set of postulates that seemed to be drawn directly from the facts of French history. The idea that society was an organic unity, made somehow by God, was fundamental to all political action. The law was of divine origin; custom, tradition, and usage were regarded as sacred. Men no more assumed that they could give a constitution to society than that they could, to quote De Maistre, give weight or extension to mass. The *Honnête Homme* who provided the ideal for the society accepted his lot with a Christian fatalism that testified to his faith in God and his conviction that the world was a vale of tears through which men must pass to reach the kingdom of heaven. Such an idea might have caused a disassociation in society had it been the mirror for the nineteenth and twentieth centuries, but in the seventeenth and eighteenth it created no difficulties.

In the eighteenth century, however, there was an intellectual revolution that had great influence in the upper classes of society; in the following century it affected the whole of the nation. The revolution can best be described by its catchword: *L'esprit géométrique*. It was the same Cartesianism that had provided the guidepost for so many of the great minds whose scientific labors in the seventeenth century became the intellectual capital of the succeeding period. This *esprit géométrique*, generalized in the eighteenth century, became the very foundation of French thought. Fontenelle, its high priest, explained that any work—be it in science, philosophy, morals, or esthetics— would be better, all things being equal, if it were written by the hand of a geometer. It was an idea that easily sank into the French mind; the French language with its exact syntax and its controlled vocabulary undoubtedly facilitated its widespread acceptance.

The basic postulate of this Cartesian philosophy is a belief in a mechanical world that is subject to law. The assumption that the world of nature and of men is a machine was buttressed by a second postulate, namely, that if it worked properly, it would be friendly to man. The Creator was thus assumed to be benevolent. This mechanistic rationalism is really not dissimilar to the Thomistic or Aristotelian, except in that it rests on different postulates and does not assume teleological causation. Like Newton, who discovered the time-machine of the universe, the Cartesian philosopher failed to understand that the world has a history, and, therefore, that the key to many of its mysteries can be understood only in terms of process. If one assumes a static entity, a mechanistic organization, it is easy to believe that the evils of the world can be eradicated by adjusting the mechanism. This conception led to an inordinate confidence in the efficacy of constitutional form and reform. With a limited postulate, politicians and theorists erected little worlds within the greater one in hopes of creating a world more nearly suited to their needs.

Men have no difficulty in assuming that what they believe to be true is in fact true; this human failing made it possible for men to find that the aspirations and hopes of their own group were political absolutes that should forthwith be written into the laws of the land. Thus the law ceased to be a traditional thing written by God, by the wisdom of the race, or by the General Will, and the entailed inheritance of society became a political football, subject to the vicissitudes of election or revolution. As early as 1790 Burke warned the French of the evils inherent in their fulsome acceptance of the geometric conception of politics; and the history of the nineteenth century unhappily bore out his doleful predictions. When men can no longer agree upon their common tradition, belief in a mechanistic structure of society can easily create a pathological situation.

A second line of thought, also growing out of the thinking of the eighteenth century, added to the disorder when it was combined with Cartesian cosmology. This was the idea that morals, manners, and customs are relative. Between 1600 and 1800 travelers and philosophers pondered the fact that variations in values were determined by differences in culture, tradition, and geography. When applied to politics, this conception of moral relativism became individualism and liberalism; when liberalism is applied to a community, however, its members must not forget either Aristotle's insistence that man is a political animal and that man outside of society is less than an animal, or Bodin's sage counsel that there must be a "greatest good" in each society. In other words, differences in moral values can be tolerated as long as there is a core of unanimity that will hold the community together. Failure to understand this fact, as we in the United States are recognizing today when we legislate against certain Communistic activity, may end in disorder. In France this moral relativism has justified disregard for all traditions. Péguy, writing in 1910, lamented the breakdown of the community of the old France, the France of his youth that still had the core of French civilization and tradition; his belief that it was already destroyed was too harsh a judgment, but the process at work seemed to justify his pessimism.

It is with extreme reluctance that I reach the conclusion that the enlightenment of the eighteenth century must share the responsibility for the disorders of the twentieth. The men of Voltaire's generation labored honestly to free the human spirit from the tyranny of ignorance, prejudice, and fear. They are not to be blamed for their postulates any more than we can be blamed for our own. The disorder is not of their making, but rather the result of continued use of their ideas long after new evidence had undermined the postulates upon which those ideas rested. Bergson was undoubtedly right when he argued so vehemently against Cartesianism, and Jacques Maritain is probably right when he insists that France must find a new axis for her social life. Unless it is found, the disorder may well become progressively worse.

There is at least one further factor that deserves serious consideration in this discussion of the basic postulates of French society. French national feeling—that is, their conception of themselves and their role in Europe—came into bloom at a time when France was a leading political and military power on the Continent, and it requires but little insight to understand that the nineteenth and twentieth centuries have deeply injured the pride of a great people. Between 1815 and 1914, with the exception of a few years under Napoleon III, the basic treaty law of Europe assumed French weakness and defeat. Even limited understanding of the July Revolution, the rise of Louis Napoleon, and the popularity of leaders like Boulanger, will testify eloquently to the gap between reality and national aspiration. Furthermore, the victory of 1919 merely emphasized that gap. It was won by a coalition, and when the coalition no longer sustained it, the victory turned to gall and wormwood. Unlike Swedes, Danes, or Dutchmen, the French—from the little people in the country whose forefathers were at Austerlitz, Jena, and Friedland, to the old families in the châteaux who try to remember the white flag of Henry IV—were psychologically unprepared to recognize their nation as a second-rate power. On the morrow of the defeat of 1870, the French began to rebuild the army and the navy: the nation never questioned the wisdom of this action. From that time down to the catastrophe of 1940, in face of a relative decline in population and a marked inferiority in industrial strength, the French government, no matter what might be its political complexion, persisted in the program of competitive military preparations. Nor were French ambitions confined to Europe alone; the fleet and the colonial empire were both indicative of a bid for world as well as European power. The military retrenchments of the past few years might indicate that France is ready to acknowledge the implications of the terrible defeat of 1940 and the readjustments of power in the modern age, but speeches in the Chamber, articles in the press, and the opinions of men on the street all indicate that the French face reality frankly, but are not yet ready to accept freely the full consequences of their position in the world.

It is a tragedy when a great man loses his strength and his personality; it is a catastrophe when a nation loses its assurance. To me the tragic pathos of the French problem can be summed up in a remark made by my hostess in a Parisian pension in 1937 when she called my attention to the notice about the air-raid shelter for the neighborhood. "Over there [in Germany]," she said with a choke in her voice, "the shelters will be safe; ours will be faulty." She wanted to be proud of the nation for which her husband had given up his life in 1916; she wanted to believe in the community that had given her nurture, but she had lost faith and with it her nerve. These simple words are dramatic evidence of the failure of the *élan vital* of a great people.

3

++

THE CONCEPT OF ÉLAN VITAL:

A RATIONALIZATION OF WEAKNESS

JOHN BOWDITCH

++

WHEN, as in the preceding chapter, one compares the France of the age of Louis XIV with the France of the Third Republic, he cannot fail to be impressed by the contrast between a social organism that responded well to the requirements of a seventeenth-century agrarian society and one that has at least partially failed to rise to the challenge of the predominantly industrial age of our twentieth century. France seemed to fit the earlier period; she appears out of step in the later one. Now, if one uses the expression in a broad sense and equates possession of *élan vital* with the measure of success a society exhibits in adapting itself to and taking advantage of its environment, then he can urge that Frenchmen living in the age of Louis XIV, or of Napoleon, when France boasted all the outward symbols of power and most of the inward signs of self-confidence, possessed an ample store of *élan vital,* whereas our twentieth-century Frenchman, who has lived through the tragedy of June 1940 and the Vichy years, has reason to fear that his supply of the precious elixir has been dangerously reduced. The preceding chapter has treated the problem in this broad framework; the present one will be confined to a more limited period when the contrast between past strength and present uncertainty was not so evident as it is today and when the concept of *élan vital* had a special historical significance.

When we speak of our industrial age, with its concomitants of big business and assembly-line production methods, of big government and regimented peoples, of huge, mechanized armies, however far back we push its origins or early manifestations, we are speaking of what is properly a twentieth-century phenomenon. Was it mere coincidence that the concept of *élan vital* was given currency just in the years from the turn of the last century to the outbreak of war in 1914 when Frenchmen were first becoming truly aware of the impact of the industrial age and of the growing contrast between their country's stabilized population and *routinière* business methods on the one hand and the burgeoning strength of its rivals on the other? I do not think so. Rather, I should like to suggest that when French labor leaders of those years, for instance, boasted of the *élan révolutionnaire* of their fellow workers or French military writers gloried in the *furia française* exhibited by their countrymen on hypothetical battlefields, they were, in effect, fabricating myths as a means of escape from the unpleasant task of coming to terms with the hard realities of their twentieth-century world. In this sense, the timely appearance of the mystical notion that Frenchmen in general, and certain Frenchmen in particular, were endowed with some sort of vital impulse or creative will to action, may be treated both as an unconscious rationalization for what were immediate material deficiencies and as a symptom of that lack of confidence in their institutions, the full effects of which have become apparent only in our time.

It will be noted that in employing French expressions of the concept of *élan vital* use will be made of such terms as *élan révolutionnaire* and *furia française*. The point is perhaps a minor one, but before dealing with the myths created by Frenchmen, it would be in order to point out that non-French writers have been guilty of fabricating something of a myth in the use they have made of the expression *élan vital*. True, the term can be traced directly to Bergson's *Creative Evolution,* a work that appeared appropriately in 1906; and since Bergsonism, with its emphasis on intuition at the expense of intellect, with its glorification of the will over reason, pervaded the intellectual atmosphere of the period, there seems to be some warrant for associating his "vital impulse" with contemporaneous expressions of belief in certain inherent spiritual and moral qualities of the French race or genius, but it does involve taking liberties with the French term. While it is fair to say that the French used the *concept* in much the sense attributed to them, they failed, at least so far as the present writer has been able to discover, to employ the *term* itself in other than a narrow, strictly philosophical context. The popular literature is full of references to the *élan* of the Frenchman; it says nothing about *élan vital*. Once this reservation has been made, however, we may proceed on the assumption that the concept, if not the term, was widely and popularly used by Frenchmen, particularly in the first years of the twentieth century.

Of those groups that leaned heavily on the concept of *élan vital*,

I shall concentrate my attention on two: one properly identified with
the French Left, the other less clearly identified with the Right. The
first was composed of those workers who subscribed to the doctrine
of revolutionary syndicalism,* a philosophy of labor action that came
to fruition just after the turn of the century and which remained the
official ideology of the French General Confederation of Labor (the
CGT) to the outbreak of war in 1914. Today, if revolutionary syndicalism has only a small following in French labor circles, the conditions that made possible the emergence of the philosophy and that
once made it popular have by no means entirely disappeared. The second group was made up of army officers, military theorists, and publicists who gloried in the doctrine of *l'offensive à outrance*. It is with
this group that non-French writers have generally linked the concept
of *élan vital*. Some of its members could claim to be republicans in
politics, but most were at least distrustful of democracy, and many
were openly hostile to the Third Republic. Today, they and their
counterparts swell the ranks of the De Gaullists.

The French labor theorists of the CGT made use of the *élan révolutionnaire* of the French worker, first of all, to explain, in a sense
favorable to themselves, the difference between the French type of
labor organizations and tactics and those developed by the English
and German trade-unionists. Where the methodical Germans and
stolid Englishmen constructed large centralized labor organizations
with relatively high dues and substantial strike and other benefits, the
French were content with loose, federalist organizations in which, to
paraphrase the syndicalists, the individual retained his full autonomy
within the union, the union within the federation or *Bourse du
travail,* and the latter organizations within the CGT. The dues paid
by the French workers were only a fraction of those paid by the English or German members, and most French unions or federations
lacked the funds to support a strike of any duration. It was accepted
syndicalist practice that more often than not strikes would be spontaneous in origin and would be supported by voluntary subscrip-
tions, communal soup kitchens, and other improvised methods. Far
from admitting any disadvantage in the absence of internal discipline
or in the anarchic character of such tactics, the revolutionary syndicalists made positive virtues of them. They set out to prove to their own
satisfaction that by such methods French unions had secured greater
benefits than had the larger and wealthier British and German organizations. The key to their success, to quote a syndicalist writer, lay
"in the *élan*, in the revolutionary attitude, in the aggressive vigor"

---

* For further discussion of revolutionary syndicalism see Chapter 16, on Georges Sorel.

of the French strikers.[1] Thus, if we are to believe the revolutionary syndicalists, the *furor gallicae* of the French workers would more than compensate for Teutonic discipline or English pounds sterling.

If the Frenchman could be counted upon to exhibit more *élan vital* than the Germans or English, it was also true, according to the revolutionary syndicalists, that only a small percentage of Frenchmen possessed it in any large measure. From this recognition of the existence of an élite among the workers, followed the doctrine that creative activity is the work of minorities upon whom must fall the burden of providing inspiration and direction to what would otherwise remain an inchoate mass. It also followed that federalist principles of organization, as exemplified in the structure of the CGT, which served to open the way for minority influence, were to be defended at the expense of democratic methods based on the principle of majority rule. "Progress, as the whole of our history demonstrates," wrote one revolutionary syndicalist, "is the consequence of the revolutionary efforts of conscious minorities. Organized democracy snuffs out minorities in favor of sheep-like and conservative majorities. Thus democracy with its universal suffrage and its political sovereignty ends by cementing the economic slavery of the working class." [2] Or, as another writer, who was attacking the "authoritarian," "hierarchical" character of democratic society, put it, "One does not revolt by delegation. The collective revolt supposes the participation of the entire mass carried along by the *élan* of a minority which from the beginning sets the example." [3]

Finally, the revolutionary syndicalists fell back on the *élan* of the French worker to justify their special brand of labor tactics. If disciplined organizations, large strike funds, and support of political parties were all to be condemned because they led to a conservative standpatism, a solution must be sought that would be more compatible with the "temperament" of the French worker. They found it in "direct action." In its broadest sense, direct action meant any action in which the workers relied on their own institutions and their own strength; as such, it need not involve other than peaceful, legal methods. But when it came to describing the various forms of direct action, such as boycotts, sabotage, strikes, and above all, the general strike, the revolutionary syndicalists could seldom refrain from alluding, in one way or another, to the utility of force. The writer who suggested that all progress was the work of conscious minorities also argued

---

[1] Émile Pouget, *La Confédération générale du travail* (Paris, 1908), pp. 41, 42.
[2] Émile Pouget, *Les Bases du syndicalisme* (Paris, n.d.), p. 18.
[3] M. Pierrot, *Syndicalisme et révolution* (2nd ed., Paris, 1908), p. 12.

that "all real progress has been obtained by force." [4] Strikes, one would gather from syndicalist writings, were of less interest because of the material benefits they brought than because of their moral effect in arousing the fighting instincts of the worker; they were likely to succeed only to the extent the workers were prepared to ignore the dictates of bourgeois legality. The terminology of the battlefield was as dear to the revolutionary syndicalists as to the military theorists.

No doubt the writers quoted above were sincere when they waxed enthusiastic about the revolutionary ardor of the French worker, about the stimulus provided by active minorities, or about the efficacy of force. It is reasonable to assume they were not intentionally fabricating a myth, as Sorel was to suggest with regard to the general strike. At least, unlike Sorel and others of the intellectuals who professed a sympathy for a philosophy of violence, these labor theorists were members of the working class or could claim that they had derived their inspiration from direct participation in the labor movement. None the less, when one relates theory to fact, one can hardly escape the conclusion that revolutionary syndicalism was little more than a rationalization for what, in terms of the twentieth-century industrial age, were serious weaknesses in the structure of the French labor movement and in the psychological attitude of the French worker.

The extreme decentralization, the tendency toward atomism, exhibited at all levels of the CGT, was hardly a matter of choice to the leadership. The truth was that French workers were very irregular about paying even the low dues charged by their unions, and any attempts to enforce discipline were likely to be followed by wholesale desertions. The federations and the CGT faced the same problem with regard to their constituent bodies, only in a more exaggerated form. The unions saw to it that the bulk of the dues paid by their members stayed in the local treasury, and they treated directives from the central bodies as no more than suggestions which could be disobeyed at will. Little was done to change these conditions before 1914, and it is perhaps not surprising that men who had grown up within the system should have defended it.

One can account for some of this emphasis on federalism within the CGT by pointing out that that organization did not represent a fair cross-section of the French economy. Those areas, such as the North and East, where heavy industry predominated, and those occupations, such as mining, metallurgy, and textiles, in which the large factory and mechanized production were becoming the rule, were inadequately represented in the CGT compared to regions (such as Paris and the Center) and occupations (such as the metal trades,

[4] *La Voix du peuple,* April 13, 1902.

leather goods, woodworking, and the like) in which the small establishment and the craft spirit remained strong. Hence the habits and prejudices of the highly individualistic craft worker, who had every reason to fear and resent the new industrial age, played a disproportionate role in the shaping of revolutionary syndicalist thought.

But the craft worker, as such, was not alone responsible. Nearly all French workers, including those in heavy industry, were reluctant to delegate authority to union officials or to pay dues, particularly to see those dues paid over to a national body. A British delegate to one of the congresses of the First International remarked that the French delegates were always ready to raise their hands when it came to passing a motion, but that they were equally slow to put them in their pockets when it came time to offer a contribution. When the issue of pooling strike funds was raised in 1905 at a congress of glassworkers, one of the delegates said, in effect: "Why should we turn over our funds for some other union to spend?" [5] The myopic provincialism evident in such a remark was not easy to break down; and, in the face of it, the argument that modern labor unions must match the methods of modern business struck no responsive chords.

The advocacy of direct action methods, and especially the exaltation of force, on the part of the revolutionary syndicalists also may be accounted for in large part as a rationalization for conditions over which the leaders had no control. When funds and a disciplined organization are lacking to a body of workers on strike, as was too often the case in French labor disputes, violence is apt to occur, not because of an exhibition of élan révolutionnaire on the part of either leaders or followers, but more likely because of hunger and exasperation. That such violence usually worked against the interests of the workers, as was repeatedly demonstrated during the strikes that marked the years 1906 to 1910, was but one of the facts the revolutionary syndicalists refused to face.

On the other hand, there can be little doubt that some of the bitterness that characterized many of the strikes in the decade before 1914 sprang from a feeling on the part of large numbers of French workers that they had nothing to hope for either from their government, as represented by the Third Republic, or from the economic system as represented by the employing class. It would be easy to exaggerate the amount of support given to the noisy campaign conducted by the CGT against militarism and patriotism were it not for the lesson of what happened in 1914, but one can believe that there was a widespread cynicism in French labor circles about the value of democratic institutions. Likewise, there is some evidence that French

[5] Charles Rist, "Chronique ouvrière," *Revue d'économie politique,* xx (1906), 233.

workers were losing faith in the capacity of their employers to meet the challenge of the machine age. Before the Paris Exposition of 1900 opened, it was pointed out in the labor press that the Exposition would "certainly exhibit a great technical revolution," and that French industry, "still too bound by tradition," would be "confronted with the marvelous machines of England, of Germany, and, above all, of the United States." [6] A similar lack of confidence in the technical proficiency of French industrial enterprises was reflected in a syndicalist pamphlet on the Taylor System of scientific management. In addition to attacking the backwardness of French industry, the author went on to make an unfavorable comparison between the social philosophies of the American and French businessman. He charged that, whereas American employers had the vision to share some of the profits of the Taylor System with their workers through shorter hours and higher pay, French employers who had experimented with the system had merely used time studies to speed up production and had given their employees no compensation whatever. If these statements can be considered at all typical of the sentiment of French workers, is it any wonder that they looked to Proudhon or to Bakunin rather than to Samuel Smiles or Horatio Alger for inspiration?

Though we can dismiss the revolutionary syndicalist use of the concept of *élan vital* as little more than a rationalization or a myth which served no useful purpose other than to gloss over the weaknesses of the French labor organizations, we cannot dismiss so easily the conclusion that the popular appeal of revolutionary syndicalism was symptomatic of lack of faith on the part of many Frenchmen in the future of their economic and political institutions. Even if one assumes that a certain amount of the revolutionary spirit is both natural and appropriate to the Left, the fact that the French Left produced a philosophy so out of step with a twentieth-century world is enough to provoke misgivings. This early development of an antiparliamentarian, hostile attitude toward the Third Republic on the part of many French workers has contributed in no small measure to the lack of assurance with which French democracy has met the economic and social strains to which it has been subjected in the last two decades.

If we turn now to the army officers and military theorists who popularized the doctrine of the offensive and who paved the way for, or took part in, the so-called "Young Turk" revolution of 1911 when the extremists of that school won control of French military planning, we find an amazingly close parallel to the use of *élan vital* made by the revolutionary syndicalists. Just as the latter expected the *élan révolutionnaire* of the French worker more than to compensate for

[6] *La Petite République,* February 1, 1900.

German discipline, so the Young Turks played upon the moral superiority of the French troops over their Teutonic rivals; where the revolutionary syndicalists relied on an élite to carry along the mass of the French workers, the Young Turks urged the importance of "quality," as measured by the size of the "active" army, at the expense of "quantity," as measured by the reserves; and, finally, the exaltation of direct action by the revolutionary syndicalists found its counterpart in the military theorists' stress on *l'attaque brusquée,* symbolized by the bayonet charge.

The inherent fighting qualities of the French soldier were utilized by the French military theorists both to justify their doctrine of the offensive and to build up confidence in a French victory, even against possible odds. The superiority of the offensive was not made to stand on the moral factor alone; Foch, for instance, managed to convince himself and his students that all the advantages of improved armaments would go to the attacker—but Foch was above all a believer in the importance of moral superiority. Captain Gilbert, the leading exponent of the offensive in the 'nineties and the spiritual godfather of the Young Turks, in an attack on a statement of Clausewitz favorable to the defense, argued that "the offensive doubles the energy of the troops," [7] and he then expatiated on the excitable temperament of the French which made them particularly suited for offensive actions. It was Gilbert who popularized the phrase *furia française.* For an example of how French *élan vital* would compensate for German material advantages, we can turn to General Langlois, editor of the military review patronized by the Young Turks. In an article written in 1907 comparing the effective strengths of the German and French armies, he noted a slight advantage for the Germans (the French, he confessed, had only 57 per cent as much artillery). "But," he wrote, "if we compare the value of the personnel, the individual values, we have an incontestable advantage over our neighbors," and he concluded, "Germany will always have the advantage of us in numbers . . . , but we can compensate for that advantage by utilizing the precious qualities of race that are peculiar to us. . . ." [8]

The association of the offensive spirit with an élite was of even greater importance to the Young Turks. After 1870, the length of service in the army was reduced to five years in 1872, to three years in 1889, then to two years in 1905. With each of these reductions the relative importance of the professional element in the army was lowered and that of the democratic reserves was raised; in fact, except for the officer element, this process went so far that it was necessary

[7] Quoted by Jean Jaurès, *L'Armée nouvelle* (Paris, 1915), p. 134.
[8] "Notre situation militaire," *Revue des deux mondes,* XLI (October 15, 1907), 780, 793.

for those who believed in the professional army to transfer their af-
fections to the field or active army. In the mobilization plan of 1889
the active army and the reserves were given equal value, but once
the school of the offensive began to win converts, its devotees, who
preached the necessity of "quality" as opposed to "quantity," succeeded in relegating the reserves to an increasingly subordinate position. Captain Gilbert decided that it was the active army that would
remain "the true, the only offensive instrument," [9] and that reserves
would prove useful only to hold the ground that had been won or
to secure a line of retreat. It was only after the Young Turks had
come into power and after the campaign for the three-year-service
law had begun, however, that the theory of an élite corps took on
the aura of dogma. "The armies of reservists are armies of decadence,"
exclaimed one general, "they are an indication that the nation lacks
the virility to accept courageously the tax of active service the circumstances require." [10] Or to quote Le Temps, "It is above all with
the active army that the first victories will be won, and it will be the
first victories that will give the country the élan and the enthusiasm
to continue the struggle." [11]

From the theory of an élite, as represented by the active army, one
passes easily to the assumption that le premier choc of red-pantalooned
Frenchmen charging with fixed bayonets against the solid ranks of
gray-coated Germans would, once war had broken out, quickly decide the issue. Jules Romains in his novel Verdun depicts two young
French officers, veterans of months of trench fighting, theorizing about
the next move in the grand strategy of the war. When pressed for his
opinion, one of the two strikes a dramatic pose, thrusts out his fist,
and growls, "When the time comes, we shall charge the foe and let
cold steel decide." [12] By the time of Verdun, the phrase, attributed to
Foch, had become the stock gibe to throw at anyone who ventured
to suggest that the high command had a plan, but in 1912 and 1913
the charge with cold steel was sacred to the Young Turks. It was
reported that at the French maneuvers of 1913 any officer who did not
put his head down and charge ahead was considered lacking in nerve.
Let us listen, if you will, to Commandant Driant speaking before the
French Chamber in December 1912: "With the fickle psychology of
the crowds which today constitute the armed nation, the victorious
army will be the one that, disdaining reserves and fortresses, will first
hurl itself at the throat of the adversary, and will, as a result, acquire

[9] Quoted by Jaurès, op. cit., p. 126.
[10] Quoted by J. Monteilhet, Les Institutions militaires de la France (Paris, 1926), p. 268.
[11] ibid., p. 272.
[12] Jules Romains, Verdun, trans. by Gerald Hopkins (New York, 1939), p. 66.

that moral superiority that takes control of events. And nothing says that it will be necessary to have hundreds of thousands of men. The first great battle will decide the whole war, and wars will be short. It is necessary that the conception of the offensive penetrate the soul of our nation." [13]

The tragic consequences of such oratorical nonsense hardly need emphasis. When war came, not only did the vaunted offensive plan of the Young Turks collapse after a few murderous charges, but officers and men who had been given no training and no equipment for defensive action found themselves in full retreat before a German army that had disobeyed the rules of the game by using reserves as front-line troops. Because the French high command counted army corps only on the basis of actives, it refused to credit the reports of the German units sweeping through Belgium with results that were nearly disastrous. When the war of maneuver turned into a war of trenches and continuous fronts, the French found themselves short of machine guns, entirely without high-trajectory artillery, and psychologically, at least at the higher levels, unprepared for the new conditions. For the next fifteen months the French high command could devise no better plan than a series of ever more costly offensives; then it fell back on a war of attrition, the kind of war France could least afford. That France was saved was not due to the *furia françese* of her élite troops, but to the Teutonic doggedness of her lousy, grimy reserves who used their bayonets to open meat cans or to scrape the mud off their boots.*

In searching for the explanation for the Young Turks' escape into the mystical, the numerical inferiority of the French must be given a large place. By the end of the nineteenth century, the French were faced by a declining birth rate and an aging population, whereas the Germans were at a peak in their growth. As a result, in 1914 France had less than 8 million men of military age, while the Germans had 15 millions.† In a war of masses it could be anticipated that France would be at a serious disadvantage. But because the Germans failed to train all their potential reserves, the French were able, with the passage of the three-year law, to achieve an active army equal to that of their rival. Thus, to follow the comfortable rationalizing of the Young Turks, in a short offensive war, a bit of Gallic *élan vital* should suffice to bring victory.

A similar line of reasoning may be applied with regard to the problem of materiel. In any prolonged contest involving the productive

---

* Concerning French military theories since the First World War see below, Chapters 23–25.

† Regarding population changes as a factor in French security see Chapter 18.

[13] Monteilhet, *op. cit.*, p. 269.

resources of the two countries, Germany, with its superiority in heavy industry, would be ahead; in a short war, the advantage would be of little consequence. In actual fact, the two armies reflected the differences in their countries' economies from the outset. A nice comparison may be drawn between the French reliance on the light, rapid-firing 75, clearly a quality weapon, and the German supply of medium howitzers and Big Berthas, the one the product of an economy that favored light industry, the other the product of the giant Krupp foundries. It might be argued that had France possessed the Ruhr, French military men might have been more impressed with the usefulness of firepower and less bewitched by *élan vital*. In any case, we have here another instance of the unwillingness of certain Frenchmen to comprehend that they were living in the twentieth century. Instead of matching the German artillery, which would not have been difficult in that period, the Young Turks decided that machine guns were defensive weapons and artillery would not be needed to prepare infantry attacks, hence neither would be required in large quantities.

A more serious charge that can be laid against the French staff and the conservative journals that helped to popularize the program of the military men was that their doctrines were founded on a basic distrust of those democratic principles on which the Third Republic rested. Their philosophy was succinctly formulated by Thiers in 1872 when, in backing a retention of the old seven-year term of service, he stated, "I do not want a compulsory service . . . that would put a gun at the shoulder of all the Socialists; I want a firm, disciplined professional army, capable of making us respected without and within, strictly limited in size, but superior in quality." [14] France and her army had changed much since 1872, but it may be questioned whether there had been any comparable change in the professional army men and in the conservative element of the bourgeoisie who controlled the organs of opinion. Had they possessed more faith in the common people, had they been able to come to terms with the requirements of the industrial world, they might have developed a military theory more in keeping with the needs of the France they unquestionably thought they were serving. Instead they were led into fabricating a myth that was as far removed from reality as that of the revolutionary syndicalists they so thoroughly despised.

By concentrating attention on a restricted period of time and on but two elements of French society, I have no doubt been guilty of some distortion. On the other hand, that two groups so widely separated as the revolutionary syndicalists and aristocratic army officers

[14] Quoted by Monteilhet, *op. cit.*, p. 145.

should each have seized upon the mystical concept we have labeled *élan vital* and should have used it in much the same way to escape from the world in which they, and France, were living is worth emphasis.

Furthermore, if these two groups did not represent the whole or necessarily the best of France, it must not be assumed that their influence was negligible. One need only mention Georges Sorel and his disciples Édouard Berth and Hubert Lagardelle to indicate that revolutionary syndicalism had adherents outside as well as within the labor movement; the language of the Young Turks was echoed by ultranationalists ranging all the way from the naïve Agathons [15] of the younger generation to the more dogmatic Maurrases and Daudets of the Action Française. It has been suggested that modern France has suffered from too much eighteenth-century rationalism, that it would benefit from a bit of Bergsonian mysticism; the present study would rather indicate that if a unifying *mystique* has been lacking, part of the reason has been just the willingness of important elements of France to turn their backs on the age in which they lived and to employ myths, such as the concept of *élan vital*, as a means of escaping from rather than coping with their problems.

---

[15] Agathon (Henri Massis and Alfred Tarde, two university students) produced a popular book, *Les Jeunes Gens d'aujourd'hui* (Paris, 1913), which carried as part of its subtitle, "The Taste for Action." The work, incidentally, was crowned by the French Academy.

4

+++

THE DESICCATION
OF THE BOURGEOIS SPIRIT

JOHN B. CHRISTOPHER

+++

"FOR more than a century," wrote Léon Blum in 1941, "everything that has happened in France suggests that the bourgeoisie has been using up its sap." [1] French analysts and politicians of almost every persuasion have echoed Blum's judgment. They have agreed that the defeat of 1940 revealed not only the incompetence of the General Staff but also the declining capacity, if not the moral bankruptcy, of the governing class. On the fellow-traveling Left, Pierre Cot found that the increasing concentration of wealth was pushing the bourgeoisie inevitably toward fascism. [2] On the Right, "Rémy," once a sympathizer with the Action Française and more recently a political lieutenant of De Gaulle, drew the following lesson from his experience in the Resistance: "The Psalmist (who in his day probably belonged to a secret intelligence network) wrote: 'God shows the little regard He has for the riches of this world by the worth of those to whom He has given them.' My companions in the Network belonged to different classes socially and carried on various professions. But they all had one characteristic in common. If they had money, they attached but relative importance to it. They were not bourgeois." [3] And "Pertinax" asked, at the conclusion of *The Gravediggers of France:* "Why did that liberal bourgeoisie which had supplied the Republic with so many good servants suddenly become sterile?" [4]

[1] *For All Mankind* (New York, 1946), p. 71.
[2] *The Triumph of Treason* (Chicago, 1944), pp. 46–47, 60–73.
[3] "Rémy" (Gilbert Renault-Roulier), *Memoirs of a Secret Agent of Free France, I: The Silent Company* (New York, 1948), p. 180.
[4] "Pertinax" (André Géraud), *The Gravediggers of France* (Garden City, N.Y., 1944), p. 578.

This chapter seeks to answer the question raised by "Pertinax." It proposes to examine the symptoms of desiccation in the bourgeois spirit and then to evaluate some of the possible causes. One cautionary remark can go almost without saying. The following pages pass some rather harsh judgments on the French bourgeois spirit. These judgments are not intended to dim the luster of French culture; they are concerned exclusively with the economic and political record of the bourgeoisie. Equally harsh conclusions may be reached about elements of the bourgeoisie in almost any industrial nation. The demoralization of the German bourgeoisie in the 1920's and 1930's, for instance, was undoubtedly more catastrophic than was the comparable demoralization in France. The fact remains, however, that of all the Atlantic democracies the French experienced the greatest difficulty in adjusting to the facts of twentieth-century economic life. It is the thesis of this chapter that this maladjustment resulted above all from the peculiar inflexibility of the French bourgeois spirit.*

First of all, a definition is in order. "Bourgeois," as used by the French, is a treacherous word; the wisest translators do not attempt to give it an English equivalent. It may be employed in a complimentary sense, pejoratively, or merely neutrally. It may praise a solid and satisfying mode of existence, as in *confort bourgeois*. It may condemn a whole series of vices, from cultural philistinism to the narrow selfishness and materialism denounced so picturesquely by "Rémy." Or it may simply describe, without judging, the status and the attitudes of a very large and ill-defined segment of French society. This chapter employs the term "bourgeois" primarily in its neutral and descriptive connotation, but inevitably with some suggestions of the moral overtones and nuances of the French word.

No one social class monopolized the bourgeois spirit under the Third Republic. Both men of property and would-be men of property took the bourgeois outlook. It was adopted by professional men, by civil servants, by *rentiers,* by land-owning peasants, and even by some wage-earning workers. It is a truism that almost every American considers himself a member of the middle class. It is perhaps almost equally true that the majority of Frenchmen regarded themselves as bourgeois or potential bourgeois under the Third Republic. In 1930 André Siegfried found the bourgeois spirit "everywhere latent" in France.[5]

* The reader will find this theme developed at greater length, with special reference to the French businessman, in Chapter 19.

[5] André Siegfried, *France: A Study in Nationality* (New Haven, 1930), p. 6. See also Blum, *For All Mankind*, pp. 15, 67–97; Albert Guérard, *The France of Tomorrow* (Cambridge, Mass., 1942), Chap. VII; Marc Bloch, *Strange Defeat* (London, 1949), pp. 138–40, 162–65.

This latent bourgeois spirit was not the simple capitalist devil of the Marxists. Even Léon Blum admitted that the bourgeoisie had once been "upright and honest, patient and prudent, modest and decent, thrifty and reasonable." [6] These virtues, however, became decidedly shopworn after 1900. The once "upright and honest" bourgeois were acquiring an unenviable reputation for tax-evasion. They carried thrift and prudence to the point where they failed to keep French industry and agriculture abreast of technological improvements. The collapse of 1940 was not the first sign of bourgeois desiccation; it was simply the last and most dramatic symptom of an illness which had already become chronic.

II

During the last three decades of the Third Republic French technology progressed at a feeble pace compared to the brisk tempo set by the economic giants—the United States, Germany, and Great Britain. The few attempts in the direction of large-scale capitalist farming during World War I did not succeed. Farmers were reluctant to invest in the chemical fertilizers, the tractors, and the other paraphernalia of mechanized agriculture. By the 1930's French farm output was the lowest per acre in northwestern Europe. Moreover, agricultural production was unbalanced: there were consistent surpluses of grains, wine, and industrial beets, and repeated shortages of fruits and vegetables.[7]

The organization of retail trade, too, revealed the obsolete pattern of a very large number of very small units. Cooperatives, chain stores and the *prix unique* ("five-and-tens"), not to mention super-markets, were few and far between. Food products moved from the small farmer to the small retailer through an expensive series of middlemen. The farmer sold at a relatively low price, while the ultimate consumer paid a relatively high one.[8]

The Third Republic, above all, was the victim of a stunted industrial revolution. For a time it appeared that World War I had obliged the French to catch up with the industrial pacemakers. Arnold J.

---

[6] Blum, *op. cit.* p. 93.

[7] Charles Morazé, *La France bourgeoise* (Paris, 1946), pp. 183–87; Michel Augé-Laribé and Pierre Pinot, *Agriculture and Food Supply in France During the War* (New Haven, 1927); Charles Bettelheim, *Bilan de l'économie française, 1919–1946* (Paris, 1947), pp. 7–31; Jean Fourastié and Henri Montet, *L'Économie française dans le monde* (Paris, 1946), pp. 63–65, 132–33; J. H. Clapham, *The Economic Development of France and Germany, 1815–1914* (Cambridge, Eng., 1921), Chap. VIII; Pierre Fromont, "La Production agricole," in *La France économique de 1939 à 1946* [*Annuaire de la vie économique française*, 18e Année] (Paris, n.d.), pp. 393–436.

[8] Morazé, *op. cit.*, pp. 191–92; Jacques Audient, "Le Paysan? Non: l'intermédiaire," *Esprit*, XVII (January 1949), 57–59.

Toynbee wrote in 1933: "In the fifteenth year after the Armistice it is already evident that it has profited France handsomely to have had her hand forced by devastation. . . . In this compulsory renovation of her industrial plant, France has been compelled to make an inestimably valuable capital investment. Moreover, her gain is not to be measured in crude terms of iron and steel and bricks and mortar. A new apparatus involves a new technique; and a new technique involves a new spirit." [9]

The new technique and the new spirit praised by Toynbee constituted the exception, however, not the rule, in the 1930's. Only a handful of industries—notably paper, rubber, and automobiles—really kept up to date technologically. Cotton textiles, leather, construction, and metallurgy all lagged far behind. France's output of bauxite, for instance, was eight times that of Germany, but its production of finished aluminum was only a quarter of the German. French iron ore cost only one-third as much as American ore, and French wages were comparatively low, but the price of sheet iron was as high in France as it was in the United States. Handicapped especially by inadequate supplies of coal, France did not possess the natural resources for industrial development on the German or the British scale. Yet the French bourgeois commanded sufficient fiscal resources to press industrialization both further and faster than they actually did. If these fiscal resources had been fully mobilized, France doubtless could never have become an industrial giant, but it could have ceased to be an industrial pygmy.[10]

The failure to make this investment was a most arresting symptom of bourgeois reluctance to face up to economic facts. Addressing a meeting of the Nord Railway Company in 1905, Baron Alphonse de Rothschild deplored the "languor" and "inertia" affecting business activity in France. "Money," he said, "has never been more plentiful. . . . Why is this money not utilized for the development of commerce and industry?" [11] One reason was the steadily increasing rate

[9] Arnold J. Toynbee, *A Study of History* (2nd ed., London, 1935), II, 107–8.

[10] D. S. Landes, "French Entrepreneurship and Industrial Growth in the Nineteenth Century," *Journal of Economic History*, IX (1949), 49–61; Clapham, *Economic Development of France and Germany*, pp. 232–60; Fourastié and Montet, *L'Économie française, passim;* W. F. Ogburn and W. Jaffé, *Economic Development of Post-War France* (New York, 1929); Colin Clark, *The Conditions of Economic Progress* (London, 1940), pp. 99, 148; Shepard B. Clough, "Retardative Factors in French Economic Development in the Nineteenth and Twentieth Centuries," *Journal of Economic History*, VI (1946), supplement, 91–102; Bettelheim, *Bilan de l'économie française*, pp. 32–53, 143–48; Georges Boris, "Réformes de la Quatrième République," *La Nef*, VI (December 1949–January 1950), 69–70; Edgar Beigel, "France and National Planning," *Political Science Quarterly*, LXII (1947), 383.

[11] "Lysis" (Eugène Letailleur), *Contre l'oligarchie financière en France* (11th ed., Paris, n.d.), p. 121.

of French investment in foreign securities before 1914. On the eve
of World War I these foreign securities accounted for 36 per cent of
the investments of Frenchmen.[12]

The First World War forced the liquidation of the bulk of French
foreign holdings. In the 1920's a new interest in the potentialities of
French enterprises arose, forming part of the new spirit noted by
Toynbee. The new interest, however, like the new spirit, vanished
during the 1930's. The danger signals, in fact, had already become evident before the onset of the Great Depression. The inflationary crisis
in the mid-'20's had caused an impressive flight of French capital
abroad. The flight of capital became virtually a mass desertion in the
1930's, especially during the era of the Popular Front. Furthermore,
the proportion of capital remaining in France which was invested in
private undertakings dropped abruptly. More and more the French
investor, if he placed his money at home, put it in government bonds
and in other obligations of the state. In 1936, to cite the most dramatic
instance, the total of new private borrowing amounted to less than
one-tenth the total of new government borrowing. Throughout the
1930's the rate of new investment in French industry scarcely covered
the cost of replacing existing equipment as it wore out. Money was
not made available for modernization and expansion. Paul Reynaud
complained: "The creative spirit and the taste for risk have all but
disappeared." [13]

Bourgeois aversion to taxation became evident and pronounced
during the legislative debates on the graduated income tax even prior
to 1914. The distinguished economist, Paul Leroy-Beaulieu, predicted in 1907 that ". . . a tax of this kind would poison the whole
life of a democracy; it would spread defiance everywhere, cause capital
to flee . . . ; it would be the onset of a struggle to the death between
the treasury and the taxpayers. . . ." [14]

In this "struggle to the death" the Third Republic fought on the
losing side. The government finally imposed an income tax in 1916; it
levied additional new taxes to meet the tremendous financial demands

12 Harry D. White, *The French International Accounts, 1880–1913* (Cambridge, Mass.,
1933); "Lysis," *op. cit.;* Margaret G. Myers, *Paris as a Financial Center* (New York, 1936),
pp. 135–36; Yves Guyot, "The Amount, Direction and Nature of French Investment,"
Annals of the American Academy of Political and Social Science, LXVIII (1916), 36–54.

13 As quoted by Henry Ehrmann, "The Blum Experiment and the Fall of France,"
Foreign Affairs, XX (1941), 157. See also Eleanor L. Dulles, *The French Franc, 1914–
1928* (New York, 1929), pp. 45–46, 412–14; Myers, *op. cit.,* p. 141; J. H. Rogers, *The
Process of Inflation in France* (New York, 1929), pp. 224–25; Ogburn and Jaffé, *Economic
Development of Post-War France,* pp. 90–92; Morazé, *France bourgeoise,* pp. 201–2;
Henri Sée, *Histoire économique de la France* (Paris, 1942), II, 247, 272, 360–61; Bet-
telheim, *Bilan de l'économie française,* pp. 113–17.

14 *L'Économiste français,* February 16, 1907.

of World War I and of postwar reconstruction. But it never persuaded or compelled the bourgeoisie to pay a fair share of the burden. It could collect the income tax effectively only from wage-earners and salaried employees whose revenues could easily be checked. While the precise extent of tax-evasion cannot, of course, be determined, there seems no reason to doubt that it was widespread. Almost every commentator on the subject, French or non-French, conservative or otherwise, has accused French farmers of consistently falsifying the reports of their revenues and profits and has alleged that many companies, shopkeepers, and professional men kept special sets of rigged books to show to the tax-collector. Charles Péguy called nonpayment of taxes the "dream of every Frenchman." Like the privileged orders of the Old Régime, the French bourgeois appeared to regard their partial exemption from taxation as a natural prerogative.[15]

The citizens of the Third Republic performed their military obligations dutifully and courageously. But, confronted with economic obligations to the nation, the bourgeois spirit rebelled. It turned pessimistic, defensive, cowardly. When Frenchmen detected a threat to their pocketbooks, they appeared more fearful of their own government and of their own compatriots than of any foreign enemy. The fears of the bourgeois mounted and multiplied in the 1920's and 1930's. They feared for their own fortunes and for the welfare of their children. They were afraid of the power of organized labor, and at the same time they were unwilling to sustain the power of private capital through adequate new investments. They feared the Bolshevik and the tax-collector with nearly equal intensity. They denied to a large extent the social and economic implications of democracy, and some of them, the future supporters of the Vichy government, abandoned political democracy to advocate a more or less fascistic authoritarianism.

The bourgeois spirit, in sum, manifested a growing *crise de confiance,* a waning confidence in the democratic republic. It exhibited an accumulating *incivisme,* or lack of civic-mindedness. It was atomis-

[15] Siegfried, *France,* p. 18; R. M. Haig, *The Public Finances of Post-War France* (New York, 1929); Gaston Jèze and Henri Truchy, *The War Finances of France* (New Haven, 1927), pp. 222–27; George Peel, *The Financial Crisis of France* (London, 1925); Pierre Dieterlen and Charles Rist, *The Monetary Problem of France* (New York, 1948), especially p. 45; the special number of *Esprit* on *"Incivisme"* (XVII, No. 1 [January 1949]); Eric Johnston, "How America Can Avoid Socialism," *Fortune,* XXXIX (February 1949), 118–20; "Pertinax" (André Géraud), "France Gets to Her Feet," *Foreign Affairs,* XXVII (1949), esp. p. 394; Delbert A. Snider, "French Monetary and Fiscal Policies since the Liberation," *American Economic Review,* XXXVIII (1948), 309–27; and the testimony of David Bruce before the U.S. Senate Foreign Relations Committee, February 11, 1949, as reported in *News from France* (New York: Information Division of French Embassy), March 10, 1949.

tic; it no longer partook of the general will. The gap widened between *"ils"* and *"nous"*—between "them," the hostile state, and "us," its actual and potential victims.[16]

III

Why was the civic sense of the bourgeoisie so blunted, so under-developed? Why did the bourgeois spirit shrivel up in the alien climate of the twentieth century? In examining this question two different avenues of approach have usually been employed. One approach may be called determinist. For the determinists the decisive cause of bourgeois desiccation is to be sought in some single overriding factor, demographic or economic, political or geographical. The other avenue lies through the analysis of the complex traits which compose the psychology, the character, and the inheritance of Frenchmen.

This latter point of view, represented most conspicuously by André Siegfried, may be called traditionalist or historical. It emphasizes the extraordinary individualism of the French. France, it explains, was singularly ill-equipped to deal with a world which science and industry were constantly knitting more tightly together, and in which a greater and greater degree of cooperation was essential. Over the centuries the French bourgeois spirit had been formed in a decidedly egotistical mold. It carried individualism to the point where, paradoxically, it lost some of its individualistic capacity to adjust to new conditions. It lacked the social-mindedness of the Anglo-Saxon spirit and the stern Protestant call to duty. It lacked the resilience and the community feeling which enabled the British and the Americans to adapt themselves more readily to the Industrial Revolution. The strongest tradition of the French bourgeoisie was the tradition of 1789, the tradition of revolt against despotic authority. Yet the bourgeois also revolted against the social turbulence which issued from the great Revolution. They desired liberty, yet they also desired order. In crasser terms, they wanted to be free to make money, to conserve it and to pass it along to their descendants; and they wanted to be free from the social disorders and changes which might jeopardize this process. From the

16 Gabriel Dheur, " 'Ils' et Nous," *Esprit,* XVII (January 1949), 50–52. See also the other articles in this special issue of *Esprit* on *"Incivisme"*; Paul Einzig, *France's Crisis* (London, 1934), Chap. VII; David Thomson, *Democracy in France* (London, 1946), Chap. V; François Goguel, *La Politique des partis sous la Troisième République* (Paris, 1946), II, 331–32; Haig, *Public Finances of Post-War France,* p. 4; Charles A. Micaud, "The Outlook for Democracy in France," *Virginia Quarterly Review,* XXIII (1947), 369–83; A. F. Wills, "Report on France," *Fortnightly* (July 1949), pp. 14–19; and the speech of Robert Schuman at Poitiers, April 18, 1948, as reported in a *Document* of the Information Division of the French Embassy (New York, May 1948).

bourgeois standpoint, the French Revolution confirmed one drastic social change—the termination of the Old Régime—and made a ban on further drastic changes imperative. It "froze" the bourgeois spirit.

The traditionalists ultimately extend their inquiry beyond 1789. The twofold aspiration, to liberty and to order, they point out, was centuries old. The theoretically absolute monarchy of the seventeenth and eighteenth centuries was unable to cope with the practical reality of the demand for liberty expressed in the form of tax-evasion. The Christian tradition of the Middle Ages stressed the necessity of order and by affirming the sanctity of the family seemed to lend a sacred character to the property of the family and of the individuals composing it. M. Siegfried asserts that ". . . deep heart-searching reveals that every essential of our national character already existed at the time of the Revolution. . . ." [17]

Determinist explanations of bourgeois decline may be grouped conveniently under seven headings: (i) geographical, (ii) political, (iii) diplomatic, (iv) financial, (v) educational, (vi) demographic, and (vii) Marxian. Each explanation ultimately unmasks its own single villain. From the Marxian approach, of course, the villain is the capitalist system. From the demographic, it is the birth rate, which began declining earlier and dropped further in France than it did in almost any other country. Obviously this phenomenon is open to interpretation as a very literal manifestation of declining *élan vital*.

The five remaining avenues of determinist inquiry require somewhat fuller exploration. Geographical explanations argue that the accidents of nature controlled the fate of the French bourgeoisie. The general straightness of the coastline and the shortage of good harbors blighted maritime development. The shortage of coal crippled heavy industry. In contrast, the variety and the wealth of agricultural resources allowed farming to retain a good measure of its medieval preponderance in the French economy.[18]

The political explanations accuse the government of the Third Republic of diverting the French economy from its normal course of development. According to this hypothesis, whenever new forms of enterprise were undertaken, the vested interests protested, and the state stepped in to make France safe for the old order. Thus small and

[17] Siegfried, *France*, p. 2. See also Maillaud, *France*, p. 41; George Peel, *The Financial Crisis of France* (London, 1925), pp. 15 ff.; Einzig, *op. cit.*, pp. 15–16; Dieterlen and Rist, *The Monetary Problem of France*, p. 23; Haig, *op. cit.*, p. 20; Charles Seignobos, *Histoire sincère de la nation française* (Paris, 1937), pp. 498–99; Blum, *For All Mankind*, pp. 94–95; Jacques-René Rabier, "Qu'est-ce que l'incivisme?" *Esprit*, XVII (January 1949), 5–14; Micaud, "Outlook for Democracy in France," *loc. cit.*, pp. 369–83.

[18] Fourastié and Montet, *L'Économie française dans le monde*, p. 127; Bettelheim, *Bilan de l'économie française*, pp. 143–47; Arthur L. Dunham, reviewing Charles Morazé, "La France bourgeoise," in *Journal of Economic History*, VI (1946), 197–99.

costly stores remained the chief outlets for retail trade because legislation drastically restricted the expansion of the "five-and-ten," the
chain stores, and the department stores. From the 1880's on, protective tariffs enabled French agriculture to live increasingly in a
kind of economic hothouse and impeded the shift of farm workers
to other kinds of employment more in keeping with the Industrial
Revolution. Furthermore, the hypothesis argues, the state for a variety
of reasons blocked normal channels of investment. For strategic reasons, it urged investors to purchase Russian, rather than French,
securities before 1914. It required that private and postal savings
deposits be committed to the official *Caisse des Dépôts et Consigna-
tions,* and then, up to 1931, it directed the *Caisse* to limit its investments to official and semi-official issues. After 1914, in order to offset
the wartime and postwar budgetary deficits, it virtually demanded
that investors give priority to government securities.[19]

The argument charging the blame to diplomacy asserts that the
cabinets of the Third Republic forced France to live beyond its
means. Perhaps the spirit of *revanche* offered the cabinets no alternative; in any case, it is argued, the results were ruinous. Money which
would have been far better employed in developing the economy
at home was poured into unprofitable colonial ventures. Vast sums
went to shore up military alliances with countries like Russia and
Poland, which promptly collapsed in time of war. The French spirit
of enterprise became the hapless victim of power politics.[20]

The argument concerning the banks transforms the bourgeois into
the victims of questionable practice by high finance. A few great
banks, it is charged, directed the placement of a large part of French
private investments. Prior to 1914 they funneled it abroad in ever-
increasing volume because the sale of foreign securities permitted
them to take larger brokerage fees, as high as 19 per cent of the face
value of some issues. Moreover, a few of the great bankers had political motives. They deliberately aimed to weaken the economy of
the democratic régime which they increasingly detested and to
strengthen that of the tsarist absolutism which they admired. Both
before and after 1914, the argument goes on, the bankers deliberately
starved small French enterprises. They consistently denied them

19 Bettelheim, *op. cit.,* pp. 172–77; Clapham, *Economic Development,* pp. 180–83;
Myers, *Paris as a Financial Center,* Chap. III; Rogers, *The Process of Inflation,* pp. 29–
30; Clough, "Retardative Factors in French Economic Development," *loc. cit.,* pp. 91–102.
20 S. H. Roberts, *History of French Colonial Policy, 1870–1925* (2 vols., London, 1929);
S. B. Clough, *France: A History of National Economics, 1789–1939* (New York, 1939),
pp. 327–30, and "Retardative Factors in French Economic Development," *loc. cit.;* G.
Peel, *The Economic Crisis of France* (London, 1937), Chaps. XVI–XVIII; Herbert Feis,
Europe the World's Banker (New Haven, 1930), Chap. V; Bettelheim, *op. cit.,* p. 170;
Guyot, "The Amount, Direction and Nature of French Investment," *loc. cit.,* pp. 36–54.

credit on the grounds that they were poor risks. They argued that enterprises controlled by a single family could not be trusted to have efficient management, and that the secrecy traditional in French business life made it impossible to obtain accurate and necessary information on production and accounting methods. A study of French banks led Herbert Feis to conclude that "The banking system facilitated the contented and routine ways of French economic life. It did not through determined leadership impart to industry a drive toward constant improvement, toward 'efficiency' and technical change." [21]

The educational explanation, finally, asserts that the secondary schools, the universities, and the professional schools all made it their business to preserve the contented and routine ways of French economic life. Both the technical schools and the *lycées* are blamed for having shamefully neglected the social sciences. Consequently, they turned forth annually a large number of economic illiterates, the future leaders of France who were only dimly aware of the basic issues of twentieth-century life. Moreover, the indictment continues, the upper reaches of the educational system were thoroughly undemocratic. Because of the tuition fees charged by the *lycées* even a secondary education was not open to all the talents. It was available only to those who could afford it. Because only graduates of the institutions of higher learning could hope to enter the bourgeois professions par excellence—the law, medicine, the upper levels of the civil service—the educational system was simply a device for making the bourgeoisie a self-perpetuating and closed corporation, cut off from the transfusions of new blood which it badly needed.[22]

IV

Both broad avenues of investigation, the determinist and the traditionalist, are suggestive. Both uncover a measure of the truth, a large measure in the case of the traditionalist explanation. But neither of them quite hits the nail squarely on the head. The determinists are suspect if only because historians are inclined to prefer multiple to unitary causation, and to mistrust the singling-out of any one force as *the* villain. Furthermore, as students of the decline of

21 Feis, *op. cit.*, p. 43. See also "Lysis," *Contre l'oligarchie financière;* White, *French International Accounts,* Chaps. XII–XIII; Myers, *Paris as a Financial Center,* pp. 113–36; Bettelheim, *op. cit.,* pp. 95–101; Landes, "French Entrepreneurship," *loc. cit.,* pp. 45–61; *Interviews on the Banking and Currency Systems of England, Scotland, France, Germany, Switzerland, and Italy* [National Monetary Commission: U.S. Senate Document, No. 405] (Washington, 1910).

22 Bloch, *Strange Defeat,* pp. 153–56; Fourastié and Montet, *L'Économie française dans le monde,* pp. 32–33; Blum, *For All Mankind,* pp. 74–75.

civilizations are aware, nothing is harder than to disentangle the causes of decline from the symptoms of decline, nothing easier than to mistake the symptom for the cause.

Determinist explanations of French bourgeois desiccation often fall into this difficulty. The decline in the birth rate bespoke conscious planning more than it did a decline in physical fertility beyond human control. The bourgeoisie may have starved itself by a one-sided and undemocratic education, but the British educational system, although the target of very similar criticisms, imparted to its graduates a much stronger sense of civic responsibility. The bourgeoisie may have been ruined by the villainy of bankers and by the folly of the Ministry of Finance and the Quai d'Orsay, but was it not thus the victim of institutions which it itself had created and which it itself managed? Did not responsibility rest ultimately with the mechanic rather than with the machinery?

Geography, on the other hand, was obviously a cause rather than a symptom of the French economic malaise. While the accidents of nature assuredly contributed heavily to the slowness of industrial development, they were hardly directly responsible for the desiccation of the bourgeois spirit. They occupied a most important position in the stage setting, but they did not play the central role in the drama. Something more than an awareness of the coal deficiency entered into the bourgeois aversion to investment in French industry.

Of all the determinist explanations, the Marxist hypothesis is the most enlightening one. The Third Republic did indeed witness the class struggle in the increasingly bitter "cold war" between capital and labor. The emergence of an industrial proletariat did indeed alarm many bourgeois. And yet the Marxian explanation leaves too much unexplained. Entirely too many little businesses survived where the dialectic decreed an inexorable movement toward a few big businesses. There was underproduction in some key sectors of the economy where there should have been inevitable overproduction. Above all, too many Frenchmen behaved in un-Marxian fashion—wealthy men not motivated solely by economics, and poor men refusing to act as though they were the "have-nots." Léon Blum exempted from his strictures on bourgeois selfishness "whole groups belonging to the more cultured section of the old liberal and Catholic bourgeoisie." [23] At the onset of World War II Marc Bloch noted apprehensively that organized labor had an "inevitable preoccupation with wage-claims," an outlook "limited to immediate issues of petty profit." "Could anything," he inquired, "have been more *kleinbürgerlich,* more *petit*

23 *For All Mankind,* p. 96.

bourgeois, than the attitude adopted in the last few years . . . by most of the big unions?" [24]

The traditionalist explanation introduces the complex human variables neglected by the Marxists and by the other determinists. What it does not do very satisfactorily is to pin down in time the operation of these factors. It does not really account for the fact that unmistakable symptoms of bourgeois desiccation appeared during the decade before 1914, rather than a generation earlier or later. Why was it that bourgeois unwillingness to pay an income tax and bourgeois reluctance to invest in French enterprise became acute issues just as the Third Republic was reaching the mid-point of its career?

The most satisfactory answer is offered by David Thomson in his study, *Democracy in France:* "The story of the Third Republic falls into two equal parts . . . : and the watershed falls about the year 1905. The thirty-five years between 1870 and 1905 were spent, in a sense, in liquidating the past—in thrashing out the old conflicts between Church and State, clerical and anti-clerical, Monarchy and Republic, militarism and parliamentarism. . . . The thirty-five years between 1905 and 1940 were spent, in a sense, in seeking a working compromise within the now established parliamentary Republic between new social forces. . . . Dynastic, ecclesiastical and militarist issues were replaced by social and economic issues. . . ." [25]

The speed with which the old issues were settled caught the bourgeoisie off guard. A rapid series of events—the failure of Boulanger (1889), the vindication of Dreyfus (beginning in 1899), and the final separation of Church and State (1905)—assured the victory of a democratic, anticlerical republic. These were issues which the bourgeois spirit really understood. They were the direct legacy of 1789 and could be stated in the familiar terms of liberty and individualism. The bourgeois spirit did not, however, fully understand the social and economic issues which were now thrust forward. The traditional concepts of liberty and individualism proved to be inadequate. The only article of the bourgeois credo which now applied was the insistence on order—a static concept, implying at most a minimum of social and economic change.[26]

[24] *Strange Defeat,* pp. 138–39.
[25] *Democracy in France,* p. 72.
[26] See, above all, Thomson, *op. cit.,* Chap. v; Morazé, *France bourgeoise,* Chaps. III–IV and conclusions; and Goguel, *La Politique des partis,* I, especially pp. 44, 82, 98–99. See further Siegfried, *France,* pp. 39 ff.; Guérard, *France of Tomorrow,* pp. 138–40, 150; Bloch, *Strange Defeat,* pp. 163–65; Cot, *Triumph of Treason,* p. 73; Clough, *France,* p. 360; Georges Gurvich, "The Social Structure of Pre-War France," *American Journal of*

The bourgeois spirit turned negative as soon as it traversed the watershed of 1905. Thus the Clemenceau cabinet of 1906–1909 failed to make good on its promise to secure from the Chamber legislation establishing the income tax, the eight-hour working day, and the elementary measures of social security which seemed obvious remedies for the new social and economic problems. Baffled by these new problems, the bourgeois political world tried to pretend that they did not exist. It continued to expend much of its energy on the more familiar but now less urgent questions of army reform and the status of the Church. "Anticlericalism," Albert Guérard has asserted, "was the stock in trade of the bourgeois radicals, their sole *raison d'être*. Hence the fierceness with which they kept whipping that poor horse long after it was dead." [27]

Shortly before 1914 a spokesman for the great banks listed some reasons why so many able young Frenchmen refused to go into industry: "the possibility that mill-hands may go on strike abruptly without preliminary notice"; "the freedom given to strikers to thwart by violence those who want to work"; "the undisciplined spirit, the denial of any concept of social hierarchy." [28] One could almost hear the bourgeois command to close ranks and take up defensive positions. Indeed, Jules Romains later asserted in his novel, *Verdun*, that World War I was a "tacit choice made by humanity between war and revolution," and that the governing class said in effect: "Only at the price of war, heavy though it may be, only by the re-establishment of discipline and by the safety-valve to passions which it will provide, can we hope to maintain the present social order." [29]

Events after 1914 accelerated and intensified the process of desiccation which had begun before 1914. The Red Revolution in Russia, followed by the organization of the French Communist Party and of the Communist wing of the French labor movement, terrified the bourgeoisie into making more and more insistent demands for order. The postwar inflation, by pauperizing many bourgeois, particularly the *rentiers*, sapped their vitality still more and hardened their negative reactions to the issue of social reform. The Great Depression, though it was actually not so severe in France as it was in many industrial countries, drained away much of the remaining reserve of bourgeois confidence. When American prosperity ended in 1929, Albert Guérard has remarked, "The bourgeois world felt that the

Sociology, XLVIII (1943), 536; André Mayer, "La Crise de structure de la société française," *The French Review*, XVI (1942), 11–15; Micaud, "The Outlook for Democracy in France," *loc. cit.*, pp. 369–83.

27 *The France of Tomorrow*, p. 150. See also Goguel, *op. cit.*, I, 193–95.
28 "Testis" as quoted by "Lysis," *Contre l'oligarchie financière*, p. 288.
29 Jules Romains, *Verdun* (New York, 1939), pp. 46–47.

Eternal Verities were not self-sustaining, and that it was high time to organize in their defense." [30]

The rise of Hitler brought the *crise de confiance* to a head. The "new order" of Germany, together with the corporatism of Mussolini's Italy, hypnotized at least a fraction of the French bourgeoisie into believing that some form of Fascism offered the only practicable alternative to Communism. Many French bourgeois did not assume this "either-or" attitude, did not say, "Better Hitler than Léon Blum." The trouble was that they did not assume any positive or consistent stand before the Nazi menace. They seemed unprepared for everything—for the Rhineland coup of 1936, for the brief reprieve of Munich, for the tedium of the "phony war," and for the Blitzkrieg of May and June 1940. The advent of the Third Reich had virtually paralyzed the will of a bourgeoisie which was already largely demoralized. [31]

Thus the road away from the watershed of 1905 went downhill all the way to World War II. One final question is sure to be put at this point. Has the downward road continued during the ten years since 1940, or has World War II acted as a new watershed, redirecting and reorienting the course of the French bourgeois spirit?

Certainly the process of defeat, liberation, and postwar inflation has jarred the French people into realizing, as they never realized before, the extent of their technological backwardness. The realization has been expressed officially in the Monnet Plan for the modernization of the French economy, and unofficially in the half-mocking song with which the Paris *chansonniers* saluted the victorious American army in 1944—"*Quel matériel!*" But plans are one thing, and persistent and successful implementation of them is something else again. Remembering Toynbee's misplaced enthusiasm for the "new technique" and "new spirit" which supposedly pervaded France after World War I, historians are bound to be very cautious about passing optimistic judgments on events since 1944. It seems as yet too early to determine whether the bourgeois spirit has taken a new lease on life, whether, in Blum's phrase, the sap has begun to run again.

[30] *The France of Tomorrow*, p. 153.
[31] Goguel, *La Politique des partis*, II, 321–44; Louis Levine (Lewis Lorwin), "The French Point of View," Chap. x in H. G. Moulton and C. Lewis, *The French Debt Problem* (New York, 1925); Charles A. Micaud, *The French Right and Nazi Germany* (Durham, N.C., 1943), pp. 223–27; Jacques Maritain, *À travers le désastre* (New York, 1941), Chap. II; Blum, *For All Mankind*, pp. 78–81; Siegfried, *France*, pp. 62 ff.; Dulles, *The French Franc*, pp. 49–51; Guérard, *The France of Tomorrow*, p. 153; "Pertinax," *Gravediggers*, p. 578.

III

FRENCH LETTERS AND SCIENCE

5

++

THE FRENCH INTELLECTUALS:

SITUATION AND OUTLOOK

KENNETH DOUGLAS

++

You may recall that ingenious book by Salvador de Madariaga, *Englishmen, Frenchmen, Spaniards*.[1] For the author, these three national types represent three levels, more usually considered successive in time, of human concern. The Spaniard is the savage, the man of passion, who alternates between lethargic indifference and a furious outpouring of energy. The Englishman has attained to the stage of a culture—that is to say, he is a barbarian (or the "mesomorph" of Professor Sheldon)—for whom existence is above all a struggle, an activity, whether physical or administrative. The Frenchman? He is the civilized man, who attains self-realization neither in feeling nor in doing, but in knowing; with, alas! the concomitant drawback that he has often been content to know—to know, for example, that his politicians are corrupt, while remaining insufficiently interested in the prospect of a mere concrete and tangible improvement to join with his fellows and clean out the Augean stables.

I

France, we must agree with Señor Madariaga, has been the intellectual's paradise,* if any paradise is available for a creature so constituted. To this state of affairs two factors, above all, have contributed.

---

* Professor Denis Brogan has pointed out that, in a similar sense, France is a politician's paradise as well.

[1] *Englishmen, Frenchmen, Spaniards; an Essay in Comparative Psychology* (London, 1931).

French sociability is one. For, at its best, social intercourse in France has been more than an end in itself. From the time of Madame de Rambouillet, who in the year 1620 began to receive her group of *"précieuses,"* grammarians and men of the world, the French salon has had great influence on the personal life and on the writings of dramatists, novelists, critics, and other manipulators of immaterial entities. This had advantages and, unavoidably, drawbacks. The salon became a forcing house of articulateness, on occasion of ideas—it also offered too ready an opportunity for the expenditure of spirit on trivialities. It was a boon for authors, providing them with an audience of connoisseurs and semiprofessionals. Promising fledglings could there be encouraged, their horizons widened, the bumpkin transformed into the *"honnête homme."* But in a real sense, too, the audience had the authors in its power. Whatever conflicted with the mores of polite society, whatever might seem ridiculous or extravagant to the drawingroom coterie, tended to disappear from literary productions. For two centuries (the seventeenth and eighteenth), "good taste," backed by the dreadful fear of mockery, exercised its sterile sway—and what could be in worse taste than lyric fervor, genuine originality, or force of the imagination?

French education worked hand in hand with this social conditioning and exposure to ideas. Daniel Mornet, in his *Histoire de la clarté française,*[2] traces the history of the long struggle, initiated in the seventeenth century, to develop clarity of thought and expression. He is well aware that clarity may be obtained by the sacrifice of those things that prove difficult to communicate, that the scales are weighted in favor of the banal and the commonplace. For all that, it must be one of the school's main tasks to teach straightforward expository writing, and no talk of "encouraging originality" can make up for it. The matter of oral expression as well is the concern of the French teacher; and the French, at the university level, attach an importance to the oral examination of candidates that is not approached in English-speaking countries.

The debit side of this stress on communicability has been more apparent to foreigners, with their undying prejudice against French superficiality and frivolity (to which the anguished Catholic poet Pierre Reverdy has retorted that every *intelligent* foreigner he has met is equally superficial). So let us emphasize rather the positive aspect, the fact that the French, unlike the English, talk their native language as if it were native to them, the fact that they are articulate. Without articulateness there may be men of good will, there may be saints and mystics—there will be no intellectuals. That possibility

[2] *Histoire de la clarté française, ses origines, son évolution, sa valeur* (Paris, 1929).

for the human species is most easily made a reality against a back-ground of loquacity—loquacity, it should be specified, which is not limited to certain stock phrases, and which is free to touch upon a wide range of topics. The English repugnance against "showing off," the American insistence that nothing controversial be mooted, serve to breed inoffensiveness and nothing more.

II

The French intellectuals who have left their mark have not been inoffensive, articulate in neutral gear, or satisfied to communicate the already communicated. The surest testimony to this is the French Revolution—one of the only two revolutions in world history, Professor Crane Brinton would maintain, one of the two periods when the naked idea made bold to incarnate itself. Scribblers and talkers had led up to this affirmation that men could make their own history; Napoleon impurely continued it and, for his part, showed a very lively fear of such a scribbler and inveterate conversationalist as Madame de Staël. Since the time of the French Revolution, it has seemed natural to the French to turn to professors and literary men not only for the expression but even for the enactment of their political ideals. For example: Guizot, Thiers, the poets Lamartine and Victor Hugo; the Socialist Jaurès; Blum, Herriot and Painlevé; the present * prime minister Georges Bidault.

The respect enjoyed by intellectuals confers on them a privileged position. As a consequence there is a temptation, to which more than one has yielded, to look kindly on the status quo and function as its defender. This trend was noted by Julien Benda, in the 1920's, as holding good for the imaginative writer, though not for the university professor.[3] With the overshadowing of France as a world power, French governments since the Liberation have staked all the more heavily on French culture to maintain the prestige of France abroad (while Frenchmen at home, if Jean-Paul Sartre is to be believed, seek balm in their past literary glories and in those of the present, real or fictitious, for a newly acquired inferiority complex).[4] Writers are dispatched on cultural missions to other European countries, and to America North and South, cultural counselors are "affected" to legations, information centers endeavor to keep France before the eyes of the world. In "La Nationalisation de la littérature," Sartre has

* Written in January 1950.
[3] Julien Benda, *La Trahison des clercs* (Paris, 1927).
[4] Jean-Paul Sartre, "La Nationalisation de la littérature," *Les Temps Modernes*, I, No. 2 (November 1945), 193–211; reprinted in *Situations II* (Paris, 1948), pp. 31–53.

expressed the fear that French writers may be declared national monuments, and denounces the consecration of budding authors in an unparalleled literary inflation which, he appears to think, has boosted aloft his own works also. The enrollment of writers as cultural ambassadors is not the sense he would give to the word *"engagement."*

But the writer's *engagement,* translated as enrollment or enlistment, is not necessarily in the government forces. Prewar propaganda insisted sufficiently on the presence, in France, of "two hundred families," of rulers behind the rulers. It is certain that considerable wealth and social influence belonged to people who did not accept wholeheartedly the implications of representative government. Thus the French Academy, under the Third Republic, took to its bosom the Royalist publicist Charles Maurras, who was welcomed by those Academicians of longer standing, Abel Hermant, Abel Bonnard, and Philippe Pétain, whose affection for the ideals of 1789 was almost equally uncertain. Maurras had gathered round himself and his paper, *L'Action Française,* a remarkable group of littérateurs. He and his followers, however, were skirmishers rather than regular troops, and enlistment demanded little in the way of discipline. Since the war, no Rightist intellectual group of anything like the same prominence has re-formed, although collaborationists, like Maurras himself, are again publishing, and Maurice Bardèche, the literary historian, who has a personal reason for bitterness in the execution as a collaborator of his brother-in-law Robert Brasillach, has printed pro-Nazi and anti-Semitic statements of the most shameless nature.[5]

We cannot attempt to trace here the multiple nuances with which various intellectuals lent their support to Vichy. Suffice it to say that it extended from the utter adulation of the Marshal by a René Benjamin to the briefest of acceptances, in the bewilderment of the first year of defeat, and the playing by some of a double game. Comparatively rare were those willing to become the Nazis' men, as distinct from Pétainists. Here, too, genuine conviction in some contrasts with time-serving in others who imagined that they were betting on a sure thing.

One path was open to French intellectuals as to all Frenchmen, after the defeat of 1940, a path that involved *engagement* not as enlistment—escape from France and enlistment with the Free French or Allied forces very literally signified that—but *engagement* as commitment in the first instant and commitment in every moment thereafter. For the Frenchman who took part in the Resistance was on his own, almost without intermission, as the soldier in a regular

---

[5] The French courts intervened to prevent the continued sale of M. Bardèche's book, which was entitled *Nuremberg, ou la terre promise,* and appeared in 1949.

army seldom is. He constantly had to make his own decisions, sometimes on the strength of no more than a hunch. If captured, he was assuredly on his own.

Certain writers took up arms: Jean Prévost, who was killed, André Malraux, the poet René Char. Others wrote clandestine tracts, and assisted in their printing and diffusion. Sartre—and the Catholic literary critic André Rousseaux has signaled his agreement—maintains that such writers have a feeling of inadequacy when they compare themselves with the men of the armed resistance and the railway workers, who really fought and hampered the enemy.[6] He even wonders whether the Germans did not slyly tolerate these paper blows as, all things considered, a harmless safety valve.

The Left, at one time, may have had purity of motive and intention to its credit: it could not match the Right in the rewards and the prestige made available for the intellectuals attracted to its orbit. With the definitive establishment of the U.S.S.R. and the postwar increase of Communist strength in France the intellectual can find a haven, not merely martyrdom, in the Communist Party.

"Haven" and "heaven," nevertheless, are not synonymous. The moral and intellectual distress of many an intellectual attracted to Communism, and the disarray of him who has broken with Communism, are tales that have too often been told. So I prefer to pass on to you the reflections of a French Communist, at times described as *the* or as *a* "strong man" of the Party, who considers that strange fish, the intellectual, from the point of view of party leadership. The intellectuals, declares Laurent Casanova, represent an "important fraction of the middle classes."[7] He realizes the significance of the intellectuals to the Communist Party better than he succeeds in liking them, or so it would seem. After an opening laudatory reference to Joliot-Curie, Picasso, Aragon, and Éluard, he has little but blame to distribute. Some intellectual converts make the mistake of abandoning their intellectualism and despising their former estate. "The mutilation they impose on themselves," comments Casanova, "is voluntary. It is never the doing of the Party, but by their attitude that is what they lead people to suppose. . . . They create the impression that they have replaced the spirit of principle by the spirit of dogma, the methods of free investigation by the devices of polemics."[8]

Other blunders (continues Casanova) are at their disposal. Some intellectuals wish to awaken the working classes to the beauties of litera-

[6] M. Rousseaux affirms his support of Sartre's judgment in "Bernanos et la démission de la France," *Georges Bernanos, Essais et témoignages* (Paris, 1949), p. 331.

[7] Laurent Casanova, *Le Parti Communiste, les intellectuels et la nation* (Paris, 1949), p. 10.

[8] *ibid.,* p. 49.

ture and art, with no regard for the foundations on which they must build. Yet others have the presumptuousness to want to run things for themselves. Of what type is this personage?

He is ". . . the intellectual socially characterized as such, the specialist highly competent in ideological problems, thanks to his technical training, and who by vocation jealously preserves his personal dignity. . . .

"Obviously, as our comrades see it, the working class and its Party should share with the intellectuals the leadership of the revolutionary movement, and this for reasons which directly impinge upon the revolutionary content of the tasks which the proletariat sets itself.

"A proposition which cannot be sustained for a moment, once it is formulated with entire clarity." [9]

Free discussion there must be, of course, among Party members and with outsiders susceptible to being won over. But free discussion has its dangers. "The critical examination of our work," writes Casanova, "with respect to the discussion that was initiated on the situation in the Jugoslav Communist Party, sufficed to reveal the existence of dangerous political currents, which tended to assert themselves openly." [10] And the "Amicales," the groups of Communist doctors, lawyers, etc., which had been formed during the Resistance, after the Liberation showed a distressing tendency to take decisions "apart from the regular political organisms of the Party," [11] and had to be dissolved.

For a non-Communist, at least, it would appear that the intellectual must be subtle indeed who can trace a viable path for himself between Casanova's multiple prohibitions. The simplest course, no doubt, is to write and talk of something else, and this is in fact the procedure followed by a number of literary Communists. Henri Lefebvre, who did not do so, has recently published an *"auto-critique"* in which he spurns his earlier errors.[12] Picasso goes on his way to all appearances unperturbed by Russian and French denunciations of "decadent bourgeois art."

The long series of conversions or awakenings of literary men to the Catholic faith, beginning in the late nineteenth century with Huysmans, Claudel, Brunetière, and continuing via Maritain to Psichari and, in the post-World War I period, to Cocteau and Julien Green, does not, I think, have quite the same importance today. The situation of the individual Catholic or would-be Catholic is less poignant

9 Casanova, *Le Parti Communiste*, pp. 74–75.

10 *ibid.*, p. 14.

11 *ibid.*, pp. 11–12.

12 In *La Nouvelle Critique*, No. 4, 1949. See J.-M. Domenach, "Le Parti Communiste Français et les intellectuels," *Esprit*, XVII (May 1949), 729–39.

than it then was for some, with the decline, outside Communist and logical positivist circles, of science viewed as a religion, with a greater sophistication concerning the notions of truth and proof, and with the relegation of Modernism to the limbo of lost causes. At the present moment, those Catholics in France who seem to have advanced most recklessly are the members of a small group, Les Chrétiens Progressistes, perhaps excessively ready to collaborate with Communists and to accept Communist ideas. Nevertheless the atmosphere has changed greatly since the time when Marc Sangnier's *Le Sillon,* of a progressive orientation, was obliged to suspend publication. The *Osservatore Romano* has underlined the radical opposition between capitalism and Christianity, and Emmanuel Mounier, Catholic leader of the movement "Esprit" and editor of the periodical of the same name, without risking censure can demand a social revolution. This movement, and other movements and trends within the Catholic Church, are much more significant a social factor than the adherence of any one person to the Faith. Collective action, in other words, or at least the need for it, outranks in public concern the question of individual salvation.

What political organizations since the Liberation have attracted intellectuals? There is the Rassemblement du Peuple Français, the RPF, headed by De Gaulle, which counts among its leaders the art historian and novelist, or ex-novelist, André Malraux, and Raymond Aron, author of an excellent study of the philosophy of history.[13] In spite of their distinction, it would be difficult to maintain that the intellectual component in this Rally is very strong: opposition to Communism, trust in one man, and a contempt for ready-made solutions enunciated in advance are more prominent features.*

Incomparably less political impact has been exerted by the Rassemblement Démocratique Révolutionnaire—it might even be questioned whether it has any demonstrable existence. Its most active leader is, or was, David Rousset, who in two or three volumes has undertaken the structural analysis of the world of the concentration camp.[14] Another prominent adherent was Jean-Paul Sartre. He retired from the movement late in 1949, on the grounds that under existing conditions it had no function to perform. More recently he has broken sharply with Rousset, who desires to attack exclusively

---

* The content and *mystique* of Gaullism are treated in Chapter 15.

13 Raymond Aron, *Introduction à la philosophie de l'histoire; sur les limites de l'objectivité historique* (Paris, 1938). For the author's political views, see his *Le Grand Schisme* (Paris, 1948).

14 *L'Univers concentrationnaire* (Paris, 1946), translated as *The Other Kingdom* (New York, 1947); *Les Jours de notre mort, roman* (Paris, 1947); *Le Pitre ne rit pas* (Paris, 1948).

abuses in Soviet Russia and until further notice to keep silent about them elsewhere.[15]

From the outlook of that need for collective action mentioned a paragraph or two back, we may diagnose: a pretty far-reaching frustration—except for such as would be happy to see the past live again, the past of the 1900's or of the 1920's, and who persuade themselves of the possibility of restoring the past. Some atheists and some Christians had united in calling for a revolution. But the hopes set in the Resistance rapidly faded in the years following the Liberation, and apparently few Frenchmen can see in the reformism of the English Labor Party any lesson applicable to conditions in France. A revolution with the Communists, a Communist revolution, is a conceivable order of the day. When a Mounier talks of some other revolution, when a Sartre and a Merleau-Ponty, irrevocably at odds with the Communists, nevertheless declare, "We have the same values as a Communist," [16] they may be sowing seeds for the future; they are not taking an effective political stand at this hour.

Let us pass from these thwarted strivings toward solidarity to a more traditional intellectual domain, that of reflection and debate. What, of recent years, have French intellectuals been discussing?

III

They have discussed, among other things, the writer's commitment. Sartre, with his peculiar genius for seizing and knotting the threads that previously had floated vaguely in the atmosphere, launched this theme in his preface-manifesto to the first number of *Les Temps Modernes,* in 1945,[17] and returned to it at length with his *"Qu'est-ce que la littérature?"* of 1947.[18] *"Il faut s'engager."*

Whether by good fortune or design, Sartre expressed himself with that insufferable oversimplification and one-sidedness employed by many skilled teachers in order to provoke their students to protest and so to induce an authentic tangling with the issue. Like such teachers, Sartre was more successful than if a scrupulously phrased formulation

15 M. Merleau-Ponty and J.-P. Sartre, "Les Jours de notre vie," *Les Temps Modernes,* v, No. 51 (January 1950), 1153–68.

16 *ibid.,* p. 1161.

17 Jean-Paul Sartre, "Présentation," *Les Temps Modernes,* I, No. 1 (October 1945), 1–21; reprinted in *Situations II* (Paris, 1948), pp. 9–30.

18 "Qu'est-ce que la littérature?" *Les Temps Modernes,* II, No. 17 (February 1947), 769–805; No. 18 (March 1947), 961–88; No. 19 (April 1947), 1194–218; No. 20 (May 1947), 1410–29; No. 21 (June 1947), 1607–41; III, No. 22 (July 1947), 76–114; reprinted in *Situations II* (Paris, 1948), pp. 57–330, with additional notes; translated in part: *Partisan Review,* xv, No. 1 (January 1948), 9–31; No. 3 (March 1948), 313–22; No. 5 (May 1948), 536–44; No. 6 (June 1948), 634–53.

of his thought had met with unreflecting acquiescence. The most direct statement is indeed not necessarily the surest way of attaining to the truth, and from all this commotion there seems to emerge a truth of our time, namely, that the author cannot live in an ivory tower for the simple reason that there is no ivory tower. He is under no constraint to deal immediately in his works with present-day situations, but he cannot escape from his own age and cannot live in an eternity divorced from the present moment. Consequently, and against the thesis Julien Benda had advanced in his *La Trahison des clercs*, the writer cannot be satisfied to enunciate eternal and fleshless verities ("Monsieur Benda would have us drivel on," comments Sartre), since any such disembodied truth is not truth, but a hoax. Behind this attitude lies Marx, with his demand that the abstract be made concrete, his assertion of the "unity of theory and practice." Behind Marx lie Christianity and the Incarnation. As a French forerunner may be mentioned the man whose friendship Julien Benda had shared, in spite of their divergencies: Charles Péguy, with his peasant's slowness, his almost physical weighing and testing of the words he used, who had to be satisfied to say what he wrote and write what he said, and mean it. Not for him the luxury of the intellect's leisured classes, who can understand and formulate each man's point of view better than he can himself, while avoiding for themselves the vulgarity of personal commitment. They do not meditate on Pascal's "We must wager," uttered several centuries ahead of the "We must commit ourselves" of Sartre.

More than one author has experienced shame at the thought that he is skating over the surface of things, taking less risk than if he ventured on a real skating rink. The young Montherlant sought a discipline in soccer football ("Tomfoolery," he later declared), dreamed of a new order of Samurai, and involved himself, not too profoundly, in bullfighting. Michel Leiris has striven to make the practice of literature itself no less dangerous than bullfighting by publishing confessions he would find it less painful not to make.[19] A rather specialized and Narcissistic solution.

Others have been less deviously heroic. Jean Prévost, who had combined his physical culture with an esthetic interest by adopting the view that he was sculpturing his own body, was killed fighting for the Maquis. Malraux threw himself into revolutionary action in Indo-China and China, flew for the Loyalist forces in Spain during the Civil War, fought in the Resistance, and is now master-minding for De Gaulle. His novels are closely connected with his life, not because

[19] Michel Leiris, "De la littérature considérée comme une tauromachie," *Les Temps Modernes*, I, No. 8 (May 1946), 1456–68.

he exploits his adventures but because his heroes—who greatly resemble each other and are joined by an undeniable umbilical cord to Malraux himself—seek to comprehend our "human condition" (the title of one novel), or rather, perhaps, the condition of the hero, if not of that more dubious figure, the hero-cum-adventurer. St. Exupéry earned his living as a pilot in days when risks were much greater than they are now; beyond normal flying age, he served in the French Air Force before the collapse of 1940 and, again, went on reconnaissance flights after the invasion of North Africa. He did not return from his last, supernumerary flight. Each of his books, which only an impossibly superficial reading could regard as simple accounts of a flyer's adventures, is a questioning of the sense of existence, of the relationship of constraint with freedom, of love with harshness and sacrifice. The value of these books lies in their close linking of the actual conditions of one man's life with his urge to comprehend the individual and society, the individual in society.

But cannot a writer find commitment strictly within the boundaries of his profession? Or must he resort like Leiris to some dodge, if he would do so? No. The heavens, it has been implied, might collapse, were justice done, and justice is often a matter of speaking the truth. Again, the refusal to compromise in any circumstances whatever is a stand few writers have the courage to adopt. It can cost friends, fame, and livelihood. Péguy found it so, who drove away from the *Cahiers de la Quinzaine,* his only source of income, the Socialists and Dreyfusards of his early days, while remaining at odds with the organization he had come to look on as the True Church. Indeed, had not the outbreak of war in 1914 suspended his publishing and writing, and brought about his death, his works might have found their way to the Index. Léon Bloy, some years earlier, soon found out that, while satire at the expense of small fry is considered amusing, people who count know how to institute a conspiracy of silence against their detractor; nevertheless he went on as before, and starved.[20] More recently the Royalist and Catholic Georges Bernanos heaped contumely on French Royalists and, like Bloy, on Catholics of the *bien-pensant* variety, and (although one of his sons served with the Falange) wrote in *Les Grands Cimetières sous la lune* of the nightly executions practised by the Franco forces on Majorca.[21] In 1938, disgusted by Munich, he set off at the age of fifty, together with his family, to farm in the Matto Grosso of Brazil. He returned

---

[20] See, on Léon Bloy, Albert Béguin's *Léon Bloy; a Study in Impatience* (London, 1947).

[21] Georges Bernanos, *Les Grands Cimetières sous la lune* (Paris, 1938); translated as *A Diary of My Times* (London, 1938).

to France after hostilities were over, in time to convince himself that the hopes for the future he had placed in the Resistance must be indefinitely postponed.

These are extreme situations. In all situations, however, the writer or intellectual can experience the pressing demand for genuineness, for authenticity. We shall consequently turn from commitment to consider this problem of authenticity and of its opposite, baptized "bad faith."

In our civilization, we have reached an advanced degree of sophistication, which might be defined as the knowing of things on the basis of the assumption that someone or other, sometime, took the trouble to look into them thoroughly. But one cannot evade the questions: did anyone ever? even if he did, what do *I* know, in a real sense, I and the people about me? Hence Flaubert's physical revulsion, as he claimed it was, at the mere presence of a bourgeois, and the fascinated horror of platitude which moved him to compile a "Dictionary of Received Ideas." Since his day, the increasing pressure of commercial and political propaganda, and the ceaseless stream of chatter emitted by the radio, have brought about such an inflation in language—that is, such a decline in the "purchasing power," in the grip on reality of the linguistic token—that the question has been raised of the authenticity of language itself. Is each and every use of language inevitably fraudulent and inauthentic? Consider Brice Parain, a peasant intellectual, who rapidly acquired, at the École Normale Supérieure, a suspicion of the glib tongue of the city-bred. He went on to compare the grim reality of the First World War's trenches with the patriotic discourses of the home front. Demobilized, he contrasted official mouthings and the swindle of the peace. Over a period of twenty years he has brooded on this problem of language, on language versus silence, and in *Recherches sur la nature et les fonctions du langage* distills his humble and disillusioned wisdom, while in the novel *Mort de Jean Madek* the loftiest figure is a peasant whose peculiarly rich taciturnity awakens respect and the desire to learn from him.[22]

The Second World War, with the very special circumstances of combat in occupied countries, helped to reawaken the conviction that language could, indeed, be meaningful. A single careless word could *mean* a great deal: torture and death for the speaker and his friends. These "extreme situations" provided a rigorous test for the validity

[22] *Recherches sur la nature et les fonctions du langage* (Paris, 1942); *La Mort de Jean Madek, roman* (Paris, 1945). See, on Brice Parain, Jean-Paul Sartre's "Aller et retour," *Cahiers du Sud*, xx, No. 264 (February 1944), 117–33; No. 265 (March 1944), 248–70; reprinted in *Situations I* (Paris, 1947), pp. 189–244.

of men and words alike, such as cannot readily be found in the "neither fish, flesh, fowl, nor good red herring" confusions of casual peacetime relations. The lesson will not, I think, be entirely forgotten.

But authenticity, we may feel inclined to agree with Brice Parain, is better made the goal of a silent resolution than a topic for profuse commentary. The same does not hold for the complex of questions evoked by such expressions as "ends and means," "efficacy and righteousness," "social justice and individual freedom." There are several relatively easy ways out of these dilemmas. Like both the professionals of revolution of our day, and those, the reactionaries, most bitterly and exclusively opposed to them, one may let the evidence of objective, and collective, efficiency, outweigh the trivial matters of justice and of individual righteousness. It is proclaimed, on the one side, that social justice has been realized; on the other, that individual freedom is preserved. What is baby, for the one, is bathwater for the other, and is thrown out without a qualm. Another would-be solution, of course, is retirement from the world, the maintenance of two scrupulously clean individual hands, and the renunciation of all else. Pascal reminds us that all these are pitifully inadequate ideals. "One does not show one's greatness by being at one extreme, but by touching both at the same time," a sentiment that has been clearly echoed by St. Exupéry and by Albert Camus.[23]

Let us take up the volume entitled *Humanisme et terreur*, by Maurice Merleau-Ponty.[24] Having been spewed upon with equal fervor by Communists and "liberals," to use a sufficiently vague word, it may be what we are looking for. The Communists are inevitably repulsed by Merleau-Ponty's final inability to throw in his lot with them, although in this examination of the Moscow treason trials of the 1930's he repudiates the too individualistic explanations offered by Koestler in *Darkness at Noon*,[25] and places every possible trump in Communist hands by his attempt to understand, not to criticize, like the anthropologist who seeks to grasp the basic patterns underlying the culture he is studying. The "liberals," on the other hand, would have him condemn, not understand. Yet Merleau-Ponty is driven to the conclusion that the Communists have been false to their

---

23 ". . . si je pense avec des mots qui excluent les contradictions j'éteins chez moi toute lumière."—Antoine de St.-Exupéry, *Citadelle* (Paris, 1948), p. 287. Albert Camus uses the phrase of Pascal's quoted above as an epigraph for his *Lettres à un ami allemand* (Paris, 1945).

24 *Humanisme et terreur* (Paris, 1947). This is a revised version of "Le Yogi et le prolétaire" which appeared in *Les Temps Modernes*, ii, No. 13 (October 1946), 1–29; No. 14 (November 1946), 253–87; No. 16 (January 1947), 676–711; and of "Apprendre à lire," *Les Temps Modernes*, iii, No. 22 (July 1947), 1–27.

25 Arthur Koestler, *Darkness at Noon* (New York, 1941).

ideals, a view which he holds with increasing firmness. But his thought continues to circle round the disquieting antinomy that opposes efficacy and justice, as in a recent article which attempts to arrive at a fairer appreciation of Machiavelli's political wisdom. The problem of "dirty hands" has also preoccupied Merleau-Ponty's associate Sartre, as is shown by the title and the text of his recent play.[26] Sartre has attempted, too, to solve the related difficulty: must there be division and misunderstanding between rulers and ruled? The pages of *Entretiens sur la politique* which sketch out, for the benefit of the Rassemblement Démocratique Révolutionnaire, an admirably fluid system of lateral and vertical interchanges of opinion, are touching in their endeavor to establish communication and prevent a rupture between average members and the leadership.[27] They might be worth the attention of English and American trade-unionists anxious to preserve or extend democracy in their unions.

French intellectuals have been talking of much else. But I shall consider no further themes, and pass on to a more difficult task, that of finding some common factor in the outlook of many intellectuals in the present and the recent past, some fundamental accord in the summons they address to the future.

IV

After sophistication, what? After the acquisition of immense stores of historical knowledge and every other sort of knowledge, after the cataloguing of every conceivable metaphysical speculation on man and the universe, and the shaking, by eclecticism, of its innumerable cocktails—where do we move on from there?

"Je suis l'Empire à la fin de la décadence," wrote Verlaine. That was before 1900. The suggestion will be advanced that the Modern World, the liquidator of the Middle Ages, itself came to a close around 1900.

The Modern World was distinguished by its rationalism, by the upsurge of a boundless faith in the powers of the human reason, narrowly understood. This faith sought justification in works, in the sciences and their applications. Men developed a prospective and forward-looking view, the belief that theirs was an ever-widening downstream course, marked by the offhand relinquishing of the old

[26] Jean-Paul Sartre, *Les Mains sales* (Paris, 1948); English translation in Jean-Paul Sartre, *Three Plays* (New York, 1949). Maurice Merleau-Ponty, "Note sur Machiavel," *Les Temps Modernes,* v, No. 48 (October 1949), 577–93.

[27] J.-P. Sartre, David Rousset, Gérard Rosenthal, *Entretiens sur la politique* (Paris, 1949), pp. 110, 119–22, 139–42.

and unhesitating acceptance of the newer and better vista. Scientific progress had shown the way. Everything, human beings included, could be exhaustively analyzed, classified, and held ready for exploitation. The evolvement of means for the achievement of ends, without any glance upstream toward the source and sanction of all this activity, led to the idolatrous worship of technique itself. Maritain has quoted the report of Ernst Jünger, the German nationalist but non-Nazi writer, that he had heard young Germans declare there was no ethic any more except the ethic of technical efficiency. They provided evidence, and evidence still piles up, of the monstrous outcome of such an attitude.

What is to be done? The decadence of the Roman Empire was followed by a "dark age," by the blind struggles of barbaric tribes. Is that to be our fate?

There might be a more radical extinction of human aspirations. Karl Jaspers had stated, in 1931, that *if* mankind knew of a means to make human life on earth impossible, it is certain that someone, sooner or later, would make of that possibility a reality.[28] And for us today, the vague "if" of 1931 has shuddered into a towering certitude. The human race will shortly be able to commit suicide.

Voices have called for a return to the innocence or innocent savagery of nature, to the spirituality of the Middle Ages, to the English village as it was in 1852. They have met with little response, and it may indeed be questioned whether we can recoil thus into the past.

A more hopeful note is sounded if we talk of a new beginning. The Greek word for beginning is *arkhē*. I shall try to present evidence that certain Frenchmen—but I offer no apology for introducing non-French names—are feeling their way toward the foundation of a new archaic age.

One obvious tentative approach to an archaic world view would be to ponder on the relics that survive of previous archaic cultures. And in the visual arts, in the last fifty years, there has been such an interest, for instance in Greek sculpture of the sixth century B. C. The inchoate, the barely dawning, move us more than the finished and fully explicated piece of work. Picasso, at a still early stage of his evolution, was influenced by the primitivism of negro masks. As everyone is aware, he did not remain a borrower, nor was he content to exploit this one vein. The tortured and disarranged faces and bodies of his more recent canvasses have been interpreted as reflecting the anguished disarray of our world—but if we recall Empedocles'

[28] Karl Jaspers, *Die geistige Situation der Zeit* (Berlin, Leipzig, 1931); English translation, *Man in the Modern Age* (New York, 1933).

vision of creation, when arms and legs wander about seeking each other,[29] Picasso may with equal validity be regarded as struggling to found a new universe. And this vision of the pre-Socratic Empedocles —significantly, it seems to me—is curiously repeated in the imaginings of the Belgian Henri Michaux,[30] who writes of fantastic lands no less torture-filled than the paintings of Picasso.

The German philosopher Martin Heidegger is closely followed in France. He is of the opinion that philosophy has been on the wrong track for a long time, to be precise, since the days of Plato and Aristotle. He would have us turn back to the pre-Socratic philosophers, who asked the right questions, the questions we today should strive to answer.[31] His admiration for the sayings of Heraclitus finds an echo in that of the French poet René Char, for whom Heraclitus is a model of style or of thought—how can one distinguish?[32] Char's own sybilline poetry permits the glimpse that he is concerned with founding the future, "future life within requalified man."

Modern industrial rationalization involves the division of labor, the fragmentation of human effort and, it becomes clear, of men themselves. Conversely, the archaic age knows an indifferentiation of function. Philosophy is poetry, poetry is philosophy. Empedocles philosophized in hexameters. Several of Heidegger's lectures are commentaries on poems by Hölderlin, and in his comments he takes over the words of Hölderlin.[33] The faith is at last reborn that the primary function of words is to unveil reality. Philosophical truth is sought, therefore, in the letters of Vincent Van Gogh, in the novels of Malraux and Proust, in the unclassifiable writings of St. Exupéry, in the *Duino Elegies* of Rainer Maria Rilke. Frenchmen analyze the concept of time revealed by the novels of William Faulkner.[34] Indeed, for

[29] Fragment 57: "On it [*Earth*] many foreheads without necks sprang forth, and arms wandered unattached, bereft of shoulders, and eyes strayed about alone, needing brows." Fragment 61: "Many creatures were created with a face and breast on both sides; offspring of cattle with the fronts of men, and again there arose offspring of men with heads of cattle; and [*creatures made of elements*] mixed in part from men, in part of female sex, furnished with hairy limbs."—Kathleen Freeman, *Ancilla to the Pre-Socratic Philosophers. A Complete Translation of the Fragments in Diels, Fragmente der Vorsokratiker* (Cambridge, Mass., 1948).

[30] See Henri Michaux, *L'Espace du dedans, anthologie* (Paris, 1944).

[31] See Heidegger's letter to Beaufret in his *Platons Lehre von der Wahrheit. Mit einem Brief an Jean Beaufret, Paris, über den "Humanismus"* (Bern, 1947).

[32] See *Héraclite d'Ephèse; traduction nouvelle et intégrale avec introduction et notes par Yves Battistini. Avant-propos de René Char* (Paris, 1948).

[33] Martin Heidegger, *Hölderlin und das Wesen der Dichtung*, 1936; *Hölderlins Hymne: Wie wenn am Feiertage*, 1941; *Hölderlins Gedicht: Andenken*, 1943. Translations of first and third will be found in Heidegger, *Existence and Being* (Chicago, 1949).

[34] See Jean Pouillon, *Temps et roman* (Paris, 1946); also Jean-Paul Sartre, "Sartoris," *Nouvelle Revue Française*, L, No. 293 (February 1938), 323-28; "À propos de 'Le Bruit et la fureur.' La temporalité chez Faulkner," *ibid.*, LII, No. 309 (June 1939), 1057-61;

Frenchmen, American novelists are neo-primitives who by some strange dispensation have been enabled to write, and the careful study of whose books might help oversophisticates to escape from their impasse into a fresher though more barbaric and more brutal world. The tone of some French writers reflects this immediacy, this refusal to apply some slow and civilized process of maturation to the raw vision, before it is decanted onto the page. Witness the feverish prose of Georges Bataille,[35] the intermittent fulgurations of the poetry of Char.

Philosophy is not only poetry, it is also theology. Casting aside the model of deduction offered by mathematics, which Spinoza had employed in the seventeenth century, repudiating any borrowing of inductive procedures from the physical sciences, philosophers tried to begin, and remain, at the root of things: they set out to describe what is nearest to us. And the question nearest at hand, and which required a descriptive answer, was the Psalmist's "What is man?" Like theology, philosophy's first task was to work out an "anthropology," a description of man's state.

Since philosophers have grown up within a Christian framework, it is not surprising that their answers should be akin to those of Christian orthodoxy. This is true not for confessed Christians alone, but also for Heidegger, and for the avowed atheist Sartre, in whom it is easy to trace the notions of the Fall and of Free Will and Original Sin, and the hint of a doctrine of Redemption. Nor can it be maintained that a definitive atheism is revealed in the brooding over Nietzsche's declaration that "God is dead," in view of the persistence throughout human history of the myth of a Resurrection. More specifically a Christian interest is the reflection on "last things," on eschatology and the Apocalypse: it is to be found in Léon Bloy, in Georges Bernanos, and in the Russian Orthodox theologian, for many years resident in France, Nicholas Berdiaev. Emmanuel Mounier, addressing a Unesco audience in Paris in 1946,[36] saw fit to discuss apocalyptic ages and to present them as periods of hope, of confidence, and of vigorous effort for the future. He also discovered suggestively parallel passages in the Apocalypse of John of Patmos and in an eyewitness account of the Bikini experiment.

It will no doubt help to confirm a more than lurking suspicion that rationalism is being swamped under a flood of superstitious twad-

LIII, No. 310 (July 1939), 147–51. These two studies are reprinted in Sartre's *Situations I* (Paris, 1947), pp. 7–13, 70–81.

[35] See, for example, Georges Bataille's *L'Expérience intérieure* (Paris, 1943).

[36] Emmanuel Mounier, "Entretien sur la fin du monde," *Les Conférences de l'U.N.E.S.C.O.* (Paris, 1947), pp. 11–28; English translation in *Reflections on Our Age* (New York, 1949), pp. 19–38.

dle, when I go on to say that there exists in France a marked interest in the "occult sciences"—although not, as far as I am aware, in psychic phenomena. To the extent that it remains a game for the erudite, the mere digging up of occult sources to explain the poetry of Nerval and Rimbaud, this interest may not be disturbing. But Albert Béguin, in a recent article,[37] is not content to stop there. He reaffirms that in the great ages—pre-Socratic Greece, the Renaissance in Italy and Germany, and the age of Romanticism—three tendencies go hand in hand: the decipherment of nature, from which the individual sciences are derived; the conviction that the poetic imagination serves to reveal the hidden structures of the real; and the acceptance of occult doctrines and evolvement of cosmogonic myths. A number of these interests have been brought together by that curious figure Gaston Bachelard, a reputable professor and historian of the sciences, who has not only attempted to psychoanalyze scientific procedures themselves (an act of *lèse-majesté*, doubtless, for a certain type of mind),[38] but has read an immense mass of occult works, old books of technical recipes replete with superstitions, and imaginative literature which presents itself as such. These readings have allowed him to work out the basic and, it would seem, inescapable metaphorical systems of the occidental mind. He has devoted five books, for example, to our emotional and metaphorical relations with the four elements.[39]

The following quotation from Simone Weil will perhaps induce us to look a little less harshly on these speculations: "Pythagoras. Only this mystical conception of geometry could provide the degree of attention necessary for the beginnings of this science. Moreover, is it not recognized that astronomy emerges from astrology and chemistry from alchemy? But this line of descent is interpreted as an advance, whereas there is a degradation of the attention. Transcendent astrology and alchemy are the contemplation of eternal truths in the symbols offered by the stars and the combinations of substances. Astronomy and chemistry are the degradations of this. Astrology and chemistry as magic are its even baser degradations. There is plenitude of attention only in religious attention." [40]

Another striking indication, not of the truth of occult notions, but of how hard it is to escape them, is their presence in the works of that prosaic spirit Jean-Paul Sartre. With Freud myth had already made a frontal entry into psychology. Sartre, in his adumbration of an "ex-

37 Albert Béguin, "Poetry and Occultism," *Yale French Studies,* ii, No. 2 (Fall-Winter 1949), 12–25.

38 Gaston Bachelard, *La Formation de l'esprit scientifique; contribution à une psychanalyse de la connaissance objective* (Paris, 1947).

39 Studies devoted to fire, air, and water preceded his *La Terre et les rêveries de la volonté* (Paris, 1948); *La Terre et les rêveries du repos* (Paris, 1948).

40 Simone Weil, *La Pesanteur et la grâce* (Paris, 1948), p. 153.

istential psychoanalysis" and his actual analysis of Baudelaire,[41] links
free will and destiny (though he does not use the latter term) in a way
that harks back to occult speculations. "We have no difficulty in con-
ceiving," he declares, in his "Présentation" in Les Temps Modernes,
"that a man may be a center of irreducible indeterminism, while at
the same time his situation conditions him totally." [42] The same intuition of a basic unity inspired Balzac, washed by all the occult currents of his day, who asserted that, given a glove, he could describe
the whole man.

V

French education has been a remarkable instrument of accultura-
tion, with virtues as essential today as ever they were. Nevertheless
Frenchmen, though they have no desire to demolish the old system
utterly, are ready to admit that it has fallen behind the times. Existing school buildings are overcrowded, and the funds made available
by the state allow of no very rapid expansion. The United States and
Great Britain devote a much larger percentage of their public moneys
to the cause of education than does France; indeed, French expenditures on education are shamefully low and, in percentages, have been
steadily shrinking over the past years. A particularly striking deficiency is the small number of technicians that have been trained, and
the laboratory facilities at the university level, already inadequate
before the war, now fall pathetically short of any tolerable minimum.
University students have a hard row to hoe. There are now some
129,000 students in France, over 55,000 of them in Paris,[43] as against
about half that number in prewar days. Amphitheaters and lecture
rooms are no more numerous than before, the professors, scarcely
more numerous, are swamped with work, and students complain that
these professors are "sclerotic." A great many students try to get along
on budgets that fall short of the subsistence level, and the incidence
of tuberculosis among them is significantly higher than in the general
population. Many work in order to make ends meet, and the French
have not learnt from the U.S. to consider such part-time employment
as an acceptable if not indeed desirable accompaniment to university

[41] Jean-Paul Sartre, Esquisse d'une théorie des émotions (Paris, 1939), pp. 25–29; L'Être
et le néant, essai d'ontologie phénoménologique (Paris, 1943), pp. 643–63; Baudelaire
(Paris, 1947). The first volume has been translated as The Emotions (Outline of a Theory)
(New York, 1948), and a translation of the Baudelaire volume is announced by New
Directions.
[42] See footnote 17.
[43] These are the figures for 1948–1949. When more recent figures are made available,
they will probably show a decline in numbers.

studies. These financial difficulties explain why too many students concentrate grimly on the *"chasse au diplôme,"* instead of seeing in their university years the culmination of their intellectual training. As in this country, many students are married, some have children. The lodging situation is acutely bad. A consequence of the Marthe Richard law banning brothels has been to make these *"maisons"* available for conversion into *"maisons communautaires,"* where students, we are informed, are making interesting experiments in communal living and shared responsibilities. Others are scattered over a wide area of Paris and its suburbs. In their own interest, students have banded together rather more effectively than their predecessors judged necessary; there is a student trade-union, organized as such, whose leaders claim that their efforts persuaded the government to include students in the social security set-up, and who are demanding that students be paid a salary or "pre-salary."

These paragraphs have deliberately thrown together some examples of how the shoe pinches, in present-day France. Against these sad realities may be set an admirable plan for the reconstruction of the whole educational system, a plan which in some measure is already being put into effect.

During the Occupation, groups of resisting teachers in France began to discuss the desirability of sweeping reforms in education, when the country would once more be free. Similar discussions were inaugurated in North Africa, after it had been invaded, and upon liberation an official commission was formed under the direction of the physicist Paul Langevin and the child psychologist Henri Wallon.

The report presented by this commission is extraordinarily successful in its avoidance of too one-sided an accentuation of any single factor. It stresses the development of the whole child, intellectual, physical, and moral, and a supple adaptation of training to the region and the individual (for France, this is a startling novelty). Nor should there be any slighting of manual skills and practical abilities as lower in dignity than theoretical attainments. The hours of class in the earlier grades are greatly shortened, and homework is abolished. Extracurricular activities, run by the pupils themselves, are to be encouraged, so that each one may learn the lesson of cooperation with the group, and the valuable discipline, when each child has experience of both, of directing and obeying. There are to be no formal examinations before the conclusion of secondary schooling, and the traditional *baccalauréat*, with its development of an unhealthy rivalry and sheer cramming, is to be replaced by a test which will give a better idea of the student's capacities. Each student should benefit by a general education and not receive a technical training alone. "General culture," declares the report, "represents what brings men closer and unites them, while the profession too often represents what separates them. . . . In a democratic state, where every worker is a citizen, it is indispensable that specialization should not be an obstacle to the understanding of vaster problems and that a wide and substantial culture should free men from the narrow limitations of the technician."

One interesting feature of the report is the creation of experimental "*classes nouvelles*," in which teachers, working as a team, are allowed every liberty to experiment with new methods of teaching which put the stress on "learning by doing." These new classes have been greeted enthusiastically by some, with a more qualified enthusiasm by others, although still with favor, and *Les Nouvelles Littéraires* interviewed a girl of nineteen, about to begin her university work, who expressed her entire satisfaction with the traditional methods of teaching she had experienced, declaring that scholars of the new classes might be more advanced in mathematics, but that a certain "austerity" led to better results with the classical languages. An indication that not everyone is an extrovert, and that, whatever the deplorable influence of foreign films and digests, intellectual zeal is not ready to wither away in France.[44]

The various factors which I have discussed in this paper would lend themselves, with a slightly different shading or emphasis, to either of two conflicting judgments: on the whole, things are going badly in France, or, in France, on the whole, things are going well. It is true today, as at previous stages of France's disturbed history, that collectively and generally speaking many flaws are to be observed. In the midst of this *pagaïe* are certain individuals, maybe even groups of individuals, who have achieved or who promise to achieve remarkable things. I do not feel on sufficiently familiar terms with the future to predict whether this leaven will be enough to leaven the whole lump, whether the seed will fall on fertile or on barren ground. But this I will affirm: there is leaven, there is seed.

44 For recent developments in French education, see *La Réforme de l'enseignement, Projet soumis à M. le Ministre de l'Éducation Nationale par la Commission Ministérielle d'Étude,* Ministère de l'Éducation Nationale [no date]; Roger Gal, *La Réforme de l'enseignement et les classes nouvelles* (Paris, [1946]); "Propositions de paix scolaire," special number of *Esprit,* XVII, Nos. 3–4 (March–April 1949); "La Situation étudiante française," special number of *Le Semeur,* XLVII, Nos. 6–7 (April–May 1949). I am also greatly indebted to George F. Kneller, of the Department of Education of Yale University, who let me read the manuscript of his "Education in France," prior to its publication by the Dryden Press.

Financial considerations, if nothing else, are causing the indefinite postponement of compulsory secondary education for all children, though not the abandonment of the principle. For details of the actual *projet de loi* introduced by the Minister of Education, M. Delbos, see *Le Monde* of January 13, 14, 18 and 19, 1950.

6

✦✦✦

SCIENCE AND FRENCH NATIONAL STRENGTH

HENRY E. GUERLAC

✦✦✦

IT IS NOT the purpose of this chapter to speculate concerning the ways in which scientific progress might contribute to a program of French industrial or military recovery. That is a problem for the economic or military specialist. It may be taken for granted that a flourishing state of science, as well as energy in developing its useful applications, is essential to the survival and prosperity of a modern nation and at the same time a sure index of that nation's cultural vitality. I wish simply to call attention to some notable features of the history of science in France and to some of the institutional and traditional factors which are relevant to the present situation. I shall conclude the chapter with a discussion of the recent policies and concrete proposals which the French nation has adopted since the war to reinvigorate her scientific life.

I

The man on the street and the man of science commonly give quite different meanings to the term "science." It is through its palpable, useful applications that the average person gains his only familiarity with its mysteries. Yet the majority of scientists view science not as the milch-cow of the modern world, but as a noble intellectual good, as John Tyndall once emphasized to an audience of materialistic Americans, to be "cultivated for its own sake, for the pure love of truth, rather than for the applause or profit that it brings." [1]

I emphasize this definition of science because, though it is widely expressed as an ideal, the French scientist has made it very specially his own; science to him is part of culture. It is in France that the cult

1 John Tyndall, *Six Lectures on Light* (London, 1873), p. 212.

of pure science, of ivory tower science, has been most eloquently expounded; in fact, it is from the words of Frenchmen that Tyndall documented his plea that science should be viewed in this fashion. From Cuvier, for example, he translated with Victorian stiffness a statement which perhaps puts the doctrine in extreme form:

"These grand practical innovations are the mere applications of truths of a higher order, not sought with a practical intent, but which were pursued for their own sake, and solely through an ardour for knowledge. Those who applied them could not have discovered them; those who discovered them had no inclination to pursue them to a practical end. Engaged in the high regions whither their thoughts had carried them they hardly perceived these practical issues, though born of their own deeds. These rising workshops, these peopled colonies, those ships which furrow the seas—this abundance, this luxury, this tumult—all this comes from discoveries in science, and it all remains strange to them. At the point where science merges into practice they abandon it; it concerns them no more." [2]

The advancement of science is admittedly a complex international activity; it is a rare event in the history of science which can be attributed to one man or one nation. Yet to deny national variations altogether is quite unrealistic; for there are subtle cultural tendencies which set apart the scientific achievements of every nation. The French animus in favor of pure science is just a tendency; so also is the American scientific genius which manifests itself best in engineering application, in carrying through to profitable completion the ideas of others, or in conducting research in which massive equipment, heavy financing, organized activity, and engineering skills all enter in. By comparison, England and France have a record of producing eminently important results in pure science with very modest equipment. If, further, we contrast France with England, France's achievement appears to be more theoretical and less empirical, more mathematical and less experimental, than England's.

Very possibly France's greatest contribution has not been in natural science at all, but in mathematics. It could be argued that in no other scientific field can France produce an aggregate of names as impressive as those of Viète, Descartes, Pascal, Lagrange, Laplace, Cauchy, Hermite, Henri Poincaré, Lebesgue, and d'Ocagne. But even if this is an exaggeration, the typical French achievement in the sciences seems nonetheless to be rationalistic, one of synthesis or great theoretical insight: such for example as Laplace's great masterpiece, the *Mécanique céleste;* Carnot's pioneer speculations into the nature of heat and energy; Jussieu's natural system of classifying plants; Cuvier's great

[2] Tyndall, *op. cit.*, pp. 221-22.

unifying studies in comparative anatomy and palaeontology; La-voisier's reform of chemistry. Despite the weighty instances of Claude Bernard and Pasteur, it is the Anglo-Saxons, not the French, who seem to have produced the mainly experimental men, the Franklins, the Faradays, and the Joules.

If we view matters at close range, all the countries of Europe at every period have shared in the progress of every field of science; but, taking a longer view, it is clear that different nations, in different times, have assumed the chief burden of advancing it. From about 1500 to the middle of the sixteenth century the leadership in science, as in so much else, belonged to Italy; for a brief period—from the Restoration to the death of Queen Anne—England predominated, and held a position in science she did not regain until after the middle of the nineteenth century. The ascendancy of France in science lagged behind her greatest period of literary and artistic domination; the Age of Louis XIV marked, it is true, the beginning of an official approval of science in France, but Colbert's Academy owed its greatest renown chiefly to foreigners, like Huygens, Cassini, and Olaus Roemer. The period of French scientific supremacy extends from about 1750 through the 1830's and 1840's, only temporarily interrupted by the great crisis of the Revolution. During this long hegemony, French leadership extended into every field of natural science, and Paris was sought out by students of chemistry, mathematics, natural history, and medicine from other European countries and from America. After the mid-century mark, and especially after 1870, there is an appear-ance of decline, which is partly a matter of comparative position and the swift rise of German and British scientific achievement. After the First World War a decline sets in which is indisputably real, related to the exhaustion of French resources in manpower and morale, and in part to the inadequacy of her scientific institutions and to what I shall call an intellectual devaluation of science. These last two factors we must consider briefly.

II

All aspects of intellectual and artistic life in France—fine arts, music, higher education, and scientific research—are to a large extent government-sponsored, and of course overwhelmingly concentrated in Paris, the one true center of all that, to a Frenchman, is worth while. Whatever the prevailing fashion in government the pattern has remained the same. In these conditions of work French science differed greatly from that of nineteenth-century Germany, which was government-sponsored but widely decentralized, and from that of

England where private institutions have predominated—up to and including the Royal Society itself—and where some degree of decentralization has always existed.

Most of the scientific and educational institutions of France are creations of the Revolutionary Convention, or recreations of institutions of the Old Régime. Leaving aside the Academy of Sciences, which is not a center of research, the most famous and still perhaps the most important centers of scientific work are the faculties of the University, the great special schools like Polytechnique and the Ecole Normale Supérieure, and venerable centers like the illustrious Collège de France and the Muséum d'Histoire Naturelle, which is not just a museum but a training ground and many-sided research center as well. All of these institutions except Polytechnique, which is a military establishment, are under the eye and the budgetary control of the Ministère de l'Instruction Publique.

Let us look first at the laboratory facilities which these institutions provided. The first important chemical laboratory was that associated with the Ecole Polytechnique—the famous "X" (as the Polytechnique has always been called) from which radiated French influence in mathematics and the exact sciences. This laboratory dated back to the time of Berthollet, Fourcroy, Gay-Lussac, and the other great chemists of the Napoleonic period; but it exerted its wide influence upon the spread of chemical studies in France through the great investigator and teacher, J.-B. Dumas (1800–1884). During the Second Empire, Dumas' pupils founded laboratories in all the principal educational centers just mentioned. The most famous laboratory was perhaps that of organic chemistry at the Collège de France where Marcelin Berthelot worked for nearly half a century.[3]

Laboratories of physics, modest and designed primarily to allow the professor to prepare his lecture demonstrations, existed in Polytechnique, the École Normale, the Faculté des Sciences, the Collège de France, and the Muséum d'Histoire Naturelle. At the Muséum the Becquerel family enjoyed a monopoly of the chair of physics through four generations. Here on a modest building a plaque commemorates the achievement of Henri Becquerel (1852–1909), the third in line, who ushered in the Atomic Age in 1896 by discovering the radioactivity of uranium salts.

[3] A complete list of French scientific laboratories—both teaching and research—as they existed at the close of the nineteenth century is given in Paul Melon, L'Enseignement supérieur et l'enseignement technique en France (Paris, 1893). The chemical laboratories at the École des Mines and the École Supérieure de Pharmacie are discussed at length in [Edmond] Fremy, Carnot, Jungfleisch et Terreil, Les Laboratoires de chimie (2 vols., Paris, 1881).

Until the end of the Second Empire, according to the testimony of Louis Pasteur, not a penny of the budget of the Ministère de l'Instruction Publique was earmarked for the support of research laboratories, and only an administrative fiction and official tolerance allowed the investigators to use some of the funds intended for teaching for their private research. Pasteur further pointed out that numerous laboratories and their equipment—notably those of Dumas, the physicists Foucault and Fizeau, and of the agricultural chemist Boussingault—were the private property of the scientists themselves.[4]

In many respects the most discussed laboratories in nineteenth-century Paris were those of the Collège de France in which were carried out by Magendie, Claude Bernard, Brown-Séquard, and Marey some of the noblest and most revolutionary experiments in the history of biological science. This brings us to an important point: the extraordinary inadequacy of scientific facilities during the nineteenth century. There were exceptions—for example, Frémy's chemical laboratory at the Muséum which was something of a showpiece, for he had one laboratory for his own use, one for his preparators, and one for his students. But in general there is a story of indifference and material starvation that repeats itself, not only in obscure corners, but even in the august Collège de France. The greatest figures in French science struggled against this handicap, and repeatedly demanded the sort of facilities that already existed in German and even English universities. Until 1840, the great physiologist, Magendie, had as a laboratory only a very small room which Claude Bernard, his preparator, later described as a closet that could scarcely hold both men. When in 1854 Claude Bernard became a professor at the Faculté des Sciences he was unable to secure a laboratory or provision for an assistant. A year later, when he succeeded Magendie at the Collège de France, he fell heir to what Paul Bert described as "a dark, damp tannery" and which led Bernard himself to characterize laboratories as the "tombs of scientists." In 1864 after an audience of Bernard with the Emperor, the Minister of Public Instruction, Victor Duruy, was told to give the great physiologist anything he wanted. When he mentioned a well-equipped laboratory, Duruy replied that his Imperial Majesty had in mind something more personal.[5] In 1867 Claude Bernard took his campaign to the public in his famous report on the progress of general physiology in France and in an article in

[4] Louis Pasteur, "Le Budget de la science," *Revue des cours scientifiques de la France et de l'étranger*, 5e année, No. 9. (February 1, 1868), 138.

[5] J. M. D. Olmsted, *Claude Bernard, Physiologist* (New York, 1938), pp. 63 and 75, and *passim*.

the *Revue des deux mondes*.[6] Moreover, he contrasted the obstacles his own new science had encountered in France—official neglect and the hostility of the established naturalists and anatomists—with the flourishing condition of physiological studies in Germany.

In the meantime Pasteur lent his voice and great influence. He had suffered the same sort of neglect. His first quarters at the Ecole Normale had been inconvenient and primitive in the extreme—attic rooms that were freezing in winter and unbearably hot in summer. When he finally obtained possession of a small wing, he was obliged to install his drying oven under the stairs and could reach it only on hands and knees. In 1867 he wrote directly to Louis Napoleon asking for an adequate laboratory with facilities for experiments as dangerous to health as his were likely to be. Napoleon was well disposed; so also was Duruy, but the necessary credits were nonetheless eventually refused.[7] This was a hard blow, since millions were being spent at this time (1861–1874) on the erection of the Opéra with lavish adherence to Charles Garnier's plans to make it the most sumptuous in Europe. Pasteur brought matters to a head by a brief but impassioned article published in February 1868, in which he eloquently described the "tombs of the scientists" and the material handicaps under which French science was laboring.[8] The article created a sensation and led Napoleon to call a conference on March 16, 1868, at which French science was represented by Claude Bernard, Milne-Edwards, Sainte-Claire-Deville, and Pasteur. The whole question of France's need for research laboratories was discussed, and as a consequence work was begun on a new laboratory for Pasteur at the École Normale and for Claude Bernard at the Muséum. A still more important consequence of the agitation was the creation of that unique institution known as the École Pratique des Hautes Études to be discussed below.[9]

The tragedy of neglect was repeated in the well-known case of the Curies. Pierre Curie spent nearly all of his scientific life at the École de Physique et de Chimie Industrielle de la Ville de Paris in the dreary buildings of the Collège Rollin, first as director of laboratory work,

---

[6] Claude Bernard, *Rapport sur les progrès et la marche de la physiologie générale en France* (Paris, 1867). See especially the conclusion, pp. 143–49; and his article "Le problème de la physiologie générale," *Revue des deux mondes*, LXXII (1867), 874–92.

[7] Olmsted, *op. cit.*, pp. 88–89.

[8] Pasteur, "Le Budget de la science," *loc. cit.*, pp. 137–39. Pasteur's title calls attention to the fact that while there existed a *"budget des cultes,"* there was none for science. cf. Renan's remarks in *L'Avenir de la science*, XIV.

[9] Olmsted, *op. cit.*, p. 89. Important documents concerning the burst of activity authorized by the decrees of July 1868—prepared with the approval of the leading French scientists—are to be found in Victor Duruy, *Notes et souvenirs* (Paris, 1891), Vol. I, Chap. XII; and in *L'Administration de l'instruction publique de 1863 à 1869*, Ministère de S. Exc. M. Duruy (Paris, n.d.), pp. 592–603 and 644 ff.

then as professor, with no funds and no personal laboratory, not even a room reserved entirely to himself. As much as he dared, he used the space and sums available for the teaching laboratory. His important experiments on magnetism were conducted mainly in an outside corridor running between a stairway and a laboratory. As *chef de laboratoire* for twelve years, he received roughly the salary of a factory hand of those times, about 300 francs a month.[10] The inadequate and unhealthy conditions under which Marie Curie began her work on radium and the notorious *hangar* of the rue Lhomond in which the two workers undertook the large-scale extraction from pitchblende are familiar to all. When Pierre Curie was given a chair of physics at the Sorbonne in 1900 he had no laboratory, but continued to work at the École de Physique. Two years before his death, he accepted his professorate at the Faculté des Sciences only upon condition that he be given a satisfactory laboratory.[11]

The most serious effect of this early stringency was that lack of space and of funds made it difficult for French scientists to bring advanced students into their laboratories in the German fashion. A sort of apprentice system, in which the professor was forced to confine himself to a single able student as preparator, was the usual practice. Two important institutional innovations, though wholly different in conception, were inspired by an attempt to improve laboratory facilities and increase the opportunities for advanced study in pure science. The first of these was the École Pratique des Hautes Études, established by a decree of July 31, 1868; the second was the Institut Pasteur which opened its door twenty years later.

The École Pratique, largely the achievement of Victor Duruy, grew out of the famous Napoleonic conference with the scientists. It was not a new physical creation, but consisted of machinery for giving grants-in-aid to existing research centers so that more students of high caliber could work under the immediate direction of the ablest professors in their laboratories and seminars.[12] In the physical sciences the major Paris laboratories just mentioned received important grants, but the only significant institutions outside of Paris that received aid before World War I were marine biological stations that depended upon the Sorbonne or the Faculté des Sciences, like the

[10] Marie Curie discusses her own and Pierre's hardships at length in *Pierre Curie,* trans. by Charlotte and Vernon Killogg (New York, 1923). See particularly p. 95.

[11] *ibid.,* pp. 99–100, 109–10; Eve Curie, *Madame Curie,* trans. by Vincent Sheean (New York, 1937), pp. 236–39.

[12] For the École Pratique, see Duruy, *op. cit.,* pp. 305–9; Ernest Lavisse, *Un Ministre— Victor Duruy* (1895), pp. 80–83. See also "Rapport de S. Exc. M. le Ministre à S. M. l'Empereur, précédant les deux décrets du 31 juillet 1868, relatifs aux laboratoires d'enseignement et de recherches et à la création d'une école pratique des hautes études," in *L'Administration de l'instruction publique, op. cit.,* pp. 644–48.

famous Station Maritime de Roscoff.[13] The exaggerated centralization of resources for research which had been, in Duruy's mind, one of the merits of the French system, was never seriously threatened.

The Institut Pasteur is the only wholly private scientific research institution of great importance in France; it was one of the models of our own Rockefeller Institute. After Pasteur's dramatic victory over rabies, an international subscription was launched to provide what Pasteur had long desired, a research center where he could be complete master and work according to his own methods.[14] Contributions of all sorts poured in, including gifts from the Tsar of Russia, the Emperor of Brazil, and the Sultan of Turkey. The French Chamber voted the then respectable sum of 200,000 francs. In little time, the Institut became self-supporting through the sale of sera and other by-products of its research activities. Even before World War I the Institut Pasteur was able to share equally with the University in endowing Mme. Curie's Institut de Radium, which is thus supported partly by public and partly by private funds.[15]

III

It is curious that no country in the past has written more in praise of science or has set a higher intellectual value upon scientific accomplishment than France, and yet none has been more unimaginative and parsimonious in providing scientists with the facilities and resources they require. Since the time of Condorcet, a succession of writers has emphasized the social importance of science, and the central role it was destined to play in the progress of the modern world. This thread of scientific rationalism inherited from the eighteenth century, and nurtured by the scientific successes of the nineteenth, has influenced and conditioned the thinking even of those Frenchmen who inveigh against it. It has become an important intellectual tradition to be reckoned with.

Yet, more than elsewhere, the subject of science and its importance is a controversial one in France. For brief periods England and America were divided into warring camps by the heated, but usually superficial, debates over Darwinian evolution; until recently, however, in the Anglo-Saxon world science has enjoyed a position *au-*

[13] Melon, *op. cit.*, pp. 22–29.

[14] René Vallery-Radot, *The Life of Pasteur*, trans. by Mrs. R. L. Devonshire (Garden City, N.Y., n.d.), p. 442; Louis Lumet, *Pasteur* (Paris, 1923) pp. 129–30. For a full description of the Institute, see Lumet, pp. 137 ff. On the early history of the Pasteur Institute, see Dr. Roux's address, "Le XXVe Anniversaire de l'Institut Pasteur," *Revue scientifique*, 52e année, No. 7 (February 1914), 193–204.

[15] cf. Eve Curie, *op. cit.*, pp. 285–86.

dessus de la mêlée. But in France the profound division between Right and Left, the great fissure that on every subject has divided France into two, has defined the proper attitude for the partisans on each important issue, and has not allowed science to escape. A crucial debate on the meaning and ethical significance of science has continued in France until our own time.

For the Third Republic—in the course of which so many men of scientific training at one time or other held office, men like Paul Bert, Marcelin Berthelot, Freycinet, Scheurer-Kestner, and Painlevé—for the anticlerical Third Republic, the cult of reason and science provided, as we all know, the central *mystique,* and served as a useful political blunderbuss. In his assault on the outdated medievalism of the Right, in his attacks on the clerical enemy, the good Radical Socialist appealed to the light of reason and to faith in scientific determinism. In an ascending order of subtlety and sophistication, Berthelot, Taine, and Renan made up his triumvirate of sages. In many respects the most enduring and influential statement of this doctrine is Renan's *L'Avenir de la science.* Though a rambling, ill-written work of his impassioned youth, produced in 1849, its real position in intellectual history is that of a document in the scientific disputes of the Third Republic. Renan fished it from a dusty carton in 1890 and tossed it into the boiling controversy set off by the publication of Paul Bourget's *Le Disciple.*

Renan's *L'Avenir* was an epoch-making book, sensitive and penetrating and, in a clumsy kind of way, deeply moving. Because he did not fully accept the prevailing materialism or the naïve determinism of his own time, did not present the case of science with quite the customary egotism and overconfidence, the work has survived its century and even today is a center of controversy. The faith in what science for all its philosophical limitations, its fumblings and half-knowledge, can mean for mankind, has never been more eloquently stated. The first achievements of science seem to Renan negative, critical; science has performed a useful sanitary operation by destroying the world of childlike dreams and alluring falsehoods; but the fulfillment of its great mission lies far in the future: "La science seule fera désormais les symboles; la science seule peut résoudre à l'homme les éternels problèmes dont sa nature exige impérieusement la solution." [16]

Science, says Renan, must penetrate the educational system. Since it is the work of many hands, scientific research should be coordinated and supplied with resources beyond anything yet proposed. The state

[16] *Oeuvres complètes de Ernest Renan, edition définitive établie par Henriette Psichari,* T. III, 814.

must patronize and support science as lavishly as it does the arts; but it must do so with the most complete neutrality, since liberty is the condition of scientific progress. From the government must come the great scientific workshops, the observatories, laboratories, and libraries which cannot be supplied by individual initiative.[17]

If Renan's *L'Avenir*, published belatedly in 1890, was the strongest statement on behalf of science, the outstanding attack on the prevailing cult of science was Paul Bourget's famous psychological novel, *Le Disciple*, which had appeared the year before. Until the appearance of *Le Disciple*, attacks on science had been largely confined to sporadic sorties from the ultramontanist camp. Clerical authoritarians from De Maistre and Bonald to Louis Veuillot had each claimed his pound of flesh.[18] But Paul Bourget's abandonment of the prevailing cult of scientific determinism, like Brunetière's conversion, signified a deeper and more serious cleavage in opinion than had been evident before. Bourget had been a disciple of Taine and Claude Bernard, and a member of the reigning school of naturalistic writers led by Émile Zola, which included—besides the exponent of the *roman expérimental* himself—Flaubert, Alphonse Daudet, Hector Malot, the early Huysmans, and Maupassant. Not only scientific naturalism, but the reigning psychological determinism of Taine and Ribot, attracted Bourget. It is against this, and what he believed to be its moral implications, that he at last rebelled. The tragedy of Robert Greslou, the central figure in his novel, is a consequence of the moral irresponsibility of science. Disciple of the mild, harmless philosopher Adrien Sixte, from whom he learned a rigid uncompromising psychological determinism like that of Taine, Robert Greslou becomes the tutor in a noble family, and puts these theories into practice in the scientific seduction of the sister of his young pupil. Greslou's experiments result in the suicide of his victim, his trial for murder, and his own death at the avenging hand of the girl's older brother. By means of this central figure, whom he once described as a Julien Sorel inspired by Renan rather than by Napoleon, Bourget hoped to show that scientific and philosophic ideas are not neutral but can—when they take possession of unstable minds and weak characters—become implements of disaster.[19]

[17] *Oeuvres complètes de Renan*, T. III, pp. 928–33.

[18] See, for example, Veuillot's *Odeurs de Paris*, Livre v.

[19] Albert Feuillerat, *Paul Bourget* (Paris, 1937), p. 136. Feuillerat has shown that Bourget was strongly influenced by an episode that had taken place ten years earlier, when a dairymaid had been brutally assassinated and dismembered by a psychopathic medical student who a short time before in a public lecture had appealed to the Darwinian struggle of existence to justify the murder of the weak by the strong.

In the *Revue des deux mondes,* Ferdinand Brunetière in his article "À Propos du *Disciple*" launched his campaign against the cult of science and urged the moral necessity of putting limits to man's speculative audacity, a proposal that brought heated replies from Anatole France, Ribot, Janet, and others.[20] In 1895 François de Curel made the conflict between the scientific and the religious views of the world the theme of his problem play, *La Nouvelle Idole.* The force of this great work is that it puts into action precisely the deepest conflicting elements in the French tradition. In the breast of the perplexed Dr. Donnat is fought the battle between scientific devotion and religious faith, between reason and emotion. Significantly the dilemma remains unresolved, but before the curtain falls Louise Donnat has eloquently expressed in her troubled words ideas destined to appeal with increasing force to the next literary generation. As far as its influence on literature is concerned, Brunetière's heralded "bankruptcy of science" is an accomplished fact. The fashion is changing; the new generation prefers the literature of moral responsibility, the *"culte de moi"* and the neo-traditionalism of Barrès, the romantic neo-Catholicism of Péguy; the movement summed up by Julien Benda as the *trahison des clercs.* The new generation turns away from science; Henri Bergson, whose philosophy sets such sharp limits to the legitimate pretensions of science, is that generation's prophet and savior.

IV

Some of the Catholic scientists were troubled by the conflict between their traditional faith and the cult of science. They found themselves on untenable ground between a Catholic clergy and laity generally ignorant and suspicious of science and scientific associates who were for the most part free thinkers. Louis Pasteur, in his famous *Discours de réception* delivered at the Académie Française when he succeeded the positivist scholar Littré, dutifully praised his predecessor, but stated the case of the Catholic savant when he attacked positivism and the widespread belief that science could solve all problems, moral and spiritual.[21] Catholic scientists, wishing to remain both Catholic and scientists, drew closer together. In 1875 a group of them founded the Société Scientifique de Bruxelles, an international association of scientists who wished to affirm their inflexible Catholi-

[20] A brief account of the quarrel over *Le Disciple* is to be found in *ibid.,* pp. 135–48. Brunetière's important antiscientific essays are to be found collected in his *Nouvelles questions de critique* (1898) and in his *La Science et la religion* (nouv. ed. revue, 1913).
[21] Louis Pasteur, *Discours de réception à l'académie française* (Paris, 1882). Reprinted in Pasteur Vallery-Radot (ed.), *Oeuvres de Pasteur* (Paris, 1939), VII, 326–39.

cism.[22] Their instinct that the loudly asserted incompatibility of science and faith was partly the result of a superficial philosophy of science and ignorance of its true history was to some extent borne out by events. It was precisely at this period that science was forced to abandon the simple mechanistic picture of the universe which had so long been held, and the criticism of Duhem, Mach, and Poincaré was fundamentally altering men's notion of scientific fact and scientific law. At the same time the work of Pierre Duhem and Paul Tannery was revealing how inadequate was our knowledge of the origins of modern science. Duhem's great discoveries in the medieval background of Galileo's thought was stimulated, if not motivated, by a desire to show that the official history of science of the positivists was an insubstantial myth, and that reputable science had existed in the Catholic Middle Ages.[23]

The Dreyfus affair divided the scientists as it did all professions, all groups, and even many families; but in the main the scientists tended, as one would expect, to be found among the Dreyfusards. I have in my possession one of those early printed petitions circulated in the Latin Quarter on behalf of Dreyfus. A number of leading scientific names appear on it. Émile Duclaux, biographer of Pasteur and director of the Pasteur Institute, and Édouard Grimaux, the professor at Polytechnique who wrote the standard life of Lavoisier, were among the most active on behalf of Dreyfus. Many younger scientists were profoundly influenced by the *affaire*. Jean Perrin and Paul Langevin, both physicists under thirty in 1899, were members of the Socialist circle which gathered around Lucien Herr and Charles Andler at the Socialist Party bookstore opened by Péguy. Here they met Léon Blum and other young Socialists, occasionally glimpsing Jaurès himself; and here the doctrines of Renan and Berthelot experienced an important revival.[24] In the period after World War I, Perrin and Langevin took the lead in what their opponents called a *scientisme politique,* carrying on a campaign for ideas not greatly different from those of Renan, but with Socialist overtones: for a moral and intellectual liberation through science; for a progressive rationalization of

[22] The members included such distinguished scientific figures as the mathematicians Hermite, Humbert, Camille Jourdan, and d'Ocagne; the sociologist LePlay; and Louis Pasteur. On the Society, see Maurice d'Ocagne, *Hommes et choses de science—propos familiers,* 2e sér. (Paris, 1932), 163 and 182; *Annales de la Société scientifique de Bruxelles, Table analytique . . . Précédée de l'histoire documentaire de la Société scientifique* (Louvain, 1904).

[23] It is of some significance in this connection that both Paul Tannery and Pierre Duhem, the two leading founders of the history of science movement, were members of the *Société scientifique de Bruxelles.*

[24] See the preface by Léon Blum in Jean Perrin, *La Science et l'espérance* (Paris, 1948).

the inherited evils of society with emphasis upon what Langevin called the "human value of science."

These doctrines came into sharp conflict with the views of the Catholic scientists. In the 1920's and 1930's the ideological battle over science continued unabated. The attack on modernism gave rise to some debates of great interest and importance for the philosophy of science, but the net result was nonetheless an atmosphere not at all favorable to the popularity of science.

Generally, the position of the Catholic scientists was moderate and enlightened, compared at least with the attacks of Brunetière and his forerunners, but it involved both a devaluation and a sharp circumscription of science. It was an encircling, not a frontal movement, intended to confine science and its method to the laboratory, surrounding it with a *cordon sanitaire* to prevent it from spreading into the sensitive areas of life. In the first place, the prestige of science must be strictly limited to the natural sciences; it should not be allowed to inflate the confidence of the moral and social studies. Sociology is particularly dangerous, hence the scorching attack leveled at Durkheim by the rector of the Faculty of Philosophy of Louvain.[25] In the second place, science cannot do the work of philosophy. Here Bergson's intuitionism, and the rise of scientific phenomenalism—the denial that science can deal with ultimate reality and the notion that it deals only with the relations between phenomena—provided a powerful, if often double-edged, weapon. Lastly, the great development of modern physics, with its seeming abandonment of strict determinism, was a godsend to those who wish to deflate and devalue science by pointing to the inadequacy of the "eternal laws" of which the nineteenth century made so much. The epithet *scientisme* was coined to fit the doctrine of those who wished, by contrast, to inflate the importance of science—specifically, men like Perrin and Langevin.[26]

These views which I have summarized are well expressed in Louis de Launay's *L'Église et la science* (1936), which appeared just as *scientisme* was being adopted as an official policy by the Front Populaire. How welcome these views were to controversialists of the Right is evident from the long and effusive front-page review which Léon Daudet devoted to it in the notorious *Candide*. A more recent presentation of this view is the symposium entitled, significantly, *L'Avenir de la science*,[27] which appeared in a series of eminently Catholic books

[25] M. Deploige, *Le Conflit de la morale et de la sociologie* (Paris, 1911).

[26] The expression was given currency by the work of a Catholic physician, Jean Fiolle, *Science et scientisme* (2 vols., Paris, 1936).

[27] Louis de Broglie, André Thérive, *et al.*, *L'Avenir de la science* (Paris, 1941).

during the time of Vichy. It is an outright attack—as the title implies—on the tradition of Renan and on the presumption of science, or rather of the *scientistes*. It is introduced by an able and moderate essay on the state of physics by Prince Louis de Broglie, of whose scientific accomplishments we shall soon speak. His discussion of the insubstantial foundations of modern physics sets the stage for the violent attacks that follow: of the R.P. Sertillanges on the *scientisme* of Renan and his kind; and of Raymond Charmet on modernism and the whole French rationalist tradition. M. Charmet finds the cause of the fall of France to be the same as the fall of Greece—for, as everyone knows, France is the Greece of modern Europe. In both cases, the decline is attributable to excessive intellectuality and loquacity and what he sums up as the *"culte obscur de la raison claire,"* whose most dangerous expositors were Descartes and Renan.

This attack from the Right upon the scientific humanism preached by the men of the Left is not avowedly antiscientific. It does not wish to destroy science, but to tame it and disqualify it for any very profound intellectual mission in the modern world. By an odd coincidence, the Catholic philosophers of science appear rather narrowly materialistic, for they would reduce science to its useful applications. "La science pratique," writes one of them, "est peut-être la vraie science." It is plain to see that this negativist mood is not such as to lure the best young intellects into science; it may well have been a very real factor in the decline of French scientific achievement in our own time, by encouraging an indifference and contempt for science among young men whose background happens to be Catholic and conservative. A decline has undoubtedly taken place, but I do not want to exaggerate it. Let us at this point search for signs of real vitality in the scientific picture.

V

To illustrate my point that French achievements in science, while no longer leading the world, still play an essential part in world scientific progress, I shall take my examples from pure science, from the history of modern atomic physics, where we will find a great French name at each of the three stages that were traversed in penetrating into the mysteries of atomic structure. These three stages are: (1) the proof of the existence of atoms and molecules; (2) the exploration of the electronic outer shell of atoms; (3) the penetration into the atomic nucleus. By a convenient historical accident, this will introduce us to the three principal personalities who are responsible for the great postwar scientific effort in France, Jean Perrin, Louis de Broglie, and Frédéric Joliot.

As late as 1895 there were still many who considered the hypothesis of atoms and molecules merely a convenient fiction. In this year Jean Perrin, a young preparator at the École Normale, entered upon a research career that was largely devoted to marshaling unassailable proof of the existence of atoms and molecules. From his studies of Brownian movement—the perpetual and irregular dance of microscopic particles suspended in a fluid—and of the properties of thin soap films, Perrin was able about 1910 to determine the sizes and numbers of atoms and molecules, and supply independent quantitative confirmation of the molecular nature of fluids. Perrin's general treatise *Les Atomes* (1921) brought together the most important proofs and to all intents and purposes ended a long-standing argument.

Perrin took little part in the succession of discoveries which showed that the atoms were not the hard, unyielding particles of early speculation but complex microcosms with electrified particles, the electrons, rotating about a central core, work we associate with the name of J. J. Thomson, Niels Bohr, Max Planck, and others. This brings us to our second historical stage, for in 1925 Louis de Broglie, now France's leading theoretical physicist, hit upon the idea that a moving electron, previously thought of only as a particle, might behave like a bundle of waves. The proof of De Broglie's daring hypothesis, that electrons should have the wavelike properties of light, was not long delayed, and led to that branch of modern physics known as wave mechanics.

Thus we find one French scientist contributing to understanding the properties of the atom as a whole, while a French physicist of the next generation is the first to expose the mysterious theoretical properties of the electron, half-particle and half-wave. French physicists also have had an important share—and why not, since Becquerel and the Curies were the first to reveal the inner storehouse of atomic energy?—in the fateful discovery of atomic fission, which resulted from stage three, the study of the inner core or nucleus of the atom.

The sport of atom-smashing dates from the work of Ernest Rutherford in 1919, who showed that the heavy, positively charged particles emitted by radioactive substances could be used to bombard the compact cores of other atoms. Nuclear chips seemed to be knocked off, producing actual transmutations on a minute scale. During the 1930's it was found possible to use other atomic projectiles, the protons, and accelerate them to great velocities in devices like the cyclotron.

In 1932 the problem was fundamentally advanced by the discovery in England of a hitherto unsuspected atomic particle, the neutron, which had the same mass as the proton, but no charge. The fact that the neutron was uncharged, and hence would not be repelled by the positively charged atomic nucleii, at once led Enrico Fermi to reason that neutrons would be very effective in inducing nuclear transformation in heavy elements where the repelling charges are very great. This proved to be the signpost pointing down the road to nuclear fission. It is precisely at this important moment that French science enters the nuclear picture in the persons of Frédéric Joliot and his wife, Irène Curie.

Frédéric Joliot was born in 1900 and thus was eight years younger than the Prince de Broglie, the father of wave mechanics, and a whole generation younger than his teachers, Jean Perrin and Paul Langevin. Just after World War I Joliot began work on radioactivity in the Institut de Radium. In 1926 he married his co-worker, Irène Curie, three years his senior. Together they shared in the important discovery, for which they received the Nobel Prize of 1935, that substances would be made artificially radioactive in the course of nuclear disintegration.

When in 1936 the chair of physics at the Collège de France fell vacant, Joliot was chosen to fill it. A Laboratory of Nuclear Physics was built for him with great care and at considerable expense. Its most important piece of equipment was Europe's only cyclotron. At the time it was ready for use, early in 1939, the peculiar behavior of uranium was the principal subject of discussion. In Rome, Fermi had bombarded small quantities of uranium—the heaviest element then known—with neutrons, and believed he had produced newer and heavier elements. In Germany the experiments had been repeated and extended by careful chemical analysis of the products. Starting from these results, Frédéric Joliot and his co-workers—independently of O. R. Frisch and Lise Meitner, whose work has been widely publicized—proved that what Fermi and the German workers had actually done was to bring about the rupture of the uranium atom into two approximately equal parts with the release of large amounts of energy. Still more important, in January 1939 two of Joliot's collaborators, Halban and Kowarski, demonstrated that when a uranium atom is split by neutron bombardment, other neutrons are released, which under proper conditions could be used to split still other uranium atoms. The French workers were thus among the earliest to discover that a nuclear chain-reaction, leading to the release of significant quantities of atomic energy, was theoretically possible.[28] The French government patented the use of fission neutrons, which gave them

[28] For the general reader, the best nontechnical account of the discovery of nuclear fission is in Selig Hecht, *Explaining the Atom* (1947). The scientific reader should consult L. A. Turner, "Nuclear Fission," *Reviews of Modern Physics*, Vol. 12, No. 1. This now famous review article summarizes the many papers published in the year that followed the experiments of Hahn and Strassmann.

the master patent in the field of atomic energy. The Laboratory at the Collège de France prepared at once to explore this fateful possibility, but the German invasion brought matters to a standstill, and when French resistance collapsed, Joliot dispatched Halban and Kowarski to England where during the war they made useful contributions to the Allied atomic energy program.

Let us now turn to the great scientific institutions these men were instrumental in creating.

VI

Of greatest significance for the future of science in France is the extraordinary boldness and enthusiasm with which French scientists and their associates in the government have set about providing a great central organization, the sort envisaged by Renan. This may go far to offset the present difficulties under which French scientists are obliged to work—the crowded laboratories, the obsolete equipment, the disastrous effects of inflation—and in the long run it may eradicate some of the evils which have so long afflicted French science. So little is as yet known about this organization—one of the focal points, I believe, of French postwar activity—that I shall devote the remainder of this paper to a factual account of its origins, organization, and purposes.

In conception, it is typically French—a plan of sweeping lines and bold proportions—possible only in a country where even the scientists of the Right are to some extent convinced of the necessities of national planning in the present emergency, and where a tradition of government responsibility for science is fully accepted. It breaks sharply with the *petit bourgeois,* close-fisted spirit with which science has often been treated in France. In the United States we saw the far more timid plan for our National Science Foundation fail of adoption, after passing the Senate three times. By comparison the French project, which was in full swing before the American measure was finally enacted, is bold indeed.

French attempts to modernize science date from the conclusion of World War I. Many scientists in France saw clearly at the end of that ordeal that countries faithful to habitual and conservative ways of doing things could not contend for long on equal terms with a country like Germany where science was applied, with a thoroughness unknown elsewhere, to the enhancement of every aspect of national and industrial strength. Even in England and America this comparison gave rise to an active movement to stimulate industrial research. In France the movement had to contend with a traditional distaste for applied research, with the conservatism of French industry, and with the antiscientific tendencies of the postwar generation. In a symposium called *L'Avenir de la France* published in the hour of victory, one writer called upon French scientists to leave their *"tour d'ivoire"* and help extend the benefits of science to industry.[29] In 1925 Henri Le Chatelier, well known as one who had made extensive scientific contributions to industry, published his classic *Science et industrie,* a fine theoretical analysis of the role of science in industry with vivid and ludicrous examples of the indifference of French industrialists and of their encyclopedic ignorance of the uses of science.

In the meantime, the French government took the first timid steps in the right direction by creating at Bellevue, near Meudon, a center where industrialists could receive scientific aid. The laboratories were installed in what had once been the luxurious Palace Hotel, which had briefly served as a wartime hospital, and before that as Isidora Duncan's Temple of the Dance of the Future. The laboratories were placed under a government body that was supposed to coordinate scientific and industrial research, investigate problems at the request of the government or of *sociétés industrielles,* and carry on developmental projects of public interest. The functions resembled those of the National Bureau of Standards or the British National Physical Laboratory.[30]

A similar movement, emphasizing pure or fundamental research even more than service to industry, took shape in the minds of the Socialists, who in this respect were the heirs of the old Radical Socialist party. The chief spokesman for the constructive regeneration of French science through government aid was the universally beloved and respected physicist, Jean Perrin, the ardent Socialist and lifelong friend of Léon Blum.[31] Perrin, and his still more Leftist colleague in physics, Paul Langevin, were instrumental in persuading men like Herriot, Painlevé, and Blum in 1936 that the Front Populaire should make the encouragement of science an important plank in its platform. The Blum government was induced to merge two previous offices for the assistance of pure science into a single Caisse Nationale.[32]

---

[29] Alphand, Belot, *et al., L'Avenir de la France, réformes nécessaires* (Paris, 1918).

[30] L. Quevron, "Les Laboratoires de Bellevue," *Journal des recherches du Centre National de la Recherche Scientifique, Laboratoires de Bellevue,* No. Hors Série (1946). The chapter on France in J. G. Crowther, *Science in Liberated Europe* (London, 1949), also gives some background material on Bellevue.

[31] For Perrin's views on the place of science in society, cf. Blum in Perrin. *op. cit.,* pp. xxxi–xxxiv.

[32] The *Caisse nationale de la recherche scientifique* and the two *Caisses* that preceded it are discussed in J. Delsarte, "De l'Organisation de la recherche scientifique," *Revue scientifique* (January 15, 1939), pp. 1–2, and Emmanuel Dubois, "Sur l'administration de la recherche scientifique en France," *Revue scientifique* (February 1939), pp. 68–69.

At the same time it was resolved to create a corps of government scientific workers with ranks corresponding to those of the Academic hierarchy, and to breathe life into the laboratories at Bellevue.[33]

The scientific aspect of the Blum program received considerable publicity, partly from the establishment of the post of Under-secretary of State for Scientific Research, which at Perrin's instigation was given to Mme. Irène Joliot-Curie; and partly from Perrin's creation, in connection with the famous Exposition of 1937, of the Palais de la Découverte, one of the finest science museums in existence.

Early in 1939 the physiologist Henri Laugier succeeded Perrin (who in turn had followed Mme. Joliot-Curie) at the head of the scientific program. Laugier had much to do with drafting the legislation which in October 1939, soon after the outbreak of the war, finally established a single, comprehensive research agency under the Ministry of Education, called the Centre National de la Recherche Scientifique.[34]

The debacle of 1940 and the German occupation at first demoralized and disrupted the scientific life of France. Laugier and Perrin both escaped to America, where the former became an active leader in the Free French movement and taught physiology in Canada, while Perrin became vice-president of the École Libre des Hautes Études in New York, dying in this country in 1942 at the age of 72. In France the CNRS continued a shadowy existence. A Vichy decree of March 1941 gave the organization a new charter which merged the sections of pure and applied research and channeled the efforts of the scientists into a modest attempt to serve industry.[35] Rather amazingly, the Bellevue laboratories thrived, despite the shortage of raw materials and the restrictions imposed by the Germans. Its facilities grew rapidly during the Occupation; in 1942 six new laboratories were equipped and opened; and in 1943, seven more.[36]

The scientists who remained in France took an active part in the

[33] The *Service central de la recherche scientifique* is discussed in the Delsarte and Dubois articles, *loc. cit.*, and in J. D. Bernal, *The Social Function of Science* (London, 1939), Appendix VI: "The Organization of Science in France."

[34] The best article on the CNRS and its problems is L. Kopelmanas, "Le Centre national de la recherche scientifique et les problèmes actuels de la recherche française," *Revue socialiste* (June–July 1949), pp. 120–34. Crowther, *op. cit.*, contains information on the background and early history. For the text of the decree of October 19, 1939, establishing the CNRS, see the *Journal officiel* (October 24, 1939), pp. 12594–95, or *Revue scientifique* (November-December 1939), pp. 704–5. There is a chart showing the relationship of the Centre to the general organization of government research in France as of January 1940 in the article "Visit of French Scientists," *Notes and Records of the Royal Society*, III (1940–1941), 11–21.

[35] See the "Exposé des motifs" preceding the *ordonnance* of November 2, 1945, *Journal officiel* (November 3, 1945), p. 7193.

[36] Quevron, *op. cit.*, p. 44.

underground; few of their number collaborated with the enemy. The aging Langevin, an outspoken radical of the extreme Left, closely associated with the Communists whom he later joined, became the official scientific martyr of the Resistance. In 1940, on returning to his laboratory at the Collège de France, he was arrested by the Germans and thrown into the prison of La Santé. His arrest provoked a great demonstration of students and a public protest by his colleague, Frédéric Joliot, who temporarily closed his laboratory. The arrest of Langevin—soon released and allowed to live under strict surveillance at Troyes—greatly stimulated the formation of the secret Front National Universitaire in which the scientists were very active.[37]

Joliot's Laboratory of Nuclear Physics was visited by German scientists who had instructions to remove the cyclotron and other useful apparatus to German laboratories. This was somehow avoided, but Joliot was obliged to permit German scientists to work there. This fact, which gave rise to rumors that Joliot was collaborating with the enemy, actually allowed him to carry out his underground activities behind an impenetrable screen. His laboratory became an important arsenal for the production of "Molotov cocktails" and other types of home-made explosives.[38]

Much has been made, and I believe can legitimately be made, of the influence of the Resistance experience upon the social awareness and the political education of the French scientists. Politicians and working class leaders, for their part, had learned to understand and cooperate with the scientists; the doctrines of Perrin and Langevin became important in their planning. Even those scientists who were not Socialists or who did not follow Langevin and Joliot into the Communist Party, came to share their views in these matters. As it emerged from the Resistance, the scientific program was a revival of the Front Populaire spirit. The Soviet Union had not yet fully revealed its determination to control its intellectuals and its scientists in all their activities; the Lysenko affair was only brewing; and the Left, even with the Communists, appeared to be the strongest bulwark of scientific progress.

Joliot emerged, at the war's end, the uncontested leader of the French scientists. His scientific prestige unassailable, a hero of the Resistance, a leading Communist intellectual, president of the largest Resistance group, he was entrusted by the Provisional Government with the task of mobilizing science to aid in French recovery. He took charge of the CNRS with a free hand to refashion it into a suitable

[37] René Maublanc, "French Teachers in the Resistance Movement," *Science and Society* (Winter 1947); and Crowther, *op. cit.*, pp. 51–52.
[38] Samuel A. Goudsmit, *Alsos* (New York, 1947), pp. 34–36.

instrument for the reinvigoration of French science. He brought with him men of common purpose who had served with him in the underground and who shared his conviction that a bold program of Socialist planning should be substituted for the Vichy policy of serving the industrialists. The postwar scientific program in France, while by no means the work of Socialists alone, is colored an ineluctable pink. The changes effected extralegally by Joliot and his aides were given legal sanction by a decree of November 2, 1945. In the meantime the atomic bombs had been loosed on Hiroshima and Nagasaki, and Joliot was swiftly withdrawn to direct the Commissariat of Atomic Energy.[39]

The CNRS has as its principal function the support and encouragement of pure and applied research. This is carried out in a variety of ways which I shall enumerate. But it also has a supervisory and planning function, for the charter of 1945 gives it authority "to undertake the coordination of research carried out by the government, private industry, and private individuals, by establishing liaison among the groups involved," and to organize inquiries into research being pursued in private and public laboratories.

So far, grants to individuals and laboratories and the support of a staff of professional researchers and technicians constitute the principal method of encouragement. In 1943–1944, at the close of the war in Europe, the Centre supported some 600 researchers. By 1946–1947 this number had more than doubled.[40] Those who hold nonacademic research appointments from the Centre constitute a permanent professional staff of investigators—*directeurs, maîtres,* and *chargés de recherches*—who are paid the salaries of university personnel of roughly equivalent rank. Unlike the technicians who assist them, and for whom there is also a rigid hierarchy, the investigators are not civil servants.[41]

A great many of the Centre's scientific personnel carry on their research in the laboratories of the other government-supported institutions. At present the laboratories and institutions directly run by the Centre are few but important: an Institut d'Astrophysique; the Observatoire de Haute Provence; the Grenoble Laboratory of Metallurgy; and, perhaps most important of all, the mathematical and

[39] The Commissariat was established in October 1945 (*Journal officiel* [October 31, 1945], pp. 7066 and 7079). On January 3, 1946, Joliot was named High Commissioner and Pierre Auger, Irène Joliot-Curie, and François Perrin, son of Jean, were named the other members. *Journal officiel* (January 4, 1946), p. 146.

[40] Ministère de l'Éducation Nationale, Centre National de la Recherche Scientifique, *Séance plénière du comité national de la recherche scientifique* (June 2, 1948, [Paris]), p. 19.

[41] The status of research personnel was determined by the decree of August 12, 1945. *Journal officiel* (August 21, 1945), p. 5201.

statistical laboratory of the Institut Henri Poincaré to which scientists can go for special mathematical assistance and the use of modern calculating equipment.[42] The Bellevue laboratories have remained under the control of CNRS and have steadily expanded their resources for industrial research. They have not been afraid to undertake long-range projects of potential value to the national economy. For example, there is an important project to explore the industrial uses of direct solar energy.[43]

The CNRS envisages a great expansion of the laboratory facilities under its own direct control. It hopes to establish at Strasbourg, for example, a laboratory of nuclear studies applied to biological and medical problems. The most ambitious program, however, is for the group of laboratories to be erected at Gif-sur-Yvette. Some 130 acres of wooded and open estate about twenty miles from Paris have been acquired by lease, through Joliot's activities, from a banker friend interested in physics. Plans are already under way for a great genetics laboratory, where the fidelity of some Communist scientists to the party line may be publicly tested. Beyond this there are plans for laboratories of pure and applied entomology; geological laboratories and laboratories for nuclear physics, electron optics, microchemistry, and microanalysis.[44]

Perhaps the most extraordinary aspect of the organization is that the social sciences are given a prominent place: historical, philological, and sociological studies receive virtually the same treatment as the natural sciences.[45] As Renan observed, these are precisely the kinds of investigation which need government support, for many of them have no conceivable utility except to add to the sum of human knowledge. The CNRS directly supports a Center of Sociological Studies and an Historical Institute.

In one very important respect, first things have been done first. Though the Centre has been unable to remedy the wretched economic plight of many of the country's investigators, it has tried to make up the deficit in properly trained personnel. For example, it has set up a training program at the Sorbonne to give researchers certain accessory tools of their trade. Lectures are given on applied mathe-

[42] The *laboratoire de calcul* and *laboratoire de statistique* of the Institut Henri Poincaré had a full-page letter in the January–May 1941 issue of *Revue scientifique*, inviting people to use its facilities for a small hourly fee.

[43] Felix Trombe, Marx Foex, and Charlotte Henry La Blanchetais, "Utilisation de l'énergie solaire," *Journal des recherches*, Nos. 4 and 5 (1949), 61–89.

[44] Crowther, *op. cit.*, pp. 23 and 30–31.

[45] For a list of projects supported by the CNRS in what it calls the *"sciences humaines,"* in its own and outside research centers, see the *Bulletin du CNRS*, Série B, No. 1 [1949]. By the decree of June 11, 1949, these sciences were given 144 members on the *Comité national* to 228 for the other sciences. *Journal officiel* (June 14, 1949), pp. 5866–68.

matics, scientific English, the use of electronic equipment, and the theory of measurement. Researchers of the CNRS, technicians of CNRS, and other scientific workers are admitted in that order of priority.[46] The Centre has furthermore made great efforts to promote scientific contacts with other nations, by sending scientific missions abroad, and by making it possible—this last with the assistance of American funds—for foreign scientists and scholars to come to France to take part in small work groups and colloquia.[47]

Second only to the inferior economic status of research workers, the difficulties and expense of scientific publication has been the most criticized and lamented aspect of the French situation. At first the CNRS confined itself to indirect support of scientific publication by occasional subsidies to publishers for important books and monographs. Increasingly, it has now gone into the publishing business itself. It issues a progress report, the *Bulletin du CNRS*, reporting the projects of its staff, and a *Journal des recherches*. But its most famous achievement is the great abstract journal, the *Bulletin analytique*, which reports on over four thousand periodicals and lists about 100,000 titles of articles and books annually.[48]

Perhaps a paragraph should be devoted to a brief description of the very interesting organization of the CNRS. The Centre is placed under the Minister of Education, and is administered by a director and assistant directors, appointed by the President of the Republic on the recommendation of the Minister. The director works through two administrative bodies, one concerned solely with high policy and finance, the Administrative Council; another, the National Committee of Scientific Research, which is the scientific policy-making body of CNRS.

It is this National Committee which is the most impressive feature of this organization. One-third of its members are named by the Minister of Education on the recommendation of the director; but the other two-thirds are chosen by an electoral body composed of all the scientists working in government institutions, the University, the

---

[46] *Bulletin du CNRS*, Série A, No. 1 [1949], pp. 135–37. The training program was discussed at some length in the "Exposé des motifs" preceding the *ordonnance* of November 2, 1945.

[47] cf. Émile F. Terroine, "Les Colloques internationaux du CNRS," *Revue scientifique* (November 1, 1946), pp. 496–97. *Comptes-rendus* of the first three colloquia held under the program can be found in *Revue scientifique* for November 1, 1946 (pp. 497–500). December 1–15, 1946 (pp. 621–23), and May 15, 1947 (pp. 559–63), respectively.

[48] The figures are from a broadside of the *Service des publications* of the CNRS. The *Bulletin analytique* appears in three parts: one for the physico-chemical sciences, one for the biological sciences, and one for the philosophical sciences. The first two appear monthly, the third quarterly. For a full discussion of the role of the CNRS in the publication of books and periodicals, see Kopelmanas, *loc. cit.*, pp. 120–34.

great schools, the Collège de France, and the CNRS itself; that is to say, an important fraction of the scientists in France.[49]

VII

The success of this program, which in the long run can have such a favorable influence on French economic prosperity and national prestige, depends in the immediate future upon the economic recovery of the country, and the sums which during this critical period can be spared for the CNRS from other more urgent tasks. It depends also on the continued support of scientists of all political allegiances, and on the solution of the very delicate problem of control. The democratic scheme of organization which on paper gives so much weight to scientific opinion, and the creation of a buffer organization of scientists between the politicians and the laboratory, must operate, as it is intended it shall, to prevent a restriction of liberty or the perversion of scientific purpose to the narrow and utilitarian needs of the state.

At present the picture is distinctly favorable. Though the CNRS is so much an achievement of the parties of the Left, and the voice of the French Communist Party is admittedly heard in its councils, there seems to have been no overt attempt to bias its activities and up to now government officials have left the scientific planning entirely to the qualified scientific leaders. It is widely taken to be a nonpartisan project desperately needed in the national interest, conceived in long-range terms, and no one seems to expect from it short-run economic benefits. It seems to have widespread support, and is criticized only for doing too little. If political or party control should threaten the basic freedoms of the scientist, then indeed the broad support might melt away.

The CNRS has not been openly attacked as a product of the *scientisme* of the Left. The Prince de Broglie, *secrétaire perpétuel* of the Academy of Sciences, in his public utterances has been more than generous to it. Whatever his private misgivings, he has spoken up strongly in its favor, first in an interview of 1945, again in the earnest preface he contributed in 1948—side by side with one by Léon Blum —to the posthumous essays of Jean Perrin.[50] In his tribute to a great man and a great scientist of the older generation, De Broglie gives Perrin credit for having defended French science and for helping to inspire the Centre National, which he speaks of as having already

---

[49] The latest decision available on the composition and functioning of the various parts of the administration of the CNRS was the decree of June 11, 1949.

[50] cf. Jean Dumont, "Interview with M. Louis de Broglie," *Essais et études universitaires*, I (1945), 84–98, and De Broglie's preface to Perrin. *op. cit.*

pursued a fruitful career, and which he hopes will contribute power-fully in the future to a great revival of French science.

On the other hand, however, the problem of Communist party members in high scientific councils has come to a head in France with the case of Frédéric Joliot. After his pronouncement on April 5, 1950, at the Twelfth Congress of the French Communist Party that "a truly progressive scientist will never donate a particle of his scientific knowl-edge to the purpose of making war against the Soviet Union," Joliot was summarily dismissed "with regret" by the government of Georges Bidault. Through a spokesman, M. Teitgen, M. Bidault explained on April 28 that Joliot's public statements and his unreserved acceptance of the pro-Russian resolution of the Communist Party made it im-possible to maintain him in his post as High Commissioner. This has not affected his post at the Collège de France nor, as yet, his connection with the Centre National. Nevertheless the question remains whether, and to what extent, the Centre will be affected by such an open recog-nition of the split that exists. Joliot's scientific supporters on the Com-mission—Kowarski and François Perrin among others—were prompt to protest his dismissal. The conflict between political loyalties and scientific freedom remains unresolved and is part of the larger ques-tion of the obligations of the citizen to the truth, as well as to the state, in an ideologically divided world.

It remains to be seen what the future has in store. Whether the in-dividualistic tradition of French science—in fact, of all science—can survive the new era of collective activity and government control, or whether it can survive without it, are serious questions. One thing is certain. There must be a new generation of scientists ready to make use of the new opportunities. And unless the educational tradition of France is drastically overhauled, and a general atmosphere is created that is favorable to science, the men will not be there to do the job. At the moment France badly needs some small portion of the eight-eenth century's great faith in the value of scientific knowledge. There are signs that—unfashionable though this is at present—such a re-valuation of science may be taking place.

IV

FRENCH POLITICS: THE SHIFTING

COALITION OF THE CENTER

7

+++

THE THIRD FORCE, 1870–1896

L. ARTHUR MINNICH, JR.

+++

DURING the first quarter-century of the Third Republic the "Third Force" existed only in embryo. No coalition of Center parties appeared to defend the régime against threats from both Left and Right, for no serious threat was yet apparent on the Left. During this same period, however, issues arose which forced the crystallization of beliefs, objectives, and fears of various political and social groups and which resulted in the establishment of important precedents and techniques. These issues fundamentally concerned the existence of the Republic and the formulation of governmental policy in regard to social problems.

The negotiations which resulted in the establishment of the Third Republic and the subsequent struggle to preserve it are too well known to require detailed treatment here. Its formal establishment in 1875 was effected by the narrowest of margins, the crucial decision to approve the Wallon amendment being carried by only one vote. Among this slight majority were many deputies whose allegiance to the Republic was lukewarm at best. They had been induced to approve the amendment only because no other form of government seemed possible at the time, but they so designed the institutions of the Republic as to allow a Monarchist restoration at a more convenient time. This negative aspect was clearly expressed by the one man who did most to establish the régime: "The Republic divides us least," said Thiers; and although he may not have been conscious of any implication for the future, he forecast fairly accurately the division of opinions which was to prevail throughout the life of the Third Republic.

Because of these circumstances, the existence of the Republic remained in doubt for more than a decade. On three different occasions the Monarchists rallied their forces in major efforts to regain their dominant position. In the famous crisis of *seize mai* President MacMahon's attempt to control the selection of ministers and secure a subservient Chamber proved a failure. The crisis resulted finally in MacMahon's resignation in 1879 and the election of Jules Grévy, a confirmed Republican, to the presidency. Since they had already obtained majorities in both the Chamber of Deputies and the Senate, the Republicans now had control of the three most important institutions of the régime.

The second major attempt arose during the election of 1885 when the Republicans were preoccupied with the contest among themselves for seats. On the first ballot, the plethora of Republican candidates enabled the Monarchists to obtain pluralities in numerous departments normally Republican. The threat collapsed on the second ballot, for the Republicans laid aside their differences long enough to present a united front against the enemy.

The Monarchists made their third major effort in conjunction with the "man on horseback," General Boulanger. Although his rise to prominence had its roots, awkwardly enough, in Radical politics, the Monarchists eventually became the most interested in his success and looked to him to accomplish through a coup what they had been unable to accomplish legally. The prospect of success on this occasion seemed the greater because of charges of corruption which resulted from the Wilson scandal. Boulangism collapsed in 1889, however, and the Monarchist position collapsed with it. When the Panama scandal a few years later provided an even better opportunity to attack the Republic, the Monarchists were already so discredited that they were unable to use it to their advantage.[1]

Developments of lasting significance occurred during this long period of defending the Republic. The efforts of both MacMahon and Boulanger intensified Republican distrust of authoritarian or even strong leadership. The result of *seize mai* was to vest in the Chamber the ultimate control over the executive power, yet even within the Chamber the distrust remained. Gambetta, Ferry, and Clemenceau all became suspect because of their efforts to exercise leadership in the Chamber. Instead, decisions on policy became dependent on the coalition of two or more minority groups; and that precursor of the "Third Force," the concentration ministry, came into being.[2] The election of 1885 exemplified the need for such a

---

[1] A recent concise statement of the political developments of the early years of the Third Republic may be found in J. P. T. Bury, *France, 1814–1940* (Philadelphia, 1949), Chaps. IX–XI, and François Goguel, *La Politique des partis sous la IIIe république* (Paris, 1946), Chaps. I–III. For the strength of the Republic after 1890, see esp. A. Dansette, *Les Affaires de Panama* (Paris, 1934), pp. 236 ff.

[2] For example, the Brisson ministry of 1885, composed of Opportunists and Radicals.

coalition, but it could not be depended upon when questions other than defense of the Republic were at issue. Finally, the identification of Catholicism with the Monarchist danger, and the traditional secularism of many Republicans gave rise to the initiation of an anticlerical program. Gambetta's cry of "Clericalism—there is the enemy!" constituted a rallying-point in the early 1880's for Republicans of all varieties. In addition, it occupied their attentions for a number of years and helped delay consideration of other basic but embarrassing issues.[3]

The election of 1893 marked a turning-point in the development of French politics. By that year the Republic was firmly established. The fact that it had attained an age equal to or greater than that of any other régime since 1789 was a superficial aspect of a basically sound reality. Monarchism was at its lowest ebb since 1870; and some of the Monarchists had even begun to rally to the support of the Republic in hopes that they could exert from within an influence on social and religious matters.[4] The election confirmed this situation. Almost four-fifths of the deputies elected were unquestioned supporters of the régime, and no more than sixty of the remainder favored an authoritarian régime.[5] The Republic was no longer in urgent need of defenders.

At the same time, the election revealed that social and economic problems dominated the minds of the French people, and the outcome was considered a mandate to the legislature to face those problems. Almost all the successful candidates had included in their programs promises to support social-security legislation of one type or another. A large majority of them had expressed their desire for a general reform of the tax structure to effect a more equitable distribution of the tax burden. About one-third of them had subscribed to the introduction of a tax on income or on capital or on a combination of both.[6] Even such a traditional conservative as Jean Casimir-

[3] Evelyn Acomb, *The French Laic Laws (1879–1889): The First Anticlerical Campaign of the Third French Republic* (New York, 1941), pp. 62–82; Raoul de la Grasserie, "De la dissociation et de la concentration des partis politiques," *Revue politique et parlementaire*, XXI (August 1899), 256.

[4] Parker T. Moon, *The Labor Problem and the Social Catholic Movement in France* (New York, 1921), p. 172.

[5] Because of the absence of strict party organization in France, it is not possible to present exact figures for the results of the elections. The approximations given throughout this paper agree generally with those cited by contemporary writers such as Pierre de Coubertin, *L'Évolution française sous la troisième république* (Paris, 1896), p. 269; Édouard Payen, "Chronique politique et parlementaire—France," *Annales de l'École libre des sciences politiques*, IX (1894), 640–41.

[6] Maxime Lecomte, *Les Ralliés: histoire d'un parti (1886–1898)* (Paris, 1898), pp. 239–40; G. Monod, "The Political Situation in France," *Contemporary Review*, LXIV (November 1893), 616.

Perier felt it necessary in his campaign speeches to promise action on these questions. The most striking feature of the election in this respect, however, was the extensive gain made by the Socialists. They increased their representation in the Chamber from about sixteen to fifty.

The popularity of the demand for governmental action in the social and economic field resulted in large part from the fact that the process of industrialization along with its accompanying problems had assumed major proportions in France by the 1890's. The transition from an agricultural society toward an industrial one had been progressing slowly but steadily throughout the period. This change was especially apparent in the relative decline of the number of agricultural workers to less than 50 per cent of the population [7] and in the spread of urbanization until nearly a third of the people lived in medium- or large-sized cities.[8] Apparent, too, was the growth of an urban working class characterized chiefly by its lack of economic security. Low wages, long hours, female and child labor, dangerous working conditions, and inadequate housing facilities—all the usual evils of industrialization—beset the working class.[9] No effective action to provide social security through old-age pensions, unemployment and sickness insurance, or compensation for industrial accidents had as yet been undertaken either by the state or by private enterprise. These reforms were within the realm of the possible, for industrialization had appreciably increased the national wealth,[10] but the task of improving the lot of the underprivileged remained.

Connected with the need for reform of industrial evils was the need for remodeling the tax structure. If the government were to undertake any action to remedy social ills the income from taxation would have to be increased. No national budget since 1871 had shown a surplus, and most of them had resulted in deficits. The national debt continued, consequently, to increase slowly during the last quarter of the century; and the carrying charges of the debt imposed a heavy

[7] France. Ministère du Commerce, de l'Industrie, des Postes et des Télégraphes. Direction de l'Office du Travail, *Résultats statistiques du recensement des industries et professions (dénombrement général de la population du 29 mars 1896)* (4 vols., Paris, 1899–1900), IV, viii.

[8] *ibid.*, I, 35–37.

[9] The best detailed analyses are to be found in Émile Levasseur, *Questions ouvrières et industrielles en France sous la troisième république* (Paris, 1907), esp. pp. 524–37; and W. E. Weyl, "Labor Conditions in France," *Annals of the American Academy of Political and Social Science*, XII (September 1898); see also the consular reports published by the United States Department of State under the title *Conditions of Labor in Europe, 1885* (3 vols., Washington, 1885), II, 1024–70.

[10] Levasseur, *op. cit.*, pp. 611, 616.

strain on the relatively low income of the government.[11] Moreover, the tax system contained a number of inequities which would be magnified by merely increasing the rate of existing taxes. The most glaring of these was the imposition of too much of the burden of taxation on those least able to pay. It would be difficult, if not impossible, to determine precisely what share of the burden was borne by particular classes, but it was generally agreed by Frenchmen of that era that the burden on the poor was unduly heavy. About half of the tax revenue was derived from indirect taxes on consumers goods, a practice noted for its disproportionately heavy imposition on the poorer classes. Raymond Poincaré, who was not at all radical on taxation questions, asserted that such taxes bore too heavily on the poor.[12] Maurice Block, writing for a conservative clientele, proved to his own satisfaction that the French laborer paid in taxes 10 per cent of an income which barely provided a living. Middle-income groups, he showed, paid between 9 and 11.3 per cent; and high income groups paid less than 12 per cent.[13] A reliable economist, Paul Leroy-Beaulieu, compiled statistics which showed that low-income groups, both urban and rural, paid 20 per cent of their income for taxes, whereas the average tax burden of all Frenchmen was only 14 per cent.[14] Many other inequities, such as the provisions for taxing certain securities but not others, and especially the method of evaluation based on "exterior signs," exposed the entire system to criticism.[15]

Action to remedy these conditions was considered urgent in the early 1890's in terms of both ideals and expediency. By virtue of its association with the ideals of democracy, the Republic had traditionally carried the connotation that its major concern was the welfare of the lower classes in social and economic as well as purely political matters. The First Republic had symbolized the victory of the people, and the Jacobins had organized and administered that republic at least partially so as to benefit the majority of the people. Similarly, the Second Republic had been at the outset a "social republic" devoted to improving the lot of the working class and giving all classes

11 Paul Leroy-Beaulieu, "Le Budget de 1907. Trente ans de finances françaises," *Revue des deux mondes*, XXXIV (August 15, 1906), 766–68. Summaries of the annual budgets can be found in Marcel Marion, *Histoire financière de la France depuis 1715* (6 vols., Paris, 1914–1931), Vol. VI.

12 *ibid.*, VI, 174–75.

13 Maurice Block, "L'Esprit du budget; les impôts et les revenus," *Revue politique et parlementaire*, IX (July 1896), 10.

14 Marion, *op. cit.*, VI, 171–73.

15 For a critical discussion of the entire tax structure, see Max Boucard and Gaston Jèze, *Éléments de la science des finances et de la législation financière française* (Paris, 1896).

equal status in the government. More recently, the objectives of the most zealous Republicans had included, as in Gambetta's Belleville program, a promise of action to remedy the grievances of the workingman. That the promise had not been fulfilled prior to 1893 could be rationalized by some in terms of the necessity of defending the Republic itself. After the Boulanger fiasco, however, that excuse no longer applied. Indeed, the support Boulanger had gained by promising reforms to the lower classes clarified the need for the Republicans to act.

Perhaps the most imperative reason for facing up to the problems resulted from the growing tendency of the working class to lose faith in Republican promises and turn to the development of extraparliamentary instruments for improving their condition.[16] The trade-union movement, legalized in 1884, experienced steady growth up to the end of the decade, and then underwent a period of rapid expansion during the next five years. It swelled from one thousand unions with a membership of approximately 140,000 workers in 1890 to over two thousand unions with nearly 500,000 members in 1895.[17] The establishment of the National Federation of Unions in 1886 and the initiation of a national congress of Labor Bourses in 1892 gave greater strength and unity of purpose to the movement. As the organization of syndicates became more widespread, the workers resorted more frequently to the use of the strike to attain their ends, until in 1893 the practice reached a high point of alarming proportions for that era. In that year, about 170,000 strikers participated in 634 strikes, and more than 3,000,000 man-days of labor were lost.[18] It was apparent, too, that even more extensive use of the strike was contemplated. Previously, strikes in France had all been undertaken by individual unions or by groups of unions in the same trade or locality. Beginning in 1888, however, consideration was given to the possibility of accomplishing a general strike throughout the country, and a resolution in favor of concentrating efforts upon the preparation of such a strike was approved at the Congress of Marseilles in 1892. Although a divergence of opinion on this resolution caused a split between the National Federation of Unions and the Federation of Bourses, the latter upheld the idea and devoted itself to propagation of the general strike.[19]

[16] For the extension of Socialist influence in general during the latter part of the nineteenth century, see Georges Weill, *Histoire du mouvement social en France* (3rd rev. ed., Paris, 1924), and Alexandre Zévaès, *Le Socialisme en France depuis 1871* (Paris, 1908).

[17] Édouard Dolléans, *Histoire du mouvement ouvrier* (2 vols., Paris, 1936–1939), II, 30.

[18] Levasseur, *op. cit.*, p. 700.

[19] Zévaès, "Les Débuts politiques de M. Briand," *Nouvelle Revue*, XVIII (December 15,

At the same time that the working class was developing the instrument of the strike to bring pressure on French industry, it was coming more and more under the influence of Socialist doctrines as set forth by the leaders of the several Socialist sects. The exponents of Socialism had become since 1871 the leaders of the urban working-class movement, and in later years they developed plans for bringing agricultural labor under their influence as well. Socialist doctrines attained a dominant position among existing labor organizations in 1879, and from then until the end of the century, despite the challenge of syndicalism, Socialist leadership retained its preeminence. At the beginning of the 1890's Socialist leaders emphasized parliamentary rather than revolutionary action, but the question remained open as to whether or not they would succeed in directing working-class agitation into legal channels.[20] Their first efforts were marked with success, as has been noted in connection with the election of 1893. In the local elections of the preceding year they had obtained a similar success by electing over seven hundred of their number to municipal councils and by taking over the majority in twenty-nine communes.[21]

The extent of union organization, the number of strikes, and the electoral successes of the Socialists were not sufficient in themselves to constitute an undeniable demand for reforms; but the rapid growth of the movements in the early 1890's and the probability of continued growth intensified the need. Completely apart from numbers was the need for action if democratic ideals were to be fulfilled.

It was the attitudes of the deputies and ministerial leaders toward social and financial reforms that determined the course of French politics after 1893. Although a majority in favor of reform had issued from the election, its members were spread among various political groups.[22] The Socialists and the Radical Socialists were firmly committed in favor of reforms. The Radicals, on the other hand, were just beginning to give social questions priority on their agenda, and the solidarity of the group on this matter was not yet settled. Finally, a number of the adherents of reform were nominally members of the Moderate group, which was as a whole opposed to the idea of any ex-

---

1910), 435 ff.; Auguste Pawlowski, *La Confédération générale du travail* (Paris, 1910), pp. 18–21.

[20] Hubert Lagardelle, "Les Origines du socialisme parlementaire en France," *Mouvement socialiste*, xxvi (1909), 183; Harold R. Weinstein, *Jean Jaurès; A Study of Patriotism in the French Socialist Movement* (New York, 1936), pp. 58 ff.

[21] Coubertin, *op. cit.*, pp. 404–5.

[22] This and subsequent statements concerning the composition and voting strength of the various parliamentary groups are based on A. Salles, "Les Députés sortants (1893–1898). Votes et groupements," *Revue politique et parlementaire*, xvi (April 1898), 33–79; on Alphonse Bertrand, *La Chambre de 1893* (Paris, 1893); and on the author's own research in the parliamentary records.

tensive reform program. To complicate the situation still further, sufficient Moderates had been elected to allow them to control the Chamber by themselves, provided they could agree among themselves on policy. It remained to be seen whether group loyalty or devotion to reform would be the stronger impulse among the small number of Progressive Moderates. (This group will be referred to hereafter as "Progressives," even though it involves the risk of confusion with the title "Progressist," frequently applied to a more conservative group of Moderates at the turn of the century.)

Under the leadership of pronounced conservatives like Casimir-Perier and Charles Dupuy, or of somewhat less rigid conservatives like Alexander Ribot, Raymond Poincaré, and Louis Barthou, the Moderates refused to adopt a policy that would command the support of the Progressive element and fulfill the popular demand for reform. Instead, they embarked upon a variety of policies designed to win allies for the Moderates without paying the price of major concessions of reforms. During Casimir-Perier's ministry in 1894, they undertook to conciliate the extreme Right by promising that a "new spirit" of tolerance and sympathy would pervade the administration of religious affairs. If successful, such a policy would have secured sufficient Monarchist adherents to offset the loss of the Progressives. Unfortunately for the "new spirit," the policy threatened to alienate those Moderates who, though not aggressively anticlerical, desired to maintain the status quo in religious matters. The proposal was no sooner made than it had to be abandoned.[23]

Under Dupuy, lip service was paid to the ideal of reforms, and the ministry even went so far as to introduce several measures favorable to labor and the underprivileged. Yet when the discussions became crucial, the ministry quickly withdrew from its advanced position. A third effort to consolidate a majority was attempted by Ribot who added two Radicals to his predominantly Moderate ministry and offered a program of mild anticlericalism. It proved no more successful in obscuring the issue than had its predecessors.[24]

That these three ministries could last so long as they did, or even be created, resulted from a combination of factors. Each of the minis-

---

[23] Moon, op. cit., p. 195; Édouard de Marcère, "L'Esprit nouveau," Nouvelle Revue, LXXXVIII (May 1, 1894), 5–21; A. Debidour, L'Église catholique et l'État sous la troisième république (2 vols., Paris, 1909), II, 116–17.

[24] The most complete accounts of the policies of the ministries of Casimir-Perier, Dupuy, and Ribot are presented in the monthly chronicle by Félix Roussel, "La Vie politique et parlementaire en France," Revue politique et parlementaire, Vol. II (July 1894), et seq. Briefer but more penetrating summaries are offered in the annual chronicle by Édouard Payen, "Chronique politique et parlementaire—France," Annales de l'Ecole libre des sciences politiques, IX (1894) and X (1895).

tries put forth promises of undertaking reforms, and they were given an opportunity to put their promises into effect. In each case the ministry was overthrown soon after it became obvious that no substantial reforms were forthcoming. In addition, a series of anarchist incidents, culminating in 1894 in the assassination of the President of the Republic, Sadi-Carnot, temporarily halted the movement toward reform and allowed the formation of "strong governments" which combined conservative policies with the repression of anarchism. Such a deviation made possible the election of Casimir-Perier to replace Sadi Carnot even though his leadership as president of the council had been repudiated only a month earlier.[25] But the effects of the anarchist incidents were on each occasion quickly forgotten and the parliamentary agitation for reform resumed. Finally, the conservatives were long successful in identifying reform with Socialism; and the Progressives, as well as some Radicals, hesitated to associate themselves with a movement which might redound to the credit of the Socialists, especially while there was some possibility that reforms might be effected through the medium of the Moderates.[26]

Throughout this two-year period the insistence of a majority of the deputies on having a reform program undertaken constantly reappeared. It took its most obvious form in the toppling of the Moderate ministries already discussed. At the same time, however, there occurred a movement of the Progressives away from the Moderate camp and a development of a greater willingness on their part to cooperate with the groups of the Left—Radicals, Radical Socialists, and Socialists—to accomplish the desired reforms. The departure of Godefroy Cavaignac from the Moderates was especially significant. He had risen to an influential position during the debates on the Panama affair and in 1894 commanded much respect in the Chamber and the country at large. In February 1894 he came out in favor of the progressive income tax as a measure necessary to relieve the inequities of the existing system. In subsequent months he prepared several propositions for introducing the tax on a trial basis, one of which eventually came up for debate in the Chamber. Although it was disapproved, his measure received support from 231 deputies, including 30 Progressives. In these attempts, Cavaignac was working within the Moderate party. As late as January 1895, after the demise of the second Dupuy ministry, he refused to cooperate with Léon Bourgeois and the Radicals to form a concentration government. The failure of the Ribot min-

[25] See esp. Payen, "Chronique," loc. cit., IX (1894), 642 ff.; and Étienne Dejean, "Une Première Année de législature: impressions d'un nouveau député," Nouvelle Revue, XCI (January 15, 1895), 307–8.

[26] Roussel, "Chronique," Revue politique et parlementaire, II (December 1894), 549.

istry to accomplish reforms, however, finally induced him to abandon the Moderates; by October 1895, he was considered a full-fledged
Radical and became Minister of War in the Radical ministry formed
at that time. The Moderates were considerably weakened by this
loss.[27]

A similar transition of many Progressives was associated with the
creation of the Progressive Union. Shortly after the formation of the
Dupuy ministry in May 1894, a small number of Progressives and
Radicals determined to establish a parliamentary group in opposition
to Raynal's Moderate group, the Republicans of the Government.
They adopted the name Progressive Union to express their desire for
cooperation between the Progressives and the Left. Adherents to the
new group would be allowed to continue their membership in other
groups, but they were expected to support the two planks in the program of the Union regarding social reforms and preservation of the
rights of the State in matters concerning the Church. Gustave Isambert—a Radical who had advocated a union of Republicans and extensive tax reforms since 1889, when he was first elected to the Chamber—became the spokesman of the group. At first neither large nor
influential, the Progressive Union soon attracted a membership of
more than a hundred. Although its members did not all support the
two planks on all occasions, the group was instrumental in swinging
some Moderate votes to the Left.[28]

By October 1895, it was evident that the Moderates were committed
to opposing rather than proposing reforms, that they could no longer
command a majority even under the guise of a concentration ministry, and that there did exist a majority which would support a Radical government dedicated to reform. This government was formed by
Léon Bourgeois. It was the first government of the Third Republic
to be composed exclusively from the Left of the Chamber, and it was
likewise the first to set forth a program of social and economic reforms
as the very essence of its existence. The presence of Bourgeois at the
head of the ministry confirmed this orientation. He was one of the
younger leaders among the Radicals and was not identified with the
old Radical political program. His rise to a position of prominence
should be explained partially in terms of his association with the social reform movement.[29] Indeed, he formulated in his writings and

[27] J. E. C. Bodley, *France* (2 vols., New York, 1898), II, 453; Godefroy Cavaignac, *Pour l'impôt progressif* (Paris, 1895).

[28] Salles, "Les Députés sortants," *loc. cit.*, pp. 64, 70; Gaston Maurice, *Le Parti radical* (Paris, 1929), p. 145.

[29] The most complete biography of Bourgeois is by Maurice Hamburger, *Léon Bourgeois, 1851–1925; la politique radicale socialiste, la doctrine de solidarité, l'arbitrage international et la Société des Nations* (Paris, 1932).

addresses on solidarity the philosophical principles for the social consciousness of the new Radicals.[30]

Prior to Bourgeois' adaptation and popularization of the idea of solidarity, it had frequently been used to express either unity of a group or interdependency of the parts of a group.[31] Bourgeois applied the first concept to society as a whole, and utilized the second to emphasize the interdependency of men in society. The individual could not hope to develop his capabilities effectively outside of society; rather, he was indebted to past generations, to his associates, and to society for everything that he was or hoped to become. To these ideas Bourgeois added his firm conviction that the primary function of man was to develop his capacities to the greatest possible extent, and that the function of any society was to provide each individual with full opportunity to do so. By reason of the fact of solidarity, it became the obligation of the privileged to fulfill their indebtedness to society by helping to provide the opportunity for development to the underprivileged.[32] Specifically, society should undertake to guarantee to each individual an opportunity to work for a living and to obtain from his labor a sufficient income to provide at least a minimum standard of living. A minimum of existence should also be guaranteed to those unable to work. In addition, the individual must have free access through the educational system to the fund of knowledge possessed by society, and he must have leisure time in order to utilize that knowledge up to the limits of his capabilities. Finally, the individual should be protected against the risks incurred as a member of society. These risks—unemployment, industrial accidents, and old age—would all be mutualized among the entire membership of a society.[33]

Despite the charges of socialism frequently leveled against him, Bourgeois repeatedly emphasized the role of the individual and shaped his entire program around the development of the individual. He insisted that a program of solidarity undertaken by the state would be no more than the expression of the will of the individuals. The state was the creation of men, and it could possess no superior rights over men. The fundamental question of rights was to be settled by agree-

[30] The most important of Bourgeois' works on the subject are *Solidarité* (1st ed., Paris, 1896); *L'Éducation de la démocratie française: discours prononcés de 1890 à 1896* (Paris, 1897); *La Politique de la prévoyance sociale* (2 vols., Paris, 1914–1919). *Solidarité* first appeared as a series of articles entitled "La Doctrine de la solidarité," *Nouvelle Revue*, Vols. XCIII–XCIV (March–May, 1895).

[31] Charles Recolin, "Questions d'aujourd'hui: qu'est-ce-que la solidarité?" *Revue bleue*, LI (April 8, 1893).

[32] Bourgeois, *Solidarité* (2nd ed., Paris, 1897), pp. 46 ff.

[33] Bourgeois, *La Politique de la prévoyance sociale*, pp. 197 ff.; *Essai d'une philosophie de la solidarité* (Paris, 1902), pp. 48–49, 82–93.

ment among men, not between the individual and the state. Further, many of the functions necessary to the development of the program of solidarity could be carried out by private organizations. Only where they proved incapable of accomplishing the desired objective should the state, acting for the entire society, intervene.[34]

The distinguishing feature of the Bourgeois ministry was its determination to introduce into governmental policy an effective concern for the underprivileged groups in France. In this respect it occupied a position similar to the New Deal in America or the Popular Front in France in the 1930's. In his ministerial declaration, Bourgeois promised to introduce projects for establishing a progressive tax on incomes and inheritances, for extending existing pension plans to a greater number of workers, and for fostering mutualism, insurance programs, and social security.[35] Through no fault of its own, the ministry was unable to fulfill any of these proposals during its short existence, but it repeatedly gave proof in other ways of its orientation. Several projects not mentioned in the ministerial declaration were introduced to the legislature in an effort to improve the bargaining power of labor. One was designed to foster the arbitration of labor disputes and another to penalize employers who restricted the legal right of workingmen to organize. In addition, the ministry offered its services as arbiter in the important strike at Carmaux, but the offer was rejected by the owner of the industry involved. The ministry attempted to dissuade the Senate from acting on a proposal to prevent the organization of syndicates among railroad workers and withdrew a measure to that effect which had been introduced by an earlier Moderate ministry. The Paris Labor Bourse, closed by Dupuy in 1893, was reopened by order of Bourgeois' Minister of Commerce.[36] All of these acts stood out in sharp contrast with the conservative actions of previous ministries; and they did redirect governmental policy, if only for a limited time, toward social reform.

The primary objective of the ministry, however, was to establish the progressive income tax. This measure, as introduced in February 1896, was designed to eliminate the traditional deficit in the budget, to provide a surplus which could be used for social security subventions, and to serve as a first step in correcting the inequities of the tax structure.[37] It provided for a tax of 1 per cent on that portion of

34 Bourgeois, *Solidarité*, pp. 6–7, 70 ff.; *La Politique de la prévoyance sociale*, p. 122.
35 *Journal officiel, Chambre des Députés, Débats parlementaires* (November 4, 1895), p. 2267.
36 Roussel, "Chronique," *Revue politique et parlementaire*, Vols. VI–VIII (December 1895–May 1896), offers the best summaries of the activities of the Bourgeois ministry.
37 The provisions of the project are summarized clearly by Payen, "Chronique," *loc.*

an individual's annual income between 2,500 and 5,000 francs; 2 per cent on the portion from 5,000 to 10,000; and so on up to 5 per cent on all over 50,000. Coupled with this measure was a proposal to remove the head tax and the door and window tax. Together, the two measures would have effected a moderate reduction in taxes for some 2,000,000 taxpayers and a slight reduction for 6,000,000 others. The tax bill of 300,000 Frenchmen, with incomes of 5,000 to 10,000 francs, would have been slightly increased, and that of the 200,000 with incomes of more than 10,000 francs would have been noticeably increased. In terms of revenue, the measure was not an extensive one and should be regarded primarily as a means of overcoming the deficit and as an experiment in a new method of taxation. In principle, however, the measure represented the introduction of an entirely new spirit into fiscal policies, for it began to shift the burden of taxation to those most able to bear it. In this respect it was a clear expression of the principle of solidarity.

The debates in the Chamber of Deputies on the income tax vindicated the Bourgeois ministry and those who had been agitating for reforms since the beginning of the legislature in 1893. Despite the opposition of influential Moderates like Georges Cochery, Poincaré, Méline, and that aged supporter of laissez-faire Liberalism, Léon Say, the Chamber approved the tax in principle but recommended that the method of collecting it be given additional study. The margin of this victory by the Left was only sixteen votes. Among the majority were 22 Progressives and 39 members of Isambert's Progressive Union, along with the Radicals, Radical Socialists, and Socialists. Opposed to the tax were 38 members of the Isambert group, the remaining 153 Moderates, all the Monarchists, and all the Ralliés.[38] The balance lay, as it had since the beginning of the legislature, with the small group of Progressives who were insistent on social and financial reforms.

From its inception the Bourgeois ministry had been considered by the conservatives as a threat to the established social and economic order.[39] Numerous stratagems had been tried by the Moderates to topple it before its reform program could get under way, but the majority persisted in supporting it until its program could obtain a fair hearing.

---

cit., XII (1897), 762 ff. The complete project can be found in the *Journal officiel, Chambre des Députés, Documents parlementaires* (1896), NO. 1765, pp. 45–123.

[38] *J.O., Chambre, Débats,* March 21–27, 1896.

[39] For example, see Francis Charmes, "Chronique de la quinzaine," *Revue des deux mondes,* CXXXII (December 1, 1895), 711; also A. Descubes, "Parlement," *Nouvelle Revue,* XCIX (April 15, 1896), 846–47.

Since the conservatives in the Chamber had been unable to oust the ministry or prevent the adoption of the principle of the progressive income tax, the task of getting rid of Bourgeois fell to the Senate. It was overwhelmingly conservative in its composition [40] and could easily have defeated any specific measures of reform; yet a majority of the Senators thought it necessary to act before any popular financial measure came up for debate. They had already gone so far as to vote "no confidence" in the ministry, but Bourgeois had proclaimed himself responsible only to the Chamber and continued in office. In April 1896, however, the Senate used a subterfuge to force Bourgeois into a position where he would have to resign or lay himself open to a charge of governing unconstitutionally.[41] His decision to resign brought the experiment in reform government to an end without any lasting accomplishments. Subsequently, the Moderates were able to reestablish their control under the Méline ministry through the aid of the Monarchists and of some twenty Progressives who, for reasons unknown, terminated their support of the Radicals.

The nature and the outcome of the Bourgeois ministry serve to clarify the political situation in France during the 1890's and, more specifically, on the eve of the formation of Waldeck-Rousseau's coalition ministry. The primary issue was the social question. It divided the Republicans into two camps of approximately equal strength, and there was little prospect of reconciliation so long as that issue remained paramount. Significant, too, was the constant support given to a ministry, for the first time, by the Socialists. It appeared that the Socialists, supported by their working class clientele, could become a normal parliamentary group if the Republicans would somehow agree upon undertaking a social reform program. Since the cause of reform was the more popular, the conservatives intensified their efforts to evade the issue. On the other hand, the dependence of the Méline ministry on the Monarchists tempted the Left to revive anticlerical agitation as a form of political maneuvering.[42] That issue had been relegated to the background during the earlier part of the decade, and it had been noticeably absent from the Radical program under Bourgeois. The Dreyfus affair was soon to provide new material for this otherwise secondary issue.

On a broader scale, the period 1870–1896 was important for the definitive establishment of the Republic and the emergence of a majority firmly committed to the maintenance of the Republic even at

[40] R. Saleilles, "The Development of the Present Constitution of France," *Annals of the American Academy of Political Science,* VI (1895), 44–45.

[41] Paul Lafitte, "La Politique," *Revue bleue,* V (April 18, 1896), 481–82.

[42] Charmes, "Chronique," *Revue des deux mondes,* CXXXV (June 15, 1896), 952.

the cost of putting aside internal divisions. Indeed, defense of the Republic and its occasional counterpart, anticlericalism, appeared to be the only programs on which the Republicans could agree. If a broad definition be given to the term "Third Force," its eventual creation could be anticipated on the basis of devotion to the Republic; and the negative aspect of the "Third Force" might be apprehended in view of the division over social problems.

At the end of the period, there remained a nucleus on the extreme Right interested in reestablishing an authoritarian régime. Also, a tendency developed for some Republicans, like Casimir-Perier and Méline, to cooperate with the anti-Republican faction in order to stave off social reforms, but such cooperation could continue only so long as the latter refrained from overt acts of disloyalty to the Republic. On the Left, there was not yet in being an organized party dedicated to overthrowing the Republic, but the seeds of one existed in the labor movement to the extent that it devoted itself to revolutionary syndicalism or to other extraparliamentary action. Most important for the future of France was the fact that the men of the Republic lost an opportunity to adapt their government to the new needs of an industrial society and thereby caused suspicion among the working class concerning the effectiveness of democratic, parliamentary government.

8

++

THE THIRD FORCE, 1897–1939

EDWARD WHITING FOX

++

THE term "Third Force" applied to French politics between 1897 and 1939 is obviously anachronistic. Its use can be justified, if at all, on the grounds that continuity of fact is more significant than change of terminology. If the phrase is new, the phenomenon is not. After all, every schoolboy knows that *"Gallia est omnis divisa in partes tres. . . ."*

Before tracing the roots, however, it is necessary to identify the development in its present form. Since the reestablishment of the French Republic after the Liberation, its day-to-day political existence has been hemmed in by the militant forces of Comrade Thorez and General de Gaulle. Within these narrow limits, the Republican parties, both old and new, have contended, combined, and compromised according to the ancient usages, and somehow managed to keep the Fourth Republic on the same road so long, if so precariously, traversed by the Third.

Some of the political problems, as some of the politicians, of today are new, but the basic pattern strikes any observer as singularly reminiscent of what went before. This French political necessity, or the habit, of entrusting the country's political fortunes to a Center coalition can be traced clearly for at least a half a century to the Waldeck-Rousseau government of Republican defense. The direct descent of the Third Force coalitions from the famous ministry of 1899 has been frequently remarked upon and was dramatically symbolized during the crisis of 1948 when M. Reynaud was minister of finance and dominant member of the Marie cabinet, M. Herriot, President of the Assembly, and M. Paul-Boncour, elder statesman of the Council of the Republic. These three had in common not only a desire to make the

oseph Paul-Boncour Dies;
ormer Premier of France

By Martin Weil
hington Post Staff Writer

ph Paul-Boncour, 98, a
r French premier and
al leader who was
for his passionate ad-
y of a world organiza-
or keeping the peace,
uesday in Paris.

hough he served as
er for only 40 days
19, 1932 to Jan. 28,
he was an influential
on the French politi-
ene for decades as a
st-oriented   cabinet
er and member of par-
t.

France's representative
old League of Nations
1920s and 1930s, he
t vainly to arm the
with the power to en-
sanctions against ag-
r nations.

armament of nations
possible so long as
is military rivalry," he
"Create an interna-
force   under   the
and the rivalry will
ear."

carried similar views
im when he arrived in
rancisco in the waning
s of World War II to
ent France at the con-
e that set up the
i Nations.

ace is impossible with-
permanent big stick
the Big Five (nations)
be ready to use at the
ign of aggression," he

June 26, 1945, Mr.
oncour, who was said

1935 Photo

JOSEPH PAUL-BONCOUR

to have campaigned perhaps
longer and more consist-
ently than any European
statesman for a world peace
organization, signed the UN
charter in behalf of France.

In a speech at the final
plenary session at San Fran-
cisco, he compared the
peace-keeping machinery
embodied in the UN charter
favorably with that of the
League of Nations.

But he warned that the
charter would break down if
the great powers sitting on
the Security Council failed
to remain truly united.

"In the hour when im-
mense hope rises from our
hearts," he pleaded, "let us
swear to remain faithful in
peace to this unity which
was our strength in war."

Mr. Paul-Boncour was
born on Aug. 4, 1873, to middle-class parents in the town
of Saint-Aignan. After receiving a law degree, he
began practicing in Paris,
electrifying courtrooms with
fiery oratory.

His skills at advocacy and
debate helped make a place
for him in politics. First
elected to the Chamber of
Deputies in 1909, he held office almost continuously for
the next 40 years.

Before becoming premier
in 1932, he had been minister of war. Afterwards, he
served in several cabinets as
foreign minister.

One interruption in his
political career came during
World War I when he led an
infantry battalion in combat
and won the Legion of
Honor.

In addition, in 1940 he led
a small group in parliament
in opposition to the government of Marshal Philippe
Henri Petain, which largely
cooperated with Germany.
He finally retired from politics until France was liberated.

A member of the Socialist
Party during much of his
political career, he was described as owing less to
Marxism than to the principles of the French Revolution.

He was divorced from his
wife, the former Helene Raf-
fard. They had a son and a
daughter.

Delay Seen In Probe At U. of Va.

CHARLOTTESVILLE, Va., March 31 (AP)—A security officer whose arrest of black students and faculty members touched off a controversy about racism last week at the University of Virginia has been forbidden from testifying in a university-ordered investigation of the incidents.

The commonwealth's attorneys of Albemarle County and the city of Charlottesville have directed the officer, Walter G. Chaffin, not to take part in any investigation of black professor Wesley L. Harris or Ronald D. Colbert, a black sophomore.

Albemarle County Commonwealth's Attorney Charles R. Haugh and Charlottesville Commonwealth's Attorney John T. Camblos issued the directive under prosecutor's power to limit the pretrial testimony of witnesses.

The restriction on Chaffin's participation apparently will hinder the investigation. The chairman of the university's investigating committee, Marvin K. Kellog, said that "as far as I can see, this would mean a temporary delay."

In a related development, the student council has censured President Edgar F. Shannon and his administration "for their insensitivity and ineptness in responding to reasonable requests for an investigation of complaints of harassment in the university community."

The student council resolution also supported the Kel-

FORECAST

Figures Show High Temperatures Expected For Daytime Saturday

Isolated Precipitation Not Indicated—Consult Local Forecast

Data From NATIONAL WEATHER SERVICE NOAA, U.S. Dept. of Commerce

Rain
Showers
Snow
Flurries

Associated Press

Weather

Chance of Showers High About 50

Washington: Today—Cloudy, 50 per cent chance of showers today and 20 per cent tonight. High will be around 50 with the low in the 30s. Sunday—Partly sunny, high in the 50s.

Maryland: Cloudy, high in the 40s and a chance of snow in the western portion of the state, and in the 50s in the eastern part. Sunday—Partly sunny, highs in the 40s.

Virginia: Today—Cloudy, chance of showers. High in the 40s, low in the 30s. There is a chance of snow in the mountains. Sunday—Cloudy, high in the 40s in the mountains and in the 50s elsewhere.

Lower Potomac and Chesapeake Bay: Today—Partly cloudy, northwesterly winds at 10 to 20 knots. Visibility over 5 miles.

Extended Area Outlook: Sunday through Tuesday—Rain on Sunday ending Monday. Highs will be in the upper 50s, lows in the 30s. Normal seasonal temperatures are a high of 60 and a low of 41.

The Nation Yesterday—March is going out like a lion across much of the country. Balmy weather, but with showers and thunderstorms, continued in southeastern Florida. On the other hand, chilly readings in the 30s and 40s prevail in much of the remaining East Coast states. In addition rain, with snow in the higher elevations, continued to fall throughout that region. Cool weather also was typical in the Gulf Coast states where clear skies dominated. Some frost or freezing temperatures were expected in the northern portions of those states. Further north there were a variety of weather conditions. A little snow was whitening portions of the central Rockies, and some light showers dampened much of the northern Pacific Coast region. Elsewhere through in the west fair skies and warm temperatures were the rule. The mercury hit 60 degrees at Great

the eastern half of the land but v in the West.

Major Map Features: At 7 p.m. Yesterday—A cold front trailed low well east of New Jersey another low east of South Caro central Florida. Another cold curved from a low over so Illinois through northern Texas to Colorado. A low lay just south of Bay, Canada. Highs were centere western North Dakota and Texas.

Predicted Map Positions: For (EST) Today—A cold front will tra a low over northeast Montana to Oregon. Another low will be s over West Virginia. Highs w located over eastern Texas and Ut

Almanac Data: Sun rises, 5:53 sets, 6:31 p.m.; moon rises, 9:40 sets 6:48 a.m.

Tides: High, 9:34 a.m. and 9:5 low, 3:59 a.m. and 4:33 p.m. H low tides at the following poin be obtained by subtracting the ho dicated from the tides above: Ar (3¼), Bloody Point Lighthouse Deale, Md. (4½), Colonial Bea Norfolk (11½), Virginia Beach (1 mon's Island (6½), Point Lookout

Air Pollution Reading: The ma hourly average of sulfur dioxide 2 p.m. yesterday was .06 parts p lion. (Note: a readng of .15 or h considered undesirable.)

The National Weather Service fo that the Potomac River stage a Falls would remain near 4.2 feet today.

Washington Data: At 7 p.m. Ye —Highest temperature since 7 a degrees, at 1:30 p.m. Lowest te ture since midnight, 45 degrees a.m. Record high temperature for 83 degrees, in 1918. Record lo perature for today, 15 degrees, i Excess of temperature since Ma 24 degrees. Excess of temperatur Jan. 1, 42 degrees. Relative hu

Republic work, but the fact that all three were personal protégés of René Waldeck-Rousseau.

The Third Force in 1948 as in 1899 was composed of defenders of private property and advocates of social progress, of Republican Catholics and Republican anticlericals, all of whom, no matter what their disagreements, believed that the first need of France was to preserve the constitutional structure, as well as the national state of mind, within which honest differences of political means and social ends could be resolved. That the Republic has been frequently and vociferously defended is known to all. What is sometimes overlooked is the monotonous regularity with which these efforts met success. Like Sieyès, it survived. In 1939 it was the oldest régime governing a major power on the continent of Europe. And now beneath the refurbished title of the Fourth Republic can be read the weathered lettering of the Third, as one reads "Chambre des Députés" behind the gilt "Assemblée Nationale" across the porch of the Palais Bourbon.

A régime which has endured for eighty years and survived the victory of 1918, the defeat of 1940, and the peace which intervened, must correspond in some organic way to the traditions and aspirations of its citizens.[1] If such correspondence does in fact exist, the question is why the Republic has created such a vivid impression of instability or even insecurity in its daily life. Historians have been tempted to stress its day-to-day disturbances rather than decade-to-decade endurance; and hence much speculation has been expended on accounting for its apparently hopeless weakness.

The standard explanations are all familiar. Puritans from west of the Hudson and east of the Rhine have liked to attribute this political instability to the essential levity of the French character. Ideologues, including many Frenchmen, have attributed the same manifestations to a deep and irreparable split in the French *esprit* stemming from the violent days of the great Revolution. Political scientists have usually found the cause of weakness in the technical inadequacies of the constitution or the failure of the French to develop a two-party system in the approved English and American manner. Moralists on the Right explain the weakness in terms of lack of discipline, while moralists on the Left attribute the same phenomenon to a lack of social responsibility and concern for human values. In all probability each of these factors has some place in a thorough analysis of the problem, but merely jumbled together they do not constitute a theory with which to explain the historical conditions which confront us.

[1] Maurice Reclus, *Grandeur de "La Troisième" de Gambetta à Poincaré* (Paris, 1948), p. 154.

The hypothesis which is needed, if we are to understand the roots of the Third Force, is one which will explain why a government apparently so unstable survived so many crises; why ministries so transitory perpetuated major statesmen in, or regularly returned them to, the same positions for a decade at a time; why a country supposedly split between Red and Black, or progress and order, managed to hold together under the disintegrating force of a world depression and a second world war; why a régime which had satisfied no one, impressed no one, except with its inefficiencies, should after fifty months of eclipse under enemy occupation be restored in substance; and why in spite of the fact that it provides the no man's land for the cold war between East and West, it is still in existence and still the most important free government on the Eurasian Continent.

Toward the formulation of such a hypothesis I should propose that the basic division in French politics has been drawn along economic class lines; that in the period before 1914, the great bourgeois were unprepared to make the concessions necessary to ameliorate the conditions of the industrial proletariat; and that after 1918 the problems of financial adjustment and national defense precluded the practicality of a thoroughgoing program of social legislation. As a corollary to this I should add that, granted the insolubility of the economic problem, the majority of voters and political leaders regularly chose to evade the problem rather than to face it and risk the hopeless disruption of the national order. The expression of this determination is occasionally clear and can be traced in the discontinuous series of Center coalitions which ruled the destinies of France in most of its major crises from the beginning of the century to the present.

In his brilliant analysis of French party politics, M. François Goguel advances the thesis that the difficulties of the Third Republic stem from a deep division in the *esprit publique* between an *esprit d'ordre établi* and an *esprit du mouvement*.[2] This is not to posit the existence of a France in which every boy that's born alive was "either a little Liberal or else a little Conservative," because, as M. Goguel points out, not only were Frenchmen divided into two camps, but many individual Frenchmen were themselves divided in allegiance between both camps. On some issues they voted for order and on some for progress. The Radical Socialists, while against the established order of the Church, were prepared to defend the established order of the franc. In actual politics this translated itself into a system not merely of two parties, but a system of two wings within each of two parties. The proponents of order tended to work together in elections as did their opponents who favored progress; but once in the Cham-

[2] *La Politique des partis sous la IIIe République* (Paris, 1946).

ber, neither group found it easy to develop a coherent policy. In every-day affairs, it frequently seemed more practical to the French politi-cians to work with members of a wing of the other party than with those of the other wing of their own.

Although practical coalitions could often be effected to deal with foreign affairs or economic development or educational reform, the chances were good that a coalition able to agree on one set of problems would find itself disintegrating when confronted with another. In the long run, of course, this did not prevent essentially the same elements from participating in succeeding ministries. It has been maintained that the membership of Third Republic cabinets was more consistent than that of most other great parliamentary régimes of recent times. But that this continuity did exist in fact makes it more, rather than less, difficult to explain the irresponsibility and insecurity which so often marked the course of the French executive.

M. Goguel attributes this paralysis to the deep and irreconcilable nature of the split in the *esprit publique*. The apostles both of order and of progress, he maintains, fought each political campaign with the aim of totally annihilating the opposition, a purpose he believes to be inconsistent with the democratic process.[3] To those brought up on the brotherly give-and-take of American politics, this last judgment may not be entirely convincing. Nor is it wholly satisfying to those who have been impressed by the essential loyalty to the Republic which has been demonstrated again and again: in support of Waldeck-Rousseau in 1899, of Clemenceau in 1917, of Poincaré repeatedly throughout the 1920's as well as in the Resistance during the first half of the 1940's, and the persistent if precarious survival of the present régime as the century enters its second half.

There is another possible explanation of this phenomenon of continued and bitter attacks upon the Republic from within the body politic of France. The business of governing being frequently en-trusted to a Center coalition, there never developed a loyal opposition to which dissatisfied voters could turn. Moreover, the separate tasks of operating the government and maintaining the régime became in-extricably confused. Thus for lack of an established focus for loyal opposition to the government, the temporary dissidents and malcon-tents were driven to support the irresponsible enemies of the régime as the only practical means of expressing their dissatisfaction.[4] This

[3] *ibid.*, pp. 25–29.

[4] Mme. Caroline Rémy Guebhard (Séverine, pseud.), *Notes d'une frondeuse de la boulange au Panama* (Paris, 1894), p. 19, "Boulangism was disgust, not with the Re-public, but 'your' republic, the republic which your friends have made." Also Paul Laffitte, "Leçon du boulangisme," *Revue bleu,* XLVIII (1891), 481–82, and the Marquis de Castellane, "1789–1889—les conservateurs," *Nouvelle revue,* LVI (1889), 525.

created a special and highly significant pattern of political action which can be illustrated by the anecdote of Boulanger and Aurélien Scholl. According to Mr. Denis Brogan, at least, the General encountered the boulevardier during the height of the campaign and demanded to know if Scholl were with him. "Right up to the seventeenth Brumaire" was the reply.[5]

It is more than possible that this accounts for the speed with which crises and *affaires* developed and collapsed throughout the entire existence of the Third Republic. Opposition within a governing coalition meant ministerial collapse. And though this occurred frequently enough, it was usually followed by governmental reconstitution. Serious opposition was regularly forced outside the Center group and found its only point of leverage within the irreconcilables of Right or Left.

The sudden movement to vote in a general pledged "to sweep the rascals out" indicated, according to the shrewdest observers of the time, nothing more than a desire to sweep the rascals out. In a day of party coups, it is difficult to peruse the records of 1889 and not read into its events a widespread desire to sacrifice the Republic to some form of martial order. The election returns of that year, however, should pour the same cold water on such ideas today as they did on the hopes of the political adventurers who made up the General's entourage. The forces of reaction were defeated, as they were again after the similar fiasco of Panama and still again after the witches' sabbath of the Dreyfus case.

The evils inherent in this *politique du dix-sept brumaire* are easy enough to see. In the first place, it committed nuisances with disturbing regularity. In the second place, it provided a potential nucleus of temporary support for the undeserving prophets and prospectors of the political extremes. Much worse than either, however, it allowed the holders of office to neglect or even evade their chief responsibilities. Without a loyal opposition to oversee and call them to account, they depended for discipline on their own near friends and neighbors, a situation uncomfortable for both. When such discipline was not provided, the credit of the régime suffered and the opposition increased until sooner or later a new crisis arose.

Instead of facing the consequences of ministerial irresponsibility, the ministers wrapped themselves in the tricolor and took up their defense behind the sacred barricade of the Republic. It is true this procedure did not always save the individuals concerned, but for an amazingly long time it did preserve the political system which, de-

[5] D. W. Brogan, *France under the Republic. The Development of Modern France (1870–1939)* (New York, 1940), p. 212.

spite all pretensions to the contrary, was not identical with the Republic.

The Republic which had divided Frenchmen least in 1873 had become by 1893 the factor which unified them most. It was an acceptance of this fact which underlay the *ralliement,* as it also underlay the sweeping Republican victory at the polls in 1893. As Mr. Minnich has pointed out, this preponderance of power embarrassed the victors and rapidly prepared the way for a serious attempt at social legislation.[6] That the Bourgeois ministry failed to achieve its program is perhaps not too important. The significance of these developments for our purpose lies in the violent reaction which the program evoked.

The possible similarity between the Bourgeois doctrine of *solidarité* and the philosophy of the Roosevelt New Deal is certainly paralleled by a more striking similarity of class antagonism aroused by a program of bold, if overdue, reforms. At this point the comparison ceases to be useful because the American Republicans had to endure Mr. Roosevelt and survive on the single hope that if they were very good they might someday do the same things in a better way. The Moderates in the French Chamber and Senate in 1895–1897 faced no such bleak if pious prospect. It lay within their power to block the social program and forestall its reintroduction for an apparently indefinite time. The blocking was handled with expedition but the forestalling, as it turned out, became highly complicated.

After Bourgeois' fall, Méline formed a ministry which might have been called the government of capitalist defense. The voting strength of the opposing factions was closely balanced in the Chamber. The advantage lay with the ministers and the extra powers of persuasion which were their traditional perquisites of office. So long as Méline maintained his cabinet, the income and inheritance taxes and the good works of *solidarité* were all safely out of the question. But if the Radical Socialists could once bring him down, there remained the possibility that they could reconstitute the Bourgeois government, reintroduce the taxes and social legislation, and possibly, if not probably, impose both on a most unwilling upper bourgeoisie.[7]

In this situation Méline played for time and the Radical Socialists and their allies probed for soft spots in his ministerial defenses. One of the possible weaknesses they discovered was the un-republican leniency shown a wealthy traitor named Captain Alfred Dreyfus. From that point the superficial aspects of the story unwind along the lines

[6] See the foregoing chapter in this volume.

[7] Georges Lachapelle, *Le Ministère Méline, deux années de politique intérieure et extérieure, 1896–1897* (Paris, 1928), p. 33.

of the old familiar maze to a conclusion of sorts with the vindication of the much-abused if equally misunderstood victim of the petty intrigues of the General Staff. Obscured beneath this drama lay another development which still can be but faintly traced.

The election of fifty Socialists in '93, the paralysis of the Moderate majority in '94, and the attempt at tax reform in '95, taken together, had convinced at least a few of the Republic's most able politicians that the threatening crisis was dangerous in the extreme. Every Western European country has faced the necessity of reconciling the implications of the great nineteenth-century revolutions of politics and industry. Fiscal questions and social reforms were becoming more and more important in the deliberations of the French chambers. Redistribution of the tax load and the development of social security had been supported by 19 deputies in 1881 and by 211 in 1889. But to judge by the fate of the Bourgeois program, at least, the country was not prepared to face the issue squarely and work out a general solution. In 1895, André Lebon, writing in the *Nouvelle Revue,* stated the case with startling clarity, pointing out that neither side in the economic struggle was willing to concede or compromise, but that the *haute bourgeoisie* in particular was unprepared to accept its new social obligations. It was one thing, he said, to defend the Republic and another to increase a tax or shorten working hours.[8] Within a year, M. Lebon, himself, provided important corroborative evidence for this thesis by devising the constitutional maneuver which precipitated the fall of the Bourgeois ministry. M. Lebon, having analyzed the crucial weakness of French party politics with penetrating candor, had proceeded to act the part of a militant defender of the economically privileged class from which he came.[9]

At almost the same time another slightly older representative of the bourgeois oligarchy manifested an equally acute comprehension of the political situation of his country. In 1895 Waldeck-Rousseau, who had withdrawn from politics four years before, reentered the political arena with a series of famous speeches intended not only to warn Frenchmen of the menace of the new Socialist Left, but also to mark out a program of Republican action. Son of a Republican deputy of 1848, raised a Breton Catholic, and by profession a corporation lawyer, Waldeck-Rousseau was admirably qualified to defend the existing régime both in its Republican constitution and its conservative bourgeois concentration of wealth and power. This, beyond

---

[8] "L'Esprit public en France, ses conditions et ses progrès," XCVII, 277–300.

[9] Robert David, *La Troisième République, soixante ans de politiques et d'histoire, de 1871 à nos jours* (Paris, 1934), pp. 217–20.

doubt, he wished to do, but his speeches revealed a breadth of statesmanship which recognized the necessity of accepting social responsibility as both the price and the justification of social privilege.[10]

The evidence leads inescapably to the conclusion that Waldeck-Rousseau was seriously preoccupied with the problem of Republican defense before he or any other political leader had sensed a threat to the régime in the case of Captain Dreyfus. His speeches of 1895–1897 on *L'Idéal républicain, Les Transformations sociales et les garanties de la société, Le Socialisme et l'état, Critique de la théorie collectiviste et de l'impôt sur le revenu,* and *Conserver et progresser,* to mention only a few, all point in the same direction. Add to this Waldeck-Rousseau's formation of the Grand Cercle Républicain in Paris, and his interest in a number of provincial *cercles,* together with hints from scattered editorials in the Paris press: all suggest the outlines of a campaign to create a concentration of conservative Republican power capable of ruling the country and avoiding a head-on clash of irreconcilable economic interests.[11]

The extent to which Waldeck-Rousseau consciously mapped such a campaign, or the exact shape the plan may have taken in his mind, can probably not be determined until his personal papers become available in 1954.[12] It is impossible to read his speeches without accepting the sincerity of his devotion to the Republican régime and his deep concern for the need of social legislation. It is also impossible to underestimate the strength of his anti-Socialist convictions. Much more difficult to determine, however, is the extent to which he calculated the disrupting impact of a Center group (which would include the Radical Socialists, perhaps even a few Socialists) upon the forces of the Left.

As early as the beginning of 1897 there were hints in the Paris press that Waldeck-Rousseau was assuming a role of importance in the leadership of the moderate Republican forces. But his plans, whatever they were, were not destined to be worked out in normal political circumstances. By November, the Dreyfus case had broken out of its judicial bounds. Every account insists that this crisis cut the soul of France to the very quick, and even today the recollection of the *affaire* can still strike sparks. For our purposes, however, there seems to be reason to question the political depth of these superficial manifestations. For all the excitement concerning the guilt and innocence of

[10] J. Ernest-Charles, *Waldeck-Rousseau* (Paris, n.d.), *passim.*
[11] René Waldeck-Rousseau, *Pour la République (1883–1903)* (Paris, 1904), *passim.*
[12] These papers were deposited in the Institute not to be opened until fifty years after his death.

the victim or the relative merits of *raison d'état* and *droit des hommes,* these issues failed to become effective in the political life of the country.[13]

The general election of 1898 was in no sense a referendum for or against Dreyfus. In fact, the *affaire* was an open campaign issue in very few parts of France except the departments of North Africa. Nor does the fiasco of Déroulède's attempted coup lend weight to the thesis that the Republican régime was actually in danger. Even the malign influence of the Church would seem to have been overestimated if its helplessness before the anticlerical campaign, culminating in separation of Church and state, is to be accepted as relevant evidence. In fact, there is very little specific evidence which would suggest that the inflamed passions of the Dreyfus crisis derived directly from important political convictions. In the mid-twentieth century, when all issues are political, it is difficult to reconstruct a pattern of violent civil strife conducted almost wholly on a moral plane, but there have been other examples of this phenomenon somewhat closer to our own experience, the Sacco-Vanzetti case for one.

It was at the height of the crisis in 1899 that Waldeck-Rousseau formed his ministry of Republican defense. Whatever his intentions had been in 1897, there is no question that in 1899 his first job was to liquidate the Dreyfus affair as rapidly as possible. His handling of this delicate task and the acceptance of his leadership by the country at large both testify to the quality of his statesmanship. Whether in the midst of this crisis he consciously defended the economic order along with the political constitution would be difficult to say. But it is on the record that Millerand's participation in the ministry did split the Socialists and further postponed a concerted leftwing attack on the positions of social privilege. It was because Guesde had foreseen this result that he opposed the ministerial cooperation which he feared would discredit political action in the workers' eyes.[14]

The great strikes of 1906–1909 may have vindicated Guesde's judgment, but they did not seriously menace the Republic or even significantly modify the privileges of the most moderate Republicans. In 1910 at a congress of the Ligue des Droits de l'Homme, called to celebrate the tenth anniversary of the victory of the Dreyfusards, Francis de Pressensé said, "In reality, we were defeated. We obtained the reparation of an individual injustice; but for the rest what did we achieve? . . . Social inequality has only grown." [15]

[13] A. Soulier, *L'Instabilité ministèrielle sous la IIIe République* (Paris, 1939).

[14] Georges Weill, *Histoire du mouvement social en France, 1852–1924* (Paris, 1924), p. 322.

[15] Georges Michon, *La Préparation à la guerre, la loi de trois ans (1910–1914)* (Paris, 1935), p. 55.

During this period, dependence on a government of Republican concentration developed into something approaching a confirmed habit. In 1909 the Socialists withdrew from the concentration, but the Radical Socialists did not. Briand's appeasement may have reduced the resentments of the Right but it did not produce tangible results in social legislation and therefore failed to disarm the militants of the Left. As a result the parties of progress fought and won the election of 1914 on class lines under a slogan of "No enemies to the Left." The coalition included the Radicals, the Radical Socialists, and the Socialists, and their platform included promises of electoral reform, the introduction of an income tax, and an extension of military service. The alliance held firm during the election, but once the deputies assembled in the Chamber the Radicals and even the Radical Socialists opposed the income tax; and the Socialists opposed the three-year military service law. The victors were saved from this impasse of conflicting promises by the outbreak of war.[16]

France was unified in 1914 even if the political groups within the Chamber were not, and it seems doubtful that Jaurès could have held the workers out of the mobilization. But victory in 1918 brought the Republicans face-to-face with staggering problems of reconstruction in the postwar world and with a long overdue account of social reform for which twenty years of Republican defense and a habit of political compromise by evasion proved to be an unfortunate preparation. The political problems of the postwar period were so different from those which preceded 1914 that it might seem impractical to draw useful comparisons between the two. But in spite of the differences, both fundamental and superficial, there were some elements of continuity.

In the twenty years which by courtesy are referred to as the peace, France was on four occasions governed by a solid concentration of Right or Left.[17] Though at first glance this might seem to be a marked change from the experiences of the first years of the century, the difference was more apparent than real. What appeared to be an alternation between governments of order and progress, turns out on close inspection to have been shifts from attempted rule by concentration of Right or Left to compromise through Center coalitions. It hardly need be urged that this was not the rise and fall of rival parties in the Anglo-Saxon manner. The reasons for this failure to develop close-knit parties of Left and Right were similar to those that mo-

[16] Goguel, *op. cit.*, pp. 129 ff.; and Soulier, *op. cit.*, pp. 427–30. From 1899 to 1909 there were only five ministries formed, but between 1909 and 1914, there were nine.

[17] Soulier, *op. cit.*, pp. 448 ff., and Goguel, *op. cit.*, *passim;* Bloc National 1920–1924; Cartel des Gauches 1924–1926, Union National 1928–1930, Front Populaire 1936–1938.

tivated Waldeck-Rousseau's formation of the government of Republican defense. Although the political alignments of the country had been modified by the ordeal of war, this modification did not eliminate either the deep split along social lines or the fact of disloyal opposition.[18]

The sentimental Royalists, it is true, had finally disappeared, but their place was taken by the proto-Fascists, and even though these latter did not become politically significant until 1934, they had to be taken into account as potential enemies of the régime. There was, perhaps, some justification for the tendency to accept the Socialists with less reservation as loyal members of the Republic. There was no question, however, that the postwar Communists—who were regularly represented in the Chamber after 1924—were militant revolutionaries dedicated to the destruction of the existing order and the philosophy upon which it was based.

The ordinary political business of the Republic had to be done by the groups between these two extremes. In the early 1920's this hardly narrowed the field appreciably, but the existence of anti-Republican elements on either wing precluded the possibility of a government solidly based on Left or Right. And as the Communists and eventually the Fascists grew in strength, the necessity of Republican defense became more clear and pressing and the possibility of a two-party system more remote.

Even before this had become a decisive factor, however, an apparent vacillation among the Republicans themselves had reestablished the dependence on a shifting coalition from Center-Right to Center-Left. For all the bewildering complexity of *couloirs politiques,* as practiced in the Chamber, the character of the shifts can be followed in the votes of the Radicals and Radical Socialists. The parties of order, those groups which sat on the Right and tended to follow Poincaré, stood for a vigorous foreign policy and a preservation of the economic status quo, including the stability of the franc. The party of progress on the Left, at least the Socialists, stood for social reform and international good will. The Radical Socialists, who were largely responsible for the organization of the victory of the Cartel des Gauches in 1924, found, in the course of the next two years, that they were not prepared to follow their own leader, Herriot, into the rough waters of financial insecurity. It was they who made possible Poincaré's salvation of the franc, just as it was they who backed Briand in his policy of Locarno.[19]

The superficial manifestation of this situation was a ministerial instability with a shift of emphasis in the cabinet from Right to Left

18 Goguel, *op. cit.,* pp. 156–64.
19 *ibid.,* pp. 191, 204.

and Left to Right again. Much of the instability, of course, was illusory. For nearly ten years the French government pursued a relatively consistent policy within a number of major fields. If the chief one on the agenda was foreign policy, the Radical Socialists would vote on the Left, giving that side a majority. If the business was financial, they would swing the majority to the Right.

There was, of course, no lack of political struggle within and without the Chamber, but it became more and more a struggle for place and position rather than of principle. Throughout this decade of euphoria, the chief desire of the majority of Frenchmen seemed to be for a return to a stable world, and to the "majority of this majority" stability meant first, the maintenance of the Republic, and after that, simultaneous maintenance of a stable currency and a stable peace.

The tragedy for France was that stability in either of these two areas was a virtual impossibility in the postwar world. From the vantage point of the present, it is inconceivable that the currency of any major participant in the war could have gone unscathed, and it is beyond reasonable doubt that the structure of the League, of Locarno, and the Briand-Kellogg Pact was anything more than the product of some millions of feverishly hopeful imaginations. In attempting to develop simultaneously these two policies of stability of the franc and peace by negotiation, France was doomed not only to ultimate failure but to immediate frustration as well. Serious efforts to stabilize the currency on a balanced budget meant curtailing expenditures for national defense as well as social reform. National security, if it was possible at all, would have necessitated heavy outlays not only of money but of manpower. Neither would conceivably have been agreed to by the Socialists without heavy compensation in social legislation. The total cost for such an over-all program would have been beyond the grasp of the French imagination if not of the country's resources.

The only way out of this vice of circumstances was intellectual escapism. The phrase "Maginot mentality" suggests the character of the aberration that swept the country; but, needless to say, there were many other manifestations of mass flight from reality. Though a realist in foreign policy, Poincaré was probably a victim of delusion when he hoped to maintain a balanced budget. Briand was the great prophet of salvation by self-hypnosis, and significantly the country accepted his gospel in foreign policy. In a stable and civilized world France might have worked out her economic and social salvation. It was almost inevitable that she posit such a hypothetical world if she could not create one.

Difficult as it is to see what effective political course France might have followed in the 1920's, the problems which confronted her in the 1930's were, if anything, more overwhelming. During the brief years when the world economy and international community fell to pieces, French politics were being entrusted to a new set of leaders. Briand and Poincaré disappeared almost simultaneously with the order which they had symbolized; and whatever their merits or defects had been, their successors were clearly lesser men, just as the problems which they faced were immeasurably greater.

In reviewing the final years before the war, it is difficult to find any useful pattern in French politics. The sixth of February, 1934, for all of its ominous violence, did not bring the Republic down. Growing out of the misdeeds of a coalition ministry that had been unable to subject itself to the salutary surveillance of a vigorous loyal opposition, the crisis revealed alarming weakness in the government. But even more, it proved a lack of strength and coherent program in the Fascist elements within the country.

Survival, in this case, was hardly victory; the great celebration of July 14, 1935, which launched the Front Populaire, offered no solid base for hope of better days. For France, there was no possible salvation until Hitler was destroyed. Perhaps the final tragedy of the Third Republic is best symbolized in the cruel dilemma of Léon Blum who, backed by an apparently overwhelming majority, attempted to effect the long-overdue social program just at the point at which the country's greater need was not reduction of working hours but an increase in plane production. M. Blum could not possibly have saved the Third Republic, but there is a decided possibility that his reforms served the Fourth Republic well. And obviously, there is now no more future for the Fourth Republic than there was for the Third unless international tensions can be reduced.

In the meantime, the Third Force is maintaining the Republic against the day when the issues of the cold war are resolved, and the world is once again safe for democratic republics. Not only is the maintenance of the French Republic essential to the preservation of the West; it is entirely possible that France will be forced to provide the practical formula for democratic action in the modern world. In this, the Third Force will necessarily provide the lead. If it draws on the statesmanlike example of Waldeck-Rousseau, it will defend the Republic first. But if it does the whole job it will progress, as he was unable to, beyond this first essential phase, to the second and, perhaps, more significant one of reconciling social responsibility with Republican defense.

9

✦✦✦

THE THIRD FORCE TODAY

CHARLES A. MICAUD

✦✦✦

THE Third Force recalls Abbé Sieyès' famous definition of the Third Estate: "What is the Third Estate? Nothing. What should it be? Everything." In one sense there is no Third Force. The attempts of Léon Blum and his colleagues to create a committee for common action among the parties in the coalition failed. The term itself is now seldom used, and there is little popular support behind a Third Force *mystique*.

That the Third Force should be everything is obvious from the nature of the two other forces, which represent an essentially disloyal as well as a formidable opposition. Lack of consensus has prevented the government from exercising vigorous, consistent, and creative leadership.[1]

Until February 1950 the Third Force could be defined as the parliamentary coalition ruling France. This coalition was composed of the Socialist SFIO, the Catholic MRP, and a number of individuals belonging to smaller groups; its cohesive force was its opposition to both Communism and neo-Gaullism. Afterwards, the Socialists' temporary withdrawal from the coalition cabinet further reduced the scope and significance of the Third Force but did not change its *raison d'être*: it remained a coalition for Republican defense that would not have been viable without the indirect support of the SFIO. Although no longer in the government, the Socialists were still a pillar of the Third Force.

Future textbooks will probably tell us that the Third Force was born in November 1947, following the municipal elections, and that

[1] See Leo Hamon, "Origines et chances de la troisième force," *Politique,* nouv. sér., V (February 1948), 101 ff. Also the chronicles of *Politique* for January and March 1948. For a Gaullist point of view on the Third Force, see Raymond Aron, *Le Grand Schisme* (Paris, 1948), and Jacques Debru-Bridel, *Les Partis contre de Gaulle* (Paris, 1948).

Léon Blum gave it its name. Actually he did not, nor can the exact date of birth be established.

The father was General de Gaulle himself.* He began it all by quitting his post in January 1946 on the pretext that his mission had been accomplished, which many doubted. He then took the lead in opposing the second constitutional draft, thus crossing his Rubicon. On both occasions the MRP defied him, at no small risk to themselves, and thus prefaced the coming to life of the Third Force. De Gaulle's next step was the formation of the RPF and the delivery of a series of famous speeches against the régime, a direct challenge to parliamentary democracy that Socialists, MRP's, and other groups met firmly. The final step was the victory of the RPF in the municipal elections, which gave some plausibility to the General's demand for dissolution of the National Assembly and new elections. Once more the challenge was met and the Third Force, as a coalition for Republican defense, came into official existence.[2]

In the meantime, on May 4, 1947, the Communists had been ejected without ceremony from the Ramadier government, following their equivocal position on the Renault strikes and the wage policy of the cabinet. At first rather frustrated, they came to take pride in their new role in the Opposition. Soon after the creation of the Cominform, Thorez apologized for past errors and stressed the wisdom of the new strategy.

The Third Force was born in defeat: the municipal elections, however interpreted, could hardly be called a victory for the Center parties. The MRP lost about two-thirds of their former electors; the Socialists could compliment themselves only on the number of Socialist mayors who had been elected, a tactical advantage due to the presence of the Extremes rather than to their own strength. This generalization can be applied to the Third Force itself: its very existence and ability to survive is due to the pressure of the two Extremes more than to its own dynamism—a statement made by P. E. Flandin back in 1935 concerning the Third Force of his day, which has some relevance today. The most thoroughly beaten party was the MRP, yet it was an MRP leader, Robert Schuman, who was given the burden and privilege of leading the government of France.

Ramadier had declined the honor, in part because of MRP's gentle pressure. After him, Léon Blum tried his hand, but taking for granted the reality of a Third Force, he neglected to establish a *"hiérarchie des urgences."* Too many deputies were offended by what they con-

---

* The political position of General de Gaulle and of "Gaullism" are treated below in Chapter 15.
[2] See *L'Année politique* (1947), pp. 215 ff.

sidered lack of discrimination and good taste. They voted him down. M. Schuman proved to be the right moderator. Not only was he respected as a calm, honest, and diligent statesman, but he represented a position closer to the attitudes and expectations of most Frenchmen—the Center coalition was finding its real *"assiette"* by expanding toward the Right. A common denominator could be found more easily through Schuman than through Blum. He received a large majority for his investiture, a smaller one when he presented his cabinet, and a still smaller one when it came time to pay the bill— that is, to agree on the so-called Mayer Plan.

The fact that the Third Force was born in defeat and in danger explains its character. The Communist-inspired strikes of the fall threatened French economy and the life of the Republic. The government had to act vigorously to crush the offensive. Thus the Third Force had to be primarily a coalition against the Communist menace, which forced the government to make advances to the hesitant deputies in the no-man's-land between neo-Gaullism and the Third Force. This was a condition of survival, but it was also a grave handicap, for the *travaillisme* dear to many Socialists and MRP's—"the something new and something reasonable" which De Gaulle himself had advocated in the honeymoon days of 1944 and 1945—was out of the question.[3] *Travaillisme* had to yield to Republican defense; a positive program of reconstruction and social justice gave way to a negative program of survival. It meant in practice a forced cohabitation between those of opposed economic and social doctrines, a *mariage de raison* between incompatibles.

This was unfortunate. For the conflict between liberalism and *dirigisme,* between Radicals and Socialists, led to lack of continuity, to contradictions, and inefficiency—above all, to lack of active popular support. A surreptitiously conservative policy was adopted, for which the Socialists got the blame from the workers and none of the credit from the investors. There was no way out for the Socialists: Republican defense demands a sacrifice of principles and of votes. The *cure d'opposition* about which many Socialists dreamed would have produced a crisis which was insoluble by any means short of M. de Gaulle's return on his own terms.[*]

The small but strategically essential support given by some Radicals, UDSR's, and independents such as Paul Reynaud, allowed them to run the show in so far as finance and national economy were con-

---

[*] Concerning the position of the Socialists in the party conflicts of this period see Chapter 11.

[3] See *Politique,* v (January 1948), 63 ff.; (February 1948), pp. 101 ff., 148 ff.; (March 1948), pp. 235 ff.; and *Esprit,* Vol. xv (December 1947).

cerned. Some of these liberals realized the need for compromises with the Socialists; others did not. Typical of this position is the *Revue politique et parlementaire;* in the issue of February 1948 it admitted that the *plan Mayer* in itself is sound enough but unfortunately unworkable. For confidence is lacking and confidence can be reestablished only if controls and nationalization are suppressed, if unadulterated liberalism is put into practice. Otherwise, *"les sacrifices seraient vains."* This absolutism, incidentally, contrasts with the more realistic position taken by the British Tories toward the welfare state.

The situation was complicated by the division within the ranks of the leftist Union. Although united on the principles of economic liberalism, the Radicals split over the question of the régime, a majority following M. Herriot, champion of the Third Force, a minority M. Daladier, sympathetic to De Gaulle. "Political bigamy," lamented Herriot, but he was unable to bring about party discipline on this all-important issue. Only in bigamy could the Radical party prosper. This, of course, gave ambitious men, such as M. Pleven, their chance to try to establish a rapprochement between the Third Force and De Gaulle—in effect weakening the resistance of the Center and adding to the general confusion.

Thus two conditions were lacking that would have made for a cohesive and effective coalition government: agreement on major issues, and party discipline. Much has been written on the basic differences between the Third and Fourth Republics: the new electoral system and the reflex of *"voter utile,"* it is said, have led to the formation of large and disciplined parties.[4] A deputy no longer dares to rebel against the leadership of his party, lest he not find his name on the electoral list at the next election. This is true enough of the Big Three —Communists, MRP, and Socialists—notwithstanding the conflict in the latter party between the *Comité directeur,* representing the more doctrinaire *militants,* and the parliamentary group, representing the electors and generally aware of unpleasant political necessities.[5]

But party discipline largely stops at the right of the MRP. The smaller groups, anxious to keep everyone within the party satisfied, have been incapable of presenting a united front on many issues. If the government could always count on some 150 MRP deputies and 100 Socialists, it was still fortunate to have on its side a majority of Radicals and one-half of the UDSR, depending on the issues at stake.

[4] See François Goguel, "Les Partis sous la 4e République," *Politique,* IV (October 1947), 685 ff.; and Leo Hamon, "Le Régime politique de la 4e République," *Politique,* IV (June 1947), 385 ff.

[5] This awkward situation, incidentally, was ended in December 1949, at the last extraordinary congress of the party. *Le Monde,* December 13, December 16, 1949.

The point could be made that France suffers not from the rigidity imposed by disciplined parties—as has often been said, and perhaps rightly so at the time of the Big Three government—but from too great elasticity, due to the lack of discipline of the smaller parties.

Had the Socialists and MRP constituted a majority in parliament, France would probably have had a stable and efficient government, for both parties are disciplined and show a large measure of agreement on economic and social issues. The other issues remain—military expenditures, Catholic schools, colonial policy—but have been of secondary importance. Perhaps they could have been kept in the pocket of each party, agitated only at the right time for electoral purposes. The remarkable thing is not that the clerical issue remains, but that it has not prevented a loyal and active cooperation between Socialists and Catholics.

Thus the Radicals appear to be the villains. This is not to say that they are wrong in preaching liberalism or that the Socialists are right in demanding a planned and controlled economy. Perhaps either policy carried out with enough consistency and forcefulness would have proved successful. But both could not be pursued at the same time by a coalition divided against itself. The compromise reached combined the worst features of each doctrine: it made for inefficient controls by the administration, and yet for lack of confidence on the part of the investors and the taxpayers.[6]

The greatest handicap of the Third Force has been the impossibility of forming another type of coalition. A realignment of parties on economic and social issues was prevented by the very presence of two powerful Extremes. Enforced cohabitation of Radicals and Socialists was the result of a lack of an acceptable alternative. The bond that held the Third Force together was a negative one—the fear of an authoritarian or totalitarian régime, should one of the parties in the coalition pass to the opposition. Significantly, the Socialists' withdrawal from the cabinet has proved to be not a *cure d'opposition* but, at best, a *cure d'abstention*. They have the government at their mercy, but they cannot afford to overthrow it.

In this connection, the ministerial crises of the last two years should not be taken, and in France were not taken, too seriously. They were a means of letting off steam, of putting pressure on one or the other co-members of the coalition, of finding a new *assiette* a little more or a little less to the Right. To some extent they represented a childish gesture of resentment: we do not like this policy and we will prove it to you militants and electors by backing out. But everyone knew

[6] Paul Fraisse, "La Crise d'automne," *Esprit*, XVII (November 1949), 833 ff. On the incoherence of the Radicals' policy, see *Le Monde*, December 29, December 30, 1949.

that the play had to go on. The fact that the Socialists managed to accept M. Reynaud and his program for a time is more remarkable than the fact that they could not do so for very long.

It is paradoxical that five years after the Liberation, the upper bourgeoisie, condemned in 1944 and 1945 as unworthy of leadership, should now be more influential than before the war. It has been quick to realize the importance of winning friends and influencing people, now that the state plays such an essential economic role. Industrial lobbies are most effective in blocking legislation and in obtaining compensations and advantages. Selfish interests can be rationalized to appear as conditions of national progress. To take a single example: A wealthy glass manufacturer was told by a friend at the time the price of glass had been doubled, "Now, at last, you can raise the wages of your workers." "Oh, impossible," he answered, "that would be inflation!" Thus the scandal can continue of prices at the coefficient 20, and wages at the coefficient 12.[7] The result is mass dissatisfaction, the appeal of Communism, and indirectly the appeal of neo-Gaullism, viewed as the best rampart against revolution.

Not only the workers, but salaried employees and people with fixed incomes are embittered by the unfair distribution of national wealth. They see the "conspicuous consumption" of the *nouveaux riches* of the black market, of industrialists and middlemen, and—until recently —of many farmers. Expectations created by the Liberation have been frustrated, inequalities maintained or created that do not appear necessary, sacrifices imposed on some and not others.

But the government, pressed by the challenge of the Extremes, has been incapable of decisive action against inflation. The two most important reforms in connection with the budget, and thus in connection with the problem of inflation—reform of the tax system, which is complicated, inefficient, unfair; and reform of administration, which has too many people doing too little—could not be undertaken except in a superficial way. There were many technical obstacles to genuine reforms, and there was, above all, a political obstacle: the government could not afford to step on too many toes if it wanted to survive. Farmers, middlemen, public servants were among its supporters, and the Communists and the Gaullists were ready to comfort them and to excite them, as they showed early in 1948 when the Mayer Plan was launched. Since the two Extremes do not represent a loyal opposition, they can capitalize on all mistakes, and be as demagogic

---

[7] This discrepancy is somewhat reduced by the increase in social security benefits borne largely by the employer. It is difficult, however, to measure the incidence of these benefits on the real income of the workers or to determine their psychological consequences. Higher nominal wages may well appear to workers and salaried employees as more desirable.

as they please; they can thus prevent the adoption of measures that are unpopular, however imperative.

Lack of effective action to redress injustices could only increase tensions and with them the temptation to use the coercive apparatus of the state against manifestations of displeasure. It became a question of suppressing Communist-inspired agitation rather than of alleviating the problems that made this agitation effective. A certain insensitivity to wrongs developed out of the fears inspired by public clamor. Many measures advocated by the CGT were automatically turned down as Communist-inspired; even the Force Ouvrière borrowed this negative outlook. Thus the fight against a party turned out to be waged at the expense of a class. The Communist Party could only benefit from this situation, since it could further identify the interests of the workers with those of Communism. A negative policy of physical containment came to take the place of positive action for improved distribution (just as the Atlantic Treaty might replace the Marshall Plan, at least in part, as the primary instrument of defense against Communism).[8]

Moreover, the Extremes benefited by their strategic position. Each created conditions—fear, insecurity—that justified its existence and its premises. The Communists could point to the dialectics involved, the inevitability of the Fascist stage of decadent monopoly capitalism; the Gaullists appeared justified in posing as the protectors of Western civilization. Many were those who voted not for the Extreme they liked best, but for the one they feared least, the one which seemed to offer the best protection against the most imminent danger. Thus the two Extremes could feed on each other: each had a vested interest in strengthening the other, since that was a condition of its own growth. The RPF's main successes have been in the cities and industrial areas where Communism was also strong. Similarly, the Communists have benefited here and there from the fear of Reaction. We have all heard the thesis frequently put forward of the Communists' Machiavellian, if questionable, strategy of bringing about a Gaullist victory in the hope that it would expedite their own ultimate triumph. The fact remains that a process of polarization did take place in 1948, particularly in cities and industrial areas, that can be explained by mutual intimidation and fear.[9]

[8] See E. Mounier, "Devant nous," *Esprit*, xv (December 1947), 940 ff.

[9] At the election of Versailles-Ouest on February 15, 1948, the Communist Party obtained 43.1 per cent of the votes, as against 32.9 per cent in 1947. SFIO and MRP candidates withdrew at the second ballot, giving the RPF a majority. At Épernay on April 11, 1948, the Communist Party obtained 37.9 per cent of the votes, as against 29.9 per cent in 1947. The SFIO had only 9 per cent (14.5 per cent in 1947). At Firminy the Communist Party raised its share of the vote from 39.5 per cent in October 1947 to 46.1 per cent in December 1948; the Third Force passed from 31.8 per cent to 26.4 per cent.

The Extremes can capitalize on emotions and prejudices, leaving
the unfortunate Center to continue its appeal to reason with diminishing success. They can unveil the picture of the millennium to come.
Escapism—whether the futurism of the Communists or the archaism
of De Gaulle—is unfortunately more attractive than the recollection
of sordid realities and appeals to daily responsibilities.

A number of observers have noted the demoralization of many
Frenchmen, a certain cynicism or *"je m'en foutisme";* for there seems
to be little hope for social peace, prosperity, harmony—and morale
and morality are closely linked. If hope is not present, effort has little
meaning. Tax-evasion and other forms of antisocial conduct are justified by the convenient belief that sacrifices would be in vain. The
Republic can be charged with all evils so long as it remains unable
to inspire active loyalty. The Third Force, lacking a *mystique,* appears to most as a *"combinaison politicienne,"* as De Gaulle labeled
it, and the Extremes have an easy task in mobilizing the younger people who are eager to fight for a cause. The distribution of age groups
among the Third forces is significant in this respect.

The philosophy of the Third Force, as expressed by Blum, Hauriou,
Maritain, and others, is a sober and mature one, holding forth no
promise of a sudden paradise and demanding constant effort and
patience.[10] In a period of stress and struggle, national and international, it finds it difficult to compete with the short-cut to happiness
presented by the Communists or with the simple institutional remedy
presented by De Gaulle. The very need for social peace through
solidarity and faith actually helps the Extremes which make solidarity impossible. The dividing forces feed upon the dread of division—
for they offer the easy way to national unity.

The attempts to teach the citizen his responsibility by having him
participate in policy decisions at the local as well as at the national
level have been courageously made by Catholics and Socialists, but
it is a most difficult undertaking. A highly centralized administration
has for many generations created the dichotomy of Sovereign State
and Sovereign Individual—of an order imposed from above and a
freedom asserted from below. The concept of responsible freedom,
slowly acquired by the Englishman through the practice of self-rule,
is unknown to many Frenchmen. It is up to the State, not to the Community, to bring order and justice: it is *their* business, not *my* business.

It is even questionable whether a tolerant, realistic, and social outlook can be created so long as the conflict of ideologies remains what
it is. The British people can afford to be pragmatic, since they hap-

10 See Albert Gortais, "La Signification politique du Congrès de Toulouse," *Politique,*
v (July–August 1948), 612 ff. See also his *Démocratie et libération* (Paris, 1947).

pen to agree on common premises and ultimate values. For the French, political religions are necessary weapons of attack and defense; they also preclude a calm and realistic appraisal of common needs. Every problem is examined through the colored glasses of one's own ideology. Class and party interests and values obscure those of the community at large.

II

All this is not to be taken as a condemnation of the Third Force, but as a general statement of the difficulties it faces. In spite of these difficulties the government has done a creditable job. It has courageously, if not altogether effectively, attacked some of the dangerous problems, such as inflation, the black market, taxation, administrative reforms, and nationalization. It has continued to put into practice the ambitious, perhaps overambitious, Monnet Plan and has helped French economy to recover. What credit can be given the government for recovery is open to question. The ERP certainly played a major part, and perhaps the rise of industrial and agricultural production happened in spite of, rather than because of, governmental action or inaction. In any case, the prestige of the Third Force has benefited from improved economic conditions.

In the international field, the successive governments have faced the weakened power position of France with growing realism. The concept of the "grandeur and prestige" of France lyrically described by De Gaulle has been replaced by a more sober acceptance of realities. The problem of national defense and welfare has been regarded from a reluctantly nationalistic viewpoint. This applies less to colonial policy than to the policy of economic, military, and political cooperation with the West. There is some evidence that the Third Force would welcome the creation of a federated Europe. The enormous difficulties that its realization presents do not prevent its usefulness as a myth, perhaps the most useful myth to oppose the Communist millennium and the Gaullist promise of salvation by constitutional reform. There is a growing awareness that France is no longer an adequate unit of defense and welfare, that a new formula must be found, short of world government, to establish a modicum of stability and security in an atomic age and a bipolar world.

The main accomplishment of the Third Force has been its demonstration of an ability to survive. The government has shown calmness, discrimination, and courage in its handling of a most difficult and dangerous situation. By proving that it could cope with revolutionary strike movements, it reestablished the authority of the state and hence diminished the appeal of the RPF. It is possible that neo-Gaullism has to be either very strong or practically non-existent, that a weak RPF would lose its reason for being. Hence the weakening of the Rassemblement in the last two years might conceivably assume the proportions of a rout. Another weakness of the RPF is the mounting resentment of a large section of big business and finance, which sees in the General an obstacle to the trend toward economic liberalism that has manifested itself elsewhere. If it were not for the General, a Right-Center coalition might well have come into being, leaving the Socialists in the opposition, and giving capital an even better chance. An authoritarian régime is only a lesser evil for many capitalists, notwithstanding the Marxian analysis.

Should the RPF pass away, it would be arithmetically possible to constitute a Right-Center coalition and allow the Socialists to take their *cure d'opposition*. For whatever the past justification for making a bid to the Right, sooner or later a bid will have to be made to the Left—that is, an attempt be made to reconquer the workers, peasants, and intellectuals now on the Communist bandwagon. Perhaps it is too late for the Socialist Party to compete with the Communist. The wrinkled old lady may have lost all her charms and be unable to discover the Fountain of Youth. In that case, another Socialist party may be created between SFIO and Communists. There are indications of at least a need for such a party in the so-called Fourth Force, a strange coalition of personalists, existentialists, revolutionary syndicalists, anarchists, Trotskyites, and Titoists. The formula appeals at present only to intellectuals, but a new party may find working class support, thanks to Communist and Soviet mistakes.

Perhaps many voters for the Communist ticket may be made to realize that catastrophic change is unlikely (except through the atomic bomb) and that peaceful change is being prevented by the Communist party itself. In a very real sense, a vote for the party is not a *"vote utile,"* but as negative as a vote for the RPF. Thanks to the party, the working class is largely absent from the determination of national policy, an absence which upsets the balance between the social forces of the country to the benefit of conservative elements.

III

In France past memories preclude a presidential system of government. A one-party or corporative system is obviously undesirable. So is a two-party system, since the minority would have little reason to trust the majority. A three-party system would be a fine solution, corresponding to the main positions on economic and social issues:

a progressive Center in alliance with either a conservative Right or a Socialist Left would be able to act alternatively as an engine or as a brake. However, this is out of the question, if only because of the presence of two irreconcilable Extremes, not to mention the reluctance of parties to commit suicide.

Under these conditions, the multiparty system appears inevitable, but it must allow for efficient leadership. Two conditions are necessary for a coalition to be efficient: disciplined parties and agreement on major issues. A third condition is a sufficient weakening of the Extremes to admit an acceptable alternative. Only then can a homogeneous coalition representing either liberalism or plannism be formed.

The MRP, however weakened, is likely to hold the balance of power for some time to come: its past performance indicates that it can be realistic and pragmatic enough to ally itself now with the conservatives, now with the Socialists. The *parti-charnière* would prevent too abrupt changes of economic policy and create an atmosphere of stability, yet not of immobility.

The more immediate problem is that of the electoral reform to which much talk and some thought are being devoted. The problem is perhaps insoluble, for the need to weaken the Extremes condemns proportional representation, while the need to keep party discipline precludes the uninominal system of the Third Republic. M. Blum made proposals to combine both systems which may well combine the disadvantages of each. In *Esprit,* in January 1950, F. Goguel wrote one of his stimulating articles on electoral reform—coming out in favor of a list system of proportional representation with two ballots, the first requiring an absolute majority for election, the second a relative majority. It is to be feared, however, that few deputies would be elected on the first ballot, and that on the second the Extremes might benefit by the embarrassing choice left to the electors. Fear of Communism may lead to Gaullism, and vice versa.

Some Socialists and Catholics have advocated a close electoral alliance of SFIO and MRP; some even have proposed their fusion into a single party. It is doubtful whether this solution would appeal to the leftwing Socialists or the rightwing Catholics, since *"voter utile"* may not be the major motivation of anticlericals and anti-Marxists. If a Third Force coalition is created, it may be good for electoral purposes, but bad for the purpose of obtaining a cohesive majority. For such an electoral coalition would weaken the authority of party leadership and add to the confusion over economic and social issues.

Electoral gadgets thus seem to offer as little promise as constitutional gadgets—including the right of dissolution.

For the problem is deeper: it is not the machinery that creates a

consensus, but rather the other way around. This does not mean that
the machinery is totally irrelevant, but that it has very definite limitations. To put too much faith in the virtue of institutions is another
form of escapism.[11]

IV

Seen in historical perspective, the present division of French politics into three forces is not an accident, or an unhappy consequence
of the war. The thesis can be advanced that France, ever since the
Revolution, has seen the competition of three major ideologies corresponding to the three forces of today. These may be called authoritarian, equalitarian, and libertarian, since the dominant value in
each was respectively authority, equality, and liberty. Each ideology
took several forms and included several idea-systems according to
period, circumstance, and clientele. Their coexistence created conditions that maintained the appeal of Extreme Right and Extreme Left
and prevented the Center, whenever in power, from exercising effective leadership.

The authoritarian system of values included two main currents,
traditionalist and Bonapartist, which tended to merge under the banner of integral nationalism. They had in common the belief in a
leader, an élite, and a creed; they both reflected a passionate need for
order in a frozen hierarchical society, an order that was to be imposed
by force if necessary. This need betrayed a deep sense of insecurity,
perhaps born of failure. Many conservatives felt that they had been
unable to retain the faith of the masses in their own leadership and
became inclined to impose their rule in order to keep their threatened
privileges.

It was in times of crisis, when people felt insecure, that the authoritarian movement gathered strength, as in 1848, when Louis Napoleon
led the party of Order. Under the Third Republic many conservatives
were reluctant Republicans, easily susceptible to the appeal of the
strong man who would protect them from real and imaginary dangers.
This was particularly true after World War I, when the authoritarian
ideology grew under the double impact of international Communism
and Fascism. Fortunately the division among the Leagues, the absence
of an undisputed leader, and the indifference of peasant and *petits
bourgeois* saved France from Fascism, if not from defeat. Mussolini,

---

[11] " 'Change the institutions and all will be well,' we are told. This is the old belief
in *'politique d'abord,'* based on the illusion that there can be perfect institutions. The
leadership principle and the faith in a miracle only increase this tendency, all the more
dangerous since it develops in the people the spirit of *démission* which is the death of
democracy." Albert Gortais to the Congress of Toulouse, *Le Monde*, May 8, 1948.

Franco, and even Hitler had found many supporters among Rightist elements. After the defeat of 1940 Pétain appeared to them as a savior, and a few years after the Liberation most of them rallied behind De Gaulle.

The main appeal of the authoritarian movement seems to have been fear of social upheaval. But this fear fed upon itself: a reactionary position could only encourage the revolutionary movement, the strength of which in turn justified the premises of the authoritarians. Each Extreme found in the presence of the other sufficient food for its own growth.

The equalitarian ideology which took the form of orthodox Marxism and revolutionary syndicalism, before becoming Communism, was anchored in an emotional basis: exclusive emphasis on equality, to be obtained through catastrophic change, betrays a deep sense of "injustice," just as the appeal of order for the Rightists betrayed a sense of insecurity. For it was the moral appeal in Karl Marx, not the intellectual structure he erected, that was convincing. He presented to people who felt unfairly treated by society both the promise of a millennium in a just order and the means of realizing it. To the working class, in particular, the memories of the June days of 1848 and of the Commune of 1871 added to the resentment caused by the indifference of the ruling classes to the plight of the workers. Unlike those in Great Britain, trade-unions in France remained weak and ineffective. Social legislation was inadequate. But one reason for this unhappy state of affairs was the systematic opposition of the Socialists to cooperation with bourgeois parties. Guesde prevented Jaurès from leading a reformist party similar to the Labor Party in Britain. Not until after World War I did the split occur between the revolutionary wing of SFIO, now the Communist Party, and the humanistic reformist wing under Blum's leadership.

What characterizes the equalitarian ideology is thus its subordination of freedom to the goal of equality. Until the classless society is established, it is said, freedom is but a bourgeois luxury, formal democracy an institutional device to protect the bourgeois monopoly of power. Peaceful change is by definition impossible; only a violent revolution can bring about the good society—an article of faith that fitted well the traditional French belief in progress through barricades. This belief led to a course of action that further strengthened the faith in revolution. Trade-unions that were to be first of all instruments for the conquest of power had a limited appeal for the workers and of course for the employers. Nor was social legislation forthcoming, since the workers had no way of exercising effective political pressure through a party that was in perpetual opposition to the government. The revolutionary temper kept feeding on the indifference of the middle classes for which it was partly responsible.

Between these two extremes, the liberal democratic ideology found it difficult to develop and mature. Two conditions for successful democracy were lacking that were present in England: a set of institutions, mainly the two-party system, that had gradually evolved and presented early enough a satisfactory machinery for peaceful change, and a set of attitudes developed during the formative period of democracy that enabled the British people to face the need for compromises in a spirit of realism and tolerance. Given the luck of an early consensus, the process of gradualism that maintained the consensus could take place: for each reform strengthened the security of the privileged classes, since it bolstered social cohesion and the sense of self-realization of the nonprivileged who saw clearly the constitutional road to progress. Freedom, redefined to fit new needs, could maintain its appeal, since the system could grant enough security and "justice."

In France institutional continuity had been abruptly ended by the Revolution of 1789. Hardly had freedom been proclaimed, than it had to be sacrificed for the sake of Republican defense. A cycle of Revolution-Reaction was started in 1789 that dominated two-thirds of the nineteenth century. The attempts made by the Restoration and the July monarchy to reconcile the authority of the state with the freedom of the individual failed. Each new régime felt obliged to maintain itself by force and by corruption, neither of which encouraged loyalty and responsibility toward the state. Each régime was forced to keep the highly centralized, omnipotent, omnicompetent administration which prevented the citizen from learning about self-rule. Freedom for the libertarians meant freedom-with-anarchy rather than freedom-with-responsibility. It was also freedom-with-equality, the belief that liberty meant equality under the law, the absence of privilege.

The Third Republic, too, had to use the weapon of the centralized state against its enemies of the Right and the Left. Several consequences ensued. Paradoxically, the strong state necessary to protect the Republic made for a weak government, since weakness was considered necessary to protect the individual against possible abuses of power. The main duty of the deputy was to keep watch over the government and through it over the permanent bureaucracy. To overthrow the government periodically was considered a Republican duty. The multiparty system itself was reassuring, since it prevented a possible concentration of power and rendered a coalition government harmless. But weak and unstable governments also made for a congenital inability to face important issues, to draw up a long-range program and to implement it.

The immobility of the coalition government, which prevented a re-alignment of parties on economic and social issues, was largely the result of the lack of an acceptable alternative. The Center could maintain itself in power because the Right was untrustworthy and the Left was uncooperative. Since the Dreyfus affair, the Radicals could govern France with the support of either Center-Right or Center-Left. They were in a convenient position to play the Left against the Right when at election time they appealed to Republican solidarity, and the Right against the Left when, once elected, they appealed to the defense of the franc. The anticlerical issue having proved its electoral usefulness, it was unnecessary to face the dangerous economic and social issues. The *raison d'être* of the Radicals was Republican defense; it was sufficient for the party to exist and unnecessary, even dangerous, for it to create. For the peasant proprietors and *petits bourgeois* who voted Radical were profoundly uninterested in the problems created by the machine and deeply suspicious of both capital and labor. The workers, whose votes were not sought for, were without means of having their demands realized. French economy suffered, since the Center was anxious to protect agricultural interests to the detriment of the industrial development of the country as well as at the expense of the living standards of the whole population.

In England there were enough reformers within each party to make possible a process of revaluation that kept the supreme value of freedom meaningful to all; freedom came to mean the maximum development of all men's potentialities, real equality of opportunity, even at the expense of existing privileges. In France this process of revaluation was blocked by fears and prejudices. Catholic reformers, such as De Mun and La Tour du Pin, often remained authoritarian after they became convinced of the need for social reforms. A tendency toward paternalism and corporativism took the place of the process of revaluation in England. Similarly, Republicans could find in anticlericalism the basis of a good conscience, and Marxists remained convinced that nothing short of the classless society would do. A realignment of parties on economic and social issues was prevented by the appeal of myths and symbols that retained the old divisions and old misunderstandings.

Frenchmen have often stressed their political intelligence, as contrasted with British muddleheadedness and opportunism. If the test of political intelligence is the ability of a people to face new realities, discuss them in a realistic manner and take steps accordingly, then the British, it must be said, have shown greater political intelligence than the French. The principles to which the French are attached reflect both intellectual rigidity—owing perhaps to the influence of the educational system—and emotional volatility, both of which are a consequence of the conflict described above. It would be legitimate to speak of this as an escapist attitude, for the supposed principles involved were often irrelevant and inapplicable to new conditions. They belonged to an electoral vocabulary that was expected of every candidate, but not binding upon him, if only because people voted not for a governmental team, as in England, but at best for a part of a team, the composition of which was unknown to the voters at election time. The apparently greater choice offered by the many parties in France was not an effective choice, since the program of the government-to-be was established not before elections for ratification by the people, but afterwards among parliamentary groups without direct responsibility to the electorate.

One result was general indifference toward the business of government, in spite of the national habit of discussing political principles. Politics had a bad name, since it involved compromises that clashed with the principles proclaimed at election time. The citizen felt that his entire civic duty was discharged by his going to the polls once every four years. Having done his duty, he was free to criticize a government that was never of his own choice—since he did not vote for that particular coalition—and even to cheat the state to the best of his ability.

Lack of civic responsibility does not reflect a tendency to amorality. It must be looked upon less as a matter of morals, than as a matter of morale, the reflection of an unsatisfactory legal order, for which it is not considered worthwhile to make sacrifices. To a large extent, it is a reflex of individual defense corresponding to the reflex of collective defense that characterizes the reactionary and the revolutionary ideology. This reflex justifies the role of the omnipotent state as the dispenser of order; it is the apparent justification, but also the basic fallacy, of the authoritarian solution.

There is no easy way out. In the absence of a psychological foundation for successful democracy in France, institutional devices appear to be of little avail. Decentralization, more direct participation of the citizen in public affairs (particularly at the local level), education in civic responsibility of the peasant and of the bourgeois, essential reforms in the tax system and administration, greater participation in politics by trade-unions and cooperatives are of much greater importance than spectacular constitutional reforms that would leave the basic problem unsolved and perhaps make its solution impossible.

10

++

THE CHRISTIAN DEMOCRATS

IN MODERN FRANCE

ROBERT F. BYRNES

++

THE sudden appearance of the Mouvement Républicain Populaire (MRP) constituted one of the most surprising features of immediate postwar developments in France. Hardly more than two years old and lacking an established party apparatus and a solid party organization, the MRP in the elections for the first Constitutional Assembly received 4,500,000 votes and elected 150 deputies. For a political group which, significantly, called itself a movement and not a party, this was a remarkable triumph. Moreover, the emergence of a democratic Center party which was Catholic was hailed both in France and in the rest of the democratic world as evidence of a fine beginning for the Fourth Republic, with most Catholics reconciled to the Republic and with three large parties dominating the entire political scene. Developments within France since 1945 have dampened this early enthusiasm considerably, but these contemporary Christian Democrats still constitute a major political power and one of the principal elements of democratic vitality in France.

I

Even though this is an irreligious age and though most minds have been shaped by ideas and attitudes which during the past two centuries have denied or restricted the significance of religion, there is still no issue more explosive than that which blends religion and politics. The bitterness and violence with which religion is included in political campaigns or excluded from them is not limited to France, or even to countries where Catholicism is the religion of the majority, or where the Catholic Church has ever had a predominant influence or privileged position. Even in the United States, the union of religion and politics has been a dangerous and threatening force. Those in the nineteenth century, for example, who wished to restrict immigration to Protestant groups and to limit the political liberties and rights of some of their fellow Americans were clearly a threat to the maintenance and development of democracy in America. Perhaps the finest illustration of the threat apparent in the union of politics and religion in this country is that all groups and parties which label themselves "Christian" are immediately known as anti-Semitic, anti-Catholic, and, of course, antidemocratic.

The true aim of the Catholic, or of any Christian,[1] in this world is the attainment of eternal life in Heaven. As a consequence, in theory at least, life in this world has only a temporary, minor interest, and the true Catholic should be interested only in his eternal salvation. However, although life in this world is of only secondary concern, the Catholic, even in theory, has a direct interest in society and in the state. The Catholic's duty is not only to attain eternal salvation for himself but also to spread the truth and thereby to enable all others to attain salvation too. Since a Catholic has a wider interest and a wider obligation than his own soul, society and the civil government are of concern to the Catholic and to the Catholic Church.

Briefly, the role of the state is to provide conditions which make it possible and even easy for the individual and the Church to fulfill their duties. The ideal position, so far as any zealous Christian is concerned, is the presence of a state system devoted to the ends of the Church and a secular arm of the Church. Thus, there have been periods in the history of various Christian denominations within various countries—such as the Anglican Church in England, the Russian Orthodox Church in Russia, and the Catholic Church in Spain—where the state on behalf of the dominant Church persecuted and crushed minority groups holding religious beliefs which differed from those of the established Church and the majority group.

The Catholic Church has lived and operated under many different political régimes. Although there is a definite Catholic theory of society, "there is no Catholic theory of the state." The Catholic Church is not committed to any particular form of civil government, so long as it is free to carry on its own mission and so long as fundamental

---

[1] The Christian Democratic parties which have appeared at various times in modern French history are parties formed by Catholics. This paper, therefore, is a discussion of French Catholics. The use of the word "Christian" to apply to these groups or to the entire issue does not mean that there are no other Christians but Catholics in France, that the Catholics alone are Christian, or that the French Catholics alone constitute those French Christians who are also democrats.

human rights are guaranteed. As Cardinal Newman once wrote, "Christianity is at once a philosophy, a political power, and a religious rite. Truth is the guiding principle of theology and theological inquiries; devotion and edification of worship; and of government, expedience." In other words, for the Catholic Church there is "a dependent variability of political values." [2]

However, churches once established in positions of supreme power have used another Christian tenet to justify and to solidify that position and to establish the conviction that a particular form of government has the special blessing of the Church. All Christians believe, in theory, that God is the source of all power, that all power by nature thus has a divine character. Resistance to the established power is thus represented as resistance against the will of God. This Christian belief concerning the source and nature of political power, and the fact that only recently in modern times have political democracies appeared, have led to the mistaken assumption by many Christians, particularly Catholics, and by many critics of Catholicism or of the tenets of the political philosophies shared by many leading Catholics, that the Catholic Church prefers and even desires monarchical or even autocratic political systems. Traditions and philosophies die slowly in countries where a church has once held supreme power, but, nevertheless, the history of the past two centuries in particular has led many Catholics to return to the original philosophical principle: no one form of state and no one state system has any special blessing from the Church, so long as the Church is allowed to fulfill its mission.

Catholic political thought has rather naturally reflected in general the societies in which Catholics have lived. Catholics in increasingly democratic states during the past two centuries have therefore seen clearly that a democracy is as legitimate in the view of Christian political theory as a monarchy, provided it does not persecute the Church. As a matter of fact, many Catholics, especially in France, England, and the United States, have come to believe that a political and social democracy is a far more logical consummation of Christian beliefs concerning the nature of man than a monarchical or autocratic society. Millions of French Catholics even before the French Revolution sought a more democratic government for France, and during the nineteenth century there began the ferment which led to the formation during the 1890's of the first Christian Democratic party in France. The MRP, which is far more democratic politically and so-

---

[2] Gabriel A. Almond, "The Political Ideas of Christian Democracy," *Journal of Politics*, x (1948), 750; W. J. Fitzgerald, "The Idea of Democracy in Contemporary Catholicism," *Review of Religion*, xii (1948), 150.

cially than its predecessors, represents a further stage in this development, which may ultimately prove to be the salvation of the Catholic
Church in France as well as of democracy there.

For many Frenchmen, educated in the anticlerical and even anti-
Christian tradition, the combination of words, Christian and Democrat, is a contradiction in terms. For most Americans, the combination of terms represents a natural and even inevitable alliance. The
principal reason for this important distinction lies in the fact that
American political thought and institutions derive mainly from the
English system and tradition, in which the influence of Judaism and
of Christianity has been great. The French democratic tradition, however, derives in large part from the French Revolution, which, in seeking to free politics from the clergy and to establish the supremacy
of the lay state over all religions, also undermined Christianity itself.
An English or American democrat therefore finds that Christianity
is a part of his democratic inheritance, while a French democrat often
believes that democracy can be secure only when the Church, if not
Christianity, is crippled or even destroyed.

The French Christian Democrats are those Catholics who refuse
to accept this assumption, or its reverse, that the Church will be secure only when democracy in France is crippled or destroyed. While
remaining Catholic, they believe and assert that the Church should
break its alliance with ancient privilege and return to the people and
the Republic. They have been resolute supporters and critics of both
the Third Republic and the Fourth Republic. Their aim has been
to give France a government which was democratic and Catholic and
which was interested in the rights and welfare of all Frenchmen.
Neither in their programs nor in their action have they been consistently democratic, but that applies also to other democratic parties
in other democracies. They have suffered heavily from the political
and intellectual tradition common to almost all French Catholics
in the nineteenth century, but they have made remarkable progress,
especially during the last fifty years.

II

The significance of the Christian Democrats in modern France can
be understood and evaluated best if related not only to the background of French history but also to the development of similar movements in other countries. None of the Christian Democrats or Christian Socialists has sought to establish a Christian society. They aim
to reform society in the light of Christian ethics. These movements

or parties developed in every case as a revolt against the obvious social and moral evils created by the Industrial Revolution and the attitude toward those evils shown by liberal and conservative governments. They have attacked and rejected the individualism and emphasis on selfish personal interest which is so basic a part of capitalism, and they have insisted that Christian ethics be applied to the political and social order. This attitude has gone far beyond the concept of charity, but it has not yet reached to Socialism, at least not to the definition of Socialism generally accepted in the Western world. At the same time, most of the Christian Democratic or Christian Socialist parties have failed to attain a clear understanding even of political democracy. These movements or parties in France, Germany, and Austria until the Second World War often were anti-Semitic, and in the attitude of both the English groups and of Sturzo's Italian party there was a clear failure to reject consistently the remnants of aristocratic and even autocratic ideas. However, in every case the criticism made by each of these parties of the existing social systems was valid and valuable, and the social classes involved took important steps toward bridging the gaps between organized Christianity and political and social democracy.

The first Christian Democratic or Christian Socialist movement outside France developed in England shortly after the Revolution of 1848. There the critique of British industrialism and of the new society by Carlyle, Coleridge, and the Chartists influenced a few serious-minded Anglicans, led by Ludlow, Maurice, and Kingsley, to try to eliminate the gross evils and to awaken Englishmen to their Christian duties. These men sought, briefly, to apply Christian ethics to social problems, to educate the workers, to foster cooperatives, and to save the reputation of religion in England by awakening the middle class to its Christian obligations. This movement failed by 1855, and somewhat similar attempts in the 1870's and 1880's also were unsuccessful.

Protestantism in Germany was even less fortunate, for the Christian Socialist Workers' Party, formed in 1878 by the court chaplain, Adolf Stoecker, was never Christian, democratic, or Socialist. Stoecker founded the party to wean the Berlin workers from Socialism, and it soon became a middle-class crusade weapon against the Socialists and Jews. It was particularly strong, especially in the capital, from 1881 to 1884, and at one time it collected 300,000 names on a petition to the German government asking that Jews be excluded from all national schools, universities, and public offices. This Protestant party collapsed almost as quickly as it had appeared, but the German Catholic version of the Christian Democratic movement was far more successful and influential.[3]

The Center Party had roots in Bavaria even before 1848, and after the failure of the Liberals to unify Germany the German Catholics organized and worked for the unification of the country. When unification was achieved, this party therefore developed quickly into a major national political group. Supported by millions of agricultural and industrial workers, by large sections of the middle class, and by many women, the Center Party profited from the political situation to hold the balance between the Right and the Left. This party was one of the largest and most influential during both the Empire and the Weimar Republic. It was one of the most genuinely democratic parties in modern Germany, and although it suffered from generally conservative leadership, as most confessional parties do, it was a bulwark of German democracy throughout these years.

Christian Democracy or Christian Socialism in Austria has a far less enviable record. This Catholic group was formed originally by Dr. Karl Lueger, who was, with Joseph Chamberlain, one of the pioneers of "municipal socialism." As mayor of Vienna from 1896 through 1910, Lueger made the city "the most 'socialized' and best administered city" of the era. Lueger showed great ability, too, in organizing a nationalist party which was conservative, and at the same time he offered a social reform program sufficiently dynamic to attract at least the lower middle class. He used anti-Semitism to bind the party together, and the Christian Socialists maintained their rule in Vienna and in Austria from 1895 until 1938.

The price of this "success" was, of course, the failure of Christianity, democracy, and Austria, for the party founded by Lueger was never either truly Christian or Socialist. Hitler described Lueger as "the greatest German mayor of all time." It was in Lueger's Vienna that Hitler became acquainted with what he called "the Jewish problem." The Christian Socialist newspaper, the *Volksblatt*, was the source of many of Hitler's beliefs. As a young man, Hitler sold this newspaper and the party's pamphlets on the streets of Vienna.[4]

Christian Democracy developed later in Italy than in most other western European countries. There it was a Catholic priest, Don Luigi Sturzo, who after the close of the First World War persuaded the Pope to allow Catholics to participate again in Italian politics. Advocating a policy of political and social reform, decentralization,

[3] Walter Frank, *Hofprediger Adolf Stoecker und die christlichsoziale Bewegung* (Berlin, 1928), pp. 39–375; Carlton J. H. Hayes, *A Generation of Materialism, 1871–1900* (New York, 1941), p. 262.

[4] Adolf Hitler, *Mein Kampf* (New York, 1939), pp. 72–78, 88, 124–30; Konrad Heiden, *Der Fuehrer* (Boston, 1944), pp. 62–66.

and freedom of education, Sturzo collected millions of Catholic votes for his Popular Party. The movement was divided and then destroyed by Mussolini, however, and Don Sturzo fled Italy and the Fascists. The Christian Democratic movement in Italy after the Second World War has developed in part in the Sturzo tradition, but the responsibilities of office and the influx of groups neither really Christian nor democratic has made the party very conservative.

It is clear from this brief survey that Christian Democracy outside of France during the past century has been unsuccessful. Whether Protestant or Catholic, the parties have been defeated by suspicion on the Right and the Left, by the general shallowness of the practical Christianity and democracy of many of their members, and by their identification with the upper and middle classes and those classes' interests. The only instances where the Christian Democrats obtained power for any significant period represent defeats more than victories, for the parties successful were neither truly democratic nor truly Christian.

III

Post-Revolutionary Christian Democracy in France really begins with Lamennais, whose life and career illustrate the difficulties facing a Catholic who sought to embrace democracy in the nineteenth century in France. Buffeted and bruised by the French Revolution, most Catholics in France turned toward the papacy and tradition after 1815. Lamennais himself early in his career as a priest was a fervent monarchist and ultramontane, and it was only after the stupidity of Charles X had shown him how complete a disaster might ensue from alliance with the monarchy that he became radical and democratic. His newspaper, *Avenir*, had "God and Liberty" as its motto, and Lamennais hoped to free the Church from the state, and then turn its interest toward the mass of oppressed. One of his followers once wrote, "Freedom, and freedom only, is what the Church needs," and the emphasis in Lamennais' thought as a Christian Democrat is on freedom of education, freedom of the press, freedom of association, and freedom of worship. Since he came to believe that only a republic could provide justice and freedom, he became a Republican and urged all French Catholics to follow him. These beliefs and his general aggressive attitude irritated and alarmed the conservative Catholic leaders and masses.

Lamennais failed. His movement was repudiated and condemned by the Pope. Although many Catholics remained Republican and greeted the Second Republic in 1848, the political philosophies of Bonald and De Maistre were those generally accepted by French

Catholic leaders. Lamennais himself left the Church, refusing to return even as he lay dying in 1854. Nevertheless, his influence among French Catholics has been enormous, and the ideas and attitudes he expressed in the early 1830's are now those generally held by most French Catholics. Even Cardinal Baudrillart, who was later, as a very old man, to welcome and support Vichy, wrote in 1903 that Lamennais was "the man who is at the beginning of the intellectual movement of the French clergy and at the source of all great movements at the end of the nineteenth century."

The defeat of the Christian Democrats under the July Monarchy gave intellectual predominance over French Catholics to the antidemocratic forces. As a result, when the Second Republic's Falloux Law of 1850 allowed freedom of education, the increasing number of Catholic schools spread an authoritarian, ultramontane philosophy based on De Maistre and Bonald. The policy of Napoleon III in Italy made religion more than ever a pressing political issue, so that the Third Republic at its origin inherited a religious-political issue almost as sharp as it had been in 1792. The Republicans thus assumed that to be a democrat one had also to be anticlerical and agnostic, or even atheistic. Therefore, when the Republicans obtained full control of the Republic, they proceeded to strip all power from what they believed an exclusive and irreconcilable Catholic Church. The vigor and even the brutality with which this was done raised the level of the controversy to a new fierceness and made it increasingly difficult for a Catholic to accept the Republic.[5]

When it became clear to most Frenchmen that the Third Republic was popular and secure, the attitude Catholics should adopt toward the government became a very pressing issue. By about 1890, French Catholics were dividing into three frequently shifting groups. Most of these Catholics sought to obtain a government in France which should give to the Catholic Church a position and influence similar to that which it had enjoyed before the Revolution. Unhappily, they differed widely as to what form of government that should be, how it should be obtained, and what kind of political and social program it should have, once established.

Thus, the Tory or extreme Catholics were devoted to a laissez-faire social philosophy and to a fond belief in benevolent paternalism. They were generally also monarchists, although after 1883 monarchism was more a pious hope than a practical program. They resented

<hr/>

[5] René Rémond, *Lamennais* (Paris, 1948), pp. 17–21, 34–47; Waldemar Gurian, "Lamennais," *Review of Politics*, IX (1947), 206–7, 223–29; David Thomson, *Democracy in France. The Third Republic* (London, 1946), pp. 28–34, 127–29, 135–45; Almond, *loc. cit.*, pp. 738–39.

the industrialization of France and the concomitant rise of another layer of the middle class. Politically, they were very strongly Catholic, although their views and actions in political affairs generally betrayed little real Christian feeling or understanding. Almost all of this group sought to overthrow the Republic during the Dreyfus affair, and it provided much of the money for such authoritarian, antidemocratic organizations as the Action Française. This group, buttressed by other conservatives who have joined it since 1919, has been one of the most stable and dangerous in the history of modern France. It generally supported Vichy, although there were exceptions, and although the mass of the support from the Right for Vichy was by no means clearly Catholic.

The Social Catholics at this time did not differ greatly from the Tory Catholics in political views, for their leaders until the early 1890's were convinced monarchists and those Social Catholics who did adopt the Republic then were generally "reluctant Republicans." The Social Catholics, however, had been seriously influenced by Le Play, and they did believe in the necessity for and the efficacy of practical social legislation to mend the social system and to keep the workers contented. They recognized the industrialization of France as an established fact which could perhaps be directed and controlled by the old ruling classes, but which could certainly not be resisted. They were almost as paternalistic as the Tory Catholics, but they were also more realistic. Much of the very essence of conservatism at its best can be found in the policies of this group. This group was divided by the Dreyfus affair, most of the Social Catholics drifting further to the Right. The appearance of Communism after the First World War quite effectively prevented the maintenance of a movement such as this, almost all of the Social Catholics being driven into joining the Tory Catholics.

There were some French Catholics, however, who by 1890 resolutely and vigorously supported and embraced the Third Republic and the democratic principles upon which it was based. They followed Lamennais in seeking to break the Church alliance with privilege and to acquire popular, mass support from the great mass of Frenchmen. They attacked monopolistic abuse and financial corruption. They recognized that most of the workers were Republican and that it was the duty of the Church and her priests to wean the workers from revolutionary Socialism with a Catholic program of social reform. The leaders of this movement were in great part sincere young Catholic priests and journalists, all anxious to ally the Church with the people in a powerful social party. They were a great source of alarm to the conservative Catholics, for their newspapers and congresses paid little respect to privilege or propertied interests and advocated a real Catholic social democracy. This led to a fear of "another Lamennais" on the Right, while the Republicans and Socialists on the Left were genuinely suspicious of the sincerity of the democratic beliefs of the Christian Democrats.

Pope Leo XIII by 1890 had reached the same decision as the French Christian Democrats, for he "had contemplated, like a new Ezekiel, the valley of dry bones of French Royalist politics and had decided that (barring a political miracle) the cause of the Most Christian King was as dead as that of the Most Serene Republic of Venice." He therefore instituted the policy of *ralliement,* which simply recognized that the great majority of the French people had freely accepted the Republican form of government and that the Church should follow its traditional principle of adapting itself to the government in power. This policy would free the Church and French Catholics from the dead body of monarchism in France and would allow the Catholics to exert far more influence upon the government than the hostile attitude thus far followed had permitted. This policy would, if successful, also soften ultimately the very strong anticlericalism of the French Radicals and Socialists and would lead to the establishment of a more firm foundation for the Third Republic.[6]

IV

The development of the Christian Democratic movement in France during the 1890's can perhaps best be described through an account of the activities and the ideas of one of the able young Catholic priests who became convinced that the Catholic Church had to accept the Republic and political democracy and to promote genuine social reform if it were to continue to thrive. Father Paul Naudet was born in Bordeaux in 1859 and became a professor in a seminary near Bordeaux after his ordination in 1883. He became a stanch Republican and defender of Republican institutions, although the anti-Masonic campaign of the 1880's and Édouard Drumont's writings made him an anti-Semite also. Naudet was never a rabid anti-Semite, however, and in the Dreyfus affair his colleagues were disappointed by his lack of vehemence as an anti-Dreyfusard. As a matter of fact, Father Nau-

---

[6] Georges Weill, *Histoire du mouvement social en France, 1852–1914* (Paris, 1929), pp. 409–24; Denis W. Brogan, *The Development of Modern France* (London, 1940), pp. 257–67; Waldemar Gurian, *Die politischen und sozialen Ideen des französischen Katholizismus* (Munich, 1928), pp. 239–94; Antonin Debidour, *L'Église catholique et l'État sous la Troisième République, 1870–1906* (Paris, 1906–1909), II, 1–78; Dominique Cardinal Ferrata, *Mémoires. Ma Nonciature en France* (Paris, 1922), *passim,* especially pp. 11–31, 66, 77–148, 204–55; Father Édouard Lecanuet, *La Vie de l'Église sous Léon XIII* (Paris, 1930), pp. 610–20; Parker T. Moon, *The Labor Problem and the Social Catholic Movement in France* (New York, 1921), pp. 175, 365–67, 445.

det's newspaper, *Justice sociale,* was the first Catholic newspaper to publish letters favorable to Dreyfus, and it also became an instrument for the Catholic Committee for the Defense of Justice.

While a supporter of the Republic and an advocate of extensive social reform, Father Naudet was an eager opponent of Socialism. His first public address was delivered in 1891 in a working-class suburb of Bordeaux on the connection which should exist between the priest and the worker. A handsome man and an excellent orator, Father Naudet debated successfully on a number of occasions with Jules Guesde and other Socialists. His speeches were so successful that he soon received invitations to address groups of workers, largely Catholic, all over France. In July 1893 he founded in Bordeaux a newspaper, *Justice sociale,* to carry the message of Leo XIII's *Rerum Novarum* to the workers. In this newspaper and in the addresses he delivered during the second half of 1893, he formulated clearly for the first time in France the Christian Democratic doctrine. After he had developed this program, he moved the paper to Paris in January 1894 and rapidly became one of the most influential priests and journalists in the capital. *Justice sociale* remained one of the principal organs of French Catholic social thought from 1893 until 1908, when it foundered during the crisis over modernism.

In October 1894, Father Naudet was named editor of *Le Monde,* which had then only 2,500 subscribers. His success in almost doubling the circulation within a few months, as well as the collapse of this newspaper in July 1896, are alike tributes to his ability as a journalist and to his honesty and perseverance as a believer in the Third Republic and in the need for social change. The principal issue over which *Le Monde* failed was the tax on the property of religious orders passed in March 1895. This was fought before passage and resisted after passage by the conservative Catholics, while Father Naudet denounced the Right for the attitude toward the legislation of the Republic which these actions demonstrated. This stand, in addition to Father Naudet's advocacy of seminary reform, praise of the more democratic American Catholic laity and clergy, and promotion of social legislation, effectively destroyed *Le Monde.* Father Fesch, the city editor of this newspaper, became so disillusioned over the stubbornness, stupidity, and power of the French Right that he abandoned the Christian Democratic movement at that time, but Father Naudet became a more ardent Christian Democrat and continued to fight for over another decade.[7]

[7] Robert Cornilleau, *L'Abbé Naudet* (Paris, 1934), pp. 9–63, 73–98, 144; Léon Chaine, *Les Catholiques français et leurs difficultés actuelles devant l'opinion* (Lyon, 1908), pp. 297–98.

The Christian Democratic movement of the 1890's in France reached its peak in its first congress, held in Lyon during the last week of November in 1896. Widely advertised, bitterly attacked by the Socialists and the conservatives alike, and a cause of much friction among the clergy, this congress attracted 6,000 representatives of anti-Semitic clubs, Father Garnier's political Union Nationale, separate Christian Democratic groups, and associations formed by individual newspapers throughout France. It lasted a week, and it benefited enormously from the fact that so many of its members were journalists.

However, the convocation of this assembly revealed that there was no national Christian Democratic organization, no clear formulation of policy or doctrine, and no simple method of determining who the Christian Democrats were. As a consequence, the principal organizer decided that the congress, "although highly Catholic and Republican," should make an appeal to "all men of good will who wish to join in the common aim of national liberation." The convention was described officially as "less a fusion than a federation of movements and ideas of all those who for Christ, the People, and Liberty work for the triumph of real democracy." The congress was, therefore, really not a national congress of the Christian Democrats, for there was no agreement on policy or organization either before or after it had met. It was a collection of representatives of many groups, all Catholic and all critical of the French social system, but without general agreement as to the political and economic policies which should be adopted to remedy the deficiencies they witnessed. In other words, like other similar movements in modern history, Christian Democracy in France was more certain of what it opposed than of what it proposed.

Thus, one day of the congress was set aside for Father Garnier's Union Nationale; another day was provided for the Catholic press, regardless of the political and economic views of the newspapers represented; a third day was devoted to a study of anti-Semitism, two days to "social reform," another day to Freemasonry. La Tour du Pin, certainly not a Christian Democrat, sent a delegation and had a speech read. There were representatives from such diverse organizations as the Young Catholics' Club of Marseille, the Paris chapter of the National Students' Anti-Semitic League, the Poitevin Anti-Semitic League of Small Businessmen, and the Lille Catholic Workers' Club. There were no clear debates and no committee meetings to define issues or policies. The representatives returned to their homes after a flooded week of talk with no national organization and no clearly defined policies.

There were, for instance, ten speeches on the day devoted to the established enemy of all French Catholics, Freemasonry, all of which reiterated the old charges concerning the evil power and the internationalism of "the evil order." The conclusion reached at the end of all the oration was that Freemasonry should be countered by propaganda, that this propaganda should always be documented, and that the order should be fought by electoral action "in every way possible." No organization was established, no positive concrete philosophy was defined and adopted, and nothing was added to the entire campaign which had not already been discussed at length since 1865.

The sessions most important for the future of the Christian Democratic party and most revealing to the modern student were those which dealt with "social reform." Anti-Semitism and Catholicism had served very effectively to draw the movement and the congress together, but these two binding forces were essentially negative. Christian Democracy needed to devise some positive and workable political and economic policies to knit the disparate groups together more closely and to attract other elements of French society. This the movement did not succeed in accomplishing. Lueger at the same time in Austria was conquering with a combination of Catholicism and "city Socialism." The French Christian Democrats borrowed the conception of a political and social party from their Austrian and German friends, but they did not succeed in cementing the groups they collected even briefly with a concrete program.

The social reform program approved at the close of the congress was neither so vague nor so impractical as the suggestions made by the speakers. However, these proposals are proof that Mouthon was correct in describing the Christian Democratic party as conservative. The principal suggestions in this statement were the protection of small business, the abolition of night work and employment of women, a ten-hour day and a six-day week, the establishment under state law of insurance and pension systems, the formation of committees including both workers and employees to study labor problems, and the election of regional parliaments to represent agriculture and industry. In addition, all Catholics were urged to unite in one political party, presumably the Christian Democratic party, and representation of professional interests in Parliament was supported. The program adopted by the second congress, in 1897, added the progressive income tax, laws on "speculation and usury," the referendum, and a clearer statement concerning corporatism.[8]

---

[8] *Congrès national de la Démocratie Chrétienne, 1896* (Lyon, 1897), pp. 33–93, 98–247, 277–306; Father Henri Delassus, *La Démocratie chrétienne, parti et école* (pamphlet)

The nature of the social program which the Christian Democrats developed in 1896 was, of course, one of the principal reasons the movement collapsed so quickly. The movement contained so many diverse social groups that no attainable positive platform which would attract mass support could be or was devised. The Christian Democratic party failed because it was bound together only by Catholicism and anti-Semitism, both ordinarily strong cohesive forces, but even together in this instance unable to counter the effect of the centrifugal forces. The pressure which destroyed the movement came from the Right, for the extreme conservatives were shocked and terrified to see Catholics, including large numbers of priests, join a movement which accepted "the slut" and which on occasion called itself Christian Socialist, even though it was in no sense a Socialist party.

This conservative opposition was ably and vigorously—even viciously—led by *Autorité* and *Vérité* in Paris and by such provincial journals as the *Semaine religieuse de Cambrai*, edited by Father Henri Delassus, himself an anti-Semite albeit a very conservative one. Aroused by the political and social ideas of the Christian Democrats, alarmed by the tolerance shown toward other Christian religions, and seeing in a priest such as Father Naudet or Father Gayraud another potential Lamennais, they used every means to discredit and smash the movement. They were aided in their designs by the strong participation in the movement of hundreds of Catholic priests and by the foolish decision of Berne and Mouthon to invite Drumont and some of his more rowdy comrades to the first congress.

It is evident from many sources that a number of Catholic priests in the 1890's were developing political and social ideas of their own, and, in some cases, entering politics advocating political and economic changes for France. This had happened often before, of course, but there was a great fear lest another Lamennais appear, particularly since most of the young priests who were becoming political proposed ideas considered radical and even revolutionary by their elders, especially those in the hierarchy. This caused great dissatisfaction and alarm, and some bishops by the fall of 1896 were seeking a means by which they might reasonably and without criticism forbid their priests to participate in the Christian Democratic movement.

The Christian Democrats escaped trouble before the first congress by adopting a technique familiar then to all Catholic authors and ad-

(Paris, 1911); François Mouthon, *Du Bluff au chantage. Les grandes campagnes du Matin* (Paris, 1908), preface, p. v; Édouard Drumont, *Nos maîtres, la tyrannie maçonnique* (Paris, 1899), pp. 134–36; Albert Houlin, *La Crise*, quoted by Chaine, *op. cit.*, pp. 619–21; Lecanuet, *op. cit.*, p. 245; Cornilleau, *op. cit.*, pp. 105–7; *Libre Parole Illustrée*, July 22, 1893, August 8–August 29, 1896, October 24–December 12, 1896; *Univers*, November 1–December 10, 1896.

ministrators, that of obtaining a letter of approval from the Pope or someone close to him and securing support from other dignitaries of the Church. As a consequence, it was difficult for critics in the hierarchy to forbid priests to attend the meetings. However, several embarrassing and disturbing episodes which occurred at the congress gave Church leaders an opportunity to criticize the movement openly and thus contribute to the subsequent failure of the entire campaign. A clash between a crowd of delegates and the Lyon police, several attacks upon the Catholic conservatives made at the congress, and Drumont's open criticism of Cardinal Couillé led the cardinal to urge all the priests in the diocese to abandon Christian Democracy. Subsequent violent editorials against the cardinal drove many Christian Democrats from the movement. Less than half as many priests attended the second convention in 1897. When Berne and Mouthon denounced the cardinal and the episcopacy for this during 1898, the cardinal forbade the clergy to read the leading Christian Democratic paper, *France libre*.

Christian Democracy then fell into the hands of Father Garnier, the Union Nationale, and the politicians who sought to use the movement as a means of winning election to the Chamber of Deputies. Except for Father Garnier, all of the leaders in the 1898 congress were men who had earlier been deputies as Bonapartists or Boulangists, or men who were to use the Christian Democratic forces and the Dreyfus affair tension to acquire brief notoriety in the Chamber. The 1898 congress was attended by only 1,500, and the movement disappeared completely after the fifth congress in Paris on July 14, 1900.

Thus, Christian Democracy in France was a dismal failure in the 1890's. The causes for this disaster were numerous, but the decisive one was the absence of a true understanding and appreciation of political and social democracy among the Christian Democrats themselves. Many of the priests involved, although they wanted "a twentieth-century altar" for the twentieth-century state, were too ignorant and uncritical and had been persecuted too long by their own educational system as well as by Republican politics to become true democrats. The large number of small businessmen in the movement had the same feelings; they believed that the Freemasons, the Jews, and, the Tory Conservatives alone were the cause of their plight. The journalists involved were only "frustrated esthetes," generally convinced that they had remarkable abilities which the régime was blunting and ignoring and seeking only a system which would give them true recognition.

The development of the French Christian Democrats later, particularly just before and after the Second World War, owed much to the sounder comprehension of democracy by the Christian Democrats themselves, as well as to the weakening of anticlerical suspicion and a growing tolerance of democratic ideals and practices by some elements of the Catholic Right. Marc Sangnier's *Sillon* movement appeared too early to profit from this development, and the noisy Action Française drained away from democracy some of the more shallow of these early Christian Democrats. By 1925 or 1930, however, a new group of Christian Democrats was ready to enter the field, this time better prepared and profiting, too, from far more auspicious circumstances.[9]

The separation of the Church and state in France in 1905 proved ultimately a blessing to the Church. Free from state interference and state control (even the anticlericals admitted that the Republic had nominated inferior bishops and generally monarchists at that), the Church became an independent institution. Progress has been slow. The Church in France was and is very poor; the hierarchy has been marked to a degree still noticeable by the conditions under which the Church operated during the nineteenth century; there are insufficient priests; and the army of anticlerical "lay missionaries" in the public school system has helped perpetuate a climate of opinion hostile to the Church. Yet even by 1914 it was quite clear that the era of violent opposition to the Church was over and that time had softened and blurred the conflicting ideas of the two camps.

V

Between the world wars, Catholicism and the Catholic Church in France increased in general popularity, power, and influence. The reasons for this are numerous, and some of them help also to explain why more Catholics became at least reconciled to the Third Republic and democracy, laying the foundations on which the MRP rests. Perhaps the most important reason of all was the blow dealt by history since 1914 to the philosophical assumptions behind the drive against the Church and religion in the nineteenth century. The disasters of the twentieth century have weakened confidence in the ability of man to stride forward unaided, and this confidence has been weakened even among the intellectuals who led the campaigns earlier. At the same time that this was happening, many Frenchmen began to notice again that the Catholic Church was an integral part of their

9 Alfred Gendrot (Jean Drault, *pseud.*), *Drumont, La France juive et la Libre Parole* (Paris, 1935), pp. 192–93; Father Paul Fesch, *L'Année sociale et économique en France et à l'étranger* (Paris, 1899), pp. 81–88; Agnes Siegfried, *L'Abbé Fremont, 1852–1912* (Paris, 1932), II, 73–74; *Congrès national,* pp. 6–25, 95–97, 214–15; Chaine, *op. cit.,* pp. 620–21; Cornilleau, *op. cit.,* pp. 111–25; Lecanuet, *op. cit.,* pp. 625–50; Debidour, *op. cit.,* II, 165.

national history and life. The patriotic role of many priests during the First World War, the presence of so many devout Catholics among the outstanding generals of the war, and the national loyalty of the Church and of leading churchmen in the occupied areas all gave renewed prestige to the Church. The colonial contribution of men and materials to the French war effort increased French appreciation of the missionary orders, while political realities led in 1921 to the restoration of diplomatic relations with the Vatican. The sanctification of Joan of Arc strengthened the nationalist appeal of the Church, and the increasingly serious social problems and Communist exploitation of the crises drove many conservatives into a renewed appreciation of its social value.[10]

This last development, of course, was a very serious one both for the Third Republic and the Catholic Church. The postwar reaction benefited the Church, but it benefited also the extreme conservative and royalist groups who sought to use religion and the Church for their own personal ends. The tradition of conflict between the Republic and the Church, the presence in the hierarchy of so many members of the upper classes hostile by tradition to the Republic, and the social and economic control wielded by these conservatives and reactionaries over political parties and over the press gave them great power.

While the swing to the Right in France pushed the reactionaries back into the Church, there began to grow again, almost unnoticed, a new Christian Democratic movement. Founded now on a new appreciation of individualism and humanism and on a renewed desire to ally the Church with the workers, the peasants, and the poor, this movement also owed much to the tradition of Lamennais and Marc Sangnier. Its foundations were more secure than those of any earlier movement, for by 1930 France was dotted with Catholic Action groups and trade-unions which indirectly provided political material. No one of these organizations or units in itself was large, but together they contributed a solid core for the future.

Thus, the CFTC (French Federation of Christian Workers), founded in France just after the First World War, organized Catholic workers. This organization joined the Catholic workers' international organization, founded in 1908, and advocated also full co-operation with all other trade-unions. Although the CFTC never had more than 500,000 members at any time before the Second World War, it did organize Catholic workers in democratic unions with a

[10] Ernest Dimnet, *France Herself Again* (London, 1914), pp. 356–77; Yves Simon, *La Grande Crise de la République* (Montreal, 1941), pp. 68–74; Denis Gwynn, *The Catholic Reaction in France* (London, 1925), *passim;* Debidour, *op. cit.,* II, 20–22; Thomson, *op. cit.,* pp. 142–45.

clear program of social reform. It was nonpolitical even after the Second World War, but its membership generally supported the Popular Democrats and the Young Republic, the Catholic democratic and progressive political groups.

Catholic Action groups were probably at least as significant as the CFTC. The Jeunesse Ouvrière Chrétienne, or JOC, founded in 1927, had 400,000 lively members at the close of the Second World War in Europe and had become a fountainhead of other similar movements for Catholic students, agricultural workers, fishermen, etc. These youth movements urged their members to work as individuals to create a Christian environment, but they did help to strengthen the CFTC as well as the political arms of the Catholic democrats. They also stimulated the clergy, some of whom had an important role in founding these groups, into a more active—even a missionary—role among the workers and peasants. The aim of these units was to return the workers to the Church, for as Pius XI said, "The great scandal of the Church in the nineteenth century is not that she lost so many workers, but that she lost the working class." [11]

The Démocrates Populaires and the Jeune République have been crowded out of the history of the 1930's by the more dashing, colorful, and violent Rightists' leagues and parties. Although many conservative Catholics were among those Frenchmen who helped to weaken and destroy the Republic during the developing national and international crisis, these Christian Democrats remained true to their principles and to democracy. The Jeune République's four deputies supported the Popular Front in 1936, and the Démocrates Populaires supported Blum's last desperate effort to hold the Popular Front together in 1938. Both of these groups refused to cooperate with Fascist parties throughout the 1930's. L'Aube, the newspaper of the Popular Democrats, supported the Loyalists throughout the Spanish Civil War. Georges Bidault, later one of the most prominent MRP leaders, led this party to oppose Munich in 1938, and throughout the 1930's it supported international law and collective security.

The actions of prominent Catholic intellectuals, some of whom were not members of either of these political parties, also helped to weaken the identity of Catholicism with reaction and to maintain a vital link between the Catholics and the other democratic groups. One manifesto in 1934 attacked the rise of Fascism in France and helped to check the movement toward Fascism of Catholics whose

11 Henry W. Ehrmann, "Political Forces in Present-Day France," Social Research, xv (1948), 159–60; R. C. Gorman, "The Church in France," Catholic World, CLXVI (1947), 79–80; Claire Bishop, France Alive (New York, 1947), pp. 25–37; James O. Supple, "What and Why are the Jocists," Christian Century, LXIV (1947), 898–900; Dorothy M. Pickles, France Between the Republics (London, 1946), appendix.

principal fears were of Communism. Another manifesto in 1935 denounced the Italian invasion of Ethiopia, and a third in 1936 protested bitterly against Nazi bombing in Spain. Jacques Maritain ridiculed Franco's declaration of a Holy War, while Mauriac pointed out to French Catholics that the Basque Catholics were among Franco's first victims.[12]

The MRP and the postwar Catholic renaissance derive from this small but vital prewar democratic stock and from the splendid Resistance role of the democratic and progressive Catholic organizations. Many of the Catholic hierarchy gave open support to Pétain, and many Catholics in France voiced their deep appreciation of Vichy rule. However, most of the priests did not follow the hierarchy in acceptance of Vichy. The role of the Catholic clergy, including many of the hierarchy, in opposing anti-Semitism and in hiding and caring for the Jews has been widely recognized. CFTC leaders joined representatives of the CGT in opposing Vichy's labor charter, and the Catholic unions had splendid Resistance records. Catholic newspapers and journals were among the leading critics of Vichy and were among the first to be driven underground, where they constituted a large and effective organ of the Resistance. Many of the leaders of the Démocrates Populaires and the Jeune République were Resistance heroes, and the membership of these parties provided some of the core of the most able underground groups. The integrity of the resistance of these Catholics not only provided a moral stimulus to the Catholic groups, but also convinced the Left that at least some Catholics had become progressive democrats, thus making possible the spirit of high cooperation which marked the first months after the Liberation.[13]

At the close of the war in Europe, the Christian Democrats did not appear to have a very bright future in France. Even in 1936, the Démocrates Populaires had polled only 350,000 votes. The party never had even twenty deputies in the Chamber, and the party's daily newspaper, *L'Aube*, in 1936 sold only 15,000 copies each day. Moreover, the MRP had been formed during the war as a movement, not a political party. Conceived in 1941 by a young Catholic student Resistance leader, the MRP was originally intended to organize "spiritual"

---

[12] Charles A. Micaud, *The French Right and Nazi Germany, 1933–1939* (Durham, 1943), pp. 113, 127–29, 146; Gordon Wright, *The Reshaping of French Democracy* (New York, 1948), pp. 16–17, 193; Alexander Werth, *The Twilight of France, 1933–1940* (London, 1942), pp. 101, 345; François Goguel, *La Politique des partis sous la Troisième République* (Paris, 1946), II, 169–70; Claude Julien, "Christian Democracy in France," *Commonweal*, XLVIII (1948), 589; Simon, *op. cit.*, pp. 55–60, 85–90, 106–32, 141–49.

[13] Lt. Colonel Pierre Tissier, *The Government of Vichy* (London, 1942), pp. 127–29, 178–81; Pickles, *op. cit.*, pp. 34, 93–95.

forces in France, to draw the Catholics away from conservatism, and to erect a powerful, nondenominational humanist Left-Center. Before young Gilbert Dru's death in the Resistance, he had convinced Georges Bidault and other Catholic Resistance leaders. Dru edited the underground *Cahiers du témoignage chrétien* and the *Cahiers de notre jeunesse,* which helped to spread his ideas and to coordinate the Catholic democrats. The MRP group at the time of Liberation, though, was small and poorly organized, and it lacked even plans for its future. However, although in August 1945 it had only 100,000 dues-paying members, it polled 4,500,000 votes in the October 1945 elections to the First Constituent Assembly.[14]

VI

An analysis of the strengths and weaknesses of the MRP will complete this study of the Christian Democrats in modern France, for it will reveal the resources as well as the limitations behind the party and its policy. Actually, the most significant reason for the sudden rise of the MRP was the vacuum left in French politics at the end of the war by the great weakness of the Radical Socialists and of the entire Right. The Radical Socialists, who had been the governing or controlling party so often in France since before the First World War, were shackled in 1944 and 1945 by their immediate prewar record, while the Right suffered from the same defect as well as from extensive collaboration with Vichy. The strength of the MRP was thus a double weakness, for the small but lively Christian Democratic core was almost overwhelmed by a mass of new adherents who supported the MRP because it alone could serve them at that time. This mass not only helped to transform the MRP more definitely from a movement to a party, but furthermore it converted it from a movement dominated by spiritual and moral impulses to one engaged in the old French political game. This mass was only a temporary accession, too, for as soon as the vacuum ceased to exist the MRP lost its attraction.

Other strengths of the MRP were more solid and convincing. The fruits of the work done during the 1930's and under the Occupation by the CFTC and the Catholic Action organizations, especially among the youth, were harvested after the Second World War. Many of the leaders and most of the elected deputies of the new party were young men who had come through the ranks of these organizations, and the educated, disciplined core of the MRP derived from the same sources.

[14] Pickles, *op. cit.,* p. 89; Wright, *op. cit.,* pp. 34–36, 73–76; Julien, *loc. cit.,* pp. 590–91; Ehrmann, *loc. cit.,* pp. 160–61.

This background helps also to explain MRP emphasis on strong organization and the education of its members, which were to prove significant attributes, particularly for combat with the older, highly centralized Socialist and Communist parties. In addition, some areas of France, notably Brittany and Lorraine, which had been Popular Democrat centers, brought their power into the new fold.

The MRP also benefited from the experience concerning political and social problems acquired by its predecessors. The lessons of the Popular Democrats and the Young Republic in political and social democracy and those learned by the CFTC were inherited by the MRP. Thus, the Catholic party accepted the principle of a directed and semicollectivized economy, while the CFTC in 1948 urged radical tax reforms, the reorganization of the land-parceling system, planned compulsory production schedules, and government control of food, trade, profits, and prices.

A final strength of the MRP is its leadership. It includes a high proportion of experienced lawyers, professors, journalists, and businessmen, sincere believers in Christian Democracy because of the training they acquired before the Second World War and because of the insight they obtained during the Occupation. They are also generally political neophytes, so that they have clear reputations and a fresh approach which often are lacking in the leadership of the established parties. This particular advantage, however, is offset in part by the fact that these unblemished leaders are also inexperienced in the ways of French politics.

Perhaps the most serious weakness of the MRP is its status as a Catholic party. Any Catholic party in France is a prisoner of the history of the last one hundred and fifty years. The suspicion and resentment on both sides has declined during the last half-century, but one's attitude toward the Church and its existence and power is still the dividing line in French politics. Thus, the Socialists, the chief ally of the MRP in any left-center Third Force, have remained suspicious of a party mainly Catholic.[15] The major disagreements are over the Church's role in education, the relative rate of speed and vigor of collectivization, and the attitude of the MRP toward Catholics and others who supported Vichy.

The basic difficulty, however, is suspicion, from which no Catholic party, however radical, will ever be quite free. It must always be remembered that anticlericalism in modern French history has had a

[15] Perhaps the clearest illustration of this kind of suspicion was voiced by the German Social Democrat, Schumacher, about the German Christian Democrats: "There is a clerical and reactionary wing which determines policy, and a clerical and 'socializing' wing which handles the advertising." Elie Baussart, "Responsabilités des partis démocrates Chrétiens," *Esprit*, XVI (1947), 919.

longer and more successful career than clericalism has had: it has been called "the only continuous policy in modern French history." The Radical Socialists used anticlericalism with great effect as a party program for more than three decades after the separation had effectively ended the Church's direct political power. Fear of the Church is so deeply ingrained in the Socialist and Communist Left and has so often been used as a political technique that the slogan and symbol are still worth millions of votes. Thus, cooperation or close association with the MRP opens the Socialists to attack from the Communists, who can and do denounce them for being the tool of the Church and, therefore, of reaction. Since anticlericalism has worked its way down the social scale until the working class is now the main depository, this effectively limits the Socialists and therefore weakens the so-called Third Force.

Another limiting weakness of the Christian Democratic movement in the Fourth Republic is its social composition. A party which polled 4,500,000 votes in October 1945 and 28.2 per cent of all of the votes cast in June 1946 is surely a mass party. Moreover, although it is widely assumed that the Communists and Socialists control the workers' votes, the MRP has strong influence among the working classes. Thus, in October 1945, the MRP elected three deputies from radical Saint-Étienne and elected more deputies from the northern coal-mining areas than the Communists. As a matter of fact, the CFTC in 1949 was at least as strong a workers' movement as the Force Ouvrière, the non-Communist movement which left the CGT in December 1947. The CFTC had 800,000 members in 1948, and its policy was frequently as radical as that of the Communist-controlled CGT itself.

Nevertheless, the MRP does suffer from inclusion of so many members of the middle classes. This has resulted in the high quality of leadership during the immediate postwar years, but it has also tended to make the party more conservative and to decrease its understanding of and interest in the need for immediate social reform. As the party's organization has become established, the workers have had greater difficulty in obtaining a hearing. Moreover, since the philosophy of the MRP is fundamentally Christian, the party is more interested in reforms than in revolution, or even radical changes. The ethical approach to social problems does not generally produce immediate material results, and results are the chief interests now of all French workers. Indeed, as most MRP leaders would readily admit, a confessional party is always dangerously exposed in politics. Religions and churches should attempt to exert moral and spiritual influence over individuals, not operate through political parties open to attack from every angle and subject to every passing influence.[16]

The final and perhaps the decisive weakness of the MRP is the presence and policy of General de Gaulle. The General has served several useful functions for the MRP, but his program and his power are now clear threats to the very existence of democracy in France. One of the reasons for the original sudden rise of the MRP in 1945 was the assumption made by many Frenchmen that it was the "party of fidelity," that it represented the General's views. In the late summer and fall of 1946, however, the threatening program of De Gaulle forced the MRP to unite with the other democratic parties to guard the Republic against De Gaulle, thus losing those followers of De Gaulle who were then in its ranks. In the June 5, 1946, elections, the MRP was the largest single party in France, but the General's stand reduced it to second place in the elections the following November. The persistence of national and international crises has continued to drain strength from the MRP and from the Socialists and, apparently, to increase the number of those on the Right and on the Left who consider salvation more likely under a dictatorial government.

There is, of course, some truth in the claims that the MRP has lost only those who had accepted it because there was no satisfactory party on the Right, and that De Gaulle has served a useful service in cleansing the MRP. The party has benefited, too, from having De Gaulle on its Right as a "lightning rod" to draw the attacks of the Left. De Gaulle has also split the clergy, leaving to the MRP the democratic majority and attaching to himself the more conservative and nationalistic minority. This has weakened criticism of the MRP as a conservative, Church-dominated party.

However, the political activity of De Gaulle has been disastrous in other ways. The very presence of a conservative and authoritarian party which has an appeal to Catholics has dissolved some of the hard-won gains of the past fifty years and has also turned the clock of French politics back again to the nineteenth century. This has reintroduced the old issues and thereby strengthened the power of the extreme Right as well as of the extreme Left. The more the old issues and passions have dominated the political scene, the less opportunity there has been of accomplishing adequate political and social reform. Since the MRP and the Third Force itself can maintain themselves

---

[16] Wright, *op. cit.*, pp. 73–77, 93–96, 105–6, 185–88, 208–11, 225–30; Pickles, *op. cit.*, pp. 170, 227, 240–42; Ehrmann, *loc. cit.*, pp. 159–60; George H. Dunne, "Socialism and Socialism," *Commonweal*, XLIII (1945), 134–39.

and prosper only by providing the changes France has delayed for so very long, this temporizing and procrastination can only sharpen the domestic crisis and make more likely the introduction into power of one of the extremes. During the past three years, the presence of De Gaulle has thus contributed to the gradual swing to the Right in French politics. Although De Gaulle and the RPF have not been able to profit directly from this swing to the Right because there has been no general election—indeed, the De Gaulle movement as an organized political force apparently has been in a decline for some time, in spite of this trend—the swing to the Right has hastened both the conservatism and the decline of the MRP. Even one of the founders of the MRP, disgusted as early as 1948 with its maneuvering, described it as "a Catholic ghetto."

Behind the appeal and the power of De Gaulle, of course, lies the most basic and serious weakness of the Third Force, the Christian Democrats, and of French democracy itself. This flaw is, paradoxically, one of the glories and strengths of France: her amazing social stability. "France has gone through several revolutions since 1789 and through countless changes of cabinet since 1870; but she has had very few drastic reforms. Her social, economic, administrative, and bureaucratic structure has remained virtually unchanged since Napoleon I." As a result, the identical issues have remained predominant through all of her modern history. France, like much of the American South, has been "looking backward," neglecting to resolve issues, until the solution when it has come has been hasty, arbitrary, and often violent. This remarkable social stability has not only delayed advance in the most revolutionary age the world has seen, but, in perpetuating the grip of the old classes and the old leaders, it has increased provincialism and even isolationism in France.

It is this social stability, strengthening rooted old beliefs, which explains the slowness and feebleness of democratic developments among French Catholics. There has been little study of the philosophy of democracy in any of the democratic countries, but there has been more thought about political democracy and the assumptions on which it is based in France than in any other Western European country. The philosophy, the ideas, in other words, are present. It is not Catholicism as such which prevents development. One has only to examine the political attitudes and policies of Catholics whose parents or grandparents came to the United States from France, Italy, Hungary, Germany, Spain, or Ireland to realize the effect made within a few, brief generations by transfer to a democratic, constantly changing society. It is primarily this social stability and the hold of political tradition which have weakened and withered the progress of democracy among Catholics in France.[17]

The Christian Democratic movement in France is weak again today politically, in spite of the high promise of 1945 and 1946. The wisdom of the development of confessional parties in a democracy is doubtful in any case. However, given the desperate necessity, the record of the Christian Democrats in France has only to be compared with those of similar parties in other Western European countries to indicate the advanced position of the French, in spite of their weaknesses and failures. The MRP has remained active in its drive for more political and social democracy in France; it has stoutly resisted the temptation of De Gaulle; it has remained stanchly anti-Fascist; it has not been acquired by other groups, as has happened in Italy; it has fought anti-Semitism, which was endorsed by the German Protestant and Austrian Catholic groups; it has progressed far beyond the sentimental preachings of the early English Christian Democrats; it has, above all, contributed heavily, even though at great cost to itself, to the survival of democracy in France. Since a peaceful solution to the problems facing the Fourth Republic will determine to a large degree whether Continental Western Europe can remain democratic, this has been of very great significance.

Christian Democracy in France extends, of course, beyond the MRP, and its contributions are not limited to the political and social sphere alone. The MRP has made a valuable critique of capitalism from an ethical point of view, and it has indicated new means by which the individual may be safeguarded from the monolithic, totalitarian state. Nevertheless, the development of missionary work among the French workers by a growing number of devoted priests may ultimately have far greater significance for France than even the vital, self-destructive holding operation conducted by the MRP. The new humanism defined and developed by such progressive Catholic organs as *Esprit* which are critical of the MRP and the Third Force may help to return France to reliance upon those values and principles which alone make the Western world worth saving. The refreshing spirit of the critical mind, the high appreciation for the dignity of every man, the zeal for true social equality and for a true brotherhood of men, the respect for the rule of law and the rights of each individual under law, the interest in the individual personality—all these principles, all these values and attitudes fundamental to the Western tradition are being reexamined and revived by these Chris-

[17] Henri Peyre, "The French Situation: A French View," *Political Science Quarterly*, LIX (1944), 380–81; Thomson, *op. cit.*, p. 172; Julien, *loc. cit.*, p. 592.

tian Democrats. If the Fourth Republic can remain sturdy, from them may come ultimately the new humanism, this time a Christian humanism, to reduce the state and again raise man to the status from which he has been reduced everywhere by the forces and ideas dominant throughout modern history.[18]

[18] W. J. Fitzgerald, "The Idea of Democracy in Contemporary Catholicism," *Review of Religion*, XII (1948), 148–65; Sally W. Cassidy, "Catholic Revival," *Catholic World*, CLXIX (1949), 52–56; Emmanuel Mounier, "Le Communisme devant nous," *Esprit*, XIV (1946), 164–90; Jean Lacroix, "La Troisième Force," *Esprit*, XV (1947), 928–39; Maurice Didier, "Coordonnées de la politique du Centre," *Esprit*, XV (1947), 924–27; Emmanuel Mounier, "Le Décret du Saint-Office," *Esprit*, XVII (1949), 305–14.

V

FRENCH POLITICS:

THE LEFT AND THE RIGHT

11

+++

THE DECLINE OF

THE SOCIALIST PARTY *

HENRY W. EHRMANN

+++

"Mère, voici vos fils qui se sont tant battus; ils sont prêts à nouveau pour le plus beau des combats, celui de la liberté et de la fraternité humaine. . . ."—CHARLES PÉGUY

"Quand c'est l'égoisme qui renverse les tyrans, il ne sait que se partager les dépouilles du tyran."—BENJAMIN CONSTANT

JUST as the Radicals typified the Third Republic at its apogee, so the Socialist Party has been a faithful expression of the hopes and harassments that have filled the infant years of the Fourth Republic. On the eve of Liberation a reborn Socialist movement was hailed by many as guardian and guarantor of French regeneration. When after early false starts the new republic was stumbling, when old divisions reappeared and republican liberties were threatened anew, the Socialist Party appeared as the wrecker of earlier expectations. That the SFIO was often only the victim of developments which it was unable to control might well be the judgment of history. To its contemporaries, friends and foes alike, the Socialist Party bears a main share of responsibility for all that has happened since the heady days of Liberation.

I

Socialist leaders have frankly acknowledged that at the time of the national debacle in 1940 the record of the SFIO was hardly a reason

* The author is obliged to the Council on Research and Creative Work of the University of Colorado for a grant-in-aid enabling him to secure many of the materials on which this paper is based. He also wishes to express his gratitude to his friend Professor James Sandoe, Order Librarian, for his patience and understanding in assembling a documentation at times difficult to obtain.

for pride.[1] While it is true that 45 per cent of the negative votes cast by the mock National Assembly at the Vichy Casino came from courageous Socialists, it is also true that out of 175 Socialist deputies and senators, only 37 voted against the granting of powers to Pétain. The absence of Jacobin-Jaurèsian patriotism which Léon Blum deplored was not only, as he maintained, a consequence of internal dissensions. Even if the party had not been divided between advocates and enemies of appeasement, it would hardly have been in a position to mobilize the people *in extremis*. For it lacked transmission belts to the masses and it appeared to a bewildered and despairing nation as an integral part of the faltering régime.

The number of Socialists who participated in the Resistance movement was considerable, their role as organizers and underground publicists often important. But the Socialist Party as such remained inconspicuous, uncertain as to which forms of organization would be best fitted to meet the exigencies of a regained legality. There was concern that by reforming the ranks of the party too early, one might dampen the fervor for a broad humanitarian socialism present among the members of the Resistance.[2]

There is no room here to analyze to what extent the *mystique* of the Resistance movement and its programs, such as the manifesto of the Conseil National de la Resistance, presented an amalgam of the traditional strands of French Socialism. Much of it reads like an attempt at adapting the contradictory and often mutually exclusive ideas of Fourier, Saint-Simon, Proudhon, Marx, and Jaurès to the conditions of modern France.[3] At many levels of the Resistance the members were held together not alone by a patriotic hatred for the invader, but by a well-nigh instinctive and always intense feeling of revolt against the forces that had immolated human dignity. That meant a simultaneous fight against contemporary totalitarianism absolutizing state and race, and against the memories of the "old order" generating social frustration and incapable of political integration.

---

[1] See e.g. Léon Blum, *For All Mankind* (New York, 1946), esp. pp. 106 ff.; Vincent Auriol, *Hier . . . demain* (Paris, 1945), I, 128–37.

[2] For certain limitations of Socialist action in the Resistance, see the testimony of one of the participants of the Resistance movement, Joseph Rovan, "Responsabilités des sociaux-démocrates," *Esprit*, xv (1947), 902 ff. For a good over-all picture of Socialist activities in the Resistance, see Alfred Spire, *Inventaire des socialismes français contemporains* (Paris, 1945), esp. pp. 89 ff., 109–11; Dorothy Pickles, *France Between the Republics* (London, 1946), pp. 98–102; and, with many details as to names and organizations, Paul Marabuto, *Les Partis politiques et les mouvements sociaux sous la IVe République* (Paris, 1948), pp. 115, 240–42.

[3] On the general Socialist philosophy of the Resistance movement, see André Hauriou, *Vers une doctrine de la Résistance, Le Socialisme humaniste* (Paris, 1944).

The meeting ground for traditionalists, liberals, revolutionaries, the devout and the nonbeliever, was a spiritual synthesis which despite being vague seemed nevertheless to provide the cohesion that previously had never been found.[4]

By its name, by a somewhat dim remembrance of its former propaganda, by certain notions of its leader (his almost Biblical fortitude in captivity evoked feelings of warmth his presence had never been able to rouse), the Socialist Party seemed predestined to become the standard-bearer of whatever concrete solutions humanitarian socialism would have to propose.

When before the Liberation Léon Blum and his most outstanding collaborators formulated their precise prescription for the future organization and action of the Socialist movement, their recommendations signified in fact a radical departure from the past of the SFIO. To provide for the French working class the experience of a strong social-welfare state, making the trade-unions and the parliamentary system close allies in the fight against economic insecurity, was a concept calling for the establishment of a stable and altogether nonsectarian labor party following closely the pattern of British Labor. In its first manifesto to the French people, the SFIO boasted of a thorough reorganization that would qualify it as a "great republican, democratic, and revolutionary force in the nation." [5] Hopes seemed to know no bounds.

"Socialism is the master of the hour," exclaimed Léon Blum in a speech at the 1945 convention of his party—a speech which now sounds altogether pathetic.[6]

II

The problem which is usually labeled one of "working class unity," but which is really that of denying to the Communist Party an influence over any sizable sector of public opinion, had to be among the first preoccupations of the Socialists.

The clamoring for a new élite was general after the capitulation of the bourgeoisie in 1940. The Vichy interlude only confirmed the widespread belief that national leadership would have to be provided by classes not yet compromised by the wielding of official power.

[4] See the remarkable conclusion in François Goguel, *La Politique des partis sous la IIIe République* (Paris, 1946), II, 335–39.

[5] See *Le Populaire*, November 14, 1944.

[6] *ibid.*, August 14, 1945. Privately Léon Blum is known to have expressed himself far less optimistically about the situation which he witnessed after his return from Nazi imprisonment: see Howard K. Smith, *The State of Europe* (New York, 1949), p. 151.

The organized working class seemed to be all the more eminently qualified since, when compared with the rural population, the workers had been, with the exception of the short-lived Popular Front, the stepchildren of the Third Republic. The first post-Liberation elections appeared to indicate that public opinion was ready to acknowledge the need for a new national leadership; on the electoral map of France, Socialists and Communists together filled the place traditionally held by what has been called the *parti du mouvement* (as opposed to the *parti de l'ordre*) of the Third Republic.[7] Comparisons that have been made with the election of 1849 show both the amazing stability of political divisions over a century, and the position which the so-called "Marxist Left" had conquered in the sentiment of the traditionally Jacobin-Republican electorate.[8]

Now, both the organization of the working class as one of the main pillars of a social welfare state and the needed simplification and strengthening of the party system called for the creation of the broad labor party envisaged by the Socialists. But such a labor party could never come into being as long as there was, competing for the same clientele, a Communist Party, which Blum had described in 1941 by the phrase, since widely quoted, "a foreign nationalist party."[9]

Before the Liberation, Vincent Auriol and Léon Blum had admitted that the future would be dark indeed not only for the Socialist movement but for the new Republic as long as there was a strong Communist Party depending for its policy upon considerations dictated from the outside. Both Socialist leaders had tried to persuade themselves somewhat in the manner of Coué that there would no longer be a Communist Party of the prewar type. They affected an oversimplified belief that merely because the Communists had altered their attitude toward the question of national defense, the character of the Communist Party had undergone a fundamental change.

It turned out otherwise: in the first postwar election the Communists commanded a vote of 5 millions, as against 4.6 millions for the SFIO. Moreover, they acquired almost immediately a solid hold on millions of trade-union members. Finally, Communist leaders declared, long before their party's secession from the tripartite government, that initial slogans of a "battle for production" and nationalistic enthusiasm for a "French renascence" would hold good

---

[7] Goguel, *op. cit., passim.*

[8] For a careful analysis of the election results in this regard, see Ernest Labrousse, "La Montée du socialisme," *La Revue socialiste,* Nouv. sér., No. 1 (1946), 26 ff., and "Géographie du socialisme," *ibid.,* No. 2, 137–48.

[9] Blum, *op. cit.,* p. 113. For an interesting comment on this significant passage in Blum's book, see A. Rossi, *Physiologie du parti communiste français* (Paris, 1948), pp. 343–57, 446–47.

only as long as the international situation warranted them.[10] As a result, earlier assumptions and hopes for creating a new labor party, and thereby a new political instrument, had already collapsed.

The alternative then open for the SFIO was either to seek the stabilization of the Republic by entering into a coalition with non-Socialist parties, or to seek "unification" with the Communists. At all times, even immediately after the Liberation and at the most impatient of all party conventions, that of 1946, the two major factions dominating the Socialist Party since 1945 have rejected with overwhelming majorities the self-liquidation of Socialism by either unification or *unité d'action* with the Communist Party. The Committee of Entente established between the Communists and the SFIO under the impact of Resistance sentimentality has never had the sympathies of any of the Socialist leaders.[11] *Nenniism* has been all but nonexistent in France. The point has sometimes been made that the SFIO was unable to evolve into a reliable labor party devoted to social reform, because its left wing never dared to give up the idea of working-class unity and hence did not take a determined enough stand against the Communists. Such reproaches fail to perceive that the pledges to "ultimate" unity which the Leftish faction reiterated from time to time were merely declamatory.[12] Moreover it is obviously impossible to create a labor party without the active support of the working class. Why such support failed to materialize will be dismissed subsequently.

The apparently erratic policy which at times the SFIO had followed toward Communism was most of all a reaction to the series of successive defeats at the polls and a vain attempt to regain lost ground. When in October 1945 the electorate had relegated the Socialists to third place, this was understood as a disapproval of the alliance which the SFIO had entered into with the Union Démocratique et Socialiste de la Résistance, uniting Socialists, leaders of the Catholic trade-union movement, and future De Gaullists like Malraux and Capitant. When the first draft of the constitution supported solely by the Left was rejected by the voters, the party reacted by launching attacks against the Communists. Often changes in tactics

[10] For details, see Henry W. Ehrmann, "French Labor Goes Left," *Foreign Affairs*, XXV (1946–47), 465–76.

[11] For the official post-Liberation attitude of the Communist Party toward the problem of unity with the SFIO, see *L'Humanité*, June 27, 1945.

[12] For a typical criticism of the SFIO as being too indulgent toward the "Leftish" sympathies of its more radical wing, see Tr., "Tour d'horizon," *Revue politique et parlementaire*, CXCI (1947), 273. For the very reserved attitude toward Communism shown by the present Secretary General of the SFIO and the spokesman of the Leftish faction, see Guy Mollet, "Examen de conscience," *La Revue socialiste*, Nouv. sér., No. 6 (1946), 657–62.

were motivated by a constant fear of the SFIO of appearing to the working class at large as being part of the anti-Communist camp.[13] In France, anti-Communism means hostility to the working class, since the Communist Party has from its early days been able to appeal to the almost atavistic feeling of *ouvriérisme*, the deeply ingrained instinctive class consciousness of the workers. Why in the past the SFIO, except in the northern region, had never qualified as a party satisfying the need for *ouvriériste* solidarity cannot be explained here. It might only be noted that today not a single member of the Comité Directeur of the party comes from a working-class family. (For the leaders of the Communist Party the over-all picture is radically different.)

A Socialist leader like Léon Blum seems never to have had a full understanding of the fundamental distrust of the French workers for the bourgeois, including the bourgeois who had joined the Socialist movement. At the national party convention of 1945, Blum tried to put the delegates at ease about the influx of middle-class elements into the party. He maintained that the middle class and working class following of the Socialist Party would be mutually strengthening, increasing the over-all effectiveness of the organization. Such an analysis might be correct for the British Labor Party. It misses an essential characteristic of the French working-class movement.

Obviously, its wavering policies since the Liberation have not saved the SFIO from the stigma of anti-Communism. But here again, developments uncontrollable by the Socialists have played the major role—first among them, of course, the polarization of all of Europe and of every European country into a Communist and anti-Communist bloc. Other factors only added to the dilemma. The well-known French "habit of historical thinking" [14] (a habit which Communist propaganda has exploited with a masterly hand) has permitted constant association of the role of Jules Moch, the Socialist Minister of Interior, with that of Clemenceau during the first decade of the century. Just as the "Tiger," after breaking up strikes by police measures, boasted of being "the first cop" of France and was then hated by the working classes, M. Moch has now attracted violent indignation from the same side.

An analysis of the election results of 1945 and 1946 reveals, however, that long before M. Moch's show of force with the Communist

---

[13] Only 35 per cent of the Socialist voters approved, late in 1947, the liquidation of Communism proposed by De Gaulle, with 50 per cent opposed to it and the remainder undecided. See Institut Français d'Opinion Publique, *Sondages,* x (1948), 5–6.

[14] David Thomson, *Democracy in France* (London, New York, 1946), p. 52.

trade-unions, his party had lost what little working-class following it had mustered after the Liberation.[15] Since then such developments seem only to have been accentuated. "The workers have walked out of the SFIO on tiptoes, as one leaves the chamber of a dying man," a former Socialist deputy wrote.[16] The war of religion which the Communist Party has been fighting against the Socialists for the souls of the French worker has been won by the Communists, inasmuch as they have deprived their competitors of any working-class following. (This does not necessarily mean that there is today in France a solid rallying of the working class to Communism. Complaints about a relapse of the workers into political apathy and cynicism are fairly general and occasionally reflected in the Communist press.[17])

By now the Socialist Party, because of its composition as well as because of its political action, has no influence over even those organized parts of the working class which are not controlled by the Communist Party, such as the cooperative movement and the workers' mutual insurance societies.[18] Socialist "cells" in the plants, the Groupes Socialistes d'Entreprises—never very strong, not even during the heyday of the Popular Front—are all but nonexistent today. While there are cordial relations between the Party and the Force Ouvrière, it is doubtful how much, if any, working-class strength Force Ouvrière possesses.*

Thus the Socialist Party is left with a following of teachers, of professional and other white-collar workers, and of *fonctionnaires*, usually of the lower ranks but with an occasional representative of the highly skilled bureaucratic "technocracy." Since the end of the war, the Socialist Party has been unable to attract any of the outstanding intellectuals of the country, another sign of weakness in the eyes of many a Frenchman and something of a disgrace for a party that once recruited its distinguished members from among the laureates of the

---

* For details concerning the Force Ouvrière, see the following chapter by Val R. Lorwin.

15 See François Goguel, "Géographie du référendum au 13 octobre et des élections du 10 novembre 1946," *Esprit,* xv (1947), 237 ff.

16 Jean Rous, "De la crise du socialisme au renouveau démocratique et révolutionnaire," *ibid.,* xviii (1950), 315.

17 For a very impressive testimony to this point, see "Enquête sur la France désorientée," *ibid.,* xvi (1948), 41–75, esp. the letters written by present or former Socialists such as Mlle. Saulnier, Pierre Boujut, Charles Jullien (pp. 52–58), André Foussard (pp. 72–74). A public opinion survey indicated that in October 1948 only 47 per cent of the working-class population favored the readmission of the Communists to the cabinet, while 40 per cent were opposed (for the population at large the figures were 35 and 55 per cent respectively). See *Sondages,* xi (1949), 16–17.

18 See Pierre Giraud, "Au coeur de l'action ouvrière—le problème de l'efficience," *La Revue socialiste,* Nouv. sér., No. 30 (1949), 253 ff.

École Normale.[19] During the last two years the desertion of party members from the SFIO has also extended to representatives of the rural and urban middle classes. It is precisely because of the likely further weakening of the Socialist grip on these groups that new elections might turn the gradual decline of the party into what an official magazine of the SFIO has called a possible *déroute*.[20]

The regional distribution of Communist gains and Socialist losses in the elections of 1945 and 1946 shows that the Communists had already made major inroads into the rural strongholds of the SFIO, a matter which will be dealt with elsewhere.* In the cities and towns a great number of shopkeepers and small businessmen had, in 1936, identified themselves with the Popular Front and with what then seemed its efficient core, the SFIO. At that time, the difficulties which the depression, characterized by overproduction, had created for the lower middle classes apparently justified the propaganda of the Popular Front against the restrictive practices of the "trusts," and against the "200 families." In the immediate postwar elections there was no reason for these groups to change their allegiance; it was due to this following alone that in 1945 the SFIO could still be included among the "Big Three" of the French party system.

Since then, the character of the postwar economic crisis, inflationary instead of deflationary as in the 1930's, has profoundly affected the position of the middle classes.[21] Small business, especially all kinds of middlemen, have on the whole greatly, though probably only temporarily, profited from the economic disruption. Their feelings of insecurity about the future have easily been turned into a bitter opposition against any form of planned economy and any kind of governmental interference designed to put an end to the prevailing "free for all." On the other hand, those living on a fixed income were economically crushed by the inflation. They saw on the social ladder below them a working class with a drastically lowered living standard, and immediately above them the profiteers of the crisis. Hence, they came to dread being drawn definitely into the ranks of the proletariat and preferred to identify themselves with the advocates of laissez-faire, even when their own social and economic position hardly justified such a stand.

---

* See Chapter 13.

[19] For a not altogether friendly but interesting description of the earlier relationship between *normaliens* and the Socialist Party, see Hubert Bourgin, *De Jaurès à Léon Blum. L'École normale et la politique* (Paris, 1938).

[20] See the very searching article by Lucien Guignon, "Alerte au parti socialiste," *La Revue socialiste*, Nouv. sér., No. 10 (1947), 467.

[21] For an excellent analysis of these changes, see Dominique Olivier, "Conjoncture économique du néo-fascisme," *Esprit*, xv (1947), 867 ff.

Whether the lower middle classes might become the followers of a neo-Fascist movement (a path they were unwilling to tread in 1934) cannot be discussed here. But it is quite obvious that they can hardly form the solid backbone of a Socialist Party.

III

From its earliest days to the present, the SFIO has devoted a greater amount of discussion than any other European Socialist party to the question of whether and under which conditions governmental responsibilities might be assumed before the D-day of Socialist revolution. A variety of factors have turned this problem into a source of permanent torment for French Socialists. The loose structure of all parties to their right encouraged such careers as Millerand's, Briand's, and Laval's and provoked a constant fear of renegades. The emphasis which Jaurès placed on the value of Republican institutions for the emancipation of the working class, and the criticism he voiced against Marxian notions of the class character of the state, made palatable the thought of participating in bourgeois governments. Simultaneously, the inability of establishing that permanent relationship to working-class organizations which other social democratic parties have never lacked, resulted in permanent frustration. All this found expression in continuous sophisticated and subtle discussions about the dangers and opportunities of "power." For such discussions Léon Blum was by temperament and training superbly gifted, but they attracted to the SFIO a leadership fundamentally different from that of the party's fellow members in the Socialist International.

The question of governmental participation by the Socialists was posed anew and with particular acuity by the contradictory situation which has arisen since Liberation. The initial weakening of French capitalism leading to extended nationalizations and a generous social security legislation was followed by a constant regression of Socialist strength in the electorate.[22] To preserve the earlier gains by remaining in the councils of government appeared as important as it was precarious. The two-front attack on the Fourth Republic from the Right and the Left seemed to throw upon the SFIO the obligation of defending the badly shaken democracy. All but delighted to follow in the footsteps of as indefatigable a Republican as Jean Jaurès had been, the Socialists are fighting in the person of De Gaulle the shadows of

[22] Sympathies for the SFIO seem to have been stabilized at about a maximum of 16 per cent of the electorate. (See *Sondages*, x [1948], 172.) This figure should not only be compared with the 24 per cent of votes obtained by the Socialists in 1945 and the 20 per cent in the elections of 1936, but with the much higher hopes of Resistance days.

General Revanche and of the clerico-military reaction of Dreyfus days.[23]

"The revolution in France has not started," wrote Léon Blum in 1947; and he went on to explain in terms very similar to those formulated by Jaurès half a century earlier how in the modern democratic state which is "detaching itself progressively from capitalism" the Socialist Party might assume governmental responsibilities "in order to establish favorable conditions for the creation of a socialist society." [24] What the French Socialists fail to perceive (as did the German Social Democrats of the Weimar Republic before them) is that such an approach makes the existing Republic a transitory phenomenon, and that in an age of "decisionism" a merely transitory scheme is not apt to generate much ardor.[25]

In fact, the trying tests to which the SFIO has been subjected while participating in the governments of the Fourth Republic have borne no similarity to Léon Blum's theoretical considerations. The traditional French preference for a weak executive has been mentioned to explain why in spite, or rather because of, its continuous decline, the Socialist Party was never without representation in the cabinet between 1944 and February 1950.[26] Immediately after the most decisive electoral defeat which the SFIO has suffered so far, a necessarily short-lived but singularly successful all-Socialist cabinet was formed.

The difficulties which the Socialist Party has encountered while sharing governmental responsibilities had a number of causes:

1. The unwillingness to abandon the cabinets of the so-called "Third Force" was constantly motivated by the necessity of denying to the two antidemocratic blocs the path to power. While tactics dictated by a "plague o' both your houses" promise turbulent times under any circumstance, they result in a particularly frustrating political experience when the forces occupying the middle ground are heterogeneous and disunited. The divergences which separate the SFIO from Radical-Socialists and the MRP have been discussed in an earlier paper.* It might be added that among the very same members

---

* Chapter 9.

[23] For a typical statement on the objectives of Socialist participation in the governments of the Fourth Republic by a prominent Socialist, and quoting Léon Blum on a comparison between Boulanger and De Gaulle, see Étienne Weill-Raynal, "Le Problème de la majorité gouvernementale," La Revue socialiste, Nouv. sér., No. 16 (1947), 537–53, and esp. p. 549.

[24] Léon Blum, "Exercice et conquête du pouvoir," ibid., No. 15, 385–95.

[25] cf. Franz Neumann, Behemoth (Toronto, New York, London, 1944), pp. 29–30, for the situation, in some respects strikingly analogous, under the Weimar Republic.

[26] See Raymond Aron, Le Grand Schisme (Paris, 1948), p. 188. The Socialists were dropped by Bidault in February 1950 but returned to the Cabinet under Pleven in July of the same year.

of the Socialist Party who have a true phobia of both Gaullism and Stalinism, the formula of the "Third Force" has aroused suspicion instead of enthusiasm. Directives from the national headquarters to make the Third Force a "living reality" on the local or departmental level have simply been ignored.[27] One of the reasons for such an attitude is the traditional, almost fanatical devotion of the Socialist *militant* to a somewhat outworn, but nonetheless intransigent, formula of anticlericalism. *Laïcisme* is evidently losing in general appeal and has been criticized by some Socialist leaders,[28] but it still prevents SFIO members from engaging in frank political collaboration even with the socialist elements of the MRP.

2. The failure to obtain extraparliamentary support for its present tactics has resulted in reducing the SFIO to a purely parliamentarian factor in the political life of the country. Hence, the party appears from yet another side as the heir of Radical Socialist inefficiency and opportunism. Ramadier might be considered as the most typical representative of an outmoded species of Radical politicians. His popularity, especially with the working class and even with Socialist Party members, has been at all times extremely low.[29]

The decline of parliament during the last decades of the Third Republic had substantially weakened the political role of the Radical Socialist Party, since its center of gravity lay in the two houses of parliament. In the Fourth Republic, and in spite of constitutional provisions against decree-laws, the importance of the National Assembly has further dwindled. The often lamented deterioration of parliamentary debates in contemporary France is only an outward sign of a shift of power away from parliament. Under such conditions, the reduction of the SFIO to an exclusively parliamentarian force has cast on the Socialist Party the same disgrace of shallow verbosity which characterized Radicalism before the downfall of the Third Republic. That the Socialist Party was in danger of falling into the pitfalls of the Radicals had been foreseen by none other than Léon Blum as early as 1918.[30]

[27] In the fall of 1947, 57 per cent of a representative sample of Socialist voters declared that they would not vote for a party which would try to group all of the elements represented in the Third Force and place itself between the Communists and De Gaulle. Only 20 per cent were willing to vote for such a party. See *Sondages*, IX (1947), 249.

[28] See e.g. Auriol, *op. cit.*, I, 326–29. Public opinion polls show that in January 1947, 61 per cent of the general and 50 per cent of the working class population were in favor of permitting parochial schools, while only 27 and 37 per cent respectively took the traditional anticlerical attitude of giving the monopoly of instruction to the public nondenominational schools. See *Sondages*, XI (1949), 44–45.

[29] In the fall of 1947, 56 per cent of the voters were dissatisfied with Ramadier; among the working class his sympathizers numbered only 11 per cent. *ibid.*, IX (1947), 202.

[30] For a sharp criticism of the turn of the SFIO toward traditional Radicalism, see Guignon, *loc cit.*, p. 612; Gaston Goldchild, "Nous n'étions pas dans le coup," *La Revue*

3. Because of their desire to preserve the social and mildly collectivistic features of earlier legislation, the Socialists have become in the eyes of the public the protagonists of a planned economy and the advocates of sweeping nationalizations. Actually, French Socialists (as well as the prewar plan of the CGT) have strenuously endeavored to devise solutions which would prevent bureaucratic rigidity in nationalized industries.[31] Vincent Auriol, writing before the Liberation and well aware of the bureaucratic pattern of political and economic institutions in France, warned explicitly against such dangers. He proposed an imitation of the British public corporation and indulged in rather sweeping generalities about "economic federalism" in the tradition of Proudhon and the Paul-Boncour of old.[32] Moreover, certain earlier proposals for nationalization had been designed as remedies for the ills of an economy characterized by an oversupply of goods. They have now been put into practice under conditions made painful by insufficient production.[33] But here again fine distinctions have proved unable to distribute responsibilities. The general wrath against *dirigisme*,[34] which is strengthening the hand of the Radicals and is at the same time unscrupulously exploited by the Communists, has altogether turned against the SFIO. Some of its technically able leaders like André Philip, Tanguy-Prigent, and Robert Lacoste have, in spite of their remarkable Resistance record, discredited themselves and their party by their doctrinaire approach to the problem of economic controls.

The rift between foes and friends of *dirigisme* dividing "all Gaul" runs through the Socialist Party itself and thereby adds further to the difficulties of formulating a dynamic policy.[35] That advocates of a return to laissez-faire economics become ever more numerous and vocal in an organization devoted to the tenets of Socialism is partly due to the shift in the class basis of the party. It is also the expression

socialiste, Nouv. sér., No. 7 (1947), 104–8; and one of the most despairing articles written about the evolution of the Fourth Republic, Jean-Marie Domenach, "De la Résistance au radicalisme," *Esprit,* XVI (1948), 441 ff.

[31] See e.g. Jules Moch, "Le Parti socialiste au peuple de France," quoted in Spire, *op. cit.,* pp. 126–27.

[32] Auriol, *op. cit.,* I, 175, 190 ff.

[33] Interestingly to this point is Lucien Laurat, *Déchéance de l'Europe. Capitalisme et socialisme devant l'héritage de la guerre* (Paris, 1948), p. 113.

[34] In 1947, 67 per cent of the population advocated a return to a free market economy without rationing or price fixing. In regard to this question, the opinion of the working class hardly differed from that of the general population. See *Sondages,* IX (1947), 171, and Service de Sondages et Statistiques, *Sondages de l'opinion publique française,* No. 38 (1947), 569–71.

[35] For the divergences within the party, see Tr., "Tour d'horizon," *Revue politique et parlementaire,* CXCIV (1948), 304; F. Lefrançais, "À la veille des élections: L'Heure du dernier choix," *La Revue socialiste,* Nouv. sér., No. 5 (1946), 601–15; and Aron, *op. cit.,* pp. 289–90.

of bitter disappointment over the results of nationalization and extended social security legislation. Instead of forming the cells of a democratic socialist order of the future or at least providing stepping-stones toward fuller economic democracy, the hoped-for welfare state has led to a widely resented bureaucratic regimentation (and often to extensive Communist prebends).

By its indecision, which results at times in mere verbal opposition to the easing of economic controls, and at other occasions in justification of all regulatory policies initiated by a Socialist cabinet minister, the party is losing further support alternately to the Right and to the Left. The secretary of the party, M. Guy Mollet, is left with the sad consolation that the polarization of society, hence "objective factors of history," are constantly helping the enemies of Socialism to turn against the SFIO every discontent hailing from whatever camp.[36] The Communists, on the other hand, seem to derive strength from the violence of attacks directed against them by conservatives and reactionaries.

When the Socialist Party is made the chief culprit of economic and administrative chaos, it is usually overlooked that Socialist cabinet ministers have held posts which gave more apparent than real power of direction. In the Fourth Republic, just as in the times of Rouvier, the Ministry of Finance commands and shapes economic policies, a fact that seems to be singularly well hidden from public knowledge.[37] Except for a short interlude of exactly one week during the Schuman cabinet in September 1948, the Socialists have never furnished the coalition governments with a Minister of Finance, but had to leave this post to their conservative colleagues. Socialist cabinet members have been exposed to popular displeasure as Ministers of National Economy or of Industrial Production, posts more highly publicized than influential which even under the Monnet Plan have never been properly organized.

Vanishing strength and failing cohesion of their party have constantly diminished the Socialist weight within the governmental coalition. The resulting popular dissatisfaction is in turn further sapping Socialist influence. The moment might soon come when the question of Socialist participation in future cabinets will be decided in the negative, not because a SFIO convention refuses to give further sanction to such collaboration, but because other political forces conclude that the usefulness of the Socialists has come to an end.[38]

[36] Mollet, *loc. cit.,* p. 659.
[37] On this point, see Olivier, *loc. cit.,* p. 873.
[38] Note that this paper was read on February 2, 1950, two days before M. Bidault formed the first "Socialist-free" cabinet since the Liberation.

IV

On the eve of the municipal elections of 1947 an observer, not at all unfriendly to Socialism, concluded: "If the Socialist Party today has no longer the method of a Marx, nor the faith of a Jaurès, nor the austerity of a Guesde, what is left for it? Power, undoubtedly. . . ." [39] Since then, power too has been all but lost.

The developments here described have had serious repercussions on the internal life and the organization of the SFIO.[40] Both horizontally and vertically a rift—or, rather, rifts—have appeared that have condemned the party as such to inactivity, caused the utter disappointment of the members, and thereby contributed to a constant hemorrhage of membership. The vertical rift has been at several levels: there exists estrangement between the upper strata of the party functionaries, such as the national and departmental officers who attend the official party gatherings, and the *militants;* within the local sections, between the more active *militants* and the mere dues-paying members; and between the party membership and the Socialist voter. At every one of these levels, problems are raised that are of no consequence to the others; indeed, the problems are formulated in a language that is different from one category to the next. Under these conditions, the written and spoken word has lost effectiveness and meaning. The notorious insufficiency of material means which the Socialist Party could use for propaganda purposes has only added to the existing difficulties. And the more the party member feels left alone, the less there is incentive to become active within the organization or simply to remain a party member.

According to official figures, which may well be padded, the dues-paying membership declined from 370,000 at the end of 1945 to 156,-000 four years later. The central party organ, *Le Populaire,* a mere shadow of its prewar self, is said to have at present a total printing of 12,000 to 15,000 copies, with no more than 3,000 sold in Paris.[41] The official theoretical magazine of the party is anemic to the point that for lack of funds it has to interrupt publication time and again.

The horizontal rift appears in Paris as well as in the provinces. When in 1946 the majority-minority relationship of the factions

[39] Jacques Fauvet, "Le Parti socialiste n'est pas un glaive mais un bouclier," *Le Monde,* October 4, 1947.

[40] Very detailed and most interesting to this point is Mlle. Saulnier in "Enquête sur la France désorientée," *loc. cit.,* pp. 52–54; also Mollet, *loc. cit.,* pp. 660–61, and Marabuto, *op. cit.,* pp. 132–34.

[41] See also Michel Rouzé, "Destin de la S.F.I.O.," *Action,* September 8, 1949, and Roger A. Priouret, *La République des partis* (Paris, 1947), pp. 235–36.

within the executive committee was reversed and instead of Daniel Mayer, faithful acolyte of Léon Blum, Guy Mollet became Secretary General, he was supposed to represent the Socialist *militants* as against the parliamentary representatives. In his own estimate, he is a devotee of Marxism rather than of Socialist humanism. Actually, he and his colleagues have been isolated in both directions: unable to establish contacts with the party echelons below them, they also are separated by activities, outlook, and temperament from their fellow party members in the Palais-Bourbon and the ministerial offices. Similar differences exist between the party federations of various *départements*. In party gatherings the delegates of the relatively strong federations of the Nord and the Haute Vienne, to give but two examples, usually express viewpoints opposed to those of the weaker or more rural party federations. The situation has reached a point where observers have spoken of the SFIO as being a federation of Socialist parties rather than one Socialist Party. That this further diminishes the effectiveness of the party is quite obvious. At the annual conventions, there is a noticeable progressive decline both of ardor and of talent.[42]

With a mixture of Guesdist belief in the well-nigh automatic Socialist victory and of self-pity—a psychological attitude quite characteristic of the present Socialist leadership—Guy Mollet has occasionally boasted that "in all our meetings our ideas receive the approval of the audience. The whole country is actually convinced of the correctness of our basic position. . . . But," he adds in melancholy fashion, "the voter doubts our efficiency." [43] Such a lack of faith in the party's effectiveness explains in part why there is an almost complete absence of youth among the inscribed membership. As far as there is political activity at all among the young, they have joined the Communists, the RPF, and even the MRP. As could be expected, the sympathies of the younger age group among the working class electorate are far more on the side of the Communists than of the SFIO.[44]

In the midst of so much confusion and frustration, constant efforts have been made at elaborating a new doctrine of Democratic Socialism. If earlier hopes of replacing the old SFIO by a new broader labor party had come true, theoretical discussions might have been relegated to the restricted circle of a French Fabian movement. The progressive reduction of Socialist strength has further accentuated the somewhat sectarian character for which the SFIO was known in pre-

[42] On the 40th and 41st National Congress of the SFIO, see especially *Le Populaire*, July 1–6, 1948, and July 14–19, 1949.

[43] Mollet, *loc. cit.*, p. 662. For an interesting characterization of the present Secretary General of the SFIO, see Priouret, *op. cit.*, pp. 219 ff.

[44] See *Sondages*, X (1948), 59, 70.

war days. Discussions about the theoretical foundations of Socialist action have hence been given undue weight. The party spokesmen who are carrying on the discussions frankly admit that they hope to find in a new fundamental approach the explanation of past failures and the means of correcting regretted mistakes. But because of the rift which has been described those who represent the SFIO in the political life of the nation are less and less guided by theoretical considerations.

It has rightly been maintained that the accidents of his career which threw Jaurès into the field of practical politics (accidents which Jaurès never truly regretted) deprived French Socialism of the theoretical contribution of an extremely lucid mind. If he had not devoted a good part of his unusual energy to the daily business of a deputy, he could have contributed greatly to the elaboration of modern Socialist thought.[45] However uncontested his leadership was during his lifetime, at his death Jaurès left to his party a heritage heavy with liabilities. At least in part because of Jaurès' example, the abler adepts of French Socialism were frankly more interested in the business of getting votes than in elaborating a Socialist theory. This spelled weakness rather than strength in a country where reform movements of whatever temperament have always searched after a system which would give satisfactory intellectual expression to their practical aspirations.

For those who made an attempt at elaborating the doctrine of a twentieth-century French socialism, Jaurès' spiritual legacy was rather one of confusion, however lucid his own writings had been. The master's passionate belief in unity enabled him to reconcile many apparently conflicting concepts, such as patriotism and internationalism, revolution and peaceful change, historical materialism and humanitarian ideals, critique of imperialism and praise of the Franco-Russian alliance. For his epigones there remained just as many contradictions which each in turn, according to his inclination, presented as the absolute truth until the discussions about the correct interpretation of Jaurèsian thought turned into sterile disputes.

The brilliant dialectics of Léon Blum were never able to dispel the haze of unreality that enveloped the discussions among French Socialists between the two World Wars. There was on his part an ardent attempt to overcome the dichotomy between the practical politician and the Socialist thinker. His authenticated remark after the

---

[45] See Roger Soltau, *French Political Thought in the Nineteenth Century* (New Haven, 1931), pp. 436-38. For recent re-evaluations of Jean Jaurès, see D. W. Brogan, *French Personalities and Problems* (New York, 1947), pp. 95-98, and Henry W. Ehrmann, "Jean Jaurès—Last of the Great Tribunes," *Social Research*, XVI (1949), 332-43.

victory of the Popular Front at the polls in 1936: "A new man must emerge in me," is psychologically quite revealing.[46] There was also, especially in his book written in captivity and in his subsequent writings, an effort to tap the humanist wells of Marxist thought. There he hoped to find a synthesis between basic Socialist concepts such as the belief in class war and the concern for human dignity. It is true that his endeavors took occasionally an altogether scholastic turn. It seemed, for instance, all-important to him that in the postwar statutes of the SFIO, the party was described as devoting its efforts to an *action de classe* rather than to the *lutte de classe*. Indeed Blum sought to prove that his was the correct translation of Marxian notions.[47]

Léon Blum's thinking—and in this regard he never changed after he entered the Socialist camp—is characterized by a belief in the perfectability of the human race and in its continuous progress toward complete emancipation from all shackles. Blum shared his overestimation of the moral forces present in the labor movement and his unalterable political and philosophical optimism with the entire leadership and many of the *militants* of the SFIO.[48] However contemptuously men like Guy Mollet and his friends might defend themselves in the name of Marxism against any concepts of a "socialist humanism," their basic attitudes are hardly different from those of Léon Blum. Indeed those are concepts characteristic not alone of French Socialism but of the entire *parti du mouvement* that has formed the antitraditionalist bloc in the Third Republic.

Today, after attempts at a more pragmatic approach to efficient politics have failed, the SFIO seems to be the only remaining political force faithful to the traditions of rationalism once vivid in the *parti du mouvement*. To its left are the Communists whose Stalinist philosophy, if philosophy it is, appears impregnated with a deep pessimism about the educability of the masses. The French Communist Party does not hesitate to indulge in an increasingly irrational appeal to followers and sympathizers. To its immediate right are the remnants of the MRP, among them sincere socialists who are, however,

---

[46] See Goguel, *La Politique des partis*, II, 281. For an interesting evaluation of the not very significant contribution of Léon Blum to Socialist thought and of the important differences between him and Jaurès, see Claude Harmel, *Lettre à Léon Blum sur le socialisme et la paix* (Paris, 1949), esp. pp. 89–91, 135–37, and 212–13.

[47] Léon Blum, "Notes sur la doctrine," *La Revue socialiste*, Nouv. sér., No. 3 (1946), 257–61.

[48] By his general outlook and personality Léon Blum fits perfectly the clear-sighted description of the bourgeois leader in the Socialist movement given by Robert Michels; *Political Parties. A Sociological Study of the Oligarchical Tendencies of Modern Democracy* (New York, 1915), pp. 252 ff. For a very interesting psychological remark on Léon Blum's "fundamental sophistication," see J.(ean) F.(raisse), "Journal à plusieurs voix," *Esprit*, XVII (1949), 705–6.

by temperament and *mystique* skeptical about the possible achievements of mundane existence.

Reflecting on the odious spectacle of the Dreyfus affair, Jules Guesde, in an access of despair, exclaimed: "What are we going to do one day, what are the Socialists going to do with a human race so degraded and dejected? We will come too late, the human material will be vitiated when our time has come to build our edifice." [49] Perhaps we are faced here with the deeper causes for the failure of Democratic Socialism in France. Since Guesde wrote, energies have been wasted by two wars, faith has been dulled by upsurges of hope too often followed by disappointment, self-confidence has been exhausted by the inability of overcoming the deficiency in civic spirit.

It is quite characteristic and frankly pathetic to read today with what anxiety the present President of the Republic recommended from his confinement in Vichy France that institutional changes destined to transform the political mores be introduced immediately after the country's liberation from the enemy. He feared that if this opportunity passed, it would be too late and new threats to republican liberties were bound to arise.[50]

Not much is to be gained from speculations as to whether the historical moment of vindication has definitely passed for the French Socialist Party or whether its decline is reversible. In the motherland of Socialist thought, Socialism might well survive even if the SFIO should find itself reduced to an impotent sect. What, if anything, does the past suggest as to the future?

From Babeuf and Saint-Simon to Marx and Lenin, Socialism had at all times a twofold countenance which in France more than in any other European country made the Socialist movement suffer from an internal contradiction. Having inherited from the revolution of 1789 the task of emancipating mankind, Socialism proposed to continue the storming of Bastilles by attacking the "bondage" to which capitalism subjected the individual. Hence the individualistic and at times frankly libertarian character of the Socialist movement.

Simultaneously Socialism suggested a new hierarchy of social and economic institutions, designed to give to the masses a feeling of security which they were rapidly losing. Hence there was an authoritarian strand in Socialism on which Louis Napoleon and his Saint-Simonist entourage endeavored to lay hold. In our own times the corporatist ideas of the neo-Socialists and of certain reformist labor leaders—as well as the builders of the Soviet state—have identified

---

[49] From a speech delivered in Lille, quoted by Michel Collinet, *La Tragédie du Marxisme* (Paris, 1948), p. 319.

[50] Auriol, *op. cit.*, I, 301.

Socialism with a highly organized system commanding and enforcing rigorous discipline.

In the "era of tyranny" which the First World War opened, the libertarian accents of Socialism, represented mostly by the SFIO, continued to appeal to the French farmers, sons of radicals and Jacobins, and to the skilled craftsmen in the cities. The operatives of mass industries, whose reactions even before 1914 alarmed the Syndicalist and Socialist élite, have looked for different values and loyalties.

That since Liberation, and in spite of the memories of the Ribbentrop-Molotov pact, the French Communists have been able to control the classes which in other European countries are in the fold of the social-democratic parties, seems to prove that the SFIO has not been successful in holding out a dynamic promise of both freedom and security.

When the French Socialists speak of liberty, they merely arouse suspicion that their vision of the future is but a return to the economic and social anarchy of the Third Republic. When they warn against the price French workers would have to pay if they were to obtain "security" on Communist terms, the Socialists' arguments are self-defeating because they cannot point to a hopeful alternative guaranteeing, along with the right to work, the dignity of full partnership in the national community. Only if and when French Socialism proves capable of pointing to such an alternative can the working class be induced to give to a non-Communist Left the solid underpinning that it sorely needs.

12

++

THE STRUGGLE

FOR CONTROL OF THE FRENCH TRADE-UNION

MOVEMENT, 1945–1949 *

VAL R. LORWIN

++

IN EVERY country of any industrial importance labor at the war's end, even more than after the First World War, emerged with heightened confidence and great expectations. Its new importance took the form in free countries of a large participation in the direction of their domestic political and economic destiny and, in other countries, of use of the labor movement as a tool for seizure of complete power by a totalitarian party.

At the time of the Liberation French labor enjoyed a position unique in its history. Numbers organized were only one manifestation of its apparent power. The unions, which all told had about two million members at the outbreak of the war, quickly enrolled a total of some six million. The CGT (Confédération Générale du Travail), with perhaps five million, was the largest and the most important mass organization in the country. The Catholic unions of the CFTC (Confédération Française des Travailleurs Chrétiens) almost doubled their prewar high of 400,000.[1]

---

* Although for four years Mr. Lorwin was with the Division of International Labor Affairs of the Department of State, and served on various United States delegations to United Nations meetings, needless to say, all opinions expressed in this paper are his own.

[1] All French trade-union membership statistics require the most critical examination, whatever their source. The unions' official claims may be closer to the truth in a period of growth or confidence than in a period of decline, such as that after the loss of a great strike. There is a brief discussion of membership statistics in the excellent volume of Henry W. Ehrmann, *French Labor: Popular Front to Liberation* (New York, 1947), p. 288, note 2. For a recent sharp criticism of membership claims by the unions, and an attempt

In the Resistance labor had been more active, and had suffered more, than any other group. This was the position symbolized in the naming of Louis Saillant, CGT secretary, to succeed Bidault as president of the Conseil National de la Résistance on Bidault's entry into the government at the Liberation of Paris. Labor received recognition at first, perhaps, even beyond its real sacrifices and its real achievements. Striving to regain national self-respect, France developed its myth of the quasi-total Resistance which, for the historical record, extolled the strikes, sabotage, and the *maquis* of labor.

Perhaps even more relevant than labor's own contribution was the collapse of the other élites. The industrial, financial, and commercial élites and their political representatives in the Right and Center parties, and the military and bureaucratic élites had, on Liberation, an almost total lack of confidence in either their power or their right to continue running the country. The country shared this lack of confidence.

The program that was to distinguish a reborn France beckoned labor to a leading role. Everybody—at least everybody who dared to write or speak—was more or less Socialist, in that already-so-distant dawn of the Fourth Republic. The new France was to be more "social." The reforms which the Resistance called for, and which Algiers had begun to write into laws, drew heavily on the prewar demands of the CGT: nationalization, national planning, workers' share in control of the economy, greater social security, a cleansing of the press, democratization of recruitment for the civil service. It was assumed that labor, which had long been asking for these reforms, would be powerful in implementing them. Even those classes which had most opposed its organization and aspirations were resigned to seeing labor play a major role in the new France. The reasons for the frustration of many of these reforms, and for labor's failure to realize its expected role, are to be found in considerable part in the story of the struggle for political control of the labor movement.

The events in the struggle for control of the trade-unions—that is, essentially, the CGT—fall into three main periods. The first was the period of Communist seizure and consolidation, from Liberation to

---

to deduce "real" membership figures, see "Quels sont les effectifs réels des syndicats ouvriers?", *L'Economie*, September 2, 1949.

The methods of collection of annual and monthly dues and payments by local unions to their departmental unions and to the central offices make the determination of actual membership extremely difficult. Interunion competition adds one more reason for the padding of membership figures. But the very concept of membership perhaps differs from that of the "solid" trade-union movements in Scandinavia, the Low Countries, Germany and Austria, and the English-speaking countries.

May 1947; then a period of realignment and struggle, from mid-1947 to late 1948; finally, a relative stabilization of positions, in late 1948 and 1949. These periods correspond also to those of international labor developments.

II

During the first period the Communists rapidly seized and consolidated control of the CGT. At the same time the international labor movement saw the dissolution of the Socialist-led International Federation of Trade Unions and the creation of the World Federation of Trade Unions (WFTU) in 1945, the rapid taking-over of the apparatus of the WFTU by the Communists and pro-Communists, and its use for Communist propaganda and the aims of Soviet foreign policy.

In France, the Communists moved with speed and force as the labor movement emerged from the underground and rebuilt its organization. They had many trained people available, and they moved into the local and national offices of the industrial federations and into the most important *unions départementales*.[2] They assumed positions immediately in the union purge committees, and purged not only collaborators but many noncollaborators who were *persona non grata* to the Communist Party. Constantly reminding workers of the sins of collaboration of some of the leading prewar anti-Communists while exalting Communist martyrs, they identified anti-Communist with anti-national and anti-working-class behavior. They gave money and attention to a great stream of party and "front" press and publications. They used their presence in the government and their position in the CGT to install party members in jobs, and party dependables in posts in nationalized industries. In the confused and critical post-Liberation months in which the union and political-party structure was reconstituted, a well-organized party interested in power had all the advantages over poorly organized competitors interested in talk and politicking.

Communist control of the CGT was first, and discreetly, shown at the initial post-Liberation meeting of its Comité Confédéral National

---

[2] The term "federation" or "industrial federation" is used here for the French *"fédération,"* or what is in the United States called a national or international union ("international" because many unions have membership in both the United States and Canada) of workers in one industry or trade—e.g., metal workers, agricultural workers, etc. The term *"union départementale"* has been left in the French, to avoid confusion: it refers to the federation by departments of the local unions of the various industries and trades. It corresponds to the state federations of the American Federation of Labor or the state industrial union councils of the Congress of Industrial Organizations.

(CCN) [3] in March 1945. The ratio of ex-Confédérés and ex-Unitaires [4] on the Bureau Confédéral, the executive of the CGT, was changed from the 5–3 established by the clandestine agreement of Le Perreux in 1943 to give the Communists parity. By the next meeting of the CCN, in September 1945, the Communists took over full control of the national machinery of the CGT. They had the CCN create another secretary-general's post (anomalous as the term may seem) for Frachon, their very able trade-union boss. This did more than make him co-equal with Jouhaux, the CGT secretary-general since 1909 who was just back from captivity in Germany, for Frachon took over the reins at the rue Lafayette (CGT headquarters), leaving to Jouhaux chiefly the honorific activities of public representation at home and on the international scene.

The Communists also insisted that the CGT take a stand in accordance with that of the Communist Party and in opposition to that of the SFIO, on the vote on the constitutional referendum. The CCN's vote on this political move showed that the Communists already had a two-to-one majority over the Socialists and pure syndicalists. (Reasons for this predominance will be discussed later in this paper.) Moreover, they already had the major industrial federations, such as the coal miners, rail, metal, chemical, textile, food trades, agricultural, and building trades workers, and the big *unions départementales,* on their side; their opponents could muster only the clerical and civil service workers, a few minor industrial unions such as the pharmacists and barbers, and small *unions départementales.*

By April 1946, at the first Congress of the CGT since 1938, the Communists had a four-to-one majority over their divided opponents. The developing opposition to the Communist majority was a mixture of several elements. The only nationally known leadership in the minority was that of the Reformists, headed by Jouhaux.[5] Some

[3] The CCN is composed of representatives of all the national federations and all the *unions départementales* (UD). The CCN is the chief authority of the CGT between biennial Congresses. At this time, in line with the strong federal tradition of the CGT, each federation and each UD had a single vote, except for the two votes of the Paris Region UD. This method of voting was altered at the 1946 Congress, as was the method of voting at CGT Congresses.

[4] The terms "Confédérés" and "Unitaires" go back to the period of the 1921–1936 split. The former were the members of the CGT; the latter the members of the CGTU (Confédération Générale du Travail Unitaire). The CGTU, originally formed by a combination of Communists and anarcho-syndicalists, gradually came to be entirely Communist in character.

[5] The term "Reformist" has been used at times in its exact sense, to designate those of gradualist rather than revolutionary outlook; at other times, more loosely, to designate the non-Communists within the CGT (even though they included some of revolutionary syndicalist views), to avoid the more cumbersome phrasing that would otherwise be needed.

of the minority were "pure" apolitical trade-unionists or syndicalists of Reformist outlook, some were Socialists in membership. Others were revolutionary syndicalists, still breathing in words the fire which had disappeared in the CGT's action after the First World War. There were a few Trotskyites. The Reformists were loosely organized around the publication and distribution of the weekly *Force ouvrière* (founded during the underground period as *Résistance ouvrière*).

The Communist majority made a show of generosity in the distribution of places on the two elected central organs of the CGT. To the disgust of the more impatient anti-Communists, the Reformist leaders accepted 15 of the 35 places on the Commission Administrative, and kept their nominal parity on the Bureau Confédéral.[6] This allowed the Communists to retain the CGT's maximum utility to themselves—its comparative respectability as a trade-union, rather than a political, body.

The Catholic CFTC had reasserted its separate position soon after Liberation. It politely declined the CGT's offer of organic unity, although professing a desire to continue the unity of action of Resistance days.[7] Although in 1944 and 1945 it was not considered proper to use such terms openly, the CFTC leaders did not want to go into an organization likely to be dominated by the Communists. It also took a position of independence vis-à-vis the MRP. Pressure from its young and Leftish minority prevented its older leadership from creating any overt ties with the MRP, or following the MRP into a stand in favor of subsidies to church schools. The post-Liberation CFTC thus avoided adding the disadvantages of ties with a confessional, predominantly middle-class party to the already great disadvantages of confessional unionism in a country where anticlericalism is a living tradition among workers.[8]

---

[6] Actually, the Communists were a majority of the Bureau, since Louis Saillant, originally chosen during the underground days as one of the Reformist members, almost always voted with the Communists even at this period. Pierre Le Brun, nominally a Radical Socialist until his expulsion from that party, representing the technicians on the CGT Bureau, had been nominated by the Communists, and voted regularly with them.

[7] Catholic policy on postwar trade-union organization has varied from country to country. The prewar Catholic unions of the Netherlands, Belgium, Luxembourg, and France have been revived as such. In Germany the Christian (Catholic-cum-Protestant) unions and in Austria the Catholic unions have so far not been revived, and the Catholics have taken part in the unified postwar unions. This they did at first in Italy, and even when they seceded from the "unified" movement in 1948, it was to set up a federation which has insisted on its nonconfessional character.

[8] The CFTC also sought to minimize its confessional character by revising its statutes to refer no longer to Catholic "social doctrine as defined in the Encyclical *De Rerum Novarum*," but simply to the "principles of Christian social morality."

III

The second period, from mid-1947 to late 1948, saw the shift in the Communist Party line internationally and, in France, the alignment of forces within the CGT and an open struggle for control of the labor movement. Internationally, in the trade-unions, this was the period of the splits in the Communist-dominated Berlin unions and the Italian General Confederation of Labor, the formation of the avowedly anti-Communist Inter-American Confederation of Workers, the first attempts to form the anti-Communist Asian Federation of Labor, the open dissension and finally the split in the WFTU.

In France, the Communist leaders were finding themselves in danger of alienating their working-class base, despite their control of the CGT apparatus. "Control" of a trade-union movement is not a mechanical matter, especially in a country of democratic traditions and undisciplined habits. The leadership has either to meet the rank and file's bread-and-butter demands or deliver some psychic goods in their place. There are, moreover, no mechanisms in France of closed shop or dues check-off by which the leadership can hold control against widespread dissatisfaction, nor has membership loyalty been built up over a period of collective bargaining and day-to-day administration of contracts and settlement of grievances in the shop.

The enthusiasm of labor for reconstruction had indeed worn thin by 1946 and early 1947, as it seemed to be the only group paying the cost. The government's repeated promises of price stabilization were received with less and less credulity; and the most hopeful attempt at stabilization, that of the Blum ministry, had just washed out.

Absorbed though they were in their high parliamentary and ministerial activities, the Communists had to adjust to the rumblings of discontent from the rank and file of the unions. Their doctrine of "produce first—make demands later" was drawing bitter comment by the workers. The attempt to sell an incentive pay system had not succeeded. Wildcat strikes were breaking out. The Renault strike (launched by the Trotskyites, and first disavowed, then taken over by the CGT) and a number of other local stoppages in the spring of 1947 vividly recalled to the Communists the risks they were running of being "outflanked on the left." For domestic reasons alone, the party line was difficult to hold; and the international line was moving to the open break between East and West which came in a few months when Molotov walked out of the Marshall Plan talks in Paris. The Communists in the CGT and parliament briskly reversed their attitude on wage demands, released their post-Liberation brake on strikes, and managed to leave the government in May 1947 on the popular issue of wage demands. With wages they coupled the question of Indo-China, for anticolonialism was a popular theme with workers even though most of them were far more preoccupied with the high cost of living than with the high cost of empire.

Within the CGT, the lines hardened further. There had already been splits in a few federations, notably the postal workers' and railwaymen's unions. Lower echelon anti-Communists urged Jouhaux and the Reformist group around him in the Bureau Confédéral to fight it out within the CGT against the Communist Party or prepare to secede. But the Reformist leaders in the CGT national office hesitated to do either. Like the average French workingman, they had an attachment to unity for its own sake: partly sentimental, partly a realistic knowledge of how the splits in French labor had enfeebled the movement in the face of employers and government. They knew all too well how weak was their own fighting potential. In 1921, Jouhaux and his friends had forced the Communists and revolutionary syndicalists to split off, and thus saved for themselves the name, offices, and paraphernalia of the CGT. They would have little money or equipment, even with the benevolence of the government and possible aid from labor movements abroad. Moreover, whatever their youthful backgrounds, most of the national leaders of the Reformists had become public figures or office functionaries, not inspired organizers or rough-and-tumble fighters. It would be hard for them to begin again at the beginning.

For all their impotence at national CGT headquarters, moreover, the Reformists still had position and stakes in a nominally unified movement. Jouhaux, whose name was regarded as necessary to a new movement, was president of the National Economic Council, a vice-president of the World Federation of Trade Unions, and—perhaps dearest to him—since 1919 French workers' delegate to the International Labor Organization. Leaving the CGT was going out of a harbor in a small boat onto an unknown sea, in the half-light. And unlike the Communists, the Reformists could get little help from the political party to which they were closest—the Socialists—for reasons which have been discussed in Professor Ehrmann's chapter.*

The reluctance of the Reformist leaders was thus understandable. In November and December, however, events forced them to leave *la vieille maison* of the CGT. The Communists launched a great wave of strikes amounting in all but name to a general strike. They hardly bothered to cover the party aim in these strikes. They demanded the return of the Communist Party to the government (on their own terms), and attacked the Marshall Plan as fiercely as they denounced

* Chapter 11.

the genuine economic grievances from which the workers were suffering. Communist tactics as well as aims made the split ineluctable. To by-pass the Reformist opposition within the Bureau Confédéral, the Communist heads of twenty major unions had set up their own strike committee and ignored the regular CGT executive. As Communist violence against those workers who opposed the strikes mounted, the hard-pressed local *militants* of the Force Ouvrière group put pressure on the national leaders to split, on pain of seeing their following melt away. The result was the creation of the new Force Ouvrière confederation (nominally called the CGT-FO) in December 1947.

Because of the common sense of French workers, the opposition of the CFTC and the FO, the courage of the railwaymen's autonomous union, and the firmness of the government, the strike wave of late 1947 collapsed. The cost for the Communists turned out to be lower than perhaps feared by some of their union leaders who may have opposed the strike action. The Communists did not lose their most valuable asset in France: the CGT was shaken but it remained the dominant labor organization even after the collapse of the strike, the loss of many members, and the split.

The FO split did take away the ability of the CGT to speak in the name of French labor, but FO itself did not attract the bulk of CGT members, and most conspicuously it failed to recruit among the workers in basic industry. Perhaps two million members simply "voted with their feet" and left the CGT. Most of them did not join FO or, as was hardly to be expected, the CFTC. The FO leaders for the most part failed to capitalize in organizational terms on the character of the strikes and the Communist leadership's responsibility for their loss. They lacked the drive, as well as the equipment, the financial and physical wherewithal, to convert CGT members' resentment into membership in the new unions instead of allowing it to turn to apathy. Moreover, as the months passed, workers tired of the political use of the CGT and became increasingly dubious of the political independence of the Force Ouvrière.

For FO became a prisoner of government policy or lack of policy. It asserted, as part of its reason for being, that it was "nonpolitical" and that it was upholding the best traditions of "apolitical syndicalism." It was embarrassed at the public rejoicing with which the Socialist Party and the conservatives hailed its formation. It rejected any overt ties with the government or the Socialist Party. But it could not do anything that would upset the government or its ever-shaky parliamentary majority. And the government, including its Socialist members, found it easier to let its friends wait for satisfaction of their demands than to worry about people who had no other place to go.

The government's constant appeals for a revival of "confidence" apparently ignored the question of confidence among workers, who were once again feeling themselves cut off from the national community.

While the Communists were demanding wage increases, FO, the CFTC, and the Confédération Générale des Cadres (CGC) formed the *"cartel de la baisse"* (of prices), and spent their energies during the critical first half of 1948 telling the workers that wage increases would be illusory and only price stabilization would increase their real income. They referred hopefully to government "policies" of price stabilization.

This was an honest and courageous position, but it was based upon an overoptimistic expectation of economic events and of government action. By the summer of 1948 prices were rising again. Just then the government chose to seek budgetary equilibrium by removing a number of price subsidies, thus further pushing up the cost of living. Said one Force Ouvrière leader, after a stormy meeting with FO delegates from the provinces: "We are right, but our followers are hungry." It was hardly necessary to add that if the followers continued to feel hungry, the leaders ceased to be either "right" or leaders. The cabinet crises of the summer were the statement of this fact on the governmental level. On the industrial organization level, the result was the frustration and falling apart of the FO-CFTC-CGC *"cartel,"* the anemic condition of FO, and the CGT's big coal strike.

The coal strike of October-November 1948 was the second great wave of CP-CGT assault on the postwar government and the recovery of France. Like the 1947 strikes, it seized upon genuine grievances for barely camouflaged political purposes. The 1948 strike did not have the extent of the walkouts of 1947, for only the coal mines were effectively tied up. Yet, in a way, the CGT leadership struck deeper this time. By pulling out the mine safety and maintenance men—a blow at the mines and the miners' future livelihood unheard of in labor history, even in the coal strike under the Occupation—and by forcing the government to use the police and troops, the Communists deepened the chasm between workers and government. (As in so many outbursts of Communist violence in Europe, it was a Socialist Minister of the Interior who took the immediate responsibility for use of the troops.)

The 1947 and 1948 strikes were no successes in ordinary trade-union terms; in terms of international Communist strategy, it is too soon to call them failures. The strikes had failed to stop the Marshall Plan or put the Communists back in the government. They showed that the Communists did not have a complete veto power over the nation's rehabilitation. By clarifying this fact, and by clarifying the relation between the Communist Party and the Republic, they reduced Communist influence within France as a whole and within the labor movement. But in the longer run, the strikes of 1947 and 1948 slowed down French recovery and hence European recovery; they weakened the confidence of Europe and the United States in the central political, economic, and military role of France; and they contributed to a further deterioration of the social fabric of the nation.

FO and the CFTC felt aggrieved that the government had let them down by refusing to act on the distortions of the wage-price relationship until the Communists forced action through the CGT. Tardy adjustments were each time more costly to the government, and the strike itself far more costly to the national economy, than the adjustments that would have been acceptable earlier. Perhaps most costly of all, the workers were being confirmed in the impression that, if action was taken at all by the government, it was due to pressure from the Communists and the CGT. The government seemed determined to keep alive and reinforce the traditional antigovernmentalism of French workers.

The price the Communists had again risked paying in 1948 in order to estrange workers from the government was that of estranging them from the unions and from the party that had launched the unsuccessful strikes. There was an increase in resentment of CGT leadership, in apathy toward unionism and a temporary loss of membership. But again the CGT organizational apparatus came through practically intact, and its rivals failed to capitalize on its losses.

IV

Viewed not in any long run but in the short term of years since the Liberation, 1949 was a period of relative stabilization in the struggle for control of the labor organizations. Internationally, this was the period of the stabilization of hostile positions, following the WFTU split in January 1949, with the foundation of the anti-Communist International Confederation of Free Trade Unions in November 1949, opposing the WFTU over most of the globe.

The CGT's survival—shaken but strong—after the loss of the two great strike movements was unprecedented in French labor history. By early 1949, its numbers had dwindled considerably, to somewhere around two million, but it was still easily the dominant organization among industrial workers and in not a single basic industry was that dominance successfully challenged. It was even a strong minority among white-collar workers and civil servants.

Moreover, the CGT showed it could survive an improvement in workers' standard of living. The improvement was not brilliant, but some there had been since the CGT-FO split. It began to look as if the "Chamber of Commerce Marxism" which had held that people would almost automatically desert Communist leadership as their stomachs were better filled was not altogether right. Perhaps the Communist hold on French workers now had an ideological character which would outlast a period of decreasing misery. On the other hand, the government had shown the will in crises to maintain order and suppress sabotage and industrial insurrection. Cabinets might again fall, or fall apart, on the wage-price issue—as that of Queuille did in October 1949—but they would fall because they could not offer minimum satisfactions to their friends, rather than because of the strikes and menaces of their enemies.

FO was for the time stabilized as a minority movement of about the same size as the CFTC. Despite the initial enthusiasm for a non-Communist, nonconfessional movement, FO had neither organized masses of the hitherto unorganized, nor drawn many of the dissatisfied CGT members. In its relations with the parties and the government, it continued to profess full independence. To make a showing of freedom from the government, it even called a couple of one-day demonstration strikes, although itself fearful that the CGT might take over and run away with them. Relations between FO and CFTC were stabilized in one way. If FO had lived up to its early promise of growth, some unification between the two confederations, or at least between FO and the Left wing of the CFTC, might have taken place. In the course of 1949, it became evident that the two would for the time being continue to go their own ways.

Gaullist relations with the labor organizations were also somewhat stabilized during this period. After long blowing hot and cold on the idea of setting up a specifically Gaullist labor confederation, the General and his advisers decided during 1949 that they would not do so. In part this was to avoid antagonizing some FO leaders who they thought might prove more or less sympathetic to them; in part it was the result of Gaullist participation in the formation of the newest labor confederation, one more which offered to bring "unity" to the French labor scene.[9] This is the CTI (Confédération du Travail In-

9 There is no space here to discuss the other interesting splinter movements (the anarcho-syndicalist Confédération Nationale du Travail or the Fédération Nationale des Syndicats Autonomes), or the important Confédération Générale des Cadres (CGC). The CGC, the most conservative of the major labor groups, has gone its separate way without political attachments. In its own field, among the supervisory and technical staffs, it is pre-eminent even in industries such as mining, where the CGT has a commanding position among the manual workers.

dépendante), founded in October 1949, largely an outgrowth of the Travail et Liberté group. Among and back of the CTI are some former Vichy labor figures and some ex-Communists, excluded from the CGT in 1944–1945, many of them highly qualified professionals in labor organization. The other main current in the CTI is that of the Gaullists.

Most Third Force labor leaders have decided that, of the two threats, the Communists are far more dangerous than the Gaullists. Moreover, of the two, De Gaulle is more likely to come to power in the foreseeable future. The General's positive appeal to workers continues low, however, despite his lively weekly sheet, *Rassemblement ouvrier,* with its attacks on the government for unfair treatment of labor, and such heroic efforts as its attempts to identify the RPF with the traditions of May Day and the Paris Commune.

V

Some reasons for Communist success in taking over, and holding, control in the dominant branch of the French trade-union movement have already been suggested. Further reasons are brought out clearly in Professor Ehrmann's chapter on the Socialist Party, and in other discussions of Communist success among various groups elsewhere in this volume. For French workers too behave like Frenchmen. In addition I should like to recapitulate—I hope without bathing in a sea of clichés—a few special reasons for French workers' continued *gauchisme* in the years since the Liberation.

The feeling of the national rebirth that aborted, of *"la révolution manquée,"* showed itself early after the Liberation, before the war was over, and among none more than among the workers. That feeling was all the deeper because of the lip service paid to labor's contributions to the Resistance and to reconstruction. It was not only a matter of what Thomson, speaking of the Commune, has called "the fascination of the revolution which might have been" [10]; it was also a feeling of resentment for the revolution that should have been.

The *"réformes de structure"* afforded little satisfaction. In the nationalized industries many of the same foremen and the same managers were still in place. The *comités d'entreprise* did not change the worker's relation to his boss; Communist attempts at political use of the *comités* discredited some of them; their economic agenda were too technical for most worker members; and it soon looked as if the committees were carrying on merely the same social welfare activities as the Vichy *comités sociaux.* There was a National Economic

[10] David Thomson, *Democracy in France: The Third Republic* (London, 1946), p. 27.

Council with a trade-union leader as its president, but workers could not see that it accomplished much.

What workers did see was the show of black-market wealth and high living and the almost universal profitability of business enterprise. In the face of their own economic difficulties, these were a sore affront to their sense of injustice. *Épuration* seemed another affront; the unions had purged their own Vichyite officials; the Socialist Party had dropped many of its deputies; the government had shot a few journalists—but apparently nobody had bothered the business or financial collaborators.

The Communists canalized with skill and persistence the resentments thus aroused, even when they were still nominally a governmental party. They focused workers' hostility on such satisfying targets as the trusts, reactionary employers, and unpurged collaborators. They offered emotionally satisfying solutions: "Tax the rich!", "Confiscate illicit profits!", "Abolish government red tape and parasitic economic bodies!", "Collect reparations!" The Communists alone sounded as if they meant to do and were doing something about injustice. And they held out to the working class a promise of power and revenge for a century of repeated betrayals.

Changes in the distribution of national income and in the wage structure, due in part to inflation, in part to social reforms, nourished feelings of resentment and insecurity. The share of wage-earners in the total national income had probably declined as compared with prewar conditions.[11] For a long time, food and other shortages emphasized the decline in the workers' position relative to that of farmers growing their own food or manufacturers or middlemen having a *quid pro quo* for black- or gray-market trading. Housing difficulties and overcrowding had grown worse. If workers came close to their prewar standards of living, it was by working longer hours and having more members of the family employed than before the war. As they read the published figures of increased production, they complained that their own real income did not increase at all proportionately to increased productivity and increased total output.

Most public discussion of wage issues has been in terms of basic and legal [12] wages, without mention of the increased social wages

[11] Changes in money and real wages, in the wage structure, and in the distribution of national income are discussed in the present writer's section (with extensive bibliography) on "France," in *Comparative Labor Movements*, ed. by Walter Galenson, to be published in 1952.

[12] "Black-market" wage payments have inevitably been an accompaniment to the setting by the government of wage scales in the vastly complicated patterns of industrial, regional, and skill categories, including the "maximum average" legal requirements within categories.

which were the chief direct gain of workers after the war. The alterations in the wage structure introduced new elements of insecurity. Young unmarried workers, generally most susceptible to radical appeals, found themselves disadvantaged because a large part of total wage-earners' income now came from allowances based on family responsibilities. The more skilled workers likewise found themselves relatively disadvantaged. Family allowances take no account of individual wage rates.

In the baroque wage structure of the inflation period, there came into account payments in kind by factory canteens and cooperatives, and a great variety of flat-sum bonuses and allowances, which further reduced hierarchic advantages. It was from the skilled workers that the Socialists used to recruit much of what industrial labor support they had. The narrowing of differentials thus not only reduced incentives to acquire training or assume added responsibility in the production process; it also stirred resentments which the Communists have been able to direct against the social order as a whole.

Employers usually get as good unions as they deserve. Since the war the Communists have won out in the labor movements of capitalist countries only in France and Italy, the two countries in which employers before the war had shown least managerial enterprise and least social responsibility and where they even had denied recognition to the unions. In defense of French employers, it may be said that the CGT's long addiction to outworn revolutionary phraseology helped frighten employers away from the bargaining table. Cause and effect can hardly be separated here; they go hand in hand.

France has never yet really tried collective bargaining. There was a brief opportunity to develop the institution immediately after the Popular Front legislation, but most employers—their hostility to labor newly sharpened by the sit-down strikes and the Matignon Agreement—refused to accept collective bargaining in good faith. Both sides soon tended to leave decisions to government arbitrators instead of trying to reach agreement on their own.

In the post-Liberation period wages continued, as during the war, to be fixed by government action. Each major adjustment in wages has been a painful political decision, after cabinet and often National Assembly debate, in the heat of political and economic pressures. After December 1946, it was legally possible for unions and employers to negotiate on issues other than wages—e.g., working conditions, health and safety, apprenticeship. But collective bargaining is stultified when the major issue is removed from the area of joint decision. (The government in February 1950 finally returned wages to the area of collective bargaining—more than three years after this was first promised, and more than a year after the removal of practically all price controls.)

The continuation of government wage-fixing turned workers' increasing hostilities primarily against the state rather than against the employers. Lack of any real collective bargaining has delayed the possible development of a workers' interest and stake in responsible trade-unionism. It has, instead, placed a premium on political action by the unions and has consequently given a great advantage to Communist organization and tactics.

The Communist Party, unlike the other parties, had operated as such during the Resistance, and it alone emerged from the underground with a functioning apparatus. From top to bottom it was better prepared than its rivals for the struggle within the CGT. Its rivals were divided among many schools of thought and talk, of whom the Socialists alone represented possible mass party competition.

At the top the Communist Party made party policy and policy for its CGT leaders a part of one unified program.[13] The Socialist Party had a national trade-union committee, but it treated the unions as independent organizations, in part because it believed in their independence, in part because of its inability to coordinate its party policy with its trade-union aims. Communists in the CGT, as in any other activity, acted in accord with party aims and discipline. The Socialists exerted almost no discipline over Socialist trade-unionists. The Communist factory cell was designed for local trade-union activity. When the Socialists attempted in 1945 to revive their *groupes socialistes d'entreprise,* the attempt was a failure.

There are no overt dissensions among Communist trade-union leaders. Within Force Ouvrière, and even in the CFTC itself, serious divisions have made their appearance. Force Ouvrière was from the start beset by division, at first between the *"autonomes,"* who had seceded before the big split, and those who had followed Jouhaux and his friends out of the CGT in December 1947. There is a conspicuous bureaucratic element in the national leadership of FO (without the advantage of a smoothly functioning bureaucracy) and this has helped crystallize a good deal of the old-style antiauthoritarian feeling among local FO leaders and members. Differences have in part been those between Paris and the provinces, between older and younger leaders, and differences of attitude toward the government in general and government policies in particular. A few of the once-dissident FO

[13] To cite a single case: the sudden demand of the CGT Bureau Confédéral for a 25 per cent wage increase, announced several days before the June 2, 1946, elections, was timed so that the CP Politburo could immediately announce its support for the CGT claim. The Socialists, unprepared, and burdened by a somewhat greater sense of cabinet responsibility, went into the elections without any real response or counterappeal.

leaders have become "bonzes" themselves. But the very failure of the organization to grow as expected, and the general decline in the position of trade unionism in French society since liberation, have limited the possibilities of recognition and absorption of dissident leaders.

Despite the extremes to which the international Communist line has forced them, the French Communists have also managed to keep the tactical initiative. They have reduced their opponents, particularly FO, to what has often looked like mere negative anti-Communism. That, for many historical reasons, has little appeal to French workers. The non-Communists were unable to seize the initiative even with the launching of the European Recovery Program. Even then, with the turn in Communist Party policy they had been waiting for, they remained on the defensive because of their own Socialist shibboleths about the nature of American capitalism and because of the workers' profound distrust of the government directing the recovery program, as well as the employers responsible for production under it.

At the split, the CGT lost the initiative for a time, but it kept the moral and organizational advantages of the "unity" slogan and position. The slogan the Communist Party has exploited in party and trade-union maneuvers since liberation; the position is valuable in any trade-union split—as it had been to the Reformists in the period after 1921. Some respected non-Communist leaders (e.g., Forgues) remained with the old Confédération, as did one important union (the printers) of traditionally Reformist character. Another major union (the teachers) withdrew, but remained autonomous rather than join FO. Most important, within the individual CGT unions, a high percentage of rank-and-filers who were far from Communists remained.

The Communists have kept the initiative on the question of war and peace which haunts France in general and no one more than its workers' families. They have hammered on the familiar themes of capitalist aggression against the "Socialist countries," the revival of an unregenerate Germany, and now on French infantry as "cannon fodder" in the North Atlantic coalition. They have in effect monopolized the use of the word "peace." Non-Communist unionists were for several years reluctant even to speak about the nature of Soviet foreign policy, or the related questions of the suppression of free trade-unions and Socialist parties in the Soviet orbit. Many, perhaps most, of them have taken a "plague o' both your houses" attitude toward the East-West conflict.[14] Their internationalism has remained vague, defensive, and without effective symbolic association.

---

[14] A single example: "We do not at all subscribe for our part to a concept which sees in the term 'free' trade-unions a sort of hitching-on of the trade-union movement to

The conservative and reactionary revival of the last two years has played into Communist hands. By moving the center of equilibrium of the Third Force governments to the right, and by encouraging a "cold intransigence" [15] among employer groups, it has menaced the basis of compromise which the CFTC and FO need for survival, while the CGT has zestfully taken the counteroffensive in the name of an embittered working class.

Increased unemployment has given the Communists another initiative. The social security reforms have not created a system of unemployment *insurance,* but have left the relief of unemployment to *assistance* programs. The amounts of unemployment assistance are pitifully inadequate. Far worse, the general insecurity of French workers gives greater significance to the numerically small increase in 1949 of unemployment and the somewhat larger increase of partial unemployment. Unemployment makes it harder to wage and win strikes, but easier to carry on propaganda based on insecurity and traditional suspicions. Communist-CGT propaganda has managed to associate unemployment with the Marshall Plan: workers do not see the millions who *might have been* unemployed without ERP. Perhaps wounded national self-esteem makes it doubly hard to visualize the more complex fact of the unemployment that foreign aid has helped to avert.

Communist trade-union leadership has been more effective than that of its competitors at all echelons. It has shown far more organizing ability, toughness, and *dynamisme*—and even flexibility—than the other organizations. For a time at least, the Communist and the CGT position and prospects were such as most effectively to attract those with leadership qualities. Even "the élite of the Jeunesse Ouvrière Chrétienne," Bernanos could then say, "slips into Marxism as the river to the sea." [16]

Union dues have always been small, irregularly and grudgingly paid, in France; they never paid for an adequate union bureaucracy. Now the Communist Party and the CGT are developing a professional and reasonably competent, if not an independent, union civil service.

The Communist leadership advantage is most conspicuous and most important in the industrial workers' unions. It is there that FO is

---

a bloc of 'liberty' which would oppose itself, in imperialist rivalries which are not ours, to another bloc, that of the U.S.S.R." From the statement of the Comité de Liaison Intersyndical de la Loire (St. Étienne), formed by representatives of the CFTC, FO, and the autonomous teachers' union, "Constations guidant la constitution du comité" (1950), p. 4.

[15] The phrase is that of Minister of State for Information Teitgen (MRP), broadcast speech, March 12, 1950.

[16] "La Trahison du démocrate chrétien," said to have been written in 1948, published posthumously in *Combat,* March 7, 1950.

weakest. FO leadership, with a few exceptions, is dominantly one of white-collar and civil service workers. The CFTC, too, is primarily white-collar in leadership. It has a few promising industrial union leaders, but most of them are young and comparatively inexperienced.

In the Communist Party itself, a high percentage of the top leaders come from working-class backgrounds. There is not a single member with a manual worker's background in the Socialist Comité Directeur. The Socialist Party, even more than before the war, is run by intellectuals and professional people, mostly of middle-class background. The French workers' deeply ingrained *ouvriérisme* attaches suspicion to the Socialists, but can forgive the Communists a great deal.

The leadership and organizational advantages of the Communists have been reinforced by their doctrinal certitudes. And their rivals, especially the Socialist Party and the Reformist union leaders, have on both scores often suffered from a feeling of inferiority vis-à-vis the Communists.

In programmatic statements or theoretical writings since liberation, the labor movement has been poor. With the Communists setting the tone, the trade-unions have been busy with polemics rather than with programs; they have hurled more slogans and less theory than in times past.

The post-Liberation CGT and its Communist leaders took over the prewar CGT program. As the Reformist Capocci complained before the split: "People tell us, 'You must modify your vocabulary, you keep using the same formulas.' But, comrades, the . . . formulas of the . . . CGT—nationalization, social security, the general interest —these are old formulas, too, which some of you opposed at one time and which are now the formulas of all of us." [17] Although in tactics the Communists have shifted to an oppositional and class struggle role, their avowed domestic program continues to be largely that of the Reformist CGT of the interwar period. Neither the CGT leaders nor the large galaxy of Communist and *communisant* intellectuals have been concerned, or free, to contribute to the theory of the labor movement.

The Reformists glumly watched the Communists take over their old program along with their organization. They have generally emancipated themselves from the dead weight of revolutionary phraseology which no longer corresponds to their own temper—indeed, it never did correspond, except inversely—and to their possibilities of action. But they have hardly attempted yet to restate their general programs

[17] CGT: *XXVIe Congrès national de Paris, Compte-rendu sténographié des débats* (Paris, 1946), p. 127.

or philosophy in the light of post-Liberation experience, or their new relations with government and with other groups in society.

The Gaullists have made some effort to develop a labor program. But so far, all that the General and those around him have produced is a concoction of medieval guild doctrine and modern Franco-Italian corporatism, with a sauce of profit-sharing; the whole is a side-dish to anti-Communism which workers have found indigestible.

An essay in recent history may be expected to conclude, amid the appropriate forms of diffidence real or feigned, with a few intimations of events to come. But this is a singularly poor moment for prediction, of the immediate or of the more distant future. In the immediate perspective, the return to collective bargaining is dependent upon a legal framework which has been only partly enacted and less implemented, and upon an industrial atmosphere which is heavy and uncertain. In the longer run, the labor movement and all of France are peculiarly exposed to the bitterest winds of international conflict. Finally, it is almost impossible to be dispassionate in assessment of trends these days; the threats are too great to a culture which we cherish because it is so clearly a source of our own and yet so intriguingly different from our own. It is as true now as when Jouhaux wrote the words in 1937,[18] but we must repeat them with less optimism: "Nous ne sommes plus dans une période d'évolution lente, de succession paisible de phénomènes transitoires."

[18] *La C.G.T.: ce qu'elle est, ce qu'elle veut* (Paris, 1937) p. 187.

13

++

COMMUNISTS AND PEASANTRY IN FRANCE

GORDON WRIGHT

++

A BRITISH journalist, interviewing Maurice Thorez after the elections of 1946, asked incredulously: "How is one to explain the influence of the French Communist Party in the countryside? . . . That is something which surpasses our understanding." It's very simple, replied Thorez genially; the peasants see that our party is the only one which has fought courageously for democracy, for peace, and for France; they know that we have devoted the greatest effort to defending peasant interests.[1]

Skeptics may detect a certain oversimplification in M. Thorez's answer, and perhaps some naïveté in his interviewer's question. Certainly modern Marxists of the Leninist-Stalinist school have never sought to hide their interest in the rural population. "Attention to the peasantry!" cried Zinoviev twenty-five years ago. ". . . A party which is still far off from the conquest of power doesn't need this slogan. But from the moment that it becomes a serious Communist party, a party of the masses, it must ask itself: what will the peasants do?"[2] Engels wrote more than half a century ago that "in order to achieve power the Party must first go from the towns into the countryside and become strong in the rural districts"; and Stalin has described the peasant problem as "one of the most vital problems of Leninism. . . . Indifference toward so important a problem . . . is an unmistakable sign of downright betrayal of Marxism."[3]

With the official doctrine so clear, one need not be surprised that the French Communists have put a high priority on their peasant action. But perhaps there is some reason for surprise in the fact

---

[1] M. Thorez, *Une Politique agricole française* (Paris, 1948), p. 4.
[2] *Bulletin communiste* (Paris, August 15, 1924), p. 795.
[3] J. Stalin, *Foundations of Leninism* (New York, 1939), pp. 71, 62.

that they have been so successful. For the French peasantry appears to have little in common with the semiproletarian rural masses of Eastern Europe and Asia or of southern Italy—the only other areas where Communist penetration in the countryside has been great. In Eastern Europe, the party could easily split the peasantry by offering land to the poorer elements; after seizing power, it could proceed at leisure to proletarianize this peasant mass. But to win over a large segment of the French peasantry, with its reputation for ferocious individualism and its petit-bourgeois outlook, was a more complex task. Most French Communists, when the party was founded in 1920, did not believe that it could be done. Many of them sympathized with Trotsky when he cried in exasperation: Why do our French comrades keep reminding us that in France the peasantry constitutes four-sevenths of the population? "Peasants are peasants, and we are the workers' party!" [4]

The progress achieved in the countryside in the past thirty years would astonish or possibly dismay those early French Communists. Yet the results still do not satisfy the party's leaders. In 1947, during a visit to Moscow, Maurice Thorez admitted that he was disappointed at the peasants' slow response to Communist appeals. (One of his Soviet listeners burst out impatiently but somewhat impractically: "Treat them like the kulaks!") [5] There are signs that Thorez is even more disappointed today, for the party's rural strength has been on the wane since 1947. How far it has slipped, and how long it may continue to slip, are still not fully clear. This chapter proposes to sketch the growth of Communist peasant action during the past thirty years; to assess the party's present influence among the peasants; and to draw some tentative conclusions as to the party's chances of attaining the goal which Stalin defined some twenty-five years ago: "to transform [the exploited majority of] the peasantry into a reserve and ally of the working class." [6]

Two facts about the French peasantry may be noted briefly at the start, for each of them has provided the Communists with an entering wedge. First, there is the old Jacobin tradition which for decades has led many peasant owners (notably in the south) to vote for the party of the extreme Left. Doubtless these peasants are moved by the comfortable feeling that it is safe to vote for Socialism since Socialism never arrives; at any rate, their conversion to Communism is a fairly simple matter. Second, there is the fact that the peasantry is much more heterogeneous than common opinion would suppose.

[4] *Bulletin communiste* (September 7, 1922), p. 689.
[5] W. B. Smith, *My Three Years in Moscow* (Philadelphia, 1950), p. 153.
[6] Stalin, *op. cit.*, p. 63.

Although statistics are shaky and contradictory, it is clear that France contains a considerable rural proletariat and semiproletariat, amounting to perhaps one-third of the total farm population if sharecroppers (*métayers*) and small tenants (*fermiers*) are added to the farm laborers.[7] Some small owners might also be classed as semiproletarian; there are many whose tiny holdings permit only marginal subsistence, although the number of these marginal farms has been steadily declining. At the other end of the scale, large farms are common enough in certain regions to lend color to the idea of a growing capitalist concentration in agriculture, and to nurture some resentment on the part of the two million small owners against their big competitors.

Communism's great successes in the countryside date from 1944 (and to a lesser degree from 1936); but these successes would not have been possible without the foundations which were painfully laid during the lean years from 1920 to 1935. The most difficult task of that early period was not the conversion of the peasants, but the conversion of the party itself to the idea of mass peasant action. As late as 1925 one prominent leader, drafted to preside over a rural party meeting, appealed to André Marty: "You've got to tell me how I ought to talk to them; these peasant comrades make me nervous." [8] Most Communists, even after accepting the need for peasant action, preferred to leave the task to a handful of "peasant specialists" headed by Jean Renaud, who chose to confuse bourgeois historians by calling himself Renaud Jean. This young ex-peasant and trench veteran constituted himself a kind of one-man agrarian committee from the start; he founded a weekly journal called *La Voix paysanne,* persuaded the party to adopt an agrarian program at its Marseilles congress in 1921, and soon won enough notoriety to get himself publicly denounced by Trotsky. In a Comintern session, Trotsky alleged that Renaud Jean was preaching the old Russian Social Revolutionary doctrine, and was attempting to make the peasants equal partners with the proletariat rather than mere recruits to be led by the workers.[9] His criticisms were echoed in Paris by Vaillant-Couturier, who described Renaud in bittersweet fashion as "a genuine dirt farmer with his roots in the soil, antimilitaristic, idealistic, practical, honest, but in the old tradition of the peasant rebels who prefer liberty to equality; haunted by the enormous

[7] The Communists claim that more than half the members of the active peasantry own no land. They estimate that there are 1,200,000 farm laborers, 800,000 tenants (of whom only 100,000 are large "capitalist" tenants), and 200,000 sharecroppers (Waldeck Rochet in *Cahiers du communisme,* 26 [June 1949], 716). It may be pointed out that "sharecropper" is perhaps too brutal a translation for the French term *métayer;* there is more stability and less social stigma attached to *métayage* than to American sharecropping.

[8] A. Marty, "Le Parti français et les paysans," *Cahiers du bolchévisme* (November 15, 1925), p. 2102.

[9] *Bulletin communiste* (July 6, 1922), pp. 531–32.

peasant problem, to the point of making it the center of the workers' revolution." [10] Renaud denied the charges, but went on insisting that most of the peasant owners as well as the rural proletariat were open to conversion.

It was not long before Renaud Jean's doctrine had become the party's doctrine. Already in 1922 his agrarian program, the Marseilles Theses, had drawn the public approval of Lenin himself. Lenin found fault with a few secondary aspects of the Theses, but called them "basically quite correct," and "on the whole, very well taken." [11] This celestial sanction made the Marseilles Theses a permanent part of the French party's scriptures. Reprinted from time to time for the guidance of the faithful (with Lenin's gloss attached), they appeared most recently in pamphlet form in the autumn of 1949.[12] Their appeal was directed not to the rural proletariat alone, but to the mass of small holders as well. Collectivization was of course set up as a long-term goal, but the emphasis was upon a guarantee of hereditary land rights to all working peasants, and a transitional program of practical reforms based on the profit motive. The Theses also sought to exploit the peasants' traditional hatred of war. As Renaud Jean put it at the time, the party's program must be flexible, not rigid: "When doctrine is in conflict with the revolution, it is the revolution which is right." [13]

Renaud's victory was consolidated in 1923 when the Comintern adopted a new slogan: "For a Workers' and Peasants' Bloc," designed to "turn the party from a sect into a mass movement." The term "peasants" was chosen in conscious preference to "poor peasants." Fortified by this change and by public praise from Zinoviev and others, Renaud could pursue his course without fear of further sniping from fellow party members. By the end of 1925, the Communists had built up a whole new apparatus of national and regional agrarian committees; they had added courses in peasant action to the curriculum of the Central Leninist School; and they had founded, alongside their union for farm laborers, a new union (the Confederation of Toiling Peasants) designed to recruit small owners, tenants, and sharecroppers.[14] In the municipal elections of 1925 the Communists registered their only notable gains in the rural villages; and in 1926 the

10 *Bulletin communiste* (October 12, 1922), pp. 780–81.
11 Article signed "Russian Communist" in *Die Kommunistische Internationale* (April 1922), pp. 71, 75.
12 *Le Parti communiste et la question paysanne* (Paris, 1949).
13 *Bulletin communiste* (November 17, 1921), p. 847.
14 This union was the outgrowth of the Fédération des Travailleurs de la Terre, founded by Marius Vazeilles in the Corrèze in 1922. For several years it scarcely existed outside a few departments in the Massif Central. *ibid.* (October 4, 1923), pp. 617–19.

party reported to the Comintern that 70 per cent of its most recent converts were peasants.[15]

Yet with all of these signs of progress, the party's peasant action was still meager indeed. A handful of "peasant specialists" could not spread themselves over 36,000 rural communes; and vigorous direct action at the grass-roots level, well planned and steadily sustained, was essential for long-range success. At a national party conference in 1925, André Marty read his comrades a severe lecture on their apathy toward the peasant question. As evidence that the peasants were ripe for action, Marty related the experience of a Communist who had lately spent his vacation in the *bistros* of a small Midi village where no party agent had ever penetrated. Shortly after the visitor returned to Paris, cantonal elections occurred in the village, and the election authorities were astounded to find 180 write-in votes for Jacques Doriot and Marcel Cachin. Go thou and do likewise, comrade, Marty implied. He also urged that party tactics be made still more flexible by adapting them to the special mentality of each group and region; and he proposed that the party concentrate on peasant grievances, no matter how petty. Some weeks earlier, for example, an unfeeling prefect had denied some peasants the right to shoot marauding crows; the party should have seized the occasion to organize a national campaign against crows and prefects. Some comrades, concluded Marty, fear that the party may bog down in peasant action; in fact, the party can never overemphasize the peasant problem.[16]

But in spite of Renaud Jean's efforts and Politburo pep-talks, the party's peasant action lost momentum after 1926. The task of building up cadres was hampered by the severe internal squabbles of the late 1920's; party membership fell steadily until it hit an all-time low of 28,000 in 1933. Another handicap was the Comintern's decision to abandon its slogan, "Workers' and Peasants' Bloc," and to renew its old stress on the class struggle in the countryside. Reports of the liquidation of the kulaks in Russia did not make it any easier to appeal to small owners who were not quite sure where the boundaries of kulak status lay. In the 1932 elections, the Communists lost half their votes in the nation; and in some rural departments, the decline was even sharper.

Then came the upturn. Farm prices, already too low in proportion to industrial prices, collapsed in 1934. As thousands of peasants sought some outlet for their discontent and some promise of salvation, the Communists rose to the occasion by proclaiming the need for a peo-

---

[15] *Cahiers du bolchévisme* (April 15, 1926), p. 938.
[16] Marty, *loc. cit.*, pp. 2099–110.

ple's front. Once again Renaud Jean and his little staff of specialists
could direct their appeal to all the peasants, and not merely to the
poorest fraction. The experience which they had gained in fifteen
years of constant, frustrating, and apparently unproductive effort was
ready at hand. These agents had learned what the peasants wanted
to hear; their program of reforms contained something for everybody,
and it was phrased in the peasants' own language. In the elections of
1936, the party's most remarkable gains were scored in farming districts. The Communists doubled their total vote, but in a number
of rural departments their gain was threefold or fourfold. The most
notable progress was made in the old Jacobin areas of the center and
south. But the Leftist tradition alone was not responsible; a strong
contributing factor was the persistent grass-roots activity which a few
party members had maintained in certain departments over a decade
or more. The results of constant direct action by able organizers with
a flair for peasant work could be seen in such departments as Lot-et-
Garonne and Corrèze. No Communist could any longer doubt the
potentialities of peasant action. There was evidence too that peasant
owners as well as the rural proletariat were susceptible to conversion.
In some small-holding areas, the Communist vote was even larger
than in regions of farm laborers and sharecroppers.

During the Popular Front era after 1936, the Communists consolidated and extended their victory. They bombarded parliament
with bills to aid the peasantry; they organized demonstrations like
National Peasants' Day; they preached peasant unity, and sought to
merge their Confederation of Toiling Peasants with the Socialists'
National Peasant Confederation. Renaud Jean, by this time one of
the titans of the party, received a standing ovation whenever he appeared at party congresses. Go to the masses! was his watchword. He
urged Communists to join that village organization which contained
a majority of the local peasants, whether reactionary or progressive
in leadership, whether called a cooperative, a union, or a hunting
and fishing club.[17] For the first time, peasant action was undertaken
on a mass scale, not merely by a few specialists.

Then came the Soviet-Nazi pact of 1939, and the whole structure
collapsed. Renaud Jean and most of those around him could not hide
their spontaneous revulsion at the news. Renaud remained in the
party; but his quasi-heresy had extensive repercussions, and disrupted
the whole agrarian organization which he had built up almost single-
handed over two decades. Renaud's brief backslide also wrecked his
own political career. After the liberation of France in 1944, the

[17] *Cahiers du bolchévisme* (January–February 1938), p. 1091.

Politburo placed him in permanent quarantine and refused to endorse him as a candidate for deputy even though his old comrades in Lot-et-Garonne stuck by him loyally. To replace him as head of the party's peasant apparatus the party promoted one of Renaud's bright young aides of prewar days: Waldeck Rochet, son of a village artisan in Saône-et-Loire, onetime truck farmer, and alumnus of Moscow's Advanced Marxist-Leninist Institute, class of 1935.

During the long years of German occupation, the Communists gradually recovered much of their shattered influence in the countryside. Their principal agency was a network of Committees of Peasant Defense and Action, which were "front" organizations led by survivors of the old Confederation of Toiling Peasants. By 1944 they had set up about 2,500 of these committees in thirty-three departments, all of them in the old centers of Communist penetration in the Massif Central and the south. The propaganda which they circulated among the farmers placed heavy stress on the patriotic and revolutionary heritage of the French peasantry. It carefully avoided the delicate issue of peasant profiteering through black-market sales to French and German buyers. Now and then, it sketched the beauties of the Soviet agrarian system, with special attention to the constitutional guarantee of individual property-holding in Russia, and the purely voluntary character of the collective farms.[18]

When the Liberation arrived, it quickly became clear that the Communists' underground activity among the peasants had been far more extensive and effective than that of any other group. They increased their advantage at once by seizing the local press in many small towns and turning a large proportion of rural newspapers into Communist organs. In October they were able to resume publication of their prewar weekly *La Terre*, with a paper allotment that allowed a circulation of 150,000. Its technical superiority over all other agricultural journals was so obvious that the Communists kept pressing continually for more newsprint to meet the public demand. The propaganda line of these early months was cleverly conceived. Above all, the Communists vigorously defended the peasants against the widespread charge that they had profiteered during the war. If the peasants were hoarding large sums in cash, declared Thorez, it was only because they had been unable to buy equipment and fertilizer for four years. In fact, Thorez added, French agriculture was worse off than it had been before the war; it needed help and encouragement, not criticism. The Communists demanded an increase in farm prices, the restriction of food imports to the barest minimum, and heavy public investment

18 A. Rossi, *Physiologie du parti communiste français* (Paris, 1948), pp. 40–45.

to modernize and mechanize the farms. After eight months of this activity (April 1945), *L'Humanité* reported that the number of party members in agricultural regions had risen by 253 per cent over 1937, and that the number of local and rural cells had more than doubled.[19]

Meanwhile a basic tactical decision had to be made: should the party seek to rebuild its prewar agricultural organization, the Confederation of Toiling Peasants; or should it play for higher stakes, and urge peasant unity in one broad confederation? The decision was for peasant unity. Late in 1944 Communist leaders of the Committees of Peasant Defense met with the founders of a new Socialist-sponsored group, the Confédération Générale d'Agriculture (CGA), and agreed on fusion under the CGA label. Within three months, every one of the Committees of Peasant Defense had been converted into a CGA local; and a powerful minority of Communists had been installed in the CGA's provisional central organs. Whether the Communists hoped to win outright majority control of the CGA, as they did soon after in the labor union field, is not clear. At the very least, they probably expected to consolidate their strong minority position in the CGA headquarters, and to win control of the local machinery in perhaps one-third of the departments. From such a strategic position, boring from within would presumably be easy, and the party's rural influence could be steadily broadened.

While the CGA was still in its formative stages, three successive national elections in thirteen months gave the Communists a chance to test and retest their rural strength. If the outcome did not fully satisfy the Politburo, at least it proved that the party had penetrated every single department of France. In the Paris region the Communists gained little over 1936; but in almost every rural district their share of the vote doubled or tripled. In Creuse and Haute-Marne, the increase was fivefold over 1936; in Morbihan, sevenfold; in Haute-Saône, eightfold. Furthermore, in most farming areas the Communists fattened their percentage from one election to the next.

A geographical breakdown of these electoral results shows that the region of deepest rural penetration continues to be the center and south. In the most recent national election (November 1946) the Communists polled one-third or more of the popular vote in thirty departments; and twenty-three of those departments lie south of the Loire. The biggest single bloc consists of eleven contiguous departments on the northern and western slopes of the Massif Central, merging into the middle Garonne Valley. Another solid strip is the Mediterranean littoral, where only one department failed to give the Communists one-third of its votes. A majority of the departments in

19 *L'Humanité*, June 30, 1945.

the Rhône-Alpine region also deserve a red star.[20] But although central and southern France are the Communist strongholds, significant progress has been made in every rural section. No area is now without its network of village cells. In the last national elections, the Communists fell below 10 per cent of the popular vote in only two of the ninety departments; and below 20 per cent in only sixteen departments—most of them in Brittany, Normandy, and the eastern frontier region.

Socially, the distribution of Communist strength is also fairly broad. No doubt the farm laborers, marginal tenant farmers, and sharecroppers are still the "reddest" of all rural elements, even though some of them (the sharecroppers of the Vendée and Mayenne, for example) still resist. But there is clear evidence of Communist penetration among the small owners and the moderately prosperous small tenants as well. The reservation must be made, however, that it is difficult to sort out the peasant vote from the small-town vote in the electoral statistics. Officially, the "rural population" includes all residents of communes with fewer than 2,000 inhabitants. A fair share of the Communists' so-called "rural" vote may come from the town-dwellers rather than from the peasants proper; and often these two groups are more antagonistic than harmonious in their outlook.[21]

Since the elections of 1945–1946, the course of events in France has cost the Communists part of their rural support. Their bitter hostility to the American aid program could not fail to sour some peasants; their loss of control over certain cabinet posts (like the Ministry of Industrial Production, which controlled the rationing of certain scarce farm implements) deprived them of useful weapons. Reports of purges and "voluntary" collectivization in the Soviet satellite states have once again aroused the fears of some potential kulaks. In the partial cantonal elections of March 1949, official statistics showed an over-all Communist decline of perhaps 20 per cent since 1945.[22] Since that time, several special elections in rural areas have also brought embarrassing setbacks. In December 1949 the Central Committee

[20] The most important bloc of departments runs from Nièvre to Lot-et-Garonne, and includes also Cher, Indre, Vienne, Allier, Creuse, Haute-Vienne, Charente, Corrèze, and Dordogne. In the Rhône-Alpine region Drôme, Isère, Savoie, Basses-Alpes, and Vaucluse gave the Communists more than one-third of their votes. On the Mediterranean coast, only the department of Aude fell slightly below one-third.

[21] L. Chevalier, Les Paysans: étude d'histoire et d'économie rurales (Paris, 1946), pp. 31–33.

[22] These elections were held in only half the cantons of France; Paris was not included. Figures compiled by the Ministry of Interior indicated that the Communists lost more than 500,000 votes in comparison to the cantonal elections of 1945 (F. Goguel in Esprit, XVII [May 1949], 695). The Communists have disputed these figures and insist that they actually gained votes in 1949. J. Duclos in Cahiers du communisme, 26 (April 1949), 403.

gathered for a long session of autocriticism, and admitted that the party's peasant action in certain areas had lost impetus. Waldeck Rochet spoke out even more bluntly in the party's monthly organ. He charged the members of many rural cells with slacking off between elections; but worse still, he accused many party members at the higher levels of continuing to show what he called "Social Democratic indifference" toward the peasant question.[23] Apparently the arduous task of educating the peasantry still lacks glamour for many city-bred proletarians, even though Leninist dogma has entrusted them with (or condemned them to) this task.

Another serious disappointment to the Communists has been their failure to get even partial control of the CGA. Their first setback came early in 1946, when the most important subdivision of the CGA was organized: the Fédération Nationale d'Exploitants (Farmers' Union), composed of owners, tenants, and sharecroppers directly engaged in working the land. This union represents the largest single segment of the rural population—the key segment, so far as political influence is concerned. The election of its local officials and of delegates to its first national convention was a severe blow to Communist hopes. Throughout most of France, there was a swing back toward the prewar peasant leaders, many of whom were political conservatives. The Communists had hoped to run Waldeck Rochet for the presidency of the new union, but they failed even to get him elected departmental president in the Saône-et-Loire. The blow was not softened by the news that Renaud Jean, exiled to the provinces in semidisgrace, had been chosen secretary-general of the Federation in Lot-et-Garonne.

Ever since that time, the Communists' battle within the CGA has been defensive rather than offensive in nature; and in general it has been a losing fight. By the end of 1947 they controlled the local machinery of the Farmers' Union in only eleven southern departments [24]; they have lost all but a handful of seats on most of the CGA's national boards, and have been threatened with complete exclusion. Their only remaining stronghold is a new subdivision of the Farmers' Union which groups tenant farmers and sharecroppers (the Section des Preneurs de Baux Ruraux). This discouraging trend has led many Communists to abandon the CGA, on the ground that it is run by reactionaries. The sulkers were recently scolded by Waldeck Rochet,

---

23 W. Rochet, "Staline et la question paysanne," *Cahiers du communisme*, 26 (December 1949), 1529–30; cf. also J. Duclos in *ibid.*, 27 (February 1950), 13.

24 N. Drogat, "Y a-t-il une crise de la C.G.A.?", *Travaux de l'Action Populaire* (January 1948), p. 36. The eleven departments were Alpes-Maritimes, Corrèze, Creuse, Haute-Garonne, Landes, Lot-et-Garonne, Lozère, Pyrénées-Orientales, Tarn-et-Garonne, Vaucluse, and Haute-Vienne. It appears that the Communists have lost control of several of these departments since 1947.

who reminded them that the duty of a good Communist is to join that organization where the mass of peasants are to be found.[25] But Rochet's own editorials in *La Terre* have hinted that the Communists may secede from the CGA if their remaining representatives are pushed off the central boards.[26] In possible preparation for such a move, the party has turned to organizing Committees of Peasant Defense alongside the CGA.

There is a certain contradiction between the Communists' rural successes in the elections and their relative weakness in the CGA. This contrast gives some support to the theory that a considerable share of the party's rural support at the polls comes from the small towns rather than from the farmers; that the electoral statistics have been interpreted in such a way as to exaggerate the party's peasant strength. A second hypothesis might be that many peasants are willing to have a Communist represent them in parliament, yet prefer to choose a hard-headed local resident with his roots in the soil to speak for them in negotiations with other interest-groups or with the government.

In spite of these anomalies, and in spite of the party's rural decline of late, Communism remains an influential force in agrarian France. Although there may be weaknesses in the party's rural cadres, Waldeck Rochet's peasant propaganda resembles that of Renaud Jean in its vigor, its continuity, and its superficial consistency. *La Terre* can plausibly describe rival party leaders as hypocrites who tell the peasants one thing and the city classes another. It can quote and requote unwary Socialists, Radicals, or Gaullists who have indiscreetly suggested that the farmers are better off than the urban classes. The Communist peasant agitators have never stumbled into these pitfalls. They have contrived to intertwine their demands for both high farm prices and lower urban food costs; for lower peasant taxes and higher public investment. They resolve all apparent contradictions by blaming everything on the industrialists and the middlemen; their solution is to demand that profits be cut and factory wages raised, in order to increase the workers' buying power and the peasants' potential market. Their aim is to play down the old hostility between country and city, and to play up the old resentment of the small farmer toward his big competitor. One of the most typical items in the Communists' program since 1947 has been their scheme for a differential wheat price in favor of 1,200,000 small producers, with the 20,000 big wheat producers (not the urban consumers) paying the piper. Their propaganda relies heavily on statistics designed to prove that farm land is unfairly distributed, and that the big capitalist farmer is steadily

25 Rochet, *loc. cit.*, p. 1529.
26 *La Terre*, January 21–28, 1949.

squeezing the little farmer out of existence. They point out that half
of the land is already controlled by only 10 per cent of the farmers,
while the other half is divided among the remaining 90 per cent.
They show, too, that large farming has pretty well taken over certain
departments to the northeast of Paris, and they predict somewhat
recklessly that the process is sure to spread to the rest of France. Who,
then, are the real expropriators? they ask. Not the Communists, but
the agrarian capitalists. "Thus it is demonstrated," concludes Waldeck Rochet virtuously, "that capitalism leads to the expropriation of
the little peasant." [27]

While the Communists have been hurt by the gradual recovery of
France since 1947, they have been helped by the gradual deterioration
of the farmer's position. Taxes were sharply increased in 1948; and
early in 1949 a sudden slump in many farm prices set in for the first
time since prewar days. Most peasants are still better off than they
were twenty years ago; but their outlook is distorted by fear of a return to the crisis years of low prices and shrinking markets. This state
of mind lends itself perfectly to the Communist line. *La Terre* blasts
the government for importing foodstuffs to force farm prices down;
it ridicules the cabinet for promising to find new foreign markets for
French produce while opening France itself to a flood of foreign
foodstuffs; it "exposes" the nefarious designs of the Americans who
allegedly aim to destroy French agriculture, and who already dare to
suggest that French farmers abandon wheat in favor of roses.[28] True,
the Communists are not alone in offering this line to the peasants;
the non-Communist leaders of the CGA are not far behind. Yet the
CGA can never manage to keep up with the Communists so long as
some of its officials support the Center coalition, favor American aid,
and retain some "bourgeois" moral scruples.

Communist hopes for the early future plainly depend on a continued deterioration in the peasants' position. Already the index of
farm prices has fallen considerably below that of industrial prices,
bringing a new "scissors crisis." For the first time in several years, farm
implements and fertilizer are going unsold for want of peasant buyers.
The end of American aid is beginning to seem uncomfortably close.
So far, this growing stress has not produced any deep political change
in the countryside; one can still contrast rural France (dominantly
Centrist in politics) with urban France (which tends to extremes of
Right or Left). But if things do get worse, the Communists alone are
fully prepared to take advantage of rising discontent. They cannot

[27] *Le Parti communiste et la question paysanne*, p. 9.
[28] The Communists allege that an American official made this suggestion during an
international conference held in Copenhagen. Thorez, *op. cit.*, p. 7.

hope to forge out of the peasantry the kind of efficient weapon which they have created within the proletariat; but that has never been their aim. The role of the peasantry is to be led, and not to lead. Already the Communists are probably strong enough in some parts of the south to neutralize their enemies in a moment of crisis. A period of prolonged economic stress would no doubt allow them to broaden their foothold, both geographically and socially. If France were to enter such a period, no one can say what proportion of the small and middle peasantry might choose the Communists in preference to a movement of the extreme Right; but there would probably be many, and there might be no third choice available.[29] French Communism is not yet in sight of the Stalinist goal of "transforming the peasantry . . . from the reserve of the bourgeoisie . . . into a reserve and ally of the working class." But it can be said that no other Western Communist party (except perhaps that of Italy) has advanced so far along the road toward that goal.

[29] In a French public opinion poll taken late in 1948, this question was asked: If you had to choose between government by a Communist bloc and by an anti-Communist bloc, which would you prefer? Fourteen per cent of the *cultivateurs* polled declared themselves for the former alternative; 66 per cent chose the latter. In the same survey, 25 per cent of the *cultivateurs* expressed a desire that the Communists be brought back into a coalition government; 64 per cent opposed it. *Sondages*, January 16, 1949.

14

++

THE COMMUNISTS

AND THE FOREIGN RELATIONS OF FRANCE

VERNON VAN DYKE

++

THE common feature of Communist proposals and demands concerning the foreign relations of France is that they support Soviet policies and oppose the major policies of the French government. The reasons for this line are to be found in obedience to the requirements of Marxism-Leninism and in the desire of Thorez and his comrades to establish a Communist-controlled government in Paris—for which a strengthening of the East and a weakening of the West is prerequisite. The principal instruments available to the Communists in the pursuit of their objectives are control over the CGT, control over a substantial number of votes in the National Assembly, and propaganda. Of these, propaganda is currently by all odds the most important, playing unceasingly on a number of related themes: that present French policy involves the subordination of France to American imperialism and therefore to the loss of national independence; that present policy promotes the revival of a reactionary, powerful, and vengeful Germany—itself a tool of the American aspirants for world hegemony; that it is leading the country to impoverishment and war; that neither the French nor foreign governments can count on the support of the French people if war with the Soviet Union should come; and that the Soviet Union is the only reliable friend and protector of France. Precisely how dangerous Communist activities are to Western hopes and plans cannot be said, but they should not—and probably will not—induce the French or other Western governments to abandon foreign policies now being pursued. Nevertheless, the situation calls for more effective counterpropaganda and for additional measures to promote the economic welfare of the French working class.

The purpose here is to develop and elaborate upon these various statements. What the Communists want, why they want it, how they are trying to get it, and what successes have been achieved or are in prospect are the central questions to be treated.

I

The platform which the French Communists advance, like most other political platforms, is a mixture of explicit demands and vague generalities. They ask for the denunciation of the Marshall Plan, the North Atlantic Pact, and all associated agreements, and for a reaffirmation of the Franco-Soviet alliance, described as the one guarantee of peace and security for France. More generally, they ask France to participate actively in all efforts tending to establish a democratic, just, and durable peace, based on respect for inter-Allied agreements and for the United Nations Charter. Following Soviet proposals, they call for the outlawry of the atomic weapon and for the conclusion of a peace pact by the Big Five—including Communist China. With regard to Germany, they demand denazification and demilitarization in accordance with the Potsdam agreement; the denunciation of agreements authorizing the formation of a West German government; and the inauguration of a policy which will safeguard French security, restore French rights to reparations, and support the so-called democratic forces of Germany. More specifically, they demand a peace settlement with Germany approved by all four of the major Allies and establishing a provisional government for the whole of Germany in which all democratic parties and organizations are represented.[1]

The plank relating to wages and industry calls for, among other things, the defense of French industry against the menace of American imperialism, and the plank relating to agriculture includes a demand for protection against foreign competition. There is a demand for an immediate termination of the war in Vietnam, for the reestablishment of normal commercial relations with the countries of central and eastern Europe, and for a "massive reduction" in military expenditures. The amount of the reduction in military expenditures usually advocated is 200 billion francs, which the Communists say represents a cut of one-third, but which would reduce expenditures explicitly labeled as "military" in the 1949 budget by 57 per cent.

The most comprehensive demand which the Communists make is for a government of democratic unity. By this they do not mean a

[1] "Appel du Comité Central du Parti Communiste Français," *Cahiers du communisme*, 26 (November 1949), 1445–47. François Billoux, "La Lutte pour l'indépendance nationale," *ibid.*, 25 (July 1948), 657. *L'Humanité*, December 10, 1949, p. 4.

government such as those in which they participated immediately
after the war; rather they would now exclude the leaders of other
parties and organize "unity from below." Bidault, Moch, Ramadier,
and Schuman are no longer acceptable as colleagues. Thorez and
Duclos want a government in which "the Communists would contribute their share, that is, the greater share of responsibility." [2] They
envisage a coalition, but it would be a Communist-dominated coalition which would implement the demands of the party both in the
domestic and in the foreign fields.

The question why the French Communists make the foreign policy
demands which they do must be answered first of all in terms of a desire to achieve their comprehensive demand—a government of democratic unity. They want to shape the foreign relations of France in
such a way as to maximize their own prospects of securing dominant
governmental power. They want to create a situation in which they
will have the greatest possible chance of overcoming the opposition
which they face, and that opposition is obviously both domestic and
foreign. It includes the French bourgeoisie and in general all those
Frenchmen who refuse to accept the Communist prescription for social ills; it includes nationalists who object to the relationship which
exists between the Communists and the Kremlin; it includes the
French government itself, which the Communists seek to overthrow;
and it includes in some degree the governments of the United States,
Britain, and other Western countries which would regard a Communist government in Paris as an instrument of the Soviet Union and
therefore a threat to their own security. Even if the French Communists were to come to power through democratic action—which is very
unlikely in the visible future—the probability is that both domestic
rebellion and foreign intervention would occur to cast them out. Certainly any attempt of the party to seize power illegally would meet
violent resistance, supported by Western governments if that should
prove to be necessary. Whatever the power relationship between the
Communists and their opponents within France, it is almost out of
the question that the resources of the party are or can be made adequate to cope with domestic and foreign opposition combined. External aid will be essential to success.

Developments in Eastern and Southeastern Europe since the war
reinforce this line of thought. Communist parties in most countries of
that region were too weak at the time of defeat or liberation to have

2 Maurice Thorez, *What Next in France?* (New York, 1948), p. 19. "Résolution du
Comité Central du PCF," *Cahiers du communisme,* 25 (December 1948), 1432. Maurice
Thorez, "Unity of Action of the People's Masses—Necessary Condition for Peace," *For
a Lasting Peace, For a People's Democracy,* October 21, 1949, p. 2.

much chance of establishing themselves in power by their own devices. Subsequent events, however, demonstrated that power brought in from abroad may be much more important to victory than power mustered at home. It is as apparent to the French Communists as it is to others that the Red Army was an indispensable element in the establishment of Communism in the present Soviet zone. Moreover, they have read the letter from the Russian party to Tito declaring it to be "unfortunate" that the Red Army did not and could not render aid in France and Italy as it did in Eastern and Southeastern Europe.[3] In these circumstances, the French Communists must hope for Soviet aid themselves, and will naturally attempt to influence the foreign relations and foreign policies of France so as to facilitate the extension of such aid.

The Communists pretend that one of their principal objectives is to preserve the Soviet Union from aggressive designs of imperialist warmongers. They describe their struggle as a struggle for peace and see threats to the peace only in the policies of the West. This line is so much at variance with the postwar record that it must conceal ulterior objectives. For the French Communists, the most important of the ulterior objectives is an improvement in the relative power position of the Soviet Union. The more fully they can succeed in this endeavor, the better will their own prospects be. Barred by circumstances from contributing much directly to Soviet power, they aim to do so indirectly by sapping the strength of the opponents of the Kremlin. Their object is, and must be, to weaken France and to weaken, divide, and if possible destroy the power of the West. Their most certain path in victory in France is to establish the dominance of the Soviet Union in Western Europe.

Doctrinal considerations reinforce this identification between the French Communists and the Soviet Union. The Communists are Marxist-Leninists, devotees of a class conception of history and progress. Guided by the alleged science of Marxism-Leninism, they not only assume that true class interests exist, but that those interests are objectively determinable. They claim to know beyond doubt what the interests of various classes are and how they can best be served, and this knowledge exists and is valid regardless of the apparent will of the individuals composing the various classes. To them, the interests of the two great classes, the proletariat and the bourgeoisie, are in most respects contradictory, and consequently a struggle for domination proceeds between the two, each seeking allies where they can be found. In this struggle, the Communists identify themselves with the

[3] *The Soviet-Yugoslav Dispute* (London: Royal Institute of International Affairs, 1948), p. 51.

proletariat. Theirs, they say, is the party of the working class, the party of the poorer peasantry, the party of those who are exploited in a capitalist society. If the proletariat and the poorer peasantry reject the Marxist-Leninist analysis of their interests, it simply indicates that they have been deceived and misled. There are no legitimate differences of opinion on the question; there are only those who promote and those who are against the interests of the exploited. Since the Communists alone know the true interests of the proletariat, they become its self-appointed vanguard, just as the Nazis became the self-appointed representatives of a master race, entitled to establish their rule by any means that may be necessary.

Endowed by Marxism-Leninism with a monopoly of true knowledge, the Communists assert that the interests of the working class everywhere coincide, and therefore they champion proletarian internationalism with a view to the ultimate establishment of a world union of socialist republics. And the touchstone of proletarian internationalism, as the Communists themselves say, is loyalty to the Land of Socialism, to the U.S.S.R., to Stalin. Loyalty to the U.S.S.R. obviously requires support for its foreign policy, and efforts to frustrate contrary policies pursued by France and other countries of the West. For a time after the war the French Communists tried hard to appear as a national party like the others, quite independent of the Kremlin, but this pretense has now been dropped. In a recent article in the Cominform journal one of the French Communist leaders, André Marty, boasted of his party's record of "absolute fidelity" to, and "unconditional solidarity" with, the Soviet Union. It has become fashionable for the Communists, comparing themselves to Thomas Paine, to claim two countries for themselves: France and the Soviet Union.[4]

It is frequently said that the French and other Communists are under "orders from Moscow." There is good justification for such a phrase, but it should be added that the relationship to Moscow is not a servile one in the sense that the French Communists are conscious of sacrificing themselves or France to alien interests. Rather, it is a partnership of mutual interest, with the French Communists necessarily taking the role of junior partners because they have less to offer.

There has, of course, been some challenge both to the proposition that the French Communists have a practical need for Soviet support and to the proposition that proletarian internationalism demands

4 André Marty, "The October Revolution and the Working People of France," *For a Lasting Peace, For a People's Democracy*, November 4, 1949, p. 2. Jean Plat, "De l'amour de la France à la fidélité à Staline," *France nouvelle*, November 5, 1949, p. 4. Jacques Duclos, "Staline et l'internationalisme prolétarien," *Cahiers du communisme*, 26 (December 1949), 1480. Georges Cogniot in *L'Humanité*, December 12, 1949, p. 3.

loyalty to Moscow. News commentators have expressed the view that Thorez and his comrades could have done much better in French elections since the war had it not been for the halo which Stalin conferred upon them, and Titoists claim that proletarian internationalism now requires resistance to the Kremlin. These considerations have no doubt had an impact on the thinking of French Communists, and may have more in the future, but it is unlikely that any drastic change in the party line will result. Whatever the situation may have been several years ago, there is no prospect that the French Communists could win power through elections in the visible future even if they became a strictly national party. Violence, or at least the threat of violence, is almost certain to be necessary if a Communist conquest of power is to occur. With this prospect in view, the Communists probably stand to gain rather than lose through an identification with the Kremlin, for the Red Army constitutes the most likely source of the military power which they need.

As to Titoism, it is quite probable that the Soviet-Yugoslav split has already alienated some Communists and fellow-travelers in France from the party. The party's Central Committee, meeting in December 1949, openly admitted that agents of Tito had penetrated the ranks, but Thorez and Duclos both denied that the party faced a crisis and that the leadership was split. The Central Committee's demand was that the Titoists be exposed and expelled, and Thorez, while calling for attention to both the quantity and the quality of the party's effectives, declared, "We are entering a period in which quality will be decisive." [5] The French Communists thus appear to be something less than 100 per cent loyal to the Kremlin's interpretation of proletarian internationalism. But if Titoists gain any significant influence, they are more likely to split the party than to capture it—more likely to weaken the party than to strengthen it. The Communist movement in France is too dependent upon Russian aid for eventual success to make the idea of a wholesale declaration of independence from Moscow attractive.

It is clear that the foreign policy demands which the French Communists make are calculated to improve the relative power position of the Soviet Union and of the Communist movement generally. The European Recovery Program, the Brussels Pact, the North Atlantic Pact, the Council of Europe, the movement for the reduction of trade barriers and for the economic and political unification of Western Europe have as their major purpose the strengthening and stabilization of the Atlantic community. If the Communists could secure the denunciation of agreements made and bring about the withdrawal of

[5] L'Humanité, December 12 and 13, 1949. New York Times, December 13, 1949, p. 4:3.

France from cooperation with the Western world, they would weaken opposition to the Soviet Union and to Communism in France and in the West generally, and thereby greatly increase the probability of an extension of Soviet and Communist power to the Atlantic Ocean.

The desire to use French foreign policy as a means of promoting the Communist cause shows up particularly in demands relating to Germany. In 1945 Thorez fixed the extirpation of Hitlerism as the objective in dealing with Germany, and then went on to specify that this would require the liquidation of the economic basis of Fascism—ultimately involving the rigorous suppression of German "trusts." In Communist parlance, the liquidation of the economic basis of Fascism and the suppression of the "trusts" means the elimination of capitalism. Insistence on the "democratization" of Germany, as the Communists interpret that word, is clearly designed to promote the achievement of the same goal. The party insists that a desire for security and justice for France motivates the demand for demilitarization and the payment of reparations, but the demand serves peculiarly Communist as well as French nationalist objectives. The demilitarization of Germany eliminates one more obstacle to the march of Soviet power toward Paris and reduces potential opposition to a seizure of power over the whole country by the SED or the German Communist Party. Agitation for the payment of reparations and denunciation of the United States, Britain, and the French government itself for abandoning alleged true interests of France in this connection are designed to serve two purposes simultaneously: to increase popular support for the party by nationalist appeals, and to create and intensify popular antagonism within France against the French and other Western governments.

With regard to the Ruhr, the Communists first joined in the official French demand for its political and economic internationalization, involving detachment from Germany. Then when Molotov denounced any dismemberment of Germany, Thorez and his comrades shifted to a demand for inter-Allied control over the Ruhr—control, they emphasized, by all the Allies. Their dominant interest has been to eliminate exclusively Western control of the Ruhr by securing the participation of the Soviet Union. The ostensible purpose has been to gain assurances that Germany will never again be able to use the Ruhr as an arsenal in war against either France or the Soviet Union, but there have no doubt been additional purposes also: if Soviet power were brought to the Ruhr and the Rhine, it could be used to promote Communism in Germany, and it would radiate strength to the Communists in France. Several years ago the Communists, after having agreed unconditionally to the conclusion of an alliance with the Soviet

Union, attempted to block the conclusion of a similar treaty with Britain, arguing that the German problem should be settled first. Aside from the implications of this stand for Germany, it was calculated to keep France and Britain divided. From the point of view of a writer in *New Times,* the treaty was part of an effort "to harness France to the chariot of British imperialism." [6]

Needless to say, the Communists oppose practically everything that the West has done in Germany since the disruption of the Allied Control Council in Berlin. Conversely, they thoroughly approve developments in the Soviet zone. The French Communists have no fear of a Germany dominated by the SED. They cite the proclamation of the SED "that in case of aggression, the German people should struggle against the aggressors and assist the Soviet army to reestablish peace." They praise the efforts of the SED to convince the German masses that friendship for the Soviet Union will be decisive to the national fate of Germany, and affirm that a Germany united in this view would offer France greater security than would military occupation. [7]

II

Propaganda is currently the major weapon which the Communists employ to get what they want. They use various appeals. Among them, the appeal to anti-German sentiment in France is prominent. There is endless repetition in Communist propaganda of the theme that under the Marshall Plan priority is given to German reconstruction at the expense of France; there are endless complaints that denazification has not occurred and that reparations are no longer paid. The Communists try to prejudice the peasants against the government by telling them that they are being asked to produce in order to feed Germans. They try to prejudice the whole people against the Council of Europe by alleging that it is a device to secure the readmission of Germany into the European community on a footing of equality. They denounce all proposals of Western federation or Western union by comparing them to the efforts of the Kaiser and of Hitler to establish a Greater Reich, adding, however, that it is the American claimants to world hegemony who now, through Germany, constitute the threat. They try to evoke sympathy for Russia and hatred for Germany by pointing to the lesson of history that "every time France is an ally of Russia, it wins wars; and every time it is not, it loses them."

---

[6] See "L'Allemagne d'abord? Non!" *Cahiers du communisme,* 25 (July 1948), 750. I. Taigin, "England and France," *New Times,* February 21, 1947, p. 9.

[7] J. B., "L'Unité allemande et la paix," *Démocratie nouvelle,* 3 (July 1949), 354. "Déclaration du Bureau Politique du PCF," *France nouvelle,* October 22, 1949, p. 5.

Europe without Russia, the Communists say, is a German-dominated
Europe. They condemn with especial ferocity all talk of rearming
Germany and including it in one way or another in the North Atlantic
defense system. Present policy, they allege, is leading to the establishment on French frontiers of a non-denazified Germany with renewed
industrial power, menacing French industry through its competition
and French security through a revival of militarism.[8] The record thus
shows that even proletarian internationalists do not hesitate to appeal
to national chauvinism in order to achieve the goals they have in view.

Another major theme in the propaganda designed to turn the
French people against cooperation with the West is that present policy
is leading to the impoverishment of France. "The Marshall Plan," says
Thorez, "can only mean poverty for [the people] while it gives reaction a free hand." Continued difficulties in the economic field, the
Communists allege, exist not in spite of but because of the Marshall
Plan. They accuse the United States of demanding the liquidation of
the nationalized sector of the French economy. They allege that the
effort to bring about a reduction in trade barriers is in reality an effort
to prevent the development of prosperity in France, to facilitate
American dumping, and to eliminate French industries which compete with those of the United States. Though the Communists cannot
deny that an increase in industrial production has occurred in France,
they contend that in general the European Recovery Program—regularly called the Marshall Plan—has weakened the French economy
more than ever. Only the capitalists have benefited, they say, while the
workers, peasants, and middle classes have suffered. This claim is
based in part on the contention that cooperation with the West requires the use of the "best part of the resources of the country" in
preparation for war, making it impossible to provide a decent standard of living for the agricultural and industrial workers.[9]

The most pervasive theme in Communist propaganda is that present French policy undermines the national independence of France.
As early as 1946, when France and the United States made a financial
arrangement which included a loan, the Communists, while voting
for the arrangement in the National Assembly, denounced it as involv-

[8] See Gilbert de Chambrun, "Un Camouflage: Le Conseil de l'Europe," Démocratie
nouvelle, 3 (June 1949), 297. Charles Haroche, "Le 'Conseil de l'Europe,' instrument des
capitalistes et de la Sainte-Alliance antisoviétique," France nouvelle, August 13, 1949, p. 8.

[9] L'Humanité, October 12, 1949, p. 3. William Grossin, "Actualité et avenir du Plan
Marshall," Démocratie nouvelle, 3 (January 1949), 28. Jean Laffitte, "Le Plan Marshall et
la Marshallisation de la France," Cahiers du communisme, 25 (October 1948), 1122 ff.
Eugène Dumaulin, "L'Économie française après deux ans de marshallisation," ibid., 26
(July 1949), 830–33.

ing American intervention in French affairs. Again in May 1947 the Communists voted to accept a loan from the World Bank while simultaneously alleging that it constituted an attack on the economic independence of France. When Ramadier dropped the Communists from the cabinet, they at first regarded the event as the result of an ordinary ministerial crisis, but after the organization of the Cominform it became the result of the "brutal intervention of American imperialists," and "an indispensable measure preliminary to the complete vassalization of France." Thorez cites statements that the readmission of Communists to the cabinet would deprive France of American aid, and concludes that French sovereignty has become an "empty word." "The French people," he says, "no longer have the right to have governments of their own choosing. From now on, the composition and orientation of French cabinets will be determined in Washington." The European Recovery Program as a whole is denounced not only as a cause of poverty, but also as an attempt to bring about the colonization of France.

The Communists also use symbols relating to national independence in their propaganda against the Brussels Pact, the North Atlantic Pact, and the Council of Europe. They tell the French people that France has renounced the formation of a command school, because strategy is to be fixed in Washington. They object to the presence of a "foreign general staff" at Fontainebleau and to the subordination of French forces to an English general, Montgomery, soon to be superseded, it is alleged, by an American. They object to the standardization of armaments because of the control which it would give to the United States. In short, they conclude, France is "in the presence of a foreign invasion" and French policy "has been strictly subordinated to the American policy of aggression."

The Council of Europe, as far as the Communists are concerned, is simply another aspect of the American attack on the independence of France and her neighbors. In the Council, they declare, "the accomplices of the kings of the dollar can hope to rule only as vassals in the sphere of influence of the United States. The ministers of the capitalist states of western Europe can only hope to play the role of managers of European subsidiaries of Yankee imperialist enterprise in a hierarchy of viceroys, governors, procurators, and prefects." According to Florimond Bonte, "The Council of Europe will have for its purpose to prepare, for the Western countries, the political and economic laws of the North Atlantic Pact. . . . The decisions which will be taken behind closed doors by the Committee of Ministers of Western Europe and ratified by its artificial appendage, the Consultative Assembly, will become law for French men and women, who will be able to do no more than to obey like slaves." [10]

III

Superficially, there would appear to be a contradiction between proletarian internationalism and a really chauvinistic insistence on the preservation of national independence and sovereignty. But the Communists easily find a theoretical basis for reconciling the two ideas. Emphasis on class, class struggle, and proletarian internationalism, they contend, is perfectly consistent with emphasis on the nation and national independence.

The initial thesis offered in support of this point of view is that the French bourgeoisie and the governing groups generally have betrayed and are betraying the nation. The bourgeoisie, according to the Communists, was patriotic as long as it was a young and rising class, as long as it was interested in the establishment and preservation of a national market. But that time has long since passed. "Industrial capital" has given way to "finance capital," and capitalism itself has reached the stage of imperialism. As a result, for the ruling class and its agents, the national idea—the idea of *la patrie*—is no longer a dominant consideration. Political control in France, and in each great capitalist country, has allegedly come to be lodged in a handful of monopolists and their agents, these monopolists being linked not so much with their own countrymen as with monopolists of other countries; they are said to be cosmopolitan in outlook and interests, detached from the nation. The sovereign nation is of interest to finance capital, to the monopolists, only to the extent that it offers an instrument for the repression of the working class and democracy at home and for the conquest of markets and the control of transportation routes abroad.

In recent years, according to the Communist analysis, fear of the people has dominated the ruling classes in Europe—fear of the rising working class and fear of the impetuous movements for liberation which shake the structure of colonial empires. The ruling classes are said to fear that their own independent national governments are no longer effective instruments for maintaining their position and privileges; and since national governments have lost their utility, the ruling classes are impelled to depart from the national framework and seek safety in international arrangements, abandoning sovereignty and independence in the process. Through the Brussels Pact and the

---

[10] Charles Tillon, "Le Plan Marshall, abandon de l'indépendance française et de la défense nationale," *ibid.*, 25 (May 1948), 481 ff. *Journal officiel, Assemblée nationale, Débats parlementaires* (July 10, 1949), pp. 4474–76 (cited hereafter as *J. O., A. N., Déb.*).

North Atlantic Pact, they create a new Holy Alliance to preserve re-actionary institutions and practices. Through the Council of Europe they seek "the protection of a kind of mutual assistance society and the support of a cartel of capitalist powers against social progress." [11]

Such treason to the nation, the Communists contend, is not new in history. The forces of reaction have always sought aid wherever it could be obtained to stop the forces of progress which threatened existing privileges. The feudal barons of France did it from the fifteenth to the seventeenth centuries. Enemies of the revolution of 1789 sought to bring about counterrevolution with the aid of the foreign princes and kings of Europe. The bourgeoisie in 1870 is said to have fraternized with Bismarck in order to massacre the proletariat of the Commune. The reactionaries of France, threatened by the Popular Front in the 1930's, endorsed the slogan, "Better Hitler than Blum," and bargained and collaborated with Hitler as a means of preserving their class privileges at the expense of France. "It is a law of history," says André Marty. "It is always the privileged classes which betray. From the moment when they are no longer strong enough to hold under the yoke the people who are breaking their chains, their only recourse is to sell themselves abroad." [12]

At the same time the French bourgeoisie is in need of foreign aid, the Yankee imperialists wish to give it—but not out of any desire to contribute to French welfare. The United States is said to face an economic crisis. It produces more than it can consume, given the capitalist relations of production. It commands more capital than it can profitably invest at home. It cannot retrench, not only because of the economic crisis which would thereupon ensue but also because retrenchment would permit the Soviet Union to forge ahead in industrial power. Therefore, to avoid a crisis and to maintain production, profits, and power, the American imperialists are driven to open up foreign markets. They are even said to endorse the slogan, "Better war than a crisis," and so plot war against the Soviet Union and the new democracies; for this war, they need allies and cannon fodder. In pursuit of markets and war, the United States regards the economic and political independence of France and its neighbors as an obstacle, and therefore proposes the Marshall Plan, the Brussels Pact, the North Atlantic Pact, and the Council of Europe as devices to bring Western Europe under its control.

With the nation thus threatened by the treason of the privileged

[11] Florimond Bonte in *J. O., A. N., Déb.* (July 10, 1949), pp. 4471 ff. Joanny Berlioz, "Une nouvelle Sainte-Alliance," *Démocratie nouvelle*, 3 (April–May 1949), 185.

[12] André Marty, "L'Outil de la victoire: le parti de Lénine et de Staline," *Cahiers du communisme*, 25 (January 1948), 47. Jean Guillon, "L'Évolution du sentiment national depuis 1848 et la notion de souveraineté nationale," *ibid.*, 25 (June 1948), 600–3.

class and by grasping and war-mongering American imperialists, it is the working class which, according to the Communists, comes to the rescue. Of course, the Communists admit that the working class, like the bourgeoisie, has a class interest to serve, but they make an important distinction. The claim is that the interests of the working class coincide with, while the interests of the bourgeoisie contradict, those of the nation. Therefore, to promote the interests of the bourgeoisie is to betray the nation; but to promote the interests of the working class is to serve the nation. Just as social and economic developments have transformed the formerly patriotic bourgeoisie into a reactionary privileged class trying to maintain itself against the interests of the nation, so has it transformed the working class into the very essence of the nation.

Communist expressions on this point vary somewhat. A writer in *Cahiers du communisme* declares that in the present period "the working class tends to become itself the nation." To him the working class is the "national class par excellence"; it is the "only authentic national class." Another writer simply declares that the working class "identifies itself" with the nation while the bourgeoisie detaches itself. A favorite expression is that the working class is *l'ossature même de la nation,* which perhaps should be translated as the blood and bones of the nation. A deputy in the National Assembly, however, goes so far as to say, "The interests of the rising class coincide in their entirety with the interests of the nation. The working class itself incarnates the national interests of the fatherland which the false élites and the ruling classes have betrayed." Another deputy quotes Saint-Simon in proclaiming that "the national party is the party of those who live by their labor, and the antinational party is the party of the capitalist parasites who live by the exploitation of the labor of others." [13]

Since the working class is the essence of the nation, and since the Communist Party is the vanguard of the working class, it follows that, in the eyes of Thorez and his comrades, policies of the party automatically reflect the interests of the nation. "Only our party," says Thorez, "has followed a truly national policy before, during, and since the war." "We are alone as a party," says Duclos, "in advancing a program which conforms to the interests of France." And according to André Marty, "Year by year, month by month, in connection with both domestic and foreign policy, it is the Communist Party which has formulated solutions which are right from the national point of view; and,

[13] *J. O., A. N., Déb.* (July 10, 1949), pp. 4476 and 4481 (Florimond Bonte and Mme. Madeleine Braun). Alfred Malleret-Joinville, "Les Communistes et la défense nationale," *Cahiers du communisme,* 26 (March 1949), 309. Joanny Berlioz, "Europe, nations, internationalisme," *ibid.,* 26 (July 1949), 815–17. Jacques Duclos, "Staline et l'internationalisme prolétarien," *ibid.,* 26 (December 1949), 1479.

by the same token, from the point of view of the interests of the workers, of the people, and of the Republic." To French Communists their
party is simultaneously "the party of the working class, the party of the
people, and the party of the nation." [14]

The Communists reveal very little of the process by which Marxism-
Leninism leads to conclusions concerning treason and patriotism.
Simply the fact that current governmental policy associates France
with Western imperialists suffices to condemn that policy as anti-
national. As to the claim that the working class is the essence of the
nation, the Communists make various supporting assertions. They
refer to the fact that the working class is numerous, but do not rest
their argument on that point. This is not a case where a majority determines the national interest, for the few charismatic interpreters of
the science of Marxism-Leninism have done that already. The "economic and political role" of the working class is "even more important" than its numbers in making it the national class. The working
class is the national class, in addition, "because it is the enemy number
one of the trusts, . . because of its unity, . . because of its sufferings
at the hands of the oppressors, because of the ardor of its struggle, and
finally because it is the rising class, the class which will put an end to
the exploitation of one nation by another and which, in giving *la
patrie* a human and fraternal content, will permit it to flower
freely." [15] In other words, just as the Communists claim to know the
"true interests" of the various classes, so do they claim to know the
"true interests" of the nation. Only those who agree with the Marxist-
Leninist view can be patriots.

From the Communist point of view, the idea of preserving national
independence and sovereignty has operational significance only in
relations with the capitalist world. It is only from the capitalist side
that threats to the nation come. Marxism-Leninism reveals somehow
that "there exists no conflict of the interests between the workers of
the different nations." Proletarian internationalism requires solidarity with the Soviet Union, but the fundamental policy of the Soviet
Union is said to be respect for national sovereignty and independence. The French Communists maintain the fiction that the Soviet
Union has in no way interfered in the internal affairs of the countries
of Eastern and Southeastern Europe or impaired their sovereignty.

[14] Maurice Thorez, *Au Service du Peuple de France* (Paris, 1947), p. 66. Marty, "L'Outil
de la victoire," *loc. cit.,* p. 49. Duclos quoted by François Billoux, "Le Grand Combat
pour le pain, la liberté, la paix et l'indépendance nationale," *Cahiers du communisme,*
25 (August 1948), 765.

[15] Jean Guillon, "L'Évolution du sentiment national depuis 1848 et la notion de
souveraineté nationale," *ibid.,* 25 (June 1948), 603. Victor Joannes, "Dans le secteur
français du camp anti-impérialiste et démocratique," *ibid.,* 25 (September 1948), 963.

They take the view that "the Soviet Union has never been and can never be an aggressor against any country," and there is to them no imperialism save capitalist imperialism. Even in the early postwar period, when the general emphasis of the Communists was still on Big Three Unity, Thorez asserted, "Only the Soviet Union supports France. The Soviet Union and our other Eastern allies are, like us, concerned with the problem of German aggression, of security, and of reparations. Other countries dream only of their hegemony." More recently, André Marty has declared that the Soviet Union is the "only country whose interests never conflict with the interests of the people of France." [16]

Not only do the Communists deny a conflict of interests between France and the Soviet Union, but they declare that France can preserve its national independence only by aligning itself with the Soviet Union. As Étienne Fajon puts it: "There is no people which cannot assure its independence, or struggle successfully to reconquer it, if it relies on the power of the Soviet Union, of the popular democracies, and of the democratic workers' movement over the world. But no independence is possible without their support. In other words, the struggle of each people for national independence is a part of the great world combat against imperialism. There is no national independence without international solidarity in the anti-imperialist camp in general and among the Communist parties in particular." [17]

The Communists admit almost openly that their championship of the idea of national independence is a matter of partisan expediency. Florimond Bonte practically said as much to the National Assembly last July in declaring that the working class defends French sovereignty "as a means to economic and political liberation." "Today," he said, "national sentiment, love of national independence, hinder the realization of plans of subjection. They impede nations from becoming easy prey to the monopoly capitalists. In these conditions . . . the idea of national sovereignty has an essentially progressive character." [18] In other words, if the French bourgeoisie can be isolated, if it can be prevented from engaging in economic and political cooperation with the non-Communist world, it will be weakened and can more easily be overthrown. According to Communist lights, progress will thereby be served. The desire to strengthen the Soviet Union indirectly by frustrating cooperation within the Atlantic community is equally apparent.

[16] *J.O., A.N., Déb.* (February 25, 1949), p. 881. Marty, "L'Outil de la victoire," *loc. cit.,* p. 50.
[17] Quoted by Billoux, "Le Grand Combat pour le pain . . . ," *loc. cit.,* p. 763.
[18] *J.O., A.N., Déb.* (July 10, 1949), p. 4472.

Another theme in Communist propaganda is that alignment with the West will not provide security for France and that France has no alliance value to the West. Communist spokesmen deny outright that the purpose of present governmental policies is security, pointing out that the Brussels Pact and the North Atlantic Pact are directed not against Germany, but against the allegedly peace-loving Soviet Union. The purpose is therefore aggressive war—war in which the United States will recruit its foot soldiers, its cannon fodder, in France. Moreover, the war envisaged does not call for the defense of France at the outset; rather, American "offensive strategy" is to abandon Continental Europe and then to reconquer it after an atomic bombardment. France is thus pictured as having everything to lose and nothing to gain by a policy of alliance with the United States.[19]

To the French government and to foreigners, the Communists say that the French people will never wage war against the Soviet Union. They grant that France has an army, but allege that though it is expensive it cannot be strong. Further, they emphasize the importance of reserves in war, and assert that reserves drawn from the French people will not fight. In fact, Thorez threatens that in case of war the Communists will stage an armed insurrection against the French government, and he declares in effect that should the Red Army ever arrive at the borders of France the Communists would welcome it into the country.[20] The Communist press does what it can to discourage the delivery of war materiel to France by playing on the possibility that it will eventually fall into Communist hands; at the same time the party urges dock workers to refuse to unload ships bearing American military aid.

IV

During the past year, propaganda along these various lines has been the principal means employed by the Communists to achieve the objectives which they have in view. The means available, however, are not limited to propaganda. Through the generalized strikes of the fall of 1947 and the great coal strike of the fall of 1948, the Communists demonstrated that their control over the trade-unions was strong and that it could be used in an effort to frustrate governmental policy. Their hold on the working class has apparently weakened some during the past two years, both in terms of membership in the unions and

19 Pierre Courtade, "La Signature du Pacte Atlantique," *Démocratie nouvelle,* 3 (April–May 1948), esp. p. 180. Joanny Berlioz, "France Says 'No!' to the Warmongers," *Labour Monthly,* 30 (November 1948), 336–43.
20 *J.O., A.N., Déb.* (February 25, 1949), pp. 881 ff.

in terms of the loyalty of the remaining members. But the losses they have suffered have apparently not meant equivalent gains for competing trade-union organizations. Persistence of the gross differential between price and wage increases provides basis for a renewal of Communist strength in the trade-unions and a revival of strike activities. Though the immediate purposes would almost necessarily be economic, extensive strikes would certainly affect the international position of France and might bring about more or less serious changes in the composition and policies of the French government.

Among the possibilities is that Communist strikes and parliamentary policies might create a situation in which De Gaulle would come to power. Several writers have suggested that this is an aim of the Communists. The argument usually presented is that if De Gaulle were to come to power he would divide France sharply between Right and Left, destroying the Third Force and giving the Communists the opportunity to establish leadership over the whole Left. Then the Communists might lead the Left in a counteroffensive against De Gaulle in order to establish the proposed government of democratic unity. Léon Blum advanced a different argument: that the Communists would like to place De Gaulle in power because his policies and temperament would most certainly obstruct cooperation among the Western countries and thus put the Soviet Union in a relatively stronger position.[21]

Certainly the strength and the policies of the Communist Party have been major factors in giving wider appeal to the Gaullist movement, and if De Gaulle should come to power he would owe his success in considerable measure to Stalin and Thorez. But it seems likely that the Communists are taking a calculated risk rather than that they are working deliberately to install De Gaulle. This estimate of the situation is based on the assumption that De Gaulle, if he did triumph, would establish a one-party or a "non-party" dictatorial régime and on the fact that wherever such régimes have been established in Europe heretofore Communist parties have been virtually crushed. If De Gaulle's anti-Communist measures were anything like as effective as were those of Mussolini, Hitler, Pilsudski, and the various Balkan dictators, the Communists would have to devote so much attention to the problem of survival that they would have little prospect of organizing an effective counteroffensive. The Kremlin has been known to demand and to secure the virtual suicide of Communist parties in the past and might do so again, but there are at least two deterrents. In the first place, a Russian demand that the Communists deliberately invite their own repression and possible extermination would accen-

21 Léon Blum, "De Gaulle and the Communists," *New Leader*, December 4, 1948, p. 9.

tuate any tendencies toward Titoist rebellion that now exist in the party. In the second place, it is not at all clear that the Communists could serve their own cause and the Soviet cause better by bringing De Gaulle to power than by continuing in their present course.

It is difficult to measure the success which the Communists have achieved and to predict the degree of success which they have in prospect. The strikes which they have led have obviously retarded French recovery. There can scarcely be any question but that the constant play on anti-German sentiment in France has retarded reconciliation between the two countries and has militated against the acceptance by France of measures looking toward the reestablishment of Germany and the entry of Germany into a Western European system. In view of Communist propaganda it would be especially difficult for the government of France to endorse rearmament in Germany and the inclusion of Germany in North Atlantic defense arrangements. It should be said, however, that anti-German sentiment in France exists quite independently of the Communists, and there is no way of knowing to what extent opposition to measures involving Germany springs from Communist propaganda and to what extent it comes from other sources.

Public opinion polls taken in France at the end of 1948 and again at the end of 1949 reveal declining support for the European Recovery Program. In 1948, 52 per cent favored the program, and in 1949 only 38 per cent. A spokesman for ECA attributed the decline in part to Communist propaganda. In addition to the 38 per cent who favored the Marshall Plan in 1949, 23 per cent thought that it had both good and bad sides; 16 per cent considered it definitely bad; and 23 per cent had no opinion.[22] The only encouraging feature of this report is either that the Communist vote has declined or that the Communists have so far failed to convince all of their own voters that the ERP is bad. Only 16 per cent definitely opposed the plan, while more than 26 per cent of the votes were cast for the Communist Party in the three national elections since the war. Doubts and opposition concerning the Marshall Plan must in some degree reflect doubts and opposition concerning the wisdom of French cooperation with the United States.

Substantial economic discontents, giving basis for Communist propaganda, still exist in France. A poll taken in July 1949 revealed that 39 per cent thought that their own personal situation was worse than it had been the year before, and only 17 per cent thought that it was better. In contrast, however, 51 per cent of those polled on a slightly different question a few months earlier thought that life in

[22] *Des Moines Register,* December 11, 1949, p. 7G. cf. *New York Times,* December 11, 1949, p. 53:1.

France was better, 32 per cent thought it unchanged, and 15 per cent thought it was worse. Sixty-two per cent of the rich, but only 44 per cent of the poor, thought that improvement had occurred.[23] The explanation of the contrasting results of the two polls apparently is that the individuals consulted felt that the country as a whole was doing better than they were themselves. Nevertheless, when 39 per cent of the population think that their lot in life has become harder, and when there in fact exists a continued discrepancy between price and wage increases, a substantial response to Communist appeals is to be expected.

Despite the prospect of continued strength for the Communists in France, the balance of internal forces and, even more, the balance of external forces is against them. They have scarcely any prospect of establishing the government of democratic unity which they propose, and little prospect of deflecting any Third Force government from present foreign policies. If their propaganda, their parliamentary maneuvers, and strikes help to bring about any drastic change in France, it is likely to involve the establishment of a Gaullist régime.

It seems possible that the strength of the Communists could be reduced considerably, most obviously by reducing the wage-price gap but also through more effective counterpropaganda. It is doubtful whether the French people are fully aware of the meaning which the Communists assign to the term democracy; it should be borne home to them that their own will would be irrelevant to governmental policy if the Communists came to power—that the Communists would implement a Stalinist conception of "true interests," whether or not it conformed to the popular will. It is also doubtful whether the French people are fully aware of the meaning and purpose of Communist appeals to the idea of national independence; it should be borne home to them that the Communists equate the working class to the nation, and that the appeal to the idea of national independence is fundamentally an appeal for revolution and for the integration of France into the Soviet system.

[23] Service de Sondages et Statistiques, "Sondages de l'opinion publique française," No. 47 (March–April 1949), 695; No. 49 (September–October 1949), 723.

15

✦✦

GAULLISM: RETROSPECT AND PROSPECT

H. STUART HUGHES

✦✦

IN THE small hours of the morning of New Year's Day 1946, General de Gaulle, president-premier of France and undisputed first citizen of his country, abruptly offered his resignation to the First Constituent Assembly. In words that carried a tone of both reproof and menace, he warned the astonished deputies that they had embarked on a wrong course:

"We have begun to reconstruct the Republic. You will continue to do so. However you do it, I think I can tell you in all conscience . . . that if you do it without taking into account the lessons of our political history of the past fifty years and, in particular, of what happened in 1940, if you do not take into account the absolute necessity for governmental authority, dignity, and responsibility, you will reach a situation such that sooner or later, I predict, you will bitterly regret having taken the road which you will have taken. . . .

"Yes, there are two conceptions. They are not reconcilable. . . .

"Do we want a government which governs or do we want an omnipotent Assembly selecting a government to accomplish its will? This second solution means a regime which we ourselves have sometimes tried, and others also have done so.

"Personally, I am convinced that it does not in any sense answer to the necessities of the country in which we live, nor to those of our era, in which problems are so numerous, so complex, so rapid, so brutal, that it appears impossible to solve them within any such constitutional framework. . . .

"The formula which is forced upon us . . . is a government which has and which bears alone—I say: alone—the entire responsibility for the executive power." [1]

[1] Charles de Gaulle, *Discours et messages: 1940–1946* (Paris, 1946), pp. 715, 716 (my translation).

Although De Gaulle's actual resignation did not come until three weeks later, his declarations on that tense New Year's Day had established a position from which there was no turning back and which virtually obliged him to withdraw from the government. To many of his followers and well-wishers his resignation came as a painful shock. Five months later, they sustained another shock when the General signalized his return to active participation in national affairs by his blunt constitutional pronouncement at Bayeux. And before another year had gone by, De Gaulle was to shake them again with his assumption of an active political role at the head of his Rassemblement du Peuple Français. To many Frenchmen, these sudden irruptions on the political scene seemed nothing but the intemperate products of frustrated personal ambition. Some saw in them the fulfillment of long-deferred hopes—others the confirmation of inherited fears. Few recognized their inner logic and historical consistency.

De Gaulle's declarations on the night of December 31, 1945, pointed both forward and back. They recalled his experiences of resistance and exile in London and Algiers. They charted his future political course. Three things in particular emerge: the suggestion of a program that linked up with a long tradition and could strike a sympathetic chord among numerous and influential segments of the French population; the exploitation of a very special personal situation and a carefully cultivated *mystique;* a consistency with the speaker's past and his actions to come.

I

It was no hard task for De Gaulle's critics to connect his forthright political declarations with the tradition summarized in the names Bonaparte–Boulanger–Pétain. Even certain of the General's friends did not deny the association. The young and ardent Jean de Borcey, related to De Gaulle both "by blood and by a faithful and fraternal affection," wrote of the liberation of France as a *"Brumaire"*—an opportunity that the General had most regrettably let slip but that fortunately had presented itself again.[2] Political observers soon noted that it was the former Pétainists who flocked in the greatest numbers in response to the new rallying-cry. The statistics of the local elections of October 1947 and March 1949 proved that there was no other party for which any considerable number of Pétainists could be voting, nor any other large constituency (except the floaters of the MRP) which was free to rally to De Gaulle. Leftist critics have exulted with impunity at the proliferation of aristocratic and wealthy names in the

[2] Jean de Borcey, *Le Gaullisme et la Résistance* (Paris, 1947), pp. 7, 28–29.

Gaullist ranks.[3] As conservative a journal as *Le Monde* has found a parallel between the urban enthusiasm for Boulanger and De Gaulle's victories in the large cities in 1947.[4] American scholars have endorsed the Bonapartist precedent.[5] All this seems proved beyond contradiction. The chord had been touched that vibrates in response to appeals to the family, religion, the army, the constituted orders of society, the state, and national unity. Those who had never accepted the Republic had again found their man. The classes, the interests, the social leaders that at moments of crisis have sought a solution in military authoritarianism, by the summer of 1947 had rallied to De Gaulle.

At the same time, those who formed the rank and file of the Free French following in the Resistance years—the Socialists and the Communists, and, to a lesser extent, the MRP—had become the General's bitterest opponents. Some observers have seen a malign illogicality in this reversal of roles, and have accused De Gaulle of opportunism, and the French Left and moderate Left of blindness during the war years. I shall take up later the charge of inconsistency. The question of the attitude of French democrats—and more particularly of the Socialists—toward De Gaulle in London and Algiers is more complex and pressing.

If one should ask a French Socialist today whether he regretted the support he gave De Gaulle in the war years, he would no doubt answer in the negative. He would recall that the General offered the only rallying-point, the only symbol of resistance, up to the very moment of Liberation. He would reconstruct the circumstances of the time—and especially the need for national unity in the face of Vichy and near-Vichy intrigue and the doubtful attitude of the United States. Above all, he would insist that it was not to the General as an individual that he had given his support, but to the Free French movement in its largest and most democratic sense. About De Gaulle himself he had always had his reservations, and he had tried to the extent of his power to counteract the influence of the General's personal entourage and to steer the movement as a whole into more democratic channels.

It is in this sense that a fair-minded critic will judge the activities of such men as Félix Gouin and André Philip in London and Algiers. Their efforts were directed toward building up the Consultative Assembly as a counterweight to De Gaulle the leader. Whether the Assembly proved in practice to be anything more than a sham

[3] For example, André Wurmser, *De Gaulle et les siens* (Paris, 1947), pp. 170–93.
[4] *Une Semaine dans le Monde,* November 1, 1947.
[5] For example, Donald C. McKay, "De Gaulle and Louis Napoleon," *Current History,* XVI (May 1949), 267–70.

is another question. Again, more of that later. In any case, as an attempt at parliamentary democracy in a situation in which a functioning parliamentary system was obviously out of the question, the Consultative Assembly became "an institution unique among the western governments-in-exile." [6]

Yet one cannot deny that the spectacle of De Gaulle-Cincinnatus abruptly transforming himself into De Gaulle-Bonaparte rather surpassed the reasoned anticipations of French parliamentary democrats. Since 1947, we have acquired a new focus on the conflicts of the Resistance period.

II

In this new focus, the stories, the rumors, that circulated in anti-Gaullist circles during the war years have taken on increased verisimilitude and a heightened actuality. The Duke Street torture chamber in London; the unexplained circumstances of the deaths of the Resistance leaders Moulin (Monsieur X) and Médéric; the machinations of the Gaullist intelligence service, the BCRA; the Cagoulard past of several of the General's closest associates and his own authoritarian leanings—to all these we are likely to give more credence than we did six or seven years ago. We may read with more approbation now Henri de Kerillis' account of his unsuccessful efforts to induce De Gaulle to undertake the rescue from captivity of such prominent pre-1940 leaders as Reynaud, Gamelin, Mandel, Daladier, and Blum, and can comprehend the reasons for the General's coolness to the proposal. We understand more clearly now the disappointment of the 100-per cent Gaullists—freely admitted by Colonel Passy himself—at Bidault's selection as chairman of the National Council of Resistance in Paris instead of a Gaullist nominee, and, after the liberation of Paris, the protracted and difficult negotiations between Bidault and the General over the reconstruction of the Provisional Government. And we see why it was a matter of vital necessity to the Algiers government that Leclerc's armored division should be on hand for the liberation of the capital—not only for reasons of national prestige but to influence the crucial political decisions that would be made there.[7]

In this perspective, also, the experience of the Algiers Consultative Assembly appears less promising than it did at the time. We recall the doubts as to whether the "mandate" of the Resistance

6 John E. Sawyer, "The Reëstablishment of the Republic; France: the De Gaulle Era," *Political Science Quarterly*, LXII (September 1947), 356.

7 On all the foregoing, see Henri de Kerillis, *De Gaulle dictateur: Une grande mystification de l'histoire* (Montreal, n.d.), pp. 53–86, 323, 256; Wurmser, *op. cit.*, pp. 180 ff., 171.

deputies was much more than a patriotic fiction, and the frequent complaint that these deputies were men of second rank, who could be spared for sterile political activity while the real Resistance leaders remained in France—even the former, critics added, had been screened for Gaullist orthodoxy before being given facilities for reaching Algiers. Tales such as these have remained on the level of gossip and polemic and still lack impartial confirmation. But as to the comedy—or scandal, if one prefers—of the election of certain overseas deputies, there is no reason for doubt; De Gaulle's personal intervention in the selection of a delegate from the French community of New York soon became common knowledge.[8] By one means or another, the Gaullist inner circle had assured itself of a safe majority.

When we think back now on the sessions of that Assembly, we realize more clearly than before that though the new institution might provide a parliamentary façade, behind it the General's personal authority remained nearly intact. His stalwarts "of the first hour"—most of whom lacked either Resistance or party standing —still held roughly half the ministries. His conduct of war and diplomacy, and more particularly his politically tinged orders to the Resistance forces in France, remained outside the Assembly's sphere of action. Meantime the Consultative occupied itself with somewhat academic projects for the reestablishment of "republican legality" on the liberation of the home country. De Gaulle's appearances before that body carried a dramatic, almost a plebiscitary tone—for all his efforts to temper his remarks to the sensibilities of old parliamentarians. And—inevitable accompaniment to these scenes—to quote Gordon Wright's elegant description, De Gaulle's "closest confidant, Gaston Palewski, . . would be seen a few feet away, always lounging against the same pillar, his thoughts masked by a smile that seemed to combine Machiavelli and Mona Lisa." [9] Palewski was a conservative and a believer in strong government; his constant attendance on De Gaulle suggested that such were the views of the inner circle and of the chief himself. The parliamentarians, the Socialists and the radical democrats, essentially remained outside.

The foregoing presents perhaps too hostile a picture. In answer, De Gaulle's defenders have always maintained that whatever imperiousness there was in his wartime conduct arose from the unavoidable necessities of his country's situation: a strong center of authority, a curbing of dissidence and half-loyalty, was required to stop the Communist drive for the *noyautage* of the whole Resistance.

8 Kerillis, *op. cit.*, pp. 325–26.
9 Gordon Wright, *The Reshaping of French Democracy* (New York, 1948), pp. 64, 129.

They add that it was De Gaulle himself who, against the wishes of many of the Resistance leaders, decided for the revival of the pre-war political parties within the French underground.[10] The two viewpoints are not entirely incompatible, and there is validity in both of them. One thing, however, is certain. Even De Gaulle's most circumspect apologists have not denied that the General and his friends sedulously exploited the circumstances of the Resistance experience to build up the *mystique* that has remained De Gaulle's most persistent attribute.

This *mystique* is the lasting legacy of the Resistance period. The Gaullist inner circle achieved a notable success in seizing a sentiment that was merely vague and diffused and concentrating it on the person of their leader. Scenes of frenzied devotion and rhythmic crowd chanting of *"Vive de Gaulle!"* became regular occurrences during and immediately following the Liberation. And already—I cite a personal experience from September of 1945—indignant old-line Republicans were protesting that the crowd should be shouting *"Vive la France!"* instead. By 1945—and indeed all through the war period—the fearful and the clairvoyant had sensed the menace of authoritarian government.

III

Thus we arrive at De Gaulle's logical consistency. There is a continuing thread that connects the boy who "before the age of twelve, . . had reached the conclusion that destiny had chosen him to guide the nation in a future hour of crisis," [11] with the soldier who labored to solve the technical problems of his country's defense, the exiled leader in London and Algiers striving to rebuild the concept of national independence and dignity around his own person, the scornful, principled opponent of the two draft constitutions of 1946, and finally, the political chief who has suffused with his spirit an equivocal mass movement. In these successive stages, one period stands out as different from the rest—the experience as a semiconstitutional chief of state from the election of the First Constituent Assembly in October 1945 to his resignation three months later. It was a position in which he was never entirely happy, if we may believe one of his apologists, who complains that this Assembly, and in particular its disciplined parties, cut the General off from the country as the Consultative had never done.[12] In retrospect, the experiment in

10 Wright, *op. cit.,* p. 35.
11 *ibid.,* p. 42.
12 Borcey, *op. cit.,* p. 50.

parliamentary constitutionalism appears as a mere episode. By re-
tiring from power and simultaneously stating his long-held constitutional convictions, De Gaulle resumed his familiar role.

These convictions, as stated in the now classic speeches of Bayeux,
Épinal, and Lille, have scarcely altered in the three succeeding years.
A recent article by Gaston Palewski—who can be presumed to be
speaking for his master—cites them as gospel.[13] Their main features
are familiar: a strong presidency; a second chamber virtually coequal
with the Assembly, and based partly on a system of corporate representation; a strict separation of legislative and executive functions;
a federal constitution for the Empire, assuring in practice the preponderance of the French state. A curious feature of this program
is its rejection of popular election for the president—presumably in
order to take some of the sting from the Bonapartist parallel. The
president is rather to be chosen by a large electoral college or series
of colleges. At the same time, the plebiscitary feature appears in
another form: in cases of grave conflict between the executive and
the legislative the president may call for a national referendum.[14]
Or, alternatively, he may dissolve the Assembly and thus bring on
new elections. This threat of dissolution is the really powerful
weapon that De Gaulle's constitutional project places in the hands of
the president.[15]

The resulting structure, Palewski explains, would be neither a
parliamentary constitution on the British model nor a full-fledged
presidential system, like the American. It would combine features
of both. Its most debatable aspect, he implies, is the president's dual
role as director of the executive, "that is, one of the [three separate]
powers," and as "arbiter between these powers." In explaining this
seeming paradox, Palewski gets to the very center of the Gaullist
concept: ". . . [the president's] supervision is to be felt chiefly in
the areas which are traditionally the sphere of the chief of state;—
those which are closely connected with his role as guardian of the
integrity of the national territory and of respect for treaties: foreign
policy, national defense, the French Union. . . ." [16]

With this, we are back to De Gaulle's earliest and most persistent
interests: the strength and integrity of the French state facing an
external menace. In the event of war, the executive authority, the
military forces, the resources of the Empire, must all be closely knit

[13] Gaston Palewski, "Pour une nouvelle Constitution," *Revue politique et parlementaire*, cxcix (December 1949), 374–75.

[14] The texts of the Bayeux and Épinal speeches are printed in *Discours et messages*,
pp. 721–27, 740–47.

[15] McKay, *loc. cit.*, p. 269.

[16] Palewski, *loc. cit.*, pp. 377, 375 (my translation).

together. In case of necessity, France overseas must be suitably organized to become again the temporary base of national resistance;
under such circumstances of crisis, no divisive nationalist agitation
in the colonies may be tolerated. And the crisis is already upon us:
qualified witnesses report that the Liberation was hardly accomplished before De Gaulle became convinced that a third world war
was inevitable—and imminent. He is resolved that never again shall
France find herself in the position of administrative and military
paralysis into which she had drifted under the constitution of 1875.

IV

There is a second central line of thought in Palewski's exegesis—
and one that serves as an introduction to the internal—as opposed
to the foreign and military—aspects of De Gaulle's program and
appeal. It is the familiar "wave of the future" argument, clothed
in technological language: the technical necessities of our time demand that power rest in "firm and sure hands." [17] This argument
recalls the General's parting blast at the First Constituent Assembly.
It also recalls the Resistance experience and one of the nearly forgotten smaller Resistance movements. In the years 1942 to 1943, the
OCM (Organisation Civile et Militaire), a group dominated by intellectuals and higher civil servants and notably loyal to De Gaulle,
had clandestinely circulated plans for the constitutional reconstruction of France. In a spirit which critics attacked as "technocratic,"
the OCM had proposed a presidential system on the American
model, with a cabinet responsible to the president alone.[18] Such a
concentration of power went beyond what De Gaulle himself currently advocates. Perhaps it was truer to the spirit and ultimate implications of the General's program than his own more modest
proposal.

A more dispassionate and closely reasoned version of the technological argument appears in a semi-academic article published a
few weeks after the launching of the RPF. Its author, Paul-Émile
Viard, deputy from Algiers and former dean of the Algiers Law
Faculty, professes to speak as an independent, saddened by the advent of political Gaullism but convinced that it answers to the needs
of his time. De Gaulle's recent gesture, he argues, "corresponds in
an imperious fashion to the evolution of present-day institutions."
Parliamentarism no longer functions; symbolic of its hollowness is
the new system whereby the whip of each parliamentary group in

17 Palewski, *loc. cit.*, p. 371.
18 Wright, *op. cit.*, p. 34.

the Assembly votes his party *en bloc*. The great organized pressure groups actually run the state, which lacks a center of administrative unity. Under these circumstances, Viard concludes, we must either return to the classic parliamentarism of the nineteenth century—liberal in politics and economics—

"Or else we shall continue to indulge in the play of parties, of established corporate bodies, of powerful trade-unions, of growing provisions for special status, of the *mystique* of numbers, and of quasi-socialist *dirigisme*. In this case, the political system will call for an executive to recreate the principle of unity.

"Within this second hypothesis—alas, the more probable!—another dilemma arises: either the reform will be carried out in an all-inclusive and rapid fashion by De Gaulle—with or without the RPF—and in this case it will be carried out under conditions of order, liberty, and harmonious political organization, or his attempt will fail and . . . the reform will be carried out just the same, sooner or later, by someone else, after crises and convulsions which the country could very well do without." [19]

V

The balancing, the reconciliation of great pressure groups by a strong executive: such is the essence of the Gaullist formula. Through the euphemisms of the General's official propaganda, this reality emerges. Is this Fascism? However much we may want to avoid an emotional and much-abused word, we must meet the question honestly. De Gaulle's critics are quite sure that he and his movement are Fascist; his supporters either deny it or evade the issue. This polemic gets us nowhere. In a case such as this, where the significant facts are established and well known, the argument may be largely verbal—a sterile dispute over an ugly label.

If we mean by Fascism the more sinister doctrines and practices that characterized the Mussolini and, in particular, the Hitler régimes—racism, predatory war, mass brutality, and a thorough-going police supervision of private life—then the epithet is undeserved, or at the least premature. These may be the eventual implications of the Gaullist program. Once in power, the General might feel obliged to resort to them. For the present, there is no compelling reason for doubting his word when he rejects them. It is even too early to say whether De Gaulle would actually scrap his own constitutional proposals and the traditional

[19] Paul-Émile Viard, "L'Inéluctable Évolution?", *Revue politique et parlementaire*, CXCI (June 1947), 201–4 (my translation).

liberties of his people and would govern France as a dictator. We should not rule out the possibility that he means what he says, that he sincerely believes his semipresidential system would equip his country with a sufficient measure of executive authority.

Yet even with this narrower—and perhaps excessively charitable —definition of Gaullism, the term Fascist may apply. If we give to the word what we might call a Latin connotation (one deriving from the experience of Italy and Spain rather than of Germany), then Fascism is practically the equivalent of the corporate state. And what has the corporate state proved to be in practice if not the balancing and integration in a nationalist sense of great pressure groups by a strong executive? We should add, of course, that in such an integration, it is the capitalist as opposed to the working class groups that win out. This is not the corporatism of Catholic theorists— although that too appears in De Gaulle's formal program in his advocacy of the "association" of workers in the ownership of factories. But traditional corporatism has by now become little more than a rather touching memory of blasted hopes. Rather than a true reconciliation of conflicting economic and social pressures, it has demonstrated itself in practice to be an admirable device for clothing the realities of class domination in the trappings of national unity.

In this sense, we may call Gaullism either Fascist or corporative as we prefer. It may be objected that this is an oversimplification— that Gaullism is a curious and personal amalgam peculiar to the General himself and to his country. But cannot the same be said of Fascism everywhere? While Fascism is a universal and international phenomenon of our century, it has never appeared twice in the same form. Peculiarities of time, national tradition, and leading personalities have marked each of its manifestations. Even in the same country, slight differences of circumstance may effect crucial changes in a Fascist movement's prospects of success. We have seen how Gaullism has been marked from the start by its leader's Resistance record and his long and consistent advocacy of a strong and coherent national policy. Thus Gaullism suggests the very opposite of that antipatriotism and collusion with the enemy which unavoidably limited the appeal of Pétainism.

Moreover, the characteristic stigmata of Fascist movements are not lacking in Gaullist tactics and the Gaullist appeal. We find the familiar defense of law and order and the old ruling classes—a position which, as J. E. Sawyer has pointed out, the General assumed as early as the moment of liberation in opposition to the revolutionary aspirations of the Resistance Left. From here, it was only a logical step for De Gaulle to stand forth as the protector of all but the most notorious of former collaborationists.[20] Coupled with this —in apparent contrast but conforming to a more subtle logic—we find the successful appeal to the salaried petty bourgeoisie, embittered by a postwar inflation in which prices have outrun incomes. Along with these class appeals, comes the familiar attack on "money" —a transparent sign of the Fascist type of manipulation when used by a party whose large capitalist source of funds is common knowledge.* We find the customary shock-troop cadres, the emotionally charged public meetings, the sudden and dramatic practice mobilizations. And—perhaps the most pervasive symptom—we recognize the lack of clear doctrine, the simple-minded or calculated political obfuscation. Anyone who needs to be convinced of Gaullism's intellectual feebleness has only to read the little book in which James Burnham records his interview with André Malraux. The latter, the intellectual *vedette* of the movement, has nothing more lucid to offer than a faith not "in programs, but only in objectives" and the "myth" of "a new human type: the liberal hero." [21] Again we bow to the shade of Georges Sorel.

VI

The final question, the prospects for De Gaulle's coming to power, is more difficult to handle than it was a year or two ago. Then a Gaullist government appeared an imminent possibility: many thought it inevitable. Since the rather surprising success of the Queuille government in maintaining itself during the winter of 1948–1949, predictions have radically altered. Now we hear on all sides that De Gaulle is "through." Even more than the French, American journalists have virtually written him off. Here again, informed observers have rushed to extremes.

It is unquestionable that De Gaulle's following has fallen off. But this has happened before and the movement has made at least a partial comeback. The history of the RPF follows an irregular wavelike curve. After reaching an initial high coincident with the municipal elections in the autumn of 1947, the wave subsided with Schuman's firm and sensible administration in the early months of 1948.

---

* In this connection it is important to point out that most French business leaders— distrustful of De Gaulle's "reliability" and of the adventurous character of his immediate associates—have to date refused to back his movement. Currently, the RPF appears to be suffering from an acute shortage of funds.

[20] Sawyer, *loc. cit.*, pp. 359–60.

[21] André Malraux and James Burnham, *The Case for De Gaulle* (New York, 1948), pp. 24, 62.

The fall of Schuman, the brief Marie-Reynaud experiment, the protracted crisis that followed, and the unsure beginnings of the Queuille government brought a Gaullist revival in the months of August and September. Public opinion statistics suggest, however, that this second wave failed to reach as high as the first. Then came the gradual increase of confidence in Queuille and an all-time Gaullist low coinciding with the cantonal elections in March 1949. Summer brought a rise of prices, autumn Queuille's fall and the hazardous launching of another government—again a gain in Gaullist confidence. Bidault has hung on, he has slipped his budget through the Assembly by the narrowest of margins, the General is in eclipse. Yet those who claim to know predict that De Gaulle's old rival will scarcely survive the spring. Again we shall see the RPF returning to the charge.*

Furthermore, part of the change in the movement's electoral strength is largely fictitious. In the elections of October 1947 most of the Radicals ran on RPF lists. A year and a half later they stood independently. In the first election, unsure of themselves and still not recovered from their 1945 debacle, they decided to ride the Gaullist crest. They went along with the General not because they were convinced of the virtues of his movement, but for tactical reasons, and more particularly because they agreed with him in opposing proportional representation and *dirigisme*.[22] Then when it appeared that the momentum of the movement had been stopped, they discreetly began to slip away. Thus, while the Gaullists might claim a near majority in the indirect elections for the Council of the Republic in the autumn of 1948, their jubilation was short-lived. Many of the senators elected with Gaullist support soon showed themselves notably independent.[23] And the following spring, when the Radicals decided to go it alone, they topped the MRP and again took up a position as a major political force.

The impact of these defections on the part of the Radicals and related groups has not been entirely to the disadvantage of the RPF. Part of what the movement has lost in numbers it has gained in cohesion. Disillusioned at the treachery of his allies, De Gaulle has announced that in the future he will depend on his "companions" and "on them alone." Presumably, this means that in the event of

* Written in January 1950. The Bidault Government fell the following June 24. Queuille became Premier on July 1 and was ousted by the Assembly the following day. René Pleven formed a government, including the Socialists, on July 11 and won the approval of the Assembly on July 13. In the Assembly elections the following June the RPF polled 21.7 percent of the popular vote and won 120-odd seats.

22 *Une Semaine dans le Monde,* October 25, 1947.
23 *The Christian Science Monitor,* January 27, 1950.

new elections for the Assembly, the RPF will not make alliances with other parties. In the same vein, the propaganda of the movement has become more combative, more nationalistic, and more demagogic—closer to the familiar Fascist model. To use the Gaullist vocabulary, it is taking shape as a "purer and harder" political weapon.[24]

De Gaulle personally has apparently not lost his confidence. He is convinced that sooner or later economic difficulties will drive the government to dissolution and general elections.[25] His *mystique* remains a potent political incalculable—and one against which even a substantial economic stabilization might prove unavailing. Nor has the technocratic argument for a strong executive lost its force. We may recall Viard's formula—either De Gaulle or someone else —under conditions of permanent crisis, in which to the nightmare of Communism has now been added the nightmare of a reviving Germany. As government after government stumbles ever more feebly along the road of improvisations, the Gaullist appeal survives— lucid in appearance if not in actuality. Observers agree that a radical political change could come virtually overnight—a "rout" either toward the General or away from him. A succession of ministerial crises could bring his old allies flocking back.* In the opposite sense, we have the memory of Boulanger—and the French scorn for the political adventurer who has missed the bus.

As the heroes—or the villains—of the outwitting of De Gaulle, the Radicals stand to gain whatever happens. An evolution toward the Right has been in progress essentially ever since the Liberation and appears likely to continue. Under these circumstances, a more conservative government could take two possible forms: a Gaullist régime or else a Right-Center parliamentary coalition, based on a return to liberal economics and the traditions of the Third Republic, with its leaders drawn from the Radical party and the conservative independents grouped around former Premier Reynaud. At the present time, the second alternative appears the more likely. This is doubtless the one that the Radicals themselves would prefer. But in either case they could make a fairly satisfactory governmental alliance. The ultimate irony of Gaullism is that the General's quixotically heroic gesture should find its most solid achievement in the revival of the most unheroic of parties.

* In the elections of June 1951 the RPF made alliances in only twelve of the election districts.

[24] *ibid.*

[25] *The New York Times,* October 28, 1949.

16

++

GEORGES SOREL: APOSTLE OF FANATICISM

SCOTT H. LYTLE

++

THE publication, in 1908, of the *Réflexions sur la violence* brought its heretofore almost unknown author, Georges Sorel, to the attention of the European intellectual. From that sudden reputation— for which the work's title alone may have been largely responsible —arose the oversimplification of Sorel's contribution characteristic of current textbooks: he wrote a book, we are told, the *Réflexions sur la violence,* in which he expounded a theory of the social myth; he was the philosopher of revolutionary syndicalism; and he had an important influence not only upon that aspect of the trade-union movement, but also upon the mind of Benito Mussolini.[1] There is a measure of truth in this capsule identification; and it possesses the persuasive virtue of simplicity. It is, however, doubly misleading. It suggests that "revolutionary syndicalist" is a sufficient label for Sorel. In fact, Sorel called himself a revolutionary syndicalist during but a fraction of his thirty-odd years as a social philosopher. It suggests, secondly, that the label "revolutionary syndicalist" is an accurate one: that Sorel's doctrine successfully accomplished its purpose of articulating the dynamic of the syndicalist movement with which it was contemporary; and that consequently we need only know the doctrine to understand the movement itself. In fact, Sorel was a "revolutionary syndicalist" *sui generis.* Indeed, his position through the years on each of the movements to which his attention and sympathy were drawn in turn was of so personal a character as to render every label suspect.

This chapter is an effort to throw some light both on the particular problem of the relationship between Sorelian syndicalism and

[1] See, for example, W. P. Hall and W. S. Davis, *The Course of Europe since Waterloo* (New York, 1947), pp. 286, 394, 414, 703.

the syndicalist movement and on the broader problem of relationship, over half a lifetime, between Sorel's evolving social theory and
the various social movements with which he strove to bring this
theory into accord. What were the prior experiences and present
aspirations which Sorel, as philosopher of contemporary practice,
brought to bear upon each of the various social movements which
his successive writings sought to describe and judge? Did he participate directly in the movement; did he, indeed, believe that such
participation would qualify him for his descriptive task? Was his
social philosophy in fact descriptive, as he claimed; did it mirror the
particular movement, or did it, rather, externalize his own aspirations for that movement? Was the *Réflexions sur la violence,* for example, an objective account of the dynamic of revolutionary syndicalism—a reflection, on the theoretical level, of contemporary
social data; or was it an idealization of that contemporary data in
the effort to make the movement what it "should be" but what it
in fact was not? Was Sorelian syndicalism, in short, the response of
theory to practice; or was it an effort, an unconscious effort, perhaps,
to bring practice into accord with personal theory?

Relevant here is another question: why did Sorel so frequently,
and on occasion so abruptly, shift his attention and sympathies from
one segment of the contemporary social scene to another? Why did
he direct them, in turn, from the older, disappearing France of the
provinces to the Guesdist orthodox Marxists of Paris; from the latter, on the level of theory, to the revisionist writings of Bernstein
and Croce, and on the level of practice, to the Jaurèsian parliamentary Socialists collaborating with the bourgeois parties in behalf of Dreyfus; and thence to the revolutionary syndicalists; and,
from the revolutionary syndicalists, to the Maurrasian antiparliamentary monarchists; and from these, after reaffirming his fidelity
to the workers' movement, to the Russian Bolsheviks? Is it that he
saw in each the instrument of moral regeneration? Is it that he was
stirred by whatever, in turn, bore the mark of power? Is it that
each, appearing latently powerful, offered a potential vehicle for a
philosopher's immortality? Was Sorel's life as a writer the tale of an
idealist whose hopes for society were repeatedly excited and then
disappointed? Or was it the tale of an egoist motivated by a personal ambition repeatedly frustrated: the ambition to serve as the
recognized prophet of whatever movement promised to become
dominant?

The answers to such questions, particularly where they have to
do with motives, belong to a no-man's-land which the historian
would be prudent to avoid. My reading of the "nobility" of Sorel's

intentions depends at least in part upon the aftertaste—not entirely pleasant—of long study of Sorel's life and writings. They remain important questions, however. By way of answer to them, I intend, first, to present Sorel the man, as he appeared to certain of his contemporaries; and, second, to sketch, within a chronological frame, the interrelationship between his life and his thought.

II

"I much liked 'le pere Sorel,' as we called him among ourselves. He was a robust old man, with a complexion fresh as a child's, white hair, a short white beard, and remarkable eyes, the color of Parma violet, which recalled to me the Vikings, his Norman ancestors." Thus is Sorel, a man of intriguing and complex character, introduced by Jérôme Tharaud, who knew him through their mutual friend, Charles Péguy, the great French moralist. Each Thursday, Tharaud recalls, Sorel would come to the office of Péguy's journal, *Cahiers de la quinzaine,* sit in its only chair, and there to any listener pour forth, quite without order, the ideas accumulated over sixty years. As soon as someone opened the door, Sorel would seize on him and draw him into his thought of that moment or, brusquely changing the subject, pass with an unbelievable ease from a description of soldiers' uniforms to a discussion of Plotinus or St. Theresa. Tharaud was impressed not only by Sorel's learning, but by the originality of his mind, which was "always prompt to separate from a subject the crusts of banality which covered it over, to discover beneath the commonplaces and ready-made ideas the living tissue of thought." Sorel reminded Tharaud of Stendhal. Where both were great amateurs of ideas, Stendhal was interested in the self-realization of an individual, Sorel in that of a social group, going "spontaneously to all that carried within it the mark of its power, a possibility for the future." In contrast to Péguy, who responded instinctively to a few profound sentiments, Sorel weighed, criticized, peeled, analyzed everything in the universe; he ratiocinated endlessly.[2]

The picture of Georges Sorel has been enlarged and filled in by other long-time friends, each of them, following Sorel's death in 1922, recalling the man they had listened to, or collaborated with, or corresponded with, from a few to many years earlier. Georges Valois was one of these: Valois who had been in turn anarchist, revo-

2 Jérôme Tharaud, *Notre cher Péguy* (2 vols., Paris, 1926), I, 255–61; II, 138–40. The Thursdays to which Tharaud refers fell within the decade of Sorel's discovery and later rejection of revolutionary syndicalism: that is, from about 1900–1910. Born in 1847, Sorel was just sixty at the time of the publication of the *Réflexions sur la violence.*

lutionary syndicalist, and monarchist; and who had known Sorel from 1898, when Sorel came each Thursday to the office of the journal *Humanité nouvelle,* where Valois was then working, and found his audience there as he was to do later at Péguy's. Another was the sociologist Pareto, with whom Sorel corresponded heavily during the years of the First World War. A third was Roberto Michels, the political scientist, who had known Sorel best just prior to the publication of the *Réflexions sur la violence* but who saw him just before his death, when he was troubled by Sorel's request for as many works of Lenin and Trotzky as possible, that they might be translated into French. René Johannet, the proto-Fascist author of *Éloge du bourgeois français,* saw Sorel at Péguy's and at Valois' and at the small Socialist bookshop of Sorel's close friends Paul and Léonie Delesalle. Hubert Lagardelle and Jean Variot collaborated with Sorel on small, sectarian journals: Lagardelle from 1905–1908 on the revolutionary syndicalist *Mouvement socialiste,* of which Lagardelle was director; and Variot from 1910–1913 on the nationalist *Indépendance.* Sorel broke from each of these magazines in turn; but whereas the earlier break led to the end of his friendship with Lagardelle, the latter did not disturb his relationship with Variot who, until the end in 1922, continued to play the role of Sorel's Boswell, jotting down the conversations later published as *Propos de Georges Sorel.* There was, finally, Édouard Berth, from about 1905 Sorel's faithful "disciple" and, if partial, the man who knew him best.[3]

Through these witnesses we see Sorel as "a somewhat old-fashioned gentleman, very bourgeois, and temperamentally much more a man of letters than a revolutionary." [4] Sorel was bourgeois in his courtesy, his studies, his relatives, his dress, his career, his income, his little house at Boulogne, his subscription to the *Journal des débats,* his economies, his disdain for men of letters, his self-distrust, his anathemas against this bourgeoisie to which he himself belonged. He had all the bourgeois gifts—industry, honesty, disinterestedness, taste for thought, love for humanity—except one, common sense; and so, born to celebrate Thiers, he extolled Lenin, and when he thought of Taine, he said Karl Marx.[5] "The basis of his character was a great moral virtue. He was horrified by dissoluteness of morals, worldly

---

[3] Georges Valois, *D'un siècle à un autre* (Paris, 1924); Vilfredo Pareto, "Georges Sorel," *Ronda,* IV (1922), 541–48; Roberto Michels (ed.), "Lettere di Georges Sorel a Roberto Michels," *Nuovi studi di diritto economia e politica,* II (1929), 288–94; René Johannet, *Éloge du bourgeois français* (Paris, 1924), Chap. XI: "Adieu à Georges Sorel"; Hubert Lagardelle, "Introduction aux lettres de G. Sorel," *Educazione fascista,* XI (1933), 229–43, 320–34, 506–18, 760–83, 956–75; Jean Variot (ed.), *Propos de Georges Sorel* (Paris, 1935); Édouard Berth, "Georges Sorel," *Clarté,* No. 21 (September 15, 1922), 495–96.

[4] Michels, *op. cit.,* II, 289, n. 4.

[5] Johannet, *op. cit.,* pp. 336–43.

superficiality, bourgeois egoism, the profound political immorality of most French statesmen. His severities with regard to the parliamentary Socialists are due precisely to the fact that he did not admit compromises. He did not admit that ambition should make a man change his doctrine." [6] His mind was learned, lively, objective. A prodigious memory enabled him to acquire an erudition comparable to that of Sainte-Beuve.[7] There was in him no pedantry; he was, rather, an affable, sprightly man, spicing his dissertations with anecdotes, tales, gossip; to listen to him was an unmixed pleasure.[8] Interested in the movements of men of his own day, he studied these with the objectivity of an entomologist; philosopher above all, he had no passion, and was never a partisan.[9]

Alongside this attractive, composite picture of an uncompromisingly moral, yet affable, social scientist, might be placed another. Lagardelle recalled Sorel to have been of hypersensitive temperament, irritable, suspicious, and timid; prone to sudden changes, contradictions, and discouragements; a man seeking the absolute, and having as his necessary destiny "hopes and deceptions and, at the end, always gloomy solitude." [10] Michels found him to be supremely intolerant; he noted particularly that Sorel profoundly distrusted the Jews, as well as idealists, whom he considered bloodthirsty beyond all political necessity.[11] Where Valois, recalling Sorel's discourses, has explained that he came simply as a savant seeking his natural audience, Michels is sharper, finding that Sorel, basically a solitary spirit, strangely could not stand solitude; a theoretician, he needed acolytes.[12] Where Variot, to whom Sorel was a political genius, was struck by his modesty, Johannet stresses his pride: "You [Sorel] compared yourself to Pythagoras, to Heraclitus, to all the great movers of crowds and minds. When I compared you to Socrates you didn't refuse the honor." [13]

And, finally, where Valois and Variot have emphasized Sorel's objectivity as a student of contemporary movements, others have offered quite another impression. Pareto has noted somewhat pompously that Sorel adopted Pareto's method of "logico-experimental reasoning" and through it reached the celebrated theory of myths, a specific illustration of his own theory of Residues; but he found Sorel, in contrast to himself, to be essentially not an experimentalist, but a

[6] Variot, *op. cit.*, pp. 128–29.

[7] *ibid.*, p. 10.

[8] Valois, *op. cit.*, pp. 133–34.

[9] *ibid.*, pp. 130–32, 135–36; Variot, *op. cit.*, pp. 10, n.1, 11–12, 258.

[10] Lagardelle, *op. cit.*, XI, 230–31.

[11] Michels, *op. cit.*, II, 289, n. 4.

[12] Valois, *op. cit.*, pp. 133–34; Michels, *op. cit.*, II, 290, n. 5.

[13] Variot, *op. cit.*, pp. 7–13, 128–29; Johannet, *op. cit.*, pp. 338–40.

man of faith, inclined to metaphysics.[14] Lagardelle has emphasized Sorel's sensitivity to the milieu: "He is a soul of fire . . . understood only through the historical milieu to which . . . it has so violently reacted. . . . His work . . . is born . . . at the mercy of circumstances. The cycle of Sorelian ideas goes not from inside out but from outside in. The inner life . . . spurts out only under the brutal shock of the external world. Sorel thinks only in terms of action." [15] This judgment by Lagardelle is in a measure confirmed by the faithful Berth: shortly after Sorel's death, he described him as a "philosopher-historian" striving to judge the events of his own time, events which he approached, however, with an intense ardor. Sorel was a "believer" in the full sense of the word, the revolutionary myth truly taking the place of religion. He was a spectator of the workers' movement, Berth added, but a spectator having a passionate sympathy. "One of the most original and freest minds of his time, Sorel's ambition was to endow the workers' movement with an ideology worthy of it and capable of raising it to the full comprehension of its historic mission. In this task he sought to discover how a new world is formed and what it is that assures the triumph of an ideology." [16]

There are contradictions in this testimony, but they must stand: Sorel was a complex and ambiguous personality. He possessed a highly developed analytical mind; but he was also an enthusiast for any movement which he judged morally fruitful. He used that mind to attack those in the current scene or in the historical past who appeared to him to be materialistically motivated rationalists; he found historical materialism useful as a method of analysis, since through its use he could argue that his current enemies (whether Jean Jaurès or St. Augustine) were not what they appeared to be, but slaves instead to ambition or economic interest; and, since some of his points were telling, he was on such occasions impressive as a political realist. On the other hand, he responded as a man of faith to such persons or movements as seemed to him to be dedicated to a selfless pursuit of the sublime; he became "objective" or realistic with regard to the revolutionary syndicalists, for example, only when they betrayed his faith in them. He was bourgeois in background, mode of life, and temperament; but he sought, through the largest part of his writings, the reputation of "servant of the proletariat." He was a man of the study, with a horror of noise, of the street, of the public square, of politics, even of all personal action [17]; but he wrote in response to activities of the external world and with a view to guiding such activities. A man of letters, he

14 Pareto, *op. cit.*, IV, 541–42.
15 Lagardelle, *op. cit.*, XI, 229.
16 Berth, *op. cit.*, No. 21, 495–96.
17 Valois, *op. cit.*, pp. 132–33.

disdained men of letters; self-appointed spokesman for those who use violence in pursuit of a social myth, he condemned idealists as bloodthirsty.

Severely critical of bourgeois egoism, of political opportunism, of those who through ambition change their doctrine, Sorel himself, though perfectly disinterested in the material sense, was egoistic as a philosopher and ambitious as a moralist. If ambition rarely led him to alter his basic doctrine, it apparently, on occasion, provoked him to transfer his sympathies from one to another possible external vehicle of that doctrine. A moralist—and this is the constant which knits his thought—he sought, not self-perfection, but the reform of society, understanding such reform in terms of his own weaknesses as well as his own virtues. He wished society to be honest, industrious, chaste, and unmaterialistic, as he himself was. He wished society to be self-sacrificing, self-confident, heroic, as he—circumspect in action, self-distrustful, and timid—would like to be but was not. He lived vicariously through the social groups which his writings damned or celebrated. His villains were projections of certain aspects of his own personality: his ambition-driven parliamentary Socialists were externalizations of himself ambitious as a philosopher; his bloodthirsty Jacobins, externalizations of his own intolerance. His heroes, on the other hand—the revolutionary syndicalists, for example—were modeled upon an idealized self. The moral self-realization of a social group provided, in short, a substitute for personal moral self-realization. At the same time, could his writings abet that self-realization, they might win for him recognition as that social group's philosopher.

III

Georges Sorel had two careers. The first was that of a civil engineer, employed by the French state in the provinces from which he had sprung. The second, which briefly overlapped the first, was that of a journalist who was essentially a philosopher-historian. As philosopher-historian, he studied the psychological history of past societies and social groups in order to understand, elucidate, and act upon the society of his own day. He focused on two questions in particular: the genesis of knowledge, and the role of the sentiments in upright moral conduct and in effective social action. The experience of his childhood and of his first career conditioned the answers to these two questions which he was to propose in the course of the second. A strict Catholic upbringing had made of Sorel a moralist who was to secularize his Catholicism while retaining the premise that upright moral behavior depends upon the pursuit of an ideal. His twenty-five years as civil engineer had prepared his affirmation that "true" knowledge consists, not in the general, abstract, Cartesian philosophy of cultured but technically ignorant administrators, but rather in the conclusions drawn from industrial practice by their underlings, technical experts like himself.[18]

These two interests—in the genesis of knowledge, and in the springs of moral conduct—became evident in his earliest writings, when Sorel, still practicing as an engineer in the provinces, began to rework his notebooks, which were based in large part upon the Greek philosophers and upon works published during his youth by the enigmatical and deeply influential Proudhon, by the sociologist Le Play, and by the historians Renan and Taine. Among these early publications, two stand out, the *Procès de Socrate* (1889) and the "Essai sur la philosophie de Proudhon" (1892). In them, in which no reference to Marx may be found, appear many anticipations of the position which Sorel would present some fifteen years later as a "return to Marx" and as revolutionary syndicalism.

In these early works, Sorel assimilated heroism to upright morality and in turn to the glory of a civilization—and showed himself anxious regarding contemporary France, which had discovered in 1870 what pretty, sentimental theories against militarism might lead to.[19] Interested in the cultivation of heroic sentiments, he recognized, following Renan, that "the sentiments have their value independent of the reality of the object which excites them." [20] He sought such a stimulus of the sentiments, and found it in the Homeric legends, in the Bible, and also, following Proudhon, in the ideal revealed through war. War "reveals to us the ideal, creates the epic, restrengthens effeminate peoples," and makes man greater than nature.[21] This stimulus, prototype of the "social poetry" Sorel would later find in Marx and of his own yet later social myth of the general strike, is, he affirmed, an ideal, an indemonstrable, since "according to a law of our nature we wish to have something indemonstrable to believe." [22] It is essential to conduct: "Man cannot do without the ideal; not only does he create it, but he tends to realize it." [23] In these initial writings, moreover, Sorel appreciated the instrumental value of a faith conjoined with violence: "Innovators can succeed only by boldness: they are a

[18] See Georges Sorel, *Illusions du progrès* (Paris, 1908), *passim*, but especially pp. 173-79. See also Gaëtan Pirou, *Georges Sorel* (Paris, 1927), pp. 19-26.
[19] G. Sorel, *Procès de Socrate* (Paris, 1889), p. 44.
[20] *ibid.*, pp. 120-22.
[21] G. Sorel, "Essai sur la philosophie de Proudhon," *Revue philosophique*, XXXIII (June 1892), 622-38; XXXIV (July 1892), 41-68. On this particular point, *ibid.*, XXXIV, 44-46.
[22] *Procès*, pp. 145-46.
[23] "Essai," *loc. cit.*, XXXIII, 638.

minority, but if they have a 'faith' they can sometimes profit. . . . The Jacobins showed themselves all the more violent the more isolated they were. They were perfectly logical. Alone they possessed the revolutionary Idea." [24]

In his attitude toward knowledge, as well, Sorel expressed from the beginning the antipathy to rationalist speculation which would be characteristic of his later thought, finding rationalism to be intimately associated with bourgeois materialism.[25] Less characteristic later, however, was his saving respect for "true" knowledge or science, found to be based (as was his own knowledge) on industrial practice, that is, on the material world.[26]

And in these early writings, finally, Sorel expounded a concept of social struggle which owed much to Proudhon but which he would later offer under a Marxian banner. In the *Procès de Socrate,* for example, Sorel indicted Socrates and his fellow-philosophers for the destruction of Athenian civilization: their teachings contributed to Athens' fall by weakening that faith in the Homeric legends which had inspired the moral greatness upon which Athenian dominance had been based. The struggle of late fifth-century Greece, Sorel continued, was only secondarily an economic struggle; it was essentially a struggle between two ethical types: the old soldier of the countryside, religious and heroic; and the clever and subtle probabilist, instructor of the increasingly materialistic Athenian bourgeoisie. Socrates was a good man, an inspired prophet who yet remained personally loyal to the old religion, and a hero in the way in which he faced death; but he bore a responsibility for the unhappy results of his teachings. His sophistries encouraged the ruin of the old military discipline and the old faith in the Homeric ideals; his theory of unisexual love contributed to the destruction of the family fabric; and his political theory promoted the replacement of the conservative military aristocracy by an aristocracy of talent.[27] With the subsequent failure of Demosthenes to awaken the ancient genius of Athenian society, "Philosophy had accomplished its work: Athenian democracy had fallen." [28] In short, Socratic rationalism, itself unable to inspire proper conduct, which requires an indemonstrable, was destructive of the old heroic faith.

And yet, while foreshadowing certain aspects of his later revolutionary doctrine, Sorel was at that time by no means a revolutionary. In his *Contribution à l'étude profane de la Bible* (1889) he affirmed that the

24 *Procès,* pp. 205–6.
25 *ibid.,* pp. 207–9, 172, 178–79.
26 "Essai," *loc. cit.,* XXXIII, 636; XXXIV, 62, 68.
27 *Procès,* especially pp. 23–73, 93–97, 230–33.
28 *ibid.,* pp. 207–9.

popularization of the Bible was a social question, not only because it could serve to initiate the people into the heroic life and to combat the deleterious tendencies of utilitarianism, but because it alone could combat the revolutionary idea.[29] And, to the older, finer civilization of Athens he compared the older civilization of the French provinces to which he yet belonged; and to the "deceitful and braggart shopkeepers' oligarchy of Athens, who governed at the countryside's expense," he compared the domination of the cities in contemporary France.[30] Upon moving to Paris, Sorel himself was to assume the revolutionary role which he had attributed to Socrates; he was to do so, however, in behalf of those heroic and quasi-religious values which he had heretofore admired in old Athens and old France, values henceforth increasingly identified with Socialism.

IV

Many years after the event Sorel was to write that he began turning toward the literature of Marxian Socialism in 1893, shortly after the election to the Chamber of a mixed group of Socialist deputies under Millerand's direction.[31] Not only did Socialism appear at that moment to be the wave of the future; but Sorel himself had recently altered both his mode of life and his place of residence and was responsive to his new environment and to the opportunities open to him, an amateur philosopher who now for the first time could devote himself wholeheartedly to a second career. The year before, he had retired, as a chief engineer and recipient of the Legion of Honor, and had settled down in Paris, there to live very modestly on a small inheritance from his mother; he had refused the pension to which his decoration had entitled him, preferring to recover his full independence.[32] No longer a representative of that older provincial society which he had previously lauded and now a stranger among the Parisian bourgeoisie whom he, bourgeois himself, continued to despise, he was ready to collaborate journalistically with the similarly antibourgeois Marxian Socialists, should the opportunity arise. Very important, moreover, to judge from his earliest Marxian works, was the Socialist claim that

[29] P. L. M. J. Perrin, *Les Idées sociales de Georges Sorel* (Alger, 1925), pp. 12–13, in which Perrin quotes from Sorel's *Contribution à l'étude profane de la Bible* (Paris, 1889). Compare Sorel's later "Germanesimo e storicismo di E. Renan," written in 1915, and published in *Critica*, XXIX (1931), 110–15, 199–207, 358–67, 430–44.

[30] *Procès*, pp. 172, 178–79.

[31] G. Sorel, "Mes raisons du syndicalisme," *Matériaux pour une théorie du prolétariat* (3rd ed., Paris, 1929), p. 249. This autobiographical sketch was based upon "Confessioni: come divenni sindicalista," *Divenire sociale* (March–May, 1910).

[32] Variot, *op. cit.*, p. 251, n. 1; Édouard Berth, *Du 'Capital' aux 'Réflexions sur la violence'* (Paris, 1932), pp. 169–70.

Marxism was a science based on a knowledge of the material world. Sorel, so lately an engineer, and now devoting himself to philosophy, could find encouragement in this claim; for it suggested that his many years as engineer were the best possible training for the construction of a philosophy not composed of empty, subjective, metaphysical speculations, but based on "true" knowledge or science.

In that year, 1893, Sorel wrote an open letter published in the *Revue philosophique*—the magazine to which he had submitted his first article back in 1886—and in it asked that Socialism be given a fair hearing on the question of its value as an economic science.[33] In 1894 he published his first major works as a Marxian Socialist in the obscure journal, *Ère nouvelle*, which did not outlive that year. He then collaborated, and very heavily indeed, in a second unsuccessful journalistic venture, *Devenir social*, which he founded with Paul Lafargue and Gabriel Deville. Thus, in the mid-1890's, Sorel associated himself with the most orthodox of representatives of the Marxian tradition, two old-time revolutionary Socialists who were, moreover, members of a Socialist fraction, dominated by Jules Guesde, which had recently acquired a new vigor.[34]

The orthodoxy of Sorel's Socialism was that of an enthusiastic neophyte who was only just becoming acquainted with a new creed —as well as with his new world of Paris—and had not yet determined his own position respecting it. He was, moreover, extraordinarily busy, in the space of about two years producing under his own name and under pseudonyms some fifty-seven articles in the *Devenir social* alone. He consequently took little part in Socialist polemics. He did, indeed, devote his strongly anticlerical "Fin du paganisme" (1894) to alerting fellow-Socialists against the dangers of sentimental or religious propaganda: anticlericalism was an issue upon which most Socialists could agree.[35] He did not, on the other hand, participate in the controversies dividing the Socialists; and (to anticipate) there is no indication that Deville's Guesdist opposition to the general strike disturbed Sorel.[36]

And yet, while Marxian orthodoxy served him, a recent convert, as his natural base, he showed himself to be a highly individualistic Marxian both in the direction of his interests and in the positions on Marxian theory to which these interests carried him. In his

33 G. Sorel, "Science et socialisme," *Revue philosophique*, xxxv (May 1893), 509–11.
34 Georges Weill, *Histoire du mouvement social en France, 1852–1914* (Paris, 1924), pp. 288–93.
35 G. Sorel, "La Fin du paganisme," *Ère nouvelle*, II (1894), 338–64; III (1894), 33–72, 170–99. For this particular point, *ibid.*, III, 174–75. This article was published, with only slight revision, as *La Ruine du monde antique* (1st ed., Paris, 1902).
36 Weill, *op. cit.*, pp. 366–67.

earliest major Marxian work, "L'Ancienne et la nouvelle méta-physique" (1894), Sorel brought the experience of an engineer to bear upon the problem of knowledge; and set forth both a position on the genesis of knowledge and a method of critical analysis. In his "Fin du paganisme" (1894) and his "Étude sur Vico" (1896) he proceeded to apply this Marxian critical method, as he called it, to the analysis of fourth-century Christian thought, in the former work, and to the philosophy of Vico, in the latter. Becoming aware, in the course of these studies, of the difficulties involved in the application of Marxian theory, and encouraged by the efforts now being made by the Italian Marxists, Antonio Labriola and Benedetto Croce, to redefine it, Sorel then devoted himself to the first of a large number of articles having to do with the proper definition of what he pre-ferred to call "historical materialism." Soon after the publication of these articles he broke with his "orthodox" Marxist collaborators, Deville and Lafargue.

Sorel introduced his "L'Ancienne et la nouvelle métaphysique" by proclaiming "the theory of Marx to be the greatest innovation introduced into philosophy for several centuries." [37] Rather than discussing that theory directly, he used this reference to it as the point of departure for a statement of his position on the genesis of scientific knowledge and on the critical method therefore appro-priate to an evaluation of any ideology or formal philosophy. Scien-tific knowledge, Sorel argued in substance, derives from industrial practice, from the "artificial milieu" which man is constantly in process of creating, and its expansion depends ultimately on the development of technology. The critic interested in appraising the scientific value of an ideology like eighteenth-century rationalism or of a formal philosophy like that of Plato must, therefore, start from a knowledge of the industrial milieu contemporary with his subject. With the aid of that knowledge he can discover the material realities upon which the philosopher's constructions of abstract con-cepts have been based, and he can, moreover, assess the validity of those concepts through his study of the care taken in their construc-tion. At the same time, Sorel continued, the critic can, by means of this approach, discover the role in that philosophy of sentimental illusions—illusions such as sometimes dominate a whole people. In what does not belong to science he may thus discover important in-dications of the emotional life of an epoch.[38]

[37] G. Sorel, D'Aristote à Marx (Paris, 1935), p. 94. This book is a reprinting of the original article, "L'Ancienne et la nouvelle métaphysique," Ere nouvelle, I (1894), 329–51, 461–82; II (1894), 51–87, 180–205.
[38] ibid., passim, especially pp. 149–51, 262–63.

The critical method here described was to serve Sorel on many subsequent intellectual forays on the battleground of ideologies: notably in his revolutionary syndicalist—and deliberately destructive—analysis of the history of rationalism to be found in his *Illusions du progrès*.[39] He would employ it, indeed, in the late 1890's, in his revisionist analysis of Marxism itself. Prior to that revision he used it, with only partial success, in his anticlerical "Fin du paganisme" (1894). The Christian theologians, Sorel argued in this work, failed to solve the problems of the late Roman Empire because their legal and economic concepts were unscientific; neglecting to think in terms of the economic milieu—a milieu which, moreover, lacked a true industrial base—the Christian doctors constructed systems of sentimental illusions which in fact merely rationalized their own material interests. Up to this point Sorel was consciously Marxian. The larger argument of this work, however, is not Marxian at all; indeed, it offers a striking analogy to that of his pre-Marxian *Procès de Socrate*. The Christian rationalists, the theologians, attacked the older traditions of service to society which had made Rome great, the traditions which the soldiers of the Roman legions had held dear; in destroying the moral fabric of society, they contributed, Sorel concluded, to the breakdown of the empire.[40]

It was this method which Sorel employed, again, in his critical analysis of Vico, whose philosophy he found to have been soundly based in its proto-Marxian recognition of the role of the technical skills in the development of knowledge—as well as in its "ideogenetic law" to the effect that general ideas are constructed in accordance with the models furnished by political practice. What marks this "Étude sur Vico" particularly, however, is the deliberate effort Sorel made in it to supplement Marxian notions with psychological considerations: in particular, with the Vichian concept of the psychological evolution of a social group from a primitive and emotional level to one which is sophisticated and scientific. His evident preference here for the primitive emotional level is a reminder of the preferences expressed in his early *Procès de Socrate;* his later *Réflexions sur la violence* is foreshadowed, as well, in his concern with what he called "the emotional tones of active groups," which are important, Sorel argued, because effective action to modify the social structure is irrational in stimulus.[41]

39 This work was originally published in *Mouvement socialiste,* Vols. XIX–XX, in 1906, shortly after the original publication of "Réflexions sur la violence" in that magazine.

40 "La Fin du paganisme," *loc. cit., passim,* but especially II, 360; III, 174, 178–79, 187–88; III, 37, 47–49.

41 G. Sorel, "Étude sur Vico," *Devenir social,* II (October–December 1896), 785–818, 906–42, 1013–47. See, especially, *ibid.,* pp. 809–13, 906–7, 910–11. See also Sorel's "Was man von Vico lernt," *Sozialistische Monatshefte,* II (June 1898), 270–72.

Contemporary with this "Étude sur Vico" were Sorel's first articles on historical materialism. Here again he argued the importance of completing Marxian theory, which he found in its present state to be metaphysically and psychologically inadequate. He went further than he had previously, however, in defining his own position on the meaning of Marx's thought. Stimulated by the works of Antonio Labriola and Benedetto Croce, he denied that Marx was an economic determinist or believed in a fatal and predetermined evolution toward an apocalypse. Since he was no determinist, Sorel continued, Marx regarded the creation of class-consciousness as the crux of the social question. He then concluded his remarks with a defense of historical materialism for its absence of the ideal, on the grounds that a reasonable ethical theory required a broad scientific base—Sorel had not yet discovered, as he was later to discover, that it contained a social myth, like the ideal a stimulus of high morality. Conceptually in large part valid, Sorel's position on historical materialism was not that of Marx; hence, unwilling to proclaim his own heresy, he seriously weakened his argument in the effort to endow his position with the sanction of Marx's authority.[42]

V

In the light of Sorel's extremely individualistic writings as a Marxist, it is not surprising to find him complaining in a letter to Croce in 1897 that "Lafargue has almost excommunicated me for expressing doubts on the division of classes" [43]; and to find him breaking with the *Devenir social* a few months later because Lafargue and Deville, still orthodox in their Marxian doctrine, had failed to take advantage of the possibilities for discussion inherent in the new positions taken by Bernstein.[44] Sorel's position on Socialism during the next five years is difficult to define, not because he failed to take part, as he had earlier, in the frequent controversies among Socialists as to the meaning of Marxism and as to participation in national politics; but rather because the positions he set forth, with characteristic fervor, contradicted one another. Broadly speaking, he was a "revisionist." He opposed those like the Guesdists in France and Kautsky in Germany who remained intransigent in doctrine while becom-

[42] G. Sorel (under pseudonym "B"), "Progrès et développement," *Devenir social,* II (March 1896), 193–208; G. Sorel, Preface, Antonio Labriola's *Essais sur la conception matérialiste de l'histoire* (Paris, 1897). Compare Benedetto Croce's "Concerning the Scientific Form of Historical Materialism," written in May 1896, which may be found in Croce's *Historical Materialism and the Economics of Karl Marx* (New York, 1914).

[43] Benedetto Croce (ed.), "Lettere di Georges Sorel a Benedetto Croce," *Critica,* xxv (1927), 50–52 (letter of December 27, 1897).

[44] G. Sorel, *Saggi di critica del Marxismo* (Milan, 1903), pp. 5–7.

ing conciliatory in the area of political practice. He was sympathetic
to those, like Saverio Merlino in Italy, Vandervelde in Belgium, and
Bernstein and Werner Sombart in Germany, who, like himself, felt
it necessary to revise the foundations of Socialist theories and to
bring them into accord with contemporary social realities.[45] Only as
he gradually formulated his own revision of Marx as "revolutionary
syndicalism" was he to become as unsympathetic to other revision-
ists as he was now hostile to the doctrinaires.

During this period, Sorel's studies—and the writings based upon
them—provided the center to which his outward life referred:
studies, on the one hand, of such contemporary social movements
as German Social Democracy and English trade-unionism; on the
other hand, in increasing detail, of the writings of Marx, which till
this time he had known in the main only at second hand. He learned
about social movements vicariously, through Socialist books and
journals, rather than through direct participation, just as he kept up
with political activity—and very faithfully—only through reports in
the press. He lived almost isolated from society, in a small room in
Boulogne, a Paris suburb. From this den he emerged occasionally
to find books in the Bibliothèque Nationale; or to make his weekly
visit to the office of the journal *Humanité nouvelle;* or, after the
turn of the century, to attend lectures by Bergson, whose friend and
admirer he became; or to participate in the sessions of the Société
de Philosophie; or, on Thursdays, to visit Charles Péguy who, like
Sorel, had responded to the cause of Dreyfus in the hopes of a moral
reawakening rather than as had others, they felt, in behalf of their
own political advantage.

During this period, Sorel corresponded with like-minded thinkers: with Lagardelle, publisher of *Mouvement socialiste;* with
Édouard Bernstein, then coming into prominence, who—for a moment at least—recognized Sorel as a kindred spirit; with Antonio
Labriola, with whom Sorel quarreled over the meaning of historical
materialism; and with Croce, with whom he would continue to correspond regularly until his death some twenty years later. From Croce
in particular he sought help in finding independent magazines,
French, German, and Italian, in which to place his articles; but he did
not at this time replace the *Devenir social* with a regular journalistic
attachment. Though lavish with advice to Lagardelle respecting the
founding of *Mouvement socialiste,* he did not join its body of editors,
according to Lagardelle, because of his exaggerated sensitivity to
the criticisms of his Bernsteinian revisionism voiced by young stu-

45 "Mes raisons du syndicalisme," *Matériaux,* pp. 250–54; G. Sorel, Preface, Saverio
Merlino's *Formes et essence du socialisme* (Paris, 1898), pp. iii–v.

dents who gravitated around the review.[46] Independent as a journalist, he was at the same time quite detached from French trade-union activity, which at this time, under the direction of the yet separate Confédération Générale du Travail (CGT) and Bourses du Travail, was becoming increasingly important and in which Sorel was becoming increasingly interested. As Sorel has indicated, what might be called his first syndicalist or trade-unionist publication, the *Avenir socialiste des syndicats* (1898), was inspired by a book of Paul de Rousiers on English trade-union development.[47]

It is in terms of this physical isolation that Sorel's reactions to the contemporary scene must be understood. He judged from afar, in the light of his own enthusiasms of the moment. He made such judgments of the contemporary scene because of a growing conviction that it was the function of the Socialist theoretician to enlighten the proletariat regarding the road it was already following in practice—indeed, even to use all the resources which propaganda can furnish so as to achieve the formation of class-consciousness.[48]

After having supported both syndicalism and political socialism, he argued in 1897 that "the whole future of Socialism resides in the autonomous development of the workers' syndicates," which he deemed capable of so well preparing the proletariat morally as to prevent the present class-struggle from leading to a destruction of civilization; and he applauded the syndicates' exclusion of such politician-intellectuals as Jaurès from their ranks, since such men wished merely to benefit themselves through strengthening the state.[49] A few months later, however, the cause of Dreyfus captured Sorel's imagination as the cause of Justice and the means of moral revival. He was among the first of a number of intellectuals to petition, in January 1898, for a revision of the trial of Dreyfus.[50] And so, while continuing to distrust the parliamentary Socialists in general, he enthusiastically supported Jaurès in particular, for Jaurès, against Socialist opposition, had similarly rallied wholeheartedly to the Dreyfus cause. Sorel found in his "admirable conduct" the finest proof that there was a Socialist ethics.[51] Indeed, he presently went even further toward what might be called the Socialist Right. Against the *"blanquistes"* under Vaillant and against the Guesdists, he sup-

[46] Lagardelle, *op. cit.*, XI, 324.

[47] "Mes raisons du syndicalisme," *Matériaux*, pp. 250–53.

[48] Preface, Merlino's *Formes et essence*, p. xxvii; *Saggi*, pp. 46–48; "Le Matérialisme historique," *Bulletin de la Société française de Philosophie*, I–III (1902), 109–14.

[49] G. Sorel, *Avenir socialiste des syndicats* (Paris, 1901), pp. 12, 14–24, 60. Written in 1897 and published originally in *Humanité nouvelle* (1898), pp. 294–307, 432–46.

[50] Berth, *Du 'Capital,'* p. 174.

[51] G. Sorel, "L'Éthique du socialisme," *Revue de métaphysique et de morale*, VII (1899), 300–1.

ported Jaurès' defense of Millerand's entry into the ministry of Waldeck-Rousseau (1899); and, a few weeks later, added that "the entry of Millerand into the ministry consecrates the cooperation of Socialism in the democratic work" and announced that "the workers have applauded." [52] Returning the following year to his book on the syndicates, Sorel wrote—in sharp contrast—a preface more ardently syndicalist than the book itself, attacking in it the policy of social peace, the Saint-Simonian ministerial Socialists, the intellectuals preoccupied with the electoral struggle, and the "disgusting" recent Socialist national congress (1900), with its *"ralliés"* to the defense of the Republic and its wealthy women revolutionaries. It was in this preface that Sorel himself first advocated the general strike, deemed by him necessary in order to prove by force that the proletariat was well enough organized to make the block of traditional institutions of the state disappear.[53] The general strike was not yet a myth for Sorel, however; it was essentially the earthbound tactic unsuccessfully defended by Fernand Pelloutier against the Guesdists some eight years before.[54]

Sorel had thus vacillated between political Socialism and syndicalism because he, a moralist become Marxian, hoped to see Socialism become the vehicle for the moral reform of society; the position taken by Jaurès regarding Dreyfus, and the workers' syndicates, had each encouraged his hopes in this regard. By 1902, however, the ambiguity in his position had disappeared. Disgusted by the quarrels among the parliamentary Socialists, he made no exceptions when he declared that the Socialist sects hoped to use the state to render life easier for their friends; he found in their abandonment of the class-struggle utopian Socialism; and he contrasted to them those wise Socialists who did excellent work without exposing themselves to degeneration and casuistry, the organizers of the Bourses du Travail.[55] Sorel was not yet a revolutionary syndicalist; but he would never again support parliamentary Socialism.

While thus haltingly striving to define his position on contemporary Socialism, Sorel was also redefining his position on the meaning of Marx; and in the course of these efforts he discovered within Marx's thought what in essence was the social myth which Sorel, later,

---

[52] Lagardelle, *op. cit.*, XI, 325–28; G. Sorel, "Préface pour Colajanni," *Matériaux*, 177–79. This preface was originally published in N. Colajanni, *Le Socialisme* (Paris, 1900). It was reprinted as Chapter X of Sorel's *Saggi*, as well as in *Matériaux*.

[53] *Avenir socialiste*, p. vi. Sorel dated this preface November 1, 1900.

[54] Francis W. Coker, *Recent Political Thought* (New York, 1934), p. 234.

[55] Lagardelle, *op. cit.*, XI, 331; G. Sorel, "Idées socialistes et faits économiques au XIXe siècle," *Revue socialiste*, XXXV (1902), 519, 528–29, 537–41; G. Sorel, Preface, Fernand Pelloutier's *Histoire des Bourses du Travail* (Paris, 1902), pp. 13–17, 27–32.

would celebrate. In a number of exegetical articles he applied his
Marxian critical method to the analysis of the body of Marx's thought.
That is, he placed Marx within his historical context in order to determine what part of his thought had scientific value, and what part
was composed of illusions inspired by historical recollections and by
hopes for the future, and of unscientific generalizations born of his
recognition of the demands of practical action.

In the course of these studies, what Sorel had originally rejected
as accidental hypotheses which did not properly belong to science
he later welcomed as myths necessary to Socialist action. In the
earlier articles, he described Marx's apocalyptic conception of a final
struggle waged by two antagonistic groups, proletariat and bourgeoisie, as an accidental—unscientific—affirmation, rather than a
fundamental thesis. Largely because of the legend of the Commune
—a legend born of, and renewed by, violence—this conception, understood in material terms, took hold of men's minds, and issued in
the brutal, anti-ethical character of contemporary Socialism. The
conception should be understood not in material terms, Sorel argued at that time, but in terms of the conflict of opposing systems of
values.[56] He elaborated on this latter note in his later articles, in
which he argued that the apocalyptic conception was of great value
when properly understood as "social poetry" useful in inspiring men's
spirits, rather than as an abstract, pseudo-scientific dogma. He maintained now, moreover, that Marx himself had in mind that very conflict of moral conceptions which was necessary if the class-struggle
was to become a reality when, in the *Communist Manifesto,* he used
the social poetry of his apocalyptic conception as an image constructed
with a view to the formation of consciences.[57]

Sorel once pronounced that "principles are things so vaporous that
one changes them in an unconscious manner." [58] Similarly did Sorel,
apparently unconsciously, shift his position on the significance of
the notion of the class-struggle. Originally he rejected it, on intellectual grounds; it was clearly not demonstrable that a final conflict would take place between two opposing classes, whatever his
erstwhile collaborators, Deville and Lafargue, might say. Moreover,
because he supported collaboration with the bourgeois parties in
behalf of Dreyfus, he opposed the employment of this "dogma" in
Socialist tactics, since it was sponsored by the Guesdist opponents
of collaboration; and he claimed to find this dogma, associated with

56 G. Sorel, "Crise du socialisme," *Revue politique et parlementaire,* xviii (1898), 597–
602; Preface, Merlino's *Formes et essence,* pp. xlii, xlv.
57 "Préface pour Colajanni," *Matériaux,* pp. 186–90; *Saggi,* pp. 13–15.
58 "La Fin du paganisme," *loc. cit.,* iii, 191.

violence, responsible for the anti-ethical character of contemporary Socialism. He could not deny its influence, however; and this impressed him, for he was searching for psychological instruments of moral regeneration. Hence gradually he adapted this notion to his own aspirations for Socialism. He rejected the notion of the class-struggle as a dogma, morally baneful as were the rationalistic sophisms of the Socratics, only to affirm it as morally fruitful "social poetry" comparable, as a moral educator, to the Homeric legends. Indeed, he did more; he convinced himself that Marx had deliberately used the "social poetry" of the class-struggle with a view to the moral, rather than material, consequences for which Sorel was hoping. Between 1893 and the end of the century, Sorel thus revised radically his conception of Marxism: what impressed him now was not its value as an economic science, but the observation that Marxism's influence on the popular masses was due above all to the attractiveness of its myths. A few years later, as an intransigent revolutionary syndicalist, Sorel was to take a further step in revising his interpretation of the notion of the class-struggle: he would declare violence, purified by its conjunction with the "myth of the general strike," to be productive of the high morality of heroism.

VI

Some years later, in 1910, following his break with revolutionary syndicalism, Sorel wrote an account of "How I Became a Syndicalist," in which he sought to identify his personal psychological development toward syndicalism with that of the workers.[59] In this account, he explained the adoption of syndicalism as the consequence of experiences undergone during the Dreyfus era: that is, from 1897 to 1905. These experiences demonstrated, first, that coordination of Socialism and democracy in behalf of Dreyfus weakened the revolutionary ideology. It had, indeed, weakened Sorel's. Second, that anticlericalism accelerated the transformation of specifically Socialist ideologies into ideologies closely resembling those employed by democracy. It had, indeed, so affected Sorel's position.[60] And, thirdly, that psychological states favorable to the development of syndicalist ideas were developing in the workers, become aware of the cupidity of their parliamentary chiefs, on the one hand, and of the value of direct action, on the other—a value demonstrated when the men of violence frightened the conservatives into forming the ministry of

[59] "Mes raisons du syndicalisme," *Matériaux*, pp. 239–86.
[60] See Sorel's "Essai sur l'État et l'Église," *Revue socialiste*, XXXIV (October 1901), 409–19, where he hailed the alliance of Socialism and democracy against the Church.

Waldeck-Rousseau. Here again the account was personal history, though it claimed to be social history as well. There was, in fact, a wave of strikes during the Waldeck-Rousseau ministry (1899–1901); but the motive would appear to have been economic, provided by the industrial prosperity of the period, rather than disgust with the Socialist chiefs.[61] Even as a personal account it must, since it is retrospective, be used with care. As late as 1903, Sorel was unsure of the psychological states of the workers, writing Croce that the "working classes are scarcely able to free themselves from the domination exercised by such men as Jaurès"; a year later he declared to Lagardelle that he had renounced writing henceforth on Socialism, which was becoming too disgusting, and that, as a distraction from it, he was returning to his studies of Renan.[62]

It was from this period of full retreat from Socialism into religious history that Sorel's doctrine of revolutionary syndicalism was to emerge in 1905, in *Divenire sociale,* the journal of the Italian syndicalist, Enrico Leone. The elements of that doctrine were already present in Sorel's thought: the opposition, on moral grounds, to contemporary society; the hostility to those who collaborate in its maintenance; the desire to see, indeed to promote, a moral reawakening, this being identified with a virility such as was displayed at Marathon by warriors inspired by Homeric legends; the conception of the essential struggle between the old world and the new world in formation as a struggle between two systems of values; the concept of the general strike; the importance of the legend, the ideal, the Marxian image, as a stimulus to moral action. These elements had yet to be combined. Sorel found his combination as he composed his *Système historique de Renan:* its explanation of the "Christian conquest" was the prototype of the argument on revolutionary syndicalism's revolutionary role to be offered, presently, in the *Réflexions sur la violence.* He made that translation, I would like to suggest, at a time when revolutionary syndicalism was most impressive in its power. In the years 1901–1905, the parliamentary Socialists, if corrupt, as he stressed, were divided into two separate parties, as he did not. The syndicalists, on the other hand, in 1902 had achieved the fusion of the Fédération des Bourses and the CGT; and in that unified national labor organization, the revolutionary syndicalists had, in September 1904, won a complete victory over the reformist syndicalist fraction.[63] Where Sorel said much of their

[61] Weill, *op. cit.,* pp. 337–38.
[62] Croce (ed.), *op. cit.,* XXVI (1928), 31–32 (letter of May 9, 1903); Lagardelle, *op. cit.,* XI, 513–15.
[63] Weill, *op. cit.,* pp. 356–67.

violence, he may have been impressed by the simple fact, neglected by him, of their present power.

In the *Système historique de Renan,* Sorel described Christianity in Vichian terms as a new beginning occurring among persons who, prepared by the apocalyptic legends prevalent in their Judean milieu, had entered a primitive, quasi-heroic, poetically creative psychological state. Later, under the impact of the persecutions and of the apocalyptic legends with which such acts of violence were associated in men's minds, that original psychological state was recreated; through such "rebeginnings," during which Christians thought in terms of an absolute scission between pagan society and their own, Christianity was able to achieve its self-realization.[64]

In the *Réflexions sur la violence,* the contemporary era replaces the era of the persecutions; the syndicalist acts of violence, the heroic acts of the Christian martyrs, with their readiness to die for the cause; the myth of the general strike, the apocalyptic myth of the Christians. From the conjunction of violence and the myth, Sorel argued, is to derive that scission of Socialism from contemporary pagan (bourgeois) society which is to permit Socialism to achieve, as Christianity once achieved, its self-realization.[65] Thus did Sorel find in "the myth of the general strike" a means of achieving a Socialist rebeginning, that myth being essentially a reformulation of the apocalyptic vision which, in the "apostolic times" of Marxian Socialism, had had so much to do with Marxism's influence over the masses. Even should syndicalism fail to achieve a Socialist society, Sorel continued, it is of great value in the moral reform of present society, since violence, purified by the myth, is an awakener of heroism.[66] In his description of the myth's function in this work, Sorel does not appear to have sought directly to inspire consciences. He writes dispassionately, in the language of a tactician, much as an officer of a general staff might write for the instruction of his field commanders. In its opposition of syndicalism to parliamentary Socialism, on the other hand, the *Réflexions* is a work of passion; it is, as it were, the expression of Sorel's private apocalyptic vision of himself in mortal rivalry with the socialist politicians, disciples of the anti-Christ, for the soul of the proletariat.

It was just as well that Sorel did not seek to inspire the masses directly. It is unlikely that more than a very few of the workers read his writings, or that those few who read them understood, or

---

[64] G. Sorel, *Le Système historique de Renan* (Paris, 1905–6), pp. 74–80, 188–90, 198–208, 312–21, 339–70.
[65] G. Sorel, *Réflexions sur la violence* (3rd ed., Paris, 1912), *passim,* especially pp. 177–79, 273–79.
[66] *ibid.,* pp. 202, 17–24.

that those who understood responded to the suggestion that, irrespective of its practical consequences, violence was worth cultivating because of the moral beauty of heroism. What he and Édouard Berth—who at this time had become Sorel's disciple—hoped to do, rather, was to inspire the leaders of the CGT, men who were writers in their own right but also, as Sorel was not, active in the practical direction of *syndicats*. Taking for granted "the immense indifference of the Socialist masses," Sorel hoped to form what he called "workers' monitors," using the offices of Lagardelle's journal, *Mouvement socialiste,* as a kind of seminary where he and Berth could strengthen in syndicalist militants the proud consciousness of a powerful ideology. At least one such "workers' monitor" was found: Victor Griffuelhes, from 1902–1909 secretary of the CGT; he was one of a group—which incidentally included also Sorel and Berth, Georges Weill and Roberto Michels, Eduard Beneš, the Italian syndicalist Arturo Labriola, and a certain Racowski who was to be a Soviet ambassador to France—which circa 1905 was meeting at Lagardelle's home for Sunday afternoon tea.[67]

Such was the tenuous character of Sorel's relationship to the syndicalist movement itself. A bond so slight would be easily severed. In 1908, the year in which the publication of the *Réflexions* in book form identified him in a lasting fashion with the syndicalist movement, Sorel severed his connection with the syndicalist *Mouvement socialiste*. As early as 1906 he had regarded as treachery the willingness of the syndicalist chiefs to write for Jaurès' *Humanité,* even though Jaurès was waging with them a common campaign against the government of Clemenceau. Again he saw them playing the game of Jaurès when they joined Jaurès in protesting the arrests of syndicalist leaders which had followed the violent demonstrations of Villeneuve St. Georges. He complained that Griffuelhes had transformed the CGT from a committee of syndicalist propaganda into a central revolutionary committee, whereas, he added, salvation lay in the sentiment of the masses rather than in the knowing maneuvers of the chiefs. He saw the *Mouvement socialiste* itself involved in the revival of reformism within the CGT. He predicted that Briand, about to come to power, would transform the CGT into a remarkably effective political machine and exercise his despotism by means of syndicalism.[68] The syndicalist chiefs themselves, in short, were following false prophets. And there is yet another factor in Sorel's turning away from the syndicalist movement: what is, in fact, the other

[67] Berth, *Du 'Capital,'* pp. 175–76; Lagardelle, *op. cit.,* XI, 778, 781–82; Michels, *op. cit.,* II, 288, n. 1.
[68] Lagardelle, *op. cit.,* XI, 774, 965–66, 969, 968.

side of the coin. Justifying to Croce his contribution of an article to a French royalist review, he ingenuously remarked: "These young men are very intelligent. As they cite my books continually, I could not refuse them a collaboration of this kind." [69]

VII

Sorel's connection with the syndicalist movement was essentially as fortuitous as it was short-lived. The movement had become strong without the doubtful benefit of Sorel's doctrines; its tactics and principles—"direct action," the general strike, the social role of the *syndicat*—had been formulated earlier and by other men; some of these tactics went back fifty years to the first International, indeed, seventy-five years to English Chartism.[70] Sorel never claimed to have been a creator of the syndicalist movement; his *Réflexions sur la violence* is, indeed, misleading in the opposite direction, in exaggerating its own lack of originality, in presenting itself as a work of observation dependent upon contemporary developments which it merely clarifies, in claiming to be a "philosophy of practice" serving as the self-awareness of an active movement regarding its role in the historical process.[71] The active movement, on the one hand, and the self-awareness which was Sorelian doctrine, on the other, did have certain common roots: direct experience with industrial practice (though, for Sorel, some fifteen years before), recollections of Proudhon, loyalty to the revolutionary interpretation of Marxian socialism, comparative poverty, attachment to a revolutionary tradition which the fortunes of French politics had kept peculiarly virile. They had common foes, too, in the bogey of centralization, the bourgeois entrepreneur, the ever-suspect politician. But that is all.

Sorel's position in life was not that of a trade-unionist; no more were his aspirations theirs, in spite of his claims. An inheritance from his mother gave Sorel enough to live on; his efforts to serve the social process through theory and through this service thereby to become a participant in it gave his life meaning. He could afford to be disinterested with regard to the economic benefits of strikes and to contemplate with equanimity materially unrewarding violence: at least, so long as the French state did not hold him responsible and take from him the Legion of Honor ribbon which he always wore in his lapel. He could, again unlike the trade-unionists, afford to appreciate the moral effects of violence and on moral

69 Croce (ed.), *op. cit.*, XXVI (1928), 108 (letter of September 18, 1908).
70 On this question, see also L. L. Lorwin's *Syndicalism in France* (New York, 1914), pp. 154–60.
71 *Réflexions*, pp. 51, 59–67, 179–82.

grounds condemn the movement's practically effective tactic of sabotage. His antimaterialistic philosophy of action was, consequently, at best very distant spiritual kin to the active movement of revolutionary syndicalism. As his own behavior would indicate, Sorel could not be in one respect the "disinterested philosopher" which he claimed to be: he could not be indifferent to the reception accorded by the active movement to the guidance which he offered it; ill-received, he turned away, to seek other vehicles for the realization of the Idea.

Sorel's connection with the syndicalist movement was fortuitous not only because it had developed without him and not only because of fundamental differences in spirit, but also because his philosophy needed that particular movement as little as it had needed his philosophy. His philosophy had developed, in largest measure, apart from his observation of the syndicalist movement; certain of its features were foreshadowed in his earliest writings, the writings of a provincial conservative unacquainted with Marxian thought. It maintained its basic outlines following Sorel's abandonment of the syndicalist movement.

Sorel abstracted from the *Réflexions sur la violence* the argument that action which is at once morally and historically effective is initiated by small groups of hero-mystics who are dominated by convictions so absolute as to cause them to forget the material considerations which men generally take into account.[72] He temporarily found the medium for such action in the anti-Republican, bourgeois, patriotic current within the French Right. Troubled over France's military and moral unpreparedness for the international conflict which he believed (ca. 1908–1913) to be at hand, he was ready to find in patriotism a "lever of energies." Still hostile to parliamentary democracy, he was ready to find in the monarchism of Charles Maurras a principle which might achieve its realization through the method of "authoritarian violence": through direct action which would galvanize the people and thereby stimulate them to the efforts necessary to overthrow the Republic.[73]

In now focusing his attention upon the means of achieving a bourgeois awakening, Sorel was not unfaithful to his earlier position; in the *Réflexions* he had expressed the hope that, as a consequence of the violent acts of their proletarian antagonists, the bourgeoisie also might again live heroically.[74] Moreover, during this nationalist phase, Sorel did not completely abandon his hopes for revolutionary syndical-

[72] As in the article, "Unité et multiplicité," written ca. 1910, and published as an appendix to the third and subsequent editions of the *Réflexions*. See, particularly, *Réflexions*, pp. 391–407.
[73] Variot, *op. cit.*, pp. 114–16.
[74] *Réflexions*, pp. 117–20.

ism in the form which he had given it. Now labeling his doctrine "Marxism in the pure state," he offered it as an alternative to monarchism, as a principle possessing the power to realize itself in practice and through which France could emerge from disorder. Sorel saw, indeed, the possibility of a struggle between these two principles, the amount of violence associated with each to determine the outcome; he predicted that Marxism was more likely to succeed, should an external war be followed (as was likely) by a civil war. In case of the probable cataclysm, Marxism—not Socialism, a sham, but Marxism in the pure state—might descend from the mountain cabin of a theoretician where alone it now existed and reassemble under the leadership of a man—for it is always necessary that there be a man whom the masses, now deceived by Jaurès, Viviani, and their like, are willing to follow.[75] Sorel, who had earlier glorified the role of anonymous heroes who work in the shadow, was indeed in one important respect modifying his doctrine. Himself no longer anonymous, but his teachings ignored, he asserted for the first time the necessity of the leadership of a man in the realization of the Idea. At this time, in 1912, he caught a glimpse of such a leader in the revolutionary Socialist editor of the Italian party journal, *Avanti:* "Our Mussolini is no ordinary socialist. Believe me: you will perhaps see him one day at the head of a sacred battalion, saluting with his épée the Italian banner. He is an Italian of the fifteenth century, a condottiere. People do not yet know it, but he is the only energetic man capable of redressing the weaknesses of government." [76]

VIII

During these prewar years Sorel was sympathetic to Paul Bourget's effort, in *Barricade,* to translate Sorelian ideas into a form useful to the instruction of the bourgeoisie. "I would be happy," he told a friend, "if this great talent could persuade the bourgeoisie to abandon, in the face of the courageous ardor of the adversary, its guilty and little glorious resignation." [77] The journal, Jean Variot's *Indépendance,* to which he contributed some dozen articles in the years 1911 and 1912, was nationalist and traditionalist. Sorel was, in this respect, completing a circle. Provoked by French unpreparedness for war, he was again asserting the antipacifist traditionalism of his very early *Procès de Socrate.* He was hardly proto-Fascist or monarchist, however. The Mussolini who interested him was still a leader in the Italian Socialist party. His own relations with the French Right were

---

[75] Variot, *op. cit.,* pp. 121–26.
[76] Pirou, *op. cit.,* pp. 52–53.
[77] *ibid.,* p. 40. Pirou's source is *Gaulois,* January 11, 1910.

largely abortive. His effort to collaborate with two members of Action Française in the founding of a new journal failed, according to Sorel's account, because they were too anxious to be in charge. "I would have been powerless," he wrote Croce, "even while having the real moral responsibility." [78] *Sic semper Sorel*. Although associated with a group known as "Cercle Proudhon," he did not join the others, including Georges Valois and Édouard Berth, in their demand for the reestablishment of hereditary monarchy.[79] He was proto-Fascist or monarchist only in this one respect. He adhered to the essence—only contingently syndicalist—of the theory set forth in his *Réflexions sur la violence*. The essence retained is the justification, on grounds both moral and pragmatic, of fanaticism, of the violent, but self-regardless, effort to realize an ideal, or a social myth, or principles. Faithful to this doctrine, Sorel responded to such movements on the Right or on the Left as appeared to embody it.

However qualified his response to the French Right was in fact, the consequent charge that he had betrayed the proletariat disturbed Sorel and provoked his break with *Indépendance*. At Easter-time, 1913, he called Variot to his book-crammed garret in Boulogne and announced his intention, explaining that he found very disagreeable the reactionary and nationalist label which *Indépendance* had acquired. Variot then reminded him that five years earlier Sorel had warned that they would be accused of being nationalist and royalist; and that they had tried, as Sorel had desired, to study the facts and as clearly as possible to write warnings. "You warn no one with your *Indépendance*," Sorel replied bitterly. "One does not warn people with magazines which have five hundred subscribers. Can I claim to warn people with books a thousand readers buy? . . . One is believed when one has been dead fifty years."

And then, as was his wont, Sorel translated this personal discouragment into philosophical terms. "Progress is only an illusion, a different form of life. . . . The failure of the centuries' enlightened minds proves that perfection is not possible, for they would have succeeded." After suggesting that *Indépendance* be abandoned completely, Sorel added: "I have one or two books to write. . . . But I have no illusions on what can carry my books to the proletariat. I will have served it without nourishing the hope that it will know my name." [80] Troubled by illness and advancing in years, Sorel wrote no further books. He did, however, collect for publication a number of earlier articles, most of them dating from the "revisionist" years. In the dedication

[78] Croce (ed.), *op. cit.*, XXVI (1928), 343 (letter of January 25, 1911).
[79] Pierre Lasserre, *Georges Sorel* (Paris, 1928), pp. 49–50; Pirou, *op. cit.*, pp. 42–45.
[80] Variot, *op. cit.*, pp. 41–44.

for this work, *Matériaux pour une théorie de prolétariat,* he referred
to himself, with suggestive inaccuracy, as "an old man who is stub-
born in remaining, as Proudhon did, a disinterested servant of the
proletariat."

The great war which soon followed plunged Sorel, rededicated to
the proletariat, into dark and bitter pessimism. He had once said that
one may judge war from two points of view: as a stimulus to disinterested heroism; as the instrument of self-interested politicians.[81] He
judged this war from the latter. He attacked with particular bitterness the position taken by the Socialists. "They have been even more
bourgeois, more ignoble, than I thought. And they have adopted a
humanitarian argot to camouflage their conduct. . . . They knew
very well that it was by no means a question of unhappy humanity,
but rather of what war is, that is to say, an excellent business for . . .
a hidden minority which grows fat on national stupidities." [82]

By the time of this attack upon the parliamentary Socialists, Sorel
had acquired an additional grievance. They were campaigning against
the Bolsheviks, his latest, and last, enthusiasm.[83] Sorel, now in his
seventies, saluted the Bolshevik revolution as "the dawn of a new
era." Intransigent idealist, he found its leader, Lenin, to resemble himself not only in wishing to reconstruct in the pure state the Marxism
which had been decomposed by parliamentary Socialism, but also in
his acceptance of the principle that every doctrine, to attain its goals,
must have violence as method—violence being understood as a state
of mind: the implacable will to achieve one's ends without compromise. Lenin, as if in recognition of the dictum voiced by Sorel as early
as 1892—man cannot do without the ideal—had known how to create
that sentiment of mysticism which gives men the strength to suffer
in order to achieve a goal. From this suffering—from "the blood of the
martyrs"—a new era comparable to that of the Athens of Marathon,
of the expansionist Roman Republic, of nascent Christianity, was to
arise, thus to realize at last the hopes of "the theoretician of syndicalism." [84] This time Sorel would not be disappointed. He died too soon.[85]

[81] *Réflexions,* pp. 246–48. Sorel drew this distinction from Proudhon's *La Guerre et
la paix.*

[82] Variot, *op. cit.,* p. 48. Conversation with Sorel during January 1921. On Sorel during
the war years, see also Pirou, *op. cit.,* pp. 47–52; Berth, *Du 'Capital,'* pp. 177–78; Édouard
Dolléans, *Proudhon* (Paris, 1948), pp. 503–5.

[83] See also James H. Meisel, "Georges Sorel's Last Myth," *Journal of Politics,* XII
(February 1950), 52–65.

[84] *Matériaux,* pp. 52–53; Variot, *op. cit.,* pp. 53–55, 78, 81–86. See also two articles by
Sorel: "Pour Lénine," *Réflexions* (4th and subsequent editions), pp. 437–54; and "La
Marche au socialisme," *Illusions du progrès* (3rd and subsequent editions), pp. 337–86.

[85] This paper was based, in large part, upon my doctoral dissertation, a study of
Georges Sorel's conception of history: "Historical Materialism and the Social Myth"
(typewritten, Cornell, 1948).

VI

SOCIAL AND ECONOMIC PROBLEMS

IN PRESENT-DAY FRANCE

17

++

STRAINS IN THE

SOCIAL STRUCTURE OF MODERN FRANCE

JOHN E. SAWYER

++

THE subject of social structure has been one of those protean problems in the study of human affairs that the historian has tended to pass by. He has traditionally paid his respects to the importance of "imponderables" but has shown a well-weathered caution about allowing himself to become involved in an area where the margins of error and uncertainty are sometimes so large. Partly as a result of this caution, research on social structure has remained fragmentary and the current goal is little more than successful approximation. The most important question is still how best to approach the problem.

Given the problem of vulnerabilities or strains in the structure of modern France, the historian is confronted by serious difficulties. The skills of his craft, while essential for examining and evaluating the evidence, offer little guidance as to how to open up the question, what ranges of data to examine, what to look for. To avoid losing himself in its imponderables with only intuitive guides, he must use some conscious frame of analysis. All such tools and schemata admittedly pose difficulties. None will exhaust or encompass the evidence in all its complexity. No one approach has a priori value. As Whitehead has put it, all analysis (or even description) involves a compromise between adequacy and clarity. The hazards of using such tools, however, must be weighed against the difficulties and hazards of *not* using them: the alternative danger of simply floundering around in the evidence. Whatever approach is used, the test is the same—its usefulness in getting at the problem, in promoting a successful compromise between adequacy and clarity.

I

This paper is frankly exploratory. It will not offer important "new research," or any full-dress formulation in the field of social theory. It will, however, advance certain hypotheses as to sources of strains in the social structure of modern France, notably those arising from the impact of bourgeois capitalism and industrialism on the existing social order; and it will approach the problem with the help of concepts and analytical tools developed by some of the newer social sciences, particularly by Max Weber and those who have carried on his work in the United States.[1] As a first step this essay will have to be concerned more with static analysis than with examining the dynamics or direction of social interaction and historical change.

The basic frame of analysis is the so-called "structural-functional" approach as developed in contemporary sociology.[2] It involves none of those overriding determinisms or teleologies that have sometimes beclouded the issues; it assumes no single causes, no Spenglerian cycles, no fixed rhythms to which the historical record must be cut.

Its starting assumption is simply that any social system has certain functional requirements for its continued operation. As a first requirement it must provide for the minimum biological and psychological needs of a sufficient proportion of its members. On the social level, it must meet at least two basically related sets of problems: those of integration and those of motivation. The diverse activities and interests of its members must be so coordinated that they do not interfere with each other to the point of breakdown, and, positively, that they mutually contribute in sufficient degree to the functioning of the whole. Similarly, a social system can operate only if enough of its members are adequately motivated to perform the roles necessary to the functioning of that system, to seek its goals and follow its standards of behavior.

The specific ways in which these functional prerequisites will be met vary from society to society; but in order that any given society may endure, these ways of doing the necessary things, these relationships, attitudes, and values, must get established in fairly stable "patterns." These patterns of acting and reacting, working and living, seeking and believing, form the structural elements in a social order.

[1] I would particularly like to express my debt here to Talcott Parsons, Francis X. Sutton, and Marion J. Levy, Jr., though they are not to be held responsible for my use or abuse of tools and concepts.

[2] More complete and sophisticated formulations than will be attempted here can be found in papers that have recently been collected in Talcott Parsons, *Essays in Social Theory, Pure and Applied* (Glencoe, Ill., 1949), and Robert K. Merton, *Social Theory and Social Structure* (Glencoe, Ill., 1949).

Where they have become so widely accepted as "legitimate" that conformity with them is generally expected and is supported by moral sanctions, they may be defined as the "institutions" of that society.

In any going society these institutions are highly interdependent. The patterning of the kinship system or of social rankings, for example, is necessarily interlocked with the economic and political patterns that prevail in that society. Common responses to shared symbols is normally one of the factors in this integration. Any important change in one set of institutions will be accompanied by changes in others, and during the transition will cause disturbing dislocations.

The term "strains" in the social structure is here used to refer to tensions, conflicts, and instabilities that arise from the institutional malintegration of a society.

Any society is subject to many different kinds of strains, and they play a fundamental part in the process of social change. While no attempt at systematic completeness is yet possible, no source of strains is more important for France than that rooted in the conflicts between historically overlapping institutional orders which contain functional and structural incompatibilities. The coexistence of such conflicting patterns can seriously disrupt both integration and motivation.[3] Strains of this type have been far more important in European history than in American, and it is on this source of strains that we will concentrate. While the significance of certain other strains, such as those within a given institutional order, cannot be ignored, it should perhaps be noted in passing that of itself the uneven distribution of rewards and power within a social system need not necessarily give rise to such strains. In stable and highly integrated societies, these inequalities may be so fully institutionalized as to be accepted as legitimate, as, for example, in the case of old-world groups proud of "knowing their place" with respect to their "betters."

Strains exist, of course, not only between different individuals and groups in the society, but within the same people. The same individual may be called upon to play conflicting roles or be placed in situations that are subject to conflicting definitions. A single Frenchman, for example, might well be exposed to the conflicting obligations and expectations of being at once a traditionalistic father and a Catholic, deferential to his social superiors, a defender of the Republic and the liberties of 1789, and an industrial worker affiliated with a Communist union.

[3] A striking example of this kind of strain is evident in the present clash between traditional Chinese family patterns rooted in a long-established social order and the functional requisites of a spreading industrialism. Recently analyzed in an excellent study by Marion J. Levy, Jr., *The Family Revolution in Modern China* (Cambridge, Mass., 1949).

Given a sufficient degree of institutional malintegration, individuals and groups cease to be motivated to the successful performance of the necessary roles (a state of things to which Durkheim's term *"anomie"* has come to be applied) and the social machinery begins to break down. The margins of tolerance, however, are fortunately large. Were they not, man would never have been able to stumble along as far as he has in maintaining the kind of societies with which we are here concerned. For no social organization as large and complex as a national state has ever been fully integrated. It must continuously adjust to strains and conflicts of interests of more or less serious proportion. This is particularly true of any society that has been changing as rapidly and fundamentally as has the modern Western world over the past few centuries.

II

It is with these general concepts about the nature of social systems and certain strains that arise within them that we will approach the structure of modern France, focusing particularly upon the institutional conflicts that have followed from economic and technological change and from the process of rationalization.

At the outset it should be recognized that these developments have had their impact on all modern Western countries; that much of what will be said applies generally to Europe; and that the strains caused by some of these changes in France have unquestionably been less than in certain other countries such as Germany. Furthermore France has undoubtedly had a greater range of outlets for internal pressures —in her politics, professions, journalism, and the like—than have many other Continental countries. These comparative references are important. Just as studies focusing on solidarity tend to discover a social lump so glued together as to appear almost eternal, so studies focused on strains tend to picture a society on the verge of explosion or at best held together only by the most fragile, fleeting kind of interconnections. Fortunately such instability is rarely the case, and certainly it was not characteristic of France in the relatively comfortable century stretching up to 1913. How much strain one sees in the period since then again depends considerably on the point of comparative reference—whether, for example, one approaches France from England or from Central Europe. Though this is not a subject that lends itself to precise measurement, these relative intensities should be borne in mind.

With certain allowances it is the thesis of this paper that the social structure of twentieth-century France is not a single, integrated social order but a combination of elements of at least three distinct and conflicting institutional orders deriving from three distinct social and economic foundations. France carried forward into the nineteenth and twentieth century two sets of institutions, two sets of attitudes whose contradictions had never been satisfactorily resolved: to be called, for convenience, the "traditional" and the "bourgeois" (used throughout in the sense of commercial and petty-bourgeois). To these has been added a third major institutional order—the "industrial"—which has major conflicts with both the previous orders and which has not been fully accepted by the various groups necessary to its successful functioning. Each of these orders—traditional, bourgeois, and industrial—has implications reaching into the basic institutions and accompanying attitudes of the society. In addition to tensions and contradictions *within* each of the three, the fact of their parallel survival—the fact that no succeeding social order has been able to demolish or absorb the conflicting aspects of the preceding orders—has produced functional and structural strains which have been of basic importance in modern French history.

We should also note here certain historical and geographical circumstances that have tended to magnify the stresses resulting from these institutional conflicts. Of prime importance are two points in which French history has contrasted sharply with that of England and the United States, if not with that of the Continent. A fact of historical timing is of great significance: that France had not yet arrived at a political and religious "settlement" before being confronted with the social problems of the modern world; that France, in a word, had not worked out the rules of the game for using and transferring political power, before the stakes of the game and therefore its tensions became vastly greater.

Closely related is the degree to which the ideological systems of modern France have tended to widen rather than bridge the differences between these social orders. As a result contemporary France has had a relative paucity of formal symbols to which all Frenchmen respond in unison. While the relative prominence of revolution and violence in modern French history has contributed to this situation, it is probably even more fundamentally a reflection of the very success of France's adjustment to *both* of the two great social orders that preceded the industrial: her position of social and cultural leadership in both the era of traditional *seigneurie,* altar, and throne, and the era of bourgeois, peasant-proprietor, and deputy. These past glories have intensified the hold of history upon France. While this constitutes no small part of her charm, it has bound individuals to traditions which are in good part divisive rather than unifying to the society as a whole. Many of the most important public symbols—Church, State, Army, Empire; Revolution, Liberty, Constitution, Paris—have very different emotional significance for different blocs of Frenchmen. Marianne, for example, has been variously depicted as a sacred image, a good woman, and a whore. Although there is, of course, a wide range of values and attitudes that *are* shared as a nation in "the French way of life," this lack of a unifying central symbol system stands out. It contrasts strikingly, for example, with the adherence commanded and function performed by these same symbols in England.

Finally the accident of geographical and international position has frequently, as today, subjected France to physical and ideological pressures that have tended to magnify whatever tensions exist. Since Bismarck's day the ever-present threat from the eastern frontier, the devastations of successive wars, and the shadow of future war have played a role in modern French history that is hard to exaggerate.[4]

In focusing upon the strains arising from this coexistence of conflicting institutional systems, we are arguing their importance, but not their sole importance. Other strains, notably in this century those within the industrial order, are important and will be discussed. Nor is it claimed that these institutional resistances alone explain the lag in French economic development. That they were extremely significant as retarding forces is clear; but so were other factors which cannot be discussed here.[5]

III

The relevant evidence of strains arising from these conflicting institutional orders is so varied and extensive that gross abstraction and selection will be necessary. Important parts of the institutional order will have to be largely excluded.

Our focus here will be on strains in what might be called France's more overt institutions. First and probably most fundamental among these are the conflicts and malintegrations that arise from the persistence of basically "feudal" elements.[6] These traditionalistic survivals

[4] For a study of this during the Nazi period, cf. Charles A. Micaud, *The French Right and Nazi Germany* (Durham, N.C., 1943).

[5] Notably the present paper necessarily neglects certain "objective" economic factors which would be fundamental to any comprehensive analysis of French economic development—the location of major industrial resources in Europe, size of the market, land and labor supply, etc.

[6] Further exploration is needed, preferably on a comparative basis, of the social and historical factors affecting this persistence of feudal institutions and attitudes, and of the adaptations that have resulted. Franklin L. Ford has contributed an excellent new chapter to this in his unpublished Ph.D. thesis, "The High Noblesse de Robe and the Regrouping of the French Aristocracy: 1715–1748" (Harvard, 1950).

tend to be obscured by the subsequent transformation of outward forms in France. Their wide penetration of contemporary French society is, however, as certain as is the radical nature of their incompatibility with some of the functional and structural requisites of *both* of the subsequent or "modern" institutional orders—the bourgeois and the industrial. The extent of these incompatibilities can be indicated by sketching as ideal types the characteristics of the traditionalistic order in contrast with the main features of both of the more modern orders, in terms of their economic sociology.

On the one hand are the institutions and attitudes of a formally stratified hereditary social order that historically grew up around a seigneurial, agricultural economy; a strongly hierarchical society in which property was tied to family and status, and political and legal authority tended to be personal and particularistic; a society built around "communal" (*Gemeinschaft*) relationships. On the other hand we have the modern social order, based on an impersonal system of production and exchange, in which rewards and statuses are ideally "open" to occupational achievement; a society in which property may be freely amassed or alienated, and legal and political authority is public and universalistic; a society tied together in important areas by relationships of rational interest (*Gesellschaft*). In the former, occupation is primarily determined by birth and is linked with kinship and status; in the latter, in response to the demands for mobility and the extensive division of labor, the occupational role has tended to be formally freed from such ties.[7]

Working out all the implications of this bare frame would disclose points of strain in almost every sphere of institutional life. It would show stresses of two principal sorts: first, those caused by the disruption of old, long-established patterns toward which people feel strong emotional attachments; second, those arising from the cramping of the "natural" growth of the new institution by strong resistances from the old. (In the discussion that follows no value judgments of any kind are intended; we are here concerned only with analyzing the phenomena.)

An example of the former can be seen in the undermining, particularly in this century, of the traditional family pattern which has persisted through the bourgeois period.[8] In this typical pattern the

[7] An elaboration of this analysis is to be found in Weber's writings, most conveniently in *Max Weber: The Theory of Social and Economic Organization*, trans. by A. M. Henderson and Talcott Parsons (New York, 1947).

[8] The material on the changing family pattern has been well explored in an unpublished Ph.D. thesis by Harry M. Johnson, "The Fall of France: An Essay on the Social Structure of France between Two Wars" (Harvard, 1949), Chap. VII. This is an interesting thesis that presents much useful information on this general area.

parent, particularly the father, was a figure of considerable authority. The family was conceived of as an enduring entity, and continuity between generations was highly emphasized. Though important areas of exception must be recognized, the child was normally raised in anticipation of a definite adult status closely derived from the relative status of the parent. His education, training, marriage, occupation, and employment tended to be arranged for accordingly by the parent.

This traditionalistic family pattern, rooted in an earlier institutional order, has been seriously challenged by new patterns which are functionally and structurally incompatible with it. The new institutions, for example, require both social and occupational mobility, and this demands the rearing of children with a "deliberate tentativeness" as to their future. In education and training, as in the greater part of their economic, political, and legal relationships, the new institutions tend to employ impersonal, universalistic criteria rather than particularistic, kinship ties. The ways in which industrialism and urbanism have disorganized and dissolved the traditional patterns are amply revealed in French fiction of this century; and by World War I Durkheim had noted (in his *La Famille conjugale*) the consequent weakening of intergenerational ties.[9]

Assaults of this kind proceeding with violence and speed against a range of traditionally held patterns and values, breaking down solidarities highly charged with emotion, can produce such strains as to cause a "fundamentalist reaction" of the kind that the Nazis exploited in Germany.[10] In France, the pace has been slower and explosive eruption less likely. The crisis as far as "public" institutions is concerned was probably passed at the time of the Dreyfus case.[11] Important areas of conflict have remained, however, and the character and symbolism of the Pétain régime were clearly conditioned by these traditionalistic survivals. In the "private" sphere they have persisted in even more widespread and deep-rooted forms; and with these survivals the further penetration of urbanism and industrialism will continue to conflict.

As an accompaniment to economic and social change, what Weber has called the "process of rationalization" has been steadily undermining traditional ways and symbols and substituting rationalized or

9 This conflict has long been familiar in immigrant communities in the United States. cf., for example, the classic study by W. I. Thomas and F. Znaniecki, *The Polish Peasant in Europe and America* (New York, 1918–1920).

10 The German case has been well analyzed in Talcott Parsons, "Max Weber and the Contemporary Political Crisis," *Review of Politics*, IV (1942), 61–76, 155–72.

11 "Public" and "private" are here used as convenient references whose meaning for the West is sufficiently clear. They are not, however, social constants. Their meaning varies according to what constitutes the primary solidarity group separating "ins" from "outs" in different societies.

pseudo-rationalized patterns. It has made itself felt in all fields, economic, political, religious, social, and intellectual, unevenly but persistently. Variations in the impact of this process have been extreme —from Parisian sophisticate to Breton peasant—but one of the resulting effects has been a corrosive criticism of old values, leaving France, as we have seen, with a slender supply of generally shared symbols about which to rally.

Examples of the second type of strain—where traditionalistic survivals have cramped the "natural" growth of modern institutions— can also be found in these family patterns. It is evident in the widespread practice of running a family business (and an unusually large proportion of all French business is family business) not in terms of maximizing profits or growth, or the institutionalized objectives of rational capitalism, but in terms of preserving the status of a family through successive generations; of trying to make the business into a family annuity. Since this phenomenon is explored elsewhere in this volume,[12] we need here only cite it as an example of strains arising from the conflict between traditionalistic patterns and certain functional requisites of expanding capitalism. In passing, it should be noted perhaps that family orientation is not in and of itself a sufficient explanation for economic lag: while the family theme is of extreme importance, the case of Japan suggests the complexity of the problem.

A deep and related source of this kind of strain lies in the survival of traditionalistic views of social stratification in the country of *Liberté, Égalité, Fraternité*. One of the central aspects of any social system is the way in which it is stratified—its criteria for establishing the relationships of superior-inferior. A system of differential rankings is a requisite of every complex society and is supported with moral sanctions that are inculcated from childhood and involve strong emotional attachments of the kind Pareto terms "sentiments." Individuals seeking recognition and distinction must do so largely in terms of the scale of values and rankings that prevails in that society. Confusion or contradictions in this scale can seriously interfere with individual behavior and motivation. Whereas, for example, Hindu society has largely oriented itself about a caste system based on birth, and American society largely about an occupational achievement scale of stratification, modern France shows deep conflicts on this score.

Assumptions of a social hierarchy based on birth remain very widely diffused in France. Like other traditionalistic attitudes, they persist not just in the Faubourg St. Germain but in circles of lawyers and civil servants, tradesmen and bankers, shop girls and peasants. André

12 cf. particularly the papers by John B. Christopher and David S. Landes.

Siegfried has analyzed their survival in virtually *all* classes of one large corner of France [13]; and Proust in *Swann's Way* unfolds a society in which Aunt Léonie has ordered a community not just according to classes, but with each family carefully placed in its niche in the hierarchy. There were indeed opportunities for individuals to rise— Odette's daughter married a Guermantes—but movement was within a tightly defined ranking system.

These attitudes, wherever they linger, clearly restrict the growth of the new institutions. They operate against social mobility, they discourage efforts to push ahead rapidly. In sociological terms they act against the distribution of rewards and status according to occupational achievement; in economic terms, against the bold and aggressive innovator. The self-made man, as has been noted, is not glorified in France. (Whether all this is to be judged good or bad is quite outside the purpose of this analysis.)

Further than this, these traditionalistic attitudes in France have operated in general against engaging in business activity, to a degree that is significantly different from the English case. The scale of values has reflected the historic attitude of a nobility which glorified land and sword, which became increasingly centered about its honorific rights and privileges as its function declined, and which as late as the eighteenth century forbade its members to engage in trade.[14] If the successful businessman does not himself divert capital into a château, he is likely to see his sons do so and to see the most talented of them move off into the bureaucracy or the professions. The result has been, beyond question, to affect the recruitment and motivation of the entrepreneurial class in ways that have seriously retarded the development of the economic order on which French prosperity in this century depends.

In other high-status occupations—such as the élite services of the state, the army, the professions, and higher education—traditionalistic attitudes have also persisted. These have been areas in which, since the ancien régime, the feudalization of the rising bourgeois has taken place. The attachment to formal hierarchy and seniority, as well as the social prestige of the professions and the higher civil service, still reflects these influences. In recent years, however—and with attendant

13 Siegfried, *Tableau politique de la France de l'ouest sous la troisième République* (Paris, 1913).

14 cf. Georges Lefebvre, *The Coming of the French Revolution*, translated by R. R. Palmer (Princeton, 1947), Chap. II. The survival of this scale of values is skillfully etched in Henry James, *The American*. David S. Landes discusses this whole problem in an excellent article on "French Entrepreneurship and Industrial Growth in the Nineteenth Century," *Journal of Economic History*, IX (1949), 54 ff.

strains—the rationalistic, competitive order open to talent has carried out increasingly successful invasions.

This ambiguity and contradiction in the criteria of status classification has probably been a more significant source of strains in modern France than has been generally realized. It has tended to create a situation in which competing groups claim the right to leadership roles, without having gained general recognition as "legitimate" leaders.[15] This confusion over the nature and basis of leadership in the society has contributed to those sharp divisions between the various elements of the French élite, to that irresponsibility of her high-status groups from which France has suffered so heavily in this century. The contrast with England is again striking.

Similar strains of varying significance are to be found at other points where the traditional and modern institutional orders meet. Among the most important of these is the whole area of "socialization"—the patterns by which each new-born barbarian is molded into working conformity with the established patterns of his society, by which he comes to absorb the culture and the standards which in large measure become the motivating forces in his own conduct. This area is quite clearly a source of deeply structured strains in French society.[15a] It is a difficult field, however, and requires close and careful treatment by qualified people with detailed information not now available. It is nevertheless a problem that someday must be faced in the study of a social order. The educational sphere would provide an important study by itself. This sample of the evidence, however, must suffice to suggest the kinds of strain that lie in this coexistence of conflicting patterns.

France thus carried forward into the age of industrialism elements of two distinct orders whose institutional conflicts may be summarized somewhat schematically: the political patterns of traditional authority, Church, and army as against the liberal-democracy of the Revolution and Republic; the economic patterns of traditional agriculture, craftsmanship, and corporatism as against bourgeois capitalism's rationalistic exchange economy; the social patterns of traditional hierarchy, status, and organism as against bourgeois individualism, equality, and opportunity.

[15] In the sense that both Mr. Churchill and Mr. Attlee, for example, were accepted without serious question as legitimate leaders in the United Kingdom. For a discussion of "legitimate" as here used, cf. Weber, *loc. cit.*, pp. 124 ff.

[15a] There is much, for instance, in the extreme complexities and ambiguities of French attitudes toward authority that is unquestionably conditioned by these patterns. Other behavior, such as the evidence of a diffuse interpersonal hostility, also suggests strains in these patterns, or at least distinctly different levels of permissible expression of hostility.

Yet nineteenth-century France, without resolving these tensions, slowly learned to live with them. Bedded in a stable class structure, the strains between the traditional and bourgeois orders have only rarely become explosive. The two orders have found that they share much in the way of respect for family, continuity, property, excellence, intellect, individuality, and such subtler components of French ways of living as find expression in conversation, gastronomy, and the relations of the sexes.

IV

At this point we must leave the strains between traditional and bourgeois, which if fundamental are also more familiar, in order to examine those arising from the impact on France and the Western world of a third institutional order, industrialism. This third institutional order conflicted seriously not only with the traditionalistic survivals from the remoter past, but also with institutions and attitudes of bourgeois capitalism *as it had taken shape in France.*

In some of its primary characteristics industrialism is not a new "order"; it shares many of the institutional forms which have been described in connection with commercial or bourgeois capitalism. Thus in France industrialism found available to it in more or less developed form an exchange economy, a "rational-legal" political order, a free property system, free labor, mobility of resources, and other of its institutional needs. Modern industrial technology carries with it, however, institutional demands of its own, deriving from its methods of production, the nature of its product, and its scale of organization. These have a total social impact that has not yet begun to be measured.

While the rationalistic bourgeois social order of commercial capitalism had cleared away many traditional restrictions, it also, by the extent of its triumph, established in France a petty-bourgeois social structure that stands to this day in serious conflict with the demands of industrialism. The concentration of social weight in the middle classes—the peasant, tradesman, artisan, official—gave the France that emerged from the Revolution an extraordinary degree of social stability. The Revolution had enshrined the little unit, the little man, the little goal (in terms of economic aspirations). He and his slogans have since been almost invulnerable. He has been *the* controlling political force. His individualistic metaphysic has permeated the social and legal fabric. A society based on assumptions of the diffusion of power and wealth was the order of the day.

Furthermore there was in the nineteenth century little to disrupt this social order, to provide the new horizons, incentives, or compulsions necessary for breaking out of these forms.[16] France had arrived at population maturity relatively early, in terms of numbers, and the rate of increase was slow. The protected home market provided relatively little in the way of dynamic demand. During critical decades high tariffs eliminated the stimulus of foreign competition in basic industries. In the pre-industrial stage France had not developed the production of staples; and the heterogeneity of individual, regional, and class consumption tastes did not encourage mass production. Being relatively self-sufficient, France was not obliged to push with vigor into large-scale foreign trade. There was no abrupt opening of new markets, and, with the exception of Lorraine ore, no sudden introduction of major new resources that might have forced the pace. By the time mass production techniques became generally available, a large part of the French entrepreneurial dynasties (including most of the Protestant families) were already "established" and more concerned with conserving than innovating[17]; and, as we have seen, social attitudes and institutions were set against the aggressive parvenu.

The result of this was that while France participated in the general economic development of the Western world to 1914, her gains were characteristically those of slow and steady accretion. There were not those spectacular rates of growth, those sudden leaps forward that might have broken through the institutional patterns of petty-bourgeois and traditionalistic resistance. The activity of the 1850's and 1860's was not general or lasting enough to fix a new pattern. France never experienced such stimuli and pressures for innovations and expansion as the United States found in its continental growth; England in the necessities and opportunities of foreign trade and in her early industrial lead; Germany in the late and sudden unification of a large national market; and all of them in the opening-up of great primary industrial resources. Nor were any of these countries so committed to a solidified institutional "set" in favor of littleness as existed in France. Elsewhere expanding horizons, fortified in Germany and England by a continuing imperial tradition which made large-scale organization familiar, eased the acceptance of the economic bigness of a growing industrialism.

In France, however, industrialism edged in only gradually, a foreign invention that had to force its way against conflicting institutional patterns. It came slowly and with real strains. As Marx observed at the mid-century, the *industrial* bourgeois had not yet come to power in France: "[Excepting Paris] . . . in the rest of France it is crowded

---

[16] cf. Shepard B. Clough, "Retardative Factors in French Economic Development," *Journal of Economic History,* Supplement VI (1946), 91–102.

[17] Landes, *loc. cit.,* p. 60.

into single, scattered industrial centers, being almost lost in the
superior number of peasants and petty bourgeois." [18] Even today the
penetration of industrialism into France is highly localized. Furthermore, the accidents of economic geography have localized it in ways
that have minimized its social impact, concentrating it on the periph-
ery—the east and north, and around the ports—with only two major
islands in the heart of France, the Paris-Rouen area and the Lyons-St.
Étienne area. The growth of urbanization has also been unusually
slow in France. Almost half of the French still live in rural areas,
another 20 per cent live in communities of less than 20,000 population, and—Paris apart—only two and a half million live in cities of
over 100,000.[19]

It could thus still be said in 1930 that, "Even after a century of intense industrial life, the social structure of France is still essentially
built up of peasants, artisans and [petty-] bourgeois." [20] The root of all
this is in the persistent survival of "the most individualistic economy
in Europe" [21]—an economic structure heavily weighted with small
units and with property ownership widely diffused among small, traditionalistic families. This institutional structure must be examined
for a moment to point up its conflicts with a modern industrial order.

In agriculture the system of tariff-protected peasant proprietorship
has survived for great parts of France, giving her the highest percentage
of "independents" in this field of any Western country. The result has
been to hold an excessive amount of labor on the land and to maintain
small, undercapitalized, unproductive units, particularly in the south
and east. After excluding parcels of less than one hectare, the 1929
figures indicate 62 per cent of the "exploitations" to be of from 1–10
hectares, 34 per cent from 10–50.[22] Augé-Laribé has estimated that
more than a quarter of the land in cultivation is too fragmentized for
economic use. Yet such is the character of the French social order that
no significant attack on this agricultural structure has ever been made.
Industrial France has not repealed its corn laws—a sharp conflict with
the needs of industrialism.

18 "The Class Struggles in France," Chap. I, printed in Émile Burns (ed.), *A Hand-
book of Marxism* (New York, 1935), p. 106. It should be noted that Paris, too, has remained a petty-bourgeois stronghold.
19 Henri Ulmer, "Structure humaine," pp. 12–16, in the extremely useful collection
of basic papers edited by Charles Rist and Gaetan Pirou, *De la France d'avant guerre
à la France d'aujourd'hui: vingt-cinq ans d'évolution de la structure économique et
sociale française* (Paris, 1939).
20 André Siegfried, *France: A Study in Nationality* (New Haven, 1930), p. 3.
21 André Mayer, "La Crise de structure de la société française," *The French Review*
(offprint, New York, 1942), p. 8.
22 Figures in this paragraph are based on Augé-Laribé, "Structure agricole," esp. pp.
119 ff., in Rist and Pirou, *op. cit.*

Even in the industrial field there is impressive evidence of the survival of small units. Though figures on numbers of establishments tend to be misleading as to the distribution of weight in an economy, they have some use for our purposes here. Of 1.6 million registered industrial establishments in the 1931 census, about 64 per cent had no paid employees and the next 34 per cent had less than ten. It is against this pattern that there have grown up at the other end of the scale in the present century the fraction of one per cent of very large enterprises. In 1931 establishments with more than 100 workers employed approximately half of all industrial wage-earners, and more than a quarter were working in establishments employing more than 500.[23]

Finally, the whole area of commerce, retail trade, communications, transportation, and public and private services has survived to a remarkable degree as a petty-bourgeois haven. This area that economists have named the tertiary industries shows perhaps the most striking pattern of small, inefficient units retarding the flow of trade and the growth of industrialism (though providing a rich and wonderful chapter in the *comédie humaine*). In most countries this is the area of highest average income per employed person, and in all the more prosperous countries it has been a field of heavy recent growth. France, however, has clung to such small-scale and uneconomic methods that costs are high and the return is low. Whereas French average real income per head of the total employed population runs about half that of the American worker or two-thirds that of the British, in this tertiary field French real income figures average less than one-fifth of the American and little more than two-fifths of the British.[24] The rule of the petty-bourgeois, by the petty-bourgeois, and for the petty-bourgeois is again reflected in the restrictive legislation and discriminatory taxation that have been imposed on department and chain store operations which threatened to upset the established order of the independent shopkeeper.

This whole set of institutional structures geared to smallness and continuity entailed a set of "attitudes" equally in conflict with the demands of industrialism. Probably the most important place to begin the examination of these attitudes is with that much abused individual, the French businessman, the feudalized-bourgeois-industrialist.

[23] cf. Henry W. Ehrmann, *The French Labor Movement from Popular Front to Liberation* (New York, 1947), pp. 10–11, and the statistical material in papers by M. Aucuy, "Structure industrielle," and J. Denuc, "Structure des entreprises," in Rist and Pirou, *op. cit.*

[24] Colin Clark, *The Conditions of Economic Progress* (London, 1940), pp. 318 ff. As orders of magnitude these figures are significant, though the assumptions and approximations involved in Clark's calculations need to be recognized. Part of the spread noted above is, of course, attributable to compositional differences, but the contrast in size of distributive units, etc., remains.

The bourgeois régime, as we have seen, never really broke the hold of traditionalistic views as to social stratification. As Defoe had noted in his day, the French businessman never gained the relative standing in terms of his own achievements that "trade" enjoyed in England; he never had a London where he and his values could reign supreme. Aggressive business behavior has in the past found only limited social rewards in French society. The more prosperous business families have indeed moved into high-status positions in time; but this has in good part followed upon assimilation with the families, or at least the ways, of hereditary prestige groups.

Direct and indirect adaptations to these surviving traditionalistic patterns have profoundly affected French entrepreneurial motivation and behavior.[25] The resulting focus on stability as against economic achievement, on assuring a regular income for the maintenance of a family status as against focus on innovation and risk, has already been mentioned. These patterns have also worked against dedication to business activity, against aggressive market behavior, against the basic drives to maximize profit and growth, to exploit competitive and technological advantage—drives that are functionally institutionalized in industrial capitalism. Traditionalisms have also contributed to the tendency to look to the state for aid, protection, and initiative.

In its turn the commercial and petty-bourgeois institutional order just reviewed has also conflicted with attitudes and behavior functionally requisite to expanding industrialism. It has furthered such contrary patterns as the preference for *rentes* as against risks, and tendencies to limited aspirations in scale and volume and investment, to passiveness with regard to technological progress and other kinds of innovation. Bettelheim quotes figures, for example, indicating that in 1928 the value of French machinery per head was less than half of the average for Europe's industrialized countries.[26] The French industrial capitalist has, in Sombart's terms, shown half of the spirit of high-capitalism, the bourgeois half—thrift, industry, calculation, etc.—but not the other half, the dynamic, driving spirit of enterprise. The few De Lessepses who did break through were historical "sports"; they were not leaders of a host of lesser men who were to consolidate their gains. (There is perhaps a symbolic truth in the fact that De Lesseps died in disgrace.) They never had sufficient numbers or influence to set

25 cf. footnotes 12 and 14 above, as well as material published by the Research Center for Entrepreneurial History in *Change and the Entrepreneur* (Cambridge, Mass., 1949), and my forthcoming "The Entrepreneur and the Social Order: France and the United States," in William Miller (ed.), *Men and Business* (Cambridge, Mass., 1951).

26 Charles Bettelheim, *Bilan de l'économie française, 1919–1946* (Paris, 1947), p. 46; cf. also Part II. Any analysis of the full causes of this, in addition to going further into the figures, would have to go beyond the factors considered in this paper.

a new pattern. It might be argued, to use other terms, that what industrial capitalism really required was the classic nineteenth-century model of a Schumpeterian entrepreneur—a creative risk-taking innovator operating on credit; that what it got in France was primarily a Weberian entrepreneur, engaged in a rational process of increasing his wealth through compound interest, saving and reinvesting (though, for the majority, doing so without benefit of Weber's fortifying Protestant ethic).[27]

The French businessman has in general accommodated his behavior to these mixed bourgeois and traditional patterns. He has tended to conduct his business according to their norms. In the present century certain tendencies to break out of this frame have been periodically interrupted by war; and the industrial bourgeois has been further made cautious by inflation, depression, and the growing hostility of the community. Partly—though by no means wholly—as a result of these conflicting institutional patterns, industrialism has not realized its potential in France. It has suffered from what might be called traditional and bourgeois "cramps." French society has accordingly experienced far more of its social problems than of its economic product.[28]

Industrialism has also brought deep conflict with the behavioral and motivational patterns of the French worker—the second element in the community most directly involved in the functioning of the system. Typically still close to his place of birth and his rural roots, attached to the traditions and relative independence of skilled craftsmanship, he has shown deep-lying resistances to the demands of mass production—standardization, speed, quantity, uniformity—and to the pressures of industrial organization—bigness, discipline, regularity, pace. Industrialism's demand for occupational mobility has also conflicted with the intense attachments that most Frenchmen, and particularly home-owning Frenchmen, feel for their own little corner of France.

Nor has the French worker found for these institutional strains any compensatory hope of sharing in a new order of abundance. The French entrepreneur had rarely caught the imagination of his workers with the idea that they would benefit by any new gains in productivity; and there is evidence that by 1900 French workers had already little confidence in the willingness or capacity of the employers to keep up with technological progress.[29] Having thus had to absorb the strains of conflicting institutions, together with those inherent in the labor role in modern society—insecurity, low status, etc.—without any such

[27] Weber, to be sure, attributes something of a restless, limitless seeking to his entrepreneur, but his emphasis is such as to make the above contrast meaningful.

[28] For figures on the cessation of economic growth in France in this century in terms of real income per head of the occupied population, cf. Clark, *op. cit.*, pp. 98–109, 146–48.

[29] cf. the article by John Bowditch in this volume.

compensating gain in his economic well-being as his American counterpart, the French worker has in our century found less and less reason to look with hope to French capitalism or to the bourgeois
Republic.

The French worker's long attachment to the loose organization and
heroic myth of syndicalism unquestionably reflects elements of "romantic protest" against these institutional conflicts, against the demands of industrial capitalism. Long after English and German labor
had turned to large centralized unions or political parties, the French
worker still clung to syndicalism's *action directe,* to loose federations,
spontaneous strikes, and improvised resources. Only slowly and with
serious strains has French labor come to accept the kind and scale of
organization that industrialism begets, and then only under a banner
of frank rebellion against the existing régime, a banner of socialist
collectivism.

Finally, we should recognize that patterns of resistance to industrialism are diffused throughout French society. The evidence can only be
suggested: the fact that Frenchmen have different gods and goals—
that production or even standards of living have never been the
primary objective of French society; that, except in terms of military
effort, collective accomplishment has not occupied the place given it in
Anglo-Saxon countries; the dislike of bigness *qua* bigness; the rejection of quantitative values; the taste for the particular, the individual,
the hand product; the repulsion of the intellectual for the products of
industrialism (of which Duhamel's *Scènes de la vie future* is a harsh
example); the prestige of the arts and the professions; the nonpracti-
cal orientation of French education, including technical education;
the reluctance of even the engineer to think in terms of mass production; the traditional hostility of the French army to tank, truck, plane,
and mechanic; the willingness of the consumer to treat shopping as a
social recreation for which a price must be paid; the endless readiness
to repair and conserve, as against an economic order built around
abundance and waste.

It might not be too much to say that all groups in France necessary
to the successful functioning of industrialism—entrepreneur, lawyer,
technician, artisan, retailer, customer, peasant, and bureaucrat—have
in greater or less degree been shaped by earlier institutional patterns
which cause them serious strains in adjusting to the industrial order.
Yet industrialism is here to stay, and it has forced upon France the
problems of bigness. The growth and nature of the new institutional
structures that have followed from industrialism are sufficiently familiar to need no elaboration; it is enough to emphasize the institutional
malintegrations that have resulted.

No democratic society has solved the problem of how to handle big economic and social units and concentrations of monopoly power—in capital, labor, or wherever they appear. The French petty-bourgeois social order, founded on assumptions of small units and diffused power, and historically distrustful of the fisc and the strong executive, seems to have been particularly unable to comprehend or contain them. The social machinery for integrating and regulating these new aggregates of power has been completely inadequate.[30] Many of the big institutional structures of industrialism have, as it were, grown up outside of the formal institutions of the bourgeois Republic rather than within them. Radically incompatible with the existing order, they have tended to go their separate ways as tensions mounted. On the one hand, rapidly growing big industry and finance, organizing itself into powerful associations, has turned to the Right against the Republic in time of crisis. On the other, working class and intellectual groups, in protest against industrial capitalism, have looked to the Left for a new institutional order.[31] In our times these splits have been intensified by war and inflation, by world tensions between East and West, and by the problem of Communism. It is a period in history profoundly unfavorable to major institutions and patterns and classes of the bourgeois phase.

V

Structures in which the locus of power does not coincide with responsibility are inherently unstable. France has a certain negative stability in her peasantry, her surviving Center, and in the fact that neither Right nor Left appears strong enough to upset the equilibrium; yet the problems of explosive class antagonisms and deep institutional malintegrations remain. The sum of the strains produced by these new institutional structures crashing around in the fragile forms of bourgeois France cannot yet be measured; but it is an impressive reason for learning more than we now know about the nature of the strains in French society.

One approach has been attempted here. It has involved a somewhat cumbrous scaffolding and hypotheses for which the evidence is admittedly incomplete. But it is an approach that seemed to open up aspects of the social structure of modern Frence and throw light on certain fundamental problems of her recent history—problems such as the

[30] On one aspect of this, cf. remarks of Alfred Sauvy in Rist and Pirou, *op. cit.*, pp. 299 f.

[31] Certain of these problems are pointed up in John E. Sawyer, "The Reëstablishment of the Republic in France: The De Gaulle Era, 1944–1945," *Political Science Quarterly*, LXII (1947), 354–67.

depth and persistence of the Left-Right cleavage, including particularly the alignments and involvements in crises such as those of Dreyfus
and Vichy; the contradictions of militant democracy and individualism with deep conservatism and the lurking readiness of large groups
to accept a symbol of authority such as Napoleon, Pétain or De Gaulle;
the chronic instability of ministries, yet the stability of the middle class
hold on the social order and political machinery of the Third Republic; the squeeze put on the liberal, individualist position in our time by
traditionalistic reaction and Leftist protest; the economic behavior
and attitudes of French businessmen, investors, and workers; the vigor
of anticapitalist, antibourgeois, antiparliamentary sentiment on both
extremes; the hostility of major groups to the economic and cultural
output of American capitalism; the divisions and vulnerability of
France in the world crisis of this century. To the extent that it offers
insights into problems such as these and suggests possibilities of comparative analysis of social structure, it may not be a wholly unfruitful
approach for further historical investigation.

18

++

POPULATION AND

POPULATION TRENDS IN MODERN FRANCE *

DUDLEY KIRK

++

FRANCE is often regarded as the classic country of depopulation. For two hundred years the dangers of depopulation have been a favorite theme of those concerned about the future of France. Lack of population is commonly given as a major cause of French weakness in a crowded and rapidly growing Europe. France has often been termed a demographic vacuum in a teeming continent.[1]

There are important elements of truth in this. But it is also true that at the moment, 1950, the population of France is larger and increasing more each year than ever before in her recorded history. Indeed, France today is growing more rapidly than several of her neighbors. It is the purpose of this chapter to examine the nature of this postwar anomaly and to evaluate its significance for the place of France in contemporary Europe.

Let us first consider the historical trends that have so greatly changed the position of France in Europe over the past one hundred and fifty years.

I

The France of Napoleon was exceeded in population only by Tsarist Russia, which apparently passed France in population sometime in the

* The views expressed in this paper are those of the author and do not necessarily reflect those of the Department of State.

[1] In 1767, Abbé Jaubert wrote a book entitled *Des causes de la dépopulation et des moyens d'y remédier*. Since then dozens of books have been written on this subject. The historical literature is extensively cited and interpreted by Joseph J. Spengler in *France Faces Depopulation* (Durham, North Carolina, 1938).

eighteenth century. France then was not only the most populous country of Western Europe, but she further enjoyed the advantages of
political unification as against Germany and Italy and of greater
cultural homogeneity as compared with polyglot Austria-Hungary.
Within her present boundaries she had about 15 per cent of Europe's
people.

Population Growth 1800-1949

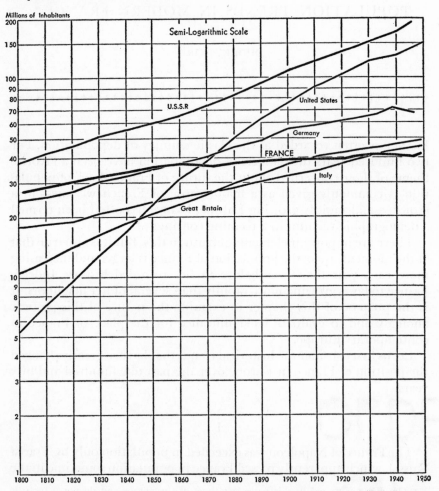

FIGURE 1. Population growth in France and selected countries, 1800–
1949. The data refer to the areas as of the dates given, except that for
Germany and Italy prior to 1871 the figures relate to the territories
as of 1871–1914

As may be observed in Figure 1, France had been passed in population by the United States and by the German Empire in 1870, by the United Kingdom about 1900, and by Italy about 1930. In 1939, Daladier's France stood fifth rather than second in Europe. The France of 1939 had only 7.3 per cent of the total population of Europe and the Soviet Union.

It is sometimes overlooked that this demographic decline of France was *relative* rather than absolute. Unlike Ireland, which is a country of true depopulation, France has not experienced sustained population loss. She simply failed to grow as rapidly as the rest of Europe. Since 1800 Europe has experienced perhaps the greatest population expansion in the history of the world. France shared only mildly in this expansion.

During the nineteenth century France grew by 12,000,000 or 44 per cent. In the same period Great Britain increased 26,000,000 (more than 3 times), Germany 32,000,000, Austria-Hungary 23,000,000, and European Russia some 70,000,000. Europe as a whole more than doubled despite heavy emigration and despite lagging growth in Ireland, in France, and in southern Europe.

The slow growth of France was certainly not the result of poverty or of catastrophe. France was generally more advanced both economically and culturally than her neighbors. France did not experience the devastating famines in the middle of the century which so decimated the populations of Ireland and the Palatinate and which set in motion the great overseas migrations from these areas.

The explanation of the slower rate of growth in France lies in the gradual decline of the birth rate at a time when the remainder of Europe still maintained the primitive levels of fertility characteristic of pre-industrial societies. While statistical evidence is not abundant, French observers have generally agreed that the decline in fertility was attributable to voluntary control in the form of contraception (especially onanism) and abortion. The desire to limit family size has been ascribed to a wide diversity of causes. Perhaps the most widespread is the theory of LePlay, who traced fertility declines in France to the adoption during the Revolution of testamentary provisions of the French Civil Code, which require parents to bequeath specified portions of their property to each child (e.g. to divide agricultural holdings among all children). Concern over possible division of the family holdings is presumed to explain the declines in the birth rate in the nineteenth century, which did in fact appear early in the rural areas.

More in keeping with current demographic thinking are the views of Leroy-Beaulieu and his school of thought, that the decline in fertility was associated with the rise in a complex of factors which he called "civilization." Civilization included the growth of cities, the rise of the middle class, the spread of education and material comforts, the extension of leisure, the soaring of individual and family ambition, the possibility open to all of rising in the social scale. According to this school of thought birth rates were lower in France because she was more advanced.[2]

Whatever its causes, there was a slow but persistent decline in the birth rate and in the rate of population growth during the nineteenth century. By 1860, 37 departments of France had net reproduction rates below the level of replacement; by 1890 more than half of the departments (49 of a total 87) were not replacing themselves, and the deserted village was becoming a common thing in France.[3]

The essential weakness of the French demographic position appeared under the strain of the First World War. In that conflict France lost 1,320,000 military dead, and 240,000 excess civilian deaths. An almost equally important numerical loss was the deficit of births—births that would have occurred in the absence of war. The total population deficit of France in the First World War therefore amounted to over 3,000,000 people. This loss amounted to 7 to 8 per cent of the 1914 population.

The French losses were by no means unique or unusual in the First World War. The total population deficits in Germany, in Italy, and in Austria-Hungary were of comparable or even greater magnitude.[4] But these countries had large reserves of children and young people to replace war casualties. France had not. Further, the comparatively high birth rate in these countries enabled them quickly to overcome their war losses. The recuperative power of Germany is illustrated by the fact that by 1930 Germany had already exceeded her 1910 population —this despite heavy war casualties and the loss of some 7,000,000 people in the ceded territories. France was able to recoup her losses only with the annexation of Alsace-Lorraine and the additions of heavy immigration in the early 1920's.

II

During the interwar years France continued to slip behind her neighbors in population growth. Over the period from 1920 to 1939 the French population rose about 2.7 millions or 7 per cent. This rate

[2] This view is expressed with varying emphases in the following well-known works: J. Bertillon, La Dépopulation de la France (Paris, 1911); P. Leroy-Beaulieu, La Question de la population (Paris, 1913); E. Levasseur, La Population française (Paris, 1898–92, 3 vols.).

[3] France, Statistique générale, Études démographiques, No. 1, "Reproduction nette en Europe depuis l'origine des statistiques de l'état civil."

[4] cf. comparative data assembled by the author in Frank W. Notestein, et al., The Future Population of Europe and the Soviet Union (Geneva, 1944), Chap. III.

of growth was only half that of Germany (in the 1937 territory), less than one-half that of Italy, and less than one-fourth that of Eastern Europe.

The slender margin of growth in France was achieved only by virtue of a very large immigration. At least four-fifths of the French increase was assignable to the huge movement of population into France during the 1920's, when France replaced the United States as the greatest country of European immigration. This immigration was particularly valuable to France because it consisted chiefly of young men of ages which compensated for the military casualties of the First World War.

The economic depression of the 1930's brought both a decline in the birth rate and a cessation of mass immigration. As a result the French population was almost stationary in the decade. From 1935 there was a small excess of deaths over births, and there was every reason to suppose that true depopulation was setting in at last. Barring further immigration, the continuation of interwar trends suggested a decline in the French population from 41.2 millions in 1940 to 40.3 in 1950, 39.0 in 1960, and 36.9 in 1970.[5]

It was a gloomy outlook for France. In terms of prime military manpower, the progressive deterioration of the French position is illustrated by the historical trends in the number of males at ages 20 to 34 (Table 1). At the time of the Franco-Prussian War, France and Germany had approximately equal manpower of prime military age. At the outbreak of World War II France had less than half as many men as Germany in this age group.

Table 1

MALES AGED 20–34 IN FRANCE AND GERMANY
(millions)

PERIODS	FRANCE *	GERMANY *
Franco-Prussian War	4.4 (1866)	4.7 (1871)
World War I	4.5 (1911)	7.7 (1910)
World War II	4.3 (1940)	9.4 (1939)

* Territories of dates given: The figure for Germany (1939) in her 1937 territory was 8.3 million.

There was some consolation for France in that she was no longer alone among European powers in facing the threat of depopulation, since the postwar period witnessed a very rapid decline of the birth rate in other Western countries as well. In several of these the annual net reproduction rates in the 1930's were even lower than in France. But in these neighboring countries the populations were continuing

5 Notestein, *et al., op. cit.,* p. 56.

to grow, owing to their favorable age distributions; there was a concentration of population in the young adult ages—the ages to which most births and few deaths occur. In Western Europe generally there was serious concern about the prospects of a declining population. Projections of interwar trends indicated, for example, that population declines in England and Wales would soon begin and would closely parallel those of France.

But in these other countries people were talking about the *threat* of depopulation; in France, it had actually begun. Furthermore, in Germany, reemployment and pronatalist population measures after 1933 had resulted in a major recovery in the German birth rate.

During the interwar period depopulation was a source of much publicly expressed anxiety in France. For many years it had been a growing practice among French industries to pay family allowances—that is, to provide supplements to wages or incomes on behalf of dependent children. During the interwar period this practice spread widely in France. To the extent that this constituted a pronatalist policy, it was, as one author had suggested, an attempt "to buy babies at bargain prices." [6] The average allowance amounted to only a very small percentage of the cost of rearing a child.

Agitation for public measures to relieve the economic burdens of child-bearing and child care culminated in 1939 in the *Code de la Famille*. This Code provided, for the first time, a comprehensive system of family allowances covering the greater part of the French population. The Code had not come into full effect when war broke out and it of course had no appreciable effect on the demographic position of France before the Second World War.

III

It is not surprising that most French leaders greatly feared the bloodletting of another World War. France's defeat in 1940, the transportation of some million and one-half French military prisoners into the Reich, five years of enemy occupation, the drafting of many Frenchmen for forced labor in Germany—one might have feared that these would give the *coup de grace* to France as a great power.

All of these indeed took their toll. The losses and their causes are detailed in Table 2. The records show that 92,000 French troops fell in the field in the campaigns of 1939–1940. Some 58,000 more were killed in the armies of liberation in the period 1940 to 1945, fighting in North Africa, in Italy, in metropolitan France, and elsewhere. The French Resistance suffered a loss of some 20,000. Sixty thousand died

6 David V. Glass, *Population Policies and Movements in Europe* (Oxford, 1940) p. 371.

in aerial bombardments, and as many more were lost in land operations and massacres. An estimated 30,000 were executed with various degrees of formality. Some 280,000 in addition died outside of France as prisoners of war, as political and racial deportees, as forced laborers, and even as French drafted into the Wehrmacht, the latter of course being almost entirely French citizens from German-speaking Alsace-Lorraine.

Table 2

BALANCE OF THE FRENCH POPULATION FOR THE PERIOD 1936–1946
(figures in thousands)

		TOTAL	FRENCH	ALIEN
POPULATION, CENSUS OF MARCH 8, 1936		41,610	39,450	2,160
Live births	+6,036 ⎱ −550			
"Normal" deaths	−6,586 ⎰			
Military dead				
Campaign of 1939–40	−92 ⎱ −150			
Armies of liberation	−58 ⎰			
"French Forces of the Interior"	−20			
Civilian deaths in war operations				
Bombardments	−60 ⎫			
Land operations, massacres	−60 ⎬ −150			
Executed	−30 ⎭		−1,060	−90
Deaths of French retained by the enemy outside of France				
Prisoners of war	−40 ⎫			
Deportees—political	−60 ⎪			
—racial	−100 ⎪			
Laborers	−40 ⎬ −280			
French drafted in the Wehrmacht —killed	−30 ⎪			
—disappeared	−10 ⎭			
Naturalizations			+200	−200
Other acquisitions of French nationality			+20	−20
Children of alien fathers who acquired French citizenship at birth			+250	−250
Excess of immigration		+320	+250	+70
POPULATION, CENSUS OF MARCH 10, 1946		40,780	39,110	1,670

Source: Adapted from France, Direction de la Statistique Générale, *Premiers résultats du recensement général—10 mars 1946* (Paris, 1947), p. 18.

In addition to these direct losses there was an excess of deaths over births in the period 1936 to 1946 of some 550,000. These were not by any means entirely attributable to the war. Deaths were already ex-

ceeding births in France by some 30,000 a year before the war, so that
in the decade under consideration there might normally have been
anticipated a natural decline of some 300,000. In other words, perhaps 250,000 surplus "normal" deaths could be assigned to the war.

In net balance there was an excess of deaths over births amounting
to some 1,150,000 between 1936 and 1946, chiefly as a result of the war.
This loss was partially balanced by a net immigration of some 320,000.
Of these an estimated 250,000 were Frenchmen returning to metropolitan France from the colonies and from foreign countries. In addition there was a net immigration of 70,000 foreigners as the result of
favorable economic conditions in the period 1936 to 1939 and as a
result of the influx of Spanish refugees at the beginning of 1939.
About 250,000 foreigners, 150,000 of whom were Italians, are believed to have left French soil as a result of the war.

Population losses of World War II were large but they were not, as
in the First World War, catastrophic. A surprising feature of the recent war in France, as in other Western European countries, was the
extent to which the birth rate held up despite the hardships of war
and the absence from home of large numbers of men in the army or
as prisoners of war. Even during the war itself, in the dark days of the
Occupation, the number of births in France had risen above what
would have been theoretically anticipated on the basis of the continuation of prewar fertility. Taking the years 1939 through 1945, there
were some 250,000 more births in France than would have been expected at prewar fertility. The deviation of the wartime experience
from the prewar trend is clearly evident in Figure 2, which shows the
very marked contrast in this regard between the First and Second
World Wars. Similarly the civilian death rate was kept under much
better control during the Second World War. There were serious increases in mortality, particularly in infant mortality and in certain of
the wasting diseases such as tuberculosis. But as is likewise evident
from Figure 2 the peaks of the death rate in the Second World War
were very moderate as compared with those experienced in the First
World War. In fact these wartime peaks did not exceed the "normal"
levels of mortality prevailing at the beginning of the century.

Biologically speaking, France emerged from the Second World
War in much less battered condition than she did from the Pyrrhic
victory of the First World War. In this regard she did not differ very
much from the other major countries of Western Europe. British
losses were comparatively small; Italian losses were much less than
in the First World War; only the smaller neutrals of the First World
War that were overrun by the Nazis in 1940 experienced greater
losses in the recent conflict. On the other hand the French experience

contrasts favorably with what happened to Germany. France's ancient enemy lost at least three and one-half million military killed, at least 700,000 civilians who lost their lives directly as a result of war, and a still undetermined number of prisoners of war who will not return.

The resistance of the French population to the impact of war augured well for the future biological survival of the French people. This portent was fully realized in the first postwar years.

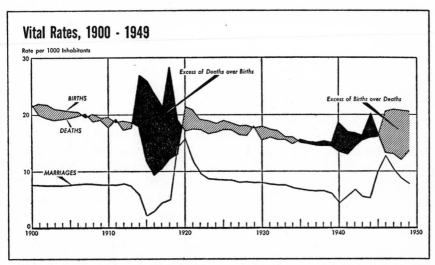

Vital Rates, 1900 - 1949

FIGURE 2. Birth rates, death rates, and marriage rates in France, 1900–1949

IV

In the five years since the close of the war in Europe, France has experienced a major reversal of previous demographic trends. Despite the ideological discouragement, the ignominy of defeat, the political and economic confusion—despite these apparently negative factors, the French population has shown a surprising biological recovery.

As might have been anticipated, the number of marriages rose very markedly with the return of the prisoners of war and the reestablishment of more normal peacetime conditions. There obviously was a deficit in marriages during the war and there was undoubtedly a very substantial backlog of marriages postponed as a result of poor economic conditions in the 1930's. Since 1946 there has been an understandable decline in the number of new marriages but even in 1949 the marriage rate remained appreciably above prewar levels.

Not unnaturally, the tremendous increase in marriages was

followed by a rapid resurgence in the birth rate after the war. The numbers of births in the years 1947, 1948, and 1949 are the highest reported in France in half a century. And the birth rate per 1,000 population, as indicated in Figure 2, has been sustained at levels not experienced in France since the early 1920's.

Perhaps most significant of all, the natural increase of France, that is, the excess of births over deaths, is now and has been for the past three years the highest ever recorded in the history of the country. In other words, not only has the postwar birth rate in France been relatively high, but deaths have dipped to new lows.

The recovery of births in France after the war is obviously in part related to the return of prisoners of war from Germany, the return of persons drafted for forced labor, and to the renewal of normal family life. It is reasonable to suppose, however, that there were more fundamental causes, particularly in view of the stronger force of this recovery following the Second World War as compared with the First. It is obvious, for example, that the high level of marriages and births is in part associated with the conditions of full employment prevailing in France since the war. In marked contrast with the 1930's, postwar France has experienced an acute labor shortage. Economic security was readily available to any person willing and able to perform useful labor.

We may even carry this argument further to the level of basic ideological point of view held by the majority of the population. The French themselves have seen in the experience of the war and the early postwar years an eclipse of classic individualism, the system of values that placed maximum importance on the development of the individual as opposed to the dominating influence of the group. Governmental planning, rationing, and social measures have resulted in a social régime which emphasizes very different personal and group values from those of classic individualism.

More specifically, this reorientation of basic attitudes has been reflected in measures to increase social security in France, which has made substantial progress toward becoming a welfare state. As related to the population this has taken the form of action in organization and action in legislation. France now has a department of ministerial rank concerned with the state of the population—La Ministère de la Santé Publique et de la Population. Within this ministry there has been established the National Institute of Demographic Studies, which now includes the largest group of research demographers in any one institution in the world. This institute, under the direction of Alfred Sauvy, has embarked upon an ambitious series of studies of the causes of specific population phenomena, and of measures to combat depopulation.[7]

Action in legislation has as its basis the above-mentioned *Code de la Famille* of 1939. The basis of French policy in regard to population is the family allowance system, by which gainfully occupied persons are given supplements to their wages or income on behalf of dependent children in their care. It is not possible to make a simple statement of how the system operates. It is complex and varies in its application to different occupational groups; it gives weight also to the number of wage-earners in the family. Also, owing to inflation in France and the rapidly changing value of the allowances, it is very difficult to state precisely what the allowances mean in terms of real consumption. As an example, however, we may take the additions to income received by a wage-earner in industry or commerce, with one wage-earner in the family, making a salary of 200,000 francs (a comparatively low income). According to the 1947 legislation, the "take-home" pay of such a worker is increased by 7.5 per cent for the first child, 22.4 per cent for two children, 38.3 per cent for three children, 49.1 per cent for four, and 60.3 per cent for five.[8] Since the family allowance is a fixed amount for all levels of income, it favors persons of lower income. The payments are greatest on behalf of second and third children, so that the family allowance system favors the medium-sized families and, to a lesser extent, the larger families. In this it may be contrasted with the family allowances of the United Kingdom in which a fixed amount is paid for all children after the first. The latter system obviously favors the poorer families, but not necessarily the larger families.

The French have been inclined to attribute the high level of the postwar birth rate to the family allowance system. It is difficult to obtain direct evidence to substantiate this belief. As in the United States, which has no family allowance system, the postwar "baby-boom" appears to be primarily a function of increase in the number of first, second, and third births, and only in a minor way the result of more really large families.[9] While it seems entirely plausible that family allowances should have contributed to the recovery in the French birth rate, it is certain that full employment and basic changes in family attitudes have likewise played a role. It still remains to be

[7] Since 1946, the Institute has published a quarterly journal, *Population*, which is an indispensable source for students of French demographic problems.

[8] J. Bourgeois-Pichat, "La Situation démographique de la Grande-Bretagne. Comparaison avec celle de la France" (2nd part) in *Population*, January–March 1949.

[9] J. Bourgeois-Pichat, "Où en est la natalité française" in *Population*, January–March 1950.

seen whether the recovery is permanent or whether, as in Britain and Sweden, which also have broad family allowances, the birth rate will fall back toward prewar levels.

Although of somewhat lesser importance than formerly, immigration still remains an important factor in French population growth. For the years 1946–1949 the excess of births over deaths in France amounted to 1,275,000. The total increase is estimated to be 1,645,000, leaving a margin of some 370,000 to be accounted for by immigration. But whereas about four-fifths of the increase of the French population in the interwar period was attributable to immigration, since the Second World War the position of the two factors of births and immigration in French population growth has been almost exactly reversed. Nevertheless, the role of the foreign worker in French life and in the French economy continues to be large. As noted above (Table 2) the number of foreigners in 1946 had declined some 500,000 as against the last prewar census in 1936, but this decline was entirely due to naturalization and to deaths—inevitably a foreign population dies out if it is not replaced from abroad.

Despite labor shortages and extensive discussion of the problem, immigration into France since the war has been on a comparatively small scale. Information on the postwar movements is not very precise. The newly established Office of Immigration has been set up to promote certain desired immigration and to provide for the location and employment of immigrants. But its records do not include immigrants from all countries, and emigration from France may go unrecorded. In addition there has been a significant amount of clandestine immigration into France from Italy. In view of all these factors it is not possible to make a very definite statement of the migratory movements. It is estimated, however, that in the years 1946–1949 there was a net immigration of about 350,000. Of this some 220,000 were foreign workers, some 60,000 members of their families, and rather more than 100,000 the net balance of Algerian immigration. Subtracted from this are about 50,000 Poles who have been repatriated into the new Poland.[10]

Of the workers who legally or illegally immigrated into France about two-thirds were Italian, some 30,000 were Germans, and 27,000 were displaced persons. Of the members of families rather less than half were Italian, rather less than one-fourth German, and about one-third displaced persons. In total in the years 1946 to 1949 it is estimated that there was a net immigration of about 160,000 Italians,

[10] Louis Henry and Jacques Voranger, "La Situation démographique" in *Population*, October–December 1949, pp. 737–42. See also Louis Chevalier, "Bilan d'une immigration" in *Population*, January–March 1950.

40,000 Germans, and 45,000 displaced persons. The small number of displaced persons received is particularly striking in a country that has spoken so loudly of its need for immigrants. Actually, for political reasons, France has been reluctant to take displaced persons. Rather interesting is the fact that she has taken almost as many civilian Germans as she has victims of Nazi oppression. But the bulk of postwar immigration into France has been Italian.

The comparatively low level of French immigration since the war is attributable to three causes: (1) the use of German prisoners in the first postwar years. Immediately after the war France temporarily absorbed 700,000 German prisoners of war. Over 500,000 of these were placed in the civilian economy and formed an essential part of the French labor force during the first three years of reconstruction. (2) The development of an understandable xenophobia. The prevailing French attitude is hostile to immigration. In a recent public opinion survey in France only 25 per cent declared themselves to be in favor of mass immigration, while 63 per cent recorded themselves as opposed (12 per cent expressed no opinion). There were widely divergent reactions as regards different nationalities: 67 per cent favored Belgians, 51 per cent Swiss, 31 per cent Dutch, 20 per cent Italians, 16 per cent Spaniards, 15 per cent displaced persons, 11 per cent North Africans, and 7 per cent Germans.[11] (3) The responsibility of the Ministry of Labor for immigration. This Ministry is naturally responsive to the needs of labor, especially with regard to its protection from foreign competition. It has not been so responsive to more general demographic considerations.[12] Though the postwar period has been one of full employment, there is a prevalent view that unemployment and reduced economic activity will inevitably return. This basic fear of unemployment has counseled great caution in bringing foreign workers and their families to France. A high proportion of the immigrants are workers with no fixed ties in France—an expendable force should depression strike. This caution has been reinforced by the extreme housing shortage in France, particularly in areas of critical industries.

V

The age structure of the French population, shown in Figure 3, is both heritage of the past and portent of the future. It is a truly battle-scarred population. The military dead of 1914–1918 have left a much

[11] Alain Girard, "Le Problème démographique et l'évolution du sentiment public" in *Population*, April–June 1950, pp. 339–40.

[12] cf. Alfred Sauvy, "Besoins et possibilités de l'immigration française" in *Population*, April–June 1950, and Paul Vincent, "Vieillissement de la population, retraites et immigration," *op. cit.*, April–June 1946.

reduced quota of males born before 1900 and now at ages 50 to 70. The birth deficits of the same war have left a deep indentation at ages 30 to 34. The recovery of births after the First World War, the sharply falling birth rate in the depression, the depressive effects of World War II, the biological recovery of postwar France—all have left their mark on the structure of the population.

Of decisive importance in determining the basic shape of the population pyramid is the fact that France has been a country of low birth rates for three or four generations. The French population is the oldest in the world, with a median age of 35. It has the highest proportion of old people over age 65 (11.3 per cent). It has an old working force, though owing to the decimation of men in World War I there is less of a problem of older workers than otherwise would have occurred. A different problem, however, is presented by the excess of women at these and older ages. More than any other country in the world, France literally deserves the title "a country of old women." The average age of females in France is about 37 years, as compared with about 30 in the United States.

This is a rather dolorous description. But to say that France is the oldest population in the world does not mean that it is a country without children or, for that matter, without young women. France has a heavy burden of old age; it has a disproportionate number of women in the older age groups; it has a disproportionate number of older workers. But the picture is by no means wholly black. In contrast with the first years after the First World War the proportion of males and females in the child-bearing ages is relatively equal and hence favorable to a large number of births. And the last few years have given the population pyramid of France a solid base in its large number of young children.

If the present structure of the French population is not especially strong, France can at least take consolation that in the twentieth century her neighbors have experienced a demographic evolution that was almost uniquely French in the nineteenth century. What was common only to France has now become common to most of Europe. The twentieth-century decline of both birth and death rates was notably less marked in France than in the remainder of the continent. In 1949, despite an unfavorable age distribution, France had a higher birth rate than any of her immediate neighbors with the single exception of Spain. For the first time France recorded a higher birth rate than Italy, which has been so long renowned as a country of large families.

Furthermore, if we compare the French population of 1950 with that of Germany as recorded in the 1946 census of that country (Fig-

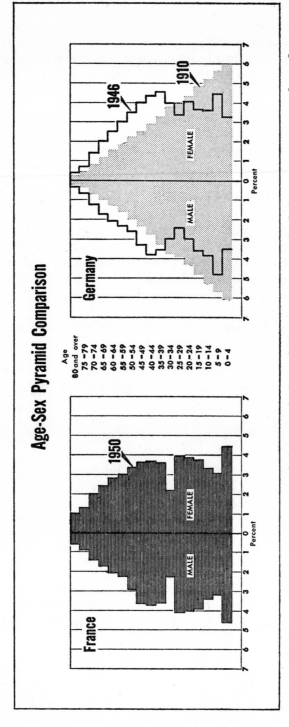

FIGURE 3. Age-sex structure of the population of France, 1950, and of Germany, 1910 and 1946

ure 3), it will be evident the extent to which French nonparticipation
in the more violent and bloody aspects of the conflict are reflected in
the lower war losses, in a lesser deficit of males, and in the healthy increase in the number of children which form the base of the population pyramid.

VI

From the vantage point of the United States and viewing France by
itself—France appears to be a rather densely populated country. She
is about four times as thickly populated in relation to area as is the
United States. At the French density of population the United States
would have to support some 600,000,000! Even at the same density in
relation to arable land, the United States could support close to 400,-
000,000. (See Table 3.) Viewed in reverse, the French population
would have to be reduced to about 16,000,000 to achieve the same
ratio of population to arable land as exists in the United States.

Table 3

RATIOS OF POPULATION TO ARABLE LAND, FRANCE AND SELECTED
COUNTRIES, 1948

COUNTRY	ARABLE LAND (000 hectares)	POPULATION (millions)	PER CAPITA hectares	acres
France	20,976	41.5	.5	1.2
Belgium	1,008	8.6	.1	.3
Germany *	13,686	68.3	.2	.5
Italy	16,986	45.7	.4	.9
United States	177,178	146.6	1.2	3.0

* Present de facto boundaries
Source: *Yearbook of Food and Agriculture Statistics, 1949*, Vol. I, Production (FAO,
1949).

The effects of population trends on economic prosperity are not
definitively known. Whether per capita output would be smaller or
larger at given population sizes is an academic question. Much more
important are the dynamic aspects of economic cycles and changes in
technology. Also, within broad limits, the direction and rate of population change may be more important than absolute population size.
France has already experienced cessation of population growth and
has already therefore felt its effects. Certainly there have been limited
opportunities for domestic investment. It is entirely possible that the
cessation of population growth is a partial explanation of the comparatively backward technology of the country. Certainly the biolog-

ical age of the population is a factor—this is strongly suggested by the fact that the most important new and rationalized industries were established after the First World War only with the help of young, mobile foreign labor.

The economic pros and cons of population growth are mixed. Population growth is some insurance against the direct impact of depressions, since a growing population means an expanding market and a minimum of risk to entrepreneurs. Furthermore, a growing population offers to entrepreneurs the possibility of increasing specialization with resultant saving in mass production for a mass market. On the other hand, rising standards of living have made the basic influence of the growing population of less importance. Variations in the value and pattern of per capita consumption are now quite as important as numbers of consumers. The further a standard of living rises above the purely biological necessities of existence, the larger is the proportion of consumption of luxury and semi-luxury goods and the less automatic will be the effect of population changes on the economy.

Viewing the economy of France by itself there would seem to be nothing catastrophic about a stationary or even a declining population. The most important consequences of depopulation are probably not the changes in absolute number but rather the inevitable consequence of a population heavily burdened with old people and older workers, with the rigidities and stagnation that the preponderance of such elements in the population strongly suggest.

But France does not exist in either an economic or a political vacuum. As the result of 150 years of differential growth the remainder of Europe is heavily populated as compared to France. In the European context France is a demographic vacuum, a state of affairs which has been intensified rather than reduced by the war. France was the only country west of the Iron Curtain with a smaller population at the end than at the beginning of the conflict. As a result of the great westward thrust of the Slavs, many millions of refugees were piled into Germany, Austria and, to a lesser extent, Italy. This great westward wave of refugees stopped at the borders of France, and only insignificant numbers of displaced persons and Germans have been admitted.

An examination of Table 3 will indicate the real pressures that exist from across the Rhine and across the Alps. France has better than one acre of arable land per person; Germany as a whole has one-half an acre per person, and the amount of land per person is still less in the industrial United Kingdom and United States Zones. Italy has only about three-fourths the acreage per person that France has, and as an average the cropland in Italy is inferior to that of France. Because

of population pressure Italians cultivate mountainsides and other
marginal lands that would not be cultivated in France. France has
even greater superiority in comparison with such heavily industrialized countries as the United Kingdom, Belgium, and the Netherlands,
which have derived much of their wealth from overseas commerce.

Because of her comparatively low population density and low economic productivity France faces dangers of persistent population
pressure on her borders. Because of her low industrial production she
is also not in a good position to defend her lands against crowded
neighbors. Regardless of economic considerations the French feel the
need of a larger population for political reasons. To the French the
problem is less a question of ends than of means.

VII

There are three ways of accelerating French population growth:
(1) by increasing the birth rate; (2) by reducing the death rate; (3) by
increased immigration.

The prospects for the first are not good. The family allowance system, now generally applied in France, probably has helped to raise
the birth rate and to check rapid recession to prewar levels. As noted
above, the French postwar birth rate has been maintained at a higher
level and has not fallen as much from postwar peaks as the birth rate
in neighboring countries.

But there are good reasons for predicting some recession from present levels. The abnormally large number of marriages in the first postwar years has resulted in catching up on marriages postponed from the
war and even the prewar period. The acute labor shortages and consequent economic security of employment may even have induced some
drawing on the future—that is, marriages may be taking place now
that would under more "normal" circumstances have been postponed.
In any event, the marriage rate in 1948 and 1949 fell very markedly
and is now approaching the prewar "normal." Since the rise of the
birth rate has been to an important extent the result of first births following marriages, it is obvious that there is now an important influence raising the birth rate that may shortly cease to operate. Unless
average family size in France becomes larger by virtue of an increased
number of second and third and further births the birth rate in France
will inevitably go down.

A further biological influence is the coming to the ages of maturity
of the age groups born in the depression, when the birth rate was falling very rapidly. In other words, the human capital of young adults
that produces most of the children will be declining in the next few

years. When all these factors are taken into consideration it seems most probable that the birth rate in France will decline somewhat from its comparatively high present level. At the same time it seems unlikely that, barring extensive unemployment, the birth rate will return to the low figures of the 1930's.

In France, more than in most Western countries, the reduction of deaths offers an important possibility of improving the vital balance. Attention in France has been called with humiliation to the fact that infant mortality in that generally advanced country is actually higher than among Negroes in the United States. It is estimated that the provision of an adequate and safe milk supply alone could result in the reduction of the infant mortality rate by half each year, with an annual saving of some 20,000 lives.

Another weak point in French mortality is the rather extraordinarily high mortality among adult males in the prime of life. Notable in this regard are the very high death rates from tuberculosis, among the highest of the civilized countries of the world. Interestingly enough, there has been some persistent agitation of a prohibitionist or a temperance nature deriving from the excessive mortality of adult males. Among French demographers there has been some tendency to ascribe this high death rate to "alcoholism," and articles on the high consumption of alcohol in France have found favor in recent years. Whatever the causes of the present situation, it is unquestionably true that a substantial saving of lives is possible in France, particularly among males. A successful effort in this regard would lengthen the working span and increase the health of older workers, upon whom France must inevitably rely.

However, savings of population resulting from a reduction of deaths in France, no matter how desirable from humanitarian and other considerations, cannot solve the French population problem. A maintenance of continued excess of births over deaths in the modern situation is more dependent upon the birth rate than upon the death rate. In the psychological and social climate of contemporary France it seems highly improbable that the present level of natural increase can be substantially raised. At the present time France is growing through natural increase at the rate of about .7 per cent per year. While this growth represents reassuring evidence of the French capacity for survival, it obviously will not change the basic demographic position of France in the immediate future. Present growth through an excess of births over deaths will not be reflected in a larger labor force until fifteen to twenty years hence.

If France is to experience truly rapid population growth she can obtain it from only one source: immigration. This was the French solution of the 1920's. But at that time France was able to draw recruits from all of Europe, from the countries of agricultural overpopulation in the East as well as from her neighbors of the West. It was possible to introduce mass migrants of rather pale political coloration, people who did not come as potential fifth columnists or as self-conscious bearers of national cultures. Today the Iron Curtain has shut off all mass migration on a voluntary basis to the West. The countries of Northern Europe, which might under different circumstances supply France with a technically capable and industrious group of immigrants, have themselves experienced major declines in birth rates and are themselves much concerned about maintaining or increasing the size of their populations.

The three major potential sources of population for France today are Germany, Italy, and Africa. Large German immigration is feared for political reasons. French attitudes even toward Italian immigration are generally negative. Despite Franco-Italian agreements with reference to immigration, only some 150,000 Italians have been admitted to France since the war, and the total balance of immigration has amounted to only about 100,000 a year—this in a period of acute labor shortage in France. Now, with some relaxation of the manpower shortage, conditions are much less favorable to mass immigration and there would seem to be a general acceptance in Europe of the difficulties of intra-European migration in the contemporary scene. The prospects for large scale immigration into France in particular are not very bright. In order to alter significantly her demographic position with reference to her neighbors France would have to accept really large numbers of immigrants: let us say, for example, 10 million Germans and Italians in the next few years. Given the existing political and social climate of Europe, peaceful migration on such a scale is unthinkable.

If we accept this conclusion we are driven to the further conclusion that demographic rearmament by itself is neither possible nor wise. France has shown an encouraging biological revival in the postwar period. If sustained, this revival promises in the course of time to establish a much more favorable population structure in France and to provide the economic and social benefits that a moderate population growth may provide in a country of reasonably adequate resources. It can furnish the human resource base for active participation and leadership in Western European affairs. But no foreseeable growth of the French population could furnish the demographic basis for the revival of French hegemony in Europe. Population and population growth are one of the primary factors of a nation's political and military power. The disadvantages at which France has operated vis-à-vis

Germany and other states during the past seventy years are likely to persist and hence to limit the revival of France as a great power. And, as is shown in Chapter 26, conditions in the French Empire are not favorable to any substantial drafts of manpower from French Africa for service in Europe or the Far East. As in 1914 and in 1939, France must stand or fall partly on her own efforts and partly upon the effective help she can receive from her allies.

19

++

FRENCH BUSINESS

AND THE BUSINESSMAN: A SOCIAL

AND CULTURAL ANALYSIS *

DAVID S. LANDES

++

WHEN the French Mission of the European Recovery Program totted up its results at the end of the first year of operation, the discovery was made that the contribution of so many new machines plus so many tons of coal and raw materials had not added up to the sum of products anticipated. This deficiency cropped up again and again in the case of firms which had apparently had the benefit of every facility and incentive to efficient production. And yet our economists and technicians had presumably taken into account all the variables involved. What was wrong?

It was soon clear that one very important element had been left out of the equation, the imponderable "human factor." The whole thing simply boiled down to this: given the same machines and the same funds as an American, the French businessman will not use them in the same way or for the same ends.[1]

* The argument and materials presented in this chapter are derived primarily from personal observation and conversation during nineteen months of study in Paris and the provinces. While this research was concerned with the role of the French businessman in the nineteenth century, it provided an unusual opportunity to meet some of the twentieth-century variety on a rather intimate and candid basis. I should like to take this occasion to express my thanks to the Sheldon Fund of Harvard University and to the Committee on Research in Economic History of the Social Science Research Council for the financial assistance that made this work possible.

[1] For the purpose of a brief comparison, the United States has seemed preferable to countries like Germany or England whose backgrounds are far more like that of France, precisely because the marked contrast is ideally suited to bring out the pattern of French business activity. Here, however, a word of caution is in order. If the over-all contrast is marked—although far from antithetical—the differences between France and the United

The peculiarity of the French entrepreneurial pattern, this problem of aims and attitudes, is by no means new from the point of view of historiography.[2] The French have long rather felt than understood it.[3] Foreign studies of the French society and economy have sometimes been aware of the problem to the extent of a few lines, or perhaps even several pages, which usually treat more of symptoms than of the disease.[4] And of course, there is always the convenient or, in all justice, the indispensable fare-thee-well that runs roughly, "But this consideration takes us beyond the scope of the present work . . . ," leaving the reader with some uncooked and well-nigh indigestible food for thought.

This is understandable. Subjects like this are somewhat disagreeable, for they lend themselves little, if at all, to a precise, statistical approach. Yet the significance of the "human factor" is such as to outweigh considerations of congeniality. As our government's representatives have empirically discovered, the effort to study it must be made. And while I do not think that a short essay of this nature can possibly do justice to so complicated a subject, a brief analysis of the role, actual and potential, of the French entrepreneur should prove enlightening and useful, if only for heuristic purposes.[5]

I

Consider first the structure of the firm, the fundamental unit of business activity. It is widely known, to the point of being almost a truism, that the typical French business is small.[6] What is less often

---

States, so far as the component elements of the pattern are concerned, are essentially a matter of degree. Two entirely unlike cakes may both contain milk; the point is, how much, and in combination with what other ingredients.

[2] For the assumptions underlying this humanistic interpretation of an economic problem, see T. Parsons, *The Structure of Social Action* (New York and London, 1936).

[3] During the nineteenth century, many French writers felt it necessary to point up the lack of initiative and enterprise of their own businessmen as against those of other countries. At first the paragon of entrepreneurial virtue was England, but the defeat of 1870 coupled with the remarkable industrialization of imperial Germany led to a whole literature of unfavorable comparisons of France with the Reich.

[4] Thus W. Sombart, *The Quintessence of Capitalism* (New York, 1915), pp. 136–40. cf. W. Bowden, M. Karpovich, and A. P. Usher, *An Economic History of Europe Since 1750* (New York, 1937), pp. 457 f.

[5] The briefness of this paper necessarily precludes an account of the regional and individual variations within the system to be described. The existence of such variations on a theme, as it were, by no means vitiates the theme. I cannot subscribe to any pluralistic interpretation of social behavior that implies that individual action is random, whether derived from some more or less whimsical soul within, or from a rationalistic reaction to personal problems taken *in vacuo*. Were individual behavior random in either sense, we might just as well throw the social sciences out the window.

[6] Perhaps the most convenient picture is given by P. George, "Étude statistique des dimensions des établissements industriels," in G. Dessus, P. George, and J. Weulersse,

realized is that most businesses are family-structured in a way that has generally been associated with precapitalist economies. They are inextricably united economically in the sense that business treasury and household purse are simply one, just as national treasuries were once inseparable from the king's personal fortune. In such a firm it is standard operating procedure for each of the partners and often all the relatives who so wish to leave their disposable funds with the business, just as Americans would deposit their money in a bank. An interest of 5 or 6 per cent is generally paid on these more or less current accounts, while the "depositors" pass by the cashier whenever they need money, even though it be only petty change to cover some daily expense. Each has his account book, duly kept up with all the other records by the apparently overworked accountant. In the nineteenth century, when the franc was still a franc, it was not unusual to draw eighty centimes for postage or ten francs for food, all carefully entered in the ledger. Nowadays, of course, the wife may take ten or twenty thousand francs for her week's expenditures, but the system remains the same.[7]

Such economic unity exists because of the profound social ties of family with firm. The latter is the material basis for the prestige and status of the former, just as the domain was the material foundation of status in an earlier age. The business is not an end in itself, nor is its purpose to be found in any such independent ideal as production or service. It exists by and for the family, and the honor, the reputation, the wealth of the one are the honor, wealth, and reputation of the other.[8] The word *maison* has retained business connotations long since lost by our word "house." It is this bond that accounts for the astonishing solidarity shown by French families when the integrity or the stability of the firm is imperiled; even today, the social register or

Matériaux pour une géographie volontaire de l'industrie française (Paris, 1949), pp. 129–43. One can only regret that more recent figures are not yet available to supplement the prewar censuses on which the article is based. For comparable statistics on American industry, see U.S. Dept. of Commerce, *Census of Manufactures*, "Wage Earners and Wages in Establishments Classified According to Number of Wage Earners: 1937" (offset, dated July 7, 1939), pp. 2–3.

[7] See on this point Max Weber, *General Economic History* (London, n.d.), pp. 226 ff., who implies that this unity, characteristic of European enterprise in the late medieval and early modern period—he cites the Medici as an example—disappears with further economic development and sophistication.

[8] Note in this connection the French attitude toward bankruptcy, which was long considered almost a hereditary stain on a family's reputation. The classical picture is given by Balzac in *Grandeur et décadence de César Birotteau*. In contrast, the American attitude has generally been one of tolerance, to the point where at certain times and in certain places, one or two failures have been looked on as an almost indispensable preliminary to a successful business career. On the contrast in this respect between the United States and Europe, especially England, see Gilbert Burck, "The American Genius for Bankruptcy," *Fortune*, XXXVII (April 1948), 130 ff.

family tree is often a better credit reference than the most profitable series of annual statements.[9]

To be sure, the industrial development of the past 150 years has inevitably affected the structure of business enterprise, giving rise to large, impersonal corporations in certain sectors of the economy, notably public utilities and heavy industries like metallurgy. But even in such fields, the role of the private firm remains impressive. Thus in the steel industry, where the requirements of production encourage, indeed impose, concentrations of capital beyond the means of most family fortunes, the largest company of all, Les Petits-Fils de François de Wendel, the biggest tool-maker, Peugeot, and perhaps the leading specialist in alloy steels, Holtzer, are all family businesses. And the greatest company of machine builders and engineers, Le Creusot, despite the fact that its shares are actively traded on the exchange, remains a partnership in which the active partners have been drawn for over one hundred years exclusively from the Schneider family. The very business form of which Le Creusot is one of the outstanding examples, the *commandite par actions,* is proof of the desire to get outside capital without yielding personal and family control and responsibility.[10] It should be noted, moreover, that the nationalization of the strongest groups of corporatively organized business—the big banks, the coal mines, gas and electricity, and the railroads—has cut down considerably that portion of the sector of free enterprise that falls outside the family-type firm.[11]

[9] This system of family effort and family rewards is only one aspect of a generalized group basis for status distinctions within French society as a whole. In other words, compared with the United States, for example, the position of the individual is less dependent on such things as personal activity or achievement than on the position of the kinship group. As a member of the *Académie Française* remarked of one of his colleagues, famous in a field even more honorific than business: "I sometimes wonder if the Prince de Broglie is more proud to be one of the world's great mathematicians and the winner of a Nobel prize, or simply a Broglie."

[10] The *commandite par actions* is a form of sleeping partnership whose distinguishing characteristic is the representation of ownership, as opposed to management, by stock negotiable in the market. The active partners, as might be expected, are in sole charge of operations and are liable to the full extent of their fortunes for any debts incurred by the company. This type of firm has also been popular in Germany, where it is known as a *Kommanditgesellschaft auf Aktien.* It is interesting to note that although the same form of business organization is provided for by statute in various states of the United States, it has to all intents and purposes never been used.

[11] According to the Ministère du Commerce et de l'Industrie, there were in France at the end of 1939, 151,044 partnerships of various types as against 43,078 corporations. (*Annuaire statistique,* 1946, résumé rétrospectif, p. 70.) cf. also for the trend, "Sociétés commerciales," *Larousse commercial,* p. 1196. As a point of comparison, there were in the United States in 1936, 530,779 corporations and 237,367 partnerships, with the former gaining every year. (U.S. Temporary National Economic Committee, *Verbatim Record of the Proceedings* [Washington: Bureau of National Affairs, 1939], I, Reference

338 DAVID S. LANDES

In such a system, the compulsive urge toward growth inherent in business for the sake of business is either diluted or absent. The family firm, large or small, is run like a household or, more specifically, a bourgeois household. The primary concern is to live well within one's means, saving as much as possible. Translated into business terms, the main objective is to avoid use of credit and to make the highest rate of profit possible on a given turnover; to amortize expenses rapidly and build up huge reserves; and to finance expansion out of such reserves, or by what the French call *auto-financement*.[12]

The retardative effect of this emphasis on conservation and consolidation is reinforced by an all-overriding concern for family independence. The French entrepreneur is inclined, if anything, to postpone possibilities for development, simply because expansion might sooner or later compel recourse to outside capital and seriously, if not definitively, compromise the exclusive character of the enterprise.[13] For the same reason, profits are often sacrificed to an over-integration extremely harmful to efficient production—the manufacturer does not like to rely on outside help or cooperation. The system of subcontractors and suppliers that creates in American industry a sort of division of labor on the factory level is still relatively neglected in France.

There is even a tendency in some cases to turn down chances for growth outright, on the theory that the firm is earning enough and that additional profits are not worth any additional effort. This particular variation, by no means uncommon, is quite alien to the thinking of most Americans, as indicated by the standard reaction of the tourist: "But don't they want to make money?" The answer is, of course, that they do, enough to give them what they want in life. "As for making money just to make money," says the pretty *charcutière*,

Data Section, p. 59.) Such figures, of course, can only give a two-dimensional picture, as it were. For the strategic importance of the corporation in France and its role in given sectors of the economy, see the *Annuaire Chaix* of the leading joint-stock companies. Note above all the limited number of such firms in manufacturing, especially in industries producing consumers' goods.

12 The semi-invisibility of this all-important form of capital formation has led analysts of the French investment picture either to neglect it entirely or to accord it short shrift in studies devoted almost exclusively to corporation finance and government investment. cf. the treatment of C. Bettelheim, *Bilan de l'économie française, 1919–1946* (Paris, 1947), pp. 113–17. And yet even in the case of corporations, self-financing has always played a more important role than the more obvious and measurable techniques of stock and bond issues.

13 It has long been a favorite sport of historians to whip the French banks for the inadequacy and parsimony of medium- and long-term credits to industry. To a certain extent such criticism is justified, but there is good reason to believe that the real culprit is industry itself, in that, at least until quite recently, no successful firm, hence no good risk, wanted any part of bank credit. This, of course, does not include the discount of short-term commercial paper.

"and giving yourself so much trouble that you have no time for pleasure later on, good heavens, I'd rather fold my arms . . . ." [14]

To be sure, the entrepreneurial pattern just described has its compensations. The French family firm, when successful, is, if I may be permitted two contrasting images, as solid as the rock precisely because it is almost drowned in its own liquidity. It can hold its prices and survive all but the most severe depressions, a fact reflected by the comparative flatness of the cyclical curve of French business activity. Throughout the nineteenth century, the literature abounds in references to France's good fortune in not being subject to the acute crises that periodically swept England and the United States.

Unfortunately, the knife cuts both ways, and this excessive prudence, this overwhelming concern with security, means less initiative and dynamism on the upswing. Confronted with an expanding economy, the French producer still does not go out and find or make new markets; he waits for them to come to him. Prior to 1914, this drawback was not nearly so critical as it proved to be later. Once the World War had permanently changed France's economic problem from one of conservation and leisurely growth to one of reconstruction and replacement, this lack of dynamism became a force for retardation and strangulation. This was the more true because the simultaneous collapse of the franc, after over one hundred years of stability, was utterly demoralizing in a society whose greatest economic virtue was thrift.

II

The survival and prosperity of the family type of enterprise imply in themselves a certain relationship between this traditional sector of the economy and the sector composed of corporations. The latter, generally possessed of superior financial resources and controlled by technicians whose kinship ties and family problems are totally divorced from the management of the firm, theoretically should long since have driven many of these obsolete family units from the field and forced the others to convert to forms better adapted to the needs of modern business.

Yet such has obviously not been the case. An analysis of business

[14] Émile Zola, *Le Ventre de Paris.* cf. also François Coppée's delightful poem, "Petit-Bourgeois." This subsistence production, as it might be called, is apparently equally alien to the thinking of most economists and economic historians, who continue to base their analyses on the classical assumption that the end of business enterprise is to maximize profit. And yet enough examples exist to the contrary in both advanced and primitive economies to indicate that the supposed rule is the exception, and that the famous diminishing returns embrace social and cultural considerations that often diminish far more rapidly than pecuniary ones.

concentration in France clearly reveals the coexistence within most industries of (1) a few powerful firms employing a substantial portion of the labor force, and a veritable swarm of small units often occupying well under half the total men in the field; and (2) a few modern regions characterized by bigger plants and more efficient techniques, and many more or less backward areas in which the small workshop and semi-artisanal methods still hold sway. This friendly cohabitation of lion and lamb suggests that these supposedly natural enemies have somehow found a remarkable *modus vivendi,* or—to put it into economic terms—that the time-honored mechanism of competition has been less than effective in France.[15]

The explanation of this *modus vivendi* must be sought in a combination of several factors. To begin with, the nature of the market accessible to the French producer is in many respects decidedly encouraging to small enterprise, and consequently limits severely the extent to which big business can throw its weight around. This market has always been relatively restricted to the home population, a population that to all intents and purposes has remained static for the past one hundred years. French businessmen are quick to remind critics that much of America's rapid economic development simply reflects the demands of a rapidly growing mass of consumers.[16] There is certainly justice in the argument, but even more important in the case is the pattern of consumption of the forty million people the French entrepreneur must satisfy.

In the first place, at least two important sections of the French population are not in a position to buy anything more than the barest essentials: (1) the vast majority of workers—industrial, commercial, and agricultural—who earn less than $40 a month in base pay [17]; and (2)

---

[15] See the above-cited article by George, "Études statistiques des dimensions des établissements industriels," pp. 113, 115, 116–18, 133, 135, and *passim.* George is especially struck by this co-existence of big and small in the metal-working industries, where one-third of the working force in 1936 was employed in plants of over 500 men (average 1,600), and one-third in a *"poussière de petits établissements"* of 10 to 25 men each. In seeking to explain this phenomenon, however, George offers another example of the economist apparently unable to free himself from the traditional assumptions, in this case that of more or less perfect competition.

[16] In the 150 years from 1800 to the present, the population of France has increased about 45 per cent, from 28,250,000 to about 41,000,000. That of the United States has jumped over 2,700 per cent, from 5,300,000 to almost 150,000,000. As for the French overseas territories, their role as an important outlet for French manufactured products still lies in the future. See preceding chapter by Dudley Kirk on population factors in modern France.

[17] This is supplemented by certain social security benefits, plus family allotments which in the last analysis barely keep a growing family from being swamped. On workers' wages and budgets, see the *Bulletin de la statistique générale de la France,* supplements of January–March and July–September, 1949. On p. 37 of the earlier number, there is a useful bibliography of similar surveys of family budgets. For more detailed

those self-supporting farmers whose small plots provide little surplus to exchange for manufactured goods.[18] In other words, those people who would unquestionably provide the best market for cheap, well made standardized articles, are largely unable to buy them.[19]

In the second place, the average Frenchman buys far less in proportion to his means than his American counterpart. Quantitative conspicuous consumption,[20] for example, is an anomaly in a country where taxation has always been calculated on the basis of *signes extérieurs de richesse*,[21] and where it is not uncommon to find a millionaire more or less comfortably ensconced in an apartment building or home of the most impressively unprepossessing appearance. Indeed, the waste characteristic of American life is by French standards almost immoral. No Frenchman will ever understand how an American can trade in last year's car simply to have a later model.

Moreover, the very idea of living standards governing expenditures, of borrowing against the future to obtain even such seminecessities as furniture, is heresy in a country where the proverb defines a man who makes $5,000 a year and spends $5,001 as poor, and one who makes $5,000 and spends $4,999 as rich. Nor should it be thought that this attitude is confined to those whose incomes permit the luxury of such abstinence and virtue. The worker who makes $35 a month is, if anything, more fearful of debt than the businessman earning ten times as much, as those enterprisers who have tried to introduce installment buying will testify.

Finally, it would be hard to overestimate the effect of the structure of retail trade in France. As is generally known, it is highly fragmented. On the one hand, there are generally far too many outlets for a given type of merchandise—the café is the best example. On the other, there is dispersion of what would form in this country the stock in trade of a single store—the American corner grocery or delicatessen

pictures of individual cases, which make up in human interest and insight what they lose in statistical objectivity, see Sherry Mangan, "French Worker," *Fortune*, xxxviii (December 1948), pp. 102 ff., and "Condition du salarié français," *Réalités* (January 1950), pp. 36 ff. The outstanding feature of all these budgets is the high percentage of income devoted simply to nourishment, and the correspondingly insignificant expenditures for manufactured articles.

[18] In 1931, of 2,421,933 exploitations in agriculture and forestry, 1,341,112 had no hired help. (*Annuaire statistique*, 1938, p. 103.) Few of these could have yielded much surplus revenue applicable to manufactured goods.

[19] In this regard, Italy furnishes a good example of such a situation carried to an exponential power, where there is not one market, but two, one handling extremely well made but costly articles for the "haves," the other purveying necessities like food and shoddy manufactured goods to the "have-not's."

[20] As we shall see below, conspicuous consumption exists in France, but it is oriented in a distinctly different direction from the American variety.

[21] Thus, for income-tax purposes, certain *"revenus forfaitaires"* have been established on the basis of real property, domestic personnel, automobiles, etc.

equals *épicerie* plus *crémerie* plus *charcuterie* plus *boulangerie*. In France the small shop fills a vital role: as a symbol of independence and the most convenient ladder between *peuple* and *petite bourgeoisie,* it is the great ambition of thousands of salaried proletarians. The mercery clerk, the butcher's assistant, the apprentice baker, even the great professional cyclist (who holds approximately the same place in France as an all-star outfielder here), all save toward the day when they can have their own *boutique,* with the husband to work and the wife to help with the counter and handle the cash drawer. *Le petit commerce* is thus an indispensable mechanism of social mobility, and hence, paradoxically enough, of social stability.[22]

This situation, however, has inevitably imposed higher costs of distribution, hence higher prices, on the French consumer, not only because of the inefficiency mechanically inherent in excessive dispersion, but at least equally because of the spirit of the sales process. The small shop in France is a sort of caricature of the family firm already described, with the objective of high profits on a limited turnover carried to an astonishing degree. There are haberdashers who try to live on the sale of three shirts a day, restaurants which serve six meals at noon. This effort to make a lot of a little is closely associated with a short-sighted philosophy of exchange wherein each transaction is considered a unique opportunity to make money. Take while the taking is good. The customer is not there to be served, cultivated, courted, persuaded to buy what he needs, and even more, what he should need or does not need. He is there on his own initiative to satisfy self-felt wants and should pay for this satisfaction as dearly as possible. He is simply a walking purse.[23]

It goes without saying that under such conditions, the techniques of creating a market are conspicuous by their absence. There is an art to selling, but the very word "merchandising" does not exist in French. Advertising is poor and limited in scope; price-leaders are nonexistent; sales, few and feeble. Confidence between buyer and seller is seriously compromised by the refusal of the latter to accept responsi-

[22] In the sense that a certain degree of fluidity is indispensable in any Western society, given the economic and social pressures of the present day. Because of this and other considerations—the shopkeepers in France have proved an exceptionally well organized and effective political force—the small merchant has generally been carefully protected by law against the incursions of such monopolistic phenomena as department, five-and-dime, and chain stores.

[23] Of course, the introduction of the fixed price sometime in the nineteenth century has imposed certain limitations on this silent warfare, although fixed prices are not nearly so universal as one might think, even in Paris. But the fixed price simply impersonalizes the relationship; the underlying conflict, the pattern of buyer vs. seller, remains the same.

bility for the quality of his merchandise—in case of dispute, the customer is always wrong. *Caveat emptor!*

This picture, to be sure, is unfair in the sense that it gives only the dominant pattern. It would require a long digression to analyze French retail trade in all its forms and nuances. There are certainly enterprising merchants who do not proceed in the typical fashion. The fact remains, however, that to an American accustomed to commerce as conducted in the United States, most French shops are a delightful or an exasperating anachronism, depending on one's mood or point of view. Even the Parisian department stores, which once pioneered modern sales techniques, not only in France but in the world —the Bon Marché was the first *grand magasin* of all—have sunk into an inertia that has chased thousands of customers back into the small specialty shops.[24]

This traditionalistic, habit-ridden, tight-fisted system of selling acts as an effective damper on the economy as a whole. The merchant who insists on exaggerated profit, who abuses the consumer in a sellers' market and would rather let his stock lie than take a loss and clear his shelves in a buyers' market, is the bane of the manufacturer.[25] It is surprising how quickly the clogging of this multitude of small outlets can back up the stream of merchandise until the very sources are dammed. Modern mass production demands turnover above all, and French retail trade turns very slowly.

III

Of course, in all fairness, the French merchant is up against a very difficult customer.[26] In this relationship of producer, middleman, and consumer, qualitative factors are just as important as quantitative ones: the French public not only buys less than the American; it buys quite differently.

[24] The following personal experience may be taken for what it is worth. I once had occasion to ask the director of one of the largest Parisian stores, which does little if any advertising, why this was the case. The answer was that advertising would be simply a waste of money. And to my question why this was so, he replied that he did not know, that he did not care to know, that he operated purely pragmatically, and that he was not interested in *why* things do or do not work, but simply *whether* they do or do not.

[25] This dogged refusal of the French merchant to sell at a loss was most intelligently exploited by the government in its recent campaign to drive down the price of gold. By simply refusing credit to tide retailers and wholesalers over a period of stagnation, the Ministère des Finances compelled them to liquidate stocks of gold and dollars hoarded during the war years and after. As a result, gold lost about 40 per cent of its value in the few months from January to May 1949.

[26] The interplay of these two factors, sales pattern and consumption pattern, is an excellent illustration of the inextricable concatenation of elements in a socio-economic problem of this type.

Most important in this respect is the simple fact that those people who are in a position to buy have never been completely willing to accept the standardization implicit in mass production.[27] There is no need to labor the French emphasis on individuality, especially in clothing, where the *couturière* is a sacred institution and even the poorest and most overworked housewife prefers to buy fabrics—which must themselves be something different—and sew her garments to her own taste. The French do not joke about the stock American situation of two women meeting at a party or dinner wearing the same dress; it is nothing to joke about.

As a result, the entire textile industry, which is still the most important in France in terms of labor employed, and wool and silk particularly, is compelled to distribute its efforts over a fantastic gamut of new designs and materials. These fabrics, often launched by fashion and decorating houses, compete from season to season on the highly fickle basis known as "*la mode.*" In such a situation, the advantage is all with the small firm. Everything is uncertain, and woe to the producer who places his trust in big factories and mass production. It is too easy to guess wrong and starve amidst the plenty of an unsold inventory. In other words, the sort of irrational structure found in the United States only in the higher reaches of the ladies' garment industry is characteristic in France of much of the manufacture of the cloth itself.[28]

Nor is this attitude limited to light, semi-durable products like textiles or leather goods which lend themselves to a certain amount of differentiation. As regards automobiles, for example, the reproach most frequently addressed to American cars is that they are all alike. From a person accustomed to choosing between front engines and rear engines, front-wheel drive and rear-wheel drive, among motors ranging from two to twenty-six fiscal horsepower, and a remarkable variety of body styles, such an observation is not surprising. The comment generally made when comparing the mass-produced Cadillac

[27] This discussion of the qualitative consumption pattern will necessarily emphasize the bourgeois classes of society. These are the people whose pecuniary means give them a semimonopoly of the market for non-necessities, and whose social prestige endows their taste and standards with a charisma which influences to a greater or lesser degree the standards of other sections of the population. As regards these other groups, the effect of their qualitative consumption patterns is obviously limited by their pocketbooks, or, in the case of certain well-to-do farmers, by a concentration of effort and wealth toward a goal of land ownership that drastically curtails purchases of manufactured consumers' goods.

[28] On the economic effects of our consumption pattern on the structure of the American garment industry, see "Adam Smith on Fifth Avenue," *Fortune*, xxxix (January 1949), 73 ff.

with the custom-built Delahaye which costs two to three times as much, is: "Not everybody can have your Delahaye." [29]

From one point of view, therefore, France has her conspicuous consumption, but it is fundamentally different from the American. In its stress on individuality, it is aristocratically directed toward a personalization of the relationship of producer and consumer. The former works not so much for a large, amorphous market, as for a specific client or clients. There is a hint of servitude in all this: this dress was made for *me;* this car was made to *my* taste.[30] As a result, a significant portion of French effective demand is oriented toward the products of artisanal and semi-artisanal as against mass-production industry.

As already implied, this notion of difference is closely related to one of quality, both presuming extra attention and effort. The ideal of quality is almost a fetish in France, and has always been greatly stressed as a sort of compensation for the inferiority of her techniques of mass production. So much so that business and social prestige depend on it to a significant degree, and French firms will perpetuate outmoded hand techniques in order to achieve utterly trivial gains in this regard. It is an important fact that throughout the history of the French textile industry, the coarser types of cloth, which would best lend themselves to efficient large-scale production, have always been left precisely to those backward centers in no position to take advantage of these possibilities. The prosperous districts of the North and Alsace have always concentrated their efforts on the middle and higher quality lines. One could even point to firms in these areas that made their success in some less expensive article, only to abandon it when the responsibilities of wealth demanded a shift to finer things.

Furthermore, the general standard of living in France—and this is true of all classes—is far more heavily biased in the direction of services than our own. For the American, such material comforts as good plumbing, electrical appliances, and even a car, are almost necessities; if not universal, they nevertheless represent idealized needs toward which people direct their efforts. In France, that part of the income left after provision for food, shelter, and clothing is channeled not so much into durable goods as into such things as vacations, domestic help, the café, and entertainment. Service and time are too cheap to make the Frenchman buy those machines and conveniences that would represent an important field of expansion for manufacturing

[29] There is, of course, a demand for American cars, although government restrictions make it impossible to say how strong or effective it is. It is generally accepted, however, that from the standpoint of originality and style, our big luxury models leave something to be desired.

[30] This analogy was suggested to the writer by Mr. Jesse R. Pitts of Harvard University.

industry.[31] Even in the case of such a necessity as clothing, the evidence tends to show that the Frenchman not only buys less than the American, but wants far less in proportion to income.[32]

IV

The influence of this pattern of consumption on the productive process, especially the emphasis on differentiation, is greatly intensified by the family structure of most firms as described above. Since one of the primary *raisons d'être* of such a business is its stability, the tendency is to put the eggs into as many baskets as possible by turning out an abnormally wide variety of goods.[33] The shoe manufacturer will make men's, women's, and children's footwear of all types. The textile producer will turn out all sorts of weaves and mixtures, often shifting so frequently that no one type is run long enough to yield any economy of factor costs.

It might be pointed out, moreover, that this excessively mixed output, which so seriously limits the possibilities of efficient mass production, is not characteristic only of the light industries producing consumers' goods for a differentiation-conscious market. Such considerations would hardly account for the output of one hundred types of rails, joists, plates, etc., by a given steel firm. Here—and this is the second factor involved in this *modus vivendi*—another phenomenon must be taken into account, the resemblance between the entrepreneurial techniques of the large, impersonal corporation and the mod-

[31] In point of fact, it is hard to say how much the preference for personal service owes to the relative cheapness of labor—the average *maîtresse de maison* considers $20 or $25 a month for a maid exorbitant—and how much to the prestige value of domestic personnel. The French attitude toward machinery in general is an excellent illustration of the conservative force of existing behavior patterns, of the natural congeniality of familiar ways. There are progressive housewives who have purchased such devices as pressure cookers or washing machines, only to find that they had to prepare the vegetables or do the wash themselves—the maid would have no part of such new-fangled gadgets. Similarly, many a businessman is convinced that no machine can possibly do a given industrial operation as well as the traditional hand methods. This attitude has played and still plays an important role in retarding mechanization in French industry.

[32] A recent survey of the market for textiles and clothing showed not only a remarkably low per-capita consumption of such goods, but—even more significant for our purposes —a general agreement on the part of those questioned that this low consumption was not the result of excessive prices. The only exception was sheets, where almost half felt that the cost was too high. "Une Enquête par sondage sur le marché des textiles," *Bulletin de la statistique générale de la France*, xxxvi (Supplement of July–September 1948), 250–62. It is worth noting in this respect that linen has always been considered in France a form of wealth, to be saved and passed on from one generation to another like silver and dinnerware, and hence possesses exceptional prestige value.

[33] This diversification of output in an effort to reduce risk should be carefully distinguished from the desire to guarantee independence by what is often excessive integration. See p. 338 above.

est family-based firm, to the point where one is sometimes tempted to describe the former as the latter writ large.

Nor is this surprising, when one recalls that all the normative standards of good management and successful operation are derived from traditions established when the family-structured firm was almost alone and unchallenged. For the one, as for the other, the virtues have always been prudence and a sense of proportion, and the end has remained security and solidity. From the start, the prosperous corporations have amortized assets as quickly as possible, often writing the largest items off to profit and loss, and hoarded enormous reserves against the day when a depression might make it necessary to compress sales far below the break-even point in order to maintain prices. Like the small partnership or individual firm, they have always used obsolete equipment side by side with the latest devices and warped their price structure to cover both.[34] And also like the former, their ultimate goal has been and is the highest *rate* of profit rather than the biggest profit.

To be sure, inflation and new taxes have compelled certain modifications. No firm writes its books as it did in the good old days, nor is it possible to build up cash reserves with what is still a weak currency. Such conditions, however, have only strengthened the pressures for extra-conservative management. More than ever, the French businessman wants security. He cannot hoard franc notes, but one of the biggest manufacturers in the field can still stock wood and coal stoves against future price rises at a time when the demand is insatiable. And if this expedient is closed to the weaver of wool or cotton, exposed as he is to frequent changes in fashion that might leave his stock worthless overnight, there are still ways and means to invest money in the colonies or abroad.[35]

V

Of course, everything is relative. It would be possible to point to similar signs in American business, a new concern with security, a

[34] This, of course, is true of American firms as well, though once again to a far smaller degree. The case comes to mind of a leading French steel producer who in 1929, if not later, was using, together with the most modern types of hydraulic press, water-driven tail hammers of the sort used in the fourteenth century. *Les Établissements Jacob Holtzer* (privately printed, n.d. [1929]).

[35] The colonies form a desirable field of action, not only because the rate of profit is likely to be higher in what is still an underexploited area, but also because the colonial franc, which is worth twice as much as the metropolitan franc, is considered a more solid currency. The ideal spot, of course, is Morocco, where the special commercial régime growing out of the nineteenth-century treaties of the Western powers with the local rulers has created a minor twentieth-century business paradise.

desire to play it safe and eliminate so far as possible the elements of risk and competition. But where, in our case, such policies represent a marked departure on the ideological level from the optimistically liberal economic doctrines that prevailed almost unchallenged only a generation ago, in France—and here we have the third major element in the accommodation of big and small enterprise—these policies are the logical continuation of centuries of entrepreneurial tradition. The concept of free enterprise as developed in the England of the nineteenth century and transplanted to the United States, with its postulate of a competitive struggle for markets and drastic penalties for failure, and with its emphasis on earning more and more through producing more and more for less and less, has never really been accepted in France. Instead France—the reference here is to the prevailing current of opinion—has continued to cherish the precapitalist ideology that underlay the guild organization of the pre-Revolutionary period. This ideology may be summed up briefly as follows: every man has his place in society, should produce enough goods and services of quality to maintain his place, and has a right to the living earned in this manner. In other words, the justification of survival lies not in the ability to make a profit, but in the correct performance of a social function. In the days of the guild system, these concepts were translated into concrete measures to establish the rules of correct performance and to restrict competition and undue growth on the part of overenterprising producers. These measures, of course, were formally abolished during the Revolution,[36] but the ideas behind them proved less vulnerable to legislation and decree. One little story may well convey the idea better than a dozen paragraphs. An executive of one of the leading textile firms in France—Dollfuss, Mieg, et Cie, the internationally known DMC—discussing the consideration and respect generally accorded the successful businessman in American society, had only one comment to make: "Do you mean to tell me that you can respect a man who has become wealthy through the ruin of a dozen or more competitors? Such a man is a menace to society."

The result of this "sanction pattern" has been to create an environment hostile to the development of a capitalistic business structure. But more important for our present purpose, it has formed to a significant degree the mind of the businessman himself, who has never fully accepted the principles of risk and competition that are at the root of a free-enterprise system as we understand it. As regards risk, there is no need to elaborate here on the oft-criticized French dependence on government protection and help, which, in its almost infantile presumption of social responsibility for the prosperity of the indi-

[36] Laws of March 2–17 and June 14, 1791.

vidual firm, is to be carefully distinguished from the predatory attitude so often characteristic of American enterprise. As for competition, one of France's largest steel manufacturers, asked why no one
there had established a continuous strip mill in the 1930's, when the
new technique was revolutionizing the production of sheet steel in
the United States, replied briefly and to the point: "It would have
been pretty expensive, to begin with; but even if the money had been
available, the creation of such a mill would have entailed the closing
of most of the plants producing sheet steel by the old system. The
public would not have stood for it, the government would not have
stood for it, and that sort of thing just isn't done in French business."

Under the circumstances, it is easier for big business to live and let
live, even to protect the small, marginal producer. In the protected,
comparatively noncompetitive domestic market, it is the latter that
sets the prices, prices which are necessarily especially favorable to the
more efficient units. The same consideration holds true for those foreign firms operating in France whose resources might permit them, if
they so desired, to destroy home competition. Here, moreover, the
normal pattern is reinforced by political considerations, since the
government and the people are even less likely to accept such a monopoly in the hands of foreign capital. It is this consideration that explains a recent reference in *Le Monde* to the "sportsmanlike" behavior of Unilever in the French soap market,[37] and the policies of
such companies as Ford or Standard Oil and Shell.[38]

Here a word of caution is in order. I would not give the impression
in all this that France has never produced businessmen who in imagination and spirit of enterprise bear comparison with the greatest of
our so-called "robber barons." A mere list of names like Péreire, Tala-
bot, Schneider, Boucicaut, Révillon, and more recently, Michelin,
Renault, Citroën, Coty, and Boussac is enough to show the absurdity
of such an argument. France has always produced pioneers, but as one
observer wrote, she has an equally extraordinary talent for putting
such men in their place.[39] The point is, the innovator may innovate
all he wants. He may build great factories, install whirring machines,
turn out standardized goods, introduce new techniques of distribution. But he must not upset the applecart of vested interests. For controlling or rebuking those who refuse to abide by this simple rule,

[37] *Le Monde,* December 25–26, 1949, p. 6.

[38] It goes without saying that the above paragraph is not meant to imply that failure
and bankruptcy are unknown in French business life. There is such a thing as being too
marginal. Once again, it is a question of degree, the tolerance here being far greater
than in more competitive economies.

[39] A. Mayer, *La Crise de la structure de la société française* (offprint from *The French
Review,* New York, 1942).

there are ways and means. In the nineteenth century, the Péreire brothers were the most famous victims.[40] In this century, the best example is probably André Citroën. And in those fields like retail trade, where the powers-that-be are too fragmented to furnish any real resistance on an economic level, political pressure is at least as effective.[41]

This *modus vivendi*, this compromise between big and small, modern and traditional, has been and is a crucial factor in France's economic evolution. For not only does it create a superficially Alice-in-Wonderland situation in which the laggards more or less set the pace,[42] but in the last analysis, it places a premium on cautious and conservative as against daring and innovative enterprise by giving all the chances of survival to the former. Why take risks and make money faster, when you can follow at a safe distance, earn less to be sure, but still be there when the front runners have long since faded? "You see, cher Maître," says Larsonneau to Saccard, "you're very good when it comes to making it rain gold pieces, but you don't know how to pick them up." [43] It is no coincidence that most of the key positions in French economic life are held today by a small group, most of whom laid the foundations of their fortunes a century or more ago and have nursed them carefully and discreetly ever since—this through a period of unprecedented political, economic, and technological change.

VI

Given this human factor and its inhibitive influence on economic development, what, then, are the prospects for future improvement? Much, of course, can be done within the entrepreneurial pattern described. A recent, unpublished survey by representatives of our own Bureau of Labor Statistics indicates that an appreciable increase of

40 cf. my article on "French Entrepreneurship and Industrial Growth in the Nineteenth Century," *Journal of Economic History*, IX (1949), 52 and n. 13.

41 As already indicated, the primary purpose of this paper is to present the dominant pattern of entrepreneurial behavior in France, without undue attention to the "but's" and "however's." It would be worse than unfair, however, to give the picture of a stagnant economy totally unleavened by the ferment of innovation. The point is that French business is far from unchanging, as the above paragraph hints only too briefly, but that it proceeds according to certain rules more conservative than those of other societies in Western Europe. Every society, indeed every social or professional group, has such rules and regulations, and all have more or less effective ways and means to penalize nonconformists.

42 Superficially, in that this situation is and always has been much more common than Americans, with their orientation of free enterprise and their big business economy, tend to think. Other European economies than the French could yield even more marked examples.

43 Émile Zola, *La Curée.*

productivity could be achieved with a minimum of expenditure simply by reorganizing production so as to eliminate waste motion and time. Such waste is in itself largely a reflection of the lack of competitive pressure, but since its removal is to some degree a question of education, and since it will not hit the businessman too hard in his most sensitive point, his pocketbook, much may yet be accomplished along these lines.[44]

As for changing the fundamental pattern, that is another story. The destruction of two wars, the inflation of the past thirty-five years, and the great depression of the 1930's with its sequel of labor discontent and political instability, have if anything intensified the quest for security. Where once gentlemen's agreements more than sufficed, cartels and *syndicats* have made their appearance and, what is more, with popular and governmental blessing. French capital, labor, and government—for a desire to increase productivity does not necessarily imply a desire to increase output—are all generally committed today to a neo-Malthusianism that prefers to limit production and spread the profits and work. The businessman wants to make sure of his market; the worker wants to make sure of his job; the government wants to make sure of its votes.[45]

This new effort on the part of the entrepreneur to formalize the live-and-let-live pattern has received its most important expression in the Conseil National du Patronat, the French equivalent of the American National Association of Manufacturers. The primary aim of this organization is to establish a system of interprofessional local committees and intra-professional *syndicats* that are essentially eighteenth-century guilds in twentieth-century dress. Such groups, of course, would make some important contributions to the improvement of French industrial and business procedures. They would disseminate technical information, promote research, study foreign methods and pass the findings on to French manufacturers, regroup production so as to eliminate some of the excessive product-mix described above. They have appointed a committee on productivity to tackle this crucial problem from the employers' point of view. But all these accessory objectives will not conceal the primary aim of assign-

[44] In this connection, the worker is apt to prove a far more serious obstacle than the employer. It should be remembered that the introduction of time and motion programs, while superficially easy, involves the creation of a discipline utterly alien at present to the mentality of most French labor.

[45] In a recent analysis of the projected French antitrust law, soon to be proposed largely at American behest, M. Robert Buron, Secrétaire d'État aux Affaires économiques and head of the government office charged with preparing the measure, differentiated between good and bad agreements (*ententes*) on the following basis: "the good being those which lighten the task of the owners of small and medium enterprises." *Le Monde,* February 1, 1950, p. 4.

ing quotas and markets in such a way as to provide security for all but the most inept units.[46]

In answer to the objections and fears of American representatives on this score—and one of the major purposes of our European aid program is to eliminate just that sort of thing—M. Georges Villiers, president of the Conseil National du Patronat, points to the social upheaval that would probably result from an all-out competitive shakedown of the type logically implied by our conception of free enterprise. Probably he is right. If the hand of big business were really forced, the carnage would be sad to behold.

In the last analysis, whether or not the CNP succeeds in organizing a businessman who is notoriously averse to formal organization, especially in those fields where the family firm predominates, the traditional entrepreneurial pattern will continue to prevail in more or less undiluted form. For what is involved is a whole way of life, the values and standards of a people, a way of life embodied in the word *civilisation*. The Frenchman can and does point with pride to those traditions of leisure and quality, of individuality and taste, to that *goût*, that *raffinement* inseparably connected with an economic system as yet unperverted by mass production and standardization. Can the one be changed without sacrificing the other? After all, it takes all kinds to make the world, and it has yet to be proved that a world formed in the image of the United States would be an improvement.

The only difficulty is that this is a very hard world, and that those finer things that are the pride of France and French civilization unfortunately weigh little in the balance of power. France—and this is the heart of the matter—had neatly solved prior to 1914 the conflict between old and new, between the traditions and norms of an aristocratic culture and a petty-bourgeois economy and the iconoclastic energy of modern industrial capitalism, by the *modus vivendi* which it has been the aim of this paper to describe.[47] The only exception, and a most important one, was the increasing conflict between a new proletariat and the rest of society, but even this might well have been resolved and the worker integrated in the whole had France been able

[46] On the ideological background of this corporative movement and its development since the First World War, see G. Pirou, *Essais sur le corporatisme* (Paris, 1938); O. de Magondeaux, *Les Ententes industrielles obligatoires et le corporatisme en France* (Paris, 1937); and especially, A. Piettre, *L'Évolution des ententes industrielles en France depuis la crise* (Paris, 1936). For a good statement of the businessman's point of view, see H. L. Dubly, *Vers un ordre économique et social: Eugène Mathon, 1860–1935* (Paris, privately printed, 1946). Mathon was an outstanding textile manufacturer in a city of outstanding textile manufacturers, Roubaix.

[47] cf. John E. Sawyer, "Strains in the Social Structure of Modern France," elsewhere in this volume. This suggestive chapter provides an institutional frame of reference for further research in French economic and social history.

to work out its problems in some sort of splendid isolation—in other words, had France had time.

This, of course, was impossible. The development of the Industrial Revolution in the rest of the world, the rise of modern Germany, the growth of a politically conscious labor movement of an international character, and most recently, the nightmarish upsurge of a Communist Russia, all these have brutally posed the incompatibility of *la doulce France* with a new iron age, of aristocratic culture and petty-bourgeois values within, with industrial capitalism without. In a new atomic world, time is the most strictly rationed commodity of all. Thus the urgent, the critical dilemma hangs over France today: To change and, in changing, die; or not to change, and risk a swifter death.

20

THE FRENCH EXPERIMENT

IN NATIONALIZATION, 1944–1950

DAVID H. PINKNEY

"NATIONALIZATION" was a popular word in France in the months following the Liberation. The Resistance organizations, the three major parties, several smaller parties, and the labor federations were energetically supporting a broad program of nationalization of key industries and credit. Even General de Gaulle himself endorsed their demands. Only a small group of conservatives dared to oppose openly so popular a reform, and they were powerless to stop the momentum of the movement.

Unlike the nationalization proposals of the Popular Front in the 1930's, which were aimed merely at remedying certain specific abuses, this program was intended to effect basic reforms in the economic structure of the country. It would create in the national economy a large sector of public ownership, and the publicly owned basic industries and big banks would, it was claimed, serve as "levers of command" by which the government might direct the whole economy in the public interest. Private economic interests, particularly in banking and heavy industry, that had in the past infringed upon the state's freedom of decision would be deprived of power to put pressure upon the government.

The advocates of nationalization also expected the program to bring important direct benefits to France. It would assure the mobilization of sufficient capital to finance, and the will and energy to carry out, the immense program of postwar reconstruction and reequipment of French industry. The national companies, freed from the need to make profits for private owners, would be able to give satisfaction to workers through higher wages, as well as through a share in management, and still charge lower prices to consumers.

Before the election of a national assembly General de Gaulle refused to sanction any but a few emergency and provisional nationalization measures, and action on the program of the Resistance and the parties was left to the Constituent Assembly. Although it did not enact this entire program, the First Constituent Assembly did effect a revolution in the ownership and direction of French industry and banking. By the passage of four sweeping laws it transferred to the state the ownership of the Bank of France and the four largest deposit banks, the thirty-four largest insurance companies (which did three-fourths of the nation's insurance business), the electricity and gas industries, and the coal mines. All the laws were passed by overwhelming majorities, the opposition never being able to muster more than some sixty votes. The banks and the insurance companies retained their corporate identities, with the state as the sole stockholder, but the private coal and public utility concerns were dissolved and their holdings taken over by new, nationwide companies in both industries. Direction of the national enterprises was vested in boards of directors composed of representatives of the state, the personnel, and the consumers.[1]

In the three years following the passage of the series of major laws, enthusiasm for nationalization declined. Waning enthusiasm was first evident in the virtual stoppage in the summer of 1946 of further nationalization, although only about half of the program endorsed by the Resistance movement and the principal parties in 1944 and 1945 had been realized. The Second Constituent Assembly, sitting from June to October 1946, considered no additional major nationalization laws, and the Minister of Finance, Robert Schuman, declared in July that it was correct to speak of a "pause" in the movement.[2] That pause has now continued for more than three years. Successive governments and the parties have introduced bills which would nationalize the iron and steel industry, the merchant marine, the chemical industry, radio and television, the Berliet automobile company, civil aviation, and Parisian passenger transportation, but only the proposal on Parisian transportation has been adopted, and it was comparable neither in form nor in purpose to the laws passed by the First Constituent Assembly. The government's proposal to create a national company, Air-

[1] See David H. Pinkney, "The Nationalization of Key Industries and Credit in France after the Liberation," *Political Science Quarterly*, LXII (September 1947), 368–80.

[2] The Second Constituent Assembly did create the Société Nationale de Vente des Surplus, but it was a company organized to meet a particular emergency and its duration was limited to three years. See the Law of August 24, 1946, *Journal officiel de la République française* (hereafter referred to as *J. O.*), *Lois et décrets* . . . , 78e année (August 25, 1946), pp. 7407–8.

France, to hold and operate the airlines taken over from private owners by De Gaulle's government, was rejected in January 1948 by the National Assembly, and in place of a purely public enterprise the Assembly established a company in which the government holds a majority of voting shares but in which private capital may be invested and enjoy representation on the board of directors.[3] The two major maritime shipping companies, the Compagnie des Messageries Maritimes and the Compagnie Générale Transatlantique, were reorganized in 1948 in the same form, despite the protests of the Communists and the Socialists, who favored outright nationalization.[4]

The reaction has not been confined, however, to termination of the powerful nationalization movement of the immediate post-Liberation years. The national companies already in existence have been the object of criticism so severe and so prolonged that the Communists and even members of the Third Force governments have denounced a systematic campaign to discredit all nationalization and to bring about the return of the nationalized industries to private ownership. Actually, denationalization has never been seriously considered by the Assembly nor by any major party, but with the exception of the Régie Renault (the national automobile company) [5] and the banks and insurance companies none of the major national enterprises has escaped almost incessant criticism over the past three years.

These attacks have centered largely on failures in production, financial mismanagement, and failure to solve administrative difficulties, particularly the problems of bureaucratic and political interference in direction. They raise doubts of the wisdom of passing the nationalization laws in the unsettled months after the Liberation. The nationalizations, intended to promote the economic and political recovery of France, may, in fact, have created obstacles to it by saddling the national budget with the operating deficits of the national companies, burdening the government with tremendous new administrative difficulties, and giving the Third Force coalition an additional point of political vulnerability. Some of the criticism raises doubts of the ultimate success of nationalization of industry at any time.

---

[3] Law of June 16, 1948, *J.O., Lois,* 80e année (June 17, 1948), pp. 5863–64.

[4] Law of February 28, 1948, *J.O., Lois,* 80e année (February 29, 1948), pp. 2122–25.

[5] The Régie Nationale des Usines Renault was created by the Ordinance of January 16, 1945, to hold and operate the plants of the Société Anonyme des Usines Renault, the largest automobile company in France. They had been confiscated by the Provisional Government in the autumn of 1944 following the death of their principal owner, Louis Renault. At the time of his death he was awaiting trial for "intelligence with the enemy" during the Occupation, and his company had already been seized by the government and placed under a provisional administrator.

II

An inquiry into the validity of these criticisms should consider the actual records of the companies in the three fields in which criticism has been concentrated: production, finance, and administration. Here the inquiry will be confined largely to the major national companies created by the First Constituent Assembly that have been most severely criticized, namely, Electricité de France, Gaz de France, and the Charbonnages de France and its operating subsidiaries (the *houillères de bassin*) in the various coal basins, and to the national aeronautical companies.[6] The latter companies, with the exception of the Société Nationale d'Etudes et de Construction de Moteurs d'Aviation (hereafter referred to by its initials, SNECMA), the former Société Anonyme des Moteurs Gnome et Rhône, were not creations of the Fourth Republic but of the Popular Front. They are included here because the discussion of their shortcomings produced some of the most virulent attacks on the whole nationalization program since the Liberation.

In the field of production the critics have accused the national companies of having failed to satisfy the demand for their goods or services and of producing at excessively high cost. Each charge contains a measure of truth, but with the exception of the aircraft and aircraft engine plants the national companies have made a commendable record of production, and quantitatively the production of coal and electricity has been impressive.

The production of coal from the mines transferred to the subsidiaries of the Charbonnages was raised from 33,500,000 tons in 1945 to 47,400,000 in 1946—700,000 tons more than in the last prewar year. In 1947 and 1948 it dropped below the level of 1938, owing in part to the loss of output through strikes in those years, but preliminary reports for 1949 indicated production of about 51,000,000 tons in that year, only two million tons below the record levels established in 1929 and 1930 and well above the level of the immediate prewar years.[7] The rapid recovery in production was achieved by an increase in the number of miners, the approximation in 1947 of the output of 1938 being the work of a labor force in the mines some 40 per cent

[6] For a discussion of the operation of the nationalized banks and of the institutions established by the First Constituent Assembly for the control of banking and credit, see Margaret G. Myers, "The Nationalization of Banks in France," *Political Science Quarterly*, LXIV (June 1949), 189–210.

[7] The nationalized mines produce about 96 per cent of the coal mined in France, the remainder being produced by mining companies of "secondary importance" that were not nationalized. The production figures given in this paragraph are for the output of the nationalized mines only, and they are, consequently, smaller than the more commonly quoted figures on the total output of coal in France.

larger. The average daily production per miner, which had been 1,227 kilograms in 1938, was only 936 in 1946 and 959 in 1947. The nationalized mines have been repeatedly denounced for the inefficiency witnessed by these figures, but the management deliberately sacrificed individual efficiency to the pressing need for coal. In the postwar years the Charbonnages de France and its subsidiaries were charged with breaking the most serious bottleneck to French recovery, the shortage of coal, and they took the only course then possible to increase the supply immediately, the introduction of more workers into the mines, many of them necessarily with insufficient skill or training for their tasks. Later, as new machinery was installed, discipline improved, absenteeism was reduced, the number of workers was cut, and output per man rose, the increase being particularly noticeable after the strikes of 1948. It exceeded 1,000 kilograms in December 1948, stood at 1,127 in December 1949, and reached 1,198 in June 1950.

Within the framework of the Monnet Plan, the Charbonnages and its subsidiaries are engaged in an expansion program that includes not only increases in output but better utilization than hitherto possible of lower grades of coal. Annual production is to be raised to 60 million tons annually by 1952, and special efforts are being made to utilize the immense coal reserves in Lorraine. An especially significant experiment is the construction by the Charbonnages of a coke oven at Marienau, Department of the Moselle, in an attempt to apply commercially certain newly devised methods for the production of coke suitable for use in the iron and steel industry from combinations of Lorraine coals, heretofore useless in iron production. If successful, this process could free the Lorraine iron-ore fields from dependence on German coal.

The failure of the electric power industry to meet the demand for power is unquestioned, and the cuts in electric service each winter since the war have proclaimed the failure to almost every Frenchman. The shortage is the consequence, however, not of any failure of the Electricité de France to maintain the productivity of the prewar, private utility industry, but of the rapid increase in demand, aggravated by coal strikes in 1947 and 1948 and by exceptionally dry weather which interfered with hydroelectric generation in 1948 and 1949. In 1938 France consumed 19 billion kilowatt-hours of electricity; in 1947 the figure was 26 billions, and in 1948 it was 28½ billions. During the years of the war and the Occupation the industry's plant was not expanded, and Electricité de France has been faced not only with meeting current increases in consumption but also with making up for the accumulated discrepancy between capacity and demand. Despite the obstacles raised by shortages of coal, of equipment, and even of rainfall, the new national company has increased its production from 16 billion kilowatt-hours in 1946 to nearly 20 billions in 1948. It is, together with other producers, carrying out a vast program of expansion to raise the productive capacity of the whole industry, in which Electricité de France accounts for two-thirds of the production, to 40 billion kilowatt-hours in 1952–1953.[8]

The record of Gaz de France is similar. The demand for gas increased more rapidly than capacity to supply it, but the new national company has increased production. In 1938 the gas industry sold 1,700,000,000 cubic meters of gas. The sales of Gaz de France, adjusted to equal calorific content, were 2,253,000,000 cubic meters in 1947, and 2,400,000,000 in 1948—41 per cent more than in 1938. The company has, moreover, invested 4 billion francs in new equipment in the three-year period 1946–1948, and plans to invest 37 billion francs in the succeeding four years. The completion of the program will raise the productive capacity of the concern to 2,800,000,000 cubic meters in 1952.

The only damaging record in production is that of the national aeronautical industry. Although it is not true, as some critics implied, that since the war the industry has not turned out a single plane capable of leaving the ground, it has failed to produce planes and motors satisfactory in quality or quantity. A government commission which investigated the industry in the spring of 1947 reported that some 2,000 planes had been produced since the war, and more than one-half of them were not capable of normal and regular use, many of them being grounded because of structural defects. Even the usable portion was made up of outdated models, inferior to those which could be purchased abroad. The production of aircraft engines has been no more satisfactory. This record, which stimulated the most heated debate on nationalization in the Assembly since the Liberation, is attributable in part to low productivity and inferior workmanship, and in the cases of SNECMA and the Société Nationale de Constructions Aéronautiques du Sud-est to incompetent management. National ownership cannot be blamed, however, for the same difficulties have plagued the private sector of the industry. The ultimate source of the trouble was the dislocation of the industry, already in difficulties before the war, by four years of occupation—when only German planes and parts were built and when experiment and study of new types of planes and motors were stopped—and the failure of

8 Electric power plants belonging to the Société Nationale des Chemins de Fer Français, the Compagnie Nationale du Rhône, and the iron and steel industry were not transferred to Electricité de France.

the government in the postwar years to adopt a long-term plan for aviation. Since the government is the industry's principal customer, its failure to adopt a definite plan has forced the companies into ill-conceived programs of study of new types, and pending the determination of government policy and the completion of new models they have attempted to keep their personnel together and their plants operating by building older types of planes.

The reports of two investigating commissions and the parliamentary debates on SNECMA and on the aircraft plants have made the government and the Assembly well aware not only of the difficulties of the aeronautical industry but also of the fundamental causes of those difficulties. In July 1948 the Assembly placed SNECMA under an emergency administrator charged with reorganizing the company,[9] and a year later it passed a law on the reorganization of the whole national aeronautical industry requiring the government to prepare and present to the Assembly a five-year plan of aircraft construction and to follow it with a proposal for reorganization of the industry in coordination with this plan.[10]

III

The precise financial condition of the national companies is virtually impossible to determine. When the Accounting Commission for the Public Enterprises undertook in 1948 to examine the books of the companies, it found that delays in adopting standardized accounting procedures and in fixing the value of expropriated property made the preparation of definitive statements of financial condition impractical.[11] Nevertheless, the report of that commission does confirm that certain of the companies have been operating at a loss. Deficits can be sensationally publicized, and they have figured largely in the attack on the national companies. In fact, the financial records have

[9] Law of July 2, 1948, *J.O., Lois,* 80e année (July 3, 1948), pp. 6450–51.

[10] Law of August 2, 1949, *J.O., Lois,* 81e année (August 4, 1949), pp. 7615–16.

[11] The Commission de Vérification des Comptes des Entreprises Publiques was created by Article 58 of the Fiscal Law of January 6, 1948 (*J.O., Lois,* 80e année [January 7, 1948], pp. 199–208). It is charged with investigating not only financial accounts but also management, production records, and labor relations of the nationalized enterprises and of companies in which the state holds only a partial financial interest. A report on its findings is to be submitted annually to the National Assembly, to the Prime Minister, and to the Cour des Comptes. Its first annual report, dated July 6–7, 1949, was published in the *J.O., Annexe administrative* (August 21, 1949), pp. 369–86.

The creation of the commission reflected the conviction frequently expressed by deputies that the National Assembly was inadequately informed of the operations of the companies it had created. The Chambre des Comptes authorized by the Constituent Assembly in the laws nationalizing the electricity and gas industries and the coal mines to supervise and report on companies in those industries never actually functioned, and the Law of January 6, 1948, formally abolished it.

appeared to be the most vulnerable spot in the whole nationalization experiment.

The Charbonnages de France, Gaz de France, and SNECMA have run up large operating deficits. The Accounting Commission did not even attempt to estimate the operating losses of the Charbonnages and its subsidiaries, but the subsidies paid by the government in 1946 and in 1947 suggest their magnitude. For the second half of 1946 the state paid the national mines a subsidy of nearly 6 billion francs and in 1947 22 billions. In December 1948 M. Queuille told the Assembly that the operating deficit in 1948 would amount to 20 billion francs, and he estimated operating losses in 1949 of about 9 billion francs. Increased productivity may have cut the latter figure considerably, but the Accounting Commission reported that the management had been making inadequate allowance for depreciation, and if the depreciation account were properly increased the operating losses would be larger than officially estimated.

Gaz de France has also operated at a loss every year since its organization in 1946: 8 billion francs in 1946–1947, 10 billions in 1948 (excluding amortization charges), and an expected 20 billions in 1949. The government was obliged to pay the company subsidies of 5 billion francs in 1948 and 8 billions in 1949.

Operating deficits are likely for public utilities, whether publicly or privately owned, in periods of inflation such as France has experienced since the war, for authorization to raise rates ordinarily lags behind increases in costs. The losses of the Gaz de France were the result largely of the government's decision to keep the selling price of gas below the cost of production. In the spring of 1949, for example, the selling price was 8.1 times the price in 1938, while the cost of coal was up 23 times, other component materials 21 times, and labor 11 times. The selling price of coal was also fixed somewhat below the cost of production, but the Accounting Commission believed that reasonable improvement in productivity of labor could close the gap. It entertained no such hope for the gas industry.

In 1948 SNECMA was amassing operating losses at the rate of 79 million francs a month, and by the end of July its accumulated losses reached nearly 1½ billion francs, exceeding its combined capital and reserves. In May and June, 1948, it had to have emergency advances from the state to meet its payrolls. The special administrator placed over the company by the Law of July 2, 1948, overhauled its finances, and in his second quarterly report, in March 1949, he stated that current operating losses had been eliminated and that a forthcoming balance sheet was expected to show a small profit on operations since July.

The conspicuous operating losses of the Charbonnages, Gaz de France, and SNECMA have been publicized by the opponents of nationalization and have obscured the more successful operations of other national companies. Electricité de France had an initial operating deficit of 7 billion francs in the first year and a half of its existence, but since then it has covered all costs of operations, depreciation, and amortization. Each of the four nationalized deposit banks reported a profit for 1946, 1947, and 1948, and except in 1947 the Régie Renault has earned a profit each year since its establishment in 1944.

Another source of financial difficulties for a number of national enterprises has been a shortage of working capital. Unable to increase capital by issuing stock, the two utility companies and the coal companies have had to borrow in order to carry on current operations as well as to finance their expansion programs. In the postwar inflationary period the market for long-term bonds has been limited, especially for the bonds of the national concerns, which are suspect among investors, and the companies have been forced to contract with banks for short-term or medium-term loans. In March 1949 the operating subsidiaries of the Charbonnages had short-term or medium-term bank credits of 23½ billion francs, and Electricité de France and Gaz de France a total of 41½ billions. The repayment of these loans has been a constant preoccupation. The aeronautical companies have had similar difficulties. The Société Nationale de Constructions Aéronautiques du Sud-ouest, for example, was organized before the war with a working capital that was inadequate even then, being sufficient to cover expenditures for only three months, and it was not increased, despite the subsequent inflation. Since the war the company has been paying about 100 million francs in interest annually to government lending agencies from which it has been forced to borrow to finance day-to-day operations.

Progress is being made toward the solution of these difficulties. Beginning in 1948 the government has appropriated funds amounting to several hundred billion francs annually for long-term investment in new plant and equipment. The financial law of March 8, 1949, authorized a credit of 15 billion francs to be used by the Minister of Finance to increase the capital of the national enterprises, and the Law of August 2, 1949, on the reorganization of aeronautical industry provided for additional capital investment in the aeronautical companies. In the autumn of 1949 one of the major national companies, Electricité de France, had achieved a sufficiently strong financial position to raise 12 billion francs from a bond issue of five years' maturity offered directly to private investors.

IV

Much of the criticism of the administration of the national companies is justified. The delays in applying certain provisions of the nationalization laws have been inexplicably long. Governmental interference in management has often made a mockery of the legally prescribed autonomy of the companies. The influence of labor unions in direction has often been excessive, and the much-esteemed tripartite boards of directors have not proved satisfactory.

The most striking instances of delay in applying the nationalization laws have occurred in the electricity and gas industries. In the winter of 1946 the Constituent Assembly altered the government's project to place both the gas and electricity industries in a single national company and prescribed in the Law of April 8, 1946, the organization of two distinct companies, Electricité de France and Gaz de France. Six weeks later the government nullified this decision by sanctioning an agreement between the two companies by which Electricité de France assumed the management of Gaz de France. The Minister of Industrial Production defended the agreement as a provisional arrangement necessitated by the fact that the production and distribution of electricity and of gas were ordinarily combined in private companies and could not be immediately separated. The agreement remained in effect, however, three years later, and Gaz de France has been little more than a holding company. The Law of April 8, 1946, also prescribed that regional subsidiary companies be formed to manage the distribution of electricity and the production and distribution of gas. By the summer of 1949 they had not been established, and direction of the two vast national enterprises was centralized in a single administration in Paris, to which even matters of only local import had to be referred for decision. The same law also required the government to issue decrees defining the powers of the directors and administrators of the companies and fixing the prerogatives of the interested ministries. Three years after the passage of the law these decrees had not been issued, and the officers were functioning without a clear knowledge of their duties and authority.

The lively recriminations stirred up in 1945–1946 by the provisions for indemnification of the owners of properties expropriated by the new national companies have been kept alive by delays in settling the indemnification accounts. The Charbonnages de France did not begin delivery of indemnification bonds until the spring of 1949, and Electricité de France and Gaz de France not until January 1950, although all three companies had paid interest annually since the summer of 1947 to former stockholders eligible to receive the bonds.

These delays, even though explicable by the complexity of the task of determining the indemnities, have increased private investors' suspicion of both bad management and bad faith on the part of the national companies and have added to their difficulties in obtaining loans on the open market.

Even more damaging to the reputations of the companies than these delays has been the excessive influence of political parties and labor unions in their direction. This problem has been particularly serious in the Charbonnages de France and its subsidiaries and in the aeronautical industry. In the spring of 1948 the General Manager of the Charbonnages resigned in protest against abuses in the industry which he was powerless to remedy, including the government's permitting the mines to become a political battlefield. Marcel Paul, Communist Minister of Industrial Production, in appointing the original boards of directors of the Charbonnages and of its subsidiary companies, gave a majority of the seats to members of the Confédération Générale du Travail, which was Communist-dominated. The independence of these directors was at best doubtful, and their loyalty was divided between the company and the nation, on the one hand, and the union and the Communist Party, on the other. The danger of this conflict of loyalties was evident in the strike in the autumn of 1948, when several directors, all members of the CGT, gave orders to union members to cease security services in the mines.

Directly after the organization of the Charbonnages and its subsidiaries, the labor-dominated boards and their appointees purged the staffs of engineers and foremen of "collaborators," which too commonly meant "non-Communists," and those who remained were not given sufficient authority or backing to enforce discipline over the miners. The Statute of Miners, established by decree of the Minister of Industrial Production in June 1946, required preliminary approval by joint labor-management committees of disciplinary action against miners more severe than a warning or a fine, thereby giving the CGT additional influence over management and making the enforcement of authority more difficult. The excessive absenteeism and the low productivity in the mines referred to above was owing in part to the weakened position of foremen and engineers.

Similar political interference occurred in the aeronautical industry. The Communist Charles Tillon, as minister in charge of military aviation from 1944 to 1946, placed politically "reliable" men in key posts of the national companies, often with little regard for their technical competence, and purged non-Communists, especially among the foremen and engineers. Political considerations have not, moreover, been foreign to the direction of subsequent non-Communist air ministers. According to *Le Monde*, which cannot be accused of partisanship in favor of the Communist Party, competent men have been dismissed from the aircraft companies because they had been members of Tillon's cabinet and incompetent men retained only because they happened to be in the opposing political camp.

These difficulties of political and labor interference are now being overcome. The board of the Charbonnages has been reconstituted with labor having only the representation prescribed by law. The Statute of Miners has been modified to reduce the authority of the labor-management committees in disciplinary matters, and following the government's demonstration of strength and determination in the coal strikes of 1948, discipline in the mines has improved, the improvement being reflected in declining absenteeism and increased productivity. The Law of August 2, 1949, on the national aeronautical industry prescribes that effective measures be taken to assure the political independence of those companies.

Government interference in management of the companies is an even more serious problem because no solution to it appears to be forthcoming. The framers of the nationalization laws, fearful that the enterprises would become mere units in the national bureaucracy, were careful to prescribe that the national companies be autonomous in management and in finances. In practice, direct interference by the government has been common. The president of Electricité de France complained in 1948 that neither he nor his board of directors had control over wages, rates, or credit; in these fundamentally important matters all decisions were made by the government. The resigning general manager of the Charbonnages protested that the government made decisions on coal affecting his company without consulting him or his board and that the Minister of Industrial Production commonly gave orders directly to the subsidiary companies, ignoring the nominally superior and responsible Charbonnages. Labor unions in the national enterprises have carried complaints directly to the Minister of Industrial Production, by-passing the management, and the ministry in receiving and acting on these complaints has assumed a prerogative of management. A solution to the problem of combining reasonable autonomy for management with adequate public controls cannot be easily achieved. The experience of the Régie Renault, which has been singularly free of government interference, shows, however, that the problem is not insoluble, at least in a company in which the public interest is not so directly involved.[12]

The tripartite administrative boards of the national companies

[12] An interesting commentary on the nominal autonomy of the national companies is the decision of the Court of Appeal of Poitiers in January 1949 annulling the election of an employee of Electricité de France to a *conseil de prud'hommes* on the grounds that employees of the state are not eligible to serve on the councils. *Le Monde*, January 23–24, 1949.

have not provided the ideal direction expected of them. The direction of national enterprises by boards composed of representatives of the state, the personnel, and the consumers was originally proposed by the CGT's Labor Economic Council in 1920, and it was a prime article of faith among the advocates of nationalization in 1944–1946. The boards would assure, it was claimed, efficient direction of the companies in the interest of those most immediately concerned and in the public interest. This purpose was thwarted in some cases, notably in the Charbonnages de France and its subsidiaries, by the appointment of labor union members to represent consumers and the state, as well as the personnel, giving overrepresentation to labor and particularly to the CGT. This was a violation of the principle of tripartite representation, but even in cases where the boards were properly composed they have not functioned as expected. Each of the three groups has tended to concentrate exclusively on its own immediate interests, and the interests of the companies themselves have been neglected. Even partisans of nationalization believe that the composition of the boards should be altered. A common recommendation is that they be transformed into quadripartite boards by the inclusion of men chosen for their special competence in the field in which a particular enterprise operates and representing no special interest other than that of the company itself.

V

In the summer of 1948 the President of the Council, André Marie, declared to the National Assembly, "We wish that the nationalized companies should become for France a subject of pride and cease to be a subject of anxiety." The preceding pages have shown that the companies have, indeed, been a subject of anxiety to the government and to the Assembly; yet they have not been the liabilities depicted by their enemies, and even now some measure of pride in them is not unjustified.

The claim that the national enterprises have been a serious brake on French postwar recovery does not appear well founded. They have, in fact, made important contributions to recovery. The Charbonnages and Electricité de France widened the most serious bottlenecks in the economy by their expansion of the production of coal and electricity. One may question if in this period private enterprise could have done as well, particularly in the coal industry, for public ownership almost certainly stimulated labor to greater efforts than it would have been willing to exert for private owners, who were in disrepute after the Liberation for production failures preceding and during the war, for collaboration during the Occupation, and for anti-labor policies. The financing of reconstruction and investment in new equipment has probably been facilitated by the nationalizations. It is doubtful that private investors could (or would) supply the huge sums required, and the present National Assembly would scarcely have been willing to finance private enterprise, particularly in coal and public utilities, to the extent that it is now financing the great national companies. The deficits, often denounced as a drain on the national budget, represented largely legitimate operating costs that ultimately had to be paid either by higher prices to consumers or by subsidies, regardless of ownership.

The total record of the national companies permits a temperate optimism for the ultimate success of the whole nationalization experiment. The production and services have with few exceptions been satisfactory, and the shortcomings in this field are attributable more to inevitable postwar readjustments, to increasing demand, and, in the case of electricity, to dry weather, than to any fundamental weakness in the structure or functioning of the companies. Their financial condition appears less alarming under careful scrutiny than when sensationally exposed in parliament or press. Financial equilibrium either has been achieved or is in prospect for all except Gaz de France, and its continuing deficit is the consequence of a decision by the government that in the public interest a certain portion of the cost of gas should be borne by the taxpayers and not by the consumers. The validity of nationalization is not involved in such a decision; subsidization of *private* enterprise in similar cases has been common in France and elsewhere.

The most serious weaknesses are in administration. The problems of combining independence and initiative in management with public controls, financial responsibility of the companies' officers with state guarantees of solvency, and unity of direction with participation of diverse interests in management remain unsolved.

21

++

THE FRENCH INVESTMENT PROGRAM

AND ITS RELATION TO RESOURCE ALLOCATION

RICHARD RUGGLES

++

IN ECONOMIC usage, the term resource allocation has generally come to refer to the patterns and the degree of utilization of human and natural resources in a nation. On the one hand, the utilization of resources can be examined by areas of industrial activity. It is often useful to consider how much of a nation's energy goes into agriculture, mining, construction, manufacturing, trade, transportation, and government services, and whether or not there is full utilization of all available resources. On the other hand, the utilization of resources can also be examined in terms of the end uses to which production is put—that is, the amounts of production going into such things as food, clothing, and shelter; new productive plant and machinery; and services provided by the government. Resource allocation in these senses thus reveals the structure of the economic life of a nation.

Resource allocation patterns in both of these forms are closely interrelated with the cultural patterns of a society. There can be no significant change in the allocation of resources in an economy without simultaneous shifts in cultural patterns. And similarly, shifts in cultural patterns are usually accompanied by changing allocations of resources. Careful analyses of both together often can reveal causal relationships which are important in explaining the evolution of the society itself. For these reasons, the study of resource allocation is especially pertinent for those interested in analyzing the nature and extent of changes in a national culture.

Investment, in one sense, is nothing more than one category of the end uses of current production; it is defined as those goods which are produced in the current period but do not enter into current consumption in that period. From a slightly different point of view, investment is also those goods set aside in the current period to assist in production of future periods. This latter definition serves to point out the special significance of investment expenditure: it is the precursor of economic change. Future changes in the pattern of resource allocation can often be discovered in advance by an analysis of the current investment pattern in an economy. It is for this reason that the analysis of current investment programs is in fact often considered to be the study of future resource allocation patterns.

For France, the analysis of the investment program is especially pertinent to an understanding of the direction in which the French economy is moving. At the present time there are a number of important and interrelated economic questions which are basic to any consideration of the future of France, and for most of these questions information on the investment program is vital. Broadly speaking, these questions can be classified into three major groups. The first is whether or not France can be integrated into a larger Europe. The creation of an integrated Europe will require adaptation and structural change in each of the individual countries, and it is useful to ask whether such adaptation and structural change can be expected to occur in France. The extent to which the French economy is actually yielding to the pressure of these requirements can be measured in some degree by the current investment program. The second group of questions relates to the general problem of the level of productivity and the standard of living in France. In production and consumption of material goods, France has fallen behind many of the other nations, and the question naturally arises whether the current investment program forecasts any change in this situation. The final group of problems is that of whether or not stability, both political and economic, can be achieved in France. Insofar as stability is directly related to wage spirals and price inflation, an analysis of the current investment program is extremely useful.

These questions cannot be answered categorically. They involve quantitative analysis and forecasts far beyond the range and reliability of currently available statistics and analytical tools. However, a greater understanding of the meaning and complexity of the questions themselves is provided if they are analyzed against the backdrop of resource allocation. This chapter will undertake to provide that backdrop. The discussion will be divided into two parts. First, in order to provide a general framework for the modern French economy, it will be useful to examine the degree of resource utilization and the shift in resource allocation patterns in France during the past fifty years. Secondly, the details of the current investment program will be analyzed in terms of the impact that this program may be expected to have on the future development of the French economy.[1]

II

During the past half-century, France has enjoyed less than ten years of prosperity. The few years preceding World War I and the few years prior to the great depression of the thirties are the only periods which can in any real sense be considered years of prosperity. Aside from these two periods, the French economy has been plagued either by chronic underutilization of resources or by the aftereffects of major wars.

The first decade of the twentieth century, although not one of deep depression, was still not one of unqualified growth. Although France was to some extent benefiting from the increased industrialization of the rest of Europe, this industrialization did not automatically provide her with prosperity. French production indexes of this period are somewhat deceiving. Many of the new industries appeared to grow by leaps and bounds, simply because they were so very small in 1900. This is especially true in the mechanical engineering fields, where a tiny absolute increase showed up as a large percentage increase. In many of the more established industries—textiles, for instance—there was an actual decline in output, and in many others—for example, construction—there was no significant increase. By 1912, however, France finally reached an all-time peak in production in almost all lines.

This short period of prosperity was of course cut off by the First World War. The position of France in the war was not conducive to the building-up of a strong war economy. In fact, much of the capacity of her peacetime economy was destroyed, either by direct enemy action or by the enforced disruptions of the war which broke the threads of industrial organization binding raw material sources, labor supplies, and markets into a successfully functioning mechanism. It was not until 1923 that France was able to regain the prewar level of output.

From 1923 to 1929, France enjoyed unprecedented prosperity. The

[1] The data on industrial production indexes and employment patterns in the period 1900–1939 in the following text have been taken from the official French statistics as given in the various issues of the *Annuaire statistique*. For the period since 1939, these data have been obtained from the publications of the ECA Mission to France, *France* and *France Data Book* (February 1950). Data on gross national product, consumption, and investment levels have been obtained from *France Data Book* and from *France, Country Data Book* (ECA, Washington, April 1950). Detailed information on investment was obtained from material made available by the Commissariat General du Plan de Modernisation et d'Équipement.

general level of manufacturing production attained a level 40 per cent above what it was in 1912. Although estimates for the economy as a whole are difficult to make, it is probably true that the total output for all sectors in 1929 was about 25 per cent above the 1912 level. Taking into account the slight increase in population over this period, this is roughly equivalent to a 20 per cent per capita increase in output over this period. This may be contrasted with the per capita increase of 55 per cent in the United States over the same period.

Following the peak of 1929, France suffered a period of chronic depression which continued to the outbreak of World War II. In this period absolute total output fell to levels below those of the period before the First World War. In fact, the production level in 1939 was no higher than the level of 1912—a level at which her industrial production was 40 per cent below that of 1929. In other words, at the outbreak of World War II, France was still, in terms of the output of the whole economy, 25 per cent below the level which had been attained a decade earlier. The war, of course, plunged France much further into economic depression; in 1944 and 1945 total manufacturing output fell to 40 per cent of what it had been in 1938. As in the First World War, a considerable amount of French productive capacity was impaired by direct war damage. From surveys made by the French government, it has been estimated that the physical damage and destruction in World War II was approximately double that of World War I.

The recovery after World War II has been considerably more rapid than it was after World War I, but as yet it has not been as complete. In 1946 the industrial production index rose to about 80 per cent of what it was in 1938; it reached 100 per cent in 1947, 110 per cent in 1948, and 125 per cent in 1949. But although France is now considerably above the 1938 level, she is still not significantly above the 1929 level of production. Furthermore, it seems reasonable that in the near future the increase in output will not be as great as it has been thus far in the postwar period. In 1946 and 1947 there was considerable unutilized capacity in France, and the increase in output in this period was largely a reflection of the increasing use of resources which had been underemployed. As specific bottlenecks were broken, industries were able to get into full production. At the present time, however, the major part of any increase in output will have to come directly from increasing productivity. In other words, the productivity of people now employed will have to be raised before the output of the French economy can be increased substantially, and it may take a number of years before the 1929 level can actually be surpassed.

This chronic underutilization of resources and the effects of two

world wars have profoundly affected the evolution of the French economy. The economic development characteristic of other advanced
economies was for the most part prevented from taking place by an
almost continual state of depression, war, or recovery from war. In a
nation where unemployment and lack of effective demand are chronic,
there is little economic pressure to build up new industries or to
shift manpower out of the less efficient and into the more efficient industries. When excess capacity exists in virtually all parts of the economy it is not possible for individuals to change their occupations—to
do so would in most cases involve only changing the name of the industry in which one is unemployed. In a nation whose economy is
seriously damaged by the effects of war, on the other hand, almost all
the energy of the people must be directed to the repair of damage
and the achievement of a workable economy rather than to new economic development. For these reasons, the French economy has been
remarkably static from the point of view of evolutionary development. Over the past half-century there has been no major change in
the pattern of resource allocation. In 1900 about 42 per cent of the
labor force was employed in agriculture; today about 38 per cent is
so employed. The percentage of the labor force in France employed
in industry, despite the important industrialization that has occurred
in the last fifty years, has changed only from 35 to 37 per cent. The
white-collar group, excluding government workers, showed the greatest change; they increased from 11 to 17 per cent of the labor force.
Those employed in public service remained stable at around 7 per
cent of the labor force, and the number of domestic servants fell
almost to half, dropping from over 5 per cent of the labor force to
less than 3 per cent. This was the extent of the change in the patterns
of manpower use which have taken place in the first half of the twentieth century.

   The pattern of output in the various industrial sectors of an economy will change differently from the pattern of labor input if changes
in productivity occur at different rates in different branches of the
economy. Little direct information is available on the pattern of
French output, but from the evidence of the input pattern and some
knowledge of the relative changes in output it is possible to reconstruct a picture of the importance of the different sectors of the French
economy. Two facts are relevant here. First, there is no significant
difference between the size of the French labor force in 1929 and its
size today. Second, available evidence seems to indicate that there is
no great difference between production levels in 1929 and production
levels today. It thus is apparent that, if any over-all change in productivity has taken place, it has been relatively small. It next becomes

proper to ask whether the lack of change in the aggregate level of productivity is due to lack of change in all sectors of production or to increases and decreases in productivity canceling each other out. Preliminary analysis seems to indicate that it is the former which was in fact the case. There does not seem to have been very much change, for example, in output per worker in textile manufacturing or in the construction industry. In all probability the structure of industrial output, at least in its broader classifications, was not much different in 1929 from what it is today. The differences between the patterns of output in 1900 and 1950 are therefore probably due solely to the productivity gains which occurred in the two prosperity periods before 1929: 1910 to 1912, and 1923 to 1929. Unfortunately, sufficient information to carry out precise calculations is not available, but it seems reasonable that the greatest productivity gains would have taken place in the mechanical equipment industries, and the smallest gains in agriculture and trade.

Finally it is useful to consider what can be said about the level of consumption and investment in the French economy over the last fifty years. Interest in this area is of rather recent vintage, and for this reason data for periods prior to 1929 are not available. It is possible to say, however, that in the first thirty years of the twentieth century per capita consumption probably increased by approximately 20 to 30 per cent. The increase in manufacturing productivity was probably considerably greater than the increase of productivity in agriculture, distribution, and the service industries. By the same token it is probably true that capital formation was slightly more important in 1929 than it had been in 1900. It is true that manpower data on employment do not indicate any startling shifts. For example, about the same proportion of the labor force was employed in construction in 1900 as in 1929. However, the greater increase in productivity probably meant that in output terms the industries responsible for capital formation grew at a faster rate than the rest of the economy.

Since 1929 some official data have been compiled on both consumption and investment levels by the Commission du Bilan. According to this information, by 1949 the consumption level in France had practically regained its 1938 level, but it was still 10 per cent lower than the level existing in 1929. Investment, according to these data, in 1949 was some 50 per cent above the depressed levels of 1938, but it also fell at least 10 per cent below the 1929 level.

The question of the proportion of the total resources of France which are now being devoted to investment is somewhat less clear. Up to now, the French national accounts figures as published have generally been used to calculate the proportion of total output being devoted to gross investment. On the basis of these figures it would appear that France was devoting 20 per cent of her total output to gross investment. Relatively speaking, this would be an extremely high level of investment, inasmuch as the highest peacetime level achieved in the United States was about 17 per cent, in 1948. It is often argued that the inflation in France is the result of this high investment level that the national accounts statistics show. But the inflation in and of itself cannot be used to reason back about the level of capital formation. In all probability the French consumers became excessively liquid during the German occupation due to the shortages of consumer goods, and with the postwar readjustment it is only reasonable that an inflationary period should have occurred, irrespective of the investment level.

A more critical examination of the French national accounts figures reveals that there are major conceptual differences between what the Commission du Bilan refers to as gross investment and what is generally considered to be gross investment in an economic sense. In the first place, the French include current repair and upkeep in their figures on gross investment. Secondly, they include the government's expenditures on armament and all public works such as roads and public buildings. If the French data are adjusted to be comparable to the gross investment concept as used in this country by the Department of Commerce, the investment level in 1949 comes out to be approximately 12 or 13 per cent of total output, instead of 20 per cent.*

In other words, contrary to prevailing opinion, France is not at the present time devoting an excessive proportion of her total output to capital formation. In spite of the tremendous needs for increased capital equipment in industry and agriculture, the French investment level remains low in comparison with most other European countries. With respect to the outlook for the future, this probably means that if the current investment level is continued France should not look forward to any spectacular rise in her productivity or standard of living.

III

A detailed analysis of the investment program in a nation is vital to an understanding of the directions in which an economy is moving. This is especially true of postwar France, and for this reason it will be useful to examine the postwar investment program in France in some detail.

* For further discussion of this important point see the appendix to this chapter, which is on pp. 380–81.

Since the end of the war, the French government has had a dominant role in the investment program through the extension of credit to both public and private enterprises and through direct grants of funds for reconstruction of war damage. As late as 1948 the government provided 70 per cent of the funds used for investment. Needless to say, in connection with this provision of funds the government exerted control over the type of investments which were taking place. Government financing has been most significant, of course, in those industries and sectors directly under its control, such as coal, electricity, and transportation. In addition, government payments for repair of war damage and for low-cost public housing financed 90 per cent of the large expenditure on housing investment. Since these groups constitute the major fields of investment in an industrial economy, it is obvious that the role of the French government in investment has been large.

The inflationary aspects of this investment program are tied up with many other considerations, and a discussion of all the contributing elements would require a more extended analysis than is possible in this paper. Mr. Rosa's article in a recent issue of the *Economic Journal* deals very competently with this subject.[2] It is his considered conclusion that "none of the steps taken by the French government up to December 1948 were powerful enough to strike the major cause of continued inflationary pressure." It is Mr. Rosa's belief that "by forthright reduction of the investment projected under the Monnet Plan, and by energetic tax reform as a preface to later restoration of the investment cuts, the French may still halt their disruptive inflation before a 'bust' produces paralysis and chaos." In his view, these measures "appear to offer the only promising outline of a solution to the problem of inflation which has barred the road to French recovery."

It may well be that events will prove this line of argument correct. The lull in the progress of inflation which has occurred in the recent period may be deceptive and short-lived. In real terms, however, there is some question whether cutting the level of investment in the immediate past would have produced more real goods in the French economy. Perhaps with less investment the inflationary gap would have been less, but it is also true that the original bottlenecks in transportation, electric power, and coal production would probably still exist in France had not investment been undertaken in these fields. France was not at full employment in the immediate postwar period, and although goods were short, labor which could be used to provide investment goods was available. A lower investment rate

2 R. V. Rosa, "The Problem of French Recovery," *Economic Journal,* LIX (June 1949), 154–70.

might have resulted in less inflation, but it would also have resulted in fewer goods available for consumption and capital formation. If this is true, it then becomes necessary to face the question of how much real income and current productive capacity it is worth while to sacrifice to avoid an inflationary price rise. It is quite true that in the current period excessive accent on investment may succeed in bidding up the cost of investment goods without achieving a greater diversion of resources to investment purposes—thus at the same time producing a violent inflationary spiral. On the other hand, with reasonable controls on the use of investment resources it would seem possible to avoid by direct measures this useless bidding-up process.

There have been significant changes in the pattern of French investment in the postwar period. At first, as might have been expected, much of the investment was directed to the repair of war damage. Transportation, communications, and housing absorbed 65 per cent of total investment in 1946, whereas today they absorb only 40 per cent. Until now, there has been little reason to question the propriety of the allocation of investment. Unutilized capacity existed in most areas, and the need for investment in war damage repair, transportation, and electric power was self-evident. These were bottlenecks in the system, and as such they had to be cleared up. Today the problem of designing a proper investment program is much more complex; for the first time in twenty years France is facing the question of how and where to expand capacity, and how to raise productivity. The new decisions will determine in large measure how the resource allocation patterns in France are to be changed, and how the French economy is to be adapted to the world economy.

In terms of the major industrial groups, the 1949–1950 total investment program is divided up as follows: fuel and energy, 24 per cent; housing, 21 per cent; transportation and communications, 19 per cent; manufacturing, 16 per cent; agriculture, 16 per cent; and other investments, 4 per cent.

The investment in fuel and energy consists mostly of those items devoted to coal, electricity, and petroleum production. It is hoped that by 1952–1953 coal production in France can reach the level of 60 million tons; this contrasts with the production figures of 45 million tons in 1948 and 55 million tons in 1929. The production goal is to be accomplished without using appreciably more manpower in the coal industry. Of the total coal investment program, 40 per cent represents subsidiary activities such as housing for the miners—an investment which is necessary to retain labor in what is otherwise an undesirable occupation. Whether or not the French coal output targets represent the most efficient use of resources depends in large part on world trade. It is quite possible that the coal needs of France can be supplied better by trade with Germany, Belgium, and the United Kingdom. Even if this point were proved, however, it would not necessarily follow that the current programs of modernization and mechanization of mining are excessive.

The electricity investment program is twice the size of the coal investment program. At present electricity is the one major bottleneck still existing in France, and in many areas the lack of adequate power has seriously hampered production. The increases now being undertaken in capacity are sufficient to keep pace with the needs of industry. The present program will use up all the economically useful waterpower available in France, and future expansion will entail the setting up of thermal plants. Since many other European countries are more favorably situated than France with respect to hydroelectric power, the continued expansion of the electric power industry beyond the present program may be open to question. Alternatively, too, it may be that France can more profitably devote herself to lines of industry which do not have large power requirements.

The last major category in the fuel and energy investment program is the building of petroleum refineries. While as a long-run program it may be useful for France to import crude oil and refine it for domestic use, it is not apparent why investment in this area could not be postponed until the more pressing needs for investment elsewhere in the economy have been met. Relative to the large fixed investment required, it would appear that there are other sectors of the economy which would benefit more from this amount of new investment.

Although housing expenditure is one of the major categories of investment, it is but a drop in the bucket of France's total housing needs. France's construction activity in the past forty years has been confined mainly to the building of a few public buildings, the construction of the Maginot Line, and the repair of war damage. A stationary population, coupled with rigid rent control, has prevented the construction of low-cost housing. It is quite possible that the housing program is politically necessary, and is one of the few overt actions which the government can take to sell itself to the French people. The housing program cannot be expected to fill the vast needs of France, but it may improve political stability.

It is difficult to evaluate the investment level which is programmed for transportation and communications. The intended investments consist mainly of modernization and replacement of outdated equipment. Since the transportation system handles the freight and traffic problems of France fairly efficiently at this juncture, it is useful to ask how the improvement in equipment is expected to contribute to the increased output and productivity of the economy. It may well be that some of the investment in this industry is not of the highest priority.

A third of the contemplated investment in the manufacturing industry is scheduled to take place in iron and steel production. Production for 1952–1953 is expected to increase almost 50 per cent over current levels. To the extent that the investment in the iron and steel industry is for modernization and increased productivity, this seems to be reasonably justified. However, any question of expansion should seriously take into account the demand for steel by the French and European steel consumers and the additional supplies which will become available from other European steel producers. There are currently some signs that the French steel industry is meeting serious sales resistance. The expansion of steel capacity should not be undertaken unless it can be shown that there is a good chance of the existence of a market for steel at a price above the cost of French steel production.*

The investment programmed for other lines of manufacturing seems to be grossly inadequate, in the light of the state of French manufacturing plants. One of the main difficulties in this area, of course, is that many plant owners, both large and small, do not as yet appreciate the gains in productivity which can be achieved by the use of modern machinery and technology, and are not in a position to make investment expenditures.†

Finally, in agriculture the investment program seems somewhat overoptimistic. It is estimated that the government will be able to finance only 20 per cent of the total investment in agriculture and it is expected that the rest will be forthcoming from private individuals. Past experience has not indicated that either the initiative or the necessary funds for such private investment will be forthcoming from private sources. It cannot be denied that investment in agriculture is needed; on the contrary, what is anticipated is far too low a level of investment. In view of French agricultural methods, it is certainly evident that an increase in the total supply of foodstuffs could be achieved simultaneously with a reduction in the number of those employed in agriculture. A precondition for this achievement would be the consolidation of many of the small and inefficient farm holdings. France must make up its mind whether it wants to keep a large

---

* The argument of this paragraph is concerned with normal peacetime uses of steel products. Expansion of facilities for armament production and for increasing war potential would raise an entirely different set of considerations—considerations of imperative necessity and hence of different character.

† See David Landes's Chapter 19 on the French businessman.

peasant class, or is willing to take its place among modern industrial nations.

An examination of the total investment program over the various sectors of the economy thus reveals considerable unevenness. Those parts of the economy under direct government control appear to benefit more than the private sectors of the economy, but it is in the private sectors that investment expenditures are most needed, since it is here especially that productivity and technology are at a low ebb.

IV

At this juncture it will be useful to relate the above evaluation of the French investment program to the questions posed in the first part of this paper. With respect to the problem of whether France can be integrated into the European economy, one factor is dominant. The changes which are occurring in France are not of sufficient magnitude to necessitate any serious adaptation on the part of the other European countries. France is in the passive position of being acted upon, rather than in the active state of consciously helping to shape the future of Europe. Insofar as French plans strive for self-sufficiency, however, the balance of European trade may be further disturbed, and in those cases in which expansion is undertaken in France without due regard to other European production targets, it is quite possible that future maladjustments will result.*

With respect to living standards, it does not seem probable that any outstanding rise will be possible in the next few years. There is not nearly enough investment in manufacturing and agriculture to raise productivity to adequate levels. Furthermore, there is little evidence that such investment will be forthcoming in the near future.

Finally, it is my personal belief that the future stability of France is far more dependent on the possible gains in the standard of living which may be achieved than on the financial problems connected with the investment level. A reduction in the investment effort might reduce disposable income in the economy, but it would probably do so by a decrease in employment and in production of investment goods. The current and future political repercussions of such a measure would do far more to upset the political and economic stability of France than would the continuation of the current investment levels.

Thus, in conclusion, it seems evident that France needs to concentrate much more than she has on measures designed to increase her output and productivity.

* This paragraph was written before the announcement of the Schuman Plan for coordinating French steel production with the rest of Western Europe.

APPENDIX TO CHAPTER 21

Three major adjustments would have to be made in the French data in order to bring them into line with the U.S. data.

1. It would be necessary to add the compensation of government employees to the government consumption of goods and services and to the gross national product, so that the services of government employees will be taken into account. The French figures as they are usually presented omit the compensation of government employees entirely.

2. In the French national accounts data the concept of gross investment follows the Scandinavian definition rather than the definition used by the United States Department of Commerce. The French definition of gross investment includes repair and upkeep. The repair and upkeep carried out by the government would be considered, in the U.S. definition, as a part of the government consumption. Repair and upkeep carried out by business would be considered as being used up in the creation of current output, and would not have been included in gross national product in the first place; therefore to make the figures comparable to the U.S. definition this amount should be subtracted from the French gross national product.

3. Government expenditures on armament equipment, public works, etc., would not be included as gross investment in the U.S. definition; instead they would be classed as government consumption. Therefore gross investment would be reduced and government consumption would be increased by this amount. These adjustments have been made in the following table:

COMPOSITION OF GROSS NATIONAL PRODUCT BY EXPENDITURES IN 1949
(billions of francs)

	I PRIVATE CONSUMPTION	II GOVERNMENT CONSUMPTION	III GROSS INVESTMENT	IV NET FOREIGN BALANCE	V GROSS NATIONAL PRODUCT
A. French definition (privately produced)	5857	173	1540	−9	7561
Percentage distribution	77.4	2.3	20.4	−.1	100.0
1. Compensation of government employees		620			620
2. Current repair and upkeep		40	−450		−410

	I PRIVATE CON- SUMPTION	II GOVERN- MENT CON- SUMPTION	III GROSS INVEST- MENT	IV NET FOREIGN BALANCE	V GROSS NATIONAL PRODUCT
3. Armament and public works	___	175	−175	___	___
B. French data adjusted to U.S. definitions	5857	1008	915	−9	7771
Percentage distr.	75.3	13.0	11.8	−.1	100.0

Source: All data for the above table taken from: "Projets établiés par le rapporteur de
la Commission du Bilan," November 1949, Appendix, "Données statistiques de la France"
(mimeographed).
Line A: page 119, Les revenus des entreprises et leur emploi en 1948 et 1949.
    Column I: Item Ia, Ventes de l'économie aux particuliers.
    Column II: Item Ib, Ventes de l'économie à l'État et aux collectivités locales.
    Column III: Item Ic, Ventes de l'économie à l'État (investissements) (225) plus item
           Id, aux entreprises (investissements) (1315).
    Column IV: Item Ie, Ventes de l'économie à l'étranger et aux territoires d'outre-
           mer   930
        Item III, Recettes de l'étranger et des territoires d'outre-mer   40
        Item V, Importations   −910
        Item VIII, Revenus versés à l'étranger et aux territoires d'outre-mer −69
        Net balance of payments   −9
    Column V: Total of Columns I, II, III, IV.
Line 1:
    Column II: page 120, Les revenus des collectivités publiques et leur emploi en 1948
        et 1949. Item IVa2, Fonctionnement des services publics; dépenses
        effectuées dans la Métropole, personnel.
Line 2:
    Column II: page 155, Investissements, 1949. Item "Renouvellement, secteur public."
    Column III: page 155, Investissements, 1949. Item "Renouvellement, total."
    Column V: Total of Columns II and III.
Line 3:
    Column II and Column III: page 155, Investissements, 1949.
        Item "Investissements, public, total"   255
        Item "Renouvellement, secteur public"   −40
        Public investment other than repair and upkeep   175
Line B: Total of Lines A, 1, 2, and 3.

22

++

THE MARSHALL PLAN

AND FRENCH FOREIGN TRADE *

WARREN C. BAUM

++

IN A volume which reflects such a wide variety of interests, a general discussion of French foreign trade in relation to the European Recovery Program is more appropriate than a more detailed and technical treatment of some specific problem or problems within this very broad field. At the risk of considerable superficiality, therefore, this chapter will sketch the broad outlines of this subject with a minimum of detailed discussion of particular points.

I

We shall naturally be concerned primarily with French trade since the end of the recent war, which left in its wake many entirely new problems. In order to gain the necessary perspective, however, the pattern of French trade immediately before the war deserves brief description.

Since France has one of the best-balanced economies of Western Europe, one might suspect that foreign trade has not occupied an important part in its economic life. France is relatively well-endowed with such basic raw materials as coal, iron ore, and bauxite, has a relatively large industrial plant, and in addition is self-sufficient in many important agricultural commodities. Nevertheless, it has always occupied a major position in world trade. Before the war, France ranked fourth among the trading nations, on both an absolute and a per

---

* This paper expresses the private views of the author, and does not necessarily reflect those of the Economic Cooperation Administration. The author is indebted to Mr. Jack Boyd for assistance in the preparation of materials for this paper.

capita basis. Another indication of the importance of foreign commerce is the fact the French foreign trade represented roughly 20 to 25 per cent of the national income during the interwar period.[1]

The commodity structure of French trade is characteristic of that of an advanced industrial economy. Imports—predominantly of raw materials—normally are double the weight of exports, which are predominantly of manufactured articles. Despite large indigenous coal resources, France imports large quantities of coal, primarily of the high grade or coking varieties. Petroleum and petroleum products, cotton, wool, jute, raw hides and skins, and other textile and leather raw materials, together with coal, comprised 50 per cent of total imports by value in 1938. In addition, France imported substantial amounts of machinery and equipment of all types, especially from the United States and Germany.

Textile products in a semifinished or finished state form the largest single group of French exports, followed closely by agricultural products (such as wine, fruits, and vegetables) and chemical products, including, of course, perfumes, oils, and essences. The conventional picture of France as an exporter of luxury articles of high price and quality has become increasingly inaccurate, although, as is the case with all such generalities, it contains a considerable element of truth. The "luxury" characteristics of French exports are most clearly evidenced in its trade with the United States, which may account for the continuing popularity of this view. As a result of the acquisition of Alsace-Lorraine, however, France was before the war the largest single European exporter of iron ore, and exported large quantities of potash and phosphates as well. In addition, modern France has always exchanged a large quantity of machinery and equipment with its industrial neighbors on the basis of the specialization of labor which developed under earlier conditions of relatively free trade. Furthermore, partly as a result of the depression of the 1930's which affected the luxury trade most strongly, and partly as a result of more fundamental developments, a gradual shift in the structure of French exports from light toward heavy manufacture took place during the decade before the war.

France's principal trading partners before the war were its industrialized neighbors of Western and Central Europe. Belgium, Germany, the United Kingdom, and Italy accounted for 70 per cent of

[1] Most of the material contained in this paper is derived from sources which, although not classified, are not available to the general public and consequently cannot be footnoted to any advantage. Prewar foreign trade statistics were obtained from the *Annuaire statistique de la France* and the *Statistical Yearbook* of the League of Nations. Postwar trade statistics are based principally on the *Bulletin du commerce extérieur* of the Ministère des Finances.

French prewar exports. The United States was the leading supplier of France's import requirements, providing petroleum products, cotton, machinery, and motor vehicles; but French exports to the United States were only one-third the value of its imports. Although France had a slight trade surplus with Great Britain, it ran a considerable deficit with the rest of the sterling area, from which it received such raw materials as rubber, cotton, wool, tin, and jute.

The importance of its overseas territories to French trade deserves brief mention. Over one-fourth of all French trade passed between the metropolitan country and its overseas possessions. This trade followed the classic pattern of exchange between industrialized and undeveloped areas: French exports to the colonial empire covered almost every French manufacture and semimanufacture, including textile goods, machinery, motor vehicles, iron and steel, and chemical products. In exchange, France received important foodstuffs and raw materials, among which were wine, fruit, olive oil, and tobacco from Algeria, rice, rubber, and corn from Indo-China, peanuts and peanut oil from West Africa, cereals, phosphates, and lead from Tunisia, and cereals, wool, phosphates, iron and manganese ore from Morocco. Imports into the Metropole were substantially in excess of exports to the colonies in the 1930's.

All of these elements are reflected in the balance of payments accounts, which are the most convenient form for a summary appraisal of France's trade and payments position. The prewar balance of payments of the French Union characteristically displayed a deficit on merchandise account, and the excess of commodity imports over exports increased during the interwar period. The net invisible account, on the other hand, has always been favorable, despite a deficit in freight, insurance, and remittances from foreign workers (mostly Belgian and Italian) residing in France. The invisible surplus resulted from the substantial income received from foreign investments and the tourist traffic, both of which customarily played an important part in French trade. During the 1920's, invisible receipts more than compensated for the deficit on merchandise account and the French current accounts as a whole showed a substantial surplus. During the depression of the 1930's as the trade deficit increased, the favorable current account balance was converted into a net deficit, financed by the liquidation of foreign assets. France was thus able to sustain its level of trade only through an outflow of gold and the loss of some of its foreign investments. If these foreign assets and gold reserves had not been available, the dollar gap and other currency shortages would have assumed critical importance even before the war.

II

So much for the prewar picture. Immediately after liberation the restoration of foreign trade encountered difficulties of almost staggering proportions. Trade statistics for the year 1945 are not available in a satisfactory state, and trading relations in that period were so peculiar that they can probably best be excluded from this discussion. In 1946, the current account deficit of the French Union reached the impressive total of over $2 billion. In 1947 this deficit had been reduced only to $1,850 million.

The more important factors which account for this rapid deterioration in the payments position of France can easily be enumerated. The first, and probably the most important, explanation was the greatly increased physical requirements of France as a result of the war, most of which could only be supplied from foreign sources. The transportation network of France was badly dislocated, and the need for repair and replacement of rolling stock was urgent. The reconstruction and reequipment of France's physical plant, a good part of which had been extensively damaged during the war, or else removed by the Germans, placed demands which French productive resources were unable to fulfill. (It will be recalled that industrial activity after liberation in 1944 was only 20 per cent of prewar, and that, owing to difficulties with coal and transport, the relatively low level of production of 1938 was regained only by the first half of 1948.) Domestic agricultural production was low during the time necessary to bring mine-infested and war-devastated land back into cultivation. A succession of bad harvests further reduced crop yields and added to the need for extraordinary grain, feed, and other imports.

The loss of most of France's sources of invisible income also contributed to the large postwar trade deficits. The French deficit on shipping accounts, which had averaged only $20 million in 1937–1938, increased to over $300 million in 1947 as a result of two factors: (1) the sinking or severe damaging of a large part of France's merchant fleet during the war; and (2) the increased need for imports from the Western Hemisphere of bulky commodities with heavy freight charges—such as coal and wheat—because of reduced production and bad harvests in Europe. The tourist trade, which had provided receipts which averaged $300 million during the 1920's but declined to an average of $90 million in 1937 and 1938 as a result of the worldwide business recession and recurrent threats of war, actually was unfavorable to France by $20 million in 1946. A slight improvement in tourism was registered in 1947, with net receipts of $9 million. This reduction in tourist traffic was due in large part to the inadequacy of French tourist facilities of all kinds (the availability of hotel accommodations, passenger ships, food supplies, etc., was far below prewar). Furthermore, as a consequence of the rampant inflation in France and the general lack of confidence in the currency, the high black-market premium on "hard" foreign currencies, particularly the dollar, resulted in a diversion of the majority of tourist receipts into illegal channels. Income from foreign investments also suffered drastically as a result of the war. Investment income in 1947 was reported at $86 million, or half of the 1938 figure. This decline, which has proceeded unabated until there is now a large deficit in the interest account, can be attributed in part to the nationalization of foreign-held investments in several Eastern European countries, but principally to the rapid liquidation of all private and public investments abroad which the French government has succeeded in discovering and requisitioning.

The inflationary course of prices in France, which continued with minor interruptions through the end of 1948, has also contributed to French payments problems, and I shall have more to say on this subject later.

Several major adjustments in the structure of French trade occurred during the first two years after the war. Imports from the Western Hemisphere, including, of course, the United States, greatly increased in both absolute and relative importance. An increasing proportion of these imports were wheat, coal, and other agricultural products, minerals, and metals, at the expense of textiles, leather, and miscellaneous imports. The area pattern of exports from the French Union, however, quickly returned to prewar. Trade with Western Europe has retained its relative importance, and the diversion of exports to the Western Hemisphere which would be necessary to close the "dollar gap" has not materialized, for reasons which will be discussed further below.

A smaller proportion of French postwar exports have consisted of agricultural products, owing to reduced domestic production and the fact that many of these commodities—wines, fruits, and vegetables— are in the so-called luxury class and foreign countries have restricted their importation. This latter factor also accounts for the relative decline in exports of some types of chemical products. On the other hand, exports of machinery have increased in response to the widespread reequipment needs of Europe. The incorporation of the Saar within the French Union in 1948 has caused a further shift in favor of raw material exports.

The exchange of goods between Metropolitan France and the overseas territories has undergone marked changes. French imports from the overseas territories have been reduced because of lower production of wheat, rice, and oilseeds in these areas; French exports have risen, however, and the prewar trade deficit of Metropolitan France became a surplus in 1947, the size of which has increased steadily in subsequent years. The increase in French exports reflects in part the sheltered market which the colonies afford for high-priced French goods, but more important is the increase in French exports as a result of reconstruction and development requirements in the colonial areas and the continued struggle in Indo-China. At present, Indo-China enjoys the doubtful distinction of having the most unfavorable balance of payments in the world.[2]

As noted previously, the payments deficit of the French Union in 1946 totaled $2,100 million, consisting of a trade deficit of Metropolitan France of $1,550, an invisible deficit of $250 million, and a current account deficit of the overseas territories with the rest of the world of $300 million. In 1947 the deficit was reduced to the level of $1,850, with a total deficit for the two years of close to $4 billion. The deficit in these two years was financed in part by two Export-Import Bank loans totaling $1.2 billion, a loan from the International Bank for Reconstruction and Development of $250 million, and the U.S. Treasury loan, resulting from the Blum-Byrnes accord, of $720 million. In addition, gold reserves were liquidated to the extent of over $1 billion, more than $300 million of privately held gold and foreign exchange assets were liquidated, and net credits of about $300 million from various European countries were drawn upon.

A special word might be added about French trade with the United States and the rest of the Western Hemisphere. In 1938 the French trade deficit with the United States and other Western Hemisphere countries was very substantial, amounting to $135 million in current (1938) dollars. The 1948 trade deficit with this area totaled $885 million.[3] Converting the 1938 figures into 1948 prices, it appears that the "quantum" of French imports in 1948 was 20 per cent above 1938, while exports were only 68 per cent of the prewar level. In 1938, France could count on a small dollar invisible surplus, probably amounting to $25–50 million, to offset in part the trade deficit, although the balance of payments as a whole was clearly unfavorable to France. In 1948, on the other hand, the French net deficit on invisible account with the Western Hemisphere was over $200 million. As a result, the over-all deficit of Metropolitan France with the Western Hemisphere in 1948 amounted to $1.2 billion. In addition, there

---

[2] *New York Times*, November 10, 1949.

[3] 1948 figures were derived from Economic Commission for Europe, *Economic Survey of Europe*, 1948.

was a net deficit of the French territories of $135 million with this area.

By the autumn of 1947, the French trade deficit had reached a critical state. Gold reserves of the Bank of France and the Exchange Stabilization Fund had dwindled to below the danger point. Foreign exchange assets and available credits had been exhausted. Drastic cuts in imports were imposed, and an appeal made to the United States. The Interim Aid Act was passed, providing France with emergency assistance to the extent of some $300 million until April of 1948 when the European Recovery Program came into being.

The immediate incidence of the Marshall Plan on the French balance of payments takes two forms. What is termed "direct aid" is given to France to match the estimated deficit in the balance of payments with the dollar area. This estimate is based on a review by ECA and the Organization for European Economic Cooperation of French forecasts for all categories of its dollar payments position. Particular attention is given, of course, to a screening of the estimated needs for commodity imports and the related shipping expenditures. In addition, what is termed "indirect aid" is given to France in an amount equivalent to its estimated net payments deficit with the other participating countries. This aid is in fact allotted to France's creditors in the form of "conditional aid," to be matched by an equivalent amount of credits or "drawing rights" extended to France by its creditors in the creditor's currency.

Direct aid between April 1 and July 1, 1948, amounted to $375 million. For the fiscal year 1948–1949, France received $980 million in direct aid and $325 million in drawing rights, raising total aid for the fifteen months to almost $1.7 billion. For the current fiscal year, France is tentatively scheduled at present to receive some $675 million in direct aid and a net figure of $220 million in the form of drawing rights. These drawing rights are received from its four creditors— Belgium, the Sterling Area, Western Germany, and Italy—and total $255 million; against them must be set the $35 million of drawing rights extended by France to Turkey, Greece, Norway, Denmark, Austria, and several other countries. This figure may be subject to some revision during the balance of the year. The amount of direct aid which France will receive in the next few years is, of course, impossible to predict at this moment, but it takes no rare gifts of divination to state that even under optimistic assumptions it is not likely to exceed $500 million for 1950–1951, and $300 million for 1951–1952.

The balance of this chapter falls under three headings. First, it discusses developments in French trade since the beginning of the ERP period, and then some of the special problems which have arisen and measures adopted by France or the ECA in connection with them. Finally, it considers briefly what the French trade position is likely to be at the end of the ERP period.

III

Comparisons of the present value of trade with that of the prewar period, and value comparisons between different postwar years, are difficult to make and often quite misleading. The rapid increase in prices in France makes analyses in terms of French francs of little meaning. In converting into dollars, however, it must be remembered that between February 1948 and October 1949 the conversion rate for imports was often different from that for exports, and some imports were converted at a special rate. In addition, the import and export rates often changed on a monthly basis, if not more frequently, and the rates applicable to the United States were sometimes different from those applicable to Portugal and Switzerland, which in turn were different from those for Belgium and Italy, all of which in turn differed from the set of exchange rates used in trade with the rest of the world. For these reasons, I shall continue to use trade statistics very sparingly, and make general value comparisons only in cases where the magnitude of the real change is sufficiently pronounced to be clear despite the many statistical obscurities.

The improvement in the external trade and payments position of France during the ERP period has been striking indeed. This improvement, which has generally paralleled the course of recovery in other sectors of the French economy, has occurred principally within the past year. The current account deficit of the French Union in 1948 was $1.7 billion, approximately the same as in 1947. Of this large deficit, $1.1 billion arose from dollar trade with the Western Hemisphere, about $370 million with the Sterling Area and Belgium, and the relatively small remainder with the rest of the world. The over-all deficit of the French Union was about $800 million in 1949, a sizable reduction from the 1948 total. The whole of this deficit, moreover, was registered from trade with the dollar area. The current account with all other currency areas showed a slight surplus for the year as a whole. The balance of trade with the dollar area improved during the last half of 1949, but this change was due almost exclusively to a reduction in the level of imports as a result of the reduction in ECA aid rather than to an increase in the dollar value of exports.

One of the more interesting features of the recent improvement in French trade is the reversal of the former deficitary position with the Sterling Area. In 1948–1949 France used all but $12 million of the

$200 million of drawing right credits extended by the United Kingdom for the Sterling Area as a whole. The payments deficit of France with the Sterling Area for 1949–1950 was originally estimated at $120 million, but after the first seven months of the fiscal year France had not utilized any of these credits and had actually accumulated sizable sterling balances. The same development has occurred in France's trade with its second largest creditor, Belgium. France has not yet found it necessary to use any of the $80 million of drawing rights to be provided by Belgium. The payments deficits with Germany and Italy, the other two European creditors of France, have proceeded more or less as anticipated, although French trade with Western Germany improved substantially in recent months. Some of the reversal in France's payments position vis-à-vis Belgium and the Sterling Area is due to temporary and nonrecurring factors, such as the speculative flight from sterling preceding the devaluation of the pound and administrative difficulties in implementing the import program from Belgium. It is probable that French accounts will show a deficit with both the Sterling Area and Belgium for the fiscal year as a whole, but considerably less than the amounts originally estimated. These temporary fluctuations in French payments should not conceal the real improvement which has occurred within the ERP period, and which is based solidly on an increase in the value and volume of exports.

A substantial element in the current account deficit of the French Union with the dollar area is the deficit of the overseas territories, which amounted to $135 million in 1948 and $170 million in 1949. In addition, the overseas territories had a deficit of $70 million on current account with the rest of the world in 1948, although this was cut to $20 million in 1949. As noted previously, Metropolitan France, which before the war ran a deficit with its overseas territories, has had an increasingly large surplus of trade and invisibles since the war. For 1949–1950, it has been estimated that the deficit of Metropolitan France with foreign countries will almost exactly offset its surplus with the overseas territories. The goods and services which move in this sheltered trade, and the means of payment, are entirely different from those which account for its dollar deficit, and it goes without saying that the dollar gap could not be eliminated by reducing Metropolitan France's surplus with the overseas territories, if indeed such a reduction were possible.

Of the factors which explain the recent remarkable improvement in the French payments position, perhaps the most important is the success of the Queuille government in finally arresting the inflationary spiral of costs and prices in France. As long as inflation was a continuing problem, even frequent devaluations of the franc were unable to keep French prices competitive in world markets and it was impossible to encourage the expansion of exports when the domestic market offered such attractive opportunities for high and quick profits. The lack of confidence in the currency, which was also a factor in the internal instability, not only retarded the flow of real savings necessary for anti-inflationary budgetary financing but widened the gap between the official and black-market exchange rates, thus diverting a large proportion of tourist and other receipts into illegal channels. The comprehensive economic program of Queuille and Finance Minister Petsche included as its principal elements a greater measure of budgetary equilibrium (with a legal maximum on expenditures within each budgetary category), quantitative as well as qualitative restrictions on bank credit to both private enterprises and the state, and associated policies in the fields of price control and wage control.[4]

The Queuille program first bore fruit during 1949. The course of prices was generally downward during the first six months of 1949, bolstering the government's position in maintaining money wages constant in the face of growing opposition from the trade-unions. A combination of circumstances which developed during the course of the summer—a partly speculative rise in food prices as a result of the drought, the speculative price increases in anticipation of devaluation, and the renewed concern over strikes and wage increases— produced a rapid increase in the price level in August and September. Since that time, however, the price level has been remarkably constant and at the end of 1949 stood at approximately the level of the year before.[5]

These achievements in internal financial stability have all been encouraging, but it is clear that greater efforts will be required if they are to be maintained and consolidated. The Bidault government will be faced during the first half of 1950 with a number of major policy decisions which affect developments in internal costs and prices over the coming months, the most important of which are the implementation of the 1950 budget and the adoption of a bill to restore collective bargaining. The year 1949 was marked by a considerable improvement in budgetary financing by noninflationary methods, but some

---

[4] The release of counterpart funds by ECA has been based on agreements between the American and French governments on the economic and financial policies to be followed by the French government, and it is primarily through these agreements that ECA has participated actively in the formulation of the economic policies which contributed to the arresting of inflation in France.

[5] These favorable price developments have continued and been consolidated during the first six months of 1950.

of this improvement must be attributed to the full utilization of ECA counterpart funds for investment purposes. The declining magnitude of ECA aid and counterpart funds makes more imperative the establishment of a durable equilibrium between receipts and expenditures. The 1950 budget represents some additional progress along these lines, but the most basic problems, such as the long-delayed reform of the fiscal system, including the enforcement of existing taxes, and the reduction in the deficit of the nationalized railways, have not been squarely faced. Many important questions of budgetary financing in 1950 also remain unresolved at this juncture.

Another issue which will be of central importance in determining the success of France in maintaining the internal stability upon which further improvement in foreign trade is contingent is the restoration of collective bargaining. It remains to be seen whether any substantial wage increases will in fact result from the progress of collective bargaining under whatever bill is finally adopted, and whether these increases will create in turn a further rise in costs and prices or serve instead as incentives to greater productive efficiency on the part of both labor and management and consequently lower rather than higher costs.[6]

The increase in French output and productivity in 1948 and 1949 also contributed to the rapid reduction in France's external deficit. By the middle of 1949, the index of industrial production had risen to 130 per cent of 1938; this level is approximately equal to the prewar peak attained in 1929. This increase in total availabilities for consumption and export came about, however, principally by the elimination of coal shortages and other industrial bottlenecks. At the present time productive resources are more fully employed and much of the slack in the industrial system has been taken up. Industrial production in recent months has failed to recover fully from the seasonal decline during the summer of 1949 and during the winter of 1950 was considerably below the spring (1949) peak period. Although this decline in industrial activity is in part a reflection of the mild recession which now exists in France and the shift from a seller's to a buyer's market, it also suggests that a productive plateau may have now

[6] Subsequent to the time of presentation of this paper, the French Parliament passed collective bargaining legislation (on February 11, 1950). The newly-established collective bargaining procedures were unable to cope with the wave of strikes which broke out almost immediately, and which resulted in what has been generally regarded as a defeat for the French labor movement although wage increases of between 5 per cent and 8 per cent were applied unilaterally by employers. More recently, collective bargaining has been delayed pending a political decision on the level at which the "minimum vital" shall be fixed by the High Commission on Collective Bargaining. Some further increases in money wages in France appear to be an integral part of the economic program of the Pleven Government.

been reached. Further increases in production will, therefore, be difficult and will depend upon a more fundamental attack upon the obstacles to greater productivity in France. The French investment program (the Monnet Plan for Modernization and Reequipment) represents a major effort in this direction, although the pattern of investment is not in all cases the one which will achieve most effectively the objectives of the ERP. The investment program, moreover, must be supplemented by measures to increase the productivity of existing resources by the adoption of improved techniques, reorganization of production methods, and retraining of personnel. French progress in increasing productivity and lowering costs through measures of this type has been disappointing, although a number of technical assistance projects in this field have recently been initiated under ECA sponsorship. Recent experience with direct measures to increase productivity has revealed clearly how difficult it is to move rapidly on problems in which a basic change in deep-set and well-established cultural and business attitudes is involved.

Another aspect of the relationship between the domestic cost and price structure and the volume of international trade is the inflexibility of the price system which results from the prevalent restrictive business practices in France. Restrictive agreements which fix prices and allocate output appear to be an important characteristic of many French industries and markets. These agreements have permitted industrialists to profit handsomely during the inflationary period, but have prevented deflationary pressures from having their desired effect upon the price structure. The failure of industrial prices to decline helped to arrest the downward price movement of early 1949, and this price inflexibility, in the face of increased availabilities of consumer goods and stiffening consumer resistance to high prices, now appears to be the principal reason for the recently reduced level of industrial activity. As long as markets are protected from competition by agreements of this type, the incentives to the adoption of improved productive techniques are reduced. Moreover, there is a real danger that the benefits of increased productivity arising through the modernization of equipment will be dissipated in the form of higher profits rather than lower prices and increased domestic and foreign sales. Some increasing awareness of the importance of this problem is evident: Premier Bidault's speech of investiture included a promise to present antitrust legislation to the National Assembly. European concepts of appropriate antitrust legislation and of the desirability or undesirability of different types of cartel agreements often differ markedly from American, however. There is little reason for optimism over the immediate success which might attend any of the legislation likely to emanate from the French parliament as it is constituted at present.[7]

The other (external) side of the coin is reflected by ECA's program to increase international and domestic competition by the liberalization of intra-European trade. France has taken active leadership within the OEEC in the discussion of trade liberalization, but has had considerable difficulty in overcoming the strong resistance of protectionist groups within the country in order to live up to its commitments. In compliance with the OEEC decision of November 2, 1949, France has removed quantitative restrictions on slightly more than 50 per cent of its private trade with the other participating countries. The direct trade impact of this measure has been reduced by the simultaneous reimposition of tariffs on many of the liberated commodities.[8] It is clear that trade liberalization will have to proceed further before increased foreign competition and a wider European market are reflected in greater efficiency and lower costs within French industry, which has long been protected from external competition. Further progress will be attendant upon the ability of the French coalition government to move effectively in the face of the strong opposition which industrial and agricultural groups will undoubtedly offer.

The Franco-Italian Customs Union and the financial union among France, Italy, Belgium-Luxemburg, and the Netherlands (which has been variously christened "Fritalux," "Benefit," and "Finebel") offer additional opportunities for the removal of trade barriers and the restoration of more normal trading incentives. The Franco-Italian Customs Union appears to have been delayed by the OEEC measures of trade liberalization and the Finebel negotiations, and is certain to meet strong opposition from the representatives of some industrial and agricultural interests in the French Parliament. The latter group, which is an attempt to achieve a closer financial union among a small number of supposedly complementary economies, is still in the discussion stage, and any comments on its possible success would be premature.[9] It is clear, however, that if French industry and agricul-

---

[7] Subsequent events have confirmed this judgment. It now appears doubtful that any antitrust legislation will be passed in the near future, and the bills which have been under consideration leave a great deal to be desired.

[8] The newly imposed tariffs are part of the schedule for France approved at various postwar international tariff conferences.

[9] The Finebel proposal failed to survive the political storms, but has been replaced in effect by the more dramatic and far-reaching Schuman Plan for the pooling of the Western European steel and coal industries. If the Schuman Plan comes to fruition in the form in which it is currently (July 1950) being discussed in Paris, it will represent a major development in the economic field by the restoration of internal and external competition to these industries.

ture are exposed to international competition on any large scale as a result of the measures under consideration, basic readjustments in production methods and costs will be necessary in some of the major sectors if present markets are to be kept or expanded.

Another factor of considerable importance in determining the course of French trade since the war has been the system of exchange rates. It may be recalled that the exchange rate between the French franc and the dollar was 37.75 to 1 from May 1938 until the outbreak of the war. In November 1944, French authorities fixed a rate of 49.6 francs to the dollar. At this rate the franc was definitely over-valued in terms of most currencies, but it was apparently believed that an overvalued rate would act as a brake on rising domestic prices. Any hope that the exchange rate would be able to contain domestic inflationary pressures was clearly unrealistic, given the state of the French economy in 1944 and 1945, as subsequent events quickly demonstrated. The new rate adopted in December 1945 of 119 francs to the dollar temporarily made French prices competitive in world markets for many products, but so long as inflation was not brought under control further devaluations were inevitable.

In January 1948, following intermittent and inconclusive discussions with the International Monetary Fund, a new, complex, and highly controversial system of multiple, fluctuating exchange rates was adopted. The "official" rate of the franc to the dollar was fixed at 214 to 1, with the exchange rates for other currencies calculated at the appropriate cross-rates. At the same time, a new market was established for the franc, nominally "free" but actually influenced by the exchange control authorities. This free rate applied to all noncommercial transactions with the dollar, the Portuguese escudo, and, shortly later, the Swiss franc. The free rate was intended to encourage tourists from these currency areas to convert their foreign exchange into francs through official channels rather than the black market where the proceeds were lost to the Office des Changes. A further purpose was to encourage the voluntary repatriation of undeclared assets held abroad in the currencies in question.

In an effort to encourage exports to the United States, Portugal, and Switzerland, exporters earning dollars, escudos, or Swiss francs were permitted to exchange half of the proceeds at the official rate and half at the free rate. Importers were initially obliged to purchase their foreign exchange on the free market. This procedure was later modified and the effective rate for imports also became the average of the free and official rates, except for certain essential raw materials which were imported at the lowest of the three rates, the official rate. Since the effective rate for almost all commercial transactions with the dollar was the average rate, while cross-rates for the pound and other currencies were based on the lower or official rate, there was a theoretical possibility of commodity arbitrage at considerable profit.

Whether or not such commodity arbitrage actually developed may be debatable, but in any event the confusion attendant upon the new system, together with the failure to devaluate sufficiently relative to the pound, the Belgian franc, and other currencies, undoubtedly retarded the expansion of French exports. Despite special arrangements with Belgium and Italy which were subsequently adopted, the black-market rate for the dollar (which is an imperfect but significant indicator of the true market value of the franc) increased. The widening gap between free and black-market rates diverted tourist receipts from official channels. The trade deficit with the Sterling Area continued to deteriorate.

In October 1948, a so-called "alignment" of the franc occurred, with the approval of the International Monetary Fund. The differential for essential imports was abandoned, and the cross-rates for other currencies were raised to the level of the average rather than the official rate. An orderly system of cross-rates was thus established for commercial transactions, although for certain currencies financial transactions continued to be based on the free rate. The black-market rate for the dollar continued to rise rapidly during the last months of 1948, but principally for reasons not directly related to the external trade position of France. Paralleling the success of the Queuille government in carrying out its anti-inflationary price and credit policies, the black-market rate declined during the first six months of 1949 to within 10 to 15 per cent of the free rate, probably the narrowest margin possible under the then existing circumstances.

The devaluation of the pound in September 1949 provided the French government with the opportunity to establish a single, uniform system of exchange rates. The new rate of 350 francs to the dollar represented a substantial devaluation (22.5 per cent) from the average or commercial rate, undoubtedly dictated by the magnitude of the sterling devaluation. The effects of the devaluation cannot yet be determined with any precision, but no appreciable improvement in French trade with the dollar area has resulted to date nor is any marked improvement likely in view of the nature of American demand for French exports to the United States and the extent of devaluation of other currencies. It is highly doubtful, however, whether any franc-dollar rate which is a realistic possibility could restore equilibrium in the French balance of payments with the dollar area, for reasons which will be discussed further below. As a result of the different degree of devaluation of various currencies, the franc was devalued with respect to some currencies and appreciated in value with respect to others. On the whole, the net change in either direction with non-dollar currencies is probably very slight.

A discussion of the theoretically appropriate system of exchange rates in France would take us far afield here, and I do not pretend to the technical competence necessary to undertake such an appraisal. Nor am I yet persuaded that this type of analysis could derive an even theoretically acceptable rate under present world trading conditions. It is interesting to note, however, in connection with the most popular exchange rate theory—that of purchasing power parities— that the new franc-dollar rate is almost exactly that which a comparison of relative increases in the price levels in France and the United States between 1938 and 1949 would indicate. In any event, it would appear that considerable progress toward a realistic exchange rate has been made, and that further exchange rate adjustments of the franc at the present time are no longer an issue of primary importance.

In addition to the stimulus to exports provided by the several devaluations of the franc, specific measures to encourage exports have been adopted. Special credit facilities and credit insurance are available to exporters. Exporters to the dollar area are also permitted to retain 15 per cent and exporters to other areas 10 per cent of their export proceeds to cover such expenses as travel, selling, advertising, and in some cases the purchase of special raw materials. An additional 10 per cent may be retained to finance the purchase of equipment. More recently, a franc-dollar export board has been organized by the Conseil National du Patronat Français (the French counterpart of the National Association of Manufacturers) to serve the government in a private advisory capacity. The board is patterned after the British Dollar Export Board, and it is a fair presumption that it will give serious consideration to the British scheme to encourage advertising and market surveys by the provision of insurance against possible loss.

The export incentives adopted to date, while sound and desirable in themselves, have had disappointing results. Exports to the dollar area in 1949 were slightly more than $100 million, approximately the same amount as in 1948 and only 15 per cent of dollar imports in 1949. Some of the reasons for the failure of dollar exports to expand sufficiently can be readily observed. The French authorities have essentially regarded the dollar-export problem as one of an inadequate supply of export goods. This point of view may have been appropriate during the period of limited production, but it is becoming increasingly evident that the major obstacle to further French sales in the dollar market is a deficiency of American demand for French products at existing prices and qualities. To stimulate American demand will require a larger and more ambitious export program than has hitherto been undertaken or contemplated. Large-scale market surveys, extensive advertising, improved merchandising methods, and better-established marketing channels are all prerequisites to a substantial penetration of the American market. In addition, French exports to the United States are too often deliberately styled and priced for the luxury trade. The greatest opportunities for increased American sales would appear to be instead in the largely untapped demand of the middle-class American consumer for products which are distinctively French but produced in sufficient quantities for sale in the intermediate price field.

It should be emphasized that a very important element in French exports is the American tariff structure, which, for example, ranges between 30 and 55 per cent on many French textile products. The unduly cumbersome and complex customs procedures are also an important limitation on France's export potential. A reduction in American tariffs and simplification of customs procedure would unquestionably contribute greatly to the expansion of French exports to this country.

IV

The last section of this chapter will consider briefly some of the prospects for French trade during the remainder of the ERP period and immediately thereafter.

The present time is particularly inappropriate for the task, difficult enough under the best of circumstances, of assessing the possibilities of dollar viability within the agreed time-span of the ERP. As indicated previously, the government is confronted with basic decisions in the field of budgetary, credit, wage, and price policy which may affect materially the future course of its external trade. In addition, on the outcome of decisions which will be made during 1950 with regard to Finebel, the further liberalization of trade, and the establishment of a European Payments Union for multilateral settlements will depend to a large extent the future volume and direction of trade and the ability of France to maintain equilibrium in its European balance of payments at a high level of international trade and real income at home. The possibility that French Indo-China will be able to regain its important position in the export trade of the French Union also cannot be predicted at this juncture. Nevertheless, a few generalizations will be ventured, hedged with all the qualifications which must attend any efforts at prognostication in this field.

The official program for French recovery during the ERP period is contained in the "Long Term Program" submitted to the OEEC in October 1948. According to this program, the French gross national product in 1952–1953 is expected to reach 128 per cent of 1938 and 131 per cent of the last half of 1948. It is estimated that the increase in gross national product, which includes a consumption target of 120 per cent of 1938 (126 per cent of 1948) and an investment target of 140 per cent of 1948, will necessitate an increase in industrial production by 1952–1953 of 140 per cent over 1948 and in agricultural production of 125 per cent over the prewar average. The agricultural production goals are intended to permit France to be a substantial exporter of wheat and other products. Only a 5 per cent increase in the industrial labor force is assumed, and the average work week is not expected to lengthen. The rise in industrial production must therefore come about through a 33 per cent increase in productivity above the 1948 level as a result of new capital investment and reorganization of productive methods. Similarly, the increase in agricultural output is assumed to result from a sharp increase in the use of machinery and fertilizers, improved seed utilization, and major changes in other farming methods, rather than from wider land cultivation or an increase in the agricultural labor force.

The 1952–1953 balance of payments objectives involve the restoration of over-all balance in the current account of the French Union, at a level of imports and exports 30 to 35 per cent above 1938 in real terms. The current account of Metropolitan France is scheduled to show a net deficit of $167 million, to be offset by a net surplus of the French overseas territories on current account of an identical amount. (Included as current account items are the heavy amortization payments scheduled on France's external debt in 1952–1953.) The long-term program does not assume that France will have completely eliminated its dollar deficit by the end of the ERP period.[10] Imports from North and Central America are programmed at $365 million and shipping expenditures at $30 million, while net interest and amortization payments are estimated at $140 million. The estimates of gross dollar earnings from exports and tourism in 1952–1953 are highly optimistic, both being shown as $190 million with North and Central America. When other invisibles are added, a net deficit of $140 million in the current account of the French Union with North and Central America results.

This dollar deficit is to be offset by an equivalent surplus with other areas, but this surplus (with the possible exception of part of

---

[10] The long-term program is based on geographical rather than currency areas. It is possible that some of the trade with South America will still involve dollar settlements in 1952–1953, but the amount of these settlements cannot be predicted at this stage.

the estimated $53 million surplus with South America) will not be available to meet dollar payments unless all currencies are freely convertible into dollars, which appears highly improbable by the end of the period in question. It is expected that the French Union will have a surplus of $35 million with the participating countries and the nonparticipating Sterling Area and a surplus of $105 million with the rest of the world.

It now appears that the original production targets set forth in the long-term program will be difficult, if not impossible, to achieve by 1952–1953. This is particularly true for agricultural production, which suffered a setback along some lines as a result of the protracted drought during 1949. Moreover, the administrative and technical obstacles to the large-scale reorganization and modernization of production methods which is necessary for the magnitude of increases in agricultural production called for can only be resolved slowly and sometimes at great effort. At the present rate of increase, French agriculture may be relatively self-sufficient by 1952–1953, but without the large export surplus originally programmed. In industrial production, substantial increases above the plateau which has recently been reached will only result from a concerted attack, of which there is still little evidence, upon obsolete production methods and conservative business attitudes. The program of the overseas territories, which involves a conversion of the present substantial trade deficit into an equally substantial surplus, will not be accomplished in full, particularly if the Indo-Chinese conflict continues much longer.

The failure of France to reach the goals which were set in the long-term program should not in itself cause serious concern. It has always been recognized that the long-term program established guideposts or targets rather than specific objectives, which, if not achieved, would eliminate the possibility of French or European viability. It is evident that substantial progress in the direction of viability has already been made, and although the problems which remain are more intractable than those which have been solved, there is still a clear possibility of further progress within the balance of the ERP period. It should also be recognized that viability is not solely a function of a given level of international trade, but depends as well on complementary domestic policies which also influence the level of employment and real income. On balance, it appears that the restoration of equilibrium in France's payments position with all non-dollar areas by 1952 at a high level of international trade is well within the realm of possibility, provided that European currencies can be cleared on a multilateral basis. In fact, as has been noted, the progress already made toward this objective is impressive.

The elimination of the dollar gap is, of course, a more difficult problem concerning which there is less ground for optimism. It will be recalled that the French payments deficit with the dollar area predates the Second World War. The loss of the prewar investment and shipping income, together with the incurring of heavy postwar indebtedness which will entail large interest and amortization payments, give some indication of the magnitude of the dollar problem which has confronted France. Moreover, there is a "hard core" of imports from the United States which cannot be reduced without serious repercussions on domestic production. Cotton, petroleum and petroleum products, nonferrous metals, chemicals, and machinery and equipment are the principal components of dollar imports. The only good prospects for the replacement of American by European sources of supply of these products appears to be in machinery, and even here the possibilities are limited. The balance consists of numerous small items (tobacco, fats and oils, etc.), in which the opportunities for substantial dollar savings are relatively slight. Even under optimistic assumptions with regard to French exports to the dollar area and tourist receipts, some deficit on current account (including amortization of foreign loans) with the United States at the end of the ERP period appears to be probable. In addition, some measure of discrimination against dollar products for balance of payments reasons will still be necessary if the deficit is to be kept within manageable proportions. Under favorable circumstances, and with continued discrimination, the deficit might be in the neighborhood of $100–$150 million, although no figure can have precise meaning at this stage. This is an impressive reduction below the immediate postwar level of over $1 billion.

This figure coincides roughly with the deficit of $140 million with North and Central America estimated by France in the long-term program, although the internal composition of my estimate is quite different from that of the French. It should be emphasized, of course, that this small deficit implies a considerable reduction in the volume of imports from the United States below the present level. Although France may, under favorable circumstances, be close to independence from extraordinary foreign assistance by 1952–1953, therefore, the narrowing of the dollar gap will be achieved at a lower level of American trade than would be desirable or would exist under freer trading conditions. Moreover, viability for France and the rest of Europe will be a dynamic and continuing problem of keeping abreast of the rate of technological advance in the United States.

The persistence of a slight dollar gap beyond 1952 can hardly be taken as an indictment of the ERP or evidence of its failure. On the contrary, the experiment has been ambitious, and the progress achieved by combined European and American efforts is remarkable in many respects. It does suggest, however, that French and European trade problems are an expression of deep-seated economic, political, and cultural forces which will not yield to easy panaceas. It is the prevalance of these structural problems, not only in France but throughout Western Europe, that has led to the adoption by ECA of the program to achieve a single, competitive market through the liberalization of intra-European trade and the economic unification of Western Europe.

VII

PROBLEMS OF FRENCH SECURITY

23

++

THE MILITARY DEFEAT

OF 1940 IN RETROSPECT

RICHARD D. CHALLENER

++

"No ARMY in the world, in the geographical situation of France, could have stopped the German flood in 1940." These were the consoling words of the Canadian ambassador to France in February of 1946.[1] Radical Socialist leader Édouard Herriot, adopting this formula, has since commented that such a view has to be taken into account if anyone attempts to discover the reasons for the defeat of his country. It is his belief that since France was the "advance guard" of a world coalition which had not as yet mobilized and that since his nation lacked the space in which to retreat and regroup her armed forces, the military issue was inevitable. Furthermore, Herriot maintained, if Frenchmen would only try to attain such a perspective, they would be able to regain confidence in their military leaders and in the institutions of the Third Republic as well.[2]

But few Frenchmen have been capable of such an Olympian detachment. Since the very moment of the armistice and, especially, since the Vichy-sponsored Riom trial of 1942, the search for "the guilty" has continued. Barely six months after the speech of the Canadian diplomat, the National Constituent Assembly, with the unanimous backing of all political parties, established a parliamentary investigating commission charged with the job of discovering "the ensemble of

---

[1] Quoted in Albert Vallet, *Le Problème militaire de la IVe République* (Lyons, 1947), p. 171.

[2] For Herriot's views, see his preface to Vallet, *op. cit.*, pp. 10–11. The same view of France as an unfortunate advance guard has been expressed by the editors of the semi-official publication of the Historical Section of the General Staff, *Revue historique de l'armée* (January 1946), pp. 46–47.

political, economic, diplomatic, and military events which, from 1933 to 1945, have preceded, accompanied, and followed the armistice." This would be a formidable enough task for any group of legislators —and one which far transcends purely military considerations. It was obvious from the general debate that political motives were as important as a desire for the truth. Socialists hoped to use the commission to snare a bag of collaborators and trace the rise of the Fifth Column in France. Communists were hopeful not only that the inquiry would reveal who had blocked collective security and the Franco-Russian Alliance but also, as their spokesman phrased it, that it would reveal the manner in which French industrialists "protected by the Cagoulard general staff" had formed criminal agreements in 1936 to sabotage war production.[3]

Much of the literature on the 1940 defeat, like the parliamentary debates, is one-sided and partisan. A Swiss military writer—trying, like a good Swiss, to steer a neutral path through conflicting testimonies—observed somewhat petulantly that most of the books which "explain" the disaster seem to have been written only for the sake of proving certain predetermined points of view.[4] Perhaps the best example of this well-nigh universal tendency was the reissue after the Liberation of Paul Reynaud's short book, Le Problème militaire français. In 1937, when he was the major advocate in the Chamber of Deputies of Charles de Gaulle's then-revolutionary projects for a mechanized army of professional soldiers, Reynaud had written this book to warn his compatriots of the dire perils facing them if they failed to match German armored achievement. In 1945 Reynaud had the original reprinted; the only change appears to be a short, one-page introduction which may be summarized in four words: "I told you so."

Obviously, then, there is no dearth of opinions on the subject of the French defeat, but there is likewise little common agreement. To this day the French are not only divided among themselves on the reasons for their collapse but also confused in their explanations of it.[5] It is significant that the above-mentioned commission of inquiry has so far been unable to render any report of its findings to the Assembly and also that there has been very little scholarly work upon the subject of the defeat to match the scores of apologias and special

[3] Le Monde, August 30, 1946; for the full debate, see Journal officiel, Assemblée nationale, Débats (August 29, 1946), pp. 3389–401.

[4] Major Eddy Bauer, La Guerre des blindés (Lausanne, 1947), p. 55.

[5] A 1945 public opinion poll revealed that 31 per cent of the French people found themselves guilty, 18 per cent thought the leaders were responsible, and 13 per cent blamed politics in general. Others mentioned treason, the low birth rate, and national disunity. Saul K. Padover, "France Today," Social Research, XVI (December 1949), 493.

pleas of interested participants in the events of 1940.[6] Most opinions seem to be purely subjective or political interpretations and hence fail to attain significant conclusions. Right and Left mutually abuse one another, with most opinion reflecting the often superheated passions generated by the Popular Front, the Vichy period, and the military debacle itself. But can any nation as politically polarized as France be expected to arrive at any single or comprehensive view of a catastrophe as complete and as overwhelming as that which befell it within the short space of six bitter weeks?

The historian must nonetheless ask the question, "Why was France so easily conquered?" and seek to impose some rational pattern upon these conflicting testimonies. The greater portion of this paper is an attempt to establish some major theses which help to explain the French disaster. It will first discuss the main differences of opinion revealed in the current literature and attempt to make some reconciliation of the conflicting viewpoints. In the ensuing section a more fundamental factor will be considered—the French theory of the nature of war in the industrial age—which I believe to be the major cause of the military defeat. Throughout, primary attention will be given to military aspects of the defeat, ending with a few observations on what conclusions contemporary military theorists have drawn from the 1940 experience. It is of course undeniable that the origins of the French tragedy are deeply rooted in chronic, inherent weaknesses in her political, economic, and social structure. Indeed, in retrospect, it has frequently been argued that the collapse was but a reflection of these fundamental national infirmities. But nonetheless I believe that the military defeat itself is largely explicable in military terms and rises out of the failure to develop a theory of warfare adequate for the twentieth century. Hence, while it in no sense offers a complete explanation of the defeat, an analysis of the military debacle merits consideration by and for itself.

II

Most of the memoirs published since liberation fall into one of the two categories which were so evident at the Riom trial in 1942. That is, the political leaders insist that they were in no way responsible for the military outcome and that the Third Republic and its civil authorities provided adequate means for the defense of the na-

[6] The commission has, however, held a number of sessions at which such persons as Blum, Daladier, Gamelin, Weygand, etc., have testified. Articles in the French press indicate though that the investigation has uncovered little new information and that political considerations are still paramount in the evidence presented. For summaries, see *Le Monde*, May 23, 1947; *Le Populaire*, June 19, 1947, and July 19 and 24, 1947.

tion. Conversely, the military leaders (with the notable exception of Gamelin) maintain that it was not their failure but rather shortages of crucial equipment which produced the May disaster—and that the shortages, in turn, were not the fault of the army but of the Third Republic.

In their own defense the political heads of the pre-1940 era offer a multitude of appealing if unconvincing arguments. Former Finance Minister (now President of the Republic) Vincent Auriol has written that according to the constitution the formidable task of preparing mobilization plans, defining war doctrine, and formulating military strategy was in no way incumbent upon the civil authorities.[7] Therefore he feels that it is unjust to blame any of the military failures upon the political leadership. Controller General Robert Jacomet insists that he and Daladier not only provided 14 billion francs of credits for war materials at a time when the military chiefs had themselves asked for but 9 billion, but also that his administration completed a four-year armament program a full eight months in advance. With regard to armaments supply, he asserts, "The military administration is without reproach." [8] Both Daladier and Blum, relying upon a phrase of Gamelin, have confidently claimed that in 1940 there was "an honorable equality" between German and French arms. They never fail to insist that it was the Popular Front government which first gave serious attention to rearmament (in 1936) and that, if there were any difficulties in getting the program under way, the reason is simply that preceding war ministries, particularly that of Marshal Pétain in 1934, had neglected war industry and cut appropriations for the armed forces.[9] Indeed, so convinced of their own righteousness are some Radical Socialists that their view can be expressed in the form of a challenge to the military, such as, "We demand once again that there be published—if anyone dares—the complete list of war materials of all sorts which fell into the hands of the enemy during the war or were destroyed to escape them. The astronomical figures at which we would arrive would remove the scales from the eyes of those whom the Riom trial has not yet convinced and would absolve the Third Republic." [10]

[7] Vincent Auriol, *Hier . . . demain* (Paris, 1944), II, 53.

[8] Robert Jacomet, *L'Armement de la France, 1936–1939* (Paris, 1945), p. 322; *Le Populaire*, July 19, 1947. The view is not supportable; for a real critique, see Maurice Gamelin, *Servir* (Paris, 1946), I, 221–22; and Paul Reynaud, *La France a sauvé l'Europe* (Paris, 1947), I, 391–93. Daladier himself before and during the war did not believe this. See his *In Defense of France* (New York, 1939), pp. 117 and 55 ff., and his speech to the Chamber of Deputies on December 28, 1939, in which he said the war had prevented completing the arms program.

[9] Based on statements before the Commission d'Enquête.

[10] Vallet, *op. cit.*, p. 135.

Needless to say, many of the military hierarchy have developed diametrically opposed views. Their major emphasis is upon the overwhelming quantitative superiority of German arms, the deficiencies of French equipment, and the failure of the civil authorities to provide them with the requisite tools. For many this alone suffices to explain the disaster of French forces in Belgium and on the Meuse. A typical though harsh example of the unrepentant military view was expressed by an embittered St. Cyr graduate, Robert Darcy, in his *Oraison funèbre pour la vieille armée*. Parliament and people, he maintained, as a result of their perpetual distrust of the army, have always hampered its development by interfering in its affairs and by denying it sufficient financial credits. If, for example, the army had cadres of poor quality or quantity, it was because the politicians imposed such cadres; if attempts to reorganize the armed forces were a failure, party politics were to blame. But, despite all this, in the hours of disaster, the French people inevitably attempt to absolve their own responsibility by blaming the army and its leaders instead of themselves.[11]

The top army officials are, moreover, often at odds among themselves. Generals Georges and Gamelin, for example, have differed sharply about the wisdom of the initial movement of the French armies into Belgium on May 10. Georges, who was commander in chief on the northeastern front and thus in charge of the operation, believes that the French should have remained in defensive positions on their own frontiers because the Germans were clearly superior in tanks and planes. In his opinion, the advance into the Low Countries was a disastrous blunder which inevitably led to the loss of irreplaceable manpower and irreplaceable equipment. But Gamelin, the overall commander in chief, insists that there was no German superiority in armor and that a sound strategical plan was robbed of its value by mistakes committed by senior officers in executing it. Georges counters with the view that, whatever the errors perpetrated by officers of his command, they were inseparable from the hopeless situation

---

[11] Cited in *La Revue de défense nationale*, VIII (January 1949), 139. Memoirs by such general officers as Edmond Ruby (of the general staff of the Second Army at Sedan) or General Requin (of the Fourth Army) stress materiel shortages. The latter officer indicated his view of the hopelessness of the struggle by the very title of his book, *Combats pour l'honneur* (Paris, 1946). General L.-M. Chassin in his history of the Second World War presents the conventional interpretation when he claims that France had but 930 tanks to oppose Germany's 4,300, a virtual five-to-one German superiority which of course points up the hopelessness of the struggle. See his *Histoire de la deuxième guerre mondiale* (Paris, 1947), p. 48. Gamelin himself, it is interesting to note, sent to Reynaud on May 18, 1940, a long report on the causes of the disaster in which he took this viewpoint, but in his memoirs he specifically repudiates much of this report. *op. cit.*, III, 419 ff.

into which the army was thrown by the very nature of the maneuver.[12]

These examples, brief though they are, set the general outline of the problem. On the crucial questions of strategy and armaments there is disagreement, not to say bitterness. Can any conclusions be drawn from such a discordant chorus of strident voices? While the wisdom of strategical decisions may perhaps be referred to the decision of military analysts, the question of armament supplies can now be answered by statistics which would have been considered unbelievable a decade ago. New evidence permits more than tentative revaluations and, I believe, leads directly to some major conclusions on the causes of the French defeat.

Since the most striking feature of the German attack was the overwhelming success of her air-tank teams, this has been both the most hotly debated and most thoroughly investigated aspect of the materiel problem. It must be admitted, however, at the outset that ten years of investigation has not changed the original testimony about French airpower. Recent documented studies indicate that, at the very minimum, the Luftwaffe had a three-to-one superiority over the combined Franco-British aerial forces. Not only did the French possess no equivalent to the potent Stuka divebomber but, qualitatively, French machines were inferior to the German in every category from fighter to heavy bomber.[13] But, in the remaining categories of war equipment, new evidence supports a conclusion that the opposing armies in 1940 possessed about the same amounts of materiel. Several impartial surveys, based upon the interrogation of German generals and research in French war archives, go a long way to show that there was indeed an approximate equality between the numbers of available tanks in the May battles. Statistics may well be suspect, but it is significant that several interpretations insist that French and German forces possessed approximately four thousand tanks apiece and that, at the most, the Germans enjoyed a one-sixth superiority in armored ve-

---

[12] See Georges' preface to General Roton's *Années cruciales* (Paris, 1947), or a discussion of his views in *Informations militaires*, No. 110 (March 10, 1948), 38. Gamelin (*op. cit.*, I, 81–111) discusses the Belgian maneuver and gives his reasons for believing it to have been strategically sound. He is, however, careful to point out (p. 84) that the decision was reached at an inter-Allied political conference on September 20, 1939. and especially approved by Daladier and Chamberlain. His criticisms of the execution of the Belgian maneuver are scattered throughout Volume III of *Servir*, which deals with the conduct of the war.

[13] Colonel Paquier (Chief of the Historical Service of the Air Force), Chef de Bataillon Pierre Lyet, and Lt. Colonel de Cossé-Brissac, "Combien d'avions allemands contre combien d'avions français le 10 mai 1940?", *Revue de défense nationale*, VI (June 1948), 741–59. Colonel Paquier dealt with the problem of quality, stating flatly that "all our planes, pursuit or bombardment, were outclassed on all points by the *Luftwaffe*" (p. 745), while the latter two officers concerned themselves with quantitative problems.

hicles—one which hardly can be described as overwhelming. As regards the other weapons of the ground forces, we have Gamelin's word that the only serious inequality was in land mines and that, qualitatively, certain French weapons—like the antitank gun—were actually more effective than the Wehrmacht equivalents.[14] The conventional opinion that the French armies of 1940 were completely outnumbered in all types of equipment is thus challenged by new evidence in all fields but that of airpower, where the verdict remains unchanged.

Consequently, though they are aware of the obvious French inferiority in planes, more and more observers are concluding, as one of them expresses it, that, "It does not seem that anyone can retain as an explanation for our 1940 defeat the sole argument of the crushing inferiority of our mechanized cavalry and tank forces." [15] Likewise a reviewer for the semiofficial publication of the Ministry of National Defense receives the work of an officer of the Historical Service joyfully because his book, unlike the publications of the defeated generals, "insists upon the equality of ground forces materiel and retains only the aerial supremacy of the enemy." [16]

This may seem mere quibbling with numbers but, nonetheless, the fact that the much-maligned and supposedly inferior French war industry was able to produce (at least until 1940) quantities of armament roughly equivalent to those produced by Hitler's Germany must necessarily shift the very basis of argument. The important question becomes, not how much armament did the French have, but what

[14] The best studies are Colonel Georges Ferré, *Le Défaut de l'armure* (Paris, 1948), and Lt. Colonel de Cossé-Brissac, "Combien des chars français contre combien de chars allemands le 10 mai 1940?", *Revue de défense nationale*, v (July 1947), 75–89. The former officer, a professor of military history at the École Supérieure des Forces Armées, claims that England and France together had 4,800 tanks to only 3,800 on the German side (pp. 108, 138–39), while De Cossé-Brissac, confining his figures to modern vehicles, discovered 3,800 tanks on the German side opposed to but 3,100 on the Franco-British (p. 86). Gamelin in *Servir* (I, 160) estimates 4,000 German armored vehicles to 3,616 Franco-British. All these figures are very complicated and depend upon what bases are used in calculation. If outmoded tanks are counted, it is possible to pad the French figures considerably—even by including some 1918 models! It also depends on whether tanks are counted as of the day they left the factory or the day they were received in combat units, or whether tanks in reserve units in the interior should be counted. My estimate of 4,000 is a very rough attempt to balance these factors and probably overestimates the French figure; the German statistics are based largely on statements by General Guderian (Gamelin, *op. cit.*, III, 41–44). The British supplied 600 of the Allied total. Despite the wide variants in even these "authoritative" studies, the essential point is that all three stress a near equality in armor and attack the legend of an overwhelming German superiority. Finally, for Gamelin's estimate of the other arms and equipment, see his succinct summary in *ibid.*, III, 448–49.

[15] De Cossé-Brissac, "Combien des chars?", *loc. cit.*, p. 88.

[16] *Informations militaires*, No. 113 (May 10, 1948), 38.

use did the French high command intend to make of it and how effective was it? Such an analysis is more significant than the mere question of numbers and quantity of equipment.

On the employment of equipment, all authorities are virtually unanimous: the French war doctrine emphasized the defensive potentialities of modern arms and placed little or no faith in their value on the offense. To select again the example of armor, French theories called almost exclusively for its employment on reconnaissance missions and in close support of infantry units. As a consequence, aside from creating several armored divisions, the French command did not combine its tank battalions into larger units but instead broke them down into companies and even smaller sections. These tiny groups were then posted in defensive positions scattered along the entire front where their job was to aid the infantry defenders.[17] As a result of this dispersal of potential strength, the entire Ninth Army on the vital Sedan sector possessed a total of three tank battalions to oppose the armored corps of Guderian which alone boasted in excess of a thousand vehicles. This is one of the main reasons why observers in 1940 received the impression that German mechanized strength was much greater than that of their hapless opponent. The fault lay in dispersal rather than concentration of strength. It did not lie in hopeless numerical inferiority.

The quality of French armor, however, was inferior to that of the German. Yet here again French theoretical concepts of the mission of mechanized vehicles were largely responsible for the mechanical and technical weaknesses of armored equipment. For instance, the radius of action of French tanks was less than that of the German, their weight of armor made them slower than the Panzers, and their radio equipment was inferior. French tanks were designed to stick close to the infantry and not to engage in far-reaching offensive maneuvers in which they themselves would set the pace of attack. Moreover, German armor was integrated with artillery and antitank weapons so that on several occasions larger French armored units— which lacked this assistance—were defeated by inferior numbers of German tanks.[18] Qualitative weaknesses arose from the failure of the General Staff—and its civil advisers—to envisage any other role for mechanized equipment than the defensive.

To whatever conclusion one may come about the relative amounts of armament, one is logically and finally driven to this conclusion: the French theory of war is more important than the quantities of

[17] Ferré, *op. cit.*, pp. 104, 193.
[18] *ibid.*, pp. 116 ff., and, for an excellent analysis of the design and characteristics of French tanks, see Bauer, *op. cit.*, p. 24.

French arms as a cause of the 1940 military collapse. As a French writer expressed it sharply, "The defeat of 1940 has its roots . . . in an eclipse of French military thought during the twenty years between the two world conflicts." [19]

III

It remains to be asked, what was this fatal doctrine of war and how did it rise to such general acceptance that neither the Spanish nor the Polish campaigns made any impression on French military thinking? It is of course well known that French theories of war were founded upon an unshatterable belief in the superiority of the defense and the continuous line of fire and that, when this concept was pitted against the superior German theory of the Blitzkrieg, the latter won a clear-cut victory.[20] Even Maurice Gamelin, who makes out a fairly convincing case that he himself did not adhere to this doctrine, nevertheless confesses that his one great error was that he believed it unnecessary to make any special efforts to change the "Maginot Line complex" of his officer corps.[21] It is likewise well known that Pétain and his followers were to a very large extent responsible for the dominance of this defensive credo in the official army mind. It was their argument, based upon the successful defense of Verdun in the First World War, that an entrenched army could withstand almost any frontal assault, since the firepower of artillery and machine guns gave the defenders complete control of the battlefield.[22]

There were also many other reasons why the doctrine of the defense was attractive to the nation as a whole. It appealed to a people bled white by losses in the First World War (particularly by the rash

[19] Tony Albord, "Appel à l'imagination," *Revue de défense nationale,* IX (August–September 1949), 159. It is also noteworthy that the Vichy government permitted the publication in 1941 of a book by a Colonel M. Alerme, *Les Causes militaires de notre défaite,* in which the main argument was that France had fallen because of the erroneous war doctrines of the High Command. While Alerme's book is filled with pro-Vichy and anti-British propaganda, it nevertheless maintains that, aside from planes, the French armies were well equipped (pp. 42–43). The book was of course published a year before the Riom trial—by which time the Vichyites had formulated their own theory which absolved the military (except Gamelin) and blamed the politicians for failing to supply the army.

[20] See especially Irving Gibson, "Maginot and Liddell Hart: The Doctrine of the Defense," in E. M. Earle (ed.), *Makers of Modern Strategy* (Princeton, 1943), pp. 365–87.

[21] Gamelin, *op. cit.,* I, 237, 373–74.

[22] Reynaud (*op. cit.,* I, 191 ff., and II, 412 ff.) constructed a dossier on Pétain which is undoubtedly one of the high points of all the attacks upon the Marshal's military theories. Reynaud, who despises Pétain, makes him the scapegoat for everything and particularly endeavors to collect all the unfavorable opinions ever uttered about him by other Frenchmen; his favorite quotation is from Foch, "When there is nothing to do, it's Pétain's job." The result is a very unfair portrait of the man and his ideas, but it does lay the record bare.

offensives of 1914 and 1917), since it promised to keep loss of life at a minimum. To pacifist-inclined political groups like the Socialists, defensive warfare alone seemed legitimate. When, for example, in the mid-1930's De Gaulle and Reynaud campaigned for an armored corps of professional soldiers, the Socialists led the pack in rejecting the demand not only because of their traditional fear of pretorian guards but also because they felt such armored forces were designed solely for aggressive, offensive warfare.[23]

But there is another and more fundamental reason why the French as a nation—for it was not simply the military leaders who were responsible but the people as a whole—adopted the concept of defensive warfare. The answer lies in the theory of total war which grew up in the years after 1918. This theory was itself both a reaction against pre-1914 doctrines of war and a reflection of the impact of modern industrial techniques and economic development upon the conduct of warfare. It is also, I believe, at the very root of the reasons why France was so easily defeated in 1940.

After the disaster of 1870–1871 the French junked their professional army and adopted their own version of the Prussian nation in arms—though, of course, with considerable addition of their own republican and Revolutionary theories. In its early years the Third Republic thus accepted—at first hesitantly, later wholeheartedly—the idea of a mass army based upon universal, short-term conscription. From then until 1914 ensued a never-ending competition with Germany to obtain the greatest number of effectives. But, even as late as 1914, the concept of the nation in arms was based exclusively and solely upon the employment of manpower. Nowhere was there any conception that French economic resources—her factories or her farms—would play any vital role in the prosecution of the threatened conflict.[24] Mass armies alone were seen as the decisive factors in war. Moreover, the prevailing opinion in both military and political circles throughout all Europe was that any war which occurred would be a short war. High commands, imbued with Clausewitzean theories, confidently predicted that the first clashes would be crucial. Victory in these initial battles would give one belligerent such an immediate advantage that the remainder of the conflict might well be little more than a large-scale mopping-up action. A theorist like Ferdinand Foch believed that the very existence of these mass armies made a short war the only kind conceivable. These armies, he argued, were com-

[23] *Journal officiel, Chambre des Députés, Débats* (March 15, 1935), pp. 1022–27.

[24] How little economic preparation there was for 1914 can be strikingly seen in the testimony of government officials, military leaders, and industrialists in the postwar parliamentary investigation concerning the failure to defend the Briey mineral basin. cf. *Journal officiel, Chambre des Députés, Documents,* Annexe 6026 (1919).

posed of civilians who had come from all ranks of society. The men had been taken away from their careers and their families; civilian life must therefore cease at the outbreak of hostilities. But, deprived of its male members, no society could exist for long without complete collapse. "From all this," Foch concluded, "it comes as a consequence that war cannot last a long time. . . ." [25]

Reality, as we all know, generally failed to live up to predictions. The First World War quickly developed into an endless, remorseless war of attrition in which every possible resource of manpower, industry, agriculture, transport—in short, the total economic complex of the belligerents—was tapped for its war potential.

In the postwar years these developments had a tremendous impact upon French military thought. However, the nation did not give up its allegiance to the mass army; compulsory service remained the basis of the army and, indeed, the length of service was doubled in 1935 to check the increasing disproportion between the size of the French and German annual contingents. Manpower for military use remained of paramount importance, and many an amateur demographer, casting a frightened eye at more populous Germany, predicted military disaster because of the decline in the French birth rate.

Though the concept of the mass army remained fundamental, French military thinkers after 1918 quickly appended to it new concepts and theories arising from World War I experience. It became a commonplace to preface military literature and parliamentary military legislation with the preamble that war had now become total and that, as a consequence, it was essential to prepare well in advance for all of its economic ramifications. It would be pointless to discuss the many ideas and projects which emerged, but they were legion. [26]

Yet this concept of total war contained within itself the seed of its own destruction. The complete opposite of the pre-1914 doctrine, the newly developed theory of total war postulated the slow wearing-down of the enemy as in 1914 to 1918—in short, a war of attrition. A writer like Chief of Staff Debeney worked out the doctrine in the following form: Modern weapons had given the upper hand to the defense and it was possible to maintain an unbroken front with their support. But there now lay behind these armaments the fully de-

[25] Ferdinand Foch, *Des principes de la guerre* (Paris, 1917, and earlier eds.), p. 37.

[26] There was, however, little concrete achievement of the theories so loudly proclaimed. The first legislation designed to provide for the organization of the nation in time of war was proposed by Painlevé in the mid-twenties, but the bill did not become law until July of 1938, on the eve of the Munich crisis! Originally the bill passed the Chamber with only the Communists in opposition, but it encountered the hostility of both labor and industrial groups in the Senate and was considerably rewritten. Thereafter it languished in committees and the two houses never got together on a revised version for over a decade.

veloped and fully organized capacities of the industrial systems of the belligerent nations. Their potentialities were virtually limitless. And since it could be assumed that every nation would utilize its economic resources to the fullest extent, the stage was set for long and not short wars. For, since the front lines would remain stationary and the factories would turn out endless streams of war materials which guaranteed that stability, the only limitation on the length of a future conflict was the limitation imposed by the strength and capacity of the industrial and economic systems of the warring nations.[27]

French writers like Debeney pushed this concept to its logical conclusion. Since defensive weapons were superior and no continuous front could be shattered, it followed that no sudden attack by Germany could knock out all of the French war industry. And, with war production thus assured, it likewise followed that any future Franco-German war must become a war of attrition. If these premises were accepted—and they were—the job of French strategists became little more than that of preparing the defense and guarding against the initial attack. In this way came about the Maginot Line, which dominated the military mind to such an extent that it is not incorrect to speak of a "Maginot Line complex."

The Debeneys and the Pétains were skeptical of the advantages to be gained from either specialized tank corps or aerial fleets. They took particular pains to point out what such counterweapons of the defense as antitank and antiaircraft artillery could do to minimize the threat of a break-through. Debeney wrote in 1935, for example, that in future wars mechanized land forces would find their freedom of maneuver much more limited than in 1918, while Pétain indicated, also in 1935, that he believed it dangerous to expect very much from the independent operations of an air force. These critics insisted that it was essential to consider the total complex of the national military effort. If overemphasis was placed upon any single aspect of the national defense—such as tanks or planes—it might lead to an improper balance in the whole defense structure and imperil French security as a whole.[28] A sound, comprehensive view, indeed, but its

[27] General Debeney, *Sur la sécurité militaire de la France* (Paris, 1930), pp. 46–50, 60–61. Also General Mordacq, *Les Leçons de 1914 et la prochaine guerre* (Paris, 1937); General Maurin, *L'Armée moderne* (Paris, 1938). Debeney's *La Guerre et les hommes* (Paris, 1937) reveals the same tendencies. The "classic" work on the defense theory is General Chauvineau's notorious *Une Invasion, est-elle encore possible?* (Paris, 1939), with a highly commendatory preface by Pétain. Since Chauvineau answered his question with a resounding "No!" virtually every critic from Reynaud to Gamelin has enjoyed a field day ridiculing book and author.

[28] See Pétain's preface to Colonel P. Vauthier, *La Doctrine de guerre du Général Douhet* (Paris, 1935), and two Debeney articles in *La Revue des deux mondes,* "Encore l'armée de métier," XXVIII (July 15, 1935), 279–95, and "La Motorisation des armées modernes," XXXII (March 15, 1936), 273–91.

unfortunate corollary was a neglect of the possibilities of armor and airpower.[29] In this fashion official military theory led France to the nightmare of the Blitzkrieg, which few of the French high command had conceived possible.

Furthermore, these were the opinions of the political leaders as well as of the military hierarchy. Léon Blum was as firmly wedded to the doctrine of the continuous front as Marshal Pétain. Édouard Daladier revealed his complete acceptance of current dogma in conversations with Neville Chamberlain over the Czech problem in April of 1938. France and England, he told the British prime minister, would indeed have to bear the burden of the shock of German arms, but it was not likely that a modern nation could be put out of action by any sudden attack. Indeed, Daladier added, the experience of the Spanish civil war confirmed this, for quite often a weak screen of machine gunners behind barbed wire had been able to resist more numerous and better armed attackers. Furthermore, Daladier continued—obviously thinking of the Luftwaffe—it was doubtful if airpower could be decisive in modern war. After all, whatever importance was attached to any one factor in the national defense, it nevertheless remained true that war was a single, complex problem which required the employment of all the resources of a country.[30] . . . But, unfortunately, the whole is not always greater than any of its parts!

Finally, both political and military authorities were further guilty of confusing actual with potential war strength. Because they were so convinced of a long war and of their own safety during its prosecution, the French refused to put their laws for national organization into operation until the actual outbreak of hostilities. In 1938, for example, Daladier consistently and successfully opposed the creation of an armaments ministry. As he said to the Chamber of Deputies, "If you do this, you create in this country, from this day on, a war economy. For my part I am resolutely opposed to this conception." [31] Consequently, even if the Daladiers can point to an "honorable equality" of armaments in May 1940, it is likewise self-evident that there

[29] So often propagandized ourselves by the horde of "victory through airpower" writers, we can appreciate more of the Pétain-Debeney argument than would have been possible a few years ago when German armies appeared invincible. It is true beyond doubt that these men presented far more comprehensive and rational arguments than the enthusiasts for tanks or planes ever achieved. De Gaulle's *Vers l'armée de métier*, for example, never once deals with the possibility that his mechanized corps might be halted; his enthusiasm envisages only ever-victorious offensives. It is not hard to understand why his views were rejected in favor of the official theories which alone seemed to comprehend all possible factors.

[30] E. L. Woodward and Rohan Butler (eds.), *Documents on British Foreign Policy (1919–1939)*, 3rd series, I: 1938 (London, 1949), 205–7.

[31] *Journal officiel, Chambre des Députés, Débats* (March 22, 1938), p. 888.

might even have been a superiority if only more of these preparatory measures had been applied prior to September 1939. Moreover, even after the beginning of hostilities there was a strong tendency to plan on the basis of a war with a minimum duration of three years. Perhaps this was a prudent view, but it had as its consequence, for instance, that the French purchased raw materials from abroad rather than finished war goods. Finance Minister Paul Reynaud, fearing for the French gold reserves, drew up his foreign purchasing program on the confident assumption that it could be spaced out over three years.[32]

As a nation the French were thus guilty of transforming their otherwise sound conception of total war into the erroneous belief that defense would win the war. The rational organization of manpower and economic resources, they thought—together with the Maginot Line—assured a war of attrition. And in such a conflict they were sure time was on their side. They of course knew that German war potential far exceeded the capacities of metropolitan France, but, secure behind their continuous front of firepower, they felt confident there was sufficient time to organize the far superior resources of their own Empire and that of the British.[33] Ultimately the two Western allies would possess a crushing superiority. Meanwhile they would so weaken Germany by air and sea blockade that German power—like the Marxist state—would wither away. Then, and then only, would Allied forces even think of taking the offensive against an almost beaten foe.

IV

The war over and Germany finally defeated, what lessons have the French derived from their own disaster to use as a guide in future planning? Though the two chapters to follow will deal with these problems in more detail, a few conclusions are worthy of mention.

In the first place, the French have probably learned more from the German, British, American, and Russian experiences than simply from their own. Most discussions of future strategy or army reorganization take as their starting point events which occurred after 1940; the future is only infrequently discussed in terms of the 1940 defeat. There is a marked tendency to hide behind the skirts of the atomic bomb—to say that this is now the age of atomic warfare

[32] Paul Reynaud, *La Guerre; notre plan économique et financier* (Paris, 1939), pp. 17–18. On December 22 Daladier told the Chamber that a long war was to be expected.

[33] Reynaud, who would like to be considered the French Churchill, has had a hard time living down a statement of his in 1939: "We shall conquer because we are the stronger." His explanation to the Commission d'Enquête was that he made the statement because he was thinking of the total economic and political power of all the democracies which could have been used against Germany.

and that we have to start at that point, since most of 1940's lessons are already outmoded. This may be a sound tendency but it also reflects a disinclination to probe too far into the disagreeable past.

Secondly, many French writers have pointed out that it was superiority in armament which enabled the British and Americans not only to achieve victory but also to do so with a minimum loss of life.[34] Consequently, projected plans for national organization in time of war stress industrial mobilization, which is now considered as of equal importance with military mobilization. Theorists have conceived a new term, "national service"; its implication is that in the future men will be mobilized for service in industry as well as in the armed forces and that both types of service are of equal value to the nation. Indeed, under the theory of "national service," mobilization of men for war production might well take preference over all other obligations.[35]

As a result of the Georges-Gamelin feud and certain obvious failures in coordination in the 1940 campaign, a third conclusion of French theorists is that unification of the armed services is now a desirable goal. There is of course considerable opposition coming from air, naval, and political circles. Likewise, to strengthen the authority and responsibility of the political leadership in time of war, Article VII of the new constitution of the Fourth Republic stresses the role of the President of the Council in the direction of war. The French want no repetition of the influence which Pétain and Weygand were able to exercise on events in 1940.

Finally, since it is felt that one of the reasons France failed to recover from the Meuse disaster was a lack of space in which to retreat, there is increased consideration of the military role of North and Central Africa. As De Gaulle said to the Provisional Assembly in 1944, "It was the Empire which should have been set up as a bulwark, as an armed fortress, and as a base of operations." [36]

[34] See, for example, Édouard Daladier, writing in *Revue politique et parlementaire*, No. 590 (July 1949), 3–8, and Chassin, *op. cit.*, p. 22.

[35] See the *exposé des motifs* in *Journal officiel, Assemblée nationale, Documents parlementaires*, No. 2732 (December 18, 1947), p. 2322 (bill for organization of armed forces); *ibid.*, No. 1871 (June 30, 1947), pp. 1526 ff. (bill for organization of the nation in time of war). There is a convenient summary of the import of the proposed legislation in the *New York Times*, December 26, 1947, and in the French Ministry of National Defense publication, *Informations militaires*, No. 128 (January 25, 1949), pp. 8–12, in which an article entitled "Économie and conduite de la guerre" presents some of the conclusions of M. Paul Ramadier to a military study group. Another interesting article is General de Lattre de Tassigny, "Essai d'adoption de l'organisation militaire aux conditions futures de la guerre," *Revue de défense nationale*, IV (April 1947), 431–50.

[36] Speech to Provisional Consultative Assembly, January 19, 1944. Later De Tassigny stated that "the narrow conception of a northeastern frontier, which was itself inherited from the 'blue line of the Vosges' of 1871, must give way to a broadened conception of French security for the whole area of the French Union which alone has sufficient space for a withdrawal corresponding to modern operations." *New York Times*, April 29, 1946.

But so far all these ideas are only the thoughts of some military and political writers. They exist in the minds of men and not on paper. Why the French have failed throughout five years to translate ideas into realities is something which the following chapters will explain.

24

+++

CONTEMPORARY

CONCEPTS OF FRENCH STRATEGY

DONALD J. HARVEY

+++

THE invading legions of the Third Reich which swept across northern France in 1940 destroyed more than the French army. They shattered a strategic and tactical doctrine which the French had assiduously prepared in the interbellum period. The disillusionment of the military defeat, the ensuing political collapse of the Third Republic, and the bitter experience of the German occupation formed the background against which France emerged from the war. Since liberation, French military and civilian leaders have been engaged in formulating new strategic concepts for the security of France against actual or presumed enemies in the postwar world.

French military policy immediately following World War II was essentially oriented toward fulfilling two international tasks [1]: participation in the joint occupation of Germany, and anticipation of providing a "police force" for the United Nations.[2] The security of French interests was assured if the status quo were maintained. But the status quo was not maintained. The amity of the Allies, especially the wartime friendship of the United States and the Soviet Union, dissolved at a rapid rate after 1946. The advent of this schism and the alleged imminence of war had serious repercussions on French security. At first the French sought refuge in the possible establishment of a "bloc" or "Third Force" which would be able to arbitrate between the East and the West. Unable to maintain an isolated position,

[1] Though fraught with international implications, the military aspects of colonial pacification have remained chiefly domestic.

[2] Paul Ramadier, *Journal officiel, Assemblée nationale, débats* (June 16, 1949), p. 3431. This source hereafter cited as *J.O., A.N., déb.*

the French signed the Brussels Pact on March 17, 1948, forming with
the British and the Benelux peoples a Union of Western Europe
which was designed to coordinate political, economic, and military
efforts. Although the pact was patently directed against Russia, it
was not a tie with the United States. One year later, however, the
North Atlantic Defense Pact was signed in Washington, symboliz-
ing the final abandonment by the French of the idea of constituting
a "Third Force." Commitments to the West had become the official
and public policy. Thus, over the short period of five years, there has
been a considerable change in the problem of security. The threat
of a resurgent Germany remains very tangible to the French, but the
menace of Russian expansion has assumed paramount importance.

Within the framework of these international alignments and commitments, the military and civilian leaders of France have pondered
the delicate question of the nature of the next war. In their speculations will be found both tenuous clues and direct indications of the
contemporary concepts of French strategy.

In a future war, which would be "worldwide, total, and scientific,"
an atomic air duel between the United States and Russia would be
accompanied by the ineluctable movement of Russian land forces
toward the Atlantic in an attempt to absorb the European Continent.[3]
Most French officers view the atomic bomb as a strategic weapon,
to be used against the enemy's key agglomerations of industry, transportation, and communication. The tactical employment of atomic
weapons or guided missiles is heavily discounted.

In addition to an extension of the conventional missions of the air
arm—strategic bombing and close, tactical support of land forces—
French military men envision other air operations on a tremendous
scale. Air drops of parachute troops and landings of entire units would
become commonplace, rendering no section of a nation immune from
the virus of combat. Supplies and equipment would be moved in unprecedented quantities by air transport.[4] To an ultra-partisan of airpower like General Chassin, the world is heading toward a war "the
principal theater of which will be the air." As a consequence, he predicted "a war of robots and the disappearance of man from the fields
of battle." [5] Although General Chassin's statements appeared in an
official publication of the French Minister of the Armed Forces, the

[3] General Sabbatier (member of the Conseil Supérieur de la Guerre), "Défense nationale," *Revue des informations militaires*, No. 134 (May 10, 1949), 8. This semi-monthly,
official publication of the Minister of the Armed Forces hereafter cited as *R.I.M.*

[4] Camille Rougeron, *La Prochaine Guerre* (Paris, 1948), reviewed and quoted in *R.I.M.*,
No. 120 (September 10, 1948), 39.

[5] General L.-M. Chassin, "Caractères généraux des guerres," *R.I.M.*, No. 114 (May
25, 1948), 10.

editors disclaimed adherence to the views of the author, counseling the reader to seek the truth in the middle ground between extreme positions.

A more conservative appraisal of the impact of atomic weapons, guided missiles, and airpower on the role of land armies was voiced by General Georges Revers, the recently discarded Chief of Staff: "If it is true that the advent of the atomic era . . . will lead to a necessary overturning of former strategic concepts, the military thinkers of the great powers do not seem to have inferred the abolition of the land armies." [6] Civilian authorities like the former Minister of National Defense, M. Paul Ramadier, have made similar statements before the National Assembly. If ground troops were to participate in future conflicts, the French universally agree that they must possess a devastating measure of firepower and a high degree of mechanization. The airplane, the tank, the heavy but mobile artillery piece, and the soldier should form an integrated whole to meet the extensive air operations forecast for the next war. Speed, mobility, and power would characterize the armies of the future.

For colonial powers like France and her allies, naval units with strong air cover would be required to maintain communications and supply lines to the resources of the overseas areas. Bases in the Mediterranean, Central Atlantic, and Pacific would increase in importance in the event of land and air attacks on metropolitan France.[7]

Obviously, a future conflict of the nature described would entail a highly technical and extravagantly expensive war machine. To provide and service such a machine, two elements are essential: industrial resources and scientific research. These the French recognize as paramount in their contemporary concepts of strategy. Concerning research, General Jean de Lattre de Tassigny, the Commander-in-Chief of the land armies of the Western Union, warned that "a nation surpassed in the field of science is beaten in advance on the field of battle," [8] while M. Paul Coste-Floret, Minister of War in 1947, expressed the belief that "a nation which makes economies in scientific research in reality does not economize at all. . . ." [9]

Despite the absence of direct provisions for armament production, the Monnet Plan, the French blueprint for postwar reconstruction,

[6] General Georges Revers, "Propos sur hier et sur demain," *R.I.M.*, No. 127 (January 10, 1949), 5.

[7] Captain Lepotier, "Les Bases maritimes françaises," *Cahiers français d'information* (March 15, 1947), p. 11.

[8] General Jean de Lattre de Tassigny, "L'Armée française de transition," *R.I.M.*, No. 85 (December 20, 1946), 18.

[9] "Visite du Fieldmarshal Vicomte Montgomery en France," *R.I.M.*, No. 100 (October 10, 1947), 3. Concerning the attitude of the French Government toward scientific research see above, Chapter 6.

contained evidence of the emphasis on the industrial nature of war preparation. The text of the plan stated: "The prerequisites for modern military equipment are the augmentation of the industrial potential, the modernization of the economy, and the development of scientific research." [10] Recognizing his nation's inadequacy in the industrial power required for modern armaments, General de Lattre, among others, pointed out the need to rely upon "allies and friends." [11] Dependent upon indigenous resources, France had but a fatuous security. Of necessity, then, contemporary French strategy became coalition-conscious. Similar views held by other Western Europeans were contributory to the formulation of the Brussels Pact. More intimate economic and political cooperation would have a salutary effect on the industrial plant, the *sine qua non* for resisting aggression. M. Paul Ramadier stressed the importance to military defense of the economic stability attributable to the Brussels Pact of March 1948.[12]

Concerning the military organization created for the Western Union, the five Defense Ministers were designated to frame over-all defense policies, while the Chiefs of Staff—thirteen senior officers from the five signatory powers—were to plan over-all strategy and decide upon the size, disposition, and commanders of the combined forces. Subordinate to the Chiefs of Staff were the Permanent Military Committee and "Uniforce," the tactical command now located at Fontainebleau. The former consisted of a technical staff whose functions were to draw up military inventories, plan future war production, determine standardization procedures, and establish stock piles.[13]

The next significant development of French strategy along the lines of coalition occurred with the signing of the North Atlantic Defense Pact. In addition to the establishment of a centralized council for resolving common problems, the Atlantic Pact provided for the defense of Europe in regional components. According to a communiqué emanating from the Paris Conference of military representatives of the twelve pact powers, problems of four categories were treated: (1) elaboration of common strategic conceptions; (2) organization of production of arms and equipment; (3) formulation of general, over-all defense plans; (4) allocation to the regional groups of the details of a defense plan.[14]

[10] Quoted by *** (Anon.), "Défense de l'Europe de l'ouest," *Revue de défense nationale* (March 1949), p. 308.
[11] "La Réorganisation de l'armée," *Le Monde*, May 1-2, 1946.
[12] Quoted in "Actualité parlementaire," *R.I.M.*, No. 138 (July 10, 1949), 12.
[13] Benjamin Welles, "Defense Prepared in Western Europe," *New York Times*, February 14, 1949. Hereafter cited as *N.Y.T.*
[14] "Nouvelles de l'armée," *R.I.M.*, No. 145 (December 10, 1949), 3.

French security was not automatically provided for, however, merely by the formation of alliances or by efforts in an industrial and scientific direction. The most economically advanced nations may be overwhelmed by an enemy of lesser endowment if they have failed to translate their industrial potential and their abundant resources into an adequate military force-in-being. To a nation like France, which is directly assailable by land, air, and sea, this observation is especially pertinent. What have French strategists planned and accomplished, alone and in conjunction with the Western Union, in consideration of this fact?

Field Marshal Montgomery, the Supreme Commander of the unified forces of the Western Union, has praised in general terms the "admirable progress" in the standardization of equipment of the member nations.[15] When asked his opinion on the technical feasibility of unifying the armaments of the Atlantic Pact countries, M. Paul Ramadier dismissed complete unification as a dream. He felt that the disparity between American and European industrial equipment and techniques militated against this process. On the other hand, he continued, unification had been accelerated among those countries linked by the Brussels Pact—for example, in the harmonization of gun calibers and ammunition sizes, at least for the more conventional weapons.[16]

Although the Monnet Plan provided for no sustained use of French armament plants until 1952, light, conventional weapons for occupation duties and the Indo-Chinese war have been manufactured. Several hundred tanks purchased in Belgium were refurbished at a cost of 500 million francs and were at the disposal of the French army by June 1949.[17] Less tangible were the prototypes of various items of heavy materiel—12-ton and 55-ton tanks, jet-propelled aircraft, etc. M. Max Lejeune, the Secretary of State of the Armed Forces, claimed that some of these items would be in the production stage by 1950.[18] On a quantitative basis, the French, according to M. Montel, the chairman of the Committee of National Defense in the National Assembly, had only two armored divisions in service in December 1949, but could furnish equipment for another three.[19] To these two armored divisions must be added three full-strength infantry divisions, and an airborne and a mountain division, both under-strength. These

---

[15] Benjamin Welles, "Montgomery Cites Flaws in Defense," *N.Y.T.*, October 13, 1949.
[16] Tibor Koeves, "If France Falls, the West Is Lost," *United Nations World* (October 1949), p. 22.
[17] "Actualité parlementaire," *loc. cit.*, p. 10.
[18] Max Lejeune, *J.O., A.N., déb.* (March 3, 1949), p. 1218.
[19] Thomas J. Hamilton, "West Said to Need 60 to 80 Divisions," *N.Y.T.*, December 4, 1949.

figures would comprise the total French force in Europe in the summer of 1950.[20] In a qualitative assessment made in 1949, M. Ramadier admitted that the French had "an outmoded, outdated materiel which entails excessive maintenance costs." [21]

The recognition and explanation of this condition by French and Allied strategists may be inferred from the identical premise of the Western Union's Note of April 5, 1949, and of the communiqué of November's Atlantic Pact Conference. The premise was that production of armament and military equipment ought not to be instituted at the expense of economic recovery nor in such a way as to create an "overwhelming burden" for the countries crippled by World War II.[22] This is as much a political as a strategic decision. Dedicated as they are to the idea of an industrial potential as the base for military strength, French military men felt they must be assured of a sound economy before drawing upon it for any substantial military production. Perhaps more important, the political demand for postwar economic reconstruction was too strong to be ignored. Any sizable diversion of factors to military rather than civilian production would have been disastrous to any French political party.* Economic recovery, therefore, had to precede large-scale armament production. A partial corrective to the deficiency of French military equipment is being applied by the military aid program of the United States, whereby, in the words of M. René Pleven, the French are receiving modern materiel of their own selection.[23] Furthermore, a modification of the French attitude to rearmament production has been suggested in view of the Korean situation. In answer to a note sent by the United States to the Atlantic Pact powers concerning the reinforcement of their national security efforts, the French government has presented its tentative program.[24] This new effort would impose "new sacrifices" on the French population in the form of increased demands on manpower and financial costs of $5,714,300,000 over a period of three years. In addition to modernizing and reequipping existing divisions already aided by the MAP, this program would permit the "constitution of fifteen entirely new divisions in three years." In accordance with previous decisions, the French reiterated their desire not to institute "defense programs out

* This point is developed further in Chapter 25.
[20] "France Asks More British, U.S. Troops," *Washington Post*, August 8, 1950.
[21] Ramadier, *loc. cit.*, p. 3431.
[22] "Brussels Powers' Note April 5, 1949," *N.Y.T.*, April 9, 1949; "Nouvelles de l'armée," *loc. cit.*, p. 3.
[23] Quoted in "Chronique militaire," *R.I.M.*, No. 150 (March 10, 1950), 4.
[24] "Text of French Note Outlining Defense Plans," *N.Y.T.*, August 8, 1950.

of proportion with national possibilities" and restated the need for "outside aid of armament, raw materials and equipment. . . ." Without this assistance the French army would be incapable of fulfilling its strategic missions or its national and international obligations. General Omar Bradley attested to the importance of the French army when he labeled it the major force in the defense of Western Europe.[25]

Still in the process of reorganization, the French army has been regrouped into units (tactical groupments) corresponding to approximately one-third the size of a former division.[26] Rather than constituting thoroughly professional divisions or regiments, veterans and career men form the cadre of various units in order to train the 120,-000 annual recruits. Training has likewise undergone a revolutionary transformation, the *camp léger* of a battalion, group, or regiment replacing the *caserne* of prewar France. Of his one year with the open-air army, the recruit, regardless of his specialty or branch of service, devotes the first three months to basic military training—discipline, physical toughening, close-order drill, combat exercises, topography. During the second three months, attention is riveted upon specialized instruction in the soldier's particular branch of service. Practice on related weapons and material is also keynoted in this period. With this type of training, the French hope to furnish men to fit Paul Ramadier's specification of modern armies: "They are armies of specialists in which a long apprenticeship is necessary to learn all the tasks which modern materiel demands." [27]

If such an army can be constituted—properly trained and adequately equipped—what strategic and tactical concepts do the French maintain for its utilization? Are the fatal doctrines of the military thought of 1939 still rampant among contemporary French leaders? Does the stagnantly defensive attitude of the 1930's find influential advocates in the Fourth Republic? The reply is resoundingly in the negative. Even renegade writers, who maintain allegiance to the principle of fortifications, qualify the ideas upon which the Maginot Line was founded. These men agree that any attempt to return to the linear system of defensive fortifications would again result in disaster.[28] The tenet of a linear and static defense has thus been abandoned in favor of a defense in depth which stresses dynamic and powerful counteroffensives by mechanized, mobile and air-borne

[25] David McConnell, "Bradley Reveals French Army Will Be Key to Europe's Defense," *New York Herald Tribune*, August 11, 1949.

[26] De Lattre, *loc. cit.*, pp. 16–18.

[27] Ramadier, *loc. cit.*, p. 3431.

[28] Chef de Bataillon Rocolle, "Le Béton a-t-il trahi?", *R.I.M.*, No. 132 (March 25, 1949), 21.

units. "Rapidity of intervention" is viewed as essential to a practical defense.[29] Derived from defensive battles waged in joint army maneuvers along the Moselle during the autumn of 1949, the official lessons are highly indicative of the French military mind today. In substance, they say that a defensive operation, conducted on wide fronts, with reduced means at its disposal, ought to be resolutely aggressive and accompanied by an air arm uniting all its firepower to that of the land arms. In order to neutralize antitank barriers in difficult terrain, armored divisions must be allotted increased infantry detachments.[30]

The change in the French notion of the character of defensive warfare since World War II must be borne in mind while treating the question of Western Europe's "defense line." Neither the French nor their fellow-strategists intend to reconstruct a Maginot Line to shield the territories of the Brussels Pact nations. One French general, in fact, preferred to use the term "zone" instead of "line" in order to show the need for a defense in depth.[31] The desire to remove this "zone" as far from the Western Union's frontiers as feasible stems from the experience of two world wars and more especially from the location of the French industrial basins on the vital northern and eastern frontiers. As Henri Queuille remarked, "Once the geographical frontiers of these countries are crossed, it will be too late for America to save very much." General Charles de Gaulle advanced the macabre view that if France were invaded again, America would liberate a corpse. Repeated declarations of the intention to "defend Europe in Europe" have been made by the leading military representatives of the Brussels Pact and Atlantic Pact nations in the face of persistent rumors alleging a British desire to concentrate on insular defense.[32]

Although the precise location of the common defense line of the Western Union is naturally veiled in secrecy, the French have indicated the Rhine, if not the Elbe, as the probable sector. After stating to the National Assembly in March 1949 that the security of France has always been on the eastern frontier, M. Ramadier was asked by a deputy, "On the Rhine or on the Elbe?" "On the Rhine and on the Elbe," he replied, "as far to the east as possible." [33] Six months later, in Washington, Ramadier again proposed a line "near

[29] "Voyage du Général de Lattre de Tassigny en Suisse," *R.I.M.*, No. 100 (October 10, 1947), 5.

[30] "Manoeuvres de la Moselle," *R.I.M.*, No. 144 (November 25, 1949), 7.

[31] General P. Gérardot, "La Défense de l'Europe occidentale," *Revue de défense nationale* (October 1949), p. 293.

[32] Clifton Daniel, "De Lattre Denies Montgomery Rift," *N.Y.T.*, August 9, 1949.

[33] Ramadier, *J.O., A.N., déb.* (March 3, 1949), p. 1215.

to the borders of the Iron Curtain. . . ." Jules Moch, too, as Minister of National Defense, insisted that "it is the creation of an Elbe-Rhine position which ought to be our constant preoccupation." [34] Under the signature of "Trois Etoiles," a French general advised including the Ruhr within the defense zone because of its industries.[35] The less anonymous General de Lattre placed himself entirely in agreement with Marshal Foch's ideas on the Rhine as the "indispensable military frontier for the maintenance of peace." To him, this view has retained its efficacy and the Rhine remains "the shield of Western Europe." [36]

Inextricably bound up with any decision on this subject, but too involved and too conjectural for any intensive treatment in this chapter, is the question of the French attitude toward German military participation in the Western Union. The French are understandably ground between the horrors of a Russian advance and their time-proven experiences with German militarism. Only the future can decide whether the French will remain in a state of decisive indecision on rearming Germany. In the light of the present limited power of the Western Union without Germany, the Elbe can be but an outpost, while the Rhineland will assume the main emphasis in the territorial defense of the French and their Allies.

The preceding chapter by Mr. Challener has introduced us to General de Gaulle's sentiments on the advisability of prepared points of refuge in the French Empire. Since World War II, this theme has received a recurrent, though somewhat surreptitious, treatment by French strategists. Whether considered as a source of raw materials, natural resources, and manpower, or as a possible refuge in the event of another occupation of metropolitan France, the African areas of the French Union have been given considerable attention by a minority of military thinkers.

General Sabbatier's proposals, presuming insecurity from invasion at home, envisaged a relocation to the overseas areas of at least a portion of French wealth in the form of "laboratories, factories, tool-shops, etc." In fact, in his opinion, the economy should be so organized that the minimum means of serving the enemy's war effort would be left in metropolitan France if the French government had to flee.[37] In a similar vein, General Breuillac advocated the preparation of the French Union, especially North Africa, for the displacement from France of the government, General Staff, scientific laboratories, and

[34] Quoted in *Le Monde,* August 5, 1950.
[35] "Défense de l'Europe de l'ouest," *loc. cit.,* p. 314.
[36] De Lattre, "Foch," *R.I.M.,* No. 130 (February 25, 1949), 8.
[37] Sabbatier, *loc. cit.,* p. 10.

even the young men of military age.[38] Pleading for the industrial equipment of North Africa, a French officer pointed to newly realized mineral wealth there, and bemoaned the fact that Algeria, Tunis, and Morocco received as new capital investment only 244 billion francs for the four-year period 1946–1950, as compared with over 439 billions for metropolitan France in 1947 alone.[39] The development of air transport introduces to these military men the possibility of utilizing the hitherto inaccessible land mass of Central and West Africa as a strategic zone of dispersal and as a "bridge" to South America. They suggest that this immense area might function for France as the Siberian mass does for Russia.[40]

These various strategic proposals concerning Africa have not been without official recognition. In July 1948 a government spokesman told the National Assembly that there was no intention of withdrawing from France in the event of war, but he did acknowledge that the government was studying a plan to transfer war industries to North Africa and to other parts of the French Union.[41] A decree dated December 31, 1948, established the responsibilities of the High Commissioner of the Republic of West Africa to include the direction of the armed forces, institution of an armaments and equipment program, and economic mobilization.[42] However, the unrest in the colonies, the preoccupation with reconstruction at home, the resistance from established business interests which oppose new competitive industries in the Union, the political inexpediency of supporting projects which might imply to the electorate the abandonment of metropolitan France, the fear of endangering the French international position which stresses a rigorous defense in Europe—such are some of the factors that dampen the immediate prospects of developing the French Union as a source of strength or as a point of refuge.

The orientation toward Africa, therefore, remains but an eddy in the main stream of French strategic concepts. The chief tributaries are those which are concerned with the industrial and scientific nature of war preparation and the resultant indispensability of coalition with the Western Union and the Atlantic powers. For the security of

[38] General Breuillac, "Il faut enseigner la défense nationale," *Revue de défense nationale* (January 1949), p. 44.

[39] Colonel Georges Spillman, "L'Équipement industriel de l'Afrique du nord," *ibid.* (August-September 1949), p. 204.

[40] General A. Niessel, "Importance stratégique de l'Afrique," *Le Monde français* (September 1949), p. 430.

[41] Paul-Henri Teitgen, quoted in "French Study Plan to Shift War Plants," *N.Y.T.*, July 2, 1948.

[42] Décret No. 48–2039 of *J.O.* (January 5, 1949), quoted in *R.I.M.*, No. 128 (January 25, 1949), 6.

France and the defense of Western Europe, the prevailing French military concepts have displayed a dynamism and flexibility rarely evidenced in the prewar period, but grave economic problems and the crucial question of the internal political situation still remain. Whether France is any better prepared today than she was in 1940 to meet an attack from the east is a question which involves the fate of all Europe.

25

++

POLITICAL PARTIES

AND THE FRENCH ARMY SINCE LIBERATION

EDWARD L. KATZENBACH, JR.

++

IN A recent article in *Le Monde,* a military writer remarked that "A country has the army it merits." [1] The expression is an old one. For a hundred years at least, French politicians and the French military have been quoting one another to the effect that the army is but the reflection of the French state. But in a democracy, the strength of an army is not so much a question of merit as one of desire, desire as expressed by the people through the votes of their representatives. Certainly, it has little or nothing to do with international necessity.

In France, as in other democracies, the military problem is essentially one of domestic politics and ideologies. What is important is not so much what the generals think should be done as what the politicians think should be done. But for a French *parlement* to come to a decision on a military question is far more difficult than in other countries, for in France all such problems are so deeply enmeshed in the conflicting traditions and principles of party struggle that they are almost impossible of solution. Since the double defeat of 1870 —the defeat of the professional army of Louis Napoleon at Sedan, and that of the Republican levies of Gambetta and Freycinet in the months that followed—there has been no meeting of French minds on any military subject. It is against this background and after the equally unexpected and even more disastrous defeat of 1940 that the present generation of politicians, harassed by an inner sense of the futility of all military preparation, has faced the frustrating task of creating an army for the Fourth Republic.

Shortly after the war, André Malraux, then President de Gaulle's

[1] *Le Monde,* February 11, 1950.

Minister of Information, quoted a Gallup poll to the effect that only 70 per cent of the citizens still wanted an army and these wanted it only "because of tradition and a love of swagger." [2] Indeed, in 1945, the people in general seemed to feel that there was no other reason for an army. De Gaulle himself was working toward a large force of nineteen divisions [3] on the plea that these were necessary for the protection of the colonies, the occupation of Germany, and the contingent which France would be required to contribute to the United Nations. But to the politicians this plan seemed nothing short of ridiculous. Reflecting the attitude of their constituents, they were primarily interested in cutting military appropriations.

In September 1945, the distinguished columnist Rémy Roure posed what many felt to be the central problem which the French had to face as to the future of their army: "Shall the army of the future be a professional army, small in number, powerful by virtue of its materiel, continually on the alert? . . . Or shall it be a large army with imposing reinforcements, but of lesser technical quality?" [4] He was restating the classic question. However, in 1945, such a question was one for the theorists, not for the politicians. The question of the moment was much more basic. It was simply this: Should the army be allowed to stay the size it was, or should it be made smaller? The question was raised by a Socialist, Jean Capdeville, in an amendment demanding a flat 20 per cent cut in army expenditures; it threw the military question into the political limelight because De Gaulle, in a stormy appearance before the National Assembly late New Year's Eve 1945, demanded that it be made a matter of confidence.

The debate touched off by this Capdeville amendment is important because it gave the parties a chance to read into the record not only what they thought about the issue at hand, but also, as is usually the case with political debates, everything they thought about the sub-

---

[2] Quoted in *Journal officiel, Débats, Assemblée nationale constituante*, Dec. 31, 1945, p. 704. (Hereinafter cited as *J.O., déb., A.N.C.*, and after 1945 as *J.O., déb., A.N.*)

[3] This was in accordance with the plan developed in May and adopted in June 1945 by the National Defense Committee. For details see *Revue de défense nationale*, January–June, 1946, p. 249. In 1946 there developed another stronger argument for an army: military writers and others emphasized that the industrial potential of Germany was greater than had been thought. See, for example, Louis F. Aubert, *Sécurité de l'Occident —Ruhr, Rhin*, Paris, 1946; L. E. Magnin, "Aspects présents du problème militaire français," *Les Cahiers politiques*, May 1946; Edmond Delage, article in *Le Monde*, March 20, 1946, in which he takes for granted the necessity for an army. There was also, undoubtedly, a considerable body of opinion in France which felt that an army was "necessary to the general spiritual, moral, and material equilibrium of a nation." For a restatement of this long-prevalent belief, see General Edgard de Larminat, *L'Armée dans la nation*, Paris, 1944, p. 1.

[4] Rémy Roure, *The French Army of Tomorrow*, Doc. Série II, No. 2785E, The French Press and Information Service, September 12, 1945.

ject in general, or, more specifically, what they thought about the relationship between welfare and warfare, what they wished to spend on army materiel, and finally what sort of military structure they envisioned for the future.

Capdeville himself, with the immediate backing of André Philip speaking for the Socialist Party, and joined by Jacques Duclos and the Communists, laid the groundwork for his amendment by undertaking a generalized attack on the whole fabric of the army.[5]

One might have expected that so shortly after the Liberation the army would have been above reproach. Such was decidedly not the case. The attack was vicious. The army, Capdeville said, was wasteful and inefficient, particularly so on the administrative level. There had been scandals in petrol and food rationing, and there were recruits without training and volunteers for the Far East idling away their time with guard duty. It is interesting to note, furthermore, that just as the double defeat of 1870 set off a protracted, almost interminable struggle over military affairs in the Third Republic, so the double victory of 1945—the victory of the Free French of the Interior (FFI) on the one hand and that of the more professional army of De Gaulle on the other—became the cause of extreme bitterness in the Fourth Republic. Capdeville claimed, for example, that the Vichy elements had not been cleaned out of the army, and that the officers of De Gaulle and those who had come over from Vichy late in the war held jobs which should have gone to those (for the most part, members of the extreme Left) who had fought so valiantly within France itself. But more significant than the criticisms themselves was the fact that there was no one in the Assembly, as there always had been in the Chamber of the Third Republic, to gainsay his accusations. From an unformed, uncertain, and unpopular Right there was silence.

Partly because of the great importance of political tradition in French party life, partly because politicians are, more than other men, creatures of habit, Capdeville and the Socialists followed as their main thesis the well-worn doctrine about which the party had said so much in the 1920's and 1930's. Basically they held that welfare should precede warfare as a budgetary principle, or, to put the idea in somewhat different terms, that only an economically sound state is worth defending. It was an easily tenable and popular position in 1945, for in 1945 there was no apparent threat to French security.

Therefore the problem of reequipping the army and more particu-

[5] *J.O., déb., A.N.C.*, January 31, 1945, pp. 695 ff. See also J. Leferreux, "Naissance et vicissitudes de l'armée nouvelle," *Esprit*, July 1945, p. 187. For an interesting contrast from the point of view of the military, see General de Lattre, "L'Armée française de transition," *Hommes et mondes*, November 1946, pp. 1 ff.

larly the air force could be, and was, passed off lightly by all parties. The government was cautioned against refurbishing the armed forces with materiel which might soon become out of date. It was urged to study the problem; study cost no money. Moreover, both the Socialists and their Communist associates felt that their program of nationalization was already doing much to gear the country for war. The concept of the nation in arms set down in 1910 as Socialist gospel by Jaurès in his *L'Armée nouvelle* had been extended after the First World War to include the organization not only of the nation's manpower, but also of her industrial power for total war. Hence, the steps which were being taken to nationalize the sources of the nation's economic strength were a fulfillment of the Socialist credo for war as for peace.*

Relatively little was said during the debates as to the form and structure which the Socialists and Communists would undertake to create in the army of the Fourth Republic. Their basic tenets on this subject had already been formulated in November when the program of the Délégation des Gauches had been drawn up. The Communists had had a good deal to say on the subject, and Pierre Villon, who was to be their very capable advocate on such matters, had already had his program approved by the National Council of Resistance.⁶ The Socialists seem to have just tagged along, both parties considering themselves to be the joint trustees of the legacy of traditional republicanism. The army was to be democratic and hence popular, national and hence virtuous, conscripted and hence cheap. Indeed Villon, speaking in terms of an army which would enable France to hold her head high and also train the youth of the nation in civics and technology, sounds for all the world like Charles de Freycinet, Gambetta's military expert on the staff of *La République française* in the early 1870's. World War II apparently had reaffirmed a popular front. Apparently, too, it had brought no change in the stream of Left-wing military thought, which appeared to forget or to discount the bitter experience of 1940.

The third great party of the Liberation, the MRP (Mouvement Républicain Populaire), also unfurled its military ideology in the course of the debates. This likewise proved to be nothing more than

---

* Concerning French experience with nationalization, including that of the aircraft industry, see above Chapter 20.

⁶ Reprinted in full in General Germain Jousse, *Considérations sur l'armée de demain*, Paris, 1946. This book is the best statement of what the Communists say they want the army to be. But see the speech of Thorez at the Party Rally at Ivry, January 21–23, 1946, as reported in *L'Humanité*, and that of François Billoux at Issy-les-Moulineaux as reported in *L'Humanité*, April 26, 1946, just before he resigned his position as Minister of National Defense.

the refurbished glad rags of traditional republicanism. Party members demanded short-term obligatory service (the actual length of service being left conveniently vague); the abolition of what still passes, for purposes of political propaganda, as an officer caste; and preliminary training. "Thus," explained one of them, "will the pretorian army which we do not want, and the militia which risks compromising the nation by its lack of technical training and the slowness with which it enters combat, be avoided." [7] Their thought was traditional, and, in the light of World War II, banal. What is more immediately interesting is that, despite their tie with De Gaulle at that time, they were careful to explain that they did not in principle oppose military budget cuts.[8]

But despite the complacency of the broad phalanx of the Left— a complacency which held sway over the three great parties of the Liberation—and the silence of the Right in 1945, there were certain problems as yet unheeded which were soon to be begging solutions, solutions which have not as yet been forthcoming. Unlike the three years following the French defeat in 1870 which saw the passing of the laws reorganizing the army from top to bottom, and rebuilding it on a new, albeit none too solid, basis, five years of the Fourth Republic have accomplished relatively little in this direction. Projects have been submitted, but the pressure of events and political strife have prevented any of them from reaching the floor of the Assembly. Nevertheless, between 1945 and 1950 the whole fabric of military thought was submitted to the test of new social, economic and diplomatic strains.

That the French should reconsider the question of military security in the light of the constantly growing tension of United States–Russian relations is not surprising. But there were two specifically French problems—outgrowths, to be sure, of the general international tension—that brought the military problem, if not into clearer focus, at least into greater prominence in French political thought: one was the smoldering war in Indo-China, and the other, less remarked upon but quite as dramatic, the issue of the army as an element in the class struggle within France herself. What had saved the honor of the army in 1871 was its campaign—and it was considered as such— against the revolutionary Commune. Since the army had saved society then, society accorded the army its support. Likewise today the part played by the army in restoring order, or at least in attempting to do so, in the colonies and in France herself during the strikes of

[7] Pierre de Chévigné, *J.O., déb., A.N.C.,* January 31, 1945, p. 699.
[8] In addition to the debate cited above, see the party platform as quoted in André Siegfried, ed., *L'Année politique 1944–1945,* Paris, 1946, p. 383.

1947 and the fall of 1948, gave it a body of defenders in the policy-making group. In short, the army found its backers when France found an enemy. Of course it follows that when the army acts as the savior of one class, it becomes the enemy of another. As the breach between the classes widened in the years since the war, and a clear-cut Right, Center, and Left developed, the army became, as Frenchmen were well aware, a bone of contention between them. Hence the political position of the army became at once more secure or more precarious, depending on the predominant color scheme in the political spectrum.

Although the necessity for an army seemed to become more serious with each passing day, certain latent difficulties, embarrassing contradictions, and disturbing quandaries continued to be a passive drag on politico-military thought and effective action. Mutual distrust between political parties, between the army and the politicians, and, on the international level, between France and the other members of the Atlantic Pact may well be the key to the problem of French military security today.

Discord was caused primarily by the new positions assumed by the parties in 1947. In April, De Gaulle with the newly formed RPF (Rassemblement du Peuple Français) became a threat on the Right. In May, the Communists resigned from the government and became its avowed enemies.[9] Prior to that time the Communists had participated in the government as Ministers of Defense, Armaments, and the Air Force. Indeed when Ramadier had been questioned as to the advisability of harboring them within the body of the government, he had replied with the rhetorical question which has been bothering all Frenchmen ever since. "If we leave an important group of the people outside the body of the National Defense," he asked, "who then can say that we are assuring the defense of the country?" [10]

When the Communists ceased to be working partners within the government, they became enemies with a vengeance. And unfortunately, such is the heritage of Talleyrand—that one can betray the government in the interests of France—that they could continue to pose as patriotic in matters of national defense at the same moment that they were doing everything within their power to make that defense impossible. Their position was made clear in the course of military credit debates in the summer of 1948. They argued that the army had become the tool of French imperialism in Indo-China and the defender of French capitalism at home. They argued that it

[9] There is still a considerable number led by Pierre Villon on the large, unwieldy Commission of National Defense of the Assembly.

[10] *J.O., déb., A.N.,* January 28, 1947, p. 50.

wasted the national wealth on expendable war materiel, and that it wasted precious lives that could be used to better advantage on production. On the international level the party claimed that the army had forsaken its national identity in the Brussels Pact of April 1948 as it was later to maintain that the army had lost its independence with respect to armament in the arms standardization agreements under the Atlantic Pact.[11]

Nor was the Communist attack left on the theoretical plane. They carried their propaganda to the squad room, as had the older revolutionaries like Auguste Blanqui in the previous century, and introduced literature to the troops which the army was obliged to ban as "subversive to discipline." [12] They carried on by organizing mass meetings of the "mothers" of those being "murdered" in Indo-China. And recently, of course, they have tried to organize strikes against the handling of materiel sent to Indo-China and to France from America. In the Assembly, by introducing a continuous flow of amendments, they have made discussion of military budgets at once incomprehensible and virtually interminable. Although the material damage of Communist obstruction seems slight, there is no doubt that psychologically the Communists have undermined the faith of the French in the possibility of ever solving their problem of military security. The experience of the last war has created in the French an acute awareness of the destructive potential of the fifth column. Furthermore, it should be noted as an important parenthesis that extreme Left-wing parties, such as the Unitary Socialist Party, which deny the tie of the Communists to Moscow, nonetheless follow the Communist line in military matters.[13]

If the actions of the Communists were a deterrent to positive legislation in the long run, their immediate effect was to spur other political groups to prepare legislation, if for no other reason than to prove to their constituents that they were not being remiss in matters of national interest. When the Socialists and the MRP got down to brass tacks, however, they found that there was a greater difference in their military ideologies than one would have supposed from what they had to say on the subject just after the war. Basically they were divided on the question of the length of service which should be required under a system of universal military training. The Socialists wanted such service to be limited to one year; the Popular Republicans demanded eighteen months. The acrid history of military legisla-

---

[11] See, for example, the speech of Pierre Girardot, *J.O., déb., A.N.* (2e séance, August 6, 1948).
[12] The *Revue militaire d'information* usually carries a notation of the literature banned.
[13] Del Vayo, "Can the Left Make a Come-Back?" *Nation*, January 21, 1950.

tion in France gives ample evidence of the importance of such a difference!

In the bill which they proposed in June 1948 the Socialists argued in favor of one-year service on the grounds that "after the last war no one will contest that the prerequisite of military power is its capacity for mass production" in industry and hence military service limited to one year is necessary so as not to hinder the country's economic recovery.[14] Paul Coste-Floret, an MRP spokesman on military affairs, at the time Minister of War, was no less dogmatic when he told the Superior Council of War in July 1947 that only with 240,000 men on eighteen-month service could France carry out what she would be called upon to do.[15] There was considerable friction between the parties on the subject during March 1948, friction which developed into a momentary threat to the Third Force. If ever a legislative bill for army reorganization reaches the floor of the Assembly this basic point of disagreement will undoubtedly emerge in an intensified form.

To date, the conservative Radical Socialists have supported the MRP proposals on army matters. The RPF has kept aloof. De Gaulle, aside from an occasional remark as to the necessity for a strong army, has suggested no coherent program of army reform. Should he ever return to office, he would presumably demand the same kind and the same size of army that he advocated at the time of his resignation in January 1946. It goes without saying that his followers see no possibility for an adequate army without him. Actually there is much support of De Gaulle's ideas among men of all parties except the Communist. There would be more outspoken support if it were not that his ideas are inevitably associated with him as a politician; furthermore, such is the power of words, and such the traditional stigma attached to the very idea of a professional army that few politicians care to back the program of the author of *Toward a Professional Army*. But both De Gaulle's *Vers l'armée de métier* and Paul Reynaud's *Le Problème militaire français* (a book which shares many of the General's ideas) have been republished since the war, and have been read widely.[16] Since the war there has been a tacit agreement among the ministers that the ideas of both men be incorporated into any plan

[14] *Documents parlementaires, Assemblée nationale* (hereinafter referred to as *Docs. parls., A.N.*) Annexe No. 4377, June 1, 1948, p. 1083. In a series of excellent articles, "Les Socialistes et la défense nationale," *Le Populaire*, March 19–26, 1948, Pierre Métayer argued the Socialist position on the army.

[15] *Informations militaires,* July 1, 1947, p. 3.

[16] Charles de Gaulle, *Vers l'armée de métier,* 2d ed., Paris, 1944; Paul Reynaud, *Le Problème militaire français,* Paris, 1945. The influence of these two books may be seen in General E. de Larminat, *op. cit.,* and Albert Vallet, *Le Problème militaire de la IVe République,* Lyon, 1947.

for the reorganization of the army. Both thought in terms of a small professional group of highly trained men ready to strike in case of domestic insurrection or armed invasion by a foreign power. Furthermore, in suggesting short-term military training for all citizens, the latter, at least, paid lip service to Republican ideology which holds that obligatory service, like primary education, is the *sine qua non* of a virtuous and well-integrated democratic society.

Since the war, therefore, there has been considerable discussion of so-called *corps d'intervention,* or "task forces," usually thought of in connection with airborne troops, which would be used as a mobile striking force in case of war, and which would, in addition, provide the kind of defense in depth which an air war would require. The army organization bill presented by the government late in 1947, although it was criticized as a mere compromise by Georges Marey in *Le Monde,*[17] called for such task forces in addition to regional forces for instruction and the protection of given areas.[18] But it would require occult powers to predict how much support would be forthcoming for such ideas in the Assembly were the project ever to come up for discussion. Party tradition aside, there is much fluidity of thought on the part of individuals within the parties. One Socialist, R. A. Guesdon, reporter for the finance committee, remarked recently that "One should not consider the professional army lightly and with prejudice." He went on to add that a mass army risks becoming "a colossus with feet of clay" whose collapse would be mathematically certain. It is therefore a fact that the bulk of the army and many of those in political circles agree that "If the country cannot keep a Goliath as guardian, she must give her defender the sinewy strength of a David." [19] But even David would necessitate expenditures for armaments, which no party wants to be the first to sponsor because of the cost involved.

On the question of armaments, all the parties of the Center are in the painful dilemma of either knowingly and willfully leaving France unprepared or of spending sums which they think the nation cannot afford. The position of the Socialists is the most difficult of all, and has been since their split with the Communists in 1947. They are divided among themselves on the problem of the war in Indo-China. They consider themselves a working-class party, and yet it was one of them who, as Minister of the Interior, sent troops against the miners in 1947 and in 1948 (although he did so to protect national property),

[17] *Le Monde,* January 2, 1948.
[18] *Docs. parls., A.N.* (Annexe No. 2922, 2e séance, December 18, 1947).
[19] Jean Planchais in *Le Monde,* March 2, 1949.

and who did such a distinguished job of purging and reorganizing the forces of law and order.[20] In theory they demand that the economic welfare of the nation come before military preparedness and yet as a party they understand the Communist threat in Europe better than any other party, and therefore see with painful clarity the necessity for rearmament. When, as in the summer of 1948, a Socialist made a cut in the military budget a matter of principle, the rest followed along even when, as in the case of the Schuman ministry, it meant the overthrow of the government. But one cannot help feeling that they would prefer such issues never to be raised. Inevitably their equivocal position has lost them much support.

In a similar position on the opposite side are the Radical Socialists and other conservative groups of the coalition of the Center. As a party the Radicals are proud of their tradition of "always having voted the military credits, before the war, during the war, and after the war" [21]; but at the same time representing, as they do, those who are hardest hit by taxes, they have not taken it upon themselves to propose any systematic program of rearmament. They have contented themselves, salved their consciences, and saved their pocketbooks by the happy expedient of criticizing expenditures made by others: the expenses of nationalized industry and of an oversized bureaucracy —money which they maintain could and should be used for defense. The MRP, perhaps because they are not quite sure as to who their constituents are, vote as they feel they must vote to keep the Center hobbling along, and let it go at that.

The problem of increasing the air force provides a good example of party attitudes toward rearmament. All parties, including the Communists, declared that the percentage of the military budget allotted to the air force was too small. Despite the fact that, historically speaking, the French politician, like the French general, has spent more time discussing the problem of the soul and spirit than that of science and materiel, the last war convinced all alike of the imperative necessity for a strong air arm. Yet prior to July 1950 nothing concrete was done to provide one. Noting the slow and steady weakening of the army of the air, the reporter for the air arm said in 1948: "If we continue along the road upon which we are at present, we should not be surprised to have, at the end of 1948, an army of some 700,000

[20] For a summary of these reforms see André Géraud, "Insurrection Fades in France," *Foreign Affairs,* Vol. xviii, No. 1 (October 1949).

[21] Henri Queuille, *J. O., déb., A.N.* (2e séance, August 6, 1948), p. 4849. General Revers, in a bitter New Year's message in 1949, commented that despite "the absurd allegations of the press" the military budget, instead of increasing, had actually decreased since the war.—*Revue militaire d'information,* January 1, 1949, p. 5.

rifles and only a rare airplane." [22] The problem was given a thorough airing in the Assembly during the summer of 1949. All parties joined in a general attack on this branch of the service, a branch in which apparently there is much to criticize as regards wise expenditure of funds and similar matters. The Assembly finally decided not to grant money for experiments with prototypes or construction of planes in series until a five-year plan was submitted. This plan was to be submitted by the Air Ministry prior to September 15 on pain of being denied appropriations. Despite the fact that the deadline was missed, appropriations were voted. The plan itself was not submitted until early in 1950.[23] Calling, as it does, for 1,100 fighting planes, including 850 jets, 1,200 transport planes, and all the necessary installations needed to maintain them,[24] no action was taken on it until August 1950. All parties were willing to criticize, but there was none which would take the lead in backing even this most necessary and most basic element of any rearmament program.

Furthermore, the plan was submitted at the worst possible moment —at a time when the demands of a new budget had shocked the Assembly, when prices seemed more out of line with incomes than they had been for several years, when scandal was enlarging the wide gap which has always tended to separate the politicians from the army, when the Communists were particularly active in their campaign against the long awaited American arms, when the colonies were voicing discontent more loudly than ever, and when the news of the hydrogen bomb seemed to generate hopelessness concerning the necessity for any rearmament at all. Despite the final advent of concrete aid from across the Atlantic, hope for military security in the future seemed more remote than ever as the year 1950 began. Discord was rampant on all levels.

The scandal which shocked France was that involving the Chief-of-Staff, General Revers, and his colleague General Mast. Suspected of having released state secrets concerning Indo-China, the generals have confirmed the politicians in the distrust of army officers which has been chronic since the Boulanger and Dreyfus affairs and which was aggravated in 1940 by the 4,000-odd officers who took their re-

22 *Docs. parls., A.N.* (Annexe No. 4719, 2e séance, June 25, 1948). The quotation is from the interesting introduction to the air section of the budget.

23 "Problèmes de l'aviation de transport française," *Le Monde*, February 23, 1950.

24 When the military budget for the year 1950 came before the National Assembly, the air force again came out on the short end. Six and a half billions more than in 1949 were allotted to it, but whether, in view of higher maintenance costs and higher prices in general, this represents a real increase is debatable. At any rate, Jean Moreau, reporter for the Commission of Finances on the air force budget, felt that this sum was totally inadequate for any true reconstitution of the French air force. *Le Monde*, May 11, 1950.

venge on the Republic by following Marshal Pétain. Furthermore, the scandal favored the growth of the belief which lay at the root of much contemporary French military thought: that perhaps national defense was, after all, impractical, and even illogical, in present-day France.

Another cause for inaction was that in 1950 the French colonies no longer appeared to be the asset that they seemed to be at the time of the Liberation. Then many Frenchmen believed that the future of the country lay in the colonies, both as a source of manpower and as a strategic position of the utmost importance. But since then the French delegates from the departments across the sea have dampened the ardor of those at home with vituperative demands that the traditional "exploitation" of the colonial soldier come to an end, that equality be established between the colonial officer and soldier and their comrades of Metropolitan France.[25]

Perhaps the final deterrent to effective action was provided by the United States' decision to proceed with the building of the hydrogen bomb. French scientists have taken an even more dismal view than Americans of the possibility of defense against atomic warfare.[26] The United States' new decision seemed to confirm a rational and gloomy nation in the belief that, when all was said and done, the United States was quite as likely to be the cause of the end of the world as the Soviet Union. "Over there," remarked Le Monde editorially, "they have always been tempted to sacrifice Europe in case of invasion." [27] Under the circumstances, it is not surprising that much of French opinion prefers some kind of neutrality.[28]

One hopes that the key to the solution of the problem of military security for France lies in the Brussels Agreement and the Atlantic Pact. Perhaps it does. But it should be remembered that France is extremely distrustful of international arrangements which envision

[25] See the bitter remarks made by M. Diori Hamani of the GRDA (Groupe du Rassemblement Démocratique Africain), J.O., déb., A.N., June 10, 1949, p. 3281.

[26] See, for example, Théo Kahan and Claude Magnan, L'Énergie atomique et ses applications, Paris, 1949, Chap. XII; and also P. Genaud, L'Arme atomique, Paris, 1950.

[27] Le Monde, February 10, 1950. This is, of course, one of the points which the Communists have been making, particularly by quoting U.S. Representative Cannon. See Alfred Malleret-Joinville, J.O., déb., A.N. (2e séance, June 9, 1949), p. 3239. The same argument, but from a different tack, is that of J.-J. S. Schreiber, "La Paix américaine, est-elle possible?" (Le Monde, February 19, 20, 1950) in which he maintains that Americans seem to be in the grip of the "Munich" psychology.

[28] American newspapers made much of this stand taken by conservative, semi-official Le Monde during the last few weeks of the month of February 1950. The question was opened in 1949 by the Academician Étienne Gilson. Now as then the rebuttal is being led by Raymond Aron of Figaro, but unfortunately Aron, despite the high esteem in which he is held, has a reputation of standing virtually alone. See his excellent article: "The Atomic Bomb and Europe," Bulletin of the Atomic Scientists, April 1950, pp. 110 ff.

the possibility of including a rearmed Germany and Spain in the Atlantic community.[29]

Perhaps it is superfluous to add that the effect of political machination has disastrously lowered French army morale. Many of the army's technicians left the service shortly after the war for better-paying civilian jobs. In 1948 only one student from the Ecole Polytechnique went into the army for which that school purportedly prepares its men. General Billotte recently resigned from one of the country's highest military posts because he felt the situation of France to be so dangerous that he wanted to be free to warn his countrymen of the perils of defenselessness.[30] Perhaps most significant of all, the backbone of the army, the noncommissioned officer, is not reenlisting, and those few who do so are being sent to Indo-China with the result, so it is claimed, that the recruit at home is receiving very insufficient instruction in the much-vaunted *camps légers*.[31] Despite the extension of social security to cover military personnel, the situation of those in all ranks of the army is not a happy one. Because of the unpopularity of the war in Indo-China they have not even the traditional soldier's reward—to be a hero!

It was against this background that the invasion of Korea burst upon an astonished world. The stand taken by the United States made a profound impression on France, as elsewhere on the Continent. So did American unpreparedness as it revealed itself in the following weeks. Paris was disappointed when, during the course of a debate on foreign policy in the last week of July, Premier René Pleven said little about Korea, and took no strong stand on French policy. André Siegfried wrote pessimistically in *Figaro* that France had "fallen again to a moral level that is hardly better than that of the years 1930 to 1940, when defeat was in preparation." [32]

But in the days which followed there was a dramatic change in the attitude of the French government. At the very end of July, Jules Moch, the new Minister of Defense, a man of energy and decision, outlined a vigorous defense plan before the National Assembly.[33]

[29] For example, when signing an economic accord with Germany in November 1949, the French Assembly and, more particularly, the Council of the Republic, reaffirmed its position that the Germans should not be admitted to the Atlantic community.

[30] See his letter of resignation in *Le Monde,* February 9, 1950. He is at present working on a book, *Le Temps du choix,* parts of which have appeared in *Le Monde.*

[31] XXX, "Un cri d'alarme; où va l'armée française?" *Le Monde* (February 11, 13, 1950)—two typically dismal articles. See also the more tempered remarks on the state of the army made before the Conseil de la République, *Journal officiel, Conseil de la République,* May 9, 1950, pp. 1200–1220. Also *Esprit,* May 1950, is almost entirely devoted to a study of the French army.

[32] Quoted in Harold Callender, "Pleven Statement Disappoints Paris," *New York Times,* July 27, 1950.

[33] See *Le Monde,* July 30, 31, 1950.

By August 5, the five-year plan for rebuilding the air force had been passed by the Council of the Republic, and on August 8, M. Pleven himself came forth with an unexpectedly ambitious program embodying the remarks which M. Moch had made a few days before. In the intervening period he had apparently been reassured that the economic stability of Europe would be disturbed as little as possible by the exigencies of defense and that his program would receive ample aid from the United States. He had probably been given to understand in the most definite terms that the United States realized that economic strength remained the prerequisite of military defense, particularly in those areas where Communist fifth columns thrive on legitimate social discontent.[34] Hence he felt a measure of confidence in outlining a program which called for fifteen additional fully-equipped divisions within three years, and for a large increase in the military budget—large enough indeed to provide for the completion of the five-year plan in three years. But the French note made what may prove to be a rather more important political statement than the immediate military pronouncement: ". . . In order for this program to attain its necessary degree of efficacy," it read, "it is indispensable that each of the peoples of the Atlantic Pact have the profound conviction of participating in a common effort, oriented in a common direction, in which each partner is fully engaged and in which each benefits from the total support of the others." [35] Perhaps in this ideal of Atlantic unity the French will find what they have lacked for so long: an ideal worthy of real, sustained effort and sacrifice.

The Schuman Plan was the first step in this direction. Whatever may be said for or against this international plan for pooling resources, one thing seems quite certain: the French envisioned it as a step toward some sort of political union. M. Pleven's statement represented the next step, raising the idea from the European to the Atlantic level. It was a strong plea for a democratic world in which the symbolic trinity of Liberty, Equality, and Fraternity would be one and indivisible. There was, to be sure, no mention of German rearmament in the Pleven proposal. Nor was an increase in steel production in the Ruhr contemplated as an aid in rearming.[36] But French enmity toward her traditional enemy may be expected to diminish in direct proportion to the extent France feels it is an integral part of a political organization that is both strong and permanent. It is this new

[34] Harold Callender, "U.S., West Europe Agree on Targets," *New York Times*, July 30, 1950.

[35] From the text of the French note, *New York Times*, August 8, 1950.

[36] According to Hervé Alphand, French delegate to the permanent committee of the North Atlantic Deputies. See "France to Add 15 Divisions in Rearming Plan," *New York Herald Tribune*, August 8, 1950.

internationalism which may prove to be the road to a spiritual renaissance—given ample time, cooperation, and patience.

As an army is, in the last analysis, a spiritual phenomenon, an improvement in French morale will show itself in a willingness on the part of the majority to effect military reform. The test will come when the French Assembly considers the Prime Minister's plan. Then it will be possible to tell whether there has been a real reaction against present-day lethargy, such as there was on the occasion of the Three Year Service bill of 1913. But it must be remembered that the French army is still, as it has always been since the double defeat of 1870, the center of a mass of distrust, a sort of point of concentration of conflicting political, economic and military theories which are so ingrained in the temper of the French body politic that they will not easily be set aside. The disillusionment of the last war and the increased bitterness of party strife, resulting from the international situation on the one hand and the impoverished condition of the country on the other, have added fuel to a classic struggle. As the situation stands at present, the problem of French security continues to be politically serious, and this, in turn, seems to increase the necessity that the United States continue a heavy military and economic commitment vis-à-vis Western Europe.

VIII

FRANCE IN WORLD AFFAIRS

26

++

THE FRENCH EMPIRE TODAY

ELLEN HAMMER

++

THE FRENCH are confronted in their Empire with a crisis of power and a crisis of nationalism. They emerged from the Second World War at the nadir of their strength and prestige, to find a deep unrest in their overseas territories. To deal with it, they drew up a new blue-print of empire. An Assembly of the French Union now sits at Versailles, the Colonial Ministry has been renamed the Ministry of Overseas France, and French governors-general have given way to more euphemistically titled high commissioners. At the same time, equipped with statistics and plans, the French are out to develop their Empire on a scale it has never known before. They have accomplished much in their overseas territories since the war; but much still remains to be done. Never have French leaders hoped for more from Overseas France than they do today; yet never has France's control over its colonial peoples been more widely or more seriously challenged.

I

The network of French control touches five continents, extends over such different peoples as the Arabs and Berbers of North Africa, the Vietnamese, Cambodians and Laotians of Indochina, and the tribes of Afrique Noire. The native inhabitants far outnumber the French colonists; only in Algeria and New Caledonia are there relatively large French settlements. Elsewhere Frenchmen constitute a small minority, maintaining administrative and economic control over peoples of different cultures and at varying levels of development.

There are areas within the Empire which are among the most populous in the world, like the overcrowded Tonkinese delta in Indochina, and others, like New Caledonia, which are handicapped by a serious labor shortage. Predominantly agrarian, the Empire includes many different kinds of agriculture, ranging from the varied products of the moderate North African climate and the tropical African products grown further south, to the rice economy of Indochina and the sugar economy of the West Indies. Some of its raw materials are of vital importance in war as well as in peacetime, such as the phosphates of Morocco, the nickel and chrome of New Caledonia, the graphite of Madagascar, the rubber of Indochina. There are large sections of the Empire which produce nothing which cannot be obtained elsewhere and which sometimes, as in the case of Algerian wheat and wine, have even competed with French products.

Although the several parts of the Empire are linked by their relationship with France, they also share the problems of and are sensitive to developments in the various regions of which they are a part. In North Africa, for example, Algeria, Tunisia, and Morocco are part of the Arab world. The great majority of their indigenous population, predominantly Moslem, live according to the Koranic code and, rather than abandon their personal status under Moslem law, have rebuffed French efforts to assimilate them. As Egypt, Iraq, Syria, Lebanon, and Transjordan achieved their freedom, the eyes of most articulate nationalists in Tunisia and Morocco, and of a considerable number in Algeria, turned toward the independent Arab states as models and toward the Arab League for guidance.

The large federations of French West Africa and French Equatorial Africa, on the other hand, have no organized foci of political attraction outside their borders. African nationalism is still in its infancy. Their serious social and economic problems, which do not stop at European-drawn frontiers, have led to cooperation among the colonial powers, particularly France and Great Britain.

Parts of the Empire which are remote from France fall within the orbits of other powers. New Caledonia and Madagascar, for example —one in the Pacific, the other in the Indian Ocean—are islands in British-American waters. Cut off from France during the Second World War, New Caledonia gravitated into close political and economic relations with its neighbors, Australia and New Zealand. Its large French population, sensitive to the proximity and greater power of the two Pacific dominions, has reacted by clinging to tariff and immigration regulations which have the effect of keeping down to a minimum the interests and influence of English-speaking peoples. At the same time there has been a movement among the New Caledonian French, resulting partly from their isolation and partly from the example of Australia and New Zealand, to urge a species of dominion status for New Caledonia.[1]

Madagascar is less than 800 miles off the coast of the Union of South Africa, another member of the British Commonwealth. When British troops arrived to occupy the island in 1942, they were welcomed by the Madagascans, many of whom are Protestants, whose nationalist leaders favor closer ties with the English-speaking world.[2]

The French West Indies, along with the islands of Saint Pierre and Miquelon,[3] lie almost in the shadow of the United States. The former —Guadeloupe and Martinique—like the island of Réunion in the Indian Ocean and Guiana in South America, fall within the category of "old colonies." A heritage of the first French Empire which pre-dated the Revolution (like the communes of Senegal in Africa), hav-ing few local traditions and little indigenous civilization, they had sought assimilation even before the French were willing to grant it. They had become overlaid with French rule and their inhabitants had achieved French citizenship so long before the Second World War and had been so integrated into the legal and cultural structure of metro-politan France, as to have little political life apart from it.

The French enclaves in India also date back to an earlier period of empire-building, but they were too integral a part of the Indian community to remain entirely separate from it. The achievement of independence by India had almost immediate repercussions in French India.[4]

In Indochina, French imperial problems are also bound up with de-velopments in Asia. The Indochinese Union was created by the French in the latter half of the nineteenth century. The coastal areas, from the Chinese frontier in the north southward to the Gulf of Siam, are peopled mostly by Vietnamese, who constitute almost three-quarters of the total population of Indochina and have much in com-

---

[1] Cyril S. Belshaw, *Island Administration in the South West Pacific* (London, 1950), p. 71. Conservative French elements in New Caledonia would benefit from greater autonomy, as they are not unaware, by achieving more protection against possible liberalizing influences in France.

[2] This statement is based on interviews with Madagascan nationalists in Paris, De-cember 1949.

[3] These small islands, along with French North Africa, were singled out by one writer as the only parts of the French Empire which it would pay France to keep. He justified this choice by the fact that Saint Pierre and Miquelon are of direct aid to the French domestic fishing industry. They also are valuable for training sailors for the French navy. They are in a temperate zone and are inhabited by people of pure French descent. Constant Southworth, *The French Colonial Venture* (London, 1931), p. 163.

[4] Chandernagore which, in a plebiscite, had voted 7,463 to 114 to join India, was trans-ferred on a de facto basis to the Union of India on August 14, 1949. Referenda in the other Indian settlements, which are scheduled, have not yet taken place.

mon, ethnically and culturally, with the Chinese. West of Vietnam lie
the Indochinese countries of Cambodia and Laos, whose Buddhist
peoples are closer in race and culture to the Siamese and who are not
overly fond of the more aggressive and enterprising Vietnamese.

The French divided the Vietnamese lands into three parts, of which
only the most southerly, Cochinchina, was juridically a colony, while
Tonkin and Annam, along with Cambodia and the kingdom of Luang
Prabang in Laos, were protectorates. The French created and maintained the forms of federation in Indochina, but these were largely
administrative; they failed to create much economic or political inter-
dependence among the three peoples, who were linked chiefly by the
French administration and by the communications and other public
works built up to maintain it. Indochina is thus not a unit but a
region, and it is a part of Asia. Although the Vietnamese struggled for
centuries against Chinese domination and, as late as 1946, had rather
an unpleasant time under a temporary Chinese occupation, Vietnamese nationalists and Communists have long found active support and encouragement in China. The example of Japan also has
stimulated the growth of Vietnamese nationalism.

Geographically and culturally so disparate, the various parts of the
Empire are also at very different levels of development. Some sections,
by every accepted criterion, whether of economic development, national consciousness, or political organization, are clearly destined for
an indeterminate period of dependence. Such are the territories of
French West Africa and French Equatorial Africa. Other areas, like
the protectorates of Tunisia and Morocco, are far more advanced.
The French were not unwilling to recognize that there should be different degrees of dependence within the Empire, but beyond that they
were not prepared to go.

French colonial practice has never thrown off the imprint of the
doctrine of assimilation. This had presented Frenchmen with the
goal of transforming the native inhabitants of the Empire into fellow
Frenchmen, replacing the native cultures with French, and absorbing
the colonies into the centralized French political structure. Toward
the end of the nineteenth century, when large new areas were added to
the Empire and the gap between theory and practice had become too
obvious to be ignored, assimilation tended to give way to association.
The aim was to gallicize not the entire population, but only a native
élite, which was to be granted French citizenship and a share in the
administration of the country. But this was a change only in emphasis,
not in essentials. It was an ideological half-way house between what
the French wanted for the Empire and what they might realistically
achieve in the colonies.

The assumptions of assimilation were never abandoned. Gallicization remained the ultimate goal. Rather than build up local self-governing bodies which might evolve in the direction of autonomy, as in the British Empire, the aim was still to have the native population represented directly in the central government in Paris. The economic and military resources of the colonies were still to be subordinated strictly to the needs of the mother country. That the native élite, any more than the native population at large, might either merit or move toward self-government outside the French Empire was an alien notion, for the demand for independence ran directly counter to the entire doctrine of assimilation. It was one demand which France would not admit.

II

The French had accomplished much in their Empire by 1939. There was peace where once there had been tribal war; where once there had been only jungles, there were impressive public works. Agriculture and mining had made great strides. New economic techniques had been introduced, as had Western medicine and sanitation and Western standards of administration. As caste and tribal systems had broken down, a new concept of personal liberty had emerged. In France, people from the colonies were treated generally as the social equals of Frenchmen; and it was from republican France that the most ardent opponents of French rule had acquired many of their ideas of liberty and the rights of man. Some members of the native élites, like Félix Éboué, a native of Guiana who became governor of the Chad, had achieved high posts in the French administration. And in certain areas, a remarkable degree of integration into the body politic of metropolitan France had been accomplished; not only were natives of these regions French citizens, but they were represented in the governing bodies of the French Republic.

There was, however, another side to this picture, which left the French Empire, when war broke out, far from well equipped to deal with the shocks of defeat that lay ahead. It was all very well to talk about the 100 million Frenchmen who were the black and brown and yellow peoples of the overseas territories as well as the white people at home. But the policies of assimilation and association looked better on paper than in practice. The fact was that only a handful of the colored inhabitants of the overseas territories had acquired French citizenship.[5] Native self-government had never gone much beyond

---

[5] In the 1936 elections, of the 70 million peoples in the overseas territories, only 432,122 were qualified to vote; and a considerable proportion of these were Europeans.

the embryonic stage, and the limited representative bodies that had emerged had functioned predominantly in the economic sphere. Political and administrative power was firmly in the hands of the French, with the final court of appeal in Paris.

The French parliament was, to some extent, a source of colonial legislation, extending some laws to the colonies and passing others specifically for them, but the great majority of legislation was by ministerial decree. It was government by bureaucracy, directed from Paris. The colonial administration was dominated by Frenchmen, even at the lower echelons which in the colonies of other powers were staffed by the native population. There were, it was true, a number of local councils in the colonies, but these were largely advisory and generally forbidden to discuss political affairs.

Only in Martinique, Guadeloupe and Réunion was there anything approaching complete political assimilation. The tendency throughout the rest of the Empire, in the protectorates as in the colonies, was toward direct rule. The usual disruptive effects on indigenous societies of European rule over Asians and Africans—the breakdown of native institutions and the destruction of the traditional social fabric—were intensified by the policy of gallicization. A small colored élite had acquired French culture and customs, but the great masses had seen their own cultural patterns disregarded and dislocated, and had been given little to replace them.

Colonial public works had been paid for by native taxes and built by native labor, but the native population had little direct benefit from them. Nationalists were to complain of inadequate nutrition, housing, public assistance, education. Algerian and Tunisian nationalists voiced the grievances of many parts of the Empire when they protested that the best lands had been taken from the peasants by French economic interests; nor was Indochina alone in the Empire in having a peasantry laboring under a staggering burden of agrarian debt. The French may have introduced a concept of civil liberties where no such concept existed before; but the French police and military played a significant part in the colonial administration, and few personal liberties were secured to any of the native populations.

French capital dominated the Empire and returned the bulk of its profits to France. Foreign investments from countries other than France were not encouraged. The Paris government treated the colonies as reservoirs of foodstuffs and raw materials and as markets for French manufactured goods. Their trade was brought within the walls of the French tariff system, even when trade with neighboring and non-French countries might have been economically preferable. Industrialization was discouraged so that it would not cut into the native market for French manufactures or compete with French industry.

The Empire was under an essentially autocratic régime. Public opinion in France was uninterested in the colonies and as a rule left imperial affairs to the small group of Frenchmen who were associated with business and financial interests in the Empire and with the colonial administration. Even when reforms were proposed in France, they were rarely implemented on the spot, for Frenchmen in the colonies tended usually to be highly conservative, cut off from the free interplay of party politics at home, a minority bent upon maintaining their domination over an alien majority. The French Socialists and Communists, as well as a minority of the Radical Socialist Party, took a stand in favor of colonial reform, but few of their plans and promises were translated into action.

Discontent grew among the native populations, and nationalist movements formed. By the time of the Second World War, there were already cracks in the veneer of French rule—Indochina had witnessed a rising at Yenbay in 1930 followed by a Communist revolt; the Neo-Destour Party had been active in Tunisia, the Étoile Norde Africaine in Algeria, the Union Marocaine in Morocco, the VVS in Madagascar.

III

The collapse of France acted as a catalyst upon the prevailing discontents in the colonies. It laid bare French weakness to countries which the French had previously ruled in large part because of the illusion of power which they had created among the subject peoples. It disrupted the structure of French control and led to the broadening and consolidation of nationalist movements.

The Empire split between Pétain and De Gaulle, the bulk of it turning to Vichy because the reaction and defeatism which Pétain symbolized was shared by influential French opinion in the colonies. In Indochina the native population watched the Japanese exploit the French administration for their own ends until March 1945 when, having outlived its usefulness, it was overthrown in favor of Japanese-sponsored régimes which declared their independence. Elsewhere, Allied occupations fanned the flames of colonial nationalism. This was the case in North Africa where the Allies landed in force in November 1942, the words of the Atlantic Charter already widely publicized in their name. It was true also in Madagascar, which the British occupied in 1942 before the Free French took over. The United States particularly had an appeal for nationalists in the Empire—it had great power and great wealth and was, in addition, the traditional and articulate exponent of anti-colonialism.

In Indochina the war had brought a new unity to the Vietnamese nationalist movement. When Allied troops arrived in the country after V-J Day, they found installed in Hanoi a government which called itself the Democratic Republic of Vietnam and in which were represented people of many shades of opinion. Playing a key role in the government was the Viet Minh (Viet Nam Doc Lap Dong Minh Hoi), the Vietnam Independence League, which had been set up in 1941 by the Communists and other groups to resist both the French and the Japanese. The president of the new republic was Ho Chi Minh, the founder of the Indochinese Communist Party.

On September 2, 1945, the Democratic Republic of Vietnam issued a declaration of independence, proclaiming the unity of the three Vietnamese countries of Tonkin, Annam, and Cochinchina.[6] It never swerved from this position on territorial unity, but it did pare down its political demands as it became clear that the Vietnamese could not achieve independence by themselves. The country was divided temporarily between the British and the Chinese who arrived to take over the surrender of Japanese troops. The British supported the French in the south, and fighting broke out in September 1945 between the Vietnamese and Anglo-French forces. North of the 16th parallel, the Republic continued in power, although the Chinese forced the introduction of pro-Chinese nationalists into the government, while at the same time looting the country.

Only on February 28, 1946, did the Chinese sign a treaty agreeing to evacuate Indochina, and then only in exchange for French concessions in regard to French extraterritoriality in China, the position of the Chinese resident in Indochina, a free zone for Chinese goods at Haiphong, and special exemptions for Chinese merchandise shipped over the Haiphong-Kunming Railway.[7] The problem for the French was then to persuade the Vietnamese to allow them to enter the northern part of the country peacefully and take over authority from the Chinese; the Vietnamese, for their part, wanted to make certain that the Chinese would actually leave the country; they wanted also to achieve a breathing space in which to attend to serious economic difficulties at home. The French and the Vietnamese each gained these limited ends when, on March 6, 1946, they signed a treaty by which France recognized Vietnam as a "free state, having its govern-

---

[6] *La République*, No. 1, Hanoi, October 1, 1945. The text is translated in Harold R. Isaacs (ed.), *New Cycle in Asia* (New York, 1947), pp. 163–65.

[7] *Services français d'information, Notes documentaires et études*, No. 555. For a translation of the treaty see Isaacs, *op. cit.*, pp. 166–68.

ment, its parliament, its army and its finances, and forming part of the Indochinese Federation and the French Union" (both of which bodies had still to be defined).[8]

The French had already signed a treaty with Cambodia on January 7, 1946, and they reached a similar agreement with Laos on August 27,[9] but the Vietnamese demanded more of the forms of independence than the French were willing to grant, as well as more satisfactory assurances that Cochinchina (whose fate had been left up to a referendum) would become part of the Republic. Franco-Vietnamese negotiations broke down on these issues. Admiral Georges Thierry d'Argenlieu, the French high commissioner in Indochina, did his best to strengthen non-Republican Indochinese groups both inside and outside Vietnam, in order to counterbalance the Republic. Amid charges and countercharges of bad faith, relations between the French and the Vietnamese grew steadily worse. On November 23, 1946, at Haiphong and then on December 19, 1946, at Hanoi, they erupted into open warfare which is still going on today.[10]

The French made no serious attempts to come to terms with Ho in 1947. Before the year was out, they had declared themselves in favor of setting up an opposition government under Bao Dai, who had ruled as emperor of Annam, in name if not in fact, first under France and then under Japan. Since only a fraction of the resistance was Communist, they tried to split the non-Communist majority away from Ho, but in this they were largely unsuccessful. They put their support behind unrepresentative Vietnamese who were not unwilling to back Bao Dai. They permitted the anti-Ho groups to include Cochinchina in Vietnam and Bao Dai assumed the leadership of a new central government. But the war went on.[11]

As Communist victories continued in China, the Communists consolidated their control over the Vietnamese resistance movement.[12] In France, members of the Left and a number of intellectuals and independents urged negotiations, not with Bao Dai but with Ho, the man against whom France was fighting. But they were overruled by the Center and Right groups which made government policy. These groups, appealing for American aid in the war against Ho, presented the French war effort in Indochina as France's defense of Western

[8] *Notes documentaires et études,* No. 548; Isaacs, *op. cit.,* p. 169.

[9] *Notes documentaires et études,* No. 554. For an analysis of these treaties, see Ellen J. Hammer, "Blueprinting a New Indochina," *Pacific Affairs,* September 1948, pp. 252–263.

[10] For an account of Franco-Vietnamese negotiations, see the same author's *The Emergence of Viet Nam* (New York, 1947).

[11] Hammer, "The Bao Dai Experiment," *Pacific Affairs,* March 1950, pp. 46–58.

[12] See in this connection Milton Sacks, "The Strategy of Communism in Southeast Asia," *Pacific Affairs,* September 1950, pp. 227–47; J. R. Clémentin, "The Nationalist Dilemma in Vietnam," *ibid.,* pp. 294–310.

civilization against the menace of Communism. Closer to home, they warned that a "soft policy" in Indochina might encourage other groups in the Empire to rise against the French, notably in North Africa.

IV

Throughout North Africa, nationalist movements had consolidated their strength during the war years. In Algeria there are two major nationalist parties. One is the PPA (the Party of the Algerian People), set up before the war by Messali Hadj. As this organization is illegal it is represented on the electoral level by the Movement for the Triumph of Democratic Liberties. The other is the Democratic Union of the Algerian Manifesto, headed by Ferhat Abbas. While Messali Hadj was under arrest, Abbas was influential in drawing up the Manifesto of the Algerian People of February 10, 1943, which was signed by leading Moslems. The Manifesto called for the end of French colonialism and demanded a constitution for Algeria, guaranteeing liberty and equality for all its inhabitants regardless of race or religion; "the suppression of feudal property by a great agrarian reform and the right to well-being of the immense agricultural proletariat"; recognition of Arabic as an official language on a par with French; freedom of press and association; free and compulsory education; freedom of religion. Further, it asked "the immediate and effective participation of Algerian Moslems in the government of their country, along the lines followed by the British government and General Catroux in Syria and the government of Marshal Pétain and the Germans in Tunisia." [13]

The following year Abbas founded the Friends of the Manifesto and of Liberty and formed a common front with the PPA. On May 8, 1945, riots broke out, the demonstrators demanding a free Algeria and the liberation of Messali Hadj. These riots were a landmark in Algerian history, evidence that the nationalist movement had won the active support of hundreds of thousands of Moslems. Abbas and Messali Hadj, however, split apart after the events of May 1945 and have been unable to reestablish their alliance. Messali Hadj is the more extremist; he demands outright independence, emphasizes Islam, and is unfriendly to the introduction of Western technical education. Abbas, on the other hand, is willing to remain within the French Union and is generally more moderate. Ho Chi Minh, whom he met in Paris in 1946 and for whom he has professed a great re-

[13] *Du Manifeste à la République algérienne* (Algiers, 1948). An indictment of French rule not unlike that in the Manifesto has also been expressed by Messali Hadj. See, e.g. *Le Problème algérien. Appel aux Nations Unies* (Paris, n.d.).

spect, told him that a nationalist should turn no one away for racial or religious reasons, and this is the policy which Abbas has followed.[14]

The Communists, who separated from the French Communist Party in 1936 to form their own Algerian Federation, are weak in Algeria, as they are elsewhere throughout North Africa; the little strength they have comes from their French members. Messali Hadj and Ferhat Abbas remain the major antagonists in the Algerian nationalist movement. That Abbas lost out to his rival in the 1948 Algerian elections does not mean very much of itself, for grave doubt has been thrown on the fairness and legality of these elections.[15] But Abbas lacks the demogogic and extremist appeal of Messali Hadj and it may well be that he has lost out in popular support.

The difficulties of Algeria are complicated by the number of Frenchmen in the country. Besides the 8 million Moslems in Algeria, there are 1 million Frenchmen, and Algeria was treated before the war, albeit with many reservations, as part of metropolitan France. It was divided into three departments which, by a system weighted heavily in favor of the French inhabitants, sent representatives to the French parliament. The French population had no intention of accepting any change in the status of Algeria which might give the Moslems power at all commensurate with their numbers. Algerian nationalists protested that they were foreigners in their own land and demanded an end to the departmental status of the country.

Tunisia and Morocco, unlike Algeria, were protectorates, bound by treaties to France and ruled nominally by their own native dynasties (although ruled actually, as was the practice throughout the Empire, by Frenchmen). Relations were close between the Neo-Destour Party of Tunisia, the Istiqlal Party of Morocco and the PPA. The three were united in a North African Defense Front, located in Cairo, which worked for the expulsion of the French from all North Africa. It was a goal which had long been preached by Abd el Krim, the Moroccan nationalist, who again made the headlines in 1947 when he escaped French surveillance and turned up in Cairo, the mecca of political refugees from North Africa.

In both Tunisia and Morocco nationalists won active support from their native rulers. Moncef Bey, who reigned in Tunisia during the war, took a strong nationalist line, standing apart from both the Allies and the Axis. His refusal to permit Allied troops to move through Tunisia caused the French to remove him from office, a violation of

[14] This statement is based on an interview with Fehrat Abbas in Paris in December, 1949.

[15] See, for example, the series of articles describing the elections by Marc Zuorro in *Combat,* April 1948.

the treaty of protectorate and, as it turned out, a serious political blunder which rallied many Tunisians against France. The Tunisian nationalist party, the Neo-Destour (Constitution) Party, rejected Axis offers of collaboration, but the French refused to deal with Habib Bourguiba, its leader. He escaped to Cairo and later visited the United States, returning to Tunisia only in September 1949. He demands immediate, unconditional independence and is against any adherence to the French Union. In his words, "We do not want to be French. We are Tunisians and want to remain Tunisians." [16] The Neo-Destour Party calls for an end to the protectorate and the negotiation of a Franco-Tunisian treaty. The party is still illegal but, together with the labor union, the UGTT, it dominates the Tunisian nationalist movement. The UGTT pushes an active program of social and economic reform.

The nationalist position was laid down in a resolution of August 23, 1946, at a congress in Medina. It charged that the protectorate, which "was to have been a provisional and purely protective regime, has degenerated until today it has become a regime of colonial exploitation in which the Guardian State systematically robs the Ward both of sovereign rights and material resources; . . . instead of confining itself to its rightful sphere of control, the Guardian State has taken the place of the Ward in the conduct of public affairs and has annihilated the authority of the Tunisian administration."

The Tunisians, the resolution asserted, had been deprived of the elementary freedoms of thought, speech, association, even of travel; and of the sixty-five years of the protectorate, they had suffered more than twenty in a state of siege and passed the rest under a police state. It condemned the appropriation of the major part of the land and the budget by French colonialism, in what it called disregard of the social obligations of France. It proclaimed the will of the Tunisian people to independence and to adherence as a sovereign state to the Arab League and the United Nations. Concluding, it demanded a constituent assembly, elected by universal suffrage, to give a democratic constitution to Tunisia.[17]

The French have done little since the war to satisfy these demands. The concessions they have offered are meager by nationalist standards, not only in Tunisia, but also in Morocco. Nationalism in the latter country has been retarded by the divisions in Moroccan society and by the timidity of the townsfolk, as well as by French policy (not un-

[16] Quoted in Daniel Boisdon, *Les Institutions de l'Union Française* (Paris, 1949), p. 259.
[17] Parti Liberal Constitutionnel Tunisien Neo-Destour, Bureau d'Information, *Rapport sur la situation politique et économique en Tunisie* (mimeo.) (Paris, 1948).

known in other parts of the Empire) which tried to perpetuate differences between groups. The Berber *dahir* of 1930 (which would have put the Berber population under a régime separate from that of the Arabs, had not widespread Arab opposition forced the *dahir* to become a dead letter) has been credited with bringing the Moroccan nationalist movement into being. Lacking the relatively large and well-developed élite of Tunisia and more remote from the Arab world (from which the French made every effort to insulate Morocco), the Moroccan nationalist movement has been slower to develop popular roots.[18]

Early in the war Moroccan nationalists tended to be pro-German. Later they turned toward the United States only to be disillusioned by the unwillingness of the Americans to offer them any tangible help. On January 11, 1944, they presented a declaration of independence to the French resident-general, justifying it by France's failure to fulfil the terms of the protectorate, by Morocco's contribution to the war, and by the Atlantic Charter. The effect of the widespread arrests which followed was to gain a wider popular support for the nationalist movement. It was broadened still further when Sidi Mohammed, the sultan of Morocco, a religious as well as a secular leader, took up the banner of nationalism. At Tangier in April 1947 he made a ringing defense of the Arab League and of Morocco's right to nationhood.

Of the two major nationalist groups in Morocco, the Istiqlal (Independence) Party and the Democratic Party of Independence, the Istiqlal Party is more important. Like the Neo-Destour Party, it demands an end to the protectorate, independence, and a treaty of alliance with France. It favors democratic principles, guaranteed by a constitutional monarchy. And also—its own special problem—it wants an end to the division between French and Spanish Morocco.

The Istiqlal Party, which has no legal existence, looks to the sultan for leadership of the nationalist movement, but he is not formally a member of the party. To what extent the social program professed by the Istiqlal Party will find support among the traditional ruling class is still an open question.[19] Morocco has no separate labor movement like Tunisia, although Moroccans do participate in the European CGT. Moroccan nationalists, although far from Communist, do not

[18] Walter B. Cline, "Nationalism in Morocco," *Middle East Journal*, January 1947, pp. 18–28.

[19] The sultan has rejected the French proposals which would have granted to the Moroccans the right to form labor unions, giving as his reasons the fact that the French would not permit agricultural workers to join these unions, that they insisted on equal representation for French and Moroccan workers even though 90% of the working population was Moroccan, and that these rights would have been limited.

fear cooperation with the Communist Party, and they regard membership in the CGT as useful training for nationalist activity.[20]

Madagascar, too, represents a challenge to French rule. In Paris
two delegates of a new nationalist party, the MDRM (Mouvement
Démocratique de Rénovation Malgache), proposed a law on March
21, 1946, which would have ended the French protectorate over their
country and made it, like Vietnam, "a free state, having its own government, its parliament, its army and its finance, within the French
Union," but their proposal was rejected. Madagascar had suffered
severe economic privation during and immediately after the war, and
in March 1947 this precipitated open revolt. Tens of thousands of
Madagascans, as well as a number of the small French population of
the island, were dead before the rebellion was put down.

Little has yet been accomplished in the way of remedying the situation which gave rise to the revolt. A report read in the Assembly of
the French Union described in some detail what it called "the gravity
of the political, economic and social situation in Madagascar." [21] Members of the MDRM, which is now illegal in Madagascar, have been
calling for a Franco-Madagascan conference to discuss broader self-
government for their country. But the major accomplishment of the
French authorities so far appears to have been the arrest and condemnation of leading Madagascan nationalists on the grounds that
they were responsible for the revolt. Some people in France are talking about a second Dreyfus affair.

In tropical Africa there is no developed nationalist movement.
Many of those who are politically awake follow the French Socialist Party. Elsewhere in the Empire the Socialists have lost many
friends, for it was the Socialists who led the war against Vietnam, who
put down the Algerian disorders in 1945, and who suppressed the
revolt in Madagascar. But in Afrique Noire the Socialists have accomplished such positive reforms as a labor code and the abolition of
forced labor. The tendency among Socialists in these areas is to move
toward a more independent position within the French Socialist
Party.[22]

Not all Africans, however, are content merely with asking reforms.
In October 1946 the African Democratic Rally was formed. It worked
with the Communists, and stated as its fundamental principles: "Struggle for the political, economic and social liberation of Africa within
the framework of a French Union founded on the equality of rights

[20] This statement is based upon an interview with Moroccan nationalists in Paris,
December 1949.

[21] *Journal officiel de la République française. Débats de l'Assemblée de l'Union
française*, Séance du 20 mai 1949, pp. 550–53.

[22] Jean Rous, "Que veulent-ils?" *Esprit*, July 1949, p. 958.

and duties; Union of all Africans, whatever their ideological conceptions, their origins, their social conditions, in the war against colonialism"; and, finally, "Alliance of the democratic African forces and the democratic and progressive forces of the entire world and, first of all, with the French people, in their common struggle against imperialism." [23] The disorders precipitated by the RDA have led to French countermeasures, and in February 1950 the party was forbidden to hold meetings anywhere in French Africa.

V

There is serious discontent throughout the French Empire. Although there is disagreement as to how popular are its roots and how influential its leaders, it constitutes a threat to the French position. Letting it continue unremedied is a risk which the French can ill afford to take.

The French have not been blind to the need for some political reform. The intricate and ambitious structure of the French Union is evidence of that. They made their first moves toward it during the Second World War. If once again France were to become a great power or, indeed, any sort of power, it seemed axiomatic that she must have her Empire solidly behind her, and reform seemed the obvious answer to the restlessness which was sweeping the colonies.

Hope began to grow of an impending radical change in French imperial policy. People pointed to the conference of colonial administrators held at Brazzaville early in 1944, which laid down a set of principles for Africa, discussed the creation of a federal assembly in which the colonies would have representatives, and talked about setting up assemblies in the colonies themselves. It called for the development of the indigenous populations, for the preservation of native institutions, for native education, for a measure of industrialization and economic modernization, and for free labor. And successive months did indeed bring reforms to Africa, limitations on forced labor, a new penal code, a new plan for education.

But the men at Brazzaville also went on record with the statement: "The objectives of the civilizing work carried on by France in the colonies dispels any idea of autonomy, any possibility of evolution outside the French imperial bloc. Even the distant establishment of self-government in our colonies must be set aside." [24] Having opposed forced labor, they were not opposed to a *corvée*. They were against

---

[23] *Le Rassemblement Démocratique Africain dans la lutte anti-impérialiste* (Paris, 1948). In October 1950, the RDA members of the French Parliament announced that they had ended their association with the Communists (*Le Monde*, October 20, 1950).

[24] *Notes documentaires et études*, No. 1,131.

the teaching of native languages. The declaration of Brazzaville indicated a new concern for the development of the colonies in their own best interests and not simply as satellites of metropolitan France, but it did not go very far in implementing its own principles or in meeting native demands.

In Algeria, De Gaulle granted French citizenship to 60,000 Moslems who were allowed to keep their personal status in Moslem law. A representative council was set up in Madagascar. For Indochina came the declaration of March 24, 1945, the first official document in which the term "French Union" appeared. It offered the Indochinese the right of participation in their own government, and called for changes in economic and administrative policy. Politically, however, the declaration changed very little. A governor-general was to continue in control of Indochina, flanked by ministers appointed by and responsible to him. There was to be a federal representative assembly in which each of the Indochinese states as well as the French would be represented, but it was to be little more than advisory.[25]

All of this added up to a certain willingness on the part of the French to modify some of their methods of imperial control, but indicated no intention on their part radically to alter that control. It took a while for this to sink into the minds of nationalists in the colonies. In the first draft constitution then being drawn up by the constituent assembly was a statement that the French Union was based upon the free consent of its members. That constitution was rejected by a popular referendum in May 1946, but revolutionary ideas of empire were still in the air. When a Vietnamese delegation arrived in Paris that summer to discuss their future relations with France, they talked about a status in the French Union like that which Eire then had as a member of the British Commonwealth. In the second constituent assembly, Ferhat Abbas, like the Vietnamese and Madagascans before him, asked for the complete autonomy of Algeria within the French Union. They received their answer in the French Union provisions of the second French constitutional draft which was accepted by the French people in October 1946.

It declared that "the French Union is composed of nations and people who pool or coordinate their resources and their efforts in order to develop their respective civilizations, increase their well-being and assure their security." More specifically, the French Union was formed, on the one hand, of the French Republic, into which were integrated overseas departments and territories; and, on the other, of associated territories and associated states. Algeria and the four "old colonies" became part of France as overseas departments. On Sep-

[25] *Notes documentaires et études,* No. 548; Isaacs, *op. cit.,* pp. 159–61.

tember 20, 1947, an organic statute of Algeria was promulgated by the French Republic. Far from the Algerian Republic federated with France which Abbas had asked, it provided that "Algeria constitutes a group of departments, endowed with civil personality, financial autonomy, and a particular organization. . . ." [26] Algerian nationalists walked out of the Assembly as soon as this first article was adopted.

In the other colonies (rebaptized as overseas territories) and in the associated territories (Togoland and the Cameroons, formerly B mandates under the League of Nations, now trust territories) local elected assemblies were set up with limited economic and administrative powers.[27] No longer was the privilege of sending representatives to the government in Paris limited as under the Third Republic to the "old colonies," Algeria, Cochinchina, Senegal, and the Indian enclaves. Now all the overseas and associated territories elected representatives both to the French National Assembly and the Council of the Republic. They also filled seats in the new Assembly of the French Union.[27a]

For a number of the less developed areas of the Empire these changes, despite their obvious limitations, could be regarded as an advance. The French were very sensitive to international criticism of their colonial policies; in the United Nations they did their best to limit the powers of the Special Committee on Non-Self-Governing Territories. Evolution toward a greater degree of self-government within the French Union would be slow—too slow for Algeria and probably also for Madagascar—but the new provisions of the French Union did not close the door to further progress. Whether they have opened the door, only time and the actual experience of working within the new juridical framework can tell.

Highest in the new hierarchy of empire, however, were the old protectorates, now associated states, and for them the outlook was much less hopeful. The comparison sometimes made between dominion status in the British Commonwealth and associate statehood in the French Union is misleading, for the two have little in common. There was no place in the centralized French Union for a state such as Eire was in 1946. France insists upon retaining control over the foreign affairs and the armed forces of the associated states. It

[26] *Notes documentaires et études,* No. 738.

[27] "There was no question of giving them a legislative function, which belonged to the National Assembly, still less of granting them control over the conduct of the policy of the governor-general of the territory, he being responsible for his acts only to the government." Boisdon, *op. cit.,* p. 95.

[27a] They are generally elected under a restricted suffrage. In the French Parliament the overseas territories "do not participate on an equal footing. In effect, the natives average only one deputy for 800,000 inhabitants, the metropolitan French one for 75,000 inhabitants." François Luchaire, *Manuel de droit d'outre-mer* (Paris, 1949), p. 134.

grants them autonomy only over their domestic affairs (in practice a limited autonomy) and representation in the High Council and the Assembly, the consultative bodies of the French Union.

In the Assembly of the French Union, which met for the first time on December 10, 1947, half the members are drawn from overseas and half from metropolitan France. The Assembly brings together a diversified group of people and is a unique development in French colonial policy; its debates and proceedings have not gone unreported in the French press. It remains, however, solely an advisory body. The High Council of the French Union, also advisory, is to be composed of representatives of the French government and of the associated states and is expected to assist in the general direction of the French Union, but it is not yet in existence. There is a president of the French Union but he is also the president of the French Republic. Although the constitutional structure has been laid down for a well-knit federal organization of the Empire, it has still to become a working federalism. The real center of power in the French Union so far is, as before, in the French government.

The position of the protectorates was to be fixed by separate agreements with France, but the countries which qualify have not all, as yet, claimed associate statehood. The kings of Laos and Cambodia have both signed agreements with France, as has the Bao Dai government of Vietnam.[28] French control is still strong in Laos and Cambodia, although more veiled than in prewar days. As to the Bao Dai government, its agreement with France was expected to demonstrate that it was indeed a nationalist régime and worthy of rallying popular support; but the terms, although in some respects more than the French were willing to grant to Ho, were so restrictive as to label Bao Dai more surely than ever a French puppet whose political support is largely measured by the strength of the French army.[29] The Bey of Tunis and the Sultan of Morocco have not yet joined the French Union.

VI

The unsettled state of the Empire has not diverted the French from their economic plans for Overseas France. The recent war underlined the value of their Empire. No longer was it simply a matter of men, loans, and supplies contributed by the colonies to help metropolitan France defend itself, as in World War I. This time the mother country fell to the invader early in the war and it was the colonies—

28 *Notes et études documentaires,* No. 1295.
29 Hammer, "The Bao Dai Experiment," *loc. cit.*

or at least those which joined the Allies—which remained free and in the war. From them came French and native forces which helped to liberate France. The Mediterranean emerged not as a frontier, but as a bridge, which linked the Metropole with its African territories—with North Africa, from which the Allies moved on Europe; and with French Equatorial Africa, which included the strategically central Chad. In the Indian Ocean, Free French Madagascar was a key point of Allied strength as, in the Pacific, were New Caledonia and its vital port of Noumea. Sections of the Empire thus contributed more than ever to the defense of France, and they also offered to France's allies essential war materials and invaluable strategic advantages. In all of these respects the Empire helped to build up the international bargaining position of France at a time when the defeat of 1940 had reduced French prestige and power to a minimum.

The economic ties between France and the overseas territories were dislocated only temporarily by the war. Forty-one and eight-tenths per cent of French exports went to Overseas France in 1949, considerably more than the 25.7 per cent of imports to France supplied by the rest of the Empire.[30] The French are concerned with limiting the drain of import trades on their precious hoard of dollars. One of the major goals of the broad colonial improvement plans launched under the law of April 30, 1946, was to enable the territories overseas to step up their production of such foodstuffs as cereals and fats so that they can fill a larger proportion of their own requirements. The French would like North Africa (an exporter of cereals before the war, but now an importer) to be able to supply out of its own production the cereals that it needs and to get other necessary foodstuffs from within the Empire. They are also aiming at a certain amount of industrialization—particularly in textiles, canned goods, and cement—in Overseas France. The French want to draw foodstuffs and raw materials for themselves from within the franc zone—oils and fats, cotton and other textile raw materials, rubber, minerals, oil, timber. And, finally, they want the territories overseas to earn dollars directly, by increasing their exports to other countries.[31]

The colonies, in other words, must help themselves, thereby helping to relieve France of economic burdens, as well as aiding the mother country more directly. The aim of limited industrialization is a change from past policy, and there is a new emphasis on raising the living standards of the native populations. The French have launched ambitious projects for mineral prospecting and public works, par-

[30] Ministère de l'Économie nationale, *Bulletin mensuel de statistique d'outre-mer*, March–April 1950, p. 43.

[31] Organization for European Economic Cooperation. *Interim Report on the European Recovery Program*. Vol. II (Paris, December 30, 1948).

ticularly in North Africa. In Afrique Noire, where industry is virtually nonexistent, the emphasis is upon on-the-spot conversion of home-grown products which are essential to the African economy. Such projects were too far-reaching to be left to the whims and limited resources of French private capital. Mixed and state companies were set up, working through the FIDES (the Investment Fund for Economic and Social Development) and a Central Fund for Overseas Territories. Of the 999.6 billion francs invested in the French Union (both in France and by the mother country in Overseas France) from 1947 through 1949, 127 billion were invested in Overseas France. As the needs of metropolitan France become less pressing, it is expected that a greater proportion of the total investments will go to the Empire, the figure for 1950 being set at 90.5 billion francs for Overseas France as compared with 482 for the Metropole.[32]

French capital, however, even in combination with that contributed by Overseas France, cannot do the job alone. Much of the capital that is needed will have to come from abroad. American aid from ECA (the European Cooperation Administration) and from private investment sources will be essential. Tunisia has already been divided into three economic zones by companies prospecting for oil and only one of these concessions is being exploited by a French company; the others have been granted respectively to the Anglo-Dutch Shell Oil Company and to American Gulf Oil. Individual Frenchmen have protested vigorously against this arrangement, complaining of Anglo-American "capitulations."

Restricted by their own limited economic resources from embarking on a large-scale development of the overseas territories, the French are nevertheless reluctant to have foreigners provide much of the capital and heavy equipment they lack. They have carried over from their traditional colonial policy an unwillingness to allow private foreign capital in any large amounts into the Empire, as well as a determination to keep economic control of the Empire in their own hands, even at the risk of retarding its economic development.[33] In

[32] République française. Présidence du Conseil. Commissariat Général du Plan de Modernisation et d'Équipement. *Rapport du Commissaire générale sur le plan de modernization et d'équipement de l'Union française* (Paris, December 1949), p. 140.

[33] There seems generally to have been "some reluctance among the European nations to admit American capital into Africa, even where it is given as a grant. The reluctance springs from a number of sources: long-standing traditions of exclusiveness and a horror of the paper work inevitably involved in the maintenance of accounts which would satisfy Congress. Even more important than these factors is the fear of the colonial authorities that any large-scale investment programme might bring with it inflation and consequent social unrest. It has been estimated that for every Marshall dollar invested in these development schemes, the local authorities would have to put up the equivalent of at least $15 in their own currencies." *The Economist,* July 15, 1950, p. 114.

Algeria, for example, nationalists chafe under what they regard as the unduly limited development plans of the French. Ferhat Abbas, for one, believes that the only solution to Algeria's economic problems lies in big imports of American and Swiss capital. Certainly foreign investments are required, and on a much larger scale than heretofore. The various economic plans are still in their infancy, and the building up of underdeveloped areas to the point where they can make effective use of investments and increase their contribution to the world economy is a slow and arduous affair.

Already some nationalists in the colonies are demanding a say in the form and type of investments and business interests introduced into their territories. In Morocco, the Istiqlal Party bitterly criticized an attempt by the American and French governments to settle a disagreement over the rights of American businessmen on the grounds that no Moroccan was consulted in the negotiations. They consider all non-indigenous capital, whether French or American, as foreign and want the Moroccan state to have a majority control in any large-scale development projects. This is a trend which will surely grow, not decrease, in the future, bringing many problems in its wake. To what extent should the needs of individual areas be permitted to override the needs of metropolitan France when the two happen to clash? Can nationalist groups always be relied on for estimates of the economic needs of their countries? Will a greater degree of control by the native population over their government and economy discourage badly needed foreign investments?

VII

French economic planning cannot be carried on in a political vacuum. The French, after all, can develop the Empire only as long as they are in peaceful control of its peoples and territories. As of the present day they are not in control of all of it.

Algeria has been included within the North Atlantic Defense Pact —over the protests of North African nationalists. But the immediate problem for the French is to defend their scattered Empire not against an outside aggressor, but against a threat from inside its boundaries. When they draw up their economic and military balance sheets of empire, Indochina seems to offer much—with its rubber, rice, and coal; the large French investments in the country; the fact that it was one of the few French colonies that had an export trade balance before the war and could earn dollars for the French Empire. It was also a key military base in Southeast Asia, although it was the Japanese who used it, not the French, in World War II. All of these varying advantages have little meaning today for, far from contributing to French strength, Vietnam is a serious drain on France. More than one-quarter of the total French army is fighting in Indochina,[34] and the French are devoting half of their military budget to the Indochinese war.

In France the Communists have urged that the French army leave Indochina, but they are not alone in this, for the same opinion has been expressed in very different quarters. The prominent conservative French newspaper, *Le Monde,* published an article in its issue of June 25–26, 1950, urging the evacuation of Indochina. Maurice Duverger, the author, argued that France could not expect to hold on to its economic interests in Vietnam. The Bank of Indochina, which had dominated much of the country's economy, had already turned in preference to other areas; "the realism of business circles precedes, alas, that of political circles." Aside from the traffic in piastres, he wrote, there would be no economic future for Europeans because any nationalist Vietnamese government would impose controls on foreign enterprise. It would be cheaper to indemnify French investors for their lost investments than to fight for them. As to the possible reaction in North Africa, he suggested that either of the alternatives which would result from a French evacuation—a Communist victory or armed intervention by the United States—would hardly appeal to Arab nationalists. In any case, a departure from Vietnam would enable France to strengthen its effectives in North Africa. The French armies could be concentrated in Europe and Africa, where French essential interests lay. The way would then be open to a policy of intelligent reforms in North Africa.

The French are receiving American aid in their war against Ho Chi Minh (not as much as they would like; and along with suggestions that they grant more real independence to Bao Dai, which they do not like at all). They are taking advantage of the fact that the United States supports the war against Ho as a part of its anti-Communist policy in Asia. But no matter how the changing international situation may affect events in Indochina, the French have failed in Vietnam. Elsewhere in the Empire, grave and unsolved problems lie ahead.

France is not alone in finding its authority challenged in its Empire. Since the war, colonial peoples have been more than ever determined on change, and the colonial powers less able than ever to withhold it. India, Pakistan, Burma, Indonesia, and the Philippines have achieved independence under varying circumstances. They have

---

[34] *Journal officiel de la République française. Débats parlementaires. Assemblée nationale,* 3e Séance du 9 mai 1950, p. 3411.

not been able to dispense with outside help, any more than have many states which have been independent far longer than they. Each of the new governments has inherited the social and economic structure of a colonial area and a complex of difficulties, some resulting from the long-standing colonial relationship, others predating it. There are no panaceas for such deep-rooted problems, but it may well be that in colonial areas they cannot be solved without first granting political independence or broader autonomy, depending upon the degree of development. A combination of legal formulae and military force, in any case, as the French have had occasion to learn in recent years, is a poor substitute for far-reaching economic and political reform. It is time, perhaps, to reread the preamble of the French constitution where it is written: "The French Republic . . . will not undertake any war of conquest, and will never use its forces against the liberty of any people."

27

++

THE RELIABILITY OF

FRANCE IN THE EUROPEAN SYSTEM *

HENRY BERTRAM HILL

++

THE elements required to provide a nation with the status of a great power are difficult to assess and are often elusive. In the world of to-day only the United States and Russia are great powers in any absolute sense, but international relationships under the nation-state system are relative and dynamic and may properly be taken into consideration only as part of the total scene, both past and present. Russia and the United States, after all, share between themselves only a fraction of the world's population and economic potential, and at this point in history are poised in juxtaposition to each other. Both are influenced by, and eager to influence, the states about them. Further, while the United States has never been defeated in war since it has acquired the status of a great power, Russia has been several times so defeated, even without extensive invasion, and at least once by a single enemy.

* This paper is a frank attempt to reverse the usual approach to an estimate of the strength of France wherein the weaknesses of French government and the turbulent events of French history are dwelt upon at length. The author is aware that he is drawing the picture with broad strokes and that he is open to the charge of picking a tortuous path, or even of seeing history backwards. The conventional view, however, certainly has its pitfalls. J. R. Moreton MacDonald, writing in 1915 an introduction to the text of his *A History of France* (3 vols., London, 1915) which had been completed before the war, makes the following point: "[May I] be allowed to say how conscious I am that I have overstated the temperamental characteristics, and in particular the temperamental weaknesses of the French. The truly remarkable way in which, under the present trial, France has purified herself of her traditional vices and developed virtues which were supposed to be quite alien to her character drives one to the conclusion, not only that the temperamental qualities of nations change more rapidly than we have been accustomed to think, but also that they are often only qualities which have been foisted on nations by noisy minorities." The last sentence has little historical realism, save for the closing clause, and that clause contains much of the underlying thesis of this paper.

History has, indeed, amply demonstrated that power is an extremely subtle factor. Its acquisition in preponderance by one state has invariably invoked inhibiting reactions from other nations. The possession of strength has not necessarily been followed by the ability to reap commensurate military or diplomatic achievements. The might of today often has become the weakness of tomorrow. And, finally, just as small party groups have been able to hold most influential and rewarding positions of balance in legislative bodies, so lesser states have, by virtue of a similar location on the world stage, played roles considerably greater than their demographic and economic attributes have otherwise indicated. They have, as a matter of fact, occupied places of such importance in the strategy of diplomacy that greater powers were perforce constrained to accord them something like equal treatment. It is against the general background of such factors as these, and in recognition of the fact that Europe is still the focal area of world affairs, that the potential role of France among the powers today has to be weighed.

It is quite obvious that France, short of an unimaginable acquisition of preponderant economic stature in Europe or the equally improbable dismantling of Russia, is unlikely to regain the basic position she formerly occupied; nevertheless she has at her disposal considerable elements of strength. First, there are those factors which are concerned with geographic location and relations with other states. As long as the West retains its democratic orientation, France is the most useful and dependable foothold on the Continent. Although England would be serviceable as a general air base and as an advanced depot, it would be on the soil of France, as in the First World War, that the real trial at arms would take place in any struggle likely to arise from the present distribution of world tensions. Strategically, France provides the best avenue for a deployment into Central Europe, and her North African territories are the best non-European approaches to the Mediterranean. In less tangible matters, despite the defeat and occupation of 1940, France still has considerable prestige in Europe. Her past cultural, economic, and diplomatic relations with the lesser states of Eastern Europe have a deeper and broader history than those of any other Western nation and have left a residue which has not been eliminated by the expansion of Russian influence in the area. In Western Europe, the position of France is better, relatively, than it has been at any time since the emergence of Hitler, while the decline of Britain, deplorable as it may be in itself, has resulted in a shortening of her shadow across the Channel and in a consequent lessening of her influence on the Continent.

Second, within France itself there are visible elements of new strength. For the first time in generations the birth rate has risen and the death rate has fallen until there is a favorable margin of increase in the population.[1] Such a development is not only indicative of returning vigor; it also has psychological value to a people aspiring to leadership when confronted with the possibility of war as a test of that leadership. Another significant factor is the economic recovery of France since liberation, made with an indicative display of energy in the face of discouraging administrative indecisiveness. In almost all categories France has equaled or surpassed prewar output and there is reason to expect further progress.[2] Still possessing as the base her large degree of self-sufficiency and internal economic balance, France is, considering conditions at large, economically the most secure state in Europe.

Third, and perhaps most important as an element of strength, is the history of France. When an historian is confronted with the problem of estimating the strength of a nation he finds it of some use to weigh such matters as population, economic development, the relative power of potential enemies, and the force of current ideas, but he finds his real clues in the past. He tries to answer such questions as the following: What historic substance has the nation? Has it acquired what might be called the psychological make-up of a great power? How effectively has it recovered from earlier shocks? What has it learned from its defeats? How serious are its enduring weaknesses? It is in the answers to these questions, insofar as they can be answered, that a significant estimate of how much of whatever weight a state may have is likely to be exercised in foreign affairs. It makes small difference if a nation is thrust into a position where it can play a brilliant role in diplomacy if it has no tradition of diplomatic skill behind it. It has been remarked, indeed, that Germany's misfortune in 1919 was less that she had been defeated than that she had no Talleyrand. It matters little if a state can mobilize ten divisions or fifty if none of them fights effectively. The pages of history are filled with the accounts of the defeats of presumably superior forces. Yet conversely, defeat has been less an indicator of the absence of strength in a long-range sense than has the failure to recuperate after disaster. Recuperation in itself, however, is of little value if the ultimate aim is to repeat the disaster—that is the kind of recuperation in which Nazi

---

[1] *Population*, Vol. 4, No. 3 (July–September 1949), 534. The figures for 1948 were 20.8 births and 12.2 deaths per 1,000 people. The favorable rate is due more to increased births than to a reduction in deaths. The figures for 1939 were 14.6 births and 15.3 deaths. For a detailed discussion of French population trends, see Chapter 18 above.

[2] Lack of investment resources, however, is likely to retard the rate of development. The recovery since the war has been largely due to the fuller utilization of facilities already available.

Germany indulged. Effective recovery includes a sober analysis of all of the lessons to be learned and of all the realities involved, including the unpleasant ones. Finally, while every nation carries certain deeply imbedded historic flaws that sap its strength, it is less their conspicuousness than their vulnerability that counts—how likely these shortcomings are to make themselves felt at an awkward moment, and at what kind of a moment and for how long.

When such questions as these are used as criteria for the judgment of France today the answers, while not wholly so, are in the main favorable. In employing them as keys to determining French strength it has to be recognized that historical factors can be exaggerated beyond their true importance to the point of denying current realities; but they can also be underestimated, and such is usually done in times of great stress or change like the present. In the belief in their importance, this chapter lays considerable emphasis upon attempting to answer those questions as they pertain to France, passing quickly over the first of them and then taking principal concern with those regarding recuperative power and vulnerability.

Frenchmen are well aware of the fact that they have long played a role of some historic magnitude. Up through the centuries of conflict during which the French state was being constructed they acquired a body of traditions and experience that still form an important reservoir. France achieved its national unification prior to the age of modern nationalism and hence was spared the perfervid immaturities which often marred the public conduct of Germany and Italy during the past century. With but few aberrations, which were brief, France long occupied a major position in Europe, became accustomed to it, exercised its cruder perquisites with relative moderation, and learned its responsibilities. France also learned that status is an ephemeral thing and she generally resisted the temptation of making flamboyant gestures in violence of her traditions in the vain hope of gaining a prestige that could be properly acquired only by remaining true to character.

France had, in other words, a remarkably long and sustained record of continuity as a great power. The surface events of the French Revolution and of the Napoleonic period, as well as of the minor revolutions of the nineteenth century, should not be allowed to conceal the essential continuity of that record. The Great Revolution, though turbulent and dramatic, was essentially a groping in search of substitutes for a bankrupt ruling class and a leaderless bureaucracy during the course of which internal forces were released that could temporarily be bent to monstrous purposes by the evil genius of Napoleon. It took France a hundred years to begin to understand the meaning of the Revolution, and the governmental changes of the nineteenth century, more Parisian than French, were the convulsions along the way to that understanding. Down below the surface, in the real vitals of France, the same indigenous forces that had character- ized her institutions from the beginning of the modern period were operating with a smooth and largely uninterrupted continuity. Cer- tainly in the field of foreign affairs the greatest of these upheavals had no detrimental affects, although Napoleon, surpassing Louis XIV in ambition, embittered Europe to an extent that has ever since made the generosity of the Peace of Paris a byword. Subsequent to the Na- poleonic interlude, the residue from the Revolution was a positive benefit to France abroad.

The questions of the historical substance of France and of her ex- perience in the role of a great power do not need to be dwelt upon at length, but the question of her recuperative power does. There are numerous examples which might be cited, running back to the begin- ning of French history, but the one which best illustrates it, as well as marking the culmination of a highly important development in her institutions, is the recovery from the fate which befell her in the years right after 1870. The outlook then could hardly have been more bleak. After generations of almost uninterrupted primacy on the Con- tinent, France had been suddenly and ignominiously brought to her knees by a parvenu from Central Europe who marched at will over her territories and dictated a humiliating peace. At home, violent civil discord gutted her capital city, leaving a heritage of hate which tore open the class cleavages so recently revealed by the developing Industrial Revolution, while contending minorities struggled to resus- citate one of the several mutually exclusive régimes whose bones lay strewn across France's preceding eight decades of political history. The government of the moment, democratically formed in structure if not in substance, had been cunningly foisted on the country by Bismarck, in part in the hope of engendering weakness and confusion, and it gave every indication of living up to that expectation.

If the vantage point is shifted from the interior of France to the exterior, the picture has an even more somber appearance. None of the neutral powers seemed particularly alarmed, or even sympathetic. The German parvenu appeared to have acquired an unassailable posi- tion on the pinnacle of Europe. The Industrial Revolution, settling down in earnest in the Rhineland, sent German economic develop- ment hurtling past that of France, giving Germany an ever-increasing military preponderance. To cap it all, Bismarck entrenched his posi- tion still further in the succeeding years by constructing a system of alliances and international friendships that seemed to preclude any

French hope of foreign assistance. In short, France was broken, divided, outstripped, and isolated. A contemporary commentator might well have judged that as a great power she was through.

Yet only a generation later France could speak with a voice equal to any in Europe, and after another decade had elapsed her armies led the conquest of Germany. Following victory, she went even further and reestablished an authority on the Continent equal to that which she had held prior to the rise of Germany. How this came about is a revealing study in the art of recuperation.

In the midst of all the tragedy that marked those years, France began her rehabilitation with one piece of unintended and unrecognized good fortune. The National Assembly, which the Germans had prescribed and most of its deputies despised, happened to be the framework for the kind of government France both wanted and required; it was what returned her to the track of her tradition. To explain this requires something of a digression into the past.[3] Politically, the rise of the French middle class in the late medieval period had been characterized by its collaboration with the crown. As the more or less silent partner of the king it had, by supplying money, trained administrative personnel, and moral support, assisted him in the piecemeal destruction of the particularistic privileges of the feudal aristocracy and in the erection of a centralized state. The logical outcome of this development would have been an absolute state operated by a bourgeois bureaucracy for king and middle class, but its final growth stopped short of that point. Several factors caused the halt. First, of little significance at the moment but freighted with meaning for the future, was the fact that the best of the bureaucrats did not trust their ability to rule in the public interest under a government with no checks whatever upon it. Here, perhaps, is the one vital nexus between the traditional institutions of France, the rationalist political theorizing of the day, and the superstructure of the French state since 1875. Second, of far greater importance at the moment, the aristocracy, although it had been stripped of its local and regional powers to the advantage of the growing royal administration, had retained its economic status and social privileges, and in the second half of the eighteenth century, it attempted to utilize these to stage a counter-revolution in the cause of self-aggrandisement. It proceeded by applying pressure upon the king through the court it decorated at Versailles; it employed its connection with the higher reaches of the administration occupied by the nobility of the robe; it even tried to

[3] The interpretation given here has been presented at greater length and with pertinent references in Henry Bertram Hill, "French Constitutionalism: Old Regime and Revolutionary," *Journal of Modern History*, xxi (September 1949), 222–27.

legitimatize its objectives by inventing new constitutional powers for the *parlements*. The results of the efforts of the aristocracy were to paralyze the government, and the outcome was the Revolution of 1789.

While the Revolution liberated the peasantry and bourgeoisie economically, and gave wide currency to the liberal social ideas of the time, it achieved little in a positive constitutional sense outside the realm of the judiciary. It ended absolutism and struck down the old aristocracy; beyond that, and several brief but interesting governmental experiments, some of which were to be of future usefulness, there were few tangible results in the area of government. Napoleon was shrewd and knowing enough to draw upon those parts of France's traditions and past institutions which might be useful to him; hence he went back to the point where the conscientious bureaucrats of the eighteenth century had hesitated, and, being the master of his aristocracy rather than subservient to it, gave France a centralized bureaucracy, reaching down through a pyramidal hierarchy to every corner of the state, and controlled by no hand save his own. The rest of his governmental apparatus largely consisted of such exotic innovations as the Consular (later Imperial) representative bodies, designed as an appeasing but unrestricting sop to the republican ideals of the Revolution and destined to serve little historic purpose beyond their shadowy resurrection in the days of Napoleon III.

Time was to demonstrate that Napoleon's administrative system was built wisely and in full conformity with France's needs and traditions. His prefects were the direct lineal descendants of Richelieu's intendants and provided the state with the responsive control which Frenchmen liked better than they thought (or still think in some quarters) and which the challenging exigencies of modern international politics and war made imperative. The Revolution had cried out against such centralization and promptly destroyed it, only to discover its error quickly and begin the reconstruction that Napoleon completed. The same administrative structure with few changes has lasted ever since, has served France well, and is likely to last indefinitely—certain current tendencies to the contrary notwithstanding.[4]

After Napoleon had disappeared, however, there emerged the questions of how this centralized administration was to be controlled, and by whom. In a sharper and more clarified form, it was a resumption of the struggle of the decades just prior to 1789, when the aris-

[4] The present constitution prescribes changes in local administration. For a brief description, together with the caustic reaction of Herriot, certainly no friend of administrative authoritarianism, see Gordon Wright, *The Reshaping of French Democracy* (New York, 1948), pp. 241–42.

tocracy and the bureaucrats vied for domination over the system. Following 1815, the bureaucracy became increasingly professionalized and declassed—the more or less willing servant of whatever master might triumph. Before the Revolution such a conscientious public servant as Turgot in a groping and ill-considered fashion had hoped to place the bureaucracy, for its own good and the good of France, under the scrutiny of the courts and perhaps of provincial assemblies; after 1815 the middle class, which formerly had been without collective voice and had lacked the political self-confidence bred of experience, entered the lists against the revived aristocracy. It did so in the form of supporting a representative central government, sometimes in an insecure truce with the lower class, sometimes in an equally uneasy compromise with the nobility. This tentative nature of its position and the uncertainty of its role account in some measure for the revolutions of the first half of the nineteenth century.

Ultimately, however, the middle class had to make a definitive choice, since there was little logic and less practicability to any way-stations between aristocracy and democracy. Given the temper of France and of the times, the only publicly acceptable claim to rule it could espouse rested upon the rationalistic precepts of the eighteenth-century philosophers—precepts given a broadly democratic orientation by the Revolution of 1789 and subsequently woven deeply into French tradition. This segment of tradition had, as a matter of fact, given a sharp definition to the kind of democratic government France needed, although it had been resorted to only once and briefly, in 1848, since the prototype had first appeared back in the days of the Convention. It was government by popular assembly, direct government by the representatives of the people, possessing plenary powers unlimited by checks and balances.

In a functional sense, it was the fulfilling of this tradition that characterized the work of the establishment of the Third Republic. At the time, the stage seemed to be occupied by the noisy contenders from the rival camps of Monarchists,[5] while the constitution, when drafted, was said to provide at one and the same time a provisional régime pending the outcome of that dispute and a convenient vehicle for transporting the royal victor to power.[6] But Thiers, although he

[5] For a summary of the conspiratorial nature of the activities of the Monarchists to enthrone "Henry V" see D. W. Brogan, *France Under the Republic (1870–1939)* (New York, 1940), pp. 98–105.

[6] At this point it is common to note that the Republic was accepted in the Assembly by a majority of one vote, while ignoring the large majorities which supported the rest of the constitutional laws. See Brogan, *op. cit.*, p. 110, and M. Deslandres, *Histoire constitutionnelle de la France* (3 vols., Paris, 1932–37), III, 329–444. Also ignored is the future revolution France would have had if monarchy had been reestablished. See Brogan, pp. 102–3. As a matter of fact, the Monarchists were more Republican than they realized;

spoke negatively, came closer to reality when he said, quoting the elder De Broglie, that republicanism "is the government which divides us least." The Monarchists tried to close their ranks, but their consciences robbed them of their nerve, for they knew that, although preponderant in the Assembly, they had been chosen by the voters not for their monarchism but because they had favored peace.[7] And while they, and the reactionary wing of the middle class and of the clergy, indulged in a variety of expediencies and delaying tactics, France and her deputies learned from experience how useful and necessary to the country so unlimited a representative body was— useful because it was governing France well, and necessary because it was the capstone to the constitutional evolution that had been in progress for centuries. The only way in which the highly centralized administration, demanded by France's position in Europe, could be kept from being the tyrannical engine of some selfish minority or individual was to put it under the control of a powerful, broadly democratic, and sensitively responsive assembly. When this was done, with such concessions to the conservatives as the addition of a president and an upper house, the constitutional architecture of modern France was completed. At home, at least, France was again on sure ground, for the first time in a century. That is why she was able to make so remarkable a recovery after what had happened in 1870–1871. That is why, with growing self-assurance, she could look squarely at the problem facing her across the Rhine.[8]

In looking at that problem, France gave another indication of her maturity. She demonstrated, quite clearly, her ability to learn from experience and to recognize the stubbornness of reality. The new Germany obviously could not be tackled head-on; a different approach, in different character, had to be evolved. Pursuing that end with great subtlety and patience, taking advantage of every strategic error committed by her immature opponent, France before 1914 emerged as the central ally in a coalition arrayed against Germany.

---

almost every parliamentary tactic they employed was based upon the spirit of Republicanism and furthered its growth. See Deslandres, III, 444–46.

[7] The by-elections of July 2, 1871, to fill vacant seats in the National Assembly, were held without pressure from extraneous influences on the voters. Of the 111 deputies elected, 100 were Republicans. See Deslandres, *op. cit.*, III, 133–37.

[8] There is no intention of implying here that France was immediately conscious of her success in conforming her institutions with her traditions, or that she had established an ideal government. What had been achieved was the best possible compromise in a society that lacked the wide consensus concerning political philosophy to be found in Great Britain and the United States. Such phenomena as the Boulanger and Dreyfus affairs, as well as the crisis of February 1934, emphasize that lack of consensus. They do not prove that the Republic could not function acceptably, even in a crisis, although they do indicate that what might be called the margin of safety was somewhat narrower than in some other democracies.

While it took the intervention of the United States in the war that followed to tip the scales in France's favor, she had, certainly, successfully exploited every European resource available to her, and the influence at her disposal far exceeded her own potential when weighed directly against that of Germany.

So far, in estimating the continuing significance of France in Europe in the terms of the historical continuity of her inner substance, of her powers of recuperation, of her adaptability, and of her maturity, all questions raised have in some degree been answered, save one —namely, that of what deep-seated flaw might lie in her organic structure and there constitute a source of vulnerability. To come to the problem directly, it has long been widely held that Republican France had one serious and debilitating flaw in her constitution that revealed itself, at times in a fashion embarrassing to her foreign policy, in the form of endemic ministerial instability. On the whole, however, much more has been made of this, both by Frenchmen and by foreigners, than the circumstances have warranted. At no time in the history of the Third Republic did the cabinet's mercurial sensitivity to parliament have what could be called a fateful effect upon the course of either domestic or foreign policy until the 1930's, and by that time almost all the states of Europe had succumbed to totalitarianism or lapsed into stagnation.

Certainly the French ministerial mechanism had successfully weathered the terrific bludgeonings that fell upon it between 1914 and 1918, and its performance during the critical years of the first half of the period between the two World Wars was far from discreditable. Later, in the nerve-shattering times accompanying the rise of Hitler, it was the issue of the very existence of France, and not the nature of her constitution, that paralyzed the country. Indeed, when the Second World War and the domestic interlude of the Vichy régime had passed, and Frenchmen had a chance to overhaul the government, what did they do? They destroyed the label under which the country had gone down in defeat, and then proceeded to reconstruct the Third Republic virtually in its entirety.[9] In other words, they again demonstrated their maturity not only by remaining loyal to their traditions, but also by reestablishing the one form of government that could work in France, that would, to repeat the formula, divide them least. It was the same formula that Thiers had pronounced, a perpetual compromise between a large majority that was

[9] The best analysis of the present constitution is in Robert K. Gooch, "Recent Constitution-making in France," *American Political Science Review*, XLI (June 1947), 429–46. For a highly illuminating and competent study of the background see Gordon Wright, *op. cit.* The text of the constitution is in the *Journal officiel* for October 28, 1946.

unsure of just what kind of republic it wanted and a not negligible minority composed of those either dubious about or openly opposed to democracy. By adhering to this formula, most Frenchmen had learned from three-quarters of a century of experience that they could best get along together, as well as govern themselves, with a periodically renewed representative assembly of almost constituent powers, reflecting these divergent tendencies and directing what was virtually a temporary executive committee. A delicately poised executive is thus an inevitable and indispensable part of the structure, the only assurance of the maintenance of the compromise, just as it is the only guarantee of democracy in a monolithically administered state. As a problem, it is insoluble; as a weakness, it is mainly psychological.[10]

The psychological weakness, however, would exist even if there were a greater degree of ministerial stability, although it is heightened by the tentative nature of the tenure of every cabinet. Parliamentary democracy, indeed, offers a peculiar difficulty of its own in the realm of political symbolism. The peoples of very few modern democracies have succeeded in detaching themselves completely from the emotional need for some permanent or semipermanent symbolic headship, which must, to serve effectively, be clothed with great power or veneration. The people of the United States, by virtue of an unusually fortunate history, have been able to fill that place with a combination of a powerful presidential chief executive and a particularly successful and little-changed constitution—a sort of human and documentary duality. The British people have encased their growing democratic institutions in the mantle of the ancient monarchy and its elaborately evolved constitution, which find their symbolic embodiment in the person of the king. The French have been unable to have recourse to either of these sets of devices and, as a rather coolly logical people, have not evolved a parallel set of institutional folkways. Parliamentary government and presidential government cannot be combined, since their apparatuses are antithetical, and under the former system a president can be little more than an embellishment. The French people by temperament are not so made up that they can take such a feature with complete seriousness, while the veneration of a constitution could hardly become a cult in a country which has had more constitutions than it cares to remember. A

[10] The eminent constitutional lawyer and historian M. Deslandres, as he came to the end of the last volume of his work cited above, presented what wisdom his study had to offer (pp. 533–34). Experience indicated to him that a stronger executive and a less willful legislature were desirable, but he presented no plan to achieve these ends. His conclusions are typical of serious French authorities on the subject. There is also some point in noting how little was accomplished toward reaching the same objectives in drafting the present constitution.

king, although he could provide the proper *mystique,* has long been out of the question for France. The absence of some such symbol, admittedly, has been a temptation which has gravely tried the French on several occasions since the time of Napoleon III, but they have never succumbed. In each instance a fear for the security of the country has been the basic case of temptation; in each instance improvement in foreign and domestic affairs has brought a renewed will to spurn seduction.

It is true that, except for the events which accompanied the military defeat in 1940, no democratic government of France since 1871 has ever been subjected to internal stresses so severe as those that bear down upon the Fourth Republic today, and the problem of symbolism is again deeply involved. Now, for the first time, heavy pressure is being applied from two sides. Both of these forces are violently contrary to French tradition and to each other, and at least one of them is anti-republican. This pressure, nevertheless, is primarily a rationalization of the troubles of the moment—of low wages, lack of capital resources, poor housing, humiliation at military defeat, fear of or high regard for Russia. These are all serious enough matters, but time and good fortune, not constitutional change, offer the only means of mending them, and developments since 1947 for the most part augur well.

After this extended digression into the historical and constitutional evolution of France, made in an attempt to demonstrate the essential stability and durability of her institutions, there remains the original problem of the potential role of France among the powers today. An approach to the problem might be made by asking a further question: If the French were in so sound a condition as a result of the successful operation of the Third Republic during almost two generations, why did the international position of France deteriorate so badly in the 1930's? The question is put in this form with the specific intention of shifting the emphasis away from a preoccupation with France's internal condition as a key to her possible position in Europe and of placing it upon the heart of the matter, the distribution of power among the major states.

To establish France's position it is necessary to go back to the state of affairs with which she was confronted following her defeat in 1871. There then was no hope of recovering her lost status in Europe except by gaining powerful allies, and it was the success in the pursuit of this objective that restored her to the ranks of the major powers. Her membership in the Triple Entente accorded her an equality with even the strongest member of the Triple Alliance, and as these two rival systems were presumed to provide a balance of forces in Europe it meant that, in the event of war, nothing so disastrous as the events of 1870–1871 would be repeated.

After the First World War was over, however, it was evident that a revolution in the European state system and in the worldwide location of power had taken place. Austria-Hungary had disappeared; the United States, which had unexpectedly been called upon to play the decisive role in the war, had withdrawn from Europe; Great Britain had shortened her commitments to the Rhine, and even there they were none too firm; and Russia, now dedicated to world revolution, could never become a reliable ally. Out of the wreckage France saved what she could—a distant but continuing friendship with the United States, a series of alliances with the new states of Eastern Europe, and, somewhat later, the Locarno Agreements. Under the circumstances it was a viable system, and demonstrated its worth for a number of years. But at best it was a jerry-built arrangement, for if the British would not support France when she was supporting her Eastern allies, as the British had done when France backed Russia in the Balkans in 1914, then the system was completely dependent on the double condition of the continued disarmament of Germany and the continued quiescence of Russia. Should Germany be allowed to rearm, France's Eastern allies would be cut off, pressed, perhaps, against a resurgent Russia, and Germany's economic and manpower preponderance would again strike France down. It was an apprehensiveness about this weakness that found vent in the petulant and almost mean vindictiveness of the Ruhr episode. Yet in a larger sense the instability of the system explains the emotions of the French, if not their manners, and France was willing to be ashamed of herself when the English belatedly gave their limited guarantees at Locarno.[11]

The threat finally arose in all its sharpness in 1936, when Hitler sent the German army into the demilitarized zone along the Rhine. The French cabinet debated long, before deciding by a narrow margin not to act. The decision was in large degree made because Great Britain refused to support intervention, and France knew that in the last analysis she could depend on no one else to assist in the defense of her homeland against German aggression, should that dire possibility ever become a reality. What had been a precarious but passable security system thus became overnight a last-ditch stand, and France was reduced henceforth to trotting dejectedly at the heels of Britain.[12] It was in that year, therefore, that the deterioration of the

11 Exactly the same manifestation, arising from the same cause, is apparent in France's present policy with respect to the Saar.

12 For a good summary of the meaning of the blow to France see Brogan, *op. cit.*, pp. 697–701.

French position began, and serious reflections of it could be seen in domestic affairs as well as in foreign. Henceforth, Hitler was able to pluck the leaves from the artichoke one by one, under the admiring gaze of the French Right, until, as he thought in 1939, he could swallow the remainder with relative ease.[13]

In the Second World War another revolution in the distribution of power occurred, even more cataclysmic than the previous one. France emerged from the struggle in much the same condition she had been in 1918—badly mauled and somewhat more depleted in capital resources, but still basically sound and still having much the same potential strength. Germany was even more decisively struck down than before, but she also retained a large degree of her residual power. The real changes had taken place elsewhere. Great Britain had lost, and lost forever, much of her former substance, while Russia, now militantly on the aggressive, had swallowed up Eastern Europe and, through the domination of her share of a divided and occupied Germany, towered over the Continent. To the west across the Atlantic another colossus had emerged, the only ultimate counterpoise to Russia.

Faced with the new realities confronting her, France in trying to reconstruct her position in Europe first attempted to play the role of mediator between the East and West. It was a pathetic, if understandable, gesture toward a departed past. When this role became an obviously impossible one, and France discovered it with a quick display of resiliency, she joined the Western Democracies in forming the new *cordon sanitaire*. That expression now has a meaning beyond its original use, for France is, indeed, the new Czechoslovakia of Europe. Just as that state was the keystone to the Eastern European arch that sustained the democracies against the threat of aggression before Hitler wrecked the system, so today, after a serious retreat to the West, a similar and stronger arch has been constructed, this time with France as the keystone.[14]

Again, however, one condition imposes itself, in addition to that of continued and full support of this system by the United States, and it is the same condition as before. If Germany is ever allowed to rearm, it will lead to the same anarchy and the same misfortunes. Even the threat of German rearmament aims a severe blow at France, for she has been thrice burned in the same fire. Frenchmen believe that an armed Germany will fight in the only cause any country fights

[13] Although it approaches the problem from exactly the opposite viewpoint of the one taken in this paper, see the penetrating conclusions in C. A. Micaud, *The French Right and Nazi Germany, 1933–1939* (Durham, N.C., 1943).

[14] For the reasons why England cannot hold that position, see the remarks of Paul Henri Spaak in *New York Times,* January 15, 1950, p. 1.

for, its own, and soon or late she will find ways and means of playing the West and Russia off against each other to her own advantage, or at least to the grave disadvantage of the West.[15] Alternatively, if Germany remains disarmed, France gives every indication that she and her associates are capable of growing strong until they form a bastion against further Russian penetration sufficient to relieve many of the present demands upon the United States. Should that point be reached there can be juxtaposed to Russia's influence in Europe something perhaps firm and durable enough to incline her to undertake the negotiating of a definitive settlement. Such a settlement might be attainable on the basis of a free, united, disarmed, and non-totalitarian Germany, and constitute the beginning of the best sort of peace Europe is likely to have in the foreseeable future.[16]

If France is afforded the security that the Atlantic Pact gives promise of providing; if she is granted the position among the members of that group which her location, traditions, and substance warrant; if the movement embodied in the establishment of the Council of Europe bears fruit; if the Organization for European Economic Cooperation continues to foster the growing economic recovery in which France is playing so appreciable a part, there is little doubt but that she will again become, as she was between the passing of Bismarck and rise of Hitler, the one power in Europe capable of motivating a foreign policy guided by the realities of Continental politics. Every nation, quite naturally, has its ultimate vulnerabilities, and if the prerequisites just mentioned are not met in some degree, then France will not regain her self-confidence, and, like any country submitted to long-continued and overwhelming pressure, will turn in upon herself. All the old wounds will be reopened, class cleavages will widen, minor issues will become major, until the governing process reaches stalemate and the constitution is declared inadequate. From that the undoubted result would be revolution, which, if a revolution to the Right, would be likely to render France useless for any viable purpose in Europe, and if to the Left would directly turn the nation and the Continent into an appanage of Russia.

[15] See the excerpts from an Assembly debate in "The French National Assembly and the West-Bonn Protocol," *News from France,* Vol. v, No. 1 (January 15, 1950), 1–12.

[16] For a convincing and more complete presentation of this concept see Hajo Holborn, "The Collapse of the European Political System, 1914–45," *World Politics,* I (July 1949), 442–66.

28

+++

FRANCE AMONG THE POWERS *

FRED LATIMER HADSEL

+++

THE path of French policy—and consequently the role of France among the powers—is as strewn with imponderables as that other very famous road is paved with good intentions. Unquestionably many things could happen which would affect France's policy, such as a change not only in the government but in the composition of the National Assembly. On the other hand, even if Rightist and Gaullist forces were strengthened, the present balance of political forces would probably not shift so radically as to reverse the existing government's foreign policy.

The possibility also exists that events outside France's border might impel a reorientation of French foreign policy. Obviously a rapid unification of Germany overtly hostile to the West, a complete dissipation of the cold war, or a sudden reversion to isolation by the United States might produce such a change. These possibilities are so remote, however, that—barring unforeseen events which insurance companies wisely lump together as Acts of God—the near future will not witness events that will drastically modify France's role among the powers as it has been developing since the war.

One characteristic of current French policy is that France's interests are concentrated in Western Europe to a greater extent than they were before the war. While the United Kingdom has maintained world-wide commitments, and in fact has strengthened its ties with both the United States and the Commonwealth, France has not maintained a similar breadth of fundamental interests. This does not mean, of course, that France is indifferent to events outside of Europe. The war in Vietnam, for example, is regularly front-page news in the Parisian

* The writer prepared this paper in private capacity rather than as an employee of the Department of State. The views expressed are therefore personal rather than official.

press. Both because of historic interests and because of the large Arab population in the French Union, France is also sensitive to developments in the Near East. Whatever the outcome of events in Indochina, however, France is in the process of restricting its commitments in this area; and whatever the importance to France of the Near East, the fact that it has relinquished control over Syria and Lebanon inevitably means that the Levant no longer receives high priority in French policy. Nor does the generalization that France is preoccupied with Europe ignore or underestimate its interest in Africa, for to the French North Africa *is* a part of Western Europe, and it is only a geographic accident that prevents the physical attachment of the Algerian departments to southern France. As to the rest of Africa, French interests, though considerable, are conceived primarily in terms of what aid these areas can give to France in Europe.

The current emphasis which French foreign policy places on Western European problems reflects the direct influence these questions have on France. The French preoccupation with Western Europe is also a symptom of a certain amount of disillusionment on the part of France with the United Nations as an international security organization, and their corresponding reliance on regional arrangements. While French leadership in the League of Nations naturally disposed France to support the UN at the outset, its confidence in the UN has recently been somewhat shaken. One reason for this change appears to have been the anticolonial implications of some of the UN's resolutions which the French have recently interpreted as being intended to dissolve the older Western colonial systems. For example, in 1949, in the question of the Italian colonies and in problems relating to trusteeship and non-selfgoverning territories, France found itself in a small minority facing a combination of Latin American, Middle Eastern, and Far Eastern nations, all of which were critical of the colonial powers. Under these conditions the French have regarded some of the activities of the UN as illegal and beyond the scope of the Charter, and they recall with bitterness that period in the League's history when domination by smaller nations caused larger powers to bypass the organization.

A third characteristic of current French foreign policy is France's solid alignment with the West in opposing the expansion of Soviet influence in Europe. During the closing months of the war and for two years thereafter—while the Communist Party was in the government —France tried to avoid a schism between Russia and the West by acting as a mediator. The Franco-Soviet Treaty of December 1944 was envisaged as the first step in this policy, which on several occasions General de Gaulle, as President of the Provisional Republic, described as that of a bridge between the East and West. This policy was particularly evident in 1945–1946 during the negotiations in the Council of Foreign Ministers on the Italian and Nazi satellite peace treaties. By the end of this period, Georges Bidault, then Foreign Minister, apparently concluded that no bridge which France might hope to build could be long enough or strong enough to span the ever-widening chasm between the East and West. Since 1947, although France has made clear its decision to stand alongside the West, the French have come to consider the fact of Soviet power an accepted part of the European landscape.

Contemporary French foreign policy is further characterized by an unprecedented degree of cooperation between France and the United States. While a strong tradition of Franco-American friendship has existed since the days of Lafayette, and this country's cultural ties with France have long been close, only since the war has this relationship been bolstered by a clear realization of the over-all identity of French and American interests in Europe. Moreover, France in enlisting American aid in redressing the European balance of power has achieved something for which French statesmen sought in vain after World War I. As a result, France has come to consider the United States as another—and in this case friendly—part of the European landscape.

But underlying these various characteristics is a more fundamental trait of current French foreign policy—a trait which in large part explains France's role among the powers. France has been caught in a conflict between policies based upon the habit of historical thinking, and policies called forth by the practical necessities of the contemporary world. Such a conflict is by no means a new experience for France. David Thomson, in his extremely literate *Democracy in France,* describes the burden which the habit of historical thinking placed on France's political life during the early years of the Third Republic.[1] In that period, he points out, the French tradition of *"la grande nation"* complicated France's adjustment to such new developments in Europe as the unification of Germany and of Italy. Likewise, the recent war has produced a set of new circumstances which clash with the habits of thought which the French developed during the Third Republic. In fact, the expansion of Soviet influence, the elimination —at least for the present—of a unified Germany, the unprecedented commitments of the United States in Europe, the decline in Britain's strength, and the general military and economic weakening of Western Europe, have produced far more serious problems in adjustment than those which France faced after 1870 or 1918.

[1] (Oxford University Press, 1946), p. 92.

The resulting tensions can be found in virtually every aspect of French foreign policy. Toward the Soviet Union France might logically reflect its historic need for an ally against Central Europe, but under present circumstances French fear of Soviet expansion makes such a plan impossible. In the UN France has been torn between a desire to carry on with its traditional role in behalf of collective security and international cooperation, and the fear that the UN will undermine the French Union. With respect to the United States, the French are, on the one hand, motivated by a desire to continue their traditional policy of friendship and retain American guarantees of French security, and an equally keen desire to resist any loss in freedom of action as a result of American economic and military aid. As regards Germany, France has maintained its traditional concern with security, but it is uncertain as to the most effective method of achieving this goal, and hence is caught between a long-standing desire to render Germany powerless and a more recent tendency to rely on Allied and Franco-German cooperation. As to England, the French have not forgotten the centuries of competition, but they also realize the need for British support in coping with Continental problems. Toward Italy, France may not have entirely forgotten the squabbles which have frequently marred Italo-French relations; at the same time, it sees a basic need for closer Franco-Italian cooperation and no longer harbors bitter resentment over Mussolini's stab in the back of 1940. On the broad question of European unification, the French are keenly aware of the political necessity of such an arrangement, while also recognizing the economic obstacles which lie in its path. As for the question of military defense, some of the French feel on the basis of history that anything is better than war; others believe that such defeatism invites another war. In view of French concentration on Europe, this conflict between historic policies and present necessities may appropriately be examined in connection with French policy toward Germany and toward Europe's political unification, economic integration, and military defense.

II

In no question of French foreign policy is the conflict between traditional and current interests more evident than in that of Germany. And in no other case, perhaps, can the emphasis on historical events be more sympathetically viewed. To the French the phrase "three invasions within seventy years" is not merely an oratorical flourish. It is a grim reminder of repeated destruction, systematic exploitation, and intense humiliation. Quite understandably, therefore, the traditional

French demand for security finds expression in support of a punitive policy toward Germany. A similar policy, it should be recalled—although never as broad or as deep as that championed by France—was espoused by the United States during the immediate postwar period. By 1947, however, the United States had moved to an intermediate stage, in which it tempered corrective measures with economic assistance, and by 1949 the United States had entered more fully on a policy of assistance to the Germans and of support for the German Federal Republic.

In France, on the other hand, where fear of Germany was naturally far greater than in the United States, the support given a punitive policy has proved much more sustained. At the same time, however, French leaders have gradually become aware that the German problem could not be solved solely on the basis of narrow security considerations. More and more, the French have come to recognize their need for German coal and certain types of German trade, notably machinery and chemicals. There has also developed in France an awareness that under certain circumstances France and Germany might have a common enemy in the Soviet Union. In such a case, Germany would become an important element *in* French security, rather than a threat to that security. Moreover, the anti-German sentiment among the people of France has proved to be less than might be expected, and certainly not as great as it was five years after World War I.

No single event marks the turning-point in French efforts to solve the German dilemma on other than narrow security considerations, particularly since this effort has at best been hesitant. It was, however, during 1947 that the French government first hinted at a change. While it continued to press for the detachment of the Saar from Germany and its economic integration with France, it in fact gave up its plan for physical detachment of the Rhineland, modified its views on the Ruhr, and agreed to an increase in the level of German production. This evolution in French policy coincided with the ousting of the French Communist Party from the government. It also coincided with the realization that while French and Soviet policies toward Germany had certain outward similarities, the reasons for these similarities were quite different and furnished no basis for real cooperation. This fact was patently clear by the close of 1947, when the Soviet Union opposed French plans for the Saar and espoused the cause of a strong central German government. The evolution of French policy toward Germany was subsequently furthered by the presence of M. Robert Schuman at the Foreign Office as of July 1948. His extensive knowledge of German affairs and his ability to establish rapport with his British and American colleagues undoubtedly assisted France in modifying its German policy. Moreover, it has frequently been noted that during Schuman's tenure of office France obtained a higher proportion of its basic demands than during the previous years.

France, of course, continues to be keenly aware of the potentials of German power. For one thing, the French cannot ignore the obvious difference in population. Since the war, the birth rate of France has been four times as great as in the prewar period, but this does not mean that a marked increase over the present population figure of 42 million may be expected. France is, instead, merely holding its own as far as population is concerned, and therefore remains far behind the present Western German state, with its more than 47 million, or a unified Germany, with close to 70 million. Similarly, the French are apprehensive about the potentials of Germany's economy. Five years after the war, German iron and steel production already equals that of France and is capable of still greater expansion. Comparable French production, on the other hand, is subject to definite limitations. France must import approximately 20 per cent of its coal, and all of its oil, while the drought continues to prevent full utilization of the nation's hydroelectric power.* Although French industrial production in 1949 was the best since 1929, over-all economic output is still insufficient and productivity (in terms of man-hours required to make a given article) is lower than in Britain or Germany. The French themselves attribute their present economic weakness not only to insufficient machinery but to the restrictive practices of the producers, whose preference for cartel arrangements is well known, and to the attitude of labor, which is first of all concerned with job security and inclined to regard technological advance as a step toward unemployment. In view of these deeply rooted traditions, there is little prospect for a marked increase in French economic strength which would give France a permanent lead over Germany's heavy industries.

In the political sphere, the French are fully aware of the probability that some day Germany will again be united. Under certain conditions, this raises the specter of another Rapallo, which, in French eyes, would be tantamount to the rearming of Germany—a prospect that the French are particularly desirous of avoiding.

In view of German demographic, economic, and political potentialities France has been especially concerned, in the evolution of its policy since 1947, with the problem of the control of Germany, for it is clearly only through some system of controls that strong French public sentiment in favor of a punitive peace with Germany can be squared with

* On this point see also Chapter 20, especially pp. 358-59.

the practical considerations which demand a more constructive policy.[2]

The French policy of controlling Germany clearly depends on continuation of the occupation; effective supervision of the German government by the Allied High Commission; full operation of the International Authority of the Ruhr; and development and extension of the Military Security Board. In order to make this system of controls effective, the French government has relied on unity of action among the three Western Allies. It is only by means of this unity that France has been able to move to a more positive program on Germany, as Foreign Minister Schuman emphatically stated during the Assembly debates in November 1949.[3] Anything which undermines the unity of the three powers, therefore, automatically undermines French policy toward Germany. A clear demonstration of this fact occurred in September 1949, when the French became deeply concerned lest Britain's decision to devalue the pound crack Western Allied unity.

Given the existence of adequate controls, and the continuation of three-power unity, France may find it possible to move toward a broad rapprochement with Germany. It has an honest advocate of this point of view in M. André François-Poncet, the French High Commissioner in Germany. Representatives of some of the more responsible press, notably *Le Monde,* have also indicated on a number of occasions the need of closer relations between the two countries. In November 1949, during a meeting of the European Movement, leading French and German parliamentary leaders discussed common problems, and somewhat later a group of such leaders held another meeting for the same purpose. Both sessions, it is worth noting, received favorable comment in the moderate French press. That genuine rapprochement is as yet politically very difficult, however, is indicated by disagreement over the Saar, in which the economic interests of the French clashed with the political desires of the Germans. On the other hand, the Schuman Plan of May 1950 is based upon the belief that France and Germany can cooperate with the other steel-producing countries of Western Europe for the effective coordination of heavy industry, regardless of political differences.

In view of such problems as the Saar, cynics are inclined to point to the parallels between present French policy toward Germany and the period of the 1920's, when France failed either to encourage the Weimar Republic or to maintain adequate means of repressing Ger-

---

[2] Representative of this attitude are the essays of Louis Aubert in *Contrôle de l'Allemagne* (Paris, 1949), in which he argued for immediate and far-reaching control of the Ruhr.

[3] *Journal officiel,* November 24, 1949.

man nationalism. They not only predict the failure of French policy but the resurgence of an authoritarian Germany. The optimists point to such new elements as the effect on Germany of its complete defeat and the presence of the United States in Europe, and they insist that history will not repeat itself. The French government, for its part, admits that the policy of imposing basic controls on Germany, maintaining close cooperation with the United States and Britain, and developing Franco-German rapprochement involves many difficulties. However, they reply to their critics by pointing out that other alternatives simply do not exist.

As a matter of fact, two alternatives are, at least theoretically, available to France. General de Gaulle has called for a Franco-German "understanding." While he has not been specific as to what he means by "understanding," he has appeared to envisage a direct approach to Germany outside the framework of Western Allied unity. This alternative, however, appears unlikely in the foreseeable future, because most of the French recognize that their unilateral action would be inadequate to ensure the control of Germany. An even more unlikely alternative exists in the possibility of a genuine implementation of the Franco-Soviet Alliance. Such an alternative, however, would appear practicable only with a Communist government in France, the prospects of which are remote.

Instead, France seems firmly committed to a continuation of the policy it has developed since 1947 of supporting the agencies for the control of Germany, of continuing close cooperation with the United States and Britain, and of seeking Franco-German rapprochement. It is possible that such issues as control of the Saar or fear of German rearmament will make it difficult to carry out this policy. Nevertheless, this policy—despite all of the problems it poses—has an exceptionally sound basis, in that it combines France's traditional and deeply rooted desire for security from German aggression with the practical necessity of working with Germany in Western Europe.

III

As a result of American stimulus, the emphasis in the movement toward Western European union during the past year has been on economic integration. Nevertheless, the political aspects of European unification, while at least temporarily pushed into the background, are as essential as economic integration, and, in the case of France, antedate the recent preoccupation with economic questions.

In dealing with the problem of the political unification of Western Europe, France has been obliged—as in the case of Germany—to try to bring conflicting traditions and current interests into focus. Historically French nationalism has been the most intense in Western Europe, and because of national interests, France has experienced long periods of conflict with all of its neighbors. On the other hand, the general weakening of the nations of Western Europe as a result of the war has removed some of the reasons for this competition, and the appearance of a common enemy in the Soviet Union not only has made further rivalry appear dangerous but has impressed on many of the French the need for the political unification of Europe.

In the unification of Europe, France's postwar role has been deeply affected by the policy of the United Kingdom. It is one of the ironies of the day that at a time when Anglo-French cooperation is so essential to the well-being of Europe, relations between the two countries are less than harmonious. The bitter memories of 1940 are far from forgotten in France. From the dispute over Syria and Lebanon during the war to the devaluation of the pound in September 1949, Anglo-French relations have been subject to stresses which have unquestionably hindered the political integration of Western Europe. To a considerable extent France has either been unaware of special British problems or has misinterpreted British intentions. And the British, for their part, have misunderstood France. The London *Economist,* for example, was so irritated by the spectacle of a prolonged French cabinet crisis in the autumn of 1949 when the issues were not momentous that it raised the question of whether France was capable of taking a leading part in the regeneration of Europe.[4]

The type of approach that Britain has taken toward Europe has also undoubtedly complicated Anglo-French cooperation. Before the end of the war, the United Kingdom had considered steps toward establishing a military European arrangement. This general plan envisaged a Grand Alliance designed to maintain the military potential of the Allies after the end of hostilities. Immediate postwar European problems, however, proved to be primarily political and economic, and Britain's original plans for a military alliance were temporarily put aside. Moreover, as the split between East and West developed, the United Kingdom began to look for support to the United States rather than to France or Western Europe. Since the Fulton, Missouri, speech of Winston Churchill in March 1946, proposing an Anglo-American Alliance, was a logical outcome of this point of view, it came as much less of a shock to the British than to the American public.

Throughout 1946–1947 the British government remained hesitant to take definite steps toward political association with Europe. In addition to the feeling that Western Europe was in no position, military

[4] November 5, 1949, p. 994.

or economic, to give Britain genuine support, the Labor government was preoccupied with internal problems; Labor leaders tended to lack interest in things European; and Labor was divided as to whether to support only Socialist régimes in Western Europe or encourage all Third Force groups. It is also clear that the British government was deeply concerned with the problems raised by its ties with the Commonwealth, to say nothing of the economic problems of the sterling bloc. The British—dedicated to austerity—were also unwilling to jeopardize their plans for recovery by opening their economic system up to Continentals. Above all, it is possible that British thought, as far as European arrangements were concerned, was still predominantly in favor of military or quasi-military alliances. Such a theory is supported by the fact that concrete British action toward Western Europe during 1947–1948 was primarily limited to two military alliances: the Dunkerque Treaty of March 1947, and the Brussels Pact of March 1948. The keystone to this system, as far as the United Kingdom was concerned, was the Atlantic Pact of April 1949, inasmuch as it brought the United States into the system of Western European military guarantees. It is apparently for this series of reasons that the British refused to participate in the formulation and implementation of the Schuman Plan of May 1950 for the integration of the European steel industry.

France, on the other hand, approached the general problem of European political unification from an entirely different point of view. By geography and centuries of experience, France was forced to concern itself with Continental events to a greater degree than the government across the Channel. The French overseas possessions, moreover, were not the deterrent to Continental commitments that the British Commonwealth was, since the French Union does not contain sovereign entities, and the administration of the Union has always been centered in Paris. Furthermore no problem of currency blocs or economic ties similar to those faced by Britain in the sterling area beset France. It also appears that French leaders were inclined to view mere military arrangements, such as the British championed, as of doubtful value unless they could be bolstered by solid political understandings. French fears of British isolation or indifference at critical junctures rest, after all, on a long history, and these fears are closely related to French apprehension of German aggression.

During 1947–1948, therefore, while the British government was primarily interested in questions other than European political unification, French governmental leaders were very much preoccupied with this very problem. In various unofficial meetings, such as the Hague Conference of May 1948, leaders of the parties in power in

France were active participants while most of the British leaders who attended were representatives of the Conservative opposition. In the same way, it was the French who, through the Bidault Memorandum of July 1947 to the Brussels Treaty Powers, took the initiative in suggesting a European federal parliament with broad political and economic powers. This memorandum, as well as one submitted by the unofficial European Movement, furnished a basis for the discussion leading to the Statute of Europe of May 5, 1949. These discussions were characterized by a much-publicized tug-of-war between the British desire for a loosely organized Council with restricted duties and the French desire for a more tightly organized Council with broader powers. On paper the compromise arrived at appeared to favor the British, for the powerful Committee of Ministers could not take fundamental decisions without unanimous agreement, and the Consultative Assembly, in which no such restriction existed, could only make recommendations. As a result, influential French spokesmen did not conceal their disappointment with the proposed organization.

The experience of the Assembly's first session in August 1949, however, indicated that the organization might possess possibilities which its statute had not fully foreshadowed. The Assembly certainly proved a forceful forum for spreading the idea of a "European approach," and it also displayed possibilities for playing a role in solving European problems. On the other hand, its capacity for developing into a European parliament such as the French originally had in mind is still problematical, and developments in this connection will undoubtedly bear careful watching. In view of the enormous obstacles which must still be overcome before genuine political unification is possible, French efforts will clearly be unavailing unless the full participation of Britain is forthcoming. Certainly Paul Henri Spaak was echoing the thoughts of other Continental nations besides Belgium when he declared at Philadelphia early in 1950 that Britain could no longer expect to enjoy the role of arbiter of European disputes, but should instead "step boldly on the way to European order." [5] This basic problem was much in evidence during the second session of the Council of Europe in August 1950, when the division persisted between the bulk of the British representatives who favored a "functional" and more gradual approach to unification and many of the French, who desired early federation of Europe.

Failing full British support, France and the other Western Continental countries have remained cautious as to the eventual role of Germany in European unification. Even in the case of the Council of Europe as now established, the French National Assembly approved

[5] *New York Times*, January 15, 1950.

the admission of Germany as an associate member only on the conditions that the German Federal Republic should first declare its intention to conform to the provisions of the Council's Statute and clearly demonstrate its ability to do so.[6] In this initial stage, moreover, there is little doubt that France looks to the United Kingdom to counterbalance Germany. The need for Britain in a more advanced political union of Western Europe is, in French eyes, even more imperative. Thus until the roles of Britain and Germany in Europe are more clearly defined, the movement toward political unification faces an impasse and it is possible that the way to further unification can be opened up only by the development of economic integration.

IV

While the problems which confront France in connection with the political unification of Western Europe lie primarily in the realm of Franco-British and Franco-German relations, the issues facing the French in economic integration are chiefly domestic. Historically, France, along with the United States, has been one of the most protectionist countries in the world. Except for a none too successful experiment with low tariffs during the period extending from the Franco-British agreement of 1860 to the protectionist law of 1892, France has remained essentially in the path of Colbert. Protection of both agriculture and industry was a primary concern of the Third Republic, and there is little doubt as to the continuation of the influence of the industrial and peasant groups in France of today. Since French entrepreneurs and farmers have shown little enthusiasm for the competition which economic integration of Western Europe implies, the French government has necessarily been hampered in carrying out integration plans. Similarly, trade-union leaders, who fear unemployment, strongly oppose tariff reductions on competing products. Yet, as Le Monde has affirmed, and as recent ECA statements emphasize, France must shake off its protectionist tradition if it is to take a leading role in the economic integration of Europe.

The stimulus for economic integration has come from the United States, which, French editorial writers repeatedly remark, is far more European than the Europeans in this respect. This does not mean that the French are unaware of the value of economic integration, for the fact is that they regard this general plan as a means of giving Europe a position of greater economic equality with the United States. Nevertheless, France has encountered a number of practical obstacles

6 Journal officiel, November 26, 1949.

to economic integration, with the result that a conflict exists between the French commitment in principle and in actual practice.

The French government took its first concrete step toward economic integration when it signed a customs treaty with Italy on March 26, 1949. This accord was concluded under favorable circumstances. French and Italian industrial establishments are to a remarkable degree complementary, and good will was in evidence on both sides during the negotiations. Yet the French Economic Council has voted not to recommend its acceptance by the National Assembly and the accord has not received the necessary parliamentary approval. Doubts have arisen as to whether the avowed purposes of reducing prime costs and selling prices, raising the standard of living, and ensuring full employment can be accomplished by such a treaty. Some of the obstacles have stemmed from vested interests favoring protectionism, while other difficulties have been technical in nature. The French press reports opposition from agricultural and other workers' organizations, which fear that the unemployment besetting Italy will be transferred to France as a result of a customs union. Medium and small enterprises, the cotton industry, and the machine-tool industry are among the industrial interests which fear competition. But these are not the only obstacles. The mere technical arrangements have presented enormous problems. For example, the French system of governmental restrictive control and appellation of wine is not duplicated in Italy. Fears of overproduction and lack of control have to be satisfied before France will be able to enter a full customs union with Italy.

Partly because the customs union project continued to present difficulties, and partly as a result of Hoffman's plea in October 1949 at the OEEC meeting for further steps toward economic integration, the French government took the lead in November 1949 in proposing a conference with Benelux and Italy to develop a series of financial arrangements, looking toward a return to convertibility of currency and a coordination of economic policies. While this arrangement, dubbed Fritalux or Finabel by the press, would be more limited than the proposed Franco-Italian customs union, it would provide France with a larger cushion for some of the economic stress involved in the customs union. Although the Fritalux plan is more modest than the steps advocated by ECA, it nevertheless raises specific problems which further spotlight the obstacles which lie in the way of economic integration. For example, the Netherlands, Belgium, and France all have different currency problems, and a period of time will be required to coordinate the guilder (tied closely to the pound), a "hard" Belgian franc, and a "soft" French franc. Benelux, moreover, is essentially a low-tariff area, while France retains high tariffs, and Benelux therefore sees little value to financial arrangements until French tariffs are lowered. While France feels that the Franco-Italian customs project will be facilitated by the Fritalux financial plan, the Benelux countries feel that intra-European economic arrangements are of little value to them unless Germany is brought into the picture. As in the political field, German participation in economic integration raises the need of British participation, which is hampered by the problems of the sterling bloc.

In view of the slow progress which has been made, ECA recommended in January 1950 that a currency union be established for all of Western Europe. As far as France is concerned, it is doubtful whether the expansion of the currency union from Fritalux to Western Europe will in itself overcome French reluctance to abandon protectionism. At the same time, the combination of the Schuman Plan and a European Payments Union may provide certain of the essential requirements of active French participation in economic integration. For example, by developing the manufacture and marketing of steel on a European rather than national basis, the Schuman Plan may eventually lead to an improvement of over-all production, which would not only help solve the payments problem but build the founda tion of economic unification. Nevertheless, both the Payments Union and the Schuman Plan will involve serious economic readjustments, and it is difficult to see how France can successfully take the lead in these projects unless outside aid assists in absorbing the resultant shocks.

V

When the French turn from the problem of economic integration to the related issue of military cooperation, they find themselves agreed as to the desirability of security. On the question, however, of how this security can be achieved, a division exists in France between the defeatists, who believe that military defense is useless and will merely invoke another disaster, and those who believe that France must take the risk involved in attempting to protect itself from another invasion. The sources of the defeatists' views are easily traced. The occupation of the northern departments during World War I and all of the country during World War II has convinced certain groups that France can no longer protect itself from armed conquest. At the same time, however, other groups are convinced that another occupation would mean the end of France's free institutions, and that France at all costs must avoid being conquered by force of arms. Admitting the inability of France to repel an attack alone, these French realize that they must rely on a system of military alliance. However, exactly what form this alliance should take has not been easy for the French to decide.

In the immediate postwar period, the defense policy of General de Gaulle's government was primarily Continental, and it coincided with a period of strained political relations between France and the two Western Allies. As East-West tensions developed a shift from this attitude gradually took place. This change in French defense policy was clearly evident between the conclusion of the Dunkerque Treaty in 1947, which was not enthusiastically received by the French, and the Brussels Pact in 1948, which met with far greater French approval. Nevertheless, even the Brussels Pact provided no satisfactory answer to the French quest for military defense arrangements, since none of the signatories was adequately armed. In addition, in working out the broad outlines of strategy under the pact, the French frequently found themselves at odds with the British. In the French mind, the basic question at issue was whether Western Europe should concentrate its defenses on the Continent or on the British Isles. The initial plan of the British, which called for the establishment in London of the head-quarters of the Permanent Defense Organization, and the appoint-ment of Marshal Montgomery as chief of ground forces, was protested by the French public as an abandonment of the Continent. The sub-sequent location of the headquarters at Fontainebleau, and the ap-pointment of General de Lattre de Tassigny as chief of ground forces, thus marked a decision on Western European strategy which favored the French point of view. Even then, however, the decisions that the French should supply most of the ground forces, while the British should have responsibility for military aviation, led to French public resentment. Quite appropriately, the *chansonniers* in Paris began to ask in their songs: "What do they think we are, all feet?"

While the Brussels organization was encountering difficulties in working out its strategy, it was even more embarrassed by the lack of arms and troops. Having committed itself to defending Western Eu-rope, it found that it had precious little with which to carry out its formidable task. Throughout Western Europe it was recognized that American support in the event of war would be vital but that this support might not be available before the Continent was overrun. Hence the Atlantic Pact of April 1949 breathed life into the arrange-ments outlined under the Brussels Treaty a year earlier. By this pact the French obtained two things which they had sought in vain after World War I: a specific security arrangement for Western Europe, and a definite political commitment from the United States to assist

in carrying out that arrangement. In addition, the pact carried with
it the implication of American material aid necessary to make the
defense of Europe a reality. Assurances to this effect were given immediately after the pact's signature, in a reply which the United States
sent to a request the Brussels powers made for material and financial
assistance. The commitment was specifically met in the Military Assistance Program, passed October 6, 1949.

Details of the strategic plan being evolved under the Atlantic Pact
are, of course, secret. Press reports indicate that France and other
Continental powers will be assigned predominant responsibility for
ground action. It has further been reported that, in the realm of production, France is to emphasize small arms, attack aircraft, and medium artillery. France's part in the productive effort is by no means
negligible, since almost a quarter of its military budget for 1950 was
for arms production, and French leaders hope to increase the percentage in 1951. French initiative in the matter of the common defense of Europe was illustrated in August 1950, when its memorandum to the Atlantic Treaty countries set in motion the proposals for
an integrated force in Europe, which came out of the New York Atlantic Council session of September.

This evolution in plans for the military organization of Western
Europe plainly indicates that France's relative position has considerably improved during the past few years, and everything points toward
a continued development along the same lines. Among the unsolved
problems, however, which continue to plague the French, the question of morale overshadows all others. It has been the opinion of
those supporting the Military Assistance Program that one practical
way of building French morale is to give France arms in which it can
have confidence. There is evidence, moreover, that the French will
to resist possible Soviet aggression is improving as the shell-shock
of defeat, occupation, and liberation gradually wears off. Thus the
psychological importance of the military arms program is great, since
defeatism may be eliminated as France regains its military potential.
There is little doubt, however, that such a development will take time,
and the Military Assistance Program will not by itself provide a
panacea.

A second question is the effect of the Indochina hostilities on
France's role in the defense of Europe. The war in Indochina has been
costing France the equivalent of half its military budget, and has involved approximately 130,000 troops. Even if the Bao Dai solution for
Indochina proves successful, France will still be committed to maintaining a considerable military establishment in the Far East. The
European defense program would benefit somewhat through the re-

turn to France of officers who are badly needed in the training of recruits. At the same time, such troops as released from Indochina are needed to fill up the depleted garrisons elsewhere in the French Union. If the Bao Dai solution fails and hostilities continue, on the other hand, France is committed to even further expense in Indochina. Such a reversal, moreover, would, in the opinion of many French observers, lead to unrest elsewhere in the Union and require considerable expansion of overseas military establishments. It appears, therefore, that whatever the solution in Indochina, the outcome will not markedly strengthen France's role in the defense of Western Europe.

A third problem is that of German rearmament. While there has been relatively little talk of direct German rearmament, there has been considerable discussion of German participation in the defense of Western Europe. The Dutch press, for example, which might be expected to be especially sensitive to this question, has canvassed the various formulae by which Germany would be required to share the burden of defense without being permitted to secure military domination of Europe. Following the Korean crisis and in recognition of the need for greater defensive effort, the majority of the Western nations have come to the conclusion that German economic and military participation in European defense is essential to its eventual success. They further maintain that once an integrated army is established and after the Atlantic Treaty countries have obtained a satisfactory minimum of preparedness, the addition of German units to the common defense will not lead to German domination or necessarily recreate traditional German militarism.

As far as France is concerned, there is no doubt but that it subscribes to the task of rebuilding the armed strength of the Western Allies. There is little doubt but that German rearmament without real controls would give a *coup de grace* to Franco-German rapprochement, provide a field-day for the Communist press, and revive the very defeatism which the Military Assistance Program is designed to overcome. It appears, therefore, that France would agree to the participation of German units in the defense of Europe only most reluctantly and under conditions which assure French security.

The conflict between historical thinking and current necessities is, as we have seen, the major theme of contemporary French foreign policy. While the effects of this strain are found in every basic question with which the French government has had to deal, France has made notable strides toward harmonizing the divergent tendencies which affect its foreign policy. The extent to which France continues to resolve these conflicts will largely determine its role among the

powers. As we have also noted, however, so many obstacles remain to
further adjustment of these opposing points of view that the French
government cannot by itself be expected to surmount all of them. The
conclusion is therefore inescapable that France needs outside assistance for some time to come, and in the last analysis this means continued American support.[7]

---

[7] Although the bulk of this chapter was written in January 1950, and amended as of
September, it is believed that as of the date of printing (winter of 1951–1952), the fundamental aspects of the problem have not sufficiently changed in the interim to invalidate
the appraisal.

WHO'S WHO OF CONTRIBUTORS

WARREN C. BAUM. Principal Desk Officer for France in the Program Coordination Division, Economic Cooperation Administration, Washington, D.C. Ph.D., Harvard.

JOHN BOWDITCH. Department of History, University of Minnesota. Ph.D., Harvard. Author of pamphlets in the "American Forces in Action" series of the War Department and two volumes of *Fifth Army History.*

ROBERT F. BYRNES. Department of History, Rutgers University. Ph.D., Harvard. Author of articles in scholarly journals and of *Antisemitism in Modern France. Vol. I, The Prologue to the Dreyfus Affair* (1950).

RICHARD D. CHALLENER. Department of History, Princeton University. M.A., Columbia. At present engaged in writing a doctoral dissertation on the development of the "nation in arms" concept in the Third Republic.

JOHN B. CHRISTOPHER. Department of History, University of Rochester. Ph. D., Harvard.

KENNETH DOUGLAS. Department of French, Yale University. Ph.D., Yale. Editor of "Yale French Studies," and author of *A Critical Bibliography of Existentialism: The Paris School* (1950), and of articles in the field of French literature.

EDWARD MEAD EARLE. School of Historical Studies, Institute for Advanced Study. Ph.D., Columbia; LL.D., Princeton. Author of *Turkey, the Great Powers, and the Bagdad Railway* (1923); editor and co-author of *Makers of Modern Strategy* (1943) and *Nationalism and Internationalism* (1950).

HENRY W. EHRMANN. Department of Social Sciences, University of Colorado. Degrees in law and political science, Universities of Berlin and Freiburg. Author of *The French Labor Movement from Popular Front to Liberation* (1947), and articles on political thought and social movements in contemporary France.

EDWARD WHITING FOX. Department of History, Cornell University. Ph.D., Harvard. Editor of "The Development of Western Civilization" Series of Cornell University Press.

HENRY E. GUERLAC. Department of History, Cornell University. Ph.D., Harvard. Author of the official history of radar development, of "Vauban: The Impact of Science on War" in E. M. Earle (ed.), *Makers of Modern Strategy* (1943), and of articles on the history of science.

FRED L. HADSEL. School of Government, George Washington University, and Foreign Affairs Specialist, Office of German Political Affairs, Department of State. Ph.D., University of Chicago. Author of articles and reports on foreign affairs and the work of the United Nations.

ELLEN HAMMER. Institute of International Studies, Yale University. M.A., Columbia. Author of a forthcoming book on Indochina and of *The Emergence of Viet Nam* (1947), both published by the Institute of Pacific Relations.

DONALD J. HARVEY. M.A., Columbia. At present engaged in writing a doctoral dissertation on French military thought, 1918–1939.

HENRY BERTRAM HILL. Department of History, University of Wisconsin. Ph.D., Wisconsin. Author of articles on French constitutional history.

H. STUART HUGHES. Department of History, Harvard University. Ph.D., Harvard. Author of *An Essay for Our Times* (1950).

EDWARD L. KATZENBACH, Jr. Department of History, University of Tennessee. M.A., Princeton. Author of "War and Economics During the Franco-Prussian War of 1870–1871," *American Historical Review*.

DUDLEY KIRK. Chief of the Population Branch, Division of International and Functional Intelligence, Department of State. Author of *Europe's Population in the Interwar Years* (1946); co-author of *The Future of Population in Europe and the Soviet Union* (1944).

DAVID S. LANDES. Junior Fellow of the Society of Fellows and member of the Research Center in Entrepreneurial History, Harvard University. M.A., Harvard.

VAL R. LORWIN. Formerly with the Division of International Labor Affairs, Department of State; now engaged in a study of the contemporary French trade-union movement under the auspices of Harvard University. A.M., Ohio State.

SCOTT H. LYTLE. Department of History, University of Washington. Ph.D., Cornell.

CHARLES A. MICAUD. Woodrow Wilson School of Foreign Affairs, University of Virginia. Ph.D., Columbia. Author of *The French Right and Nazi Germany, 1933–1939: A Study of Public Opinion* (1943), *La Droite devant l'Allemagne* (1945), and articles in American and French periodicals.

L. ARTHUR MINNICH, Jr. Department of History and International Affairs, Lafayette College. Ph.D., Cornell.

DAVID H. PINKNEY. Department of History, University of Missouri. Ph.D., Harvard. Author of "Nationalization of Key Industries and Credit in France after the Liberation," *Political Science Quarterly*.

RICHARD RUGGLES. Department of Economics, Yale University. Ph.D., Harvard. Author of *National Income and Income Analysis* (1949).

JOHN E. SAWYER. Department of Economics, Harvard University. A.M. and Junior Fellow, Harvard.

ANDRÉ SIEGFRIED, LL.D., Litt.D. President, Fondation Nationale des Sciences Politiques. Member of the French Academy. Author of *Tableau des partis en France* (1927), *America Comes of Age* (1927), *England's Crisis* (1931), *Suez-Panama* (1939), *The Mediterranean* (1948).

VERNON VAN DYKE. Department of Political Science, State University of Iowa. Ph.D., Chicago. Contributor to scholarly journals and the memorandum series issued by the Institute of International Studies at Yale.

JOHN B. WOLF. Department of History, University of Minnesota. Ph.D., Minnesota. Author of *The Diplomatic History of the Bagdad Railroad* (1936), *France, 1815 to the Present* (1940), and *A History of Civilization*, with Hutton Webster (1947).

GORDON WRIGHT. Department of History, University of Oregon. Ph.D., Stanford. Author of *Raymond Poincaré and the French Presidency* (1942), and *The Reshaping of French Democracy* (1948).

GLOSSARY OF ABBREVIATIONS

CCN. Comité Confédéral National. The standing executive committee of the CGT.

CFTC. Confédération Française des Travailleurs Chrétiens. The Catholic workers' organization; second largest.

CGA. Confédération Générale d'Agriculture. The Socialist peasant organization.

CGC. Confédération Générale des Cadres. A politically independent union of supervisory and technical personnel.

CGT. Confédération Générale du Travail. The largest labor organization in France; Communist-controlled.

CNR. Conseil National de la Résistance. The central coordinating board of Resistance units in the French underground.

CNRS. Centre Nationale de la Recherche Scientifique. The central governmental administrative agency for the coordination of scientific research.

CTI. Confédération du Travail Indépendante. Controlled by Gaullists, ex-Communists, and leaders of the Vichy labor movement.

ECA. Economic Cooperation Administration. Administrative organization for the European Recovery Program.

ERP. European Recovery Program. American program for economic aid to Europe (1948–1952); also called the Marshall Plan.

FO. Force Ouvrière. Independent, but with Socialist leanings; third largest.

JOC. Jeunesse Ouvrière Chrétienne. A Catholic youth movement.

MAP. Military Assistance Program. American program under which military equipment is delivered to European members of the North Atlantic Pact.

MDRM. Mouvement Démocratique de Rénovation Malgache. Madagascan nationalist party.

MRP. Mouvement Républicain Populaire. The Catholic Center party founded after Liberation; one of the three largest parties in France.

OEEC. Organization for European Economic Cooperation. European agency for the allocation of Marshall Plan aid.

PPA. Parti du Peuple Algérien. Algerian nationalist party.

RDA. Rassemblement Démocratique Africain. Nationalist party for all of French Africa.

RPF. Rassemblement du Peuple Français. The Gaullist party.

SED. Sozialistische Einheitspartei Deutschlands. German Communist party.

SFIO. Section Française de l'Internationale Ouvrière. The French Socialist party.

SNECMA. Société Nationale d'Étude et de Construction de Moteurs d'Aviation. A government aircraft corporation.

UDSR. Union Démocratique et Socialiste de la Résistance. A small Center party headed by René Pleven.

WFTU. World Federation of Trade Unions. Communist-dominated international labor group.

INDEX